THE PROCESS OF PARENTING

THE PROCESS OF PARENTING

THIRD EDITION

JANE B. BROOKS

Mayfield Publishing Company

Mountain View Toronto London

To my grandparents and parents,
my children and their children

Library of Congress Cataloging-in-Publication Data

Brooks, Jane B.
  The process of parenting / Jane B. Brooks. — 3rd ed.
      p.   cm.
  Includes bibliographical references and index.
  ISBN 1-55934-013-4
  1. Parenting—United States. I. Title.
HQ755.8.B75 1991
649'.1—dc20   90-20499
                                                      CIP

Manufactured in the United States of America
10 9 8 7 6 5 4 3

Mayfield Publishing Company
1240 Villa Street
Mountain View, CA 94041

Sponsoring editor: Franklin C. Graham   Manuscript editor: Joan Pendleton
Typesetting: Text set 10½/12 Berkeley Oldstyle by TBH/Typecast, Inc.
Printing and Binding: R. R. Donnelley & Sons, Inc. Printed on 50# Finch Opaque.
Cover design: Gary Head   Cover Photograph: Jean Claude Lozouet/Image Bank
Text design: Diane Beasley.

Photo credits: Suzanne Arms/Jeroboam, p. 131; Elizabeth Crews, pp. 8, 76, 99, 126, 171, 180, 200,
226, 240, 266, 362, 418, 438; Sam Forencich, p. 143; Bruce Kliewe/Jeroboam, p. 29; Phiz Mezy,
p. 233; Erica Stone, pp. 18, 41, 42, 68, 285, 316; Taurus Photos/Shirley Zerberg, p. 92; Suzanne Arms
Wimberly, p. 338.

CONTENTS

CHAPTER 1

PARENTING AND THE LIFE CYCLE

CHAPTER 2

PARENTING IS A PROCESS

CHAPTER 3

ESTABLISHING CLOSE EMOTIONAL RELATIONSHIPS WITH CHILDREN   58

CHAPTER 4

MODIFYING CHILDREN'S BEHAVIOR 83

CHAPTER 5

PREGNANCY AND DELIVERY 109

CHAPTER 6

THE FIRST YEAR OF LIFE   138

CHAPTER 7

TODDLERHOOD: THE YEARS FROM ONE TO THREE

178

CHAPTER 8

THE PRESCHOOL YEARS   223

CHAPTER 9

THE ELEMENTARY SCHOOL YEARS 263

CHAPTER 12

PARENTING/WORKING   388

CHAPTER 13

SINGLE PARENTING   426

CHAPTER 14

STEPPARENTING   453

PREFACE

Parenting means loving and caring for children, helping them to grow. Parenting activity is not confined, however, only to those who produce children; it is shared with many others in our society—day care workers, coaches, teachers, and community volunteers.

This third edition of *The Process of Parenting*, like its predecessors, is written to show how parents and caregivers can translate their love and concern for children into effective parenting skills. The book strives to bring to life the world of the child, the experiences of parents, and the kinds of interactions between them that promote effective functioning and well-being for all. When people learned I was revising a book on parenting, many were genuinely curious about what could have changed in four years to require a new edition. I answered them by explaining that more and more research is available to tell us about the needs of children. More material, much of it anecdotal, describes the profound changes parents experience in the process of parenting. Most particularly, we are learning more and more about the ways people influence each other and the ways social institutions set up processes that have impact on our lives. Thus, although the effects of particular strategies of parenting may not have changed, we now know much more about the participants and the process of parenting.

To understand how children think and feel and act, this book presents information on children's physical, intellectual, and personal-social development for six age periods—infancy, toddlerhood, preschool years, elementary school years, early adolescence, and late adolescence. The tasks parents carry out to promote healthy development are discussed for children of each age.

Based on a careful review of the recent literature many topics have been updated, the treatment of children's emotional development and school experiences has been expanded, and new sections on issues relevant to minority group parents have been added. In addition to this review of the literature, I have selected seventeen outstanding researchers and clinicians in child development and personality and interviewed them about the applications of their findings to the concerns of today's parents. Thus, each chapter contains interview material from one or more researchers who discuss everyday situations that parents encounter.

The greatly expanded Instructor's Manual will, I hope, enhance the third edition's usefulness throughout the wide range of teaching situations in which *The Process of Parenting* is used. The Instructor's Manual—a small book in itself—provides for the instructor a chapter outline, supplementary lecture topics, guest speaker suggestions, and a list of audio-visual resources. To further encourage student learning, it offers elements such as provocative topics for small group discussion as well as suggestions for long and short term student projects. Finally, it includes an extensive test bank of questions for convenient test generation.

As in every activity, problems in parenting arise and demand attention. A portion of each chapter focuses on problems common to children in a specific age period or situation. Because each child is a unique individual, parents require a variety of strategies and techniques for handling problems depending on the child and the circumstances. The strategies of Haim Ginott, Thomas Gordon, and Dorothy Briggs emphasize communicating feelings and establishing relationships with children. Rudolf Dreikurs and the behaviorists emphasize ways of changing behavior. Parents can find solutions among these approaches if they adopt a problem-solving method that consists of: defining the problem exactly, making certain that the problem is the child's and not the parent's, considering alternative actions, taking action, evaluating the results, and starting again, if necessary.

The previous edition described parents' experiences and changes in the course of child rearing. This third edition expands on this theme and includes excerpts from interviews with parents about what they wish they had known before they started and about the joys and changes they have experienced in the process of parenting. This edition continues to include the adaptations of parenting techniques for working parents, single parents, and stepparents.

Helping children grow is an intense, exciting experience that exercises adults in all areas of daily functioning. Parents and caregivers develop physical stamina as they care for the newborn, who allows them little sleep. Their physical agility and speed increases as they chase toddlers. Their athletic abilities are honed as they roller skate, ride toboggans, and play baseball. Their minds, as well as their bodies, are stretched in many directions. Parents master science and math to answer questions about where the stars go in the daytime, what makes rain, and why people grow old. Then come the questions only children ask: Why can't a girl grow up and marry the dog she loves? Where are children before they are born? Emotional expressiveness, too, gets a real workout. The range of emotions is extended—joy and frustration are experienced as never before. Depth of feeling is intensified, and parents achieve incredible mood changes, going from joy to tears or from rage to delight in just moments.

In helping new life to grow, we gain for ourselves an inner vitality and a richness in all our relationships. Parenting is indeed the best all-round exercise for being human. It is my hope that this book contributes to students' understanding of the process and to parents' enjoyment of this intense activity.

ACKNOWLEDGMENTS

Writing the acknowledgments is one of the pleasures of completing a book, and there are many people to thank.

First, I thank all the researchers and clinicians who gave so generously of their time to participate in the interviews and to edit the interview excerpts. They are: Jay Belsky, Jack Block, Judy Dunn, Ellen Galinsky, Arlie Hochschild, Barbara Keogh, Claire Kopp, Anneliese Korner, Jacqueline Lerner, Richard Lerner, Susan McHale, Paul Mussen, Emily Visher, John Visher, Judith Wallerstein, Emmy Werner, and Carol Whalen.

I also thank Dr. Robert Kremers, Chief of the Department of Pediatrics of Kaiser Medical Center, for his willingness to have questionnaires about the joys of parenting distributed to parents in the waiting rooms. I thank the many anonymous parents who completed questionnaires in waiting rooms and in parenting classes. Most particularly, I express my gratitude to all those parents whom I interviewed about their joys in parenting and the ways they changed and grew through the experience. I gained invaluable insights about the parenting process from them, and their comments enliven the book immeasurably. These parents are: Wendy Clinton, Mark Clinton, Judy Davis, Robert Rosenbaum, Linda Dobson, Doug Dobson, Jill Fernald, Charles Nathan, Otie Gould, Warren Gould, Caryn Gregg, Robert Gregg, Jennifer Lillard, Michael Hoyt, Henrietta Krueger, Richard Krueger, Patricia Landman, Steven Tulkin, Chris McArtor, Robert McArtor, Kathy Malone, Jean Oakley, Susan Opsvig, Paul Opsvig, Sherry Proctor, Stewart Proctor, Iris Yotvat-Talmon, Moshe Talmon, Raymond Terwilleger, Patricia Toney, Anthony Toney, Barbara Woolmington-Smith, Craig Woolmington-Smith.

The staff at Mayfield Publishing Company deserve heartfelt gratitude for the way they have transformed the manuscript into a book. Franklin Graham, sponsoring editor, has been a consistent and enthusiastic supporter of the book, giving time and thought to ways to make the book more usable for students. His assistant, Laurel Sterrett, has been prompt and helpful in dealing with many practical details and has helped to evaluate material that could be omitted. John Harpster has helped to refine and focus the material. Mary Douglas, production coordinator, has shepherded the book to its final form with patience and care, always reassuring that everything would fall into place. Joan Pendleton has been a thoughtful, highly considerate copy editor who made clear the murky aspects of the manuscript. Special thanks go to Diane Beasley the book designer who used space so creatively and added to the esthetic style of the book. J. Eileen Gallagher-Haugh of St. Mary's College in Winona, Minnesota and Mary Forth of West Hills College in Coalinga, California reviewed the manuscript and made many useful suggestions regarding content and organization. Their fresh view of the book resulted in several improvements.

Coworkers at Kaiser Medical Center at Hayward were supportive and helpful at every step of the way. Marsha Mielke, the medical librarian, diligently tracked down and obtained articles and books. Pediatricians and pediatric advice nurses have given helpful information on parents' concerns. Staff and receptionists in the Department of Psychiatry have shown continuing interest in the project and relieved me of emergency work so I would be free to work on the book. I am most appreciative of the leadership at Kaiser. Dr. Paul Jewett, the Physician-in-Chief, Dr. Norman Weinstein, the former chief of psychiatry, and Dr. Jerome Rauch, the current chief, all promote an atmosphere in which creativity flourishes.

I again wish to thank Paul Mussen for his suggestions and interest in the project. He recommended using comments from researchers' interviews to make material more vivid for students. His concern with the social forces impinging on parenting has continued to influence my thinking.

Finally, my family and friends provided encouragement and helpful comments. I appreciate their thoughfulness and their company. My children who are grown and live away from home were, nevertheless, very much in my mind as I revised the book. In working on the book I have relived certain periods of their development. I find I learned the most important truths about parenting from my interactions with them. I believe that when I have paid attention, they have been the most excellent of teachers.

Jane B. Brooks

FOREWORD

The author of this book, Jane Brooks, has had a wide variety of professional and personal experiences that qualify her as an expert in child development. She is a scholar, researcher, and writer in the discipline of child psychology; a practicing clinician working with parents and children; and a mother. Drawing on the knowledge and insights derived from this rich background of experience, she has produced a wise and balanced book that parents will find valuable in fostering the optimal development of their children—helping them to become secure, happy, competent, self-confident, moral individuals. Dr. Brooks offers guildelines that are explicitly linked to major theorists (for example, Freud, Piaget, Erikson) and findings of scientific research in child development, so that the reader is also presented with a wealth of information on physical, cognitive, social, and emotional development. Students of human development and all who work with children professionally, as well as parents, will profit greatly from reading this book.

Brooks' approach to parenting incorporates many noteworthy features. Her coverage of the fundamental tasks and issues in childrearing is comprehensive. Included are tasks shared by all parents (for example, preparing for the birth of the infant, feeding, toilet training, adjusting to nursery school or kindergarten, the adolescent's growing interest in sex) as well as special, although common problems (such as temper tantrums, delinquency, use of drugs, and physical or mental handicaps). Critical contemporary experiences such as divorce, single parenting, and stepparenting are also treated with insight and sympathy. Brooks' suggestions for ways of dealing with these problems are reasonable, balanced, and practical; her writing is straightforward, clear, and jargon-free.

Authorities in child development generally agree that the principal theories and accumulated findings of scientific investigations are not in themselves adequate to provide a comprehensive basis for directing parents in childrearing. Given the limitations of the present state of knowledge, guidance must be based on established principles of human development *plus* the cumulative wisdom and insights of specialists who have worked systematically and successfully in child-guidance settings. Yet many, perhaps most, academically trained child psychologists pay little attention to the writing of such clinicians as Briggs, Dreikurs, Ginott, Gordon, and Spock, regarding them as unscientific "popular" psychologists. This is not true of Dr. Brooks. After careful and critical reading of their work, she concluded that, as a consequence of their vast clinical experience, these specialists have achieved some profound insights about children and have thus developed invaluable techniques for analyzing and dealing effectively with many problems that parents face. Furthermore, Brooks believes that parents themselves can successfully apply some of these techniques to resolve specific problems. Some of the experts' suggestions are therefore incorporated, with appropriate acknowledgement, where they are relevant.

The book is not doctrinaire or prescriptive, however; the author does not advise parents simply to unquestioningly adopt some "system," plan, or set of rules. On the contrary, Brooks stresses the uniqueness of each individual and family, the complex nature of parent-child relations, and the multiple determinants of problem behavior. In Brooks' view, each problem must be placed in its developmental context, evaluated in terms of the child's level of physical, cognitive, and emotional maturity. The processes of parenting are invariably bidirectional: Parents influence children *and* children influence parents. Furthermore, families do not function in isolation; each family unit is embedded in a wider network of social systems that affect its functioning. Successful childrearing depends on parents' accepting these complexities, yet also attempting to understand themselves and their children and maintaining a problem-solving orientation.

It is a pleasure to note the pervasive optimistic, yet realistic, tone of the book. The author has recognized that promotion of children's welfare and happiness is one of the highest parental goals, and she communicates her confidence that most parents *can* achieve this. Underlying this achievement is parents' deep-seated willingness to work hard and to devote thought, time, energy, and attention to their children's development and their problems. Reading this book will increase parental understanding and thus make the difficult tasks of parenting easier.

Paul Mussen
Professor Emeritus of Psychology
Former Director, Institute of Human Development
University of California, Berkeley

PARENTING AND THE LIFE CYCLE

C H A P T E R   1

Children are life in process. They are growing, usually in size, but certainly in ways of thinking, behaving, and reacting to the world about them. As they grow to maturity, they create new psychological identities. Parents participate in the growth process of their children in many ways. First, they usually contribute the physical start of life with sperm and egg carrying genetic information to form a new and unique individual. They support and nourish the growing child with food, shelter, and clothing. But most important, parents form emotional attachments and psychological bonds with children. As parents and children interact, they create family life, which introduces children to culturally approved ways of meeting needs. Parents guide children as they venture outside the family to other activities and to other people. As children reach maturity, they move outside the original family and form new ties, starting the process again by assuming the role of parents themselves.

Rearing children is perhaps the most exciting and challenging activity of adulthood. A very recent large-scale study shows that two-thirds of men and women find their family and love life the most satisfying part of life.[1] David Gutmann, a psychologist who has tested and interviewed men and women in many cultures about the impact of parenthood, writes, "For most adult humans, parenthood is still the ultimate source of the sense of meaning. For most adults the question 'What does life mean?' is automatically answered once they have children; better yet, it is no longer asked."[2]

Despite the importance of parenthood, most adults come to the experience with little preparation. Some parents have had jobs nursing or teaching that have allowed contact with children. Many parents have babysat. But few know even basic childcare practices until they are introduced to them in the last month of pregnancy as part of preparing for childbirth.

Lack of preparation makes parenting more difficult and less satisfying than it otherwise would be. This book is designed to open up the potential of parenthood by preparing people for the experience and helping parents enhance their effectiveness. It is a source of information on how children grow and develop. When parents understand what their children are experiencing, they are better able to intervene to meet children's needs. Parenting takes place in a social context that influences the process itself, and consequently we focus on parenting in single families, dual-career families, and stepfamilies. To deal with difficulties that are bound to arise in individual situations, the book presents a problem-solving approach incorporating strategies culled from many different "experts." Parents can then make choices based on their child's unique qualities and situation as well as on their own personal values.

WHAT IS PARENTING?

Parents foster all facets of children's growth. Nourishing, protecting, guiding new life through the course of development—these are the tasks of a parent. The word *process* is used in this book to emphasize that parenting is a continuing series of interactions between parent and child—a process that changes both.

The words *protecting* and *guiding* are vague. What do they mean in day-to-day life interactions? Saul Brown presents four main tasks of a family: (1) establishing basic commitments to family members, (2) providing warmth and nurturance for all members, (3) providing opportunities and encouraging the development of individuality, and (4) facilitating ego mastery and competence.[3] When these four tasks are related to the process of rearing children, we can describe the parents' main tasks as establishing warm, nurturant emotional relationships with children and providing opportunities for the development of competence and individuality. Several studies have found that a child's effectiveness is related to a strong emotional tie with a caretaker who stimulates a positive approach to other people and the world and to a consistent set of reasonable limits within which the child is free to explore and to develop skills. The challenge of parenting, then, is to relate to children in ways that stimulate their potentialities for growth and provide appropriate opportunities for experiences that develop these potentialities.

The relationship between parent and child is special, complex, and unique to each parent-child pair. Yet many factors influence the ways in which this highly personal, private relationship develops. A parent brings to the relationship all his or her experiences as a child and an adult as well as hopes and expectations for satisfaction in the relationship. The child, even when only hours old, brings to the relationship inborn characteristics, ways of reacting to the world, that will mold interactions with parents. The parent-child relationship is embedded in a specific family with other members of different ages, and the family lives in a social and cultural milieu that in turn exerts an influence on the family. The parent-child dyad is thus nested in a social group that expands as the child grows and comes into contact with school and other community activities.

FAMILY LIFE IN A CHANGING SOCIETY

Parents rear children in families, but our understanding of what families are and what they do has changed dramatically in the last twenty-five years. To get a sense of the momentous transformations that have occurred in the North American family, let us look back to a hundred years ago, when most North Americans lived on farms and in rural settings. Although the lifespan then was shorter than it is today, marriages occurred later and family size was large. In the early nineteenth century, mothers had an average of eight children. Both men and women spent most of their adult lives as active parents. Families also lived more settled lives. All family members worked together as economic producers, and children often followed in the occupational footsteps of parents. There was less geographical mobility than today, so many relatives lived close together and served as additional role models for children growing up. Parents had a clear sense of the lives they were preparing their children to live as adults and a solid core of values that were supported by the community at large.

Life was not necessarily easy in nineteenth-century North America. Since life expectancy was shorter, parenting years longer, and loss of the mother in childbirth more frequent than today, many families were disrupted by the death of a spouse. Epidemic and unpreventable illness, economic hardship, and discrimination against minorities also took their toll. Family members, however, retained strong feelings of closeness, belonging, and interdependence that provided strength and comfort at times of trouble.

Following the Industrial Revolution, as families moved to urban settings, fathers left their families to go to work and women's and children's economic labor decreased. It was a sign of the father's success that the mother could stay at home and focus on childrearing. Wives of blue-collar workers often continued to work for financial reasons. Women worked in large numbers during the Depression of the 1930s and World War II, but their labor force participation was the temporary result of hard times and not a socially approved ideal. The post–World War II days brought the flowering of what we think of as the **nuclear family**: Men were employed in a booming economy; women remained at home, rearing three or more children. Families tended to be child-centered and the principal source of warmth and affection for their members. Sex role attitudes were fixed—men were economic providers, competent and skilled in the world of work outside the home. Women were the heart of the family, nourishing children, supporting their husbands in their careers.

The 1960s were a decade of turbulence and change that disrupted this view of the family. Disagreement with government policy in many areas, the violence reflected in assassinations and war, led to wide-scale social protest. Rebellion initiated by younger people drove a wedge between youth and older adults, and families were sometimes split on issues of values and goals in life.

Other social movements also caused changes in the family. People became concerned about world population. Improvements in contraception enabled women to prevent pregnancy and enjoy sexual activity outside marriage without fear of having children. Premarital sexual activity increased, and both men and women postponed marriage. Couples began to live together, contributing to the delay in family formation.

At the same time, the women's movement grew and created an awareness of satisfactions attainable in the world outside the home. Women not only joined the labor force in increasing numbers, but they also sought higher-status occupations in business and the professions.

When these women married and had children, they stayed at work, and the work force today includes many mothers of young children. Fifty-two percent of women with children under a year work, and about two-thirds of women with children older than a year have employment outside the home.[4] Employment figures for single mothers are even higher. So the mother is no longer full-time caregiver of children, and families have adapted to her transformed role in a variety of ways.

In some families, the mother and father work different shifts so that children are continually cared for by a parent. In other families, both parents decrease work time to care for children. In still other families, the father has become the primary caregiver while the mother works outside the home. In most families, however, the mother works while children receive day care of some kind from nonfamily members, while the mother retains primary responsibility for home and children in her nonwork hours. Men are taking increasing responsibility for home chores—cooking, shopping, cleaning—but families with an equal division of responsibilities between parents for home and children are in the minority.

Although the age at first marriage has increased since the 1960s, these marriages were not necessarily more stable so that in the same period, the divorce rate began to rise. The percent of divorced men and women in the population doubled between 1970 and 1987.[5] This change has had a profound effect on both adults and children. The percentage of children living in single-parent homes rose from 11 percent in 1970 to 27 percent in 1987. Most of the children (24 percent) live with single mothers, and only a small number (3 percent) with single fathers.[6]

Though parents are divorcing, they are also marrying again, blending families in a variety of ways. Children may become part of a very much larger network of individuals whom they see regularly. For example, a child may live with her mother and stepfather and their child by their marriage, her half-sister. Every other weekend she may have as visitors in her home her stepfather's children by a previous marriage. She herself may go regularly to see her biological father, her stepmother, and her half-brother who is their child. If her stepmother has been married before, she may have stepbrothers and stepsisters whom she sees there as well. The child may have four sets of grandparents whom she sees on holidays. Thus, the family unit, as well as the number of role models, has been greatly expanded for this child.

In dual-career and single-parent families, adult caregivers outside the family play a large role in family life and become **extended family** to the child. Infants and preschoolers spend much of their waking time with these adults, who in turn affect all family members. When childcare is good, it can be an enriching experience—both for the child, who is exposed to caring adults, and for the parent, who can exchange information and get support from someone who knows the child well. Adults at school play a large role because they provide programs for preschoolers and afterschool programs for older children. Incorporating these new influences on the family is an additional family task.

Family life is becoming more varied as we continue to incorporate different **ethnic groups** in our society. Because of immigration from Asia and a higher reproductive rate in some groups, the proportion of ethnic group members is increasing. By the term *ethnic* we refer to groups of people who share a sense of communality with regard to religious, racial, national, or cultural traditions passed from one generation to another. *Ethnic* is a broader term than race, religion or place of national origin.

Although the United States is the most culturally diverse country in the world, we consider our society a "melting pot" that blends everyone together into a cohesive group with one set of values. There is evidence, however, that people retain ethnic traditions for generations. These traditions bring richness to our society.

The phrase *ethnic groups of color* refers to groups sharing racial characteristics—Afro-Americans, Hispanic-Americans, Asian-Americans, and American Indians. In 1984 social scientists considered the term *minority* unsuitable for these groups because these groups make up the majority culture in other parts of the world.[7] In 1990, social scientists find the term *minority* applies to these four groups because minority refers to a castelike group that is more or less forced to be part of the society by slavery or conquest.[8] Thus, a 1990 issue of *Child Development* is titled "A Special Issue on Minority Children."[9]

In this book we use the term *ethnic group* to refer to any group that shares a common heritage and sometimes use *minority* to refer to one of the four groups mentioned earlier. We use the term *predominant culture* or *majority culture* to refer to that set of beliefs emphasizing initiative, independence, achievement, individualism, ownership of material goods, mastery, and planning.

The main minority groups in this country now are Afro-Americans (28 million), Hispanic-Americans (19 million), Asian-Americans (10 million), and American Indians (1.5 million).[10] Just as the majority culture consists of many distinctive groups tracing their origins to different parts of Europe, so each minority group consists of several subgroups, each with its own particular set of values. For example, Hispanic-Americans from Mexico differ from Hispanic-Americans from Cuba. Asian-Americans from Vietnam have different traditions from Asian-Americans from China. The ease with which any new group fits in depends on many factors—the circumstances of the arrival in this country as well as similarity in characteristics such as color, language, and values to the majority culture. Each subgroup will have its own individual experience with the majority culture.

Nevertheless, reviews of the literature describing the attitudes and values of minority families reveal they use common strategies, though in differing degrees and combinations, to survive and flourish in the majority culture. Relying on the extended family, becoming bicultural (functioning well in more than one culture and using whatever behavior is adaptive to the situation), developing role flexibility, and drawing strength from ancestral or spiritual world views are ways to adapt traditions to a majority culture that stresses competitive individualism.[11]

Though the majority culture sometimes assumes that differences in family life mean deficiencies, Diana Baumrind points out in a discussion of cultural variations in social competence that the continued survival of Afro-American and Hispanic-American families in our highly industrialized society is "proof of their outstanding and durable competence."[12] As we move toward a new century, we do not know what qualities will be most adaptive. We may need different values and find ourselves drawing on the strengths of our minority cultures—for example, by incorporating the more cooperative approaches these groups favor.

As we shall see when we examine resources and strengths for individuals in times of trouble, the values of the extended family, role flexibility, and a spiritual orientation all promote resilience in people. Recent work suggests that the most understanding and perceptive parents are those who go through the process of integrating two cultures into a meaningful whole. Mexican-American mothers who are attached equally to their Mexican heritage and to the American culture have a broader, more understanding view of their children's development than do mothers attached to only one culture, be it Mexican or American.[13] In later chapters, we take up how parents of minority children help them individually to adapt to the different majority culture.

The National Commission on Children recently documented a tragic social change—the increasing number of children living in poverty and at risk for chronic problems like malnutrition, poor health, and school failure. The poverty rate in 1987 was 20 percent for all children, but it was higher for children of certain ethnic groups. For white children it was 15 percent, but for Afro-American children it was 45 percent and for Hispanic-American children, 39 percent.[14]

Even more disturbing are figures showing that Afro-American children experience more persistent poverty.[15] Longitudinal data from 1968 to 1982 reveal that 24 percent of Afro-American children were poor for at least ten years of the fifteen-year period, and 5 percent were poor for the entire time. Less than 1 percent of non-Afro-American children were poor for ten years and none was poor for fifteen years.

Poverty has increased with the rise in single-parent households. In 1987, the median family income for married couples with children under eighteen was $36,365, and for single mothers with children, $10,551. For single fathers, the average income was $20,967.[16] Poverty is also related to other economic changes like the decline in higher-paying manufacturing jobs, the rise in lower-paying service jobs, and changing governmental policies that have taxed low-income families more and provided fewer supportive programs.

Other social forces along with changes in work, marriage, and childbearing are affecting the contemporary North American family. Men's and women's attitudes about themselves, their children, and their goals in life have also been transformed. Summarizing polls conducted in the 1970s, Daniel Yankelovich described attitude changes in *New Rules: Searching for Self-Fulfillment in a World Turned Upside Down.*[17] Individuals, certain of the successful economy in the 1960s, became bored with hard work as the driving force in life. Young people felt they had more options than their parents, and they wanted greater meaning in life, more opportunities for self-expression. Men no longer felt they had to be the sole providers for their families. They endorsed sharing in a more equal division of responsibilities at work with women. They also endorsed women's having greater freedom to choose what they wanted.

As these new generations of North American adults searched for self-fulfillment, they had less interest in sacrificing for their children. Nearly two-thirds of parents rejected the idea that parents should stay together for the children if the parents were unhappy with each other. Two-thirds felt that parents should be free to live their own lives even if it meant spending less time with children, and about two-thirds of parents endorsed the view that they had the right to live well now even if it meant leaving less to children. But likewise parents did not expect children in turn to sacrifice for them or take on burdens for them in the future. It was as though less would be given and less expected in return.

This kaleidoscopic view of the social changes affecting North American family life and children indicates that parenthood is in transition.[18] Though we may be able to describe what has come before, it is difficult to predict what will happen as we move into the 1990s. Statistics since 1980 suggest the rates of marriages, births, and divorces have stabilized somewhat. We may witness a resurgence or blossoming of family closeness. The same two-thirds majority that endorsed reduced commitment to children in Yankelovich's survey favors "a return to more traditional standards of family life and parental responsibility."[19] How to foster closeness and warmth while maintaining the options for individual choice is the major challenge the future holds for adults.

REASONS FOR HAVING CHILDREN

Though many changes have occurred in the family settings in which children are reared, the desire for children remains constant. With greater control of contraception, however, men and women can now ask themselves *why* they want to have children before pregnancy occurs. Erik Erikson, a clinician and theorist who has described lifetime psychological development, believes adults have a basic need to create and nourish new life.[20] If they do not care for someone or something outside themselves, they become stagnant and unproductive. In the past, men have gratified generative needs by working and women by raising children. With changes in men's and women's roles, both sexes are free to express creative energies in work and at home with children.

Though children are important in people's lives, few studies have been conducted on the value of children to parents. One large 1979 survey reported the most frequent reason for having children cited by men and women of all ethnic backgrounds, parents and nonparents alike, was a desire for love, interpersonal satisfactions, and close ties to others.[21] A couple who have a child become a family unit, which is seen as a defense against loneliness, isolation, and anonymity in our society. For women, particularly, children may be primary providers of affection and warmth. Children may be seen as compensation for difficulties between the parents and for lack of affection in the marriage. In the event of divorce, they become even more important as sources of love. Some single people seem to be having children to create someone to love. Many teenagers and unmarried women have said they want a child to love because they have never really loved anyone else, and they have never had just one person to whom they could feel completely attached.

The second most frequent set of reasons was desire for stimulation, the novelty children bring to marriage. Children are lively and they keep parents young; it is exciting to see them grow and change. In addition, children may help to keep a balanced perspective in a home because they impose a routine on family life and help parents to forget outside troubles. And parents sometimes find it easier to worry about children's behavior problems than about their marriage, job, or personal problems.

A third common reason focused on parenting as a way of developing the self, linking oneself with the community. Rearing children stimulates the development of

Becoming a parent is seen by some as a defense against loneliness, isolation, and anonymity in our society. It is also a source of stimulation, novelty, and fulfillment.

personal characteristics such as selflessness, responsibility, and sensitivity. In addition, as parents care for children, they express previously untapped talents and develop new abilities. Parents become skilled storytellers, superb negotiators, and spontaneous teachers. Parenthood also expands self-concept by linking the parent to other people in a close family setting and in the larger social community. It is sometimes only because of children that adults take active roles in community activities. Children are also a link with generations yet unseen, and for some parents they provide a sense of immortality.

A fourth reason cited in the survey was to establish that they are stable adults. More than getting a job or getting married, parenthood is regarded as "proof" that an individual is a mature person. Parents, relatives, and friends expect that children will follow marriage, and adults oblige to meet social expectations. This has been particularly true for women, who are taught from childhood that their destiny and purpose in life is motherhood. As small girls they think about being mothers and form their identities in terms of loving and caring for others, particularly children.

A fifth reason was that children give parents a sense of creativity and achievement. Helping children grow, seeing them surmount the hurdles of childhood, gives parents a sense of accomplishment and competence.

A sixth group of reasons centered on parenthood as an expression of religious and moral beliefs. Many people equate motherhood with virtue and fatherhood with respect and authority. Children are viewed as manifestations of God's blessing and God's will. Individuals not connected with any formal church may consider having children a sign that they are more altruistic, less selfish, and less egocentric than those who remain childless.

A final reason for having children was economic utility. In the past, especially in agrarian societies, children were valued as laborers who contributed to the family's productivity. More recently, grown children have been the caretakers of aged parents and less fortunate relatives, but today these responsibilities are beginning to be assumed by governmental agencies. And now that the cost of raising a child through age eighteen is about $100,000 for a middle-class family in New York,[22] children are an economic burden rather than a utility.

In addition to the reasons cited in the survey, in some countries, and in some North American subcultures, children bring power to the parent, particularly to the mother. Mothers who have been subservient in the marriage relationship may, at times, have the courage to make demands for their children. Both mothers and fathers may derive a sense of power from being responsible for their children. Some adults have few opportunities to achieve power; control over children may give them their only experience of it.

Children can serve as sources of prestige and competitive advantage. Sometimes these are achieved by having many children—more than parents, brothers, or sisters had. As children grow, their achievements are sources of pride and can be compared with the achievements of children of friends and relatives. If children are valued only because of their objective achievements, they feel unimportant as individuals and the parent-child relationship is disrupted. Some children are pushed to live out the fantasies of their parents. The parent whose child does not comply with such wishes is disappointed with his own life and compounds his disappointment by diminishing the parent-child relationship.

If any of these reasons carry too heavy a weight in the decision to have children, difficulty in the parent-child relationship can occur. Yet all these motives are probably present, in varying degrees, in each family.

DECISION TO PARENT

Knowing the reasons for having children does not tell us about the process whereby parents decide to have a child. In their study of couples who had babies in their twenties, thirties, and forties, Pamela Daniels and Kathy Weingarten identified four different family-timing "scenarios."[23] About 40 percent of the sample believed in the "natural ideal": Parenthood was not a matter of thought; nature would take its course, and a child would come at the right time. A second cluster of parents, representing 29 percent of the sample, believed in "a brief wait" of two or three years

THE JOYS OF FAMILY GENERATIONS

"My mother died when my daughter was about two. My mother had saved my clothes from when I was a child, so it's fun for me to pass these things on to her and have her wear them and enjoy them. It was particularly nice to have the things because of my mother's death. It was a very great sadness not to have her here." MOTHER

"One of the nice things also, is being a part of the family, bringing her into the family and seeing all the grandparents and great-grandparents and the fuss they make over her." FATHER

"Carrying on tradition is something I like to do. My mother sewed my Halloween costumes for me and I do that for my daughter. I keep her costumes, and she talks about maybe her child wearing her costume. These are small things, but they give her a sense of tradition." MOTHER

"At her christening party, we had a tape recorder, and each guest taped a little message into the recorder. When she began to sing, she would sing into the recorder, and when her grandmother was alive, she sang the old Norwegian songs into the recorder so we have that on tape. And every year at various times, at birthdays or holidays, we would all talk into the tape recorder about what our lives had been like and what had gone on since the last time we did it. We have her singing 'Silent Night' with all the words wrong, and that has been a real thread. We have a sort of oral history, and it's a real pleasure for us." MOTHER

"Thomas Wolfe wrote *You Can't Go Home Again*, but James Agee said you do go home again in the lives of your children. It is a sort of reexperiencing what you experienced when you grew up—they're reading the same books you read, the conflicts they have are the ones you remember having with your parents, or issues

following marriage. Husband and wife could get to know each other and become established as a couple before having a baby. A third scenario was "programmatic postponement": About 20 percent of the couples postponed babies until very definite goals were accomplished—graduate school completed, career goals achieved. A fourth group of 8 percent had what was termed a "mixed script" in which husband and wife disagreed about the ideal timing. Finally, a small group of 3 percent had no idea whatsoever about parenthood and the timing of it.

These scripts suggest that most of the babies in the study were planned, but in fact only 38.9 percent of the couples made a deliberate decision to conceive at the time they did. Thirty-nine percent had unplanned pregnancies—28 percent because of ineffective use of contraceptives and 11 percent because of fertility problems. The remaining 22 percent had children without any planning one way or the other. All couples who had an unplanned child felt the nine months of pregnancy gave them an opportunity to come to terms with the baby and accept the child happily at birth. Of interest is the fact that only 5 percent of the couples found themselves unexpect-

that mattered to you as a child are issues for them. When you have time to reflect on them, they bring you back over and over again to issues in your own childhood that I guess you have a second opportunity to resolve. You have a different perspective on them than you did before." FATHER

"One of the interesting things was when we took our children back to Ohio, and before she could crawl, one used to scoot around on her rear end and tuck one knee under the other, and she wore out all the seats of her pants. Her great-grandmother was alive then and said, 'Oh, that is just the way her grandfather did it.' We never knew that and it was just amazing. One of our girls is so like her great-aunt who never had any children of her own and was such a lovely woman. It would have pleased her so much to see my daughter grow up. Our son looks like my father and is so much like him in every way. He has his build. My father always had a joke at dinner every night and our son has always loved jokes. As soon as he could read, he had joke book and was always telling us jokes at dinner. Our other son looks just exactly like his father and his grandfather." MOTHER

"One of my great joys was the first time my parents came to visit us, very proudly handing my son to my father and saying, 'Here's my boy!' That was a real highlight, a great thrill. I get choked up saying it now." FATHER

"I like having my family around. For the first time in my life, I want my mother to be here. There is a basic need to have your family around you. My husband's family and cousins are here, and I have a really strong urge to have everyone around. I was not really prepared for that." MOTHER

"Being a parent has helped me to see into myself. It's very illuminating in a personal way. It brings back a lot of memories, good and bad." FATHER

edly pregnant with their second child. Contraceptive use was more effective later in marriage.

Although most unplanned children are welcomed by the time of birth, actively unwanted children may have a more difficult time. A Swedish study of children whose mothers had requested but were denied abortions found that these unwanted children had more insecure childhoods, received more psychiatric treatment and more public assistance, engaged in more delinquent acts, and obtained less education than the wanted children with whom they were compared.[24]

Since many couples are postponing having children until they are in their thirties or forties, information on the effects of timing are important. Daniels and Weingarten found that although the number of problems parents experienced was about the same in early and late timing births, the content of the problems differed for the two groups. Those parents who had children quickly in their early twenties found themselves rearing children before they themselves had firm identities. They were less established in work roles and were generally less experienced out in the world. The partners had not had time to become thoroughly acquainted with each other and settled as a couple. This group was nurturing children before they felt mature; it had, however, less difficulty adjusting to the wife's role as mother and caregiver.

Late-timing couples had established themselves as individuals out in the world. They had work they enjoyed. They had time to focus on their relationship, to learn about each other's reactions, to establish routines of working together and accomplishing tasks. When the baby came, late-timing couples were ready to nourish new life, but they had difficulty with the disruption of their intimate connection and established ways of doing things.

Of interest is the authors' finding that many of the early-timing parents, if they had it to do all over again, would have postponed having children, whereas none of the late-timing parents would have had children earlier. Other studies support the view that when parents are older and more settled, they are frequently more attentive, more sensitive caretakers.[25] Nevertheless, Daniels and Weingarten conclude that parents' individual "readiness" to be parents is the critical factor. When individuals have a clear sense of who they are, what they like, how they relate to other people, when they can care for themselves and have established patterns of intimacy with the other parent, then they are ready to nourish new life.

Many parents may be uncertain whether they want to have children. Several books are available to help them make a decision. Judith Blackfield Cohen has written *Parenthood After Thirty? A Guide to Personal Choice,* focusing on the older parent.[26] The risks of later parenthood have decreased with greater medical knowledge, better care for the baby, and better health among older mothers. Cohen includes questionnaires and exercises to help parents focus their thinking and arrive at a decision about children.

Ellen Peck and William Granzig are authors of *The Parent Test: How to Measure and Develop Your Talent for Parenthood.*[27] They believe that every child should be planned carefully. In addition to reviewing reasons for wanting children, they present the problems of rearing children—the financial strains, the time pressures, the psychological stresses. They believe that our culture glamorizes parenting and that many people have children without really understanding what they are undertaking. These authors explore the resources, skills, interests, and motivations required for parenting, and they urge prospective parents to examine themselves to determine if they possess these qualities.

All parents need good health, psychological stability, and adequate financial resources. Peck and Granzig suggest that parents also need patience, flexibility, independence, generosity, an optimistic outlook, and a sense of humor. Will a couple mind the routines, the repetitions of rules, stories, and directions, and the frustrations of dealing with children? Will they be selfless enough to subordinate their own needs and desires to those of their children? Will they be able to care for sick children, settle disputes between siblings, teach their youngsters how to fly a kite or to value beauty and friendships? If they do not have these qualities, are they willing to develop them?

Peck and Granzig have suggestions about ways to develop interests and qualities related to successful parenting. Parents can develop knowledge and interest in children by babysitting with the children of friends, by volunteering time to recreational projects for children, by joining Big Brothers or Big Sisters, or by becoming foster parents. A couple can begin to create a lifestyle that would enhance the lives of children, perhaps by moving to an area where they would like to raise children and by saving money. They can imagine how their lives would change concretely if they had children and make some changes in the present. All these activities would help a couple see whether parenthood would be an enjoyable activity even if their scores on the tests were low. In fact, with these life changes, the scores would change, too.

Marilyn Fabe and Norma Wikler describe four factors that affect how a working mother will adapt to children: (1) the demands of her work, (2) her attitudes about her job, (3) her use of childcare, and (4) her personal reaction to motherhood.[28] Women whose jobs permitted flexibility in determining a work schedule, who could take leaves or could work part time, had an easier time adjusting to the demands of motherhood. These women, however, had to modify their attitudes toward work so that they could feel satisfied with a decreasing commitment to it, at least while their children were very young. Women who had access to good childcare, whose husbands participated in parenting, and who felt comfortable relying on others to help in caring for their children made an easier transition to parenthood. Finally, women who most wanted to have children enjoyed them the most.

Fabe and Wikler devote a significant section of their book to single women who became mothers. The success of these mothers depended in large part on their ability to build a support system that enabled them successfully to combine work and rearing children. Some lived in communes, others were able to gather support from friends and family. Although these women clearly made sacrifices to have children, they felt the rewards more than compensated for the difficulties. Some of the women worried about the effects of father-absence on their children, but most believed that the love and care of a single parent were beneficial and equal to the care provided by many divorcing families.

Most of the women who did not have children had arrived at this decision gradually. The primary reason for not having children was that the women had evolved a happy, satisfying life that included a strong commitment to work and relationships, and they did not feel the need for children. Their decisions, however, seem in part to be influenced by earlier events. Many reported difficult relationships with their own families in childhood, problems they did not want to duplicate. These women nurtured and guided people in other ways and felt they were satisfying the need to be generative through these activities.

Elizabeth Whelan suggests guidelines similar to those of Peck and Granzig for making the decision to parent or not to parent.[29] Whelan, however, stresses the very personal nature of the decision. She encourages parents to talk to older parents with similar interests, to determine their satisfactions with having children. She suggests that this should be a personal decision, rather than one based on test scores. While it is important to be aware of the problems children bring, couples must also think of the pleasures, which cannot be experienced in advance as easily as the limitations. The cuddling, hugging, loving; the warm sense of community with other people and other families; the pleasure and closeness that comes with watching children grow; the possibility of mastering upsetting experiences of our own—all these sensations are hard to duplicate in experiences with other people's children.

All the books concerning the decision to parent suggest that couples and individuals will be best prepared to make decisions about children if they (1) learn exactly what childrearing involves, (2) examine their own interests and their motivations for having children, (3) plan how they will modify their work commitments and interpersonal relations to include a child, and (4) consider relying on help from partners, childcare providers, and a support system.

All books comment on the gradual nature of the decision not to have children. One social scientist describes a four-step sequence often mentioned in the interviews presented in the books: (1) postponing children for a definite period, (2) postponing children for an indefinite period, (3) considering the possibility of not having children, and (4) making a definite decision not to have children.[30] Some women know from an early age that they do not want children, but most report going through a sequence similar to that just described.

These books say little about health as a factor in the decision. Peck and Granzig mention energy level as a prerequisite for rearing children. Many physical conditions, however, particularly if the mother has them, will result in making a decision not to have children. Women with diabetes and hypertension may want to have children but will time their pregnancies so their health is at its best. Family history of genetic diseases like Tay-Sachs disease (which results in the early and difficult death of the child) or osteogenesis imperfecta ("brittle bone" disease, which results in many breaks and early death) will be a factor in the decision. Genetic counseling can help couples who have a history of such problems to obtain information and to sort out their feelings about the information.

TEENAGE PARENTS

Although planning for parenthood has become easier in the second half of this century, the problem of unplanned teenage pregnancy has increased. In 1986, teenage mothers had about 500,000 babies; and while the number of babies is decreasing among older teens, it is increasing among children fourteen and under.[31] Approximately 60 percent of these children are born to unwed black and white mothers—a dramatic increase from the comparable figure of 15 percent in 1960. The large majority of these births are unplanned and unwanted. Further, a pattern of generational continuity is developing in which 60 percent of teenage mothers are themselves the products of teenage pregnancies.

Teenage mothers become parents under difficult conditions. Because they frequently do not get good prenatal care and are physically less mature, teenage mothers suffer more pregnancy complications and more often have babies with problems. Prematurity and low birth weight—which increase the likelihood of cerebral palsy, mental retardation, and epilepsy—occur most frequently in the babies of teenage mothers.

In addition, because teenage mothers frequently do not stay in school and complete their education, they have limited job opportunities. Many work in low-paying jobs without a chance for advancement in order to support their child. It is not surprising, then, that a large percentage of single, teenage mothers live in poverty.

The psychological immaturity of these mothers poorly prepares them to care for young children. Observers find that when their children are infants, young mothers prematurely foster independence, pushing children to hold their own bottles, sit up too early, and scramble for toys before they really can get them.[32] These mothers often tease their children as well. As infants become toddlers, however, these mothers reverse their behavior and try to control children, not letting them explore freely, not giving them choices in activities and toys.

The children may have strengths that buffer them in the situation—intelligence, adaptive temperamental qualities, the ability to cooperate with the parent easily, the ability to soothe themselves. And the mothers may find strengths that help them become good parents—emotional availability and responsivity to the child, the ability to form goals for the future and to use community resources to obtain goals.

Two kinds of programs attack the problems of teenage pregnancies: (1) those that postpone the birth of the first child by means of effective education and birth control and (2) those that help mothers once they have had children. Both programs emphasize effective birth control at the same time that teens are encouraged to develop a sense of confidence about their ability to make and carry out future goals for themselves.

TRANSITION AND ADJUSTMENT TO PARENTHOOD

The arrival of a baby changes every aspect of married life, from finances to sex life, sleeping habits, and social life. The positive changes—having a baby to love, feeling closer to the other parent, sharing the joys of the child's growth—are easy to incorporate. The negative changes require adaptation. Although many first-time parents report that nothing could have adequately prepared them for the experience, knowing what to expect in advance can still help parents cope.

We know little about how people cope with learning to be a parent and incorporating this role in their lives. Alice Rossi, a sociologist, outlines four stages in the development of the role of parent, and compares this role with two other major social roles—the marital role and the work role.[33] The four stages of a role cycle are (1) the anticipatory stage, (2) the honeymoon stage, (3) the plateau stage, and (4) the disengagement and termination stage.

During the anticipatory stage, the individual obtains training and becomes socialized to the role. For the marital role, the anticipatory stage is the engagement period. For the parental role, it is the months of pregnancy. For the work role, it is the learning, direct training, and apprenticeship period.

The honeymoon stage begins as soon as the role is assumed—just after marriage, just after the baby is born, just after the work has begun. Rossi compares the marital role with the parental role. She points out that in the parental role, a great deal of learning and adjusting occurs in the honeymoon period, but in the marital role much of the adjusting is completed during the anticipatory stage. You marry someone you know and understand, and many problems can be worked out during the engagement.

INTERVIEW
with Jay Belsky

Jay Belsky is Professor of Human Development at The Pennsylvania State University in College Park. He is the initiator and director of the Pennsylvania Infant and Family Development Project, an ongoing study of 250 firstborn children whose parents were enrolled for study when the mothers were pregnant in 1981.

What leads to improvement in the marriage after the birth of the baby?

Husbands and wives who are more educated and are older at the time they have their baby seem to do better. They have been married longer, and they have more family competence. Personality features of the parents also are related to improving—these include both husbands' and wives' self-esteem and, not surprisingly from our standpoint, what we call their interpersonal sensitivity, the degree to which they are tuned in to the emotions and feelings of others. It is easy to understand why that would buffer a marriage from deteriorating.

There are some risks associated with being too romantic, naively romantic, preceding the baby's birth, and this may reflect the fact that the couple isn't really being realistic about what being a parent is all about. These are the things we see playing a role before the baby is born.

Most of the infant data show a positive relationship; that is good marriages go with more sensitive parenting.

The plateau stage is the long middle period during which the role is carried out. In marriage, it is the years after the couple have adjusted to each other and have made a strong commitment to the marriage. In parenting, it is the period of rearing the children. And in work, it is the years of continuous occupation.

The disengagement and termination stage occurs when a role ends. In the marital role, this occurs just before a divorce or at the time of a death. In the parenting role, some adults consider it occurs when the children are fully grown and married. As one psychologist remarked, however, "Parenthood is a life sentence." If you remain active and available to your children, they may see you as a parent until you die. In the work role, this stage occurs at retirement.

Rossi points out that, until recently, there has been less conscious choice in taking on the parenting role than the marital or work roles. There are many more accidental pregnancies than there are accidental marriages or accidental careers. She examines marital relationships and points out that as long as a couple has no children and both husband and wife are working, there may be few adjustments for the couple to make. The patterns of interaction may be similar before and after marriage. In our present society the major changes in the couple's relationship come with the arrival of the first child. Thus, two major adjustments—readjustments to each other and adjustment to the infant—are made at the same time, and this makes parenthood harder.

Rossi uses the concepts of instrumentality and expressiveness to deepen our understanding of the parenting roles of men and women. **Instrumentality** refers to doing, producing, and accomplishing in an efficient way. **Expressiveness** refers to nurturance, interpersonal relatedness, harmony between people, or expression of affect toward others. Professionals have looked at families and labeled the husband/father the instrumental person because he has gone out and earned the paycheck, managed finances, developed ties with the rest of the community, and set long-term family goals. He has been a doer. The wife/mother has been considered the expressive person—the heart of the family—because she has been concerned with everyone's feelings and making sure family life runs smoothly and harmoniously. She has nurtured children and established many of the family's interpersonal ties.

As parents, both men and women must be both assertive and accommodating, both instrumental and expressive. Adults who have not developed both aspects of their personalities find that, as parents, they need to do so.

The mother's adjustment to pregnancy, birth, childcare in the first year, and the baby's functioning is predicted from her adaptation to the pregnancy itself.[34] Women who feel positive about the pregnancy, who envision themselves as confident mothers, do indeed adjust more easily to being a mother. Further, their babies seem more competent in social, motor, and cognitive skills. What predicts the mother's positive view of pregnancy? According to current research, in the main it is her own experiences with her parents as she was growing up. These relationships are not absolutely fixed; a woman who had a difficult time as a child will not necessarily be destined to repeat it. Many parents make strong, successful efforts to avoid repeating and passing on parenting behaviors they experienced as children. They feel satisfaction and pleasure at creating the family they would like to have had when they were children. Information on child growth and development and strategies for establishing relationships and positive behavior provide tools for interrupting a negative cycle that began in childhood.

Couples making the transition to parenthood sometimes experience a decline in marital satisfaction just before and after the birth of the baby. A honeymoon period occurs around the birth of the baby but it is short-lived.[35]

While parenthood is thought to cause this decline, couples without children experience a similar decline in marital satisfaction in the same time period.[36] Parenthood does not cause the decline, but it does change a couple's activities together. Following the birth, parents, in fact, spend more time together, but the time is spent on household chores and childcare. Though they have as much recreational time together as nonparents do, this time, too, is child-oriented. Women carry the major responsibility for these new activities, but in dual-earner families, husbands take on some as well. Both husbands' and wives' sex role attitudes change as they shift their activities in a more traditional direction.

Despite all these changes in their lives, parents do not differ from nonparents in their love for their partner or their overall satisfaction with the marriage even a year after the birth. Some couples reported their marriage improved after the birth. It became a shared partnership, with more working together to accomplish tasks.

This baby is likely to be more competent in social, motor, and cognitive skills if her mother felt positive about the pregnancy and her potential to be a good mother.

The most dissatisfied parents are those whose sex role attitudes do not match what they are doing. Men with traditional attitudes who do more childcare and household tasks than they want to do report more dissatisfaction. Women with traditional sex role attitudes who share more tasks and are less traditional than they want to be, are more dissatisfied in the marriage.

Parenthood brings new responsibilities that require changes in attitudes and negotiation, and so couples evolve household and childcare routines that fit their personal values and interests.

THE JOYS OF PARENTING

We have discussed the strains and changes that parenting creates but have made little mention of the many joys that children bring to their parents' lives. In a remarkable study forty years ago, Jersild and his co-workers interviewed 544 parents about the joys and problems of childrearing. They introduced the book with the following comments:

> There has been relatively little systematic study of the cheerful side of the ledger of child-rearing. Studies of characteristics that bring headaches to a parent have not been matched by surveys of characteristics that warm a parent's heart. . . . The fact that the emphasis has been so much on the negative side is perhaps no more than one should expect. Behavior that is disturbing to the parent or to others usually calls for action or for a solution of some sort, and as such it also attracts the research worker. On the other hand, what is pleasant can be enjoyed without further ado.[37]

What did Jersild and his group find when they talked to parents? They learned, that by and large parents experienced many more joys than difficulties, though the latter certainly existed. They found that children bring what parents hope they will—affection, companionship, enjoyment of the child as a special person, and delight in development and increasing competence. Jersild et al. conclude about parenthood, "Perhaps no other circumstance in life offers so many challenges to an individual's powers, so great an array of opportunities for appreciation, such a varied emotional and intellectual stimulation."[38]

In this book we will describe the many joys parents report with children of different ages, emphasizing the "cheerful side of the ledger."

MAJOR POINTS OF CHAPTER 1

Parenting is:

- nourishing, guiding, protecting children as they grow
- a process of interaction between parent and child
- a role with two major tasks of establishing warm relationships and providing limits
- an activity usually occurring in family settings

Social changes affecting family settings are:

- more effective contraception, leading to later marriage
- population control, leading to smaller families
- women's increasing commitment to work, leading to new roles for mothers and new adults in child's life
- rise in rates of divorce and remarriage, leading to changes in family living and new adults
- rise in ethnic population, leading to greater diversity in family traditions and values
- rise in poverty, leading to more stressful lives for children

People's reasons for wanting children include:

- love and affection
- stimulation
- creative outlet
- proof of adulthood
- sense of achievement
- proof of moral behavior
- economic utility
- power

Decision for parenthood involves:

- assessing parental readiness in terms of time, money, and psychological resources
- planning/not planning pregnancy—most unplanned children are wanted by the time of birth
- timing of the pregnancy—early versus late
- possibly going through stages of deciding not to have children—temporary and indefinite postponement, considering having no children, and final decision

Transition to parenthood includes:

- four stages: anticipatory, honeymoon, plateau, and termination
- less conscious choice than in work or marital roles and less possibility for divorce or termination of role
- men and women's becoming both instrumentally competent and emotionally expressive

Changes in couple's relationship after parenthood are:

- not necessarily the cause of marital decline
- in kinds of activities together, not amount of time
- manageable when parents establish routines acceptable to both and feel pleasure in their accomplishments

Joys of parenting are:

- available to all parents regardless of experience with own parents
- in large part what parents hoped they would be

ADDITIONAL READINGS

Brazelton, T. Berry. *Families: Crisis and Caring.* New York: Ballantine, 1989.
Cohen, Judith B. *Parenthood after 30? A Guide to Personal Choice.* Lexington, Mass.: D. C. Heath, 1985.

Curran, Dolores. *Stress and the Healthy Family.* Minneapolis: Winston, 1985.

Daniels, Pamela, and Weingarten, Kathy. *Sooner or Later: The Timing of Parenthood in Adult Lives.* New York: W. W. Norton, 1983.

Erikson, Erik H. *Childhood and Society.* 2nd ed. New York: W. W. Norton, 1963.

Notes

1. Lynn Smith and Bob Spichen, "Workers Crave Time with Kids," *San Francisco Chronicle,* August 13, 1990.
2. David Gutmann, "Parenthood: A Key to the Comparative Study of the Life Cycle," pp. 167–184 in *Life-Span Developmental Psychology: Normative Life Crises,* eds. Nancy Daton and Leon H. Ginsberg (New York: Academic Press, 1975), p. 170.
3. Saul L. Brown, "Functions, Tasks and Stresses of Parenting: Implications for Guidance," in *Helping Parents Help Their Children,* ed. L. Eugene Arnold (New York: Brunner/Mazel, 1978), pp. 22–34.
4. U.S. Bureau of the Census, *Statistical Abstract of the United States: 1989,* 109th ed. (Washington, D.C.: U.S. Government Printing Office, 1989).
5. Ibid.
6. Ibid.
7. Algea Harrison, Felicisima Serafica, and Harriette McAdoo, "Ethnic Families of Color," in *A Review of Child Development Research,* vol. 7, ed. Ross D. Parke (Chicago: University of Chicago Press, 1984), pp. 329–371.
8. Margaret Beale Spencer, "Development of Minority Children: An Introduction," *Child Development* 61 (1990): 267–269.
9. "Special Issue on Minority Children," *Child Development* 61 (1990): 263–589.
10. Algea O. Harrison, Melvin N. Wilson, Charles J. Pine, Samuel Q. Chan, and Raymond Buriel, "Family Ecologies of Ethnic Minority Children," *Child Development* 61 (1990): 347–362.
11. Ibid.
12. Diana Baumrind, "Subcultural Variations in Values Defining Social Competence," Society for Research in Child Development, *Papers presented at Western Regional Conference,* April 1976, p. 26.
13. Jeannie Gutierrez and Arnold Sameroff, "Determinants of Complexity in Mexican-American and Anglo-American Mothers' Conceptions of Child Development," *Child Development* 61 (1990): 384–394.
14. "Child Poverty 'Tragedy' for U.S.," *San Francisco Chronicle,* April 27, 1990.
15. Vonnie C. McLoyd, "The Impact of Economic Hardship on Black Families and Children: Psychological Distress, Parenting, and Socioemotional Development," *Child Development* 61 (1990): 311–346.
16. U.S. Bureau of the Census, *Statistical Abstract of the United States: 1989.*
17. Daniel Yankelovich, *New Rules: Searching for Self-Fulfillment in a World Turned Upside Down* (New York: Random House, 1981).
18. Alice S. Rossi, "Parenthood in Transition: From Lineage to Child to Self-Orientation," in *Parenting Across The Life Span: Biosocial Dimensions,* eds. Jane B. Lancaster, Jeanne Altmann, Alice S. Rossi, and Lonnie R. Sherrod (New York: Aldine de Gruyter, 1987), pp. 31–84.
19. Yankelovich, *New Rules,* p. 104.
20. Erik H. Erikson, *Childhood and Society,* 2nd ed. (New York: W. W. Norton, 1963).
21. Lois Wladis Hoffman and Jean Denby Manis, "The Value of Children in the United States: A New Approach to the Study of Fertility," *Journal of Marriage and the Family* 41 (1979): 583–596.
22. Caroline Bird, *The Two-Paycheck Marriage* (New York: Rawson Wade, 1979).
23. Pamela Daniels and Kathy Weingarten, *Sooner or Later: The Timing of Parenthood in Adult Lives* (New York: W. W. Norton, 1983).
24. Hans Forssman and Inga Thuwe, "One Hundred and Twenty Children Born after Application for Therapeutic Abortion Refused," *Acta Psychiatrica Scandinavia* 42 (1966): 71–88.
25. Arlene S. Ragozin, Robert B. Basham, Keith A. Crine, Mark T. Greenberg, and Nancy M. Robinson, "Effects of Maternal Age on Parenting Role," *Developmental Psychology* 18 (1982): 627–634.
26. Judith Blackfield Cohen, *Parenthood After 30? A Guide to Personal Choice* (Lexington, Mass.: D. C. Heath, 1985).

27. Ellen Peck and William Granzig, *The Parent Test: How to Measure and Develop Your Talent for Parenthood* (New York: G. P. Putnam's Sons, 1978).

28. Marilyn Fabe and Norma Wikler, *Up Against the Clock* (New York: Random House, 1979).

29. Elizabeth M. Whelan, *A Baby? . . . Maybe* (New York: Bobbs-Merrill, 1975).

30. Jean E. Veevers, "Voluntarily Childless Wives: An Exploratory Study," *Mental Health Digest* 5 (1973): 8–11.

31. Joy D. Osofsky, "Risk and Protective Factors for Teenage Mothers and Their Infants," *Newsletter of the Society for Research in Child Development,* Winter 1990.

32. Ibid.

33. Alice S. Rossi, "Transition to Parenthood," *Journal of Marriage and the Family* 30 (1968): 26–39.

34. Eleanor E. Maccoby and John A. Martin, "Socialization in the Context of the Family: Parent-Child Interaction," in *Handbook of Child Psychology,* eds. Paul H. Mussen and E. Mavis Hetherington, vol. 4: *Socialization, Personality and Social Development,* 4th ed. (New York: John Wiley, 1983), pp. 1–101.

35. Jay Belsky, Graham B. Spanier, and Michael Rovine, "Stability and Change in Marriage Across the Transition to Parenthood," *Journal of Marriage and the Family* 45 (1983): 567–577.

36. Shelley M. McDermid, Ted L. Huston, and Susan M. McHale, "Changes in Marriage Associated with the Transition to Parenthood: Individual Differences as a Function of Sex Role Attitudes and Changes in Division of Household Labor," *Journal of Marriage and the Family,* 52 (1990): 475–486.

37. Arthur T. Jersild, Ella S. Woodyard, and Charlotte del Solar, in collaboration with Ernest G. Osborne and Robert C. Challman, *Joys and Problems of Child Rearing* (New York: Bureau of Publications, Teachers College, Columbia University, 1949), pp. 1–2.

38. Ibid., p. 122.

PARENTING IS A PROCESS

CHAPTER 2

We will now focus on the process of parenting—what the participants bring to the process, how they affect each other, and what goals they strive for. Parenting is a process of interaction between parent and child. As the parent nourishes, supports, guides the child to maturity, both parent and child are changed, and that change in turn transforms the interaction between the two. Take Jody, for example—an active, curious, sixteen-month-old boy. Jody was always alert and busy, but when he began to walk and climb on furniture, his horizons expanded alarmingly. He was into everything. His mother had to give him more restrictions, say "no" more often. She lost patience with him, feeling inadequate as a mother because she could not control his behavior as well as she had in the past; when he would not listen to her, she became even more irritated. Jody cried when he couldn't climb on the table or go out as he pleased. He also cried when his mother was upset with him. Feeling guilty because he was unhappy and uncertain of what rules were realistic, his mother abandoned her restrictions. Jody became more self-determined when he saw he could get his mother to change her mind. The relationship between the two became more negative as each reacted to the behavior of the other. To make positive changes, the mother first examined her own expectations of Jody and of herself. She realized he was a small child with a high energy level and needed structure and firmness to learn very gradually how to control himself. As she became more confident in what she was doing and less frustrated with Jody, he came happier. There was little yelling and the rules were consistent so he could gradually master them. As his behavior improved, his mother in turn felt more relaxed and competent. So a positive pattern of interaction came to replace the negative one.

THE ROLE OF PARENTS

Parenting has not always been considered a process of interaction between child and parent. The role and function of a parent has changed from one generation to the next.[1] Understanding the changes serves as a starting point for understanding the role of parent in our society today. In Europe there was no concept of childhood until about the seventeenth century. If children survived infancy, they were treated as adults. They wore adult clothes, played adult games, and went off to work when they reached the age of seven or eight. Apprenticeship was the only form of schooling. Sometime in the seventeenth century there was a change, perhaps because of a decline in infant mortality, and families became closer and more concerned about the welfare of the children.

Until late in the nineteenth century, parents were most concerned about the physical survival of their children rather than about effective parenting. And even children who survived infancy could still succumb to disease at any time. Because of their precarious hold on physical life, there was great concern about the moral state of the infant and child. The doctrine of original sin suggested an evil nature that had to be subdued quickly. Parents were strict and punished the child for his or her own good.

During the early years of the twentieth century, this notion of an evil child was changed by the early behaviorists, particularly John B. Watson, a psychologist of the 1920s. He believed, as did many psychologists, that children are "blank slates" who need to learn good habits. The behaviorists stressed the importance of parenting in determining how children would develop emotionally and intellectually. Watson wrote:

> There is a sensible way of treating children. Treat them as though they were young adults. Dress them, bathe them with care and circumspection. Let your behavior always be objective and kindly firm. Never hug and kiss them, never let them sit on your lap. If you must, kiss them once on the forehead when they say good night. Shake hands with them in the morning. Give them a pat on the head if they have made an extraordinarily good job of a difficult task. Try it out. In a week's time you will find how easy it is to be perfectly objective with your child and at the same time kindly. You will be utterly ashamed of the mawkish, sentimental way you have been handling it.[2]

Although this advice now seems extreme and even absurd, it is hard to exaggerate the impact the behaviorists had, here and in England. Mothers refused to feed their children even a few minutes before the end of the prescribed 4-hour period and were afraid to hold and cuddle their babies. They were told that adherence to rigid rules was necessary if their children were not to go astray later in life.

In the 1930s and 1940s, two trends led away from such strict habit training. Drawing on Freud's insights, psychologists began to urge parents to relax and permit children to grow without frustrations and repression of impulses. Parents were encouraged to be lenient and understanding so that internal conflicts and neurotic symptoms would not develop. At the same time Arnold Gesell was publishing norms of infant and child development. On the basis of observations of healthy, upper middle-class children, Gesell concluded that the patterns for healthy growth were within the child and that, if the parents would relax, growth would occur naturally. Both Freud and Gesell stressed the importance of the natural child with natural impulses, a child who needed to be understood and gratified in certain ways. These views, in contrast with the rigid habit training of Watson, provided a welcome emphasis on the needs of the child.

In recent years we have moved away from these frameworks, for two reasons. First, research has shown that children need limits and more interference with their natural impulses than psychoanalysts in the 1930s and 1940s considered wise. We now believe that excessive parental permissiveness can create an intolerable child and that such a child will be unhappy. Second, Gesell's emphasis on the growth process underemphasized the importance of the environment and of the parents in child-rearing. Studies of children from all socioeconomic levels reveal that the environment can help or hinder the growth process within each child. If environmental factors prevent appropriate timing and sequencing of behavior development, some behaviors may never develop.

Three current developments in psychology have again altered our view of the nature of the child and the role of the parents. Jean Piaget, a Swiss psychologist, describes the many differences between a child's thinking and an adult's logic.[3] He emphasizes that children construct a view of the world based on their own experience with people and objects in the environment. Children must act in order to develop. They are curious investigators who adapt their thinking to fit their experiences, but at the same time interpret their experiences in terms of their own way of looking at the world. Piaget asserts that children proceed through a predictable series of stages of cognitive development. Parents can provide experiences and opportunities that will enable children to develop a complex view of the world.

The ethological perspective in psychology has also become an important influence in the past twenty years. Ethologists study human behavior in terms of its adaptive qualities. They are concerned with behaviors that may be built into the organism but that require environmental stimulation to develop fully. Critical periods of growth are studied to determine what happens if the environment does not permit behavior to develop. Ethologists believe that children have enormous potential and that a stimulating environment is needed if children's capacities and abilities are to develop. That environment must include people who provide the emotional bonds and the environmental experiences that trigger and nourish the child's growth.

The most recent perspective is the interactional model of growth. It emphasizes that development results from the interplay between the child and the environment. The interaction changes both contributors, resulting in turn in a new form of behavior. The environment includes not only people like parents, but other features as well. It includes geographic location. City and rural children grow up differently. The environment includes the social status of the family—the amount of money available, the physical living conditions, the values parents have. It includes ethnic background. For some children, the ethnic cultural background of their parents and grandparents has little impact on everyday life; for others, it is an important feature. Children who look different or whose behavior is different from the norm may be treated differently. The child's environment also includes school. Children spend approximately 1,000 hours a year in school once they go into first grade. The friends they meet there and the teachers they have are strong influences not only on academic learning, but also on their feelings of confidence and self-esteem. Television, a powerful agent in a child's life, makes its first appearance early in infancy and toddlerhood and is present for several hours a day thereafter.

Finally, the environment includes what we might term the "accidents" of life, events that have a strong impact on a person's life but are not under anyone's control. Natural events such as hurricanes, earthquakes, and floods can change a child's way of life overnight. Illness—of the child or other family member—changes everyone involved. Economic hardship, whether experienced on a personal level or on a broad scale, has profound effects.

In describing a process model of parenting, Jay Belsky lists three major influences on parenting: (1) the child's characteristics and individuality, (2) the parents' personal history and psychological resources, and (3) the context of stresses and supports in the parents' lives.[4] Since we have already focused on some of them, let us discuss general stresses and supports first and then examine what the child and the parent bring to the parenting process.

CONTEXT OF STRESSES AND SUPPORTS

Parenting occurs in a social context that can provide either support or stress for parents. Major sources of stress/support are the marriage, parents' social network, and work. Evidence from many different studies links the parental competence of both mother and father with the quality of the marriage. Parents who feel support from each other are sensitive, accepting, and responsive with children; conversely, parents who are unhappy with each other are nagging, critical, and restrictive with their children.

Support from friends who are compatible and accepting contributes to parental competence and well-being. Social isolation is linked with parental difficulties, as with, for example, child abuse. Work, too, influences parenting both in amount of time available for parenting and in childrearing values. Maternal employment influences family organization and parental activity. When mothers have positive attitudes toward work, they experience fewer problems in rearing children.

Economic hardship has major effects on parenting. Vonnie McLoyd has developed a model of how poverty and economic loss affect parenting behaviors and, in turn, children.[5] Poverty is accompanied by many day-to-day problems that create psychological distress for parents (see Figure 2-1). McLoyd presents statistics showing that psychological distress follows poverty rather than produces it. Parents under stress are less likely to support each other, are more irritable with children, and give them less affection. As a result, children suffer more emotional problems.

Recent research supports McLoyd's model and suggests that income level is a more powerful predictor of children's functioning than being a minority group member or living in a single-parent household.[6] Poverty, however, is linked with racial background—as we noted in Chapter 1, more Afro-American children are poor—and with living in a single-parent household. Research suggests it is poverty that accounts for many differences in functioning between white and Afro-American children. Support for people under stress from economic hardship can be achieved through a concerted societal effort to institute both public and private programs to reduce poverty.

Being a member of an ethnic minority group presents both parents and children

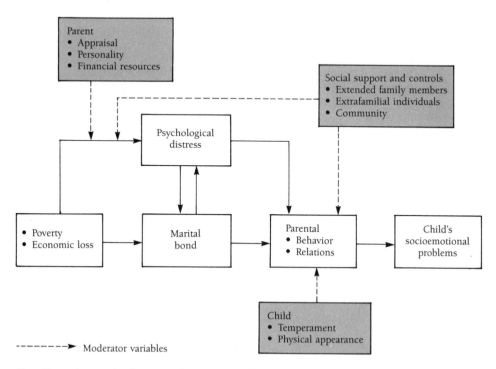

From Vonnie C. McLoyd, "The Impact of Economic Hardship on Black Families and Children: Psychological Distress, Parenting, and Socioemotional Development," *Child Development* 61 (1990): 311–346.

with the additional stress of adapting to two cultures at the same time. At times the stress may be minimal because the values, language, and color of the group are similar to that of the majority group, and individuals are easily integrated. When ethnic minority group members are discriminated against and prevented from full participation in society, then the stress is a major one. Both parents and children suffer the effects of discrimination. At the same time, they must find ways to reaffirm their own values and talents when surrounded by people who devalue them. Supports come from within the ethnic culture. An emphasis on family interdependence, strong support from friends, flexibility in taking on roles, and valuing a bicultural orientation are all helpful to individuals in this situation.[7]

Systems of support increase parental feelings of love and acceptance and provide direct assistance and guidance. Support from family and friends reduces parental stress. Children's well-being depends on our society's making changes to provide more support for parents and children.

WHAT THE CHILD BRINGS TO THE PROCESS OF PARENTING

Even as newborns, children bring individual temperamental qualities (inborn characteristic ways of reacting to the world) to the parent-child relationship. These qualities, described more fully in Chapter 6, include activity level, positive/negative mood, and approach or avoidance of new stimuli. Children also bring their own rates and patterns of growth to the parenting process. Some children are taller, heavier, quicker to develop characteristics of their age. Others of equal skill are slower, and this characteristic is very noticeable in the early years. As children grow older, they show individual differences in style and speed of doing many things—learning in school, making friends, developing skills and interests.

A child is also born with a certain position in the family—first born, middle child, last born. Birth order in turn affects the parenting process. Parents will not be as experienced with their firstborn, though initially they will have more time to spend with this child. Later borns only know family life with brothers and sisters.

The child's sex is a significant contributor to the parenting process. We know the first question asked after birth is, "Is it a boy or a girl?" Nowadays parents try to rear children with equal opportunities for experience. They want boys to be independent and self-sufficient, but also to be loving and kind with others, to be able to express their tender feelings, their empathy or sorrow at the distress of others. They want girls to be independent, self-motivated people who are also caring and kind to others.

To repeat, the child comes with his or her own temperament, patterns of growth, birth order position, and sexual gender. All these qualities affect the process of parenting.

WHAT THE PARENT BRINGS TO THE PROCESS OF PARENTING

Parents have a longer history in this world than their offspring; they bring a complex personality history and set of expectations to the process of parenting that children do not have.

Personality and Personal History

Parents, of course, have their own temperamental qualities in addition to a host of life experiences that influence the process. They also live in a specific social niche that influences the process. Parents are settled in a marriage or a stable relationship, in a work setting, in a social network with relatives and friends, all of which provide varying degrees of satisfaction. When parents feel support from each other, when they are economically and psychologically ready to have a child, the process of parenting begins on a positive note.

Parents also bring their gender to parenting. For many years psychologists focused primarily on the mother-child relationship because it was the mother who had the greatest contact with children. Only recently have they begun to observe the father-child relationship in greater detail. Findings indicate, as will be seen in later chapters, that there are differences in the ways mothers and fathers relate to children,

Parental concern and acceptance are essential ingredients in children's lives, but love must be translated into sensitive caretaking. Parents under stress from conflicts between parenting duties and personal routines do affect a baby's emotional well-being.

even when both are with the child about equal amounts of time and both have equally strong attachments to the children.

As noted in Chapter 1, parents are influenced by experiences with their own parents when they were growing up. Parents with positive experiences look forward to parenthood with confidence in their own abilities. When experiences have been difficult, parents may have trouble in precisely those problem areas as they rear their own children.

The relationship between childhood experience and adult parenting behavior is complex, however. Parents carry with them relationship histories that may be expressed in different ways with different children. The study of an unusual kind of parent-child interaction highlights this complexity. Researchers have identified "seductive" behavior on the part of mothers interacting with their toddler sons.[8]

Seductive mothers sought physical contact with the children to satisfy their own needs rather than the child's. For example, they stroked the child or squeezed the buttocks, or they engaged in sensual teasing, promising physical affection if only the child would obey. These behaviors were termed seductive because they were not in response to the child's request or need for affection, and they engaged the child in behavior that was overly stimulating. With their daughters, however, these mothers were physically aloof, hostile, rejecting, critical. These patterns make sense when one learns that almost half the seductive mothers had been sexually abused as children. Inappropriately involved physically with fathers, feeling rejected by mothers, they expressed their own relationship histories in one way with their sons and another way with their daughters.

Parents may worry if they read statements connecting childhood experiences with later adult parenting. Most parents want a fresh start with their children. They do not want to feel doomed to poor parenting by events of their own past lives. And, in fact, they are not doomed to poor parenting. Recent research reveals that parents who come to terms with their own negative childhood experiences do not repeat the unhappy interactions with their children.[9] Mothers and fathers who understand and accept their feelings that their own parents could not give them what they wanted are able to create new kinds of relationships with their sons and daughters. Parents who describe difficult times but deny any emotional reaction like anger, sadness, or frustration in response to their parents are those most likely to carry over negative patterns in their day-to-day contact because they have not worked through their feelings about their childhood.

When parents have strong feelings of dislike about some feature of their childhood and find themselves acting the same as their parents did or having trouble in the same area, they can take action. Talking to friends or relatives who also have children and know the parents' children can give a fresh view on what is happening. Sometimes just the opportunity to air feelings makes a parent feel better and return to deal with the problem more effectively. Joining a parent group, hearing the problems and views of others, can give a more balanced perspective on childrearing issues. It also helps to know that other parents have similar concerns.

As parents become more aware of childhood experiences that were full of conflict, they can take action to change the relationships. In *Making Peace with Your Own Parents,* psychiatrist Harold Bloomfield and psychologist Leonard Felder describe a variety of techniques they present in workshops.[10] Exercises and personal growth skills help individuals master the conflicted feelings and create satisfying relationships with parents. The exercises focus on becoming aware of hidden feelings, particularly buried resentments, and then learning to heal the hurts. People learn to forgive their parents for not being what they wanted them to be. Adults are then free to discover and appreciate their parents' unique qualities. Increasing communication skills makes possible a more satisfying give-and-take in current relationships with parents.

Bloomfield and Felder emphasize that creating new relationships with parents requires self-observation, awareness of others' behavior, and much practice in changing behavior patterns. Changes in parenting require the same persistence and effort as that required to master a new sport, and the effort is worth it. People who are distant and alienated from their own parents are more likely to take on their parents' negative qualities and hence are more likely to repeat the behavior they so disliked.[11]

FIGURE 2-2
A dynamic, interactional model of child and parent development

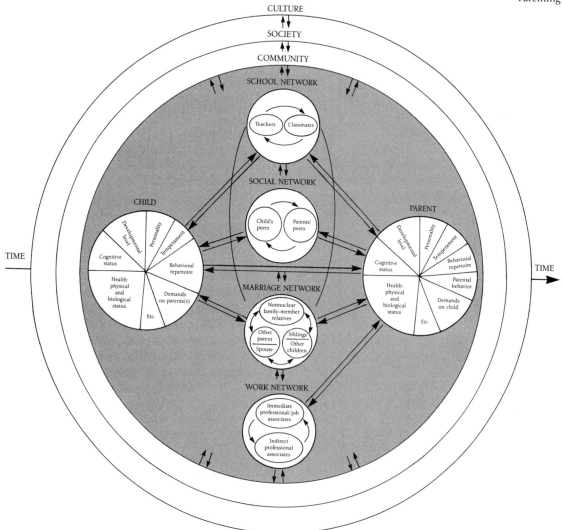

From R. Lerner, *On the Nature of Human Plasticity* (New York: Cambridge University Press, 1984), p. 144.

Goodness of Fit

Figure 2-2 shows the relationships Richard Lerner describes between the child, parent, social networks, larger community, society, and culture.[12] The arrows show how people and institutions influence each other. The child lives in a social context that makes demands on him or her and, at the same time, reacts to the child's behavior and is changed by it.

Parents and social institutions, like schools, have values and shape the child's behavior to fit these values. If the child's temperamental qualities do not fit the demands of the parents or school, then there is not a good fit between the child's individuality and the context the child lives in.

Adaptive behavior does not depend on the child's characteristics or on the environment's demands, but on the match between the two. A highly active child who lives on a farm where he works with the animals before and after school and walks a mile to the bus stop may be highly valued at home because of his great energy. He may have little trouble sitting in school because so much of his out-of-class time is active. He probably has little trouble meeting the teacher's expectations for quietness and sitting still. The social context of his daily life fits very well with his temperament.

Contrast this situation with that of an equally active child who lives in a small apartment and whose parents both work. Before and after school, he goes to the babysitter's, where he gets little outdoor time and little exercise. Instead, he watches TV. He squirms in school and gets out of his seat a lot. At home, he nags his parents to let him go out to play; but there is no supervised play space for him, and they are reluctant to let him play on the sidewalk unsupervised. His parents are irritated by his demands and the teacher's complaints about his behavior. There is not a good fit between what parents and social networks ask of the child and the child's individuality. Consequently, the child is labeled a problem at school and at home.

Parental expectations create standards that can help or block children's development, and so parents need to develop reasonable and sensitive expectations of their children.

What Parents Expect of Themselves

Most parents have high—and often unrealistic—expectations of themselves as parents. These expectations can be stumbling blocks to successful parenting, hindering rather than helping, so let us talk about them. The list of expectations discussed here is not an exhaustive one, and not all of these expectations are unrealistic. However, this discussion can help you to explore your own expectations and decide which you want to retain and which you want to discard.

Many parents expect that if they just love their children enough, they will have no problems. When problems do occur, parents are startled and uncertain about what action to take. Parental concern and acceptance are essential ingredients in children's lives, but love must be translated into sensitive caretaking. During the early years this includes the daily routines of dressing, bathing, and feeding. Toddlers and preschoolers need encouragement and stimulation. Elementary school children need help in adjusting to the outside world, and teenagers need to be allowed to make their own decisions and choices. Parents develop skills in interacting with children, and these skills enable parents to express their affection and warmth.

Many parents expect that if they devote enough time and energy and thought and caring to their children, all will go smoothly. Then they are confounded when problems occur anyway. Studies of representative samples of children report that the average child has several behavior problems at any given time. In a longitudinal sample, children had between five and six problems per year.[13] In a sample of several thousand children who were nine, ten, and eleven years old, the average child had between three and four problems.[14] Such problems, if not long-lived or intense, appear to reflect the stress that accompanies even healthy development.

Some parents expect that if they are effective, their children will be happy all the time. They believe that if children suffer or are sad they, as parents, are responsible and must quickly remedy the situation. Parents can try to design the family's living arrangements so that children are happy much of the time. But it is important to remember that many events and influences that are beyond parents' control can affect children and make them unhappy. Haim Ginott notes that parents would be unwise to remove all suffering even if they could. Children grow through such experience.

Many parents expect that they will always put their children's needs ahead of their own. The needs of children deserve special consideration, particularly in the early years when they are least able to take care of themselves. As children grow, however, much of what they may consider needs are really wants that can be deferred without harmful effects. When parents go to extremes to see that children get what they want, the children pay a price. Parents are likely to become resentful and angry at how much they are giving, and children sense this underlying hostility. Ginott remarks that parents can be a little kinder than they feel, but not much.

Another expectation many parents hold is that they will avoid all the mistakes their own parents made. Parents who wish they had had fewer limits will give their children more freedom; parents who had little real communication with their parents will engage their children in lively debates. The desire to improve on our own experiences in childhood motivates us to seek better ways to rear our children. It is just as important, however, to recognize the positive and beneficial aspects of our parents' childrearing philosophies and methods.

What Parents Expect of Their Children

Many parents have very specific expectations about the kind of people they want their children to become. Sometimes parents hope a child will grow up to be exactly like themselves and are surprised and disappointed when the child's temperament, skills, or interests are different from their own. Problems also develop when parents expect children to succeed in ways—emotional, social, professional—that they, the parents, feel they have failed. For example, a parent who lacks self-confidence may encourage a child to be aggressive and outgoing. Parenting goes more smoothly when parents think of each child as a unique and separate individual who needs to become his or her own person.

Some couples expect that children will cheerfully do as they are told. If children comply grudgingly, parents may become annoyed. Thus, sometimes parents punish, not because of disapproved behavior, but because the child's attitude is not what they wanted. Such parents expect to control the child's behavior and all of the child's thoughts, feelings, and reactions. But this kind of control severely limits a child's responsiveness.

Parents sometimes expect children to be helpless, inadequate creatures who require continual aid and direction in order to accomplish anything. They are often surprised at what babies and young children can do to meet some of their needs. The

INTERVIEW
with Ellen Galinsky

Ellen Galinsky is co-president of the Families and Work Institute in New York City. She has been director of the Work and Family Life Studies Project at the Bank Street College in New York since 1981. She was 1989–90 president of the National Association for the Education of Young Children. Ellen Galinsky is the author of The Six Stages of Parenthood (Addison Wesley, 1987) *and co-author of* The Preschool Years (Ballentine, 1991).

You have interviewed hundreds of parents about their enjoyments and difficulties as parents and how it has changed them as individuals. What are important things for parents to do to become effective parents who enjoy what they are doing?

First, look at your expectations of yourself and your children. See if they are realistic. Alter them so they fit you and your children. *The Six Stages of Parenthood* was all about parents' expectations of themselves and how these change as children grow and how important it is to understand what and how you are feeling.

Second, develop your ability to solve problems. Look at what is really bothering you and decide what you have to address first. List all your options and decide what the pluses and minuses of each are, and then take action. Don't insist that there has to be just one right solution. Think of a lot of different solutions, and if one doesn't work, try another.

Third, social support is crucial. You need people who make you feel competent, who enjoy your child, who like you. You need someone to talk to, someone you can laugh with.

Fourth, practical help is very important. When things are going crazy and you need help, you have to have someone you can call, even in the middle of the night and say, "I need you."

Fifth, being able to live in the present is very important. Being able to enjoy raindrops on a window or an ant walking across a sidewalk, putting aside work or other concerns so that these moments do not roll right past really helps parents enjoy these times with their children.

Sixth, having a sense of humor is very helpful. Taking a step back and looking at what you and your child are doing that is funny brings perspective to everything. I don't mean humor

more careful and complete studies of children's behavior document the child's capacities for complex, adaptive functioning, as we shall see in Chapter 6.

Another parental expectation is that children will understand and appreciate what parents do for them. But children often do not appreciate what parents do for them, in part because they do not have the range of experience necessary to do so. Many parents do without things they need or want to save money for piano or dance lessons, for camp, or for dental care. Just as many spend precious hours as classroom parents and scout leaders. When a child has parents who do these things and does not know parents who are not giving and generous, the child many not realize how fortunate he or she is.

Another expectation is that children will become what parents make them. Watson set the stage for this belief with the statement that, given a dozen infants, he could make of them whatever he wanted.[15] More recently, psychologists have come

in the sense of making fun of the child, but humor in the sense of seeing the funny side to the whole situation.

Seventh, understand your child's development as well as your own. Sometimes parents don't really understand young children, and they misinterpret the child's behavior; for example, worrying that a four-year-old's fantastic stories mean he will be a liar throughout his life and perhaps end up in prison.

What kinds of things are important for parents to avoid doing?

I recently interviewed a group of women whose children were grown, and I asked them what they wished they had done differently. I wanted to know this so I could do some of these things now. This is what I learned from those interviews. First, don't ignore what your child says to you. Listen to your children, really listen to what they are saying. Second, don't be judgmental. And, third, don't minimize your child's interests. Encourage what is meaningful to the child. Children have interests and ideas of their own. Support them, for example, be interested in the lemonade stand they set up or whatever else they like. Many of the children who got into drugs were children with no interests.

How would you say your work has changed you as a parent?

I've learned a lot from other parents, talking, listening to their questions. I feel through seminars and talks I am in the thick of what is happening with parents, and I really get a sense of their concerns. In each case I have learned from parents, and I use the information to help others and to help myself.

Because of my work I understand development, my own and my children's, and that is so important in helping you understand what is happening with them and with you. My own children know how important they are to me and how much I want to be a good parent.

I was a manager before, but there is nothing like dealing with a child, getting a three-year-old into a bathtub. It is different from any kind of learning that you do as a boss, or a friend, or a colleague. With children you learn things in a very profound way.

to believe that the child's temperament is an important force in determining how external stimuli, including each parent's behavior, will affect the child.

A child's characteristics determine how a parent's behavior is interpreted. For example, a sensitive child may be deeply hurt by parental criticism that her more assertive sister barely notices. The parental behavior is the same, but each child has interpreted it in terms of her own personality. Further, a child's characteristic ways of behaving will elicit particular behaviors from parents.

Each of us has our own unique expectations of ourselves and our children. Dorothy C. Briggs presents a valuable method for identifying and assessing expectations:

During the next few days, observe your behavior toward each child. Try to identify your expectations. Write each one down and look at it in the light of these questions.

Why do I have this expectation?

Where did it come from?

What's in it for me?

Is it based on my needs or my child's?

What purpose does it serve?

Does it realistically fit this particular child at this age and with this temperament and background?

Check each expectation to see if it exists to meet your hidden hungers, hangover wishes, or unfinished business. Be careful, for it is easy to camouflage a need in yourself as a need in your child.[16]

COPING WITH PARENTAL FRUSTRATION AND GUILT

When parents and children fail to live up to the parents' expectations, frustration, guilt, and general stress result. It does not take much stress on parents to make an impact on their parenting. Parents in a playroom with their children were given a simple mental task of anagrams to complete and changed their way of relating to their children when distracted by the task.[17] They gave much less positive attention to their preschoolers and were more irritable, critical, and interfering while solving the task. Since even minimal stress seems to change parent-child interactions, it is important for parents to deal with frustration and guilt as they arise.

In a book titled *Parent Burnout*, Joseph Procaccini and Mark Kiefaber[18] define burnout as "a downward drift toward physical, emotional, and spiritual exhaustion resulting from the combination of chronic high stress and perceived low personal growth and autonomy."[19] Parents feel worn out by meeting seemingly endless family needs, especially those of children, and they lose enthusiasm for parenting.

Procaccini and Kiefaber identify five stages of burnout. In the first or "Gung-Ho" stage, highly conscientious parents start parenting with enormous energy and high expectations. As the child or the parent fails to achieve what is expected, the parent moves to the second stage of "Doubts." The parent questions (1) his or her abilities to do what is needed and (2) the child's worth and acceptability. As doubts continue, resentments build up because the parent gets little positive feeling from the parenting experience. Parents then move into a third "Transition" stage, in which they can make one of two choices. They can address the doubts, change their expectations of themselves and the child, find new ways to achieve a more balanced life that reduces parental frustration, and move to a new stage of growth. If parents make no changes and continue on the same path, feeling self-critical and resentful of energy spent in what appears to be fruitless efforts, they move into the fourth stage of "Pulling Away" from the child. If they still make no changes, they move to the fifth stage, "Chronic Disenchantment," in which they feel angry, withdrawn, helpless to change.

Enthusiastic, devoted parents are those most likely to burn out because they invest so much of themselves in the parenting process and want to be perfect. The authors propose a six-week program of daily exercises to deal with burnout by substituting positive attitudes for negative ones and by changing behavior slowly (see Box 2-1). Woven into the program are eight important ingredients for reducing burnout. These are: (1) getting information about children and parenting skills from

---

BOX 2-1
DEALING WITH PARENT BURNOUT

TUESDAY

Morning

Write down your first thoughts after you wake up. Answer these questions: Do you feel irreplaceable as a parent? Do you accept parental duties out of responsibility or out of obligation? Do you secretly believe that no one else can do quite as good a job as you?

Afternoon

From yesterday's list of possible helpers, select three and imagine yourself asking them to do something for you in your role as parent.

Evening

Before you go to bed, stand in front of the mirror. Look at yourself and say, "I am not indispensable and I am comfortable asking for help because I am not superhuman."

SATURDAY

Morning

Write down your first thought after you wake up. Answer these questions: Do you dread weekends? Do you find excuses for being away from your family on weekends (such as playing golf, going to the hairdresser, working at the office, going shopping, etc.)? Have you saved up all the hassles (e.g., doing laundry, mowing the lawn, etc.) for the weekend?

Afternoon

Spend at least two hours engaged in an activity that includes the entire family, excluding watching television. Examples are: going shopping together; playing a game; taking a walk; working around the yard; running errands; and going out to eat.

Evening

Before going to bed, stand in front of the mirror and say, "It was nice enjoying spending time with my family once again." Remember, even if it is not true, say it anyway because having said it, it is more likely to come true.

Joseph Procaccini and Mark Kiefaber, *Parent Burnout* (New York: New American Library, 1984), pp. 148, 151.

---

books, (2) connecting with a significant other for support (spouse, relative, friend, minister), (3) becoming part of a small social group, (4) engaging in some goal-oriented activity (athletics, artistic pursuit, hobby), (5) gaining knowledge of self, (6) having access to money or credit, (7) developing spiritual or intellectual beliefs that provide meaning to life, and (8) maintaining self-nourishing activity. All eight are needed to buffer a parent against burnout. Note that only one ingredient, the first, bears directly on rearing children. All the rest focus on helping the parent to become a competent, integrated person and on forging interpersonal connections with other people.

Research supports the findings of Procaccini and Kiefaber.[20] Parents who received training in parenting skills and in techniques of reducing parental distress were more effective in managing their children's behavior than parents who received information only on parenting skills. As we will see, these eight ingredients are found in families who are rearing healthy children.

A mother and writer, Shirley Radl, describes a shorter program for dealing with parental guilt.[21] Guilt, or feeling responsible for some wrong-doing, is a common feeling among parents. Dr. Louise Bates Ames, who has directed studies of children at Yale University, states that most parents

> have a deep basic dread that they are somehow damaging their children. But the fact is, conscientious parents are probably causing themselves more anxiety worrying about this than they could ever visit upon their children.
>
> Naturally, if parents are very harsh, indifferent, permissive, or terribly inconsistent in dealing with their children, the chances are children may be damaged. But such parents tend not to worry about this, while paradoxically, conscientious parents do—and that they care so much tells me they are the least likely to cause any harm.[22]

How to cope with this dread feeling of wrongdoing? Shirley Radl describes the process, learned from a friend, that she used to cope with self-hatred and restore her confidence and self-esteem. Radl started with a session in which she forgave herself for all her past mistakes. She began to recall all the things she felt consciously guilty about. She began by forgiving herself for early mistakes as she was growing up because she felt these early guilts provided a basic reservoir of feeling that had to be eliminated. She said to herself, "I forgive you." After doing this she felt truly, deeply forgiven by herself.

She then began to go over her "motherhood guilt list." She divided the guilts into two piles—the ones she could control (providing good meals and good care) and the ones she could not control (birth complications, poor health). Then she began to examine her good points as a parent. She really loved her children, tried to be fair and understanding, and exerted effort toward being a good parent.

Radl began a program to improve her behavior with her children, rewarding herself when she met her goals. She discovered that to be the kind of giving mother she wanted to be, she had to look after her own needs as well. She had to get plenty of rest, eat a healthy diet, and find time for relaxation. She concluded that when parents can care for themselves, they can rear their children more happily and effectively.

Note that Radl's method involves forgiveness of her past mistakes, making choices of areas one wants to change, taking action to make the changes, and rewarding oneself for work well done.

A positive approach is to develop courage and self-confidence as a parent. As Dreikurs has written:

> The importance of courage in parents cannot be overemphasized. Whenever you feel dismayed or find yourselves thinking, "My gosh, I did it all wrong," be quick to recognize this symptom of your own discouragement; turn your attention to an academic and imper-

sonal consideration of what can be done to make matters better. When you try a new technique and it works, be glad. When you fall back into old habits, don't reproach yourself. You need to constantly reinforce your own courage, and to do so, you need the "courage to be imperfect." Recall to your mind the times that you have succeeded, and try again. Dwelling on your mistakes saps your courage. Remember, one cannot build on weakness—only on strength. Admit humbly that you are bound to make mistakes and acknowledge them without a sense of loss in your personal value. This will do much to keep your courage up. Above all, remember that we are not working for perfection, but only for improvement. Watch for the little improvements, and when you find them, relax and have faith in your ability to improve further.[23]

REASONABLE AND EFFECTIVE GOALS OF PARENTING

We have emphasized that unrealistic expectations are a source of frustration and difficulty for parents. But, parents wonder, what *are* reasonable goals in parenting? Most psychologists agree that the goal of parenting is to help children grow into responsible, self-directed adults who can care for themselves and nurture others, with an added emphasis sometimes placed on the individual's ability to contribute to society's benefit. The goals can be met by using what might be called the "building blocks" of parenting.

BUILDING BLOCKS OF PARENTING

Surveying such major parenting experts as Haim Ginott,[24] Thomas Gordon,[25] Dorothy Briggs,[26] Rudolf Dreikurs,[27] and the behaviorists[28] reveals large areas of common agreement that we can identify as basic building blocks of parenting.

Modeling

The aim of parenting is to help children develop into independent, autonomous, responsible, and self-directed adults. All strategies emphasize that parents should provide models of the characteristics they want their children to develop. If parents do not provide guidance by personal example of their major values, it is difficult for any method to help a child grow in the desired ways.

How do parents provide models for infants and toddlers? The behavior of an adult is strikingly different from that of very young children, yet mimicking of adult responses has been observed in infants who are just a few days old. When adults are completely unavailable, a baby's capacity to respond diminishes dramatically. We see this clearly in blind babies, whose initial smiling disappears because they cannot see the smiles of their parents, and in deaf babies, who cease their babbling when they do not hear sounds made by other humans. Babies need parents to model the smiles and laughter, the language and emotional responses of life.

During the early years, the quality of parental behavior is important. Parents who express warmth, happiness, consideration, and respect in their daily handling of the child, who are gentle and respond to children's needs with smiles and humor, help their children to develop a positive approach to life.

From time to time parents need to look at their own behavior through the eyes of their children to see if they are providing appropriate models. A father who is eager to be a good provider so that his family can enjoy life may work long hours at one job or take a second. The children of this father may feel that he is a remote, over-worked man who has little time for them rather than a happy, responsible father.

Trust

Parents need to have confidence that, given emotional support, their children will be able to cope well with the demands of family, friends, school, and society. When problems arise, children can learn new behavior patterns. They can meet problems and often can find solutions themselves. Parents who have this trust are able to inter-vene, in whatever ways they choose, to influence their child's behavior—to set limits, shape behaviors, and engage in mutual problem-solving sessions.

Respect

Effective parents respect their children as human beings. Even the very young child is a separate person, with individual needs and preferences, not an object to be manipulated at will. Children need to be interacted with and talked to with as much courtesy and consideration as you would expect for yourself.

Love and Discipline

Love is an essential part of the parent-child relationship. But parents who love their children are not automatically effective parents. Love must be expressed in ways that are beneficial for the children and comfortable for the parents. Remember that caring discipline is a form of love.

Communication

All the parenting strategies discussed in this book focus on communication between parent and child. Behaviorists place less emphasis on communication than other psychologists, but even they talk about the importance of expressing affection and positive feelings, smiling and hugging the child while giving material rewards. When parents and children discuss family rules, share points of view and reactions to each other, and plan joint activities, they are all participating in the creation of more com-fortable living arrangements.

Honesty

All strategies recommend that parents be honest, specific, and clear about the changes they want a child to make. They must also strive to be honest with their chil-dren. Honesty means expressing your feelings as accurately as possible and having

The aim of parenting is to help children develop into independent, autonomous, responsible, and self-directed adults. All strategies emphasize that parents should provide models of the characteristics they want their children to develop.

your words match your tone of voice, gestures, and facial expression. When parents do not match their behaviors with their words as they go about setting limits, children get mixed messages. When children get too many mixed messages, they begin to distrust what parents tell them, or they begin to distrust their own perceptions. Either result presents problems.

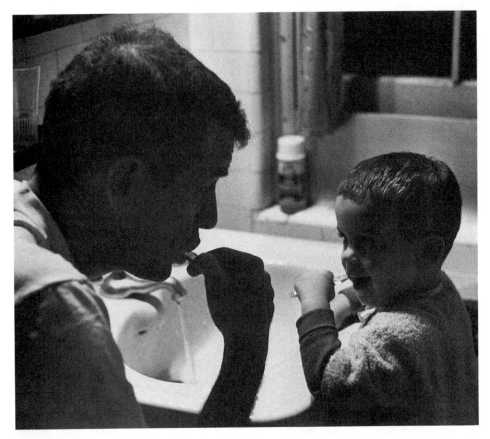

Because children observe, imitate, and model the behavior of their parents, parents have the opportunity to exert both positive and negative influence over their children.

Positive Statements

Avoid negative terms that label the child: "Janet is a lazy child," or "Jim is aggressive and obnoxious," "Linda is loud and pushy," or "Joe is sneaky and mean." Instead, be specific about the behaviors you want changed and, whenever possible, use positive terms: "I want Janet to get involved in a hobby and help me with household chores"; "I want Jim to be pleasant and sharing with his friends."

Time, Attention, Concern

Children require time—time spent talking, playing, sharing experiences. In busy adult lives, time is at a premium, yet parents must find the energy and time not only to relate to children, but also to attend, think about, and, when necessary, change their behavior as parents.

GUIDELINES FROM RESEARCH AND CHILDREN

Many studies of infant behavior reveal that "attentive, warm, stimulating, responsive, and nonrestrictive caregiving" promote healthy socioemotional and cognitive development.[29]

A critical ingredient is *involvement* with the child. What does involvement mean? It means having conversations with children, knowing what they are doing, who their friends are, where they are going, considering their opinions. Summarizing research with two longitudinal studies, Dr. Jack Block wrote, "In order for a child to become appropriately controlled, someone has to invest time and trouble. The responsibilities of parenthood take much effort and, perhaps more crucial, the proper timing of the effort. It is so often the case that when the child requires a parental response, the parent would much rather be doing something other than being a parent. The test of the good parent is that she (or he) functions parentally even when she (or he) could gain more immediate pleasures elsewhere."[30]

Children who grow up in homes with parental involvement become responsible, competent, achievement-oriented adults who are appropriately controlled and happy. Children growing up in homes where parents are self-focused and uninvolved tend to be impulsive, moody adults who find it difficult to control aggression.

Beyond parent involvement, what else is important?

Diana Baumrind has conducted careful research on the effects of parents' child-rearing practices on children's behavior.[31] The findings suggest that parents who are accepting and who also provide structure and limits have the most competent children. Baumrind identified three patterns of childrearing: (1) authoritative, (2) authoritarian, and (3) permissive.

Authoritative parents exercise firm control of the child's behavior but also emphasize the independence and individuality in the child. Although the parents have a clear notion of present and future standards of behavior for the child, they are rational, flexible, and attentive to the needs and preferences of the child. "Authoritative parents . . . balanced what they offered with what they demanded. They balanced high control with high independence-granting, high standards for maturity with much support and nurturance."[32] Their children are self-reliant and self-confident and explore their worlds with excitement and pleasure.

Authoritarian parents employ a similar firm control, but use it in an arbitrary, power-oriented way without regard for the child's individuality. They emphasize control, without nurturance or support to achieve it. Baumrind writes, "The authoritarian parent values obedience as a virtue and believes in restricting the child's autonomy. This parent values the preservation of order and traditional structure as an end in itself. He or she does not encourage verbal give and take, believing that the child should accept the parent's word for what is right."[33] Children of authoritarian parents, relative to other groups of children, are unhappy, withdrawn, inhibited, and distrustful.

Permissive parents set few limits on the child. They are accepting of the child's impulses, giving as much freedom as is possible while still maintaining physical safety. They appear cool and uninvolved. Permissive parents sometimes allow behavior that angers them, but they do not feel sufficiently comfortable with their

own anger to express it. As a result, the anger builds up to unmanageable proportions. They then lash out and are likely to hurt the child more than they want to.
Their children are the least independent and self-controlled and could be best classified as immature.

Extensive studies of self-esteem and the family and school behaviors related to it
reveal that self-esteem is an important ingredient in effective functioning. The childrearing practices that enhance the development of self-esteem resemble those used
by Baumrind's authoritative parent, who uses warm acceptance, attention to
individuality with definite limits, and high but reasonable expectations. Stanley
Coopersmith, who has studied the development of self-esteem, describes a stimulating family atmosphere as follows:

> The treatment associated with the formation of high self-esteem is much more vigorous,
> active, and contentious than is the case in families that produce children with low self-
> esteem. Rather than being a paradigm of tranquility, harmony and open-mindedness, we
> find that the high self-esteem family is notable for the high level of activity of the individ-
> ual members, strong-minded parents dealing with independent, assertive children, stricter
> enforcement of more stringent demands, and greater possibilities for open dissent and dis-
> agreement.[34]

Studies of families rearing competent children have found that members care
about each other;[35] they reach out to each other, and reach out with the expectation
that interaction will be positive. They love and respect each other, but all are individuals and all are free to be open and honest. They value individual differences and
consider many options when solving problems. Members of healthy families are
active in meeting problems and show initiative. Often they are involved in community activities. Parents respect each other as individuals and present models of
leadership to children. Power structure is clear, but parents negotiate problems when
they arise. Family members are close, but all are encouraged to be individuals who
accept responsibility for their acts. They are accurate in understanding each other,
in part because they are able to communicate feelings and ideas. Healthy families are
made up of individuals who share differing ideas and opinions in an accepting
atmosphere. Disagreements occur, but they serve primarily to broaden points of view
rather than stimulate conflict.

These families have many of the qualities Procaccini and Kiefaber encourage parents to develop as buffers against burnout. Parents are supportive of each other; family members are involved in activities, connected to community groups. They have
positive attitudes toward themselves and other people.

We must be cautious in generalizing the results of these studies to all ethnic
groups, for they were carried out primarily on white, middle-class families and children. Baumrind, for example, found that the authoritarian parenting style linked
with withdrawn, inhibited behavior in white girls, led to competent, mature behavior
in her small sample of Afro-American girls.[36] In the Afro-American culture, strict
control seemed to be interpreted as a sign of caring and involvement rather than a
sign of the cold rejection it seems to be in the white culture.

We must not assume ethnic differences in parental attitudes, values, or behavior
unless recent, well-controlled research documents them. We come upon too many

surprises in well-done studies for us to make assumptions—for example, one surprise was the finding that Chinese parents value the open expression of affection as much as Anglo-Americans do.[37]

We must be cautious in interpreting research because there are too many instances in which differences attributed to ethnic values are a matter of educational or social differences. Luis Laosa found that Mexican-American mothers used more modeling and visual cues to direct children in making a toy whereas Anglo-American mothers used questioning and praise. The ethnic differences disappeared when he had groups of mothers with equal amounts of schooling.[38]

Childrearing activities of different ethnic groups have to be understood in terms of the traditional values of the culture of origin as well as the values of the culture to which the group is adapting. When, for example, the childrearing attitudes of Chinese immigrant parents in this country are compared with the attitudes of Anglo-American parents, the Chinese immigrant parents are more controlling, more achievement-oriented, and more encouraging of independence than are Anglo-American parents. You might think they have not adapted to this country at all. Yet when the attitudes of immigrant Chinese parents are compared to those of Chinese parents on Taiwan, they are less controlling, less achievement-oriented, and less encouraging of independence. The immigrant parents have moved in the direction of absorbing the values of the majority culture. It is of interest that the Chinese seem able to encourage both strong family interdependence and individual independence. Also note that the three groups did not differ on open expression of affection.[39]

Within the limited scope of this book we cannot enumerate the characteristics of major ethnic groups and still be sensitive to social and educational differences within each group, so we shall focus on general characteristics associated with many minority groups. Minority group parents use the same techniques for socializing their children as do majority parents—modeling, reinforcement, identification—but they often use the techniques to pass on different values, different ways of doing things.[40]

These values frequently center on giving children a positive view of their own group so that they will develop a bicultural vision and carry on their own cultural traditions. Children learn that their obligations to the family and the group are of first importance. They are taught that cooperation, sharing, and reciprocating favors are primary values. Interdependence is more important than competitive individualism. As a result of learning two sets of values, minority children can become more flexible and broader in outlook.

We have looked at what researchers think is effective. But what do children want in their parents?

Interestingly, children value these same qualities of involvement and limit-setting in parents.[41] Preschoolers interviewed about the qualities of a good mommy and daddy and a bad mommy and daddy believe that good parents are physically affectionate and nurturant, especially in the area of providing food for children. In addition, good parents like to play games with their children and read to them, and they discipline them—that is, they keep children from doing things they should not, but they do not spank or slap in the face. Bad parents have the opposite qualities. They don't hug or kiss, don't fix food, don't play games. They hit and don't let you go outside. Bad parents are also described as generally irresponsible—they go through red lights, throw chairs at people, don't read the newspaper.

As children grow older, they continue to value nurturance and affection, but they also appreciate qualities reflecting psychological nurturance. Mothers' good qualities include "understanding feelings and moods," "being there when I need her," "sticking up for me." Children continue to emphasize the limit-setting behaviors in a good mother—"she makes us eat fruit and vegetables," "she yells at me when I need it"—but they want their mother to consider their needs and wishes in setting the rules. Older children still enjoy mutual recreational time—playing, joking, building things together. Finally, as children get older they appreciate the teaching activities of the good mother.

So research and children, too, tell us that, first, healthy parents have close emotional relationships with their children, regard their children positively, and give them opportunities to develop and express their own thoughts and feelings. Second, parents modify children's behavior with reasonable, firm limits that are consistently enforced. Thus, they provide structure within which the child is independent and free to initiate activities. Chapters 3 and 4 discuss these two tasks of parenting in greater detail.

PARENTAL COMPETENCE, CHILD COMPETENCE

Jay Belsky, Elliot Robins, and Wendy Gamble point to parental patience, endurance, and commitment as the important qualities underlying parental sensitivity and involvement.[42] Patience enables parents to control their feelings and impulses so they can be sensitive to the needs of the child. Endurance gives parents the energy to persist and carry out all their activities and still remain involved. Finally, commitment to children insures that parents will use patience and endurance to meet the child's needs.

Belsky et al. propose a model for predicting the probability that a child will develop competence. They consider parental resources, social supports, and the child's own characteristics the three basic factors determining the probability of child competence (see Table 2-1). When all factors are supportive, then the probability of child competence is high. When two of the three factors are supportive, there is still a good probability of child competence. For example, if a child develops a chronic illness like diabetes, but parents' personal resources are strong and the family has many relatives who provide practical help and emotional support, then the probability of child competence is high.

Conversely even when the child has many skills and positive qualities, but there is little social support and the parent is not involved, then the probability of child competence is lower. Belsky et al. believe that all can go wrong, but if the parent brings his or her personal resources to bear in behalf of the child, then there is a good chance of average child competence.

They describe the vicious cycle that sometimes occurs when, for example, a child's temperamental characteristic—low activity level, for example—can exhaust the parent's capacity for support and alienate possible social supports. Intervention can occur at any point in the cycle, however, and effect change.

TABLE 2-1
RELATIVE PROBABILITY OF A CHILD'S DEVELOPING COMPETENTLY

Probability of Child Competence	Conditions of the Parental Subsystems*		
	Parent's Personal Resources	Subsystems of Support	Child's Characteristics
High			
↑	+	+	+
│	+	+	−
│	+	−	+
│	−	+	+
│	+	−	−
│	−	+	−
│	−	−	+
↓	−	−	−
Low			

*(+) stands for supportive mode (−) stands for stressful mode.

From J. Belsky, E. Robins, and W. Gamble, "The Determinants of Parental Competence: Toward a Contextual Theory," in *Beyond The Dyad*, ed. Michael Lewis (New York: Plenum, 1984), p. 253.

PROTECTIVE FACTORS AT TIMES OF RISK

Life is unpredictable. Even the most competent parents and children experience hard times beyond their control—crippling accidents, wide-scale economic depression, personal losses through divorce or death. Michael Rutter describes the "protective factors" that help individuals respond to the crisis in an adaptive way.[43] Protective factors are not synonymous with positive, pleasurable experiences, though they may include such experiences. In some instances, manageable levels of stress help a person develop strength.

Some protective factors, like stressors themselves, are beyond the individual's control. Rutter refers to such factors as age at time of crisis, the number of negative events, an easygoing temperament that makes adaptation easier, and sex—girls are less at risk for physical hazards and for damaging psychological experiences because people are less aggressive in the presence of girls.

Nevertheless, certain protective factors can be cultivated, and so it is useful to focus on what parents can do to promote resilience in the face of adversity. Although more details are provided in Chapter 3, we present an overview here.

Two kinds of experience are helpful. The first is having a secure emotional relationship with someone who teaches you how to get along with other people. The satisfying relationship might not occur until adulthood and yet still will have a powerful, positive effect. Women who were raised in institutions but were able to make a happy marriage were similar to those who had grown up in families and never had institutional experience.

The second kind of experience is having an activity or skill that results in an accomplishment—making something, helping someone. Experiences that strengthen people's abilities to set goals and take action decrease the feelings of helplessness that are perhaps the worst part of adversity.

So, events that promote secure relationships with people and demonstrate the personal rewards of action help people cope with difficult times.

PROBLEM-SOLVING APPROACH

Just as success in adverse circumstances comes from taking planned action, so when children develop difficulties, parents have greatest success when they take action. We recommend a seven-step approach to handling difficulties.

First, parents must identify the child's behavior or concern and describe it specifically. For example, "She does not take out the garbage," not "She is lazy." Then observe when and how often the behavior takes place. Does it happen with one parent and not the other? How often does it happen? When instances are actually counted, the behavior may not occur as often as parents believe. At the end of this step parents have valuable information on the occurrence of the behavior, information that can tell them why it happens and how they can stop it.

Before taking any action, however, parents must go through a step of self-questioning to determine whether the behavior represents a real problem. Parents must ask themselves whether they are taking out frustrations in another area of their lives—marriage, work, extended family—on the child, preferring to see the child's behavior as the problem rather than something in their own lives.

If convinced that the child's behavior is really of concern, parents must ask themselves whether their expectations of the child are realistic for that child at that time. Sometimes, especially with firstborns, parents expect more than the child can do, or they may expect more than that particular child can do. The parent must also ask whether the behavior may be a child's temporary reaction to some special stress, thus not a matter of permanent concern. For example, when a new sibling comes, when the family moves, or when the child changes school, temporary changes in the child's functioning may occur as a result of stress. Although it is important to be aware of the behavior change, the parent may not want to define it as a problem but rather as a temporary indication that the child needs special support during a stressful period.

Once the parent is convinced a problem exists that requires action, the third step involves eliciting the child's point of view on the behavior. If the child is an infant, the parent will have to observe and guess what the child is thinking or feeling, a technique we will discuss further in Chapter 6. But when children are older, a parent should always get their view of what the problem is. They may have the answer to the difficulty themselves. For example, a single mother was about to bring her daughter to a counselor because she could not get her to bed at night. She decided to ask the six-year-old first what would help get her to bed. The child suggested two stories before bed and a chance to look at books in bed before sleep. The mother followed the girl's suggestion and the problem ended.

The fourth step is to pay positive attention to the child while solving the problem. When trouble strikes, parents sometimes become so frustrated that they focus narrowly on the difficulty and overlook all the child's competent, enjoyable behaviors. Thus it is important to spend leisure time with the child, playing games or going on an outing, to gain a more balanced, positive picture of the relationship with the child.

The fifth step is carrying out some intervention to change the child's behavior. Intervention may take the form of setting and enforcing a limit, but it could well be some other action. Providing encouragement when the child is discouraged in mastering new tasks and teaching a new behavior are two examples of interventions to stimulate a change. Sometimes two interventions are carried out at the same time. For example, if a child in third grade lacks friends, the parent might want to increase the child's self-confidence by getting swim lessons and inviting a friend's son over for play to give the child increased social experience.

The sixth step is evaluating the results of the intervention. How successful was it? Try the intervention for two weeks and then count the undesirable behaviors again. Has there been a decrease? If not, go on to the seventh step: starting over again with a new intervention. In the process of trying one intervention, the problem often emerges more clearly and a more effective way of dealing with it comes to mind. For example, in dealing with fights between brothers, a parent may learn that the older boy is frustrated in school and takes out his feelings on his little brother after school during the week. The problem then changes from one of sibling fights to a scholastic problem. The problem-solving approach resumes within this new framework.

To review, the problem-solving approach has seven steps:

1. Identify the problem specifically; observe when and how often it occurs.
2. Question yourself on the reality of the problem.
3. Get the child's point of view.
4. Spend pleasurable time daily with the child.
5. Carry out an intervention.
6. Evaluate the results of the intervention.
7. Start over again, if necessary.

And remember: Changing a child's behavior requires patience and practice from the parent.

A problem-solving approach to difficulties is useful because, as we saw in Chapter 1, parents' circumstances vary and may require different behaviors from the child. For example, when both parents of young children work outside the home, they may have to direct problem-solving skills to morning routines so that everyone leaves home at an early hour in a reasonable mood.

Parents may be members of religious and ethnic groups that value certain behaviors not stressed in the majority culture. A problem-solving approach enables parents to encourage their group's desired qualities. For example, American culture emphasizes developing independence and having many social ties in the community. Yet many ethnic groups value interdependence and close emotional ties with extended family members. Parents who want children to be close and depend primarily on the extended family for social activities can use problem-solving techniques to achieve these goals.

THE JOYS OF BEING A PARENT

In what way would you say being a parent has changed you as a person?

"It has changed my priorities, my perspective. I am much more protective. If I see someone driving like an idiot, I get much more upset. I feel more like a regular person, more grown up." FATHER OF TODDLER

"Now I'm officially grown up. It's kind of funny because I am a forty-year-old person who is just feeling grown up. For me, it's being less caught up in myself, more unselfish. I don't do everything I want to do all the time, and that's changing and it's okay. I used to resent that. I am less self-centered, less concerned with myself and how I'm doing, how I'm feeling, what's up. Now I am thinking more about him. For both my husband and me, I don't know whether this is going to change, but we are more oriented toward the future. We have to plan for his college, plan for our retirement; all of a sudden, it's not just living in the present; the future is there. We spend less time thinking about the past, but now we are more caught up in what is coming. That's different. We are going to be retiring when he goes off to school, and how are we going to handle all these expenses?" MOTHER OF TODDLER

"My own personal sense of the meaningfulness of life, in all aspects, has really gone through a dramatic change. It's just been so gratifying and meaningful and important to have this other little life, in a sense, in my hands, to be responsible for it. It's just been one of the best things I could have done. I am always looking forward to going home to see him. My attitude about things has changed. I'm more patient, even when I'm on my own, say, in a traffic jam, when I used to get irritable. Somehow I'm happy enough and satisfied enough with the rest of my life that it doesn't have the same effect on me. It doesn't matter." MOTHER OF TODDLER

"It has changed my sense of the past. I appreciate more of what my parents must have gone through for me. No matter what their problems or shortcomings, gee, they had to do all this for me; my mother changed all the diapers, she must have, someone did. My father was exactly the same age when I was born that I was when my son was born, so I have a sense of what it was like for him to be a certain age and be a father, even though he had an older son too. All the existential issues are taken care of." FATHER OF TODDLER

"It's that overused word, maturity. It happened for both of us, my husband and me. We look back on how our lives were before our son and afterwards. We were well-established adults, older, we had resolved all our career issues, we had nice incomes, and we were in love. Our whole lives were what we wanted every hour of every day. Along came the baby and, by choice, there was a reverse, almost 100 percent. We don't get to go out like we used to. We don't get to go on vacations or go to meetings with the same abandon that we used to; our budget is much tighter; our daily life with our son in it is much more decided by him, at times I think to a fault. We talk about problems that come up and grapple with them. It seems like an agony sometimes, but we are growing as a couple and as a family. It's very enriching." MOTHER OF TODDLER

"It has changed me for the better. It matured me, really at the core. I am much more responsible because I want to be a good example for them, provide stability for them. It has helped me to see into myself. I recall things I did as a child, and I understand better what was happening then. It has changed the kinds of things I think of as fun. I never would have found sailing on my own, and I like it a lot because he made me try it. It has changed my finances for the worse, but I can't think of a better use for the money. It has changed my whole outlook. It has made me better at my work because I understand people better." FATHER OF ELEMENTARY SCHOOL CHILD AND EARLY ADOLESCENT

"I wish I could say it has made me more patient, but it has intensified my emotions; and if something really difficult has happened, as it did today when she destroyed something I took a lot of time to make for her, because she didn't follow a simple rule, then I am amazed at how furious I feel. I almost never felt that angry at anyone before I had children. Yet a little while later, the great love I have for her makes forgiveness easy, and I sat down and started to make the whole thing over. So now I have extremes of feeling from great love to great anger." MOTHER OF ELEMENTARY SCHOOL CHILD AND EARLY ADOLESCENT

"Having children makes you more patient, more humble, better able to roll with the punches because life is not so black and white. You can't just base your life on platitudes. You have the experience of having things go, not the way you would have them go, having your children do things you would not have them do; and you have to roll with that. You learn; it either kills you or you go on, and you have a different view of life. You become more patient and, I think, more kind." MOTHER OF EARLY AND LATE ADOLESCENTS

"I want to be a good father so it makes me evaluate what I do and say; I look at mistakes as you would in any important and intense relationship, so it certainly makes me more self-examining and more aware of myself and how I am being experienced by the other person. It is also a challenge to be tolerant when I don't feel very tolerant. And I am not always tolerant; if you get me at the wrong time, I'm not very tolerant at all. But I think it's important, and it's a skill I try to develop because I think it makes for being a better parent. So in developing certain interpersonal skills, I think being a parent has helped me to become a better person." FATHER OF ELEMENTARY SCHOOL CHILD

Parents often wish there could be a single solution to each kind of problem situation—one way to handle temper tantrums, one way to deal with refusals to eat, one way to deal with teenagers' rebelliousness. There is no formula that all parents can use to raise all children. Each child is a unique individual. Differences are present at birth, as we shall see in Chapter 6, and continue to develop throughout life.

A behavior problem can originate in several ways, and the source of the problem will influence the solution. For example, a four-year-old boy may suddenly refuse to go to bed. Exploration with the child may reveal he is fearful, and reassurance about the absence of monsters may enable him to resume his regular bedtime. Another child may have the same problem, but it may stem from her need for extra attention after the arrival of a new baby brother. Her parents may decide to spend more time with her in the evening after the new baby has gone to bed for the night. Perhaps delaying the older child's bedtime for another 15 minutes spent in play may be all that is required.

A child's age is an important factor when parents are trying to determine the best approach to a particular problem. The same problem will require different approaches at different ages as well as with different children.

Each parent is also a unique individual. One parent may find unacceptable the strategy that another parent finds effective. Some parents are not comfortable with as much confusion, noise, and disorganization as others. They may insist on very clear-cut limits, regularly enforced, while other parents will prefer greater flexibility. Each parent needs to be aware of his or her own reactions to techniques and to decide which are most useful in achieving the desired family atmosphere.

The complexity of using childrearing strategies increases when we realize that children may not be learning by the strategy parents are using. Jane Loevinger, in a perceptive and humorous article, illustrates this problem with the example of a five-year-old who hits his younger brother.[44] The parent who punishes the older child with a spanking may actually be teaching that child that it is permissible to use physical aggression to obtain one's ends. The parent who uses reason and logic in dealing with the older boy may find that the child, seeing that no punishment follows hitting, is likely to do it again.

Why use a strategy—why not just do whatever comes to mind at the time? Because, says Loevinger, those children who have the most difficulties growing up and functioning are raised by parents who are impulsive, self-centered, and unable to follow a set of guidelines. "The chief value of a parental theory," writes Loevinger, "may well be in providing a model for the child of curbing one's own impulses out of regard for the future welfare of another."[45]

HOW PARENTS CHANGE

Parents and psychologists have begun to look at the parenting experience in terms of its effects on parents. How do parents change as a result of having children? Ellen Galinsky, a consultant and lecturer on child development, found herself changing after her children were born. Curious about the meaning of her feelings, she went to books and research reports to see what other parents were describing. Finding little to inform her, she began to run groups of parents of young children. She then interviewed 228 parents with different experiences of parenthood—married, divorced, step, foster, and adoptive parents. These parents did not represent a random sampling but were a broad cross-section of the population.

Galinsky divided parenthood into six stages in which parents focus their emotional and intellectual energy on the task of that period.[46] Parenting stages are different from most other stages because a parent can be in more than one stage at a time with children of different ages. The first stage, occurring in pregnancy, she terms the *image-making* stage. It is a time when parents prepare for changes in themselves and in their relationships to others. The second *nurturing* stage goes from birth to the time when the child starts to say "no," about eighteen to twenty-four months. As parents become attached to the new baby, they arrange their lives to be caregivers, balancing their own and their child's needs, setting priorities. The third *authoritative* stage lasts from the time the child is two to four or five. Parents become rulegivers and enforcers as they learn that love for children goes hand in hand with structure and order. From the child's preschool years through adolescence, parents are in the *interpretive* stage. Children are more skilled and independent, and parents establish a way of life for them. They interpret outside authorities such as teachers to children. Parents teach values and morals. In brief, they teach children what life is all about.

When their children are adolescents, parents enter the *interdependent* stage. They form new relationships with children and, though they are still authorities, their power becomes shared with children in ways it was not in past years. In the sixth *departure* stage, parents evaluate themselves as their children prepare to leave home. They see where they have succeeded and where they might have acted differently.

Galinsky summarized her views of how parenthood changes adults:

> Taking care of a small, dependent, growing person is transforming, because it brings us in touch with our baser side, it exposes our vulnerabilities as well as our nobility. We lose our sense of self, only to find it and have it change again and again. We learn to nurture and care. We struggle through defining our own rules and our own brand of being an authority. We figure out how we want to interpret the wider world, and we learn to interact with all those who affect our children. When our children are teenagers, we redefine our relationships, and then we launch them into life.
>
> Often our fantasies are laid bare, our dreams are in a constant tug of war with realities. And perhaps we grow. In the end, we have learned more about ourselves, about the cycles of life, and humanity itself. Most parents describe themselves as more responsible, more accepting, more generous than before they had children.[47]

MAJOR POINTS OF CHAPTER 2

The parenting process involves:

- a balance in the roles of disciplinarian and nurturer
- an interaction between the child, the parents, and the environment

- an environment that provides both stresses and supports
  - stresses are negative events such as economic hardship, experiencing discrimination
  - supports are positive factors such as work, marriage, extended family, friends
- a child who brings:
  - sexual gender
  - temperament
  - birth order
  - own growth patterns
- parents who bring:
  - sexual gender, birth order, temperament
  - experience with own parents
  - satisfactions/frustrations in other areas of life—marriage, work
  - expectations of themselves and their children

Goodness of fit means:

- a good match between the child's qualities and what parents and the environment demand
- parents' expectations are reasonable for this child

Coping with parental frustration and guilt means dealing with:

- parental burnout by getting information about children, developing a supportive system of people and activities to increase good feelings
- parental guilt by forgiving oneself and making specific behavior changes to remedy guilt-inducing behavior
- imperfection by developing the courage to be imperfect

All experts agree on the importance of:

- modeling
- communication
- trust in child
- honesty
- respect for child
- positive statements
- love and discipline
- time, attention, and concern

Research guidelines for parenting emphasize importance of:

- attentive, warm, stimulating caregiving in infancy
- parental involvement
- balancing parental control and demand for high standards of maturity with parental support, nurturance, and granting of independence

- encouraging and respecting the expression of the child's thoughts and feelings
- considering many options for action when differences occur
- taking account of cultural and ethnic differences in parents' values

Child competence depends on:

- social support system, child's characteristics, and parental resources
- intervening to stop any vicious cycle of negative behavior that occurs

Resilience grows in times of stress when individuals have:

- a secure, emotional relationship with someone who teaches them how to get along with people
- an activity or skill that gives a feeling of accomplishment

The seven steps of the problem-solving approach are:

- identifying the problem
- self-questioning by the parent
- eliciting the child's point of view
- spending enjoyable time with the child
- taking action
- evaluating the action
- starting again if necessary

The advantages of the problem-solving approach are:

- parents can take account of the individual characteristics of the child
- parents can retain their own goals and values for their children's behavior

As they raise children, parents go through the stages of:

- image making
- nurturing
- being authorities
- interpreting the world to children
- being interdependent with children
- departure

ADDITIONAL READINGS

Bloomfield, Harold, with Felder, Leonard. *Making Peace with Your Parents.* New York: Random House, 1983.

Galinsky, Ellen. *The Six Stages of Parenthood*. Reading, Mass.: Addison-Wesley, 1987.

Greene, Bob. *Good Morning, Merry Sunshine: A Father's Personal Journal of His Child's First Year.* New York: Penguin, 1985.

Plutzik, Roberta, and Laghi, Maria. *The Private Life of Parents*. New York: Everest House, 1983.

Procaccini, Joseph, and Kiefaber, Mark. *Parent Burnout*. New York: Doubleday, 1983.

Notes

1. John Newson and Elizabeth Newson, "Cultural Aspects of Child Rearing in the English-Speaking World," in *The Integration of a Child into a Social World*, ed. Martin M. P. Richards (London: Cambridge University Press, 1974), pp. 53–82.

2. John B. Watson, *Psychological Care of Infant and Child* (New York: W. W. Norton, 1928), pp. 81–82.

3. Herbert Ginsburg and Sylvia Opper, *Piaget's Theory of Intellectual Development* (Englewood Cliffs, N.J.: Prentice-Hall, 1969).

4. Jay Belsky, "The Determinants of Parenting: A Process Model," *Child Development* 55 (1984): 83–96.

5. Vonnie C. McLoyd, "The Impact of Economic Hardship on Black Families and Children: Psychological Distress, Parenting, and Socioemotional Development," *Child Development* 61 (1990): 311–346.

6. Charlotte J. Patterson, Janis B. Kupersmidt, and Nancy A. Vaden, "Income Level, Gender, Ethnicity, and Household Composition as Predictors of Children's School-based Competence," *Child Development* 61 (1990): 485–494.

7. Algea O. Harrison, Melvin N. Wilson, Charles J. Pine, Samuel Q. Chan, and Raymond Buriel, "Family Ecologies of Ethnic Minority Children," *Child Development* 61 (1990): 347–362.

8. L. Alan Sroufe, Deborah Jacobvitz, Sarah Mangelsdorf, Edward DeAngelo, and Mary Jo Ward, "Generational Boundary Dissolution Between Mothers and Their Preschool Children: A Relationship Systems Approach," *Child Development* 56 (1985): 317–325.

9. Mary Main, Nancy Kaplan, and Jude Cassidy, "Security in Infancy, Childhood and Adulthood: A Move to the Level of Representation," in *Growing Points of Attachment Theory and Research*, ed. Inge Bretherton and Everett Waters. Monographs of the Society for Research in Child Development,

no. 50 (1985), serial no. 209, pp. 66–104; Margaret Ricks, "The Social Transmission of Parental Behavior: Attachment Across Generations," in *Growing Points of Attachment Theory and Research*, eds. Bretherton and Waters, pp. 211–227.

10. Harold Bloomfield with Leonard Felder, *Making Peace with Your Own Parents* (New York: Random House, 1983).

11. John A. Clausen, Paul H. Mussen, and Joseph Kuypers, "Involvement, Warmth, and Parent-Child Resemblance in Three Generations," in *Present and Past in Middle Life*, ed. Dorothy H. Eichorn, John A. Clausen, Norma Haan, Marjorie P. Honzik, and Paul H. Mussen (New York: Academic Press, 1981), pp. 299–319.

12. Richard M. Lerner, *On the Nature of Human Plasticity* (New York: Cambridge University Press, 1984); Richard M. Lerner and Jacqueline V. Lerner, "Children in Their Contexts: A Goodness of Fit Model," in *Parenting Across the Life Span: Biosocial Dimensions*, ed. Jane B. Lancaster, Jeanne Altmann, Alice S. Rossi, and Lonnie R. Sherrod (New York: Aldine de Gruyter, 1987), pp. 377–404.

13. Jean W. Macfarlane, Lucile Allen, and Marjorie P. Honzik, *A Developmental Study of the Behavior Problems of Normal Children Between Twenty-One Months and Fourteen Years*, University of California Publications in Child Development, vol. 2 (Berkeley, Calif.: University of California Press, 1954).

14. R. D. Tuddenham, Jane B. Brooks, and Lucille Milkovich, "Mother's Reports of Behavior of Ten-Year-Olds: Relationships with Sex, Ethnicity, and Mother's Education," *Developmental Psychology* 10 (1974): 949–995.

15. John B. Watson, *Behaviorism* (New York: People's Publishing, 1925).

16. Dorothy C. Briggs, *Your Child's Self-Esteem* (Garden City, N.Y.: Doubleday, 1975), pp. 53, 55.

17. John U. Zussman, "Situational Determinants of Parenting Behavior: Effects of Competing Cognitive Activity," *Child Development* 51 (1980): 792–800.

18. Joseph Procaccini and Mark Kiefaber, *Parent Burnout* (New York: New American Library, 1984).

19. Ibid., p. 41.

20. Rex L. Forehand, Page B. Walley, and William M. Furey, "Prevention in the Home: Parent and Family," in *Prevention of Problems in Childhood: Psychological Research and Application,* ed. Michael C. Roberts and Lizette Peterson (New York: John Wiley, 1984), pp. 342–368.

21. Shirley Radl, "Breaking the Guilt Habit: A Joyful Mother's Guide," *Ladies' Home Journal,* May 1979.

22. Philip Zimbardo and Shirley L. Radl, *The Shy Child* (New York: McGraw-Hill, 1981), p. 30.

23. Rudolf Dreikurs with Vicki Soltz, *Children: The Challenge* (New York: Hawthorn, 1964), pp. 55–56.

24. Haim G. Ginott, *Between Parent and Child* (New York: Avon, 1969).

25. Thomas Gordon, *P.E.T. Parent Effectiveness Training* (New York: New American Library, 1975).

26. Briggs, *Your Child's Self-Esteem.*

27. Dreikurs with Soltz, *Children: The Challenge.*

28. Wesley C. Becker, *Parents Are Teachers* (Champaign, Ill.: Research Press, 1971); Robert Eimers and Robert Aitchison, *Effective Parents/Responsible Children* (New York: McGraw-Hill, 1977); John D. Krumboltz and Helen B. Krumboltz, *Changing Children's Behavior* (Englewood Cliffs, N.J.: Prentice-Hall, 1972).

29. Jay Belsky, Elliot Robins, and Wendy Gamble, "The Determinants of Parental Competence: Toward a Contextual Theory," in *Beyond The Dyad,* ed. Michael Lewis (New York: Plenum, 1984), pp. 251–280.

30. Jack Block, *Lives Through Time* (Berkeley, Calif.: Bancroft Books, 1971), p. 263.

31. Diana Baumrind, "The Development of Instrumental Competence Through Socialization," in *Minnesota Symposia on Child Psychology,* vol. 7, ed. Ann D. Pick (Minneapolis: University of Minnesota Press, 1973), pp. 3–46.

32. Ibid., p. 21.

33. Ibid., p. 13.

34. Stanley Coopersmith, *The Antecedents of Self-Esteem* (San Francisco: W. H. Freeman, 1967), pp. 252-253.

35. Jerry M. Lewis, W. Robert Beavers, John T. Gossett, and Virginia Phillips, *No Single Thread* (New York: Brunner/Mazel, 1976).

36. Baumrind, "The Development of Instrumental Competence."

37. Chin-Yau Cindy Lin and Victoria R. Fu, "A Comparison of Child-rearing Practices among Chinese, Immigrant Chinese, and Caucasian-American Parents," *Child Development* 61 (1990): 429–433.

38. Luis M. Laosa, "Maternal Teaching Strategies in Chicano and Anglo American Families: The Influence of Culture and Education on Maternal Behavior," *Child Development* 61 (1990): 759–765.

39. Lin and Fu, "A Comparison of Child-rearing Practices among Chinese, Immigrant Chinese, and Caucasian-American Parents."

40. Harrison, et al., "Family Ecologies of Ethnic Minority Children."

41. Jay D. Schaneveldt, Marguerite Fryer, and Renee Ostler, "Concepts of 'Badness' and 'Goodness' of Parents as Perceived by Nursery School Children," *The Family Coordinator* 19 (1970): 98–103; John R. Weisz, "Autonomy, Control and Other Reasons Why 'Mom Is the Greatest': A Content Analysis of Children's Mother's Day Letters," *Child Development* 51 (1980): 801–807.

42. Belsky, Robins, and Gamble, "The Determinants of Parental Competence: Toward a Contextual Theory."

43. Michael Rutter, "Resilience in the Face of Adversity: Protective Factors and Resistance to Psychiatric Disorder," *British Journal of Psychiatry* 147 (1985): 598–611.

44. Jane Loevinger, "Patterns of Parenthood as Theories of Learning," *Journal of Abnormal and Social Psychology* 59 (1959): 148–150.

45. Ibid., p. 150.

46. Ellen Galinsky, *Between Generations: The Six Stages of Parenthood* (New York: Times Books, 1981).

47. Ibid., p. 317.

ESTABLISHING CLOSE EMOTIONAL RELATIONSHIPS WITH CHILDREN

C H A P T E R 3

In the next two chapters we present basic techniques that may be applied to the two main tasks of parenting—establishing close emotional relationships with children and modifying children's behavior with fair and firm limits. In subsequent chapters we will see how the various techniques of parenting apply to different developmental stages.

In this chapter we look at how parents form close emotional relationships with children. Close emotional ties do not just evolve by themselves. Negative emotional reactions intrude and create distance. In Chapter 2, for example, we noted that frustration and guilt can arise and lead to withdrawal on the parents' part. Although very young children do not hold grievances, older children's anger and frustration tend to linger and also create distance between parent and child. In this chapter, we examine techniques for establishing and maintaining warm, close ties between parent and child and for decreasing the distance that naturally occurs from time to time.

PARENTING EXPERTS REVIEWED

This book will identify five basic strategies in performing the tasks of parenting. These were drawn from the work of Haim Ginott, Thomas Gordon, Dorothy Briggs, Rudolf Dreikurs, and the behaviorists. The work of other researchers is discussed as it bears on particular points. Ginott, Gordon, and Briggs focus on feelings. Clinical psychologist Haim Ginott conducted parent groups in the 1960s and wrote two best-selling parenting books, *Between Parent and Child*[1] and *Between Parent and Teenager.*[2] The application of Ginott's method in day-to-day life is chronicled in *Liberated Parents/Liberated Children*[3] and *How to Talk So Kids Will Listen So Kids Will Talk,*[4] by Adele Faber and Elaine Mazlish, two mothers who participated in discussion groups with Ginott for over five years. Thomas Gordon, also a psychologist, organized his principles into Parent Effectiveness Training (PET) programs given around the country. His major books are *P.E.T. Parent Effectiveness Training,*[5] *P.E.T. in Action,*[6] written with his daughter Judith Sands, and *Teaching Children Self-Discipline.*[7] Dorothy Briggs is also a psychologist and marriage, family, and child counselor who has led many parent education groups. Her book, *Your Child's Self-Esteem*,[8] focuses on how parents can help children to develop the quality that forms the basis of psychological health. Her book includes much information on the growth of the child's self-concept.

Rudolf Dreikurs, a Chicago psychiatrist, was an early researcher concerned with healthy functioning in the family who held groups for parents to improve marriages and for mothers to improve parenting skills. His major books are *The Challenge of Parenthood*[9] and, with Vicki Soltz, *Children: The Challenge.*[10]

The behaviorists are a group of psychologists who focus on changing children's behavior by means of principles found to modify behavior in experimental studies of learning. Those behaviorists whose work will be cited here include Gerald Patterson, who worked with aggressive children and wrote *Families*[11] and *Living with Children;*[12] Wesley Becker, who wrote *Parents Are Teachers;*[13] Robert Eimers and Robert Aitchison, who wrote *Effective Parents/Responsible Children;*[14] and Helen and John Krumboltz, who wrote *Changing Children's Behavior.*[15]

ATMOSPHERE OF PSYCHOLOGICAL SAFETY

Briggs describes an atmosphere of psychological safety that forms the basis for close emotional ties between parents and children. This atmosphere has six important components. The first is **trust**. Children must be able to rely on parents to meet their needs and to be open and honest with them. Parents must strive to communicate what they really mean. Parents will want to keep some of their thoughts and feelings to themselves, but they must be honest about that, too. Parents must avoid saying things they do not mean—for example, "Nothing is bothering me," when they are worried about work. Parents think they are sparing children either criticism or worry, but children are far more bothered by the discrepancy between what the parent says and the emotional state communicated by the parent's voice and behavior.

The second component of a psychologically safe atmosphere is **nonjudgment**. Parents must convey their feelings to children in a nonblaming way. To do this, Briggs suggests parents become reactors rather than judges. Instead of saying, "You're terrible," say, "I can't stand all the arguing we do." Instead of saying, "You're lazy," be specific: "I worry that the dog is not fed when you say you are going to feed her." Briggs separates the behavior from the person, so that it is possible to love children and approve of them without approving their behavior.

The third component is **cherishing** children, caring about them just because they are who they are, appreciating their special qualities. Parents cherish children when they respect them as individuals, when they focus on the child's assets rather than on shortcomings. Perhaps your daughter likes to wear unusual costumes to nursery school. When you appreciate that she likes to go to school as a ballerina, even though you wish she would go in a play outfit that permits climbing without bruises, you are cherishing your child. If a child develops a sense that she is worthwhile, then she will have greater freedom to explore and engage in activities. She will not worry about making mistakes or being criticized, because she has a strong self-image. This freedom will enable her to develop greater competence.

The fourth component is **letting children own their own feelings**. Briggs advises accepting all feelings but not approving all acts. Parents must realize that their perceptions of a situation are not the only valid reactions. Each person experiences a slightly different aspect of a situation. For example, one mother complained that her twelve-year-old daughter was sassy to her and screamed at her. The daughter felt the mother had been making fun of her, and she screamed in response to the hurt she felt. Both reactions were valid, although they were certainly different.

The fifth component is **empathy**—understanding and feeling what the other person experiences. The empathetic parent is genuinely interested in what the child feels and reflects this feeling back. Empathy is built on the belief that each person owns his or her own reactions. Thus, parents can be comfortable in reflecting back something that is quite different from what they think and feel.

> Jim played a tennis match with an older, more experienced player and bemoaned his loss in an irritated voice because he felt he should have won. His mother, who works hard for everything she has achieved, was annoyed that her son expects to do well with little practice, but nevertheless, bit her lip, and reflected that he felt he should have been able to beat the older player. To her amazement, her son said, well, he only wished he had been able to play as well as he did when rallying. If he had, then he would have beaten the other player. This seemed more realistic to the mother, who was delighted that focusing on her son's feelings had given her a new view of the situation.

The sixth component is **parents' faith in the child's capacity for growth**. Just as we believe a plant can grow, so we must trust our children to have within them the capacity for full development. But we do not wait, passively, for changes to occur. We seek ways of stimulating and encouraging development, just as a gardener fertilizes a plant. We also accept that, at times, growth may be halted or sidetracked because of unusual events. Change can be a scary experience for children. There will always be a pull toward the new and unknown, but there will also be hesitation and reluctance to give up what is familiar and trusted. At such times parents must be quietly supportive and understanding of the child's reluctance to explore a new path. Also, we must recognize that children have different growth patterns, so there may be times when our children will be out of step with their peers and especially in need of parents' support.

The environment of psychological safety leads children to feel high self-esteem based on a sense of importance and value to those they love. With high self-esteem, each child is able to explore the world with confidence and to relate to others as a unique individual worthy of respect.

Supporting Briggs's findings, research shows that babies whose mothers are accepting, sensitive, and responsive to them from the earliest days of infancy feel close, positive attachments to their mothers.[16] Babies who grow in families where they are treated as important individuals, where their needs are respected, develop into affectionate, independent toddlers who cooperate with the mother's requests. A system of mutual cooperation between mother and child is established early, so acceptance, sensitivity, and responsiveness get parent-child relations off to a good start.

COMMUNICATING FEELINGS

Briggs, Ginott, and Gordon all emphasize communication of feelings between parent and child. Why are feelings so important? Many psychologists believe that an individual's feelings are all that give life meaning. If everyone felt exactly the same way about every other person, object, or event, life would lose its color, zest, and significance. Ginott describes emotions as follows:

> Emotions are part of our genetic heritage. Fish swim, birds fly, and people feel. Sometimes we are happy, sometimes we are not; but sometimes in our life we are sure to feel anger and fear, sadness and joy, greed and guilt, lust and scorn, delight and disgust. While we are not free to choose the emotions that arise in us, we are free to choose how and when to express them, provided we know what they are. That is the crux of the problem. Many people have been educated out of knowing what their feelings are. When they hated, they were told it was only dislike. When they were afraid, they were told there was nothing to be afraid of. When they felt pain, they were advised to be brave and smile. Many of our popular songs tell us "Pretend you are happy when you are not."
>
> What is suggested in place of this pretense? Truth. Emotional education can help children to know what they feel. It is more important for a child to know what he feels than why he feels it. When he knows clearly what his feelings are, he is less likely to feel "all mixed up" inside.
>
> How can we help a child to know his feelings? We can do so by serving as a mirror to his emotions. A child learns about his physical likeness by seeing his image in a mirror. He learns about his emotional likeness by hearing his feelings reflected by us.[17]

The parent's role is to describe or feed back—to reflect—the child's feelings so that the child is able to identify her reactions. In recent years we have learned a great deal about children's emotions. We know that babies come into the world with emotions and feelings that serve as the primary signals to others of what the infant experiences and needs. Long before they have language, children express surprise, joy, fear, anger, pain, and distress by their smiles, laughs, cries, and frowns. They not only express feelings, but they are also very reactive to the feelings of those around them. A child as young as three months old ceases to play when his mother appears depressed, even if the depression is just part of a laboratory experiment. So children express and react to feelings long before they have the intellectual understanding of what different feeling states are and what events cause certain emotional states.

Infants and toddlers are eager observers, however, and even young toddlers begin to learn words for emotions and to develop ideas as to why people feel a certain way (see Chapter 7 for further details). Nevertheless, they do misunderstand and make faulty connections, and so they do need parents to feed back feelings and clarify what events produce what feelings. For example, as we'll see later in the chapter, little children often believe they are the cause of family members' anger even when adults are angry at something else; children need information from parents about the source of their irritation.

Parents help children identify emotional feelings, but they must not tell children they do not feel a particular way, or that they *should not* feel that way, or that others feel differently. When parents feed back children's feelings, children feel understood.

I N T E R V I E W
with Parents

How has being a parent changed you?

"In a social context, I have had several major revelations. We are all family. I can love these other little children just as much, and any illusions that they are my family or your family or us versus them disappear as I see the children. I guess part of that is the unconditional love. When I had a child, doors opened in my heart that I did not even know were there. There was a depth of love that I had never experienced before. Being with really innocent, loving, accepting children, realizing how vulnerable they are, how impressionable they are, takes a whole different sense of responsibility. I realize that I am working with something that is extremely important, impressionable, and fragile and also that translates, to the extent that I can do it, to adults because I realize they were children not too long ago." FATHER

"It has made me a lot more aware of communication, of people's feelings, even of talking with an adult. And I am more interested in how people feel about things, their emotions, and their lives. I have learned communication skills, empathic listening, and that helps your relationships with adults as well – allowing other adults to express feelings and to try to find out why they feel the way they do. Trying to raise my children in a healthy atmosphere has made me look at my own background, and how I was raised and why I am the way I am, and why I want them to be different from the way I am or the same. And the same with my husband. He looks at his background, why he is the way he is. When you look at yourself and when you come to terms with yourself, you are more easily able to deal with other people, people you might not like as well or don't understand. So there has been a lot of self-introspection that has gone on because I have taken a more conscious look at how children react to their environment and how they are raised. I am more patient, more understanding, but I would say that looking at myself is the most significant way I have changed." MOTHER

Children who are understood feel important and valuable as people. As their responses receive attention, their self-esteem grows. How do you go about feeding back feelings? First, pay attention and listen to hear what the feelings are, then restate what you perceive in simple language.

Active Listening

Active listening is Gordon's term for what parents do when they reflect their children's feelings. Parents listen to children's statements, pay careful attention to the feelings expressed, then make a response similar to the child's statement. If a child says she feels too dumb to learn a school subject, the parent feeds back that she feels she is not smart enough. Ginott might feed back a response about the child's fear, worry, or frustration. Gordon gives examples of feeding back responses about deeper feelings, so the difference between the two strategies is minimal. Following are Gordon's examples of active listening.

CHILD: I don't want to go to Bobby's birthday party tomorrow.
PARENT: Sounds like you and Bobby have had a problem maybe.
CHILD: I hate him, that's what. He's not fair.
PARENT: You really hate him because you feel he's been unfair somehow.
CHILD: Yeah. He never plays what I want to play.

CHILD: (Crying) I fell down on the sidewalk and scraped my knee. Oh, it's bleeding a lot! Look at it!
PARENT: You're really scared seeing all that blood.[18]

If the parent's response accurately reflects the child's feeling, the child confirms the feedback with a positive response. If the parent's interpretation is wrong, the child indicates that and has a chance to correct the misinterpretation by expanding on feelings. The parent can continue active listening and gain greater understanding of what is happening to the child.

A major advantage of active listening is that it helps children express feelings in a direct, effective way. As feelings are expressed and parents accept them, children learn they are like everyone else, and they need not fear what they feel. In the process of being understood, children gain a feeling of being loved and cherished.

A second major advantage of active listening is that, as feelings are expressed, parents and children together learn that the obvious problem is not necessarily the real or basic problem. Like the rest of us, children use defenses and sometimes start by blaming a friend, a parent, or circumstances for what they are feeling. Sometimes they deny, at first, that they are upset. As parents focus on the feelings, children gradually come to identify the underlying problem and discover what they can do about it.

Gordon tells of a teenager who insisted she did not want any dinner. When her father used active listening to get at her feelings, she revealed she did not want to eat because her stomach was in knots. She was worried and frightened that her boyfriend was going to leave her for another girl. She felt the other girl was more popular and successful with boys. She wanted to be that comfortable with boys but was afraid of making a fool of herself. After describing her feelings, she decided she would take a few chances and speak up. The father's active listening moved the conversation from a refusal to eat dinner to the daughter's statement of a serious problem and how she might handle it. As children feel understood, they feel increasingly competent and become responsible problem solvers. A positive cycle is set up, in which parents are accepting of children and trust them to behave responsibly, and children become separate persons who act independently, thus reinforcing the parents' beliefs.

A third advantage is that listening to children's feelings sometimes resolves the problem. Often when we are upset, frustrated, sad, or angry, we simply want to express the feeling and have someone respond, "Yes, that's frustrating," or "It is really painful when a friend walks off with someone else and leaves you behind." The response validates the feeling as being justified and important, and frequently that is all we want.

What qualities must parents have to do active listening? At first active listening involves more work and time than the characteristic responses of advice, criticism, or instruction. When a child says, "Oh, I'm furious at Margie!" it's easier to advise getting a new friend than to engage in a conversation about feelings. Gordon warns parents not to attempt active listening when they are hurried or when they are preoccupied. It takes time and effort to determine whether a joking comment covers up a wealth of sadness over some disappointment, whether a cutting, critical remark hides a feeling of hurt from rejection, or whether a casual remark about a success covers real pleasure at a difficult achievement. Parents need to think carefully, to phrase and time their words with sensitivity, to make the comment that will move the dialogue along and facilitate expression of true feelings. Remember that if, too often, you start such a dialogue and children begin to open up only to find that you cut them off, they will soon come to distrust these conversations and may refuse to participate.

Active listening requires persistence, patience, and a strong commitment. When you begin to use active listening, conversations may seem unnatural, stilted, even contrived. But you will improve with practice—and you can use active listening with your mate and friends as well as with children. Old habits die hard, but you will find yourself giving fewer warnings, less advice and criticism, and being a better facilitator of communication as you continue to practice active listening.

Active listening is a helpful method when it is appropriate. But there are times when it is not. If a child is asking for information rather than expressing an emotion, your response should be to provide the information or guidance to the source of information. If a child does not want to talk about feelings, you should respect the child's privacy and not probe. Similarly, if you have been using active listening and the dialogue has gone as far as the child is willing to go, then you need to recognize that it is time to stop. And finally, don't begin an active listening conversation if you are too busy or too preoccupied to stay with it and really hear and respond to the child's feelings.

Be aware of both the child's words and the behavioral clues that accompany what is said. Is the child's attitude casual, or do you sense an emotional intensity that is inconsistent with the words? Is the child fidgety, uncomfortable, withdrawn, silent, or distracted and thinking about something else? Be aware, too, of your own feelings. Are you preoccupied with a problem at work, worried about getting dinner prepared before guests arrive, or are you concerned and empathetic and ready to spend whatever time is needed for an active listening dialogue? Don't diminish the value of this tool by dulling it with overuse or misuse.

One of the mothers in Ginott's groups raised the question of reflecting back feelings of great sadness over a loss.[19] Is this wise? Does it help children? Might not such feelings overwhelm them? Ginott responded that parents must learn that suffering can strengthen a child's character. When a child is sad in response to a real loss, a parent need only sympathize, "You are sad. I understand." The child learns that the parent is a person who understands and sympathizes.

I-messages

When a parent is angry, frustrated, and irritated with a child, the parent communicates his or her feelings with an **I-message**. The I-message contains three parts: (1) a clear statement of how the parent feels, (2) a statement of the behavior that has caused the parent to feel that way, and (3) why the behavior is upsetting to the parent. For example, a parent who is frustrated with a teenager's messy room might say, "I feel upset and frustrated when I look at your messy room because the family works hard to make the house look clean and neat, and your room spoils all our efforts."

An I-message is a very effective means of communication, but one that is not, in the beginning, easy to use. You will find that you have to concentrate and practice to develop skill with I-messages. But when you are comfortable with them and they come easily, I-messages facilitate communication. I-messages help children to understand their parents as individuals. When parents use I-messages and feel free to express their individuality, they serve as models that encourage children to react openly, too.

Parents may look at their feelings and at children's behavior and discover that, after all, the behavior has no effect on them. When this happens, the reasonable parent may decide there is no need to ask the child to change the behavior. For example, many parents have been concerned about the style of their child's hair. But since this has no direct effect on them, parents do not discuss their dislike of the hairstyle and do not ask the child to change it.

Parents need to spend time analyzing their feelings and becoming more aware of exactly how they feel. Gordon points out that, often, when a parent communicates anger at a child, the parent may actually be feeling disappointment, fear, frustration, or hurt. When a child comes home an hour late, the parent may burst out in a tirade. The worry that grew into fear during the hour of waiting is transformed into relief that the child is safe, and that relief is then translated into angry words intended to prevent a recurrence of this disturbing behavior. Similarly, a parent may complain about a child's behavior when, in reality, what is disturbing the parent is a problem at work. The parent who has learned to use accurate I-messages is less likely to misplace anger and use a child or mate as a scapegoat.

What should you do if a child pays no attention to your I-messages? First, be sure you have the child's attention when you send the I-message. Don't try to communicate your feelings when the child is getting ready to rush out of the house or is already deeply immersed in some other activity. If your I-message is then ignored, send another, more forceful message. And be sure that the feeling tone matches your feelings.

I-messages have several benefits. First, when parents use I-messages, they begin to take their own needs seriously. This process benefits all family relationships because parents feel freer—more themselves—in all areas of life. Second, children learn about the parents' reaction, which they may not have understood until the I-message. Third, children have an opportunity to engage in problem solving in response to I-messages. Even very young toddlers and preschoolers have ideas, not only for themselves but also for others. Siblings often have good ideas about what may be bothering another child in the family. They think of things that might have escaped the attention of parents.

Sometimes a child responds to an I-message with an I-message. For example, when a parent describes upset and distress because the lawn is not mowed, the daughter may reply that she feels annoyed because mowing interferes with her afterschool activities. At that point, the parent must "shift gears," as Gordon terms it, and reflect back the child's frustration by using active listening.

Appreciative I-messages Gordon's techniques can be used for family interactions that do not involve conflict. He suggests that parents send appreciative I-messages. These statements consist of three parts: how the parent feels, what the child did to make the parent feel that way, and the specific effect of the behavior on the parent. For example, "When you let me know where you are, I feel relieved, because I don't have to worry about you." Appreciative I-messages can improve the quality of family life. One mother commented that she never realized how much time she spent sending I-messages of irritation, in contrast to appreciative I-messages, until one evening when her son reported that he had cleaned up a huge mess made by the dog. Often when the dog had an accident, it went unattended until the mother came home from work. She would complain about how upset she was and how it delayed her getting dinner. She later realized that, in contrast to the long period spent expressing irritation, she spent only a few seconds saying "Thank you" and expressing her appreciation. As a result she resolved in the future to be more attentive to helpful behaviors and more verbal in expressing her thanks.

Preventive I-messages Preventive I-messages are useful in heading off problems and in helping children to see that parents are fallible, too. These messages express parents' future wants or needs and give children an opportunity to respond positively. For example, if you say "I got very little sleep last night and want quiet so I can take a nap," you make it possible for them to help you. Preventive messages can be especially practical before an unusual event that may place a special strain on family members. One mother reported that within an hour after the family started out on a long driving trip, the two children, ten and thirteen, began bickering in the back seat. She stopped the car and explained they would be driving for several days, and she needed cooperation. She realized that it would be hard to be cooped up in the car, but it would be easier for everyone if they did not fight. Miraculously, she said, in five days there was hardly a single fight, and the whole family had a good time.

A parent's acceptance of the child, responsiveness to his or her needs, willingness to express positive and negative feelings, along with willingness to listen to the child's feelings—all these behaviors build more harmonious relationships among family members because individuals' feelings are respected and validated.

PROVIDING OPPORTUNITIES FOR SELF-EXPRESSION

Family relationships are most harmonious when children and parents alike have outlets for expressing feelings. Activities such as daily physical exercise, opportunities to draw, model clay, paint, and cook all serve as outlets to drain off tensions and irritations and provide individuals with additional sources of pleasure and feelings of competence. Parents are wise to see that children have a variety of outlets so that they develop many skills. Research indicates that childhood leisure activities, especially a wide variety—such as painting, reading, athletics—are more predictive of psychological health in adulthood than the child's own personality characteristics in childhood. These activities develop confidence and self-esteem that increase psychological health.[20]

Negative feelings like anger and irritation can get in the way of happy relationships. Although, as described in the previous section, there are psychological ways of dealing with anger, parents can also provide special activities to discharge these feelings directly. Young children can be encouraged to divert their energy to physical play. Preadolescents and teenagers can learn the value of physical work and exercise to drain away frustration. Cleaning a room or scrubbing a floor discharge feelings and also provide the pleasure of accomplishment. Helping children learn these techniques strengthens them as individuals and gives them resources in times of trouble. When outlets are provided for negative feelings, children feel their feelings are respected while at the same time the expression of these feelings is channeled in socially productive directions.

Parents help children express themselves when they encourage children to verbalize their thoughts and reactions on a daily basis. Making time for conversation about school, friends, activities of the day conveys to children that their reactions are important. When children are skilled at verbalizing their everyday experiences, they will be better able to talk about their feelings and frustrations at times of stress. They can learn the power of words to tell other people exactly how they feel and to resolve difficulties in an equitable way.

THE CHILD'S BASIC COMPETENCE

There are other ways to build close emotional ties with children: by expressing respect for the child's competence and by giving the child opportunities to participate in the family group as a contributing member. Dreikurs believes that children have built-in capacities to develop in healthy, effective ways.[21] Because they have a push to be active and competent, a parent's main task is to provide an environment that permits this development to occur. The child's strongest desire is to belong to a group, and from infancy the child seeks acceptance and importance within the family. The deepest fear of childhood is fear of rejection. Each child develops a unique path to family acceptance. The child accomplishes this task by using innate abilities and environmental forces to shape dynamic relationships with other family members.

Do parents usually help children discover their own strengths and abilities? No, says Dreikurs. Most often we tear down their confidence with such comments as "What a mess you make," or "I can do it for you faster," or "You are too little to set the table." Dreikurs recommends that parents use encouragement to help children develop their abilities. He defines encouragement as a "continuous process aimed at giving the child a sense of self-respect and a sense of accomplishment."[22] Encouragement is expressed by word and deed.

A parent's facial expression, tone of voice, gesture, and posture all tell children how the parent feels about them. In many different ways—warm cuddling, active play, gentle nurturing—a parent can communicate that children are worthwhile and

A child's strongest desire is to belong to a group, and from infancy the child seeks acceptance and importance within the family. By using innate abilities and environmental factors, children shape dynamic relationships with other family members.

capable of participating in social living. How does a parent provide encouragement for development? First, by respecting the child and, from infancy, permitting self-sufficiency in all possible situations. Babies, for example, are encouraged to entertain themselves; they are left alone at times to explore their fingers and toes, play with toys, and examine their surroundings. As soon as possible, they feed themselves. Very young children of one or two are included in family chores and responsibilities as soon as they show any interest in helping. Even a toddler can empty a wastebasket and carry small nonbreakable items to the dinner table. Second, by giving verbal encouragement, telling children specifically what they do well: "I like your painting with all the bright colors," "You certainly picked up all your toys quickly and that helps Daddy when he vacuums."

Parents offer encouragement when they teach children to ask for what they want. Children need to learn that parents cannot read their minds and that they must take an active role in saying what they want. As children try out new activities, parents wait until children ask for help before giving it. If children ask for help, parents can start off with aid at the beginning or request that children begin and say they will be available when children cannot proceed. When parents give encouragement, they call attention to the challenge of the task—"It's hard practicing now, but you'll master the keys and really enjoy playing the piano as you get more experience." Finally, parents emphasize children's gains. They show children how far they have come since starting the activity. Encouraging comments often refer to the completed task. But children soon learn that enjoyment comes from the process as well as from final success.

DEMOCRATIC FAMILY LIVING

Thomas Gordon and Rudolf Dreikurs both emphasize the importance of a democratic atmosphere, but each gives a slightly different meaning to the word.

In his recent book, *Teaching Children Self-Discipline,* Thomas Gordon describes his great concern about authoritarian families in which parents control children through rewards and punishments.[23] He is highly critical of parents who manipulate children in order to change them into what powerful parents think is desirable. He dislikes the concept of praise because it implies the parent judges and evaluates the child in terms of some external standard. He disapproves of punishment because it allows a powerful person to take advantage of a less powerful person, and he especially condemns physical punishment for children because it belittles them, makes them angry and fearful of the parent, and does not work.

Gordon also criticizes a permissive atmosphere of chaos and disorganization. He encourages a democratic atmosphere in which children are accepted as they are, with important needs and wishes that at times conflict with others' needs. When there is a problem, parents send I-messages, reflecting their own thoughts and feelings, and do active listening to get the child's point of view. If a solution does not arise, then parents and children engage in the mutual problem solving described in the next chapter.

Parents never dictate solutions but work cooperatively with children to form a plan that meets everyone's needs. Working together this way frees children from feeling judged, evaluated, or manipulated. Children and parents become partners in solving the hassles of life.

Dreikurs, too, believes that democratic family living provides an encouraging atmosphere in which the needs of children and parents are given equal respect and consideration. Everyone, however, has responsibilities as well. Parents provide food, shelter, clothes, and recreation for children. Children, in turn, must contribute to family functioning by doing chores and errands. Material rewards are not given for doing a particular number of chores. When mutual respect among equal individuals is the rule in a family, members work together to do the jobs that are necessary for the welfare of all. To deny children the opportunity to do their share is to deny them an essential satisfaction in life. Democratic living ensures freedom for family members but does not imply an absence of rules. Dreikurs strongly favors structure in family life and believes it provides boundaries that give a child a feeling of security.

To help children follow routines, parents serve as models. They also teach children how to do routine tasks. Parents often expect that children will be able to master self-care and household chores without any instruction, and they do not spend the time needed to teach children. How many parents have taught a child, step by step, how to make a bed or how to get dressed, then observed as the child increased in skill, giving added coaching as needed? An encouraging parent helps children to be both self-sufficient and involved with other people. Dreikurs describes the difficulties of life and insists that we prepare our children to cope with them. Life presents problems and hazards. Children who meet painful situations will learn to conquer them if their parents are not overprotective.

Even in ideal family conditions, children make mistakes and fail to accomplish what they set out to do. Parents must learn to accept mistakes without dwelling on them. Dreikurs describes parents' tendencies to overemphasize the errors children make. We want so much for children to grow up and do well that sometimes we trot at their heels, pointing out every minor mistake, telling them what they must do to improve. Under such a regime children may get the idea that they have to be perfect in order to be accepted. Far from stimulating them to action, that idea may build so much fear that the child cannot function. Dreikurs writes,

> We all make mistakes. Very few are disastrous. Many times we won't even know that a given action is a mistake until after it is done and we see the results! Sometimes we even have to make the mistake in order to find out that it is a mistake. *We must have the courage to be imperfect*—and to allow our children also to be imperfect. Only in this way can we function, progress, and grow. Our children will maintain their courage and learn more readily if we minimize the mistakes and direct their attention toward the positive. "What is to be done now that the mistake is made" leads to progress forward and stimulates courage. Making a mistake is not nearly as important as what we do about it afterward.[24]

Parents need to separate the deed from the doer when responding to mistakes. It is important to make clear that the child is not a failure but unskilled, in need of teaching. In coping with a mistake, parents need to stay problem-oriented—to look at the situation, see what needs to be done, and try to help the child function well by giving encouragement and guidance. When a junior high school student gets a poor grade in school, the parent can sit down with the child and help to figure out what the trouble is and how the child might improve. Perhaps more studying, more careful attention to deadlines for papers, or greater participation in class will result in better grades. Parents can help guide the child to select the actions that will bring improvements.

Mistakes are a natural part of life and need not have lasting ill effects. When children learn a healthy attitude towards mistakes early, they are freer to explore and act, and as a result they learn and accomplish more. A healthy attitude consists in believing mistakes are an expected part of life; they are often accidental but they do have causes and can be prevented. So children and parents can learn to look at mistakes carefully and find out what to do differently the next time. Mistakes are proofs the child is trying to do something, but may not be quite ready to achieve the goal. Mistakes are incompletions, not failures. The child can take more time learning the activity or perhaps take more time practicing to achieve the goal.

Mistakes are unfortunate in the sense that they take up time and sometimes money, but they are rarely disastrous or damaging. To the contrary, they are very often valuable experiences because a child learns what is not effective. In addition, many warm family memories center on mistakes that were made and survived.

MISBEHAVIOR: MISTAKEN GOALS

When children feel discouraged and are unable to become involved in activities and make positive contributions to the social group, they are likely to seek other ways to feel important and competent. Misbehavior results from the pursuit of goals that give feelings of importance instead of feelings of self-sufficiency and social integration. Dreikurs identifies four goals of behavior and calls them "mistaken" goals because they do not bring genuine feelings of competence and participation. These goals are attention, power, revenge, and inadequacy. The parent's task is (1) to understand which of the four mistaken goals is motivating the child's behavior and (2) to act so that the purpose is no longer achieved. Thus, the parent must understand the child's underlying feelings, but instead of reflecting back feelings, Dreikurs advises action to modify the child's behavior.

A child is seeking mistaken goals when the behavior conflicts with the needs of the situation. For example, a child may seek attention by being talkative and charming. This behavior is pleasant and endearing rather than annoying. When such behavior prevents others from talking, however, it becomes misbehavior. A child may ask his mother to play a game with him—a reasonable request. But when he insists on this attention when the mother is preparing dinner, she can assume he wants attention rather than to play a game. Where there are several children in a family, they may band together and seek attention by bickering.

When attention is denied, a child may hunt for an issue to use in the struggle for power. A three-year-old may insist she does not have to go to bed at 7:30 p.m. If she persists, running around the house and causing the mother to spend a lot of time in the chase, the child is struggling for power. Sometimes parents find it hard to tell whether a child is seeking attention or power. Dreikurs points out that children usually stop the mistaken behavior after the first request if they are seeking attention, but not if what they want is power. Attempts to stop the behavior only aggravate children, who will try all the harder for power.

When problems continue, children may intensify the power struggle and seek revenge and retaliation. Here children have lost hope of getting approval through positive behavior and feel there is nothing to lose, so revenge is sought as a means of feeling important. Children are determined to feel important even if they have to hurt others physically.

Dreikurs remarks that this kind of misbehavior is particularly sad because children who need the most encouragement are the ones most likely to be punished. Parents need to offer warm understanding and sympathetic acceptance so that children can release their own positive qualities. Unfortunately, punishment intensifies anger and guilt, leads to further attempts to provoke the parents, and sets up a vicious cycle.

Children who claim inadequacy to explain poor performance in some activity are also pursuing a mistaken goal. Dreikurs gives the example of an eight-year-old boy who was having school difficulties. The teacher told the mother he was a poor reader, was slow in all subjects, and showed no improvement despite the teacher's extra efforts. She asked the mother what he did at home. The mother replied that he did not like chores and did them so poorly that she had stopped asking him. The child had developed a low opinion of his abilities over a period of time and found it easiest to claim incompetence. Feelings of helplessness exaggerate any real or imagined problem. In such a situation, a parent can demonstrate the chores and work with children until they feel competent to function alone. Encouragement helps children persist until they are able to finish a job independently.

The behaviorists write less about relationships than other strategists. When children's behavior is of an approved nature—that is, when it meets parents' and other authorities' standards—children receive rewards in the form of approval and positive social attention. Parents feel pleased with children and the children enjoy the attention. Thus, positive family relationships flourish when parents teach children approved behaviors without scolding, blaming, or judging. Using appropriate rewards or punishments, parents have no need to resort to uncontrolled yelling, screaming, or threatening behavior.

Behaviorists also pay much less attention than the other strategists to the feelings of children and parents. They assume that positive emotional and attitudinal changes will occur as behavior changes. Behaviorists, however, do inquire into feelings to determine the most appropriate rewards and punishments. For example, they need to know children's likes and dislikes to select the most effective reinforcements for behavior. They need to know when children are fearful so they can teach new responses to the stimuli that trigger fears. They urge parents to be warm and nurturing so that their rewards will have great impact. As children grow, parental warmth, attention, approval, and praise are more powerful reinforcers than any material rewards. In the behaviorist approach, however, feelings are considered primarily as a basis for determining how to change the child's behavior. The effects of rewards and punishments depend, in part, on the characteristics of the individual who is learning. What is a reward for Suzy is not a reward for Mary; what helps Johnny learn to read does not help Jimmy. Thus, behaviorists are interested in the unique characteristics of each child.

FAMILY ANGER

We have long known that physical violence in families is a destructive force that damages children and all participants. Children who are physically abused or witness the physical abuse of others in the family themselves tend to become depressed, more aggressive, and prone to repeat the pattern as adults. We are not so aware that ordinary yelling and the angry outbursts of everyday life have destructive effects on children as well.

Mark Cummings and his co-workers have carried out a series of studies, assessing the responses of children two to nine years old when they are exposed to different forms of anger. Children respond with emotional arousal that changes heart rate and blood pressure[25] as well as the production of hormones.[26] Whether the angry interaction is actually observed or only heard from another room, or only angry silence is observed, young children react in a variety of ways.

A majority of children show signs of anger, concern, sadness, and general distress that can disrupt play, lead to increased aggressiveness, or result in attempts to end the conflict or comfort the participant. By the preschool period, definite styles of responding to anger are identifiable.[27] Some children, almost half, primarily feel distress with a strong desire to end the fights. Other children, slightly over a third, are ambivalent, revealing both high emotional arousal and upset, but at the same time reporting that they are happy. A small percentage (15 percent) give no response. The ambivalent child is the one who becomes more aggressive in behavior.

Children who are exposed to parents' fighting at home have strong physiological and social reactions to anger.[28] They are more likely to comfort the mother if she is involved in an angry exchange in a laboratory setting. The exposure to marital conflict changes the way young children relate to their own friends. Characteristically they play at a less involved level; and when anger occurs with friends, they find it very hard to handle.

Even when there is no particular distress, family members, both parents and children five to fifteen, see themselves as a major cause of angry feelings in others.[29] Fathers (for whom there is limited information since they were not questioned in as much detail) and children of all ages see themselves as the major cause of mothers' anger. Although mothers cited more general reasons like violence and poverty, when they were asked to keep diaries of what made them angry on a daily basis, they most often cited the noncompliance, destructiveness, and demanding nature of children. Thus, the children's perceptions appeared more accurate.

Children cited the family as the major source of their own anger and saw their happiness as coming from experiences outside the home with friends and personal accomplishments. In contrast, mothers thought children's happiness came from the family and their anger from other experiences. This is how mothers attribute their own feelings—the family providing major positive feelings and other experiences providing anger—and they assume children view life in the same way.

Equally important, all family members believe they can change other members' feelings even when anger is involved. The majority of children believe they can alter their mothers' feelings—68 percent say they can make happy mothers angry, 68 percent said they can make sad mothers happy, and 63 percent said they could make angry mothers happy. Here there is agreement. Mothers say children can change their feelings dramatically, but also believe that they can alter children's feelings as well. Behavioral and verbal strategies were most frequently used by adults and children, but children also included material reward strategies.

So all family members see anger as very much a part of family life. Children appear more accurate in seeing their behavior as a major cause of family anger—though on any given occasion they may be mistaken—and the family routines and demands as the major source of their own irritations.

This study supports the active listening and I-message techniques of Ginott, Gordon, and Briggs, which alter misperceptions and give accurate information so that problems are solved. When parents listen to children's complaints and underlying feelings, they learn exactly how children view situations—how angry they feel sometimes, how responsible. When parents send I-messages effectively, children learn they are not the only source of problems in their parents' lives and, indeed, are a major source of happiness and pleasure to parents. The youngest children know their positive contribution to family life, but this awareness fades as children grow older, and so parents need to help children retain their feeling of importance with I-messages to that effect. When parents use problem-solving techniques to negotiate differences leading to anger, children are less upset at the anger because it is resolved.[30]

LOVE, AFFECTION, CARING, ATTACHMENT, AND JOY

Love is the feeling parents most want to communicate to their children. Throughout this book, we make references to positive feelings of love, caring, and attachment. We consider them in greater detail here because they form the glue of close emotional ties between parents and children. The *American Heritage Dictionary* gives as first definitions of the word *love,* "an intense affection for or attachment to another based on familial or personal ties," and "a strong affection for or attachment to another person based on regard or shared experiences or interests."[31] Other definitions refer to sexual attraction and passion, brotherly love, and enthusiasms—for example, love of language or love of science. Synonyms for love include such words as devotion, affection, and infatuation, but love implies a more intense, less consciously controlled feeling than its synonyms.

When parents talk about loving their children, it is in terms of the first definition—having a strong affection for and attachment to the child. The attachment may grow slowly or may appear in full strength at birth. Parents are often surprised at the intensity of their attachment to their child. They are unprepared for how engrossing children are.

Love and caring grow as children stretch their parents' capacities to give, asking for more time, more attention, more interest. Parents express their love in many ways. Physical affection—hugs, kisses, pats—conveys love. How much physical affection parents gives depends on their own personalities and that of their child. Some parents do not feel comfortable with many physical gestures. But since the average child enjoys being touched, physically reserved parents can sometimes unlearn old habits of restraint with their children. It is wise to give some physical demonstrations of love, even if just a friendly pat or tussle of the hair, but it is unwise for parents to force themselves too much. Some children enjoy hugs and cuddles; still others prefer playful wrestling or being thrown up in the air. These differences are explored in Chapter 6.

Parents reveal their love in many other ways besides physical affection. With young children, parents reveal their caring as they go about their daily routines. Recall that in the last chapter preschoolers defined the good parent—and, presumably, the loving one—as someone who plays with children, hugs, cuddles them, looks after their needs, and protects them. As children grow older, parents reveal love in their understanding of the child, their support, their availability. A loving parent is one who is there for children and who continues to protect children and guide them to learn new behaviors.

In focusing on the giving aspects of parental love, we may forget its enjoyable, pleasurable aspects. When children are grown, devoted parents often remark, "I wish I had enjoyed them more. I was so worried about how things were going, I didn't take time to really enjoy them." Clearly, children feel loved and cared for when parents share the playful activities of life with them. In sharing interests and joyful events with children, parents' love deepens and children reap the benefits.

When we examine the nature of love, in fact, we find it a given factor in all interactions with children—in routine care, in physical affection, in play, and in parental understanding and support.

THE POWER OF POSITIVE FEELINGS

Just as there has been increased attention to the destructive aspects of ordinary angry exchanges, so there has been increased attention to the power of good feelings to make changes in both current behavior and future well-being.

In Chapter 2 we discussed protective factors at times of risk. Primary among them is the strong effect of a secure emotional relationship. Close emotional relationships bring pleasure to all family members and contribute to everyone's well-being. When people are happy, research shows, they are more concerned about others' needs.[32] Pregnant mothers who experienced warm relationships with their own parents look forward with confidence to their own mothering, and the prophecy comes true. Their babies flourish. Husbands and wives who are happily married are more effective parents. Infants with strong attachments to mothers become competent, effective toddlers and preschoolers. As we see in Chapters 4 and 9, older children with strong attachments to a parent are more likely to internalize and obey social rules.

Although closeness is enjoyable and helpful to children, some parents may not feel good about themselves or some of their own qualities, causing them to wonder if their children might not be better off remaining distant from them. They fear their children will pick up their bad qualities. Research on close and nonclose relationships among adolescents and their parents revealed that children who feel close to their parents are less likely to take on the parents' negative qualities than children who feel distant. Negative parental qualities are more potent influences on children when parents and children are not close.[33]

We can speculate that when children feel close to a parent and have some understanding of the parent as a person, they look at the undesirable quality more objectively and reject it as undesirable for themselves. When children are distant from a parent, perhaps feeling rejected by the parent, they may have less understanding of

When children are happy, they are more concerned about the needs and perspectives of others. Thus, well-being in families increases. Close relationships also serve to promote positive qualities in children.

the parent and the negative behavior, causing the children to imitate it. It can also be that imitating the parent's behavior may represent a thwarted attempt to be close to that parent.

Thus, even when parents have many self-doubts and self-criticisms, closeness with them and all their failings is still a positive experience for their children.

Good feelings come from one's own actions and successes as well as from relationships. Kirk Felsman and George Vaillant, following the development of a sample of men from early adolescence to late middle life, identify boyhood competence as an important forerunner of adult mental health. Boyhood competence—a summary measure of having part-time work, having household chores, participating in extracurricular activities, getting school grades commensurate with IQ, participating in school activities, and learning to make plans—consists of experiences Rutter described as protective factors. All bring good feelings of effectiveness. Felsman and Vaillant write, "Perhaps what is most encouraging in the collective portrait of these men's lives is their enormous capacity for recovery—evidence that the things that go right in our lives do predict future successes and the events that go wrong in our lives do not forever damn us."[34]

We do not always have a recent accomplishment to treasure, but studies reveal that if a child just thinks of some pleasant event for a short time, even as short a period as 30 seconds, then performance improves and behavior becomes more friendly, responsive, and responsible. Children resist temptation more successfully (as we shall see in Chapter 7), and they respond to unfair treatment with fairness and generosity.

Happy feelings serve as an inoculation against the effects of negative events.[35] These good feelings are not just fleetingly helpful. Longitudinal research shows that how one spends leisure time, how one has fun in childhood, is more predictive of later psychological health than the presence or absence of problems in childhood.[36] So parents are wise when they follow Dreikurs' advice to remind children of their progress and accomplishments and to build recreational activities into children's everyday lives.

MAJOR POINTS OF CHAPTER 3

Six components of an atmosphere of psychological safety for child:

- trust
- nonjudgment
- cherishing child
- letting child have own feelings
- empathy
- faith in child's ability to grow

When parents listen to child's feelings and reflect them:

- child becomes increasingly able to identify feelings
- child learns his or her own feelings are important
- child's point of view is better understood
- parent and child learn the obvious problem is not always the real problem
- problem is sometimes resolved because feelings are validated

When parents express their feelings, they send I-messages that:

- help parents clarify their own feelings
- state how the parent feels, what behavior aroused the feelings, and why the behavior affects the parent

INTERVIEW
with Emmy E. Werner

Emmy E. Werner is professor of human development and research child psychologist at the University of California, Davis. For three decades, she and colleagues Jessie Bierman and Fern French at the University of California, Berkeley, and Ruth Smith, a clinical psychologist on Kauai, have conducted the Kauai Longitudinal Study, resulting in books such as Vulnerable But Invincible, The Children of Kauai, Kauai's Children Come of Age, *and* Against All Odds.

From your experience of watching children at risk grow up on Kauai, what would you say parents can do to support children, to help maximize their child's potential? From your work with children at risk, what helps children survive and flourish even when faced with severe problems?

Let me say that, in our study, we studied the offspring of women whom we began to see at the end of the first trimester of pregnancy. We followed them during the pregnancy and delivery. We saw the children at ages one, two, and ten, late adolescence, and again at thirty to thirty-two. We have test scores, teachers' observations, and interview material at different times on these people. We have a group of children who were at high risk because of three or more factors. They were children who (1) experienced prenatal or perinatal complications, (2) grew up in poverty, and (3) lived in a dysfunctional family with one or more problems.

You ask me to comment on parenting and what parents can do, but first I would like to urge that we redefine and extend the definition of parenting to cast a wider net and include people who provide love in the lives of children. I like to talk about *alloparenting,* the parenting of children by alternate people who are not the biological parents—they can be relatives, neighbors, siblings.

In our study of vulnerable but invincible children, we found that a major protective factor was that at least one person, perhaps a biological parent, or a grandparent, or an older sibling, accepted them unconditionally. That one person made the child feel special, very, very special. These parent figures made the child feel special through acts. They conveyed their love through deeds. They acted as models for the child. They didn't pretend the child had no handicap or problem, but what they conveyed was, "You matter to me, and you are special."

Now, another theme in our findings is that the parent figure, whoever he or she was, encouraged the child to reach out to others beyond the family—to seek out a friendly neigh-

- convey a message about a problem, about a good act the parent likes, or about a possible problem in the future
- help children understand parents' wishes and points of view

Close relationships grow when parents:

- encourage the child and give the child a sense of self-respect and accomplishment by allowing as much independence as possible

bor, a parent of one of their boy or girl friends, and, thus, learn about normal parenting from other families.

The child resilient was temperamentally engaging. He or she encouraged interaction with others outside the home and was given the opportunity to relate to others.

I had no preconceptions about this protective factor, but what came through was that somewhere along the line, in the face of poverty, in the face of a handicap, faith has an abiding power. I'm not referring to faith in a narrow, denominational sense, but having someone in the family or outside of it who was saying, "Hey, you are having ups and downs, this will pass, you will get through this, and things will get better."

Another thing was that these children had an opportunity to care for themselves or others. They became nurturant and concerned, perhaps about a parent or a sibling. They practiced "required helpfulness."

Now, another protective factor is whether the children were able to develop a hobby that was a refuge and gave them respect among their peers. One of our study members said later, "If I had any doubts about whether I could make it, that hobby turned me around." The hobby was especially important as a buffer between the person and the chaos in the family. But it was not a hobby that isolated you from others; it nourished something you could share with other people.

As many of the children looked back, they describe how a positive relationship with a sibling was enduring and important. As adults they commented with surprise how supportive the relationship was and how these relationships were maintained despite great distances and despite dissimilarity in life and interests.

What do adults say they want to pass on to their own children?

Looking back as an adult, they felt some sort of structure in their life was very important. Even though the family life was chaotic, if a parent imposed some reasonable rules and regulations, it was helpful.

They emphasized faith as something to hang on to and make this clear to their children. As parents now they are quite achievement-motivated. They graduated from high school, and some went back and got additional training. They encourage their children to do well in school.

The main theme that runs through our data is the importance of a parent figure who says "you matter" and the child's ability to create his or her own environment. The children believed they could do it, someone gave them hope, and they succeeded against the odds.

- teach children how to do what is wanted so they can contribute positively to family life
- teach children to communicate their needs
- teach children a healthy attitude toward mistakes
- give many opportunities for self-expression in sports, creative activities, hobbies

- discourage the child's seeking the mistaken goals of attention, power, revenge, and inadequacy
- create a democratic family atmosphere of mutual respect and cooperation in accomplishing family tasks and resolving problems that arise

When adults express unresolved anger in the presence of children, the anger:

- disrupts children's physiological functioning
- produces feelings of sadness, anger, and guilt in children
- decreases their level of play with other children
- makes it hard for children to learn to express their own anger—some become overly passive and others become overly aggressive
- makes children feel they are the cause of anger and should fix the situation

Happiness comes from:

- feelings of love, affection, and concern others direct to us
- activities that lead to feelings of accomplishment and competence

When people are happy, they:

- show more concern for other people
- feel greater confidence in themselves and their abilities
- perform tasks better
- are more friendly and responsive to others
- respond to unfair treatment generously
- seem inoculated against future difficulties

Children under stress are resilient when:

- they have one person who feels they are special
- they are encouraged to reach out to other adults
- they have an easy temperament
- they have faith the future will be better
- they have opportunity to help others
- they develop a hobby they share with others
- they have a strong relationship with a sibling

Close family relationships:

- increase joy and pleasure in life
- promote healthy growth
- buffer members against daily frustrations and disappointments
- expand horizons as members take up new activities together

ADDITIONAL READINGS

Briggs, Dorothy. *Your Child's Self Esteem.* Garden City, N.Y.: Doubleday, 1975.

Faber, Adele, and Mazlish, Elaine. *How to Talk So Kids Will Listen and Listen So Kids Will Talk.* New York: Rawson Wade, 1980.

Ginott, Haim G. *Between Parent and Child.* New York: Avon, 1969.

Gordon, Thomas. *P.E.T. Parent Effectiveness Training.* New York: New American Library, 1975.

Gordon, Thomas. *Teaching Children Self-Discipline.* New York: Times Books, 1989.

Notes

1. Haim G. Ginott, *Between Parent and Child* (New York: Avon, 1969).
2. Haim G. Ginott, *Between Parent and Teenager* (New York: Avon, 1971).
3. Adele Faber and Elaine Mazlish, *Liberated Parents/Liberated Children* (New York: Avon, 1975).
4. Adele Faber and Elaine Mazlish, *How to Talk So Kids Will Listen and Listen So Kids Will Talk* (New York: Rawson Wade, 1980).
5. Thomas Gordon, *P.E.T. Parent Effectiveness Training* (New York: New American Library, 1975).
6. Thomas Gordon with Judith G. Sands, *P.E.T. in Action* (New York: Bantam, 1978).
7. Thomas Gordon, *Teaching Children Self-Discipline* (New York: Random House, 1989).
8. Dorothy C. Briggs, *Your Child's Self-Esteem* (Garden City, N.Y.: Doubleday, 1970).
9. Rudolf Dreikurs, *The Challenge of Parenthood,* rev. ed. (New York: Hawthorn, 1958).
10. Rudolf Dreikurs with Vicki Soltz, *Children: The Challenge* (New York: Hawthorn, 1964).
11. Gerald R. Patterson, *Families: Applications of Social Learning to Family Life,* rev. ed. (Champaign, Ill.: Research Press, 1975).
12. Gerald R. Patterson, *Living with Children,* rev. ed. (Champaign, Ill.: Research Press, 1976).
13. Wesley C. Becker, *Parents Are Teachers* (Champaign, Ill.: Research Press, 1971).
14. Robert Eimers and Robert Aitchison, *Effective Parents/Responsible Children* (New York: McGraw-Hill, 1977).
15. John D. Krumboltz and Helen B. Krumboltz, *Changing Children's Behavior* (Englewood Cliffs, N.J.: Prentice-Hall, 1972).
16. Inge Bretherton, "Attachment Theory: Retrospect and Prospect," in *Growing Points of Attachment Theory and Research,* eds. Inge Bretherton and Everett Waters, Monographs of the Society for Research in Child Development 50 (1985), serial no. 209, pp. 3–35.
17. Ginott, *Between Parent and Child,* pp. 39–40.
18. Gordon with Sands, *P.E.T. in Action,* p. 47.
19. Faber and Mazlish, *Liberated Parents/Liberated Children.*
20. Jane B. Brooks and Doris M. Elliott, "Prediction of Psychological Adjustment at Age Thirty from Leisure Time Activities and Satisfactions in Childhood," *Human Development* 14 (1971): 61–71.
21. Dreikurs with Soltz, *Children: The Challenge.*
22. Ibid., p. 39.
23. Gordon, *Teaching Children Self-Discipline.*
24. Dreikurs with Soltz, *Children: The Challenge,* p. 108.
25. Mona El-Sheikh, E. Mark Cummings, and Virginia Goetsch, "Coping with Adults' Angry Behavior: Behavioral, Physiological, and Verbal Responses in Preschoolers," *Developmental Psychology* 25 (1989): 490–498.
26. John M. Gottman and Lynn F. Katz, "Effects of Marital Discord on Young Children's Peer Interaction and Health," *Developmental Psychology* 25 (1989): 373–381.
27. E. Mark Cummings, "Coping with Background Anger in Early Childhood," *Child Development* 58 (1987): 976–984.
28. Jennifer S. Cummings, Davis S. Pellagrini, Clifford S. Notarius, and E. Mark Cummings, "Children's Responses to Adult Behavior as a Function of Marital Distress and History of Interparent Hostility," *Child Development* 60 (1989): 1035–1043.

CHAPTER 3
Establishing
Close Emotional
Relationships
with Children

29. Katherine Covell and Rona Abramovitch, "Understanding Emotion in the Family: Children's and Parents' Attributions of Happiness, Sadness, and Anger," *Child Development* 57 (1987): 985–991.

30. E. Mark Cummings, Dena Vogel, Jennifer S. Cummings, and Mona El-Sheikh, "Children's Responses to Different Forms of Expression of Anger between Adults," *Child Development* 60 (1989): 1392–1404.

31. *American Heritage Dictionary*, 2nd college ed. (Boston: Houghton Mifflin, 1982), p. 744.

32. Eleanor E. Maccoby and John A. Martin, "Socialization in the Context of the Family: Parent-Child Interaction," in *Handbook of Child Psychology*, eds. Paul H. Mussen and E. Mavis Hetherington, vol. 4: *Socialization, Personality, and Social Development*. 4th ed. (New York: John Wiley, 1983), pp. 1–101.

33. John A. Clausen, Paul H. Mussen, and Joseph Kuypers, "Involvement, Warmth, and Parent-Child Resemblance in Three Generations," in *Present and Past in Middle Life,* eds. Dorothy H. Eichorn, John A. Clausen, Norma Haan, Marjorie P. Honzik, and Paul H. Mussen (New York: Academic Press, 1981), pp. 299-319.

34. J. Kirk Felsman and George E. Vaillant, "Resilient Children as Adults," in *The Invulnerable Child,* ed. E. James Anthony and Bertram J. Cohler (New York: Guilford, 1987), p. 298.

35. Charles R. Carlson and John C. Masters, "Inoculation by Emotion: Effects of Positive Emotional States on Children's Reactions to Social Comparison," *Developmental Psychology* 22 (1986): 760–765.

36. Brooks and Elliott, "Prediction of Psychological Adjustment at Age Thirty from Leisure Time Activities and Satisfactions in Childhood."

MODIFYING CHILDREN'S BEHAVIOR

C H A P T E R 4

Children do not naturally do all the things parents want them to do. This chapter focuses on ways of shaping children's behavior so they can adapt to family and social standards. As in many other areas of parenting, parents change their own behavior to ensure children will follow guidelines. In this chapter we cover ways of (1) establishing realistic expectations, (2) structuring the environment to help children meet them, (3) teaching new, socially approved behaviors to children, (4) setting limits, and (5) enforcing limits.

KINDS OF LEARNING

Much of the information about changing children's behavior comes from psychologists who have studied the learning process. They identify three kinds of learning—classical conditioning, operant or instrumental conditioning, and observational learning. **Classical conditioning** occurs when new signals are learned for already existing responses. Classical conditioning is especially important in understanding how new responses are attached to an individual's emotional and physiological responses. In everyday life, a stimulus (trigger) is followed by a response. In Pavlov's first experiment with dogs, the sight of food caused the dog to salivate. Sight of food was called the **unconditioned stimulus** and salivating the **unconditioned response.** When a neutral stimulus, a buzzer, was paired many times with the sight of food, soon the buzzer alone triggered the response of salivating. The buzzer was called the **conditioned stimulus** because only after many pairings with food was it able to elicit the response.

We see the process of classical conditioning in everyday life when people who experience a strong emotional feeling attach that feeling to other stimuli present at the time. Later, other stimuli may trigger the emotional response. For example, a child is frightened by a barking dog who nips him playfully. The next time the child sees a barking dog, he feels frightened because he associates the barking alone with the fear that he felt when the barking was accompanied by a nip from the dog.

INTERVIEW
with Paul Mussen

Paul H. Mussen is professor emeritus of psychology at the University of California, Berkeley. He is a former director of the Institute of Human Development on the Berkeley campus. He has coauthored many books, including The Roots of Prosocial Behavior in Children *with Nancy Eisenberg in 1989. He is also an editor of* The Handbook of Child Psychology.

Parents are very interested in moral development. What can they do to promote this in their children?

With my bias, modeling is of primary importance. It is *the* single most important thing parents can do. Parents create a nurturant environment in which the child wants to imitate the parent's behavior and the parents behave in an altruistic way so that there is an identification with the parents. Parents also can try to get the child to participate when they are doing something for someone else.

Then parents use empathy-eliciting disciplinary procedures in which they make the child aware that he or she has hurt someone. In the early years with toddlers, it is a disciplinary technique that involves showing clearly and emphatically that you disapprove but at the same time, making clear that someone else was harmed by what the child has done—"You pulled her hair. Don't ever do that again. You really hurt her."

In general I think the disciplinary practices are very important. Studies show the empathy-eliciting techniques—so-called induction and reasoning as opposed to power-assertion (spanking and threatening)—are important because they focus not on punishing the child but on pointing up the consequences of what is done. So, first eliciting empathy, then later reasoning with the child are important.

Rewarding altruistic behavior when it occurs is important. The research evidence here is not as strong as one might like, but it does suggest this.

Discussing moral issues at home is critical both from the point of view of moral thinking and from the point of view of moral behavior. Older studies showed that the model's behavior was the critical thing, not what the model said. More recent studies show that verbal

Operant or **instrumental conditioning** involves forming new associations between stimuli (triggers) and responses on the basis of rewards and punishments. When a stimulus-response pattern leads to a reward or positive consequence—a cookie, a parent's smile, extra privileges—the behavior is likely to occur again. When the pattern receives no reward or leads to a negative consequence, a punishment—a parent's frown or loss of a privilege—the behavior pattern decreases. When the behavior disappears, we say it is **extinguished** or has undergone **extinction**.

Children also learn by observing **models** and imitating them. A four-year-old imitates the mother's care of a two-year-old sister and reaps the reward of a big smile from daddy. Imitation of a model will occur even when the child receives no reward. Observation of another person's behavior is enough to stimulate imitation. Children often do as we do and not as we say, because they have observed us and are imitating

responses can be helpful also. You are giving the child some codes or rules that the child can then apply later on when various situations arise. So the discussion and what, for lack of a better word, we used to call preaching—in effect, discussing problems, making principled statements—can be helpful.

Giving children assignments of responsibilities fairly early at the child's level, is also useful. For example, in the schools, a young fifth-grader can help a second-grader; and at home older siblings can help younger siblings. Having chores and assigning tasks in such a way that children get satisfaction from accepting responsibility is important.

Those are the important disciplinary techniques—modeling, a nurturant milieu so the child identifies with the modeling, reasoning, discussing rules and principles so the child can use them later, rewarding positive behavior when it occurs, and giving opportunities for satisfaction from accepting responsibility.

What are the things parents should avoid doing?

One thing to avoid is behaving immorally themselves. Another is being inconsistent—occasionally not reacting to misbehavior that harms someone else and at other times punishing it, and at still other times rewarding it. Inconsistent patterns of reaction should be avoided. Also be very alert in terms of inconsistency with respect to what the parent says and what the parent does.

In general, I feel that power-assertive techniques (like spanking) should be avoided because they produce the wrong orientation. They give the impression that authority can do whatever it wants and the rest of us just have to go along. They result in less independent moral judgment, and they make the point that aggression can be a successful means of getting what you want.

Avoid underestimating children's understanding because I think they are a lot more sensitive to these issues than we might think. And I don't think they should be babied or patronized when you are handling something. Let them be involved in making decisions. Assume that they can understand when you are trying to use inductive techniques. Parents sometimes feel they have to play down to children, and I don't think that's true.

our behavior instead of obeying our words. Research indicates that children are most likely to imitate models who are warm, nurturing, and powerful. In extreme circumstances, when there is no model of warmth and power to copy, children will imitate a hostile, rejecting figure.

Learning principles help parents teach children how to behave in approved ways. Rudolf Dreikurs commented that parents spend too little time actively instructing children in what they want them to do.[1] They seem to expect children will naturally observe what is correct. Children learn a great deal this way, but not everything. It is indeed true that a first rule of parenting is that parents model the behaviors they wish children to have. Parents, however, must go beyond this simple model and take a more active role. Before teaching children new skills and limiting behavior, parents must decide on realistic expectations for children.

ESTABLISHING REALISTIC AND APPROPRIATE EXPECTATIONS

As noted in Chapter 2, their own unrealistic expectations of children's behavior are a major source of parents' frustration. Since there is no one correct way to rear children at each stage of development, how do parents make their expectations realistic? What is realistic, given the variety of family settings that parents and children live in?

Realistic expectations are those that take into account the child's age and characteristics, family pattern of living, social standards, parents' individual characteristics, health and safety factors, and daily events. Parents use the child's age as their first guide. For example, they do not expect toddlers to conform to their every wish quickly, because they know toddlers are beginning to explore the world and assert their individuality. Parents expect more refusals at this age and are ready to be patient as children learn to master activities themselves. Parents learn what to expect at different ages by reading, going to parent groups, talking to other parents, and by experience.

Having considered the child's age, parents then consider the child's own individual characteristics. Some children develop exactly by the book and parents base their expectations on what is typical for children of that age. Other children may have special needs to take into account. For example, parents of highly active children must learn to have different expectations about how long their children can sit at a movie or musical event. Parents of shy children will have different expectations of how much support their children need when meeting new people in a strange setting. Parents of gregarious, outgoing children will have different expectations about how often friends can come to spend the night. So parents will always ask themselves whether a specific expectation is realistic for a specific child at a specific stage.

Having taken the child's special characteristics into account, parents arrive at expectations based on their own and their family's overall needs. For example, in families where mothers do not have paid employment outside the home, there may be fewer expectations about children doing their chores before they leave the house each day. In families where both parents work outside the home and children are in day care after school, it may be more important for children to do chores before school because there is little time before dinner. Or, in families with many children, expectations about sharing toys and possessions and helping each other may be much greater than in two-child families.

Then we have parents' personal expectations. Parents may expect that children will follow in their footsteps—parents who were school achievers may expect very good grades from children; athletic parents may expect children to perform well in sports. Other parents expect children to achieve what they did not—the shy parent who wants a popular child or the early-working parent who wants the child to enjoy childhood. These expectations based on parents' lives are reasonable if they can be abandoned when a child cannot or does not want to meet them. Parents have other expectations based on personal characteristics—parents who like lots of sleep may expect children to be similar; parents who do not like noise may expect very low noise levels. It is always wise for parents to reassess their expectations based on personal values to see whether they are realistic.

Parents also base expectations on their own social values and the social standards of the community. Parents of ethnic groups may have expectations about sharing or independence or about participation in extended family activities that are different from those of the predominant culture. Or parents may live in a community where the standard is participation in some kind of group activity such as Boy Scouts or Girl Scouts; parents may then expect their children to take part, too.

Expectations must be tailored to meet health and safety needs. When families live near busy streets, there will be firm expectations that very young children stay out of the streets. Health needs dictate reasonable amounts of sleep per night, a nutritious diet, toothbrushing. Children can be expected to follow these guidelines even though they do not want to.

Finally, daily events influence the nature of realistic expectations—and precisely in this area parenting becomes an art. If a child had a stressful day, expectations may have to be changed. If a child went to the dentist, had a fight with a friend, lost a pet, it may be realistic and understanding to be tolerant of the child's irritability or inability to perform chores. Similarly, a parent who had a very rough and unusual day, feeling sick with flu or meeting some unusual expense, may want a respite from the expectations of other family members.

Finally, when they assess the appropriateness of their expectations, parents must ask themselves if this is something they expect from themselves or a friend. Parents will occasionally demand that children do things they themselves do not do. For example, parents may demand that children not eat between meals, while snacking themselves and having two or three coffee breaks per day. Sloppy parents may expect neat children. When parents themselves do not perform behaviors they expect of children, they should not be surprised when children follow suit.

All these factors—child's age, special characteristics, parents' characteristics, family lifestyle, community standards, health and safety needs, daily events—influence parents' realistic expectations. In general, children do best when expectations are consistent from one day to the next, especially in matters of importance. Though parents may make occasional allowances for special events and stresses, consistent expectations for the child lead to greater compliance.

HELPING CHILDREN MEET EXPECTATIONS

Having established realistic expectations, parents help children meet them in several ways. First, they structure the child's physical environment. They have storage space for children to put away toys, they have hooks in closets at children's level of reach. They have dressers children can open and storage space marked for clothes in drawers. They have toys children can take care of.

As nearly as possible, the family house should be structured to meet children's needs. Play space outdoors is available. Furniture, rugs, decorations are selected with an active family in mind. Thomas Gordon says many parents refuse to take things off tables or put fragile objects out of children's reach because they believe children should learn early not to touch certain objects.[2] When asked, however, most of these same parents said they would quickly modify their homes if an elderly parent were coming to stay! Gordon believes that if an aging parent with mature faculties needs the home adjusted, all the more so do young children, who are not mature.

There is wide agreement that homes need to be babyproofed and childproofed. Chapter 7 presents suggestions for making the home a safe environment for children. Putting dangerous substances out of the way, having locks on drawers containing knives, clearly marking sliding glass doors—all these changes minimize the opportunities for children to harm themselves and help children lead a safe, healthy life.

A second major way parents help children meet parental expectations is by establishing a regular daily routine. A regular routine makes a habit of certain behaviors that children learn to do automatically. Regularity, as we will see in Chapter 6, has physical benefits for the child as well. Our physiological systems—including secretions of hormones, needs for sleep and food—operate on a 25-hour cycle, but we live in a 24-hour day. So, to help bodies stay in rhythm, both children and adults need a schedule for sleeping, eating, exercising at regular intervals. Human beings function at their best in this kind of routine.

Here again, however, children's individual tempos must be taken into account. Some children are slow to wake from sleep; they must have more time in the morning to get started. Other children need more time to wind down at night, so their bedtime routines may have to be started earlier than usual. Children have different patterns of eating—some eat a lot in the morning, tapering off by dinner; others have opposite patterns. A child can be expected to come to the table for some sort of food, but portions can be varied so that the child's individual needs are kept in mind.

A third way parents help children meet expectations is by monitoring the amount of stimulation children receive. For example, they schedule their children's activities in such a way that children do not become overly tired or overly excited. Parents do not take a preschool child shopping all morning and then send the child off to a birthday party in the afternoon because the child may well be irritable and overly stimulated. As holidays or vacations approach, parents try to schedule rest periods or quiet time so that children have a chance to unwind from all the excitement.

Parents also prepare children for difficult situations or changes in routine. They may calmly rehearse a visit to the dentist, letting the child practice with a doll or stuffed animal, so that the child will be much less likely to feel overwhelmed when the real event occurs. Parents can use rehearsal to prepare children for other changes in routine. For example, if parents are going on a vacation, or if a parent will not be there to pick up a child at day care, they can go over in advance what the child will do and what other caregivers will do.

REWARDS

Once parents have agreed upon realistic expectations and structured their children's environment, they reward children for appropriate behavior when it occurs. **Rewards** or positive reinforcers are actions that increase the likelihood the behavior will occur again. Rewards are always present when a behavior continues, whether we recognize them or not. Sometimes the rewards are pleasurable feelings inside the person and are not observable. For example, children run and jump because they feel good when they do it. They draw and solve puzzles often because such activities are enjoyable in themselves. Sometimes rewards are given by other people. Such external rewards fall into three general categories: **social rewards** of attention, smiles, approval, praise, physical affection; **material rewards** of food, presents, special purchases; and **privileges and activities**, such as trips, special outings to the zoo, or permission to stay up late. Parents are wise to notice the kinds of rewards that appeal to their children and to make a list of activities and privileges that are particularly appealing to each child in the family. Sometimes the reward is allowing the child to continue the pleasurable activity he or she initiated. When parents supply external rewards, behaviorists suggest they rely most heavily on social rewards because those bring the family closer together and create an atmosphere of warmth and trust. Within this category, however, individual preferences exist. Some children enjoy hugs and kisses, while others like verbal compliments.

When behavior patterns are being established, parents give rewards after each successful act. Once the behavior occurs regularly, they can give rewards only occasionally. For example, when Jimmy first started picking up his clothes and putting them in the hamper, his mother commented every day about how helpful he was. As he continued, his mother remarked on it only when he did it rapidly.

How, specifically, should rewards be given? Eimers and Aitchison have outlined seven specific steps.[3] They believe social rewards of praise and approval are more effective than material rewards because they are less costly, less formalized, and have lasting psychological benefits. Specific statements of praise and approval are informative. They may describe positive characteristics that children have not noticed about themselves, thus increasing their self-esteem and self-confidence. Following are the seven recommended steps:

1. Make eye contact with your child. Direct eye contact makes the statement a more personal one.

2. Be physically close to your child. Praise given at close range has more impact.

3. Smile. Sometimes a smile alone is praise, but it should accompany the verbal message so that the child sees your pleasure in your facial expression.

4. Comment on positive behaviors. Send I-messages, telling the child what you like about his or her behavior—"I like it when you help me carry in the groceries." Express appreciation when the child does you a favor—"Thank you for mailing my letter." Children blossom under this attention.

5. Focus on behavior, not on the child. Like all other strategists we have cited, behaviorists recommend comments on specific behaviors, not on the child's characteristics. "Doing the dishes is a big help to me, Linda, and I appreciate it," not "What a good girl you are."

6. Show affection. How we handle our bodies—our gestures, moves, tones of voice—can increase the value of the praise and make the child feel very special. Again tailor the affectionate demonstrations to the child.

7. Deliver the reward immediately. The faster the reward is given, the more effective it is.

◆

BOX 4-1
REWARD MENU

Extra snack	5 tokens	Play cards with parents	5 tokens
Extra story read	5 tokens	Play outside extra hour	10 tokens
Extra game with parents	10 tokens	Trip to park	10 tokens
Trip to library	10 tokens	Movie	15 tokens
Special dinner menu	15 tokens	Special hike	15 tokens

Sometimes praise alone is not effective. Children may not want to carry out an activity no matter how approving a parent is. A schoolchild may not like math and may refuse to work hard, even for social rewards. In this situation, tokens or a point system can be useful in motivating the child to take an interest. A token system is one in which children earn tokens or points that they can exchange for privileges or other rewards (see Box 4-1). If a child does not like math and is careless when doing homework, parents may want to establish a program in which the child can earn one token for every correctly completed math problem. At the end of the week, the child presents the homework, corrected by the math teacher, to the parent. The number of math problems correctly done determines the number of tokens earned.

As children improve their behavior, they must do more and more to obtain tokens. For example, as math improves, the child might earn only half a token for each problem correctly done in a week. Eimers and Aitchison recommend giving social rewards of approval along with tokens and eventually switching to social rewards alone.[4] When the child's math skills are firmly established, the entire system can be phased out.

Parents must be careful not to take approved behaviors for granted. They must continue to comment on the chores completed on time, the good report card, the clothes picked up. In the rush of everyday life, it is easy to forget the desirable behaviors performed by all members of the family. The sensitive parent continues to make comments on well-learned but much appreciated behavior.

Are rewards a form of bribery? This is a charge often made about the use of external rewards. Behaviorists reply that if rewards are increased when the child refuses to carry out an act, then the reward is a bribe. Giving regular rewards for desirable behavior, however, is nothing more than giving a realistic payoff, a common motivation for adults as well as children. For example, a paycheck is a payoff for work; a compliment to a coworker expresses appreciation of some positive act. Why should we not do this with our children? To the extent that behaviorists rely on social rewards of attention, smiles, and praise, they are conveying positive feelings to the children in the same way that Gordon, Ginott, and Briggs recommend. Reflection of feelings and I-messages are not considered bribes, but they are social rewards that increase communication between child and parent.

TEACHING ACCEPTABLE NEW BEHAVIORS

Because children may not spontaneously do what parents want them to do, parents must actively teach children what they desire them to do. When the behavior is already within the child's capacity, parents show the child what they want done. They move very young children through the necessary steps, verbalizing each step as they go—"This is how you put on your shirt." Parents can break the task into separate units and describe what is being done while the child does it. "First you put one arm through the sleeve. Then put the other arm through the other sleeve. Then you put your head through the opening and pull the shirt on." Parents offer encouragement and praise after each step. After the child has thoroughly learned the behavior, only occasional praise is needed.

In some situations the child is not able to carry out the behaviors the parents want to reward, so parents must *shape* the child's existing behavior. For example, suppose a parent wants her five-year-old to begin making his bed, and he does not know how. The first step for the parent is to decide what behaviors come closest to the specific behavior she wants the child to learn. Reward these. Then, as these increase in frequency, demand a higher level of performance before the reward is given. For example, in teaching bed making, a parent might initially reward the young child when the covers and spread are pulled up close to the pillow. As the child masters that skill, then the parent rewards pulling the spread over the pillow. Finally, when that is mastered, the parent rewards the child for having a smooth bed with no wrinkles and the spread over the pillow.

Shaping behavior is a useful approach with schoolchildren who get poor report cards. Parents can reward the highest passing grade on the first report card. They can contract with children for rewards after the next report card if there are specific improvements. Since report periods are usually six weeks long, parents may reward good test performance during that period or contract to give small regular rewards for teacher reports of acceptable work. Report cards are a situation where parents do not want to give a child rewards only for superb performance because they may be a very long time coming; in this situation rewarding improvements in homework and test grades may be more effective.

Theoretically, it is possible to rear children using only rewards and ignoring all misbehavior, which theoretically becomes extinguished for lack of reward. In everyday life, however, parents usually must deal with behavior that violates rules. When the child actively does something not approved, parents have two tasks before them—to state limits effectively, then enforce them.

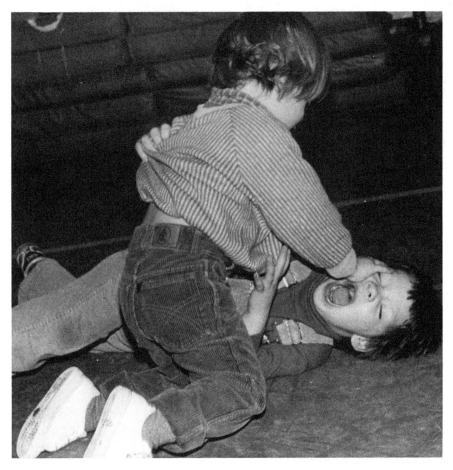

Children may not spontaneously do what parents want them to do, necessitating that parents actively teach children what they desire them to do. All siblings fight, but families differ in their tolerance of aggression. Children who are allowed to be aggressive in the home will be aggressive in preschool and school.

STATING LIMITS EFFECTIVELY

When limits are clearly stated, they are more likely to be followed. Parents make their work easier when rules are specific. Tell children exactly what you desire of them. Say, "I want you to play outside for a while"; not, "Be good this afternoon." Phrase the rule, if possible, in positive form, also stating its purpose. For example, instead of saying, "Don't drag your coat on the floor," say, "Carry your coat so it stays clean." Research shows that when parents say, "Don't" in a loud voice, followed by a few words, the child hears only the few words and continues the action.[5] "Don't jump on the sofa" leads young children to continue the jumping.

Children respond more easily when rules are phrased in an impersonal way. "Bed-time is at 8," or "Dinner at 6" is more likely to result in compliance than "You have to go to bed now," or "You have to be home for dinner at 6."

Parents get best results when they give only one rule at a time. As they give the rule, they gain the child's attention, standing close to the child with good eye contact. Young children can be walked through the desired behavior. For example, as parents say, "It's time to clean up toys," they pick up the young toddler's hand and show her how to put teddy on the shelf, guiding her hand through the movements.

When possible, give the children options. "You can have hot or cold cereal," "You can take the trash out now or right after dinner," "You can wear a raincoat or carry an umbrella." Having choices gives children some control over what is happening. Parents also give options when they prepare for changes in behavior. For example, just before dinner, a parent may prepare a child for coming in by saying, "Dinner is in five minutes," or, "In five more swings, it is time to leave the park." Children have a chance to get ready to follow the rule. Having options and having time to prepare for a change not only make it easier for children to follow rules, but also boost their self-esteem as they see their feelings and wishes respected.

Ginott suggests four steps in stating limits: (1) accept the child's wish without criticism or argument, (2) state what the rule or limit is, (3) when possible, describe how the child can obtain the wish, and (4) accept any irritation or resentment the child feels over being denied a request.[6] For example, with an elementary school child, a parent might say, "I understand that you want to watch an extra hour of TV tonight, but you know the rule is only one hour per day and you have already watched the one hour. If you want to give up tomorrow's hour, you can watch the extra hour tonight." If the child refuses to accept this, the parent can say, "I know you are unhappy you cannot watch TV tonight."

Parents might like to see many changes in their children's behavior, but parents work best with children when they can agree with each other on priorities in the rules. In most families, health and safety rules are most important. Rules about stay-ing out of the street, about always telling parents where they are, and about following curfew rules are the most important and the most carefully monitored. Also in this category are prohibitions against hurting other people and damaging them physi-cally by biting, hitting, kicking. Next are what might be termed rules that ease social living—rules that make being together easier. This category includes rules against destroying other people's property or hurting their feelings deliberately and rules of general consideration (such as being quiet when others are sleeping or being helpful with chores).

Third in priority come conventional rules—how to use a napkin and silverware, what clothes to wear, what social routines to follow. Parents sometimes place great emphasis on this area—chewing with the mouth closed, sitting up in chairs. Even young preschoolers are aware of the difference between rules that concern kindliness and basic consideration of others and rules having to do with social convention.[7] Significantly, they are more impressed with the importance of kindness to others than with social conventions. Parents are wise to accept their preschoolers' reasoning and let them master conventions at a later date.

Last on the list are rules governing behaviors that can be choices for children.

What clothes to wear, what music or records to hear, what games to play are, in most cases, matters of the child's individual preference. These choices usually carry no serious consequences. If parents believe there are consequences—such as very loud music that affects teenagers' hearing or clothing so inappropriate to the weather there is a health risk—then limits must be set. In general, however, children have autonomy in these areas of dress, play, and entertainment. Parents need not expend enormous energies getting children to do things just as they would like them to.

Once they have set priorities on the rules, parents must deal with children's failures to abide by them.

ENFORCING LIMITS

When rules have been stated clearly and children do not follow them, then parents act to enforce them. Before acting, however, parents must do two things. First, they must ask themselves whether children continue to break the rule because, in some disguised fashion, parents are rewarding the rule-breaking behavior. Parents sometimes tell children to stop running or stop teasing, but then undermine themselves with a chuckle and a shake of the head to indicate that the child has a lot of spirit and that they admire that spirit. So, the child continues. Parents must first look to see if they are rewarding behavior they do not approve.

Second, parents must be sure they are in general agreement about enforcing the rules. If there are big differences of opinion between them about enforcing the rules, parents should get off by themselves and negotiate the differences with mutual problem-solving techniques. Otherwise, any family discussions about the problem may bog down in parents' arguing with each other. When parents can agree on basic rules and enforcers and back each other up, children will learn more easily and quickly. If parents frequently disagree, they may refuse to set any consequence for a behavior until they have a chance to talk with the other parent. Though they may not be in complete agreement about all aspects of discipline, most parents can agree on the three or four rules they will be absolutely firm about. Parents have many options to choose from in enforcing limits.

Mutual Problem Solving

Using Gordon's mutual problem-solving technique is a useful first step.[8] Employing this approach, parents identify the rule breaking as a problem to them, a problem they want children to help them solve so that children, too, will be satisfied with the outcome. Parents solicit their children's opinions and work together to find a solution agreeable to all concerned. For example, when children are consistently late for dinner or do not come to the table when called, parents present this as a problem they all must solve. The underlying assumption is that the family working together can find an alternative that satisfies everyone. There are six steps to the problem-solving process: (1) defining the problem, (2) generating possible solutions, (3) evaluating possible solutions, (4) deciding on the best solution, (5) implementing the decision, and (6) follow-up evaluation.

INTERVIEW
with Parents

What are the joys of parenting for you?

"I have made deals with her. We always call it, 'Let's make a deal. This is what I want. What do you want?' We would come to some agreement, and as long as she was clear about it, she would do it. This was from early, early, early. So now on just about anything, we can negotiate. She wants to watch two programs, and we want to watch something else, and she'll come up with an idea. 'How about you let me watch this, and you tape that? Then I'll go do this.' We have tried a few democratic family meetings which is a little early, and we have done only a few, but she likes them. She'll see a problem and say, 'I think we need a meeting.'" FATHER OF PRESCHOOLER

"We don't have sidewalks, and I have always put a chain at the end of the driveway whenever he is riding his bike so he doesn't go out. The other day he got his bike out to ride and then went and put the chain up. I thought, 'Good for him! He's learning to protect himself; he's learning these adaptive skills of safety for himself.' It made me feel proud of him. It was a good moment." FATHER OF PRESCHOOLER

"Another great joy is like painting a good picture or taking a good jump shot. It's doing something that is just right for your kids. It just hits the target. It might be, after reprimanding him and sending him to his room, going up and talking to him, telling him you love him and to come downstairs now. Just knowing how good a thing that is, how appropriate it is. It may be buying the fishing rod for a child that he desperately wanted. It is the pleasure of pleasing someone you care about and pleasing him on the basis of personal knowledge you have about him." FATHER OF ELEMENTARY SCHOOL CHILDREN

Parents begin by explaining to children the exact problem that is troubling them and its effect on them and then say that they are going to try a new method to solve the problem so that everyone's needs are met. Children may be skeptical at first, thinking this may be another way for their parents to get them to behave. But as children realize that their needs are being considered, they become more active participants. Gordon advises parents and children to spend the most time on defining the nature of the problem and exchanging possible solutions.

Parents and children may disagree about a problem. Parents may feel upset by the continual mess in the kitchen on weekend mornings as children trail in one after another and get breakfast at odd times without cleaning up. The mother finds her kitchen in a mess and no one child to hold responsible. The children, in turn, may feel the problem is that Mom won't serve weekend breakfasts at a reasonable time, like 10 or 11 a.m., because she wants to be out doing errands. Active listening by everyone and willingness to hear suggestions can bring agreement.

Gordon advises that, when you start these problem-solving sessions, they should be frequent. But don't let a discussion last too long. If the list of problems is long, take the most important ones first. If a problem involves only two family members, the others don't need to participate. And remember that it is not necessary to resolve a problem the first time it is discussed. Family members should feel free to think about a problem, then discuss it together, and resolve it at the next session.

As you talk about each proposed solution, try to figure out how it will work. Once a solution is selected, consider how the results will be evaluated and make sure that you allow enough time so that it has a chance to succeed. During the process of proposing solutions and picking one, each family member needs to listen actively to the suggestions of all family members. In this situation, as in so many, family members need to be able to trust each other and to recognize each other's needs.

Sometimes children are reluctant to get involved in mutual problem solving. Gordon suggests that parents start with a problem that family members are not upset about. For example, in your first problem-solving session you could talk about how the family is going to spend the next vacation. Also, you can help the individual child to understand that the no-lose method is worthy of his participation if you start with a problem that is bothering him. If children can see, concretely, how their life is better when these talks are held, they are more likely to participate.

Once a solution is agreed on, parents may find that children don't follow through. Children break agreements for a variety of reasons—they may not have had enough experience in self-direction, they may forget, they may test the limits to see what will happen, or they may have accepted an unworkable solution just to end the session. When an agreement is broken, parents must send a strong I-message of disappointment and surprise, as soon as possible. Perhaps the child can be helped to keep the agreement. Or perhaps another problem-solving session is needed.

Parents might be tempted to build punishments into the problem-solving agreement—"If you don't carry out the garbage, your allowance is reduced by 25¢." Gordon advises against the use of penalties to enforce agreements. Parents should assume children will cooperate, instead of starting with a negative expectation expressed in the threat of punishment. Children frequently respond to trust.

The **contracting sessions** devised by behaviorists are similar to Gordon's mutual problem-solving sessions. Contracting sessions are an expansion of the token system. When parents use tokens, they may do so to change one specific behavior or to reward the child for doing a particular chore. When parents want to reach agreement on several matters, and children are also asking for some changes, the family holds a contracting session. Contracting sessions are most appropriate with elementary school children and teenagers, but verbal preschoolers can also participate.

In approaching the problem, parents need to be clear about the specific, positive behavior they want to see. You can make a list: (1) vacuuming once a week, (2) dusting once a week, (3) changing the bed once a week. Each task can be worth 30 points, and the total of 90 points can be exchanged for two car rides or staying out an extra hour on a weekend evening. You present the scheme to the teenager, who agrees to clean his or her room once a week for that number of points. Then you monitor the behavior each week and give the number of points earned.

Now let's look at a more complicated example. Suppose you wish to decrease your seven-year-old son's messiness. You decide he should do four things, hang up his coat, clean and put away his lunchbox, put away his toys, and put his dirty clothes

◆

```
BOX 4-2
BEHAVIOR LOG
```

Behavior	Sun	Mon	Tue	Wed	Thurs	Fri	Sat
1. Hang up coat							
2. Clean and put away lunchbox							
3. Put away toys							
4. Put dirty clothes in hamper							

in the hamper. The behaviors are clearly stated. Before you propose a contract, observe the boy's behavior—count how many times in a week he does these things. Eimers and Aitchison suggest a chart to record behavior over a seven-day period (Box 4-2).[9]

One mother, after observing and counting for a week, discovered that her son had hung up his coat only once and at no time put his dirty clothes in the hamper or put his toys away. When she told him what rewards he could earn with a point system, the child was excited and eager to try. Mother and child used the same form to record successful completion of each task. After the system went into effect, the mother noticed dramatic differences in the child's behavior. After seven weeks, the child was picking up his toys and putting his dirty clothes in the hamper. The system was gradually phased out after the habits were established.

Some behaviorists disapprove of elaborate programs of special incentives because they are more formalized and less personal than social rewards and can be financially costly. If a child has not responded to other strategies, however, special incentives may produce the desired results.

Natural and Logical Consequences

Suppose that mutual problem solving and contracting sessions do not work. Then a parent might try Dreikurs' natural and logical consequences.[10] A **logical consequence** is the natural outcome of misbehavior in which parents do not interfere. When children experience the logical consequences of misbehavior—for example, eating cold food because they are late for dinner—they learn to anticipate the consequences and to avoid them by not repeating the misbehavior.

Because the consequences are the result of the child's misbehavior, the child and not the parent is responsible for the child's discomfort. The violation, not the parent, brings the penalty. Instead, the parent remains friendly and undisturbed. The following incident illustrates the method of logical and natural consequences. When a three-year-old crayoned on the walls, the mother told her that they would not be able to go to the beach until she, the mother, washed off the marks. She asked the daughter to help, but after cleaning for a few minutes the girl wandered off. Every few minutes the child came back and asked when they were going to the beach. The mother replied calmly, "As soon as we get this wall cleaned." The child did not complain when she learned that it was too late to go to the beach.

Logical consequences differ from punishment in several ways. Logical consequences are directly related to what the child has done—if children do not put their clothes in the laundry, they have no clean clothes. A punishment may have no logical relationship to what the child has done—a spanking is not the direct result of being late for a meal, but is the result of the parent's authority. The method of logical consequences does not place moral blame or pass moral judgment on the child. The child has made a mistake and pays the price. The parent stands by as an adviser, rather than acting as a judge. Punishment implies that the child has committed a "wrong" act and must atone for the offense.

The method of logical consequences is not always as simple as standing by and letting the natural outcome of the act teach the child not to repeat the act. Parents must sometimes take a more active role. They must be careful not to turn the consequences into punishment by the comments they make. They must not criticize the child or angrily label the child. If a parent, for example, seems gleeful when a child suffers consequences—"You did not finish your homework and now you are paying the price! What did I tell you?"—the value of the method is lost. Children then experience the consequences as punishment, and they resent the parent's reaction.

In some situations parents will have to supply the consequences because not all misbehavior results in unpleasant outcomes. For example, when a child bites or hits another child, the consequence is a howl from the recipient. There is no discouraging consequence unless the other child takes action. Dreikurs indicates that when a child bites, a parent may want to bite back to demonstrate that a bite hurts. Similarly, if a child hits a parent hard, the mother may comment that she, too, can hit. She may then hit the child playfully, but in a way that hurts slightly. Most experts recommend against biting and hitting as being too physically aggressive and suggest restricting children to their room.

Logical consequences cannot be used when they result in danger to the child. We cannot allow children to run into the street and be hit by a car to teach them to stay out of the street. Parents can restrict children to a safe place—either to the house or to the backyard—until they have learned to stay away from the street.

Taking Action

Ginott recommends **taking action**, using some form of behavior to enforce existing limitations.[11]

When reflecting feelings, setting limits, and allowing natural consequences have not worked, parents can take action. Ginott does not believe in punishment, which he defines as a powerful person taking punitive action against a child. Taking action is different because the parent uses some form of behavior to enforce an existing limitation. For example, let's assume that house rules include not bouncing a ball in the house. If a child continues to bounce the ball after being given the choice of going outside to bounce or staying in and not bouncing, then parents act. They either send the child outside with the ball or they take the ball away and permit the child to

This boy knows he should not crowd the girl, and he uses a subtle form of aggression.
If aggression serves to get the boy what he wants, his aggressiveness will increase and
other children will imitate it. The boy's parents must take immediate steps to help the boy
control his aggression.

to remain in the house. With teenagers, parents might remove the privilege of using
the car if children do not respect the family curfew. Again, removing car privileges would
not be punishment; it would be acting to enforce the established rule. The main difference is the parent's attitude. A parent who takes action is not a punishing authority
figure but an adult who is acting to enforce the meaning of his or her words.

Punishments

These four methods may not have worked, and parents will have to use punishments. Punishment means giving a behavior a negative consequence to decrease the likelihood of its occurrence. There are a variety of punishments, requiring varying degrees of effort on the parent's part. Before describing these, let us look at six general principles for using punishments: (1) Intervene early. Do not let the situation get out of control. As soon as the rule is violated, begin to take action. (2) Stay as calm and objective as possible. Sometimes parents' upset and frustration are rewarding to the child. Parents' emotions can also distract the child from thinking about the rule violation. (3) State the rule that was violated. State it simply: do not get into arguments about it. (4) Use a *mild* negative consequence. A mild consequence has the advantage that the child often devalues the activity itself and seems more likely to resist temptation and follow the rule in the future. (5) Use negative consequences consistently. When actions are sometimes punished and sometimes not, they do not decrease. This may seem to contradict what was said earlier about taking into account daily events in establishing expectations. Daily events, however, are only rarely sufficiently stressful to change major rules. (6) Reinforce positive social behaviors as they occur afterwards; parents do not want children to receive more punishments than rewards.

These principles stand in marked contrast to what parents often do. Let us take, for example, two sisters who have begun teasing each other on a Saturday afternoon. They make faces at each other and talk about how poorly each does at school. Parents often wait, hoping the teasing will stop of its own accord. When it continues, they may say in a distracted tone, "Stop it." When the quarreling does not stop, they repeat the phrase in a louder tone of voice, adding a "Please." When one girl hits the other and the other reacts by pushing her down, parents intervene with a sudden punishment of two weeks' room restriction. The parents are busy with errands and chores, however, and do not monitor the restriction, so the girls are out of their rooms in a few hours.

In this case, the parent could have intervened quickly as the teasing escalated, suggesting that one girl go outside or both go to their rooms for a brief time. Then they could have given rewards of social attention and approval when the girls played happily together.

Following are a variety of punishments, ranging from mild to severe. First, **ignoring** might seem the easiest punishment as the parent must pay no attention to what the child says or does. It requires effort, however, as the parent must keep a neutral facial expression, look away, move away from the child, and give no verbal response or attention to what the child says or does. A parent may be tempted to look or watch the child, and this attention may be enough reward for the child to continue the behavior. To be effective punishment, then, ignoring must be complete. Ignoring is best for behaviors that may be annoying but are not harmful to anyone. For example, children's whining, sulking, or pouting behavior can be ignored. Some experts put temper tantrums in the category of behavior that is best ignored. Although a parent might start out by ignoring a temper tantrum, some children work themselves into such an emotional and physical state that they cannot bring the tantrum to an end. Children can frighten themselves with the intensity of a tantrum. Parents may then want to be more active and use the strategy of time out described later in this section.

A second punishment is **social disapproval**. Parents express in a few words, spoken in a firm voice with a disapproving facial expression, that they do not like the behavior. For example, when a child dawdles, not clearing the table after dinner, a parent can say firmly, looking directly at the child with a serious expression, "It's time for the table to be cleared." Parents sometimes make the mistake of requesting behavior in a pleading tone of voice which suggests that the child may or may not comply. Hearing this tone, children know the parent does not mean business and do not comply. Or parents may say, "I do not like your teasing your brother," while smiling or chuckling about this "devilish" behavior; and so the child, rewarded by the parents' smile and laughter, continues. Words, physical gestures, and facial expressions must consistently make the point that the behavior is not approved of for change to occur.

When children do not change behavior their parents have disapproved of, parents can institute a **consequence**—removing a privilege, using the time-out strategy, or imposing extra work. When families have contracts, children agree to carry out specified chores or behaviors in exchange for privileges. When certain behaviors do not occur, children lose privileges. For example, TV time is linked to the completion of chores or homework. When homework or chores are not finished by a certain time, there is no TV. If a child does not bring home an acceptable school report about classroom behavior, no friends may stay overnight that weekend.

Time out (Box 4-3) is a method best used for aggressive, destructive, or dangerous behaviors. It serves to stop the disapproved behavior, giving the child a chance to cool off and, sometimes, to think about the rule violation. There are variations on the time-out method: The child can be requested to sit in a chair in the corner, but many children get up. If the child is required to face the corner, parents can keep the young child in the corner for the stated time. With older children, parents may want to add the rule that if the child does not comply with time out for one parent during the day, making the presence of both parents necessary, then the child will spend twice the amount of time in time out. Parents may feel facing the corner or the wall has little negative value because the time involved is only a few minutes. Time out has symbolic value, however. It demonstrates to children that parents are in control; certain behaviors are not permitted, and children will suffer consequences if they do them. Time out excludes the child from the social group for a certain period. Even though the time is short, children dislike being excluded.

It is best to have only two or three behaviors requiring time out at any one time. Otherwise, a child may be in the corner a great deal of time for too many different things. Further, it is important that both parents and all caregivers agree on the two or three things that will lead to time out. Then the child gets consistent punishment. If one parent uses time out and one does not, or if the child gets time out at home but not at day care, the program may fail.

Many experts have found that sending a child to his or her room or being

◆

BOX 4-3
USING TIME OUT FOR MISBEHAVIOR

1. Make a request in a firm but pleasant voice. Do not beg or shout.
2. Count silently to 5. Do not let the child know you are counting.
3. If the child has not started to comply in 5 seconds, look the child in the eye and say firmly, "If you don't _____, then you are going to stand in the corner."
4. Count silently to 5. Do not let the child know you are counting.
5. If the child has not begun to comply, take the child firmly by the hand or arm and say clearly and loudly, "You did not do as you were told, so you will have to stand in the corner."
6. No matter what the child promises, begs, screams, or yells, he or she goes directly to the corner. There is no going to the bathroom or getting a drink. Do not argue with the child.
7. Face the child to the wall and say, "Now you stay here for _____ minutes." If the child leaves the corner, return the child to the corner and stand behind him or her so that leaving the corner is not possible.
8. When the time is up, say, "Now you may _____" (state the positive behavior).
9. If the unacceptable behavior recurs, start the process again.
10. Following the punishment, praise the next positive behavior with positive feedback. Never punish more than you praise.

Where should the corner be? Choose a dull corner—in the hall or dining room where there are no toys or distractions, no TV. You should be able to see the child.

How long in the corner? Young children under four can spend a few minutes. Children between the ages of five and eight can spend 5 to 10 minutes, and children over eight may require between 10 and 30 minutes. A general rule is that the child spends the same number of minutes as his or her age. While he or she is in the corner, the child misses whatever is happening—a meal, TV.

Adapted from Russell A. Barkley, *Hyperactive Children* (New York: Guilford, 1981), pp. 328–330.

grounded there for a period is not effective punishment. The child can find many enjoyable things to do there—reading, listening to the stereo, playing games. So, as children get older, extra work and chores may be substituted for grounding. One boy was consistently sent to his room for lying, where he read and listened to his tapes. His lying continued. But he decidedly disliked the negative consequence of raking leaves for 20 minutes for every lie he told, and when this punishment was given, his behavior improved.

The last punishment we will consider is **spanking**. In one study of 150 families, 148 had used spanking at least once.[12] Thus, almost all parents spank their children at some time, but there are problems with using it as a regular form of discipline. First, if parents rely heavily on spanking for discipline, children may behave well only under threat of physical punishment. When away from the spanking parents, children may run wild. Second, children who come from homes where physical punishment is frequently used tend to be more physically aggressive than their peers, and this aggressiveness creates further problems. Most parents use physical punishment only in extreme situations that involve safety—running into the street or trying to get out of a moving car.

When parents use punishments, they are sometimes thrown off track by the child's comment: "I don't care. That doesn't bother me." Parents then give up the punishment, thinking the child does not mind it. The child's comment, however, is often an attempt to save face and be in control when she feels just exactly the opposite. Some children may use the comment to get their parents to stop the punishment. So parents must not be misled by their children's statements of unconcern. Continue to apply the negative consequence.

MANAGING CHILDREN'S BEHAVIOR IN PUBLIC PLACES

Parents feel vulnerable when their children refuse to follow rules in public places. Embarrassed parents imagine that onlookers are highly critical of their attempts to control their children and judge the parents as cruel, incompetent, unloving, and unfair. Many of these imagined criticisms are thoughts they themselves have had observing parents and children before having children of their own. The experienced, effective parent is more likely to feel sympathetic, however, since almost all parents have had to deal with this situation.

Managing behavior in public places pulls together most of the principles of modifying children's behavior. First, parents fit the demands of the situation to the child's individual temperament and condition that day. If a child has a cold and is irritable, that is not the day for a family dinner at an expensive restaurant with a long wait for service; that may be the day for fast food. If a child has been active all morning, that is not the day for a long shopping trip to a department store. Before entering a public place, remind the child of the rules; if the child is young, have him or her repeat them to you. Provide the child with activities in the public place. If it is the grocery store, let the child help get the purchases off the shelf. If it is a restaurant, give the child a drawing pad and pencil to occupy time.

Parents model desired behavior. They show children how to do the approved behaviors—put a napkin in their lap, eat slowly, engage in conversation. Parents give praise and attention, perhaps even a reward, for good behavior—a special dessert, a desired food at the store. When rules are violated, the parent immediately takes action. If a child throws food at a restaurant, gets out of the chair to run around, or leaves the parent in the store, immediate action follows. Parents can express disapproval or immediately take the child to the rest room to do time out in a corner. One family solved the problem by carrying a picture of the time-out chair at home with them. When the child began to violate the rules, parents got out the picture and told the child there would be so many minutes in the chair as soon as they got home if the disapproved behavior did not cease. The behavior stopped.

THE CHALLENGE OF LEARNING

When parents have growing children, they would be wise to take up a new hobby or athletic activity periodically. Learning a new skill themselves, they can appreciate how slow the process of learning can be and how frustrating it is to want to improve and still make mistakes. Parents will gain a greater appreciation of their children's sturdiness when they realize that if learning is hard for parents with mature motor and intellectual skills, how difficult must it be for children learning many skills with bodies and minds that are still developing. Further, children are surrounded by others who seem able to do what is required rather easily. That children are as cheerful and patient as they are is a testament to their basic good nature.

DEVELOPMENTAL CHANGES AND PARENTING BEHAVIOR

We have devoted the last two chapters in a general way to two major parental tasks—establishing close emotional relationships and modifying children's behavior. How parents carry out these tasks depends in part on the child's age and developmental state, which we will trace in subsequent chapters that examine the child's development from the prenatal stage through late adolescence. Eleanor Maccoby recently described seven developmental changes that occur in children as they grow.[13] These changes affect how parents interact with their children and what parenting tasks must be carried out at each stage. They are: (1) physical growth, (2) language development, (3) control of impulsivity, (4) children's conceptions of others, (5) children's conceptions of self, (6) cognitive executive processes, and (7) autonomy. In each age period, we look at the changes that occur in these seven areas as well as in the area of emotional reactivity. At each period, we examine areas that are most in need of parental attention and focus.

Maccoby summarizes the parental tasks at each age as follows:

> In infancy, the parent's function is mainly one of caregiving, and this includes helping the infant to regulate its own bodily functions. During the preschool years, children are learning to regulate their own affective states, and parents are contributing to this, partly through their direct dealings with the child's emotional outbursts, but also by regulating the rate at which the child is exposed to new experiences. In this period, parents do a great deal of monitoring of the child's moment-to-moment activities and provide much direct feedback. During the school-aged years, the amount of direct contact between parent and child diminishes greatly; parental monitoring is more distal. In a sense, much of it involves monitoring the child's self-monitoring. The child must now join the family system as a contributor, a cooperative interactor. In simpler societies, this middle-childhood period is the time during which children begin to participate in family survival enterprises: caring for domestic animals, doing some work in the fields, getting wood and water, caring for younger children. In our own society, children's labor is not needed, and their task is to become educated. Nevertheless, they are able to contribute to the functioning of the family. In adolescence, the child is becoming heavily involved in the larger society outside the family, but the family still has the function in providing both guidance and support for the child's entrance into these larger spheres.[14]

Not only will we look at the parent's task in relation to the child, but we must also examine the stages parents themselves go through as they rear their children. We focus on parents' feelings, frustrations, and pleasures and discuss ways of maximizing the enjoyment of parenting. Parenting is a process that goes beyond meeting daily needs and solving problems. Thus, we need an overview of development so that we may nurture children to realize their full potential.

When we combine the problem-solving approach with the parental qualities and behaviors all strategies advise—modeling of desired traits, respect for the child's and one's own needs, confidence that the child can learn what is necessary, sharing of problems and solutions in family meetings—then parents can effectively foster the growth and development of their children. Each individual has a unique potential to discover and develop. Arnold Gesell and Frances Ilg state it well:

> When asked to give the very shortest definition of life, Claude Bernard, a great physiologist, answered, "Life is creation." A newborn baby is the consummate product of such creation. And he in turn is endowed with capacities for continuing creation. These capacities are expressed not only in the growth of his physique, but in the simultaneous growth of a psychological self. From the sheer standpoint of creation this psychological self must be regarded as his masterpiece. It will take a lifetime to finish, and in the first ten years he will need a great deal of help, but it will be his own product.[15]

Parents have the privilege of serving as guide and resource as their child creates a unique "psychological self."

MAJOR POINTS OF CHAPTER 4

Children learn when:

- new signals are associated with already existing responses
- new associations are made between stimuli and responses on the basis of rewards and punishments
- they observe models and imitate them

Parents set stage for learning by developing realistic expectations of the child based on:

- goals of the parent
- child's age
- child's particular characteristics and needs
- health and safety issues
- family's needs and values
- events of the day

Parents help children meet expectations when they:

- structure the physical environment with hooks for clothes, storage space for possessions
- establish a regular routine that takes account of children's tempo so they can anticipate what is going to happen and cooperate
- monitor stimulation so children are prepared for difficult situations, and are prevented from overexcitement that leads to their falling apart
- take an active role in teaching children by shaping new approved behaviors

Rewards are:

- those actions that increase the likelihood a behavior will occur again
- always present whether recognized or not
- available in many forms from social attention and approval to privileges and material rewards like money and tokens that can be exchanged for privileges
- are most useful when given in the form of positive social attention

Parents set limits most effectively when they:

- state rules as clear, objective, positive statements of what they want
- explain the purpose of the rule
- focus on the most important rules of health and safety first, then rules that ease social living
- are consistent with rules and back each other up
- discuss differences of opinion about the rules away from the children and arrive at a joint decision
- offer children options whenever possible
- give a child a chance to prepare for a new activity

When children do not follow rules, parents have many techniques for enforcing the rules. Parents can:

- use a mutual problem-solving session with all family members to arrive at a solution agreeable to all—this may or may not be put in the form of a contract
- remain detached and let the natural consequences of the act teach the child—parents may have to devise logical consequences if no natural ones arise
- take action to enforce limits, accepting the child's disappointment in not having his or her own way and showing how, if possible, the child can get his or her way
- use punishments to decrease the likelihood of the behavior's happening again—for example, ignoring, taking away privileges, time out, and rarely, if at all, spanking

Managing children's behavior in public places illustrates:

- setting realistic expectations for child
- parents' modeling of appropriate behavior
- rewarding positive behaviors
- giving negative consequences for misbehavior

How parents' behavior changes with the age of the child:

- in infancy, parents are caregivers
- in preschool, parents monitor activities and give immediate feedback
- in school years, parents help children become self-monitors who can guide their own behavior
- in adolescence, parents help children engage in the larger society

To help children develop caring, prosocial behavior, parents:

- provide a nurturant, warm home atmosphere
- are models of caring and ethical behavior the child can imitate
- use reasoning in talking about rules
- arouse the child's empathy for the distress the child has caused in another person
- involve the child in altruistic behavior
- reward caring behavior with attention
- shun power techniques like spanking
- discuss moral issues and actions so the child learns a code of rules that can be applied in new situations

ADDITIONAL READINGS

Becker, Wesley. *Parents Are Teachers*. Champaign, Ill.: Research Press, 1971.

Dinkmeyer, Don, and McKay, Gary D. *The Parent's Handbook*. Circle Pines, Minn.: American Guidance Service, 1989.

Dreikurs, Rudolf, with Soltz, Vicki. *Children: The Challenge*. New York: Hawthorn, 1964.

Nelson, Jane. *Positive Discipline*. New York: Ballantine, 1987.

Patterson, Gerald R. *Living With Children*. Rev. ed. Champaign, Ill.: Research Press, 1977.

Notes

1. Rudolf Dreikurs with Vicki Soltz, *Children: The Challenge* (New York: Hawthorn, 1964).
2. Thomas Gordon, *P.E.T. Parent Effectiveness Training* (New York: New American Library, 1975).
3. Robert Eimers and Robert Aitchison, *Effective Parents/Responsible Children* (New York: McGraw-Hill, 1977).
4. Ibid.
5. Eli Soltz, Sarah Campbell, and David

Scotko, "Verbal Control of Behavior: The Effects of Shouting," *Developmental Psychology* 19 (1983): 461–464.

6. Haim G. Ginott, *Between Parent and Child* (New York: Avon, 1969).

7. Larry P. Nucci and Elliot Turiel, "Social Interactions and the Development of Social Concepts in Preschool Children," *Child Development* 49 (1978): 400–407.

8. Gordon, *P.E.T.*

9. Eimers and Aitchison, *Effective Parents/Responsible Children.*

10. Dreikurs with Soltz, *Children: The Challenge.*

11. Ginott, *Between Parent and Child.*

12. Diana Baumrind, "The Development of Instrumental Competence through Socialization," in *Minnesota Symposia on Child Psychology,* vol. 7, ed. Ann D. Pick (Minneapolis: University of Minnesota Press, 1973), pp. 3–46.

13. Eleanor Maccoby, "Socialization and Developmental Changes," *Child Development* 55 (1984): 317–328.

14. Ibid., pp. 324–325.

15. Arnold Gesell and Frances L. Ilg, *The Child From Five to Ten* (New York: Harper & Row, 1946), p. 308.

PREGNANCY AND DELIVERY

C H A P T E R   5

Why have a chapter on pregnancy and delivery in a parenting book? Because parenting begins here. We have defined parenting as nourishing, protecting, and guiding children. Women's bodies surely nourish the developing baby in this period. Both parents begin the task of protecting the child from harmful environmental influences that can have a profound and lifelong impact on the child. Infection and exposure to damaging substances, for example, can severely damage the child's sensory, intellectual, and motor functioning.

Understanding the events of pregnancy enables prospective parents to become more effective parents. They learn the importance of leading a healthy lifestyle during the time they may be bearing children. From the second to the eighth week of pregnancy, the developing fetus is especially vulnerable as the basic organs and systems of the body are beginning to develop. The organism grows rapidly, and it is during this time that many harmful agents can produce nongenetic malformations. Unfortunately, during much of this period, the woman does not know she is pregnant and is unaware of the need for protection. By the time she discovers she is pregnant, she may have exposed her child to potential damage. We refer to the importance of both parents' living a healthy lifestyle, for men can pass infections to their wives and, in turn, to the child.

During this period, too, prospective parents begin to experience some of the changes a new baby will bring to their lives. Both mothers and fathers must adjust to the changes in the mothers' physical state—her fatigue, her nausea, her difficulty sleeping, and later her reduced activity. They begin to work together in preparation for the delivery and the baby's arrival in the home. They attend prenatal classes, and they prepare a home for the baby. Parents begin to take on the characteristics of mothers and fathers.

It is impossible to describe how any one parent will feel during pregnancy and delivery, because each person experiences so many feelings during these months and because different people feel so differently about events at this time. Although we often recognize that this is a momentous time for mothers, we must also recognize that fathers, too, have many feelings to handle. For both parents, the major tasks of

WHAT I WISH I HAD KNOWN ABOUT PREGNANCY

"I wish I had known more about the early stages of pregnancy. The baby doesn't show on the outside, but so much is going on inside to create the baby. I thought I had to prepare for the birth, but really I had to know more about the pregnancy. My wife was so tired, sometimes so nauseated. To know about all the changes in the body would have helped me to relate to her better and appreciate all that was happening." FATHER

"I wish I had known more about how crucial the choice of doctor was. I wish with the first, I had gotten more information about the whole birth process—what it means to have a birth in a hospital or a birth at home. It is so important to be informed as much as you can. Talk with your friends about birth, talk to everyone you can. I wish I had gotten as much information as I possibly could have and then gone to search for the right people to take care of me." MOTHER

"I wish I had known more about the positive parts of pregnancy. People only talk about the problems. It was such a surprise that I felt so great. I was trying to savor it, to pay attention to the different phases and to enjoy each one." MOTHER

"I wish I had started in the pregnancy to focus less on myself. I have always been so organized and focused on what I want to get done. Having a baby has been a big change in this area—thinking very much about a third person—and I think I could have got started during pregnancy being less focused on myself." FATHER

this period are to accept the new life coming into the family and to begin to form an attachment that is intensified by the child's arrival and the events of the labor and delivery.

The reactions of both the mother and the father to the coming child depend not only on the circumstances of the conception and pregnancy, but also on a host of attitudes and feelings that relate to past events. Their reactions to their bodies, themselves, each other, their own parents and childbearing experiences, as well as the number of supports they have outside the family (job satisfaction, friends) all influence parents' feelings about the coming of their child.

The mother's lifestyle particularly will change. Her body is no longer her own. She will eat certain amounts and kinds of foods, get exercise, and rest at certain intervals.

The relationship between the father and mother also changes during pregnancy. Women have a more intimate connection with the child and what is happening and, as a result, fathers may feel left out, excluded from a very important family event. However, there will be a sharing of a heightened emotional experience that brings many couples closer together. At this time, the single mother will begin to get a sense of what it is like to rear a child alone. She will not be able to talk over day-to-day changes with the father, nor will she receive emotional support from him. She should begin to build a network of friends she can call upon for long talks and for help if she needs it.

PREGNANCY

It is convenient to think of pregnancy as three periods of three months each—as three **trimesters**. Let's look at the baby's growth and development, the changes in the mother, and the parents' psychological reactions during each of these periods.

First Trimester

The union of the sperm and the egg occurs in the Fallopian tube. The fertilized egg moves down to the uterus, increasing in number of cells, and at the end of the first week implants itself in the spongy inner wall of the uterus. In the entire human lifespan the death rate is highest in the week before and after implantation.

In the first eight weeks of life, all the major organs of the body begin to develop. The heart beats from the fourth week on, and the brain and nervous system send out impulses. Sex organs begin to develop and the sex of the child is visible. Facial features—eyes, ears, nose, lips, tongue, and even the beginnings of milk teeth—are present.

By the end of twelve weeks, the baby has a well-formed body and is active, even though the mother will not feel the movements for several more weeks. The repertoire of behaviors is impressive, considering that the baby weighs only 1 ounce. The baby can kick, turn its head, curl and fan the toes, make a fist, open and close its mouth, swallow amniotic fluid, and then excrete it.

During this three-month period, the woman's body adjusts to the presence of the fetus. The hormone levels in her body change and breasts may swell. She may have early morning nausea; she may develop a ravenous appetite; she may feel more tired than usual and want frequent naps. She may have less energy than before she became pregnant, feel more emotional, cry more easily, and crave certain foods. As these changes occur, some women experience a strong sense of and unity with the natural processes of life and an increased awareness of their bodies and their femininity. A woman whose pregnancy is unexpected and unwanted, who already has all the children she wants or who has a career she values may, especially during this time, feel that the child she is carrying is an intruder.

During pregnancy the father begins to get a sense of what it is like to share his wife with a newcomer. In the first months, while the mother is preoccupied with all the physical changes taking place in her body, the father looks ahead to their growing responsibilities and both parents plan how family resources will provide for the new member.

A study of expectant fathers' changes in self-concept and in relationships to their wives and social world found three natural groupings: (1) romantically oriented fathers, (2) family-oriented fathers, and (3) career-oriented fathers.[1] The romantically oriented men were in awe of the whole process of pregnancy. They were more aware of their responsibilities as husbands and fathers during the months of pregnancy than they had been before, and more aware of the differences between being a teenager and being an adult. Family-oriented fathers accepted their new responsibilities and were eager to be fathers and family men. Pregnancy brought them closer to their wives. Also, they began to experience fatherhood before birth, in the early months of pregnancy. These men reported that they were drawn to children. One man commented that fatherhood was something that grew on him. Career-oriented fathers saw fatherhood as a chore, a burden that diminished their freedom and interfered with their careers. These men tried to ward off any change in their identities, insisting that they could be good fathers without making any changes in their behavior.

The emotional experiences of the wife and husband may differ in ways that make if difficult for them to be supportive of each other. In the first trimester, many women are involved with their changing bodies. The husband may be less aware of the physical changes his wife experiences because they are not visible to him. Talking over feelings and seeing the differences relieves tension. In families that already have a child, both parents may take all these changes in stride if the pregnancy has no complications and is wanted. In each pregnancy, however, events may occur that arouse these different kinds of concerns in each parent.

Ellen Galinsky describes the entire pregnancy periods as the **image-making state** for parents.[2] Parents form ideas of what they and the baby will be like. Galinsky has identified developmental patterns as parents go through the three trimesters. In the first trimester, parents may feel elated but worry about miscarriage. Even in these first few months, their images may clash with reality: The pregnancy did not occur as expected; it came too soon, or it was too difficult, achieved only after months of tests and trying. Parents may have planned the pregnancy but do not feel as excited as they had expected. Already, parents have to alter their images to fit the reality of what is happening.

Second Trimester

By the end of six months, the baby has grown to 14 inches in length and weighs about 1¾ pounds. Development of the systems laid down in the first trimester continues. The child is more muscular and movements are stronger. Several kinds of movements occur—slow, squirming movements, sharp kicks, and slow, hiccough-like movements that can last 15 to 30 minutes. The baby establishes a sleep-wake cycle similar to that of a newborn. The child has a favorite position for resting and when awake tumbles and rolls about. Babies can hear noises, and a loud noise or music can stimulate a spurt of activity. In the sixth month the baby develops a grip so strong that it can support its weight. This grip is stronger than it is in the newborn, although breastfeeding maintains the strong grip for a while after birth.

In the second trimester, the mother has already adjusted to the hormonal changes of pregnancy and is over the discomfort of nausea. As the baby grows, the mother's body changes shape, and she may wonder if her altered appearance makes her less attractive to her husband and to others. Research suggests that women who want and plan children are more likely to view their changing shapes as signs of womanliness and femininity and to enjoy the extra attention they receive.[3] At this time, the woman is not yet so big as to be uncomfortable. Many women report this period as the most pleasant during pregnancy.

In the fourth or fifth month, the mother has that exciting moment called quickening, when she can first feel the baby's movements. Some women describe these as

INTERVIEW
with Jay Belsky

Jay Belsky is Professor of Human Development at The Pennsylvania State University in College Park. He is the initiator and director of the Pennsylvania Infant and Family Development Project, an ongoing study of 250 firstborn children whose parents were enrolled for study when the mothers were pregnant in 1981.

You have done a great deal of research on parents making the transition to parenthood, and you have emphasized the importance of supports for parents. What would you say are major ways parents can get support for themselves?

It depends very much on the situation. In the two-parent, middle-class family, the marriage is usually the principal source of support. In traditional working-class families, the extended family may be the principal source of support. With a single, teenaged mother, it is usually her parents who are the most important source of support.

You have to think of where the person gets basic emotional satisfaction—marriage, job, extended family. That can either support parents or undermine them. For example, when a marriage that is usually a support is really distressed, then it undermines the parent's sensitivity and involvement.

Invariably, the risk of saying "Most important" points the finger at one thing or another. The most important idea that I have to offer, and I think it is very consistent with Michael Rutter's thinking about risk and protective factors, is that it is the combination of stresses and supports that is important. We can imagine a very stressful job, but we can also imagine a person whose job is not his center of being, who has a marriage that is important to him and well functioning, and then I would say that person is well buffered.

Similarly, if a person has herself together psychologically and feels good about herself and not too negative, if she has a great job that makes her feel good, but her marriage is a source of dissatisfaction, then she is possibly relatively well buffered as well. It is the profile and combination of stresses and supports that will determine how parents function, not any single factor.

---

similar to the fluttering of a butterfly or the gentle strokings of a soft glove. Mothers begin to turn their attention to the developing child and begin to form an attachment. Many women report talking to the baby and calling the baby pet names based on the movements and activity cycle. The mothers may develop fantasies about the baby, worry about the health of the child, and wonder who the child will resemble. As she focuses on the child, she withdraws energy from the outside world and from day-to-day events. Many women are preoccupied and yet serene as they think about the child.

If this is a first child, the father may be unprepared for the mother's remoteness just as he is becoming involved in the physical aspects of the pregnancy. The woman's changing shape reminds the husband of the physical changes that were not visible in the first trimester. And the father is likely to be excited when he feels the baby's movements by placing his hands on the mother's abdomen, sometimes seeing the abdomen move as the baby gives a sharp kick. The father, too, is forming an attachment, but it may not be as strong as the mother's because he does not experience the same internal physical sensations. Also, he may be jealous and annoyed at the changes the unseen baby brings to family life. The husband must share his wife's attentions with this newcomer, whether it is their first child or their fifth.

In the second trimester, Galinsky believes parents prepare for parenthood.[4] They accept the separateness of the baby from themselves. They think of the changes in their roles that will occur as they care for this child. They look back at their own childhoods, think how they want their child's life to be different, how they want to be different from their parents. If they already have a child or children, they think about the effects the coming child will have on them. Will there be enough love? If there is only one child, parents worry if they will love the second as much as the first. Parents often look carefully at their relationship with each other and how they as a couple are managing the pregnancy together. Are they working together? Are they supportive of each other? What will it be like after the baby comes? Friendship patterns also change. New friendships are formed with other parents-to-be. Old friends with other interests may fade into the background. All these issues continue to be worked through as the pregnancy goes on.

Third Trimester

In this period, the baby gains weight and makes final preparations for birth. By the seventh month the baby is sufficiently developed so that it will live if born prematurely and cared for with modern equipment. In the last three months the child gains 5 pounds or more and receives substances to immunize it against many diseases. From the mother's blood come antibodies that protect the child against all the diseases the mother has had. From the placenta comes gamma globulin to fight other diseases.

As the baby takes up more room in the uterus, there is less space for large movements. Much activity is spent practicing reflexes that will be used after birth—breathing and sucking, especially. The child sucks its thumb and breathes. Although fluid is taken in with the breath, this is not a problem because it is excreted. The infant receives oxygen from the mother's blood supply. As we noted, the child can hear and is also able to make eye movements. We do not know what the child sees before birth, although we do know that some light penetrates the womb.

Shortly before birth, the child drops down into position for the birth process. Usually the head rests against the cervix, but sometimes the buttocks are in this position. The baby is ready for birth.

Just as the baby prepares itself for birth, the parents spend the last trimester preparing for the baby's arrival. If this is a first child, parents get furniture and clothes and arrange space for the child. This is an exciting time as parents work together to create a nest. The father may paint and make things while the mother does work that is less demanding physically. Many women practice maternal behaviors on their husbands, babying them a little. Alternatively, other mothers want to be looked after and cared for during these last weeks of pregnancy. Myra Leifer, who studied pregnant women, speculates that during this time the woman is practicing both the mother's and child's behavior.[5] The mother's desire to be cared for may be intensified by her worries about her own health and safety in the delivery. Up until the last trimester, the baby's well-being has been the major focus. Now the mother becomes concerned about herself as well.

In this last trimester especially, parents expecting a first child will get a taste of the limitations a baby will bring. The mother may feel less inclined to go out socially because she is big and heavy and has less energy. She cannot sleep easily and the frequency of sexual relations may decrease.

Galinsky believes that in the last trimester, as their thoughts focus on preparation for birth, parents worry—about the difficulty of the labor and delivery, the functioning of each parent during that time (will the father be a good coach, will the mother go through without drugs?).[6] As the due date approaches, parents may feel they are on a sled zooming downhill; they cannot stop. Now there is no turning back from being a parent and, once a parent, always a parent.

Many parents have dreams or nightmares centering on the birth experience. Particularly in this trimester, women may dream of deformed or animal babies. Mothers may worry when they have such dreams. Yet a study of the content of women's dreams during the last trimester revealed that those women who had the largest percentage of dreams reflecting anxiety had shorter labors than did women whose dreams reflected less anxiety.[7] The investigators speculated that women who expressed anxiety in dreams got the feelings out of their systems and so were more relaxed and had faster deliveries.

This is also the time when parents select a pediatrician. T. Berry Brazelton, himself a pediatrician, makes some specific recommendations.[8] Find out as much as possible about the pediatrician you are considering. The county medical society, the hospital with which the doctor is affiliated, and perhaps a local medical school can provide information about the pediatrician's medical competence and whether he or she can care for the baby at the hospital where the child is to be delivered. Then consider this doctor's personal qualities. Are you comfortable with him or her? Is he or she open with you? Is he or she willing and able to answer questions? Is he or she warm? Does he or she like children? Talk to mothers whose children are cared for by this pediatrician to see how the practice is run, who cares for children when the doctor is away or emergencies arise, and whether care is available only during office hours or at other times as well. Visit the doctor in his or her office before your baby is due. If you are not comfortable, you will have a chance to find another doctor. If you decide you want this doctor to care for your child, an office visit before the birth gives you an opportunity to get to know each other before you meet in the delivery room.

The parents' confidence in the doctor is an essential ingredient of a good parent-doctor relationship and of a good child-doctor relationship. Parents communicate their trust in the doctor to the child, who is less fearful and anxious. Parents, particularly mothers, must have confidence in themselves when talking to the doctor. They need to state their worries, concerns, and views openly. Some doctors are aware that the parent-doctor relationship is awkward, but not all will take time to help parents feel at ease. Brazelton urges parents to present their feelings and reactions clearly and to be sure that the doctor listens to them.

THE JOYS OF PREGNANCY

"All my senses became more acute, more attuned. My taste in music changed. I wanted pure tones like opera singers. When I am pregnant, I want operas." MOTHER

"I had the feeling of a ripe body, full of life. There is a secret communion going on all the time within oneself. In daily life, you are walking around, whatever you are doing, you are thinking, 'Oh, there's another person inside me.' I was very conscious that whatever I heard, she heard. She was a third ear." MOTHER

"I remember looking at my wife. She looked very beautiful, more whole. There was a feeling of a larger, bigger connection created between us." FATHER

"I felt I could deserve being spoiled. I was queen for nine months and a day." MOTHER

"I remember being attended to by friends and colleagues at work. Everyone asked how things were going, and I was happy to give all the details." FATHER

"A main joy was the support of women friends. I don't know how I would have managed without them since my family weren't here." MOTHER

"I felt she deserved attention for herself and for the child for nine months. I became more accepting of her grouchiness, her pains, her weaknesses. Now I am more empathic about her moods, her ups and downs." FATHER

"I loved being pregnant. I felt good. I had no morning sickness. I felt very alive, very satisfied. It was a pleasurable time as a couple. It was a time when I got a lot of attention from my husband. All his energy got directed to me, he shopped for me to get the best, healthy foods." MOTHER

"Once we had the amnio and knew that everything was okay, we really felt we had this child—we knew the sex, we had the name. He was a person with us, but he was all taken care of. We didn't have to do anything. It was a good time. . . . People are very friendly, they pay a lot of attention, they are interested. . . . All my energy went to my wife. I was into health and wanted her to have the best nutrition, the best food." FATHER

In the third trimester, both parents may be attending childbirth classes together. As parents prepare for the arrival of the child, they may debate whether to have a home or hospital delivery. Although this choice is often made early and is a factor in selecting a doctor, parents may wait until the last trimester to make the final decision on the basis of the mother's and child's progress during the pregnancy. When making this decision, parents should be aware that most babies throughout human history have been delivered at home. Two discoveries made in the 1840s and 1850s led to more women having hospital deliveries. First, germs were discovered to cause infections and increase maternal mortality, so that a relatively germ-free atmosphere was seen as desirable. Second, the development of anesthesia led to the possibility of pain-free delivery in a hospital setting. However, although delivery in the sterile, stainless steel hospital atmosphere is considered safer for mother and child, the warmth and family support that are part of home are also important. Many parents object to having a natural process—childbirth—treated as an illness that requires medical intervention. Adequate childbirth preparation can reduce the need for medication.

Although many parents want to have their children delivered at home, most obstetricians recommend against home birth. They explain that when complications do arise, there is little time to get the technical and professional help needed. When this happens, both mother and child may suffer damage that could have been averted if both were in the hospital. Statistics in New York State from 1973 to 1976 reveal that the death rate of infants at birth was 37 per thousand in home deliveries compared to 11 per thousand in hospital deliveries.[9]

PRENATAL CARE

Throughout pregnancy the mother needs a good diet, appropriate exercise, rest, and enough sleep to maintain her own health and to provide the best possible start for the child. Pediatrician David Smith writes, in *Mothering Your Unborn Baby,* that this is a crucial time because prenatal growth is very rapid and has long-term implications for later behavior.[10] Mothers are advised to consult their doctors regarding foods, weight gain, and the need for vitamins and minerals; these recommendations change from time to time.

Cyril Young recommends moderate exercise in noncontact sports.[11] Mothers can continue regular programs of tennis, golf, swimming, and walking provided they have no complications of pregnancy and excessive fatigue does not occur. In addition, they may add exercises to tone the body for childbirth. Daily rest periods in which the mother relaxes completely are essential. Sitting or lying down with legs raised is especially helpful.

Obstetrician Clark Gillespie says that continuing work for pregnant mothers depends on the mother's health, type of work, and company policy.[12] A healthy mother can continue to work in a healthy work environment, doing work that does not involve physical agility, during late pregnancy. Pregnant women should consider not working if they have: (1) had repeated premature labor and repeated spontaneous abortions, (2) moderately severe or severe heart disease, (3) blood diseases that produce anemia, like sickle cell anemia, (4) hypertension, (5) certain categories of diabetes, and (6) certain other disabilities like chronic back problems or chronic asthma. Work places are best avoided by pregnant women if they involve: (1) radiation, unless strictly monitored, (2) exposure to anesthetic gas, (3) veterinary medicine or work in pet shops, (4) risk of hepatitis or AIDS (hospitals, laboratories), (5) risk of rubella, (6) chemical substances such as heavy metals, organic solvents, pesticides, anesthetic gases, estrogen (such as DES), and certain hydrocarbons. Because company policy sometimes discriminates against pregnant women, court action is possible when women feel unfairly treated. The decision, however, may not come in time to affect that pregnancy.

As early as possible in the pregnancy, mothers should choose an obstetrician and make an appointment. Good prenatal care is especially important for very young and older mothers. Teenage mothers are more likely to have complications during pregnancy and to deliver babies of low birth weight who are themselves at greater risk of infant mortality and neurological defects. Good prenatal care reduces the risks of problems. Mothers over thirty-five are more likely to have illness and miscarriage with the pregnancy and to deliver stillborn, underweight babies or babies with chromosomal problems like Down's syndrome. Although the older mother has a greater risk of problems than a woman in the age range of twenty to thirty-five, the risk is still small, especially if she is in good health and gets good care. Techniques for early prediction and assessment of fetal abnormality are discussed in a later section.

You should be aware that when you choose a doctor you are also choosing the place of delivery. If you want to have your baby at home, if you want to have the father present during labor and delivery, if you want a rooming-in arrangement after the baby is born, you need to select an obstetrician who will cooperate and who practices in a hospital that provides for your needs.

On the basis of information gathered during interviews with mothers and from questionnaires and a review of medical journal articles, Carole McCauley suggests the following guidelines for choosing an obstetrician:[13]

1. Talk with parents, particularly any who are nurses and have special knowledge, and consider their recommendations.

2. Be critical of the preferences of other parents—remember that they may value different qualities in a physician.

3. If you are a high-risk mother, find a doctor who has experience with mothers who have similar problems.

4. Choose a doctor you feel comfortable talking to and questioning. Don't pick a doctor who refuses to answer questions. Before committing yourself to a doctor's care, discuss with her or him all the subjects about which you are concerned—for example, prepared childbirth, father's participation, medication, and home delivery.

5. Avoid the busiest doctor in town. He or she may be a fine physician but will probably have little time for personal attention.

6. Select a doctor who is interested in learning from your questions and who has or will get all the information you need—for example, about genetic counseling.

7. Avoid any doctor who minimizes problems with words like "simply," "only," or maximizes problems with words like "never," or "all."

8. Reread your insurance policy to determine whether it covers everything you want and everything the doctor considers necessary.

Many obstetricians have firm views about the kind of childbirth classes you attend and about the role of the father during labor and delivery. If you have strong feelings about these matters, knowing how a doctor feels can help you decide whether he or she is the obstetrician for you.

HAZARDS DURING PREGNANCY

As our knowledge of fetal development increases and we learn more about how the unborn child is affected by environmental influences, the list of "don'ts" changes. For example, a few years ago, moderate alcohol use was approved; now alcohol intake is prohibited. Thus, the pregnant woman needs to be constantly aware of whether activities or foods currently approved appear to have uncomfortable side effects on her or the quality of the baby's movements. She can then decide to avoid certain experiences.

The effects of harmful influences depend on when they occur in the pregnancy. As we noted, from the second to the eighth week, the fetus is especially vulnerable, and it is during this period that many harmful agents can produce nongenetic malformations. It is particularly important, during the childbearing years, for a woman who may conceive to have a consistently healthy lifestyle.

Poor diet—either too little food or food lacking in essential vitamins and minerals—affects both child and mother. If the mother's diet does not provide enough nourishment for the child, the child draws on the mother's supply of essential elements and the mother's health suffers. If her supply is not adequate, the child has an increased risk of rickets, anemia, pneumonia, colds, and bronchitis. In addition, poor diet affects growth of the central nervous system and influences later intellectual development. Thus, the mother must be sure her diet is adequate.

The developing baby is sensitive to radiation. The effects of radiation depend on the age and the developmental status of the organism as well as on the amount of radiation. Retarded growth, including mental retardation, has been found to result from exposure of the pregnant mother to radiation. A body temperature of 103°F or more can cause problems. Such high temperatures are often associated with infection. However, pregnant women who use saunas for extended periods (Smith estimates 15 minutes or longer) are found to have more problems in pregnancy and a higher rate of miscarriage, stillborns, and premature deliveries than women who do not.

When a mother with Rh negative blood is pregnant with a baby with Rh positive blood, there is the possibility that she may receive some of the baby's blood. Her body will then have a sensitive reaction to the foreign blood and will make antibodies that can harm the unborn child by destroying the baby's red blood cells. Fortunately, the bloods rarely mix except at the time of delivery or, sometimes, in the event of miscarriage. Thus, a first Rh positive baby of an Rh negative mother is usually safe from harm. There is a substance called RhoGAM that will prevent the manufacture of antibodies in the mother if the bloods mix. When injected into the mother, RhoGAM circulates in the mother's blood and destroys the baby's positive cells, and so the mother does not manufacture the antibodies. Every Rh negative mother who gives birth to an Rh positive baby should receive this injection within 72 hours of the birth. The injection is also given at the time of miscarriage or abortion. It entirely eliminates the possibility of harm due to antibodies.

Infections are known to affect the fetus. The effects of **German measles** or **rubella**, a viral infection, depend on the stage of development when the mother contracts the disease. If rubella occurs in the sixth week, cataracts are likely to result; in the ninth week, deafness; in the fifth to tenth weeks, cardiac problems; and in the sixth to ninth weeks, dental deformities. Other infections of importance are hepatitis B, B streptococcus, influenza, mumps, and chicken pox.

Human immunodeficiency virus (HIV), the cause of acquired immunodeficiency disease syndrome (AIDS), infects an increasing number of infants and children. In 80 percent of these cases, the mother infects the child during pregnancy.[14] Women who are IV drug users or are having unprotected sexual relations with IV drug users are the primary sources of the virus in children. The women themselves may be asymptomatic and unaware they are carriers of the disease until the child is diagnosed sometime in the first few years (50 percent of cases are diagnosed in the first year of life and 80 percent in the first three years).

The virus passes in the blood and bodily secretions (breast milk), but we do not know the exact mechanisms of transmission.[15] For example, it is not clear why only one twin might contract the virus or how mothers can give birth to uninfected children after giving birth to an infected one. Exactly when in pregnancy the virus is transmitted is unknown also. When it is passed very early, there can be many facial and skull abnormalities.

Children with HIV infection are prone to the problems of infants of drug-using mothers—prematurity, low birth weight, and other birth complications.[16] Worse, they are subject to profound effects from the virus following birth. They suffer many and various forms of infection affecting many different systems of the body, including the brain. When neurologic disorder occurs, then infants may suffer varying degrees of developmental delay and behavior problems. In all, it is a very sad picture for the child, and especially sad since HIV-infected children frequently live in home environments that cannot provide the increased care these children require.

The mother's untreated **syphilis** is known to have a profound impact on the baby in the latter part of pregnancy. About 30 percent of affected fetuses die before delivery. Of those delivered, 70 percent will have the disease. Sometimes symptoms are seen at birth, but usually the child appears healthy at birth with lesions and symptoms developing later, sometimes years later.

A woman with the virus **genital herpes simplex** may infect her child when the baby passes through an infected birth canal. At present, there is no known cure for this disease, which can cause a rash on the child and, more seriously, can result in mental retardation. To avoid passage through the birth canal, the child is delivered by Caesarean section.

Cytomegalovirus infection (CID) is a rarely discussed infection that may damage as many as 1 percent of all babies in the uterus. The mother may never know she has the disease because the symptoms are fever, aches and pain. If it occurs during the first three months of pregnancy, the disease can produce deafness, mental deficiency, or growth deficiency. Research is being conducted to develop a vaccination similar to the one used for rubella.

Toxoplasmosis is a relatively rare disease acquired by eating raw meat that is infected with the organism or by contact with a cat that has eaten such meat. Pregnant mothers are advised not to clean out cat litter boxes. The disease may be barely detectable in the adult—symptoms of upper respiratory infection are reported, or no symptoms at all. This disease, however, like so many others, causes physical and mental growth deficiencies in the child.

It was long thought that many drugs, safe for mothers, were safe for babies because they did not pass through the placenta to the child. The drug Thalidomide, however, provided a dramatic example of a medication that was safe for mothers but damaging to babies. A number of women who took the drug early in pregnancy bore infants with a wide variety of malformations: cleft palate; small ears; fused fingers and toes; dislocated hips; digestive, heart, and genitourinary malformations. Most noticeable were missing arms and legs, hands and feet attached to the torso. The intelligence of those children without sensory defects appears normal.

Since that time, physicians and parents have focused more attention on the potentially damaging effects of drugs on the unborn baby. At present, the general rule is to take no prescribed or over-the-counter medication without a physician's approval. Some antibiotics, hormones, tranquilizers, antiseizure medications, and steroids are related to birth defects.

The mother's **smoking** is related to prematurity, lower birth weight, shorter length, and small head size of the child. Smoking also affects the child's heart rate and breathing in the uterus. The mother who smokes needs to realize that each time she smokes, her unborn child also has a cigarette. Studies show that children's ongoing intellectual and physical development may be hampered by the mother's smoking.

The focus of much recent attention has been the **fetal alcohol syndrome** (FAS). In the early 1970s, doctors identified a group of babies—the children of alcoholic mothers—who were stunted in growth and development, small even for their weight, and hyperactive. The faces of some of these children were deformed, with asymmetrical features, low-set eyes and small ears. Their intellectual growth was retarded. Follow-up studies of these children reveal that the damage is irreversible. When the fetal alcohol syndrome was first identified, experts believed that a steady, daily consumption of 3 to 6 ounces of alcohol by the mother was needed to produce abnormalities in the infants. More recently, smaller doses of alcohol (1 ounce per day or more, the equivalent of two beers, or 8 ounces of wine, or one or two drinks) have been related to problems in children—low birth weight, breathing/sucking difficulties, and developmental delays. Differences in children's behavior have also been found when mothers consumed around two drinks a day before pregnancy.[17] When children of these mothers were four years old and showing no other noticeable problems, they showed poorer attention and longer reaction times on certain tasks. Many other variables related to the mother's health and lifestyle were well controlled—smoking, use of other drugs, children's early home environment—and children's difficulties appeared specifically related to their mother's alcohol consumption.

Women are now advised not to drink alcohol during the times they plan to conceive. If you are pregnant, remember that the more alcohol you drink, the greater the risk that your child will have abnormalities and the more severe the abnormalities are. If you are a heavy drinker, stopping at any time can reduce the risks to the child. Alcohol appears to exert its greatest impact during the second trimester of pregnancy.

Mind-altering drugs such as **heroin, morphine, methadone, cocaine,** and **LSD** affect prenatal development. Babies of heroin and morphine addicts will be addicts at birth. These infants exhibit withdrawal symptoms—including high-pitched crying, disturbed respiration, vomiting—some of which can lead to death. Often these babies are also premature and small and so less able to survive such symptoms. Methadone, which is prescribed as a substitute for heroin, can produce more severe withdrawal symptoms for the baby than those produced by heroin. There are indications that LSD may lead to chromosomal damage, but it is difficult to carry out controlled studies because of the many other variables, such as poor diet and use of other drugs, that accompany LSD use. Smith says there is no evidence that marijuana causes damage in babies, but a very recent report indicates that marijuana "may be capable of causing miscarriages or birth defects."[18]

Babies are being born in increasing numbers to mothers who use cocaine or crack during pregnancy. These babies are more likely to experience prematurity, low birth weight, birth complications like meconium staining, and heart malformations.[19] These babies are often irritable and highly sensitive to sensory stimulation. They are at high risk for developing later behavior problems that may be partially related to the effects of cocaine on the developing brain. For example, they appear subject to problems with mood and feelings of pleasure.

All the environmental factors that affect fetal development can be described as stresses for the developing organism. An additional source of stress is emotional upheaval experienced by the mother. Emotional stress produces changes in the levels of the mother's hormones, especially adrenaline and noradrenaline, which can pass the placental barrier and be transported to the fetus. Severe anxiety in the mother during pregnancy has been associated with nausea, abortion, increased length of labor, and delivery problems. Anxious and emotionally upset mothers have babies who are more active during pregnancy and are more irritable, hyperactive, and restless following birth. Hyperactivity in infancy can influence the mother-child relationship by making childcare more difficult for an already stressed mother. Thus, women who may be least able to cope with babies deliver babies who are most difficult to nurture.

Several of the harmful agents that increase deviations and malformations in the fetus have effects before a woman knows she is pregnant. These substances pass through the placental barrier, the fine mesh of cells that separates the child's blood from that of the mother. So it is important to remember that, even though we think of the mother and child as having a symbiotic relationship during pregnancy, the child is negatively affected by many substances that are not harmful to the mother.

In utero there are profound individual differences in the effects of the dangerous substances like Thalidomide. Some babies exposed to that drug showed no effects. The effects of a given agent depend in part on the timing and the stage of fetal development at which it is experienced. For example, rubella, or German measles, has different effects at different times. Several different agents can produce the same effects; for example, several agents change the appearance of the face and the mental level of the child. On the other hand, one agent, like alcohol, can produce changes in several areas, including appearance and mental level.

When early damage to the developing organism is severe, miscarriage may occur. About 20 percent, perhaps as many as 33 percent, of all pregnancies are ended by spontaneous abortion. Roughly 28 to 33 percent of these spontaneous abortions result from chromosomal defects. Male fetuses are aborted far more often than female fetuses. About 130 to 140 boys are conceived for every 100 girls conceived;

by the time of birth the ratio of boys to girls is 105 to 100. The reasons for the high rate of abortion of male fetuses is not known.

ASSESSING FETAL HEALTH

Amniocentesis is a technique used to obtain information about the physical characteristics and health of the developing organism. It is recommended for (1) women over 35, because they have the greater risk of bearing a child with defects, (2) women who have already borne children with defects, and (3) women with family histories of birth defects. Parents who are sure they will continue the pregnancy regardless of the results of amniocentesis are advised not to have it done, because the process involves a 1 percent risk of aborting the fetus.

Amniocentesis is a simple and relatively painless procedure. A needle is inserted through the abdomen into the amniotic sac, and a small sample of fluid, which contains waste cells from the baby, is removed. The fluid and cells are then analyzed to detect sex and abnormalities in the child. The procedure, carried out when the woman is fourteen to sixteen weeks pregnant, can identify several kinds of defects: (1) defects like Down's syndrome or trisomy 21, which results from chromosomal damage and produces mental retardation; (2) defects caused by hereditary factors—hemophilia, failure of the blood to clot, and Tay-Sachs disease, a disorder that results in suffering and early death of the child; and (3) malformations in the brain and spine that occur in the course of development.

Chorionic villi sampling (CVS) is another method for detecting fetal defects. A long catheter (tube) is inserted into the vagina and then into the mother's uterus. With the guidance of an ultrasound monitor, it is then placed between the uterine lining and the chorion (fetal membrane of the placenta). Analysis of the cells obtained from the chorionic villi (projections from the fetal membrane) reveal the child's genetic make-up.

At present, the test is done at medical centers, but eventually it will be done routinely in the physician's office. CVS can be done in the eighth week of the pregnancy, earlier than an amniocentesis. Parents know the results within a week and can make decisions earlier in the pregnancy. It is considered a safe test. Although it has a slightly higher risk of complications leading to miscarriage, some believe having the information sooner is worth the risk.

If abnormalities are found, parents can then decide what to do. Treatments of intrauterine defects are not now routine, although research is being done with the goal of increasing our capacity to intervene and correct defects. If amniocentesis or CVS reveals a disorder, the parents must decide whether they will abort the child. In the case of some extreme disorders, like Tay-Sachs, the parents may have little question. Other disorders may require a more difficult decision. For example, a Down's syndrome child may live and enjoy many years. Genetic counseling on traceable genetic diseases can help parents make informed choices.

Ultrasound scanning serves several purposes. This technique uses the echoes of high-frequency, undetectable sound waves to project an outline of the developing baby on a screen. The outline of the head can be measured, and the exact age of the fetus can be learned. It is also possible to determine the number of fetuses and the placement of the placenta. Ultrasound scanning is considered safe at present, though unnecessary ultrasonic scanning is discouraged. Tests of the mother's blood and urine indicate whether hormone levels are rising appropriately. Although these levels depend on many factors, they do give some indication of fetal progress. Measure of fetal heartbeat can be made throughout pregnancy and provide additional information.

BIRTH DEFECTS

Birth or congenital defects are those present at birth for a variety of reasons. Identifiable malformations occur in two or three of every one hundred newborn babies and more frequently in boys than in girls. Not all defects are anatomical. Some are biochemical, and some are not immediately detectable. Thus, 6 to 7 percent of all one-year-old children are identified as having birth defects.

There are many kinds of birth defects. Malformations during gestation result in cleft lip, cleft palate, hare lip, spinal malformations, club foot, dislocation of the hip, and heart malformations. Often these conditions can be corrected by surgery. Hereditary disorders include hemophilia and Tay-Sachs disease. Birth injuries result in head trauma and poor oxygen supply that can have long-term consequences. Let us look at the long-term effects of two birth problems—anoxia, or lack of oxygen, and prematurity.

Anoxia, or lack of oxygen, can occur because of problems with the umbilical cord during birth or if the baby does not breathe immediately after it leaves the mother's body. Lack of oxygen during the birth process can result in brain damage, motor problems, or possibly death. One of the most thorough studies of the effects of anoxia at birth followed children for seven years and compared them with a control sample of children who did not experience anoxia.[20] Assessments at birth, at three years, and at seven years revealed changes in the effects of anoxia as the children grew older.

Initially the effects seem to be primarily sensory and motor, then intellectual, and finally social and psychological. At birth, anoxic children tend to be irritable, muscularly tense, sensitive to pain and visual stimuli, and experiencing disrupted motor functioning. At age three, they exhibit some intellectual deficit—their vocabularies are small and their ability to form concepts is impaired. Anoxic children show more neurological deviations and they are more easily distracted than the average three-year-old, but by this age they have few perceptual-motor problems. At age seven, the intellectual difficulties of anoxic children are less salient, but they are likely to have psychological problems—to be socially immature, easily distracted, and somewhat more dependent.

It is possible that parents respond to the initial motor and intellectual difficulties of an anoxic infant in ways that increase psychological pressures on the child. Sensitive caretaking can help the child compensate for these deficits, particularly when parents are aware that the problems change with age.

Research following premature children for five years indicates, too, that the quality of the caretaking influences the later effects of **prematurity**.[21] When parents are supportive and stimulating, there are minimal differences between premature children and their controls. When there is little stimulation, prematurity is associated with many problems.

Birth complications may make initial care more difficult, but sustaining, supportive, attentive childcare can help to overcome these early deficits. The child who suffers both reproductive casualty (such as malformations) and caretaking casualty (lack of stimulation and attention) suffers most. Parents cannot always reverse the physical effects of birth defects, but they can provide the attention and support that minimize the effects of these problems.

The authors of a large-scale, longitudinal study on the island of Kauai that followed children from birth to age eighteen concluded that perinatal stress (problems occurring around the time of birth)

> were consistently related to later impaired physical and psychological functioning only when combined with persistently poor environmental circumstances (e.g., chronic poverty, family instability, or maternal health problem). Children who were raised in more affluent homes, with an intact family and a well-educated mother, showed few, if any, negative effects from reproductive stress unless there was severe central nervous system impairment.[22]

PREPARATION FOR LABOR AND DELIVERY

As the third trimester approaches, parents begin to prepare for labor and delivery. They take classes, do exercises, and practice breathing in anticipation of their child's birth.

Childbirth Classes

Childbirth classes provide information about pregnancy, labor, delivery, hospital procedures, medications for pain, postpartum care of child and mother, and breastfeeding. The earliest proponent of such preparation, in the 1930s, was Grantly Dick-Read, an English physician who believed that childbirth could be free of pain, discomfort, medication, and forceps if mothers had no fear.[23] To reduce fear, he provided each patient with information about childbirth, gave her relaxing exercises to practice, and served as coach for the mother during delivery. He used the term **natural childbirth** to refer to this process. Robert Bradley, who practices in the United States, also emphasizes natural childbirth.[24] He is opposed to the mother's having any medication during pregnancy and so strongly disapproves of medication during childbirth that instructors who teach the Bradley system must demonstrate for certification that 90 percent of their students have medication-free deliveries.

Unlike Dick-Read, Bradley considers the father an important part of the childbirth experience. Bradley believes that the father's participation is essential to a satisfying birth experience, and he warmly describes the joy and caring fathers bring to the

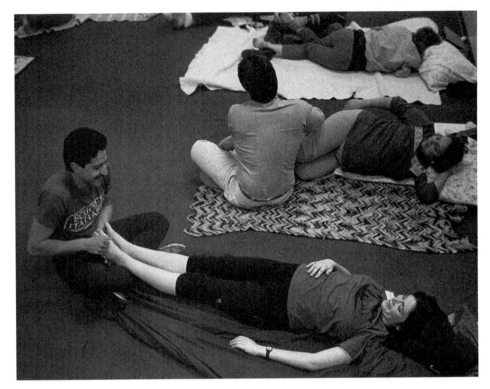

Childbirth classes provide information about pregnancy, labor, delivery, hospital procedures, medication for pain, postpartum care of the child and mother, and breast-feeding. Lamaze classes, as shown above, integrate the father into the birthing process.

experience. The term **husband-coached childbirth**, which Bradley uses to describe his method, underscores the father's role. Bradley likens the role of doctor during delivery to that of a lifeguard at a pool. The doctor's job is to stand on the sidelines and let both parents do the work, unless some unusual problem develops. Bradley's aim is joyful delivery, with the mother able to walk back to her room with her baby and husband. After a first nursing and a few hours' observation to be sure uterine bleeding is controlled, the mother and baby may go home.

In addition to providing factual information and breathing techniques, Bradley suggests relaxation techniques and visual imagery of pleasant events and experiences to further relax the mother during labor. Preparation is begun in the pregnancy, and the amount of training required depends on the particular mother and her physical condition. Although Bradley does not give medications and believes the role of doctor is a minimal one, he does believe babies should be born in hospitals in case there is a sudden difficulty and a Caesarean section is required. He does recommend, however, that the hospital provide a cozy, homelike atmosphere for delivery.

Fernand Lamaze, a French obstetrician, studied Russian methods of childbearing and combined conditioning principles with hypnotic techniques to help mothers have satisfying births. Marjorie Karmel, an enthusiastic follower, introduced his work to this country in a book, *Thank You, Dr. Lamaze*.[25] The Lamaze method is sometimes called a **psychoprophylactic** method (meaning psychological and physical preparation of instruction and practice). In contrast to Dick-Read and Bradley, Lamaze believes natural childbirth can involve pain and discomfort and that the mother must be trained and must work to handle the birth. Mothers learn to concentrate, breathe properly, and have confidence in their ability to deliver the child. Elizabeth Bing, a Lamaze teacher in the United States, likens the mother's role to that of a swimmer riding ocean waves in the surf.[26] In the beginning the swimmer may be knocked over and tossed about by the waves, but with experience and some training she learns to ride them buoyantly. Training and preparation do not begin until the last trimester, so that the mother does not become bored with the exercises.

Even before Bradley, Lamaze encouraged the presence of the father in the labor and delivery rooms, to coach the mother, help with her breathing, massage her, and give her support and confidence. Although the method stresses a natural birth and an active role for the mother in achieving this goal, Lamaze is not as opposed to medication as Bradley is.

Sheila Kitzinger, a British anthropologist and mother, has combined the work of Dick-Read and Lamaze with body exercises stressing physical fitness.[27] She emphasizes breathing and relaxation and introduces "touch-relaxation," a series of special exercises that lead to increased relaxation. Kitzinger's **psychosexual** approach views childbirth as one event in a woman's ongoing sexual life.

The most recent addition to childbirth methods is Esther Marilus' style of natural childbirth.[28] Believing that each labor and delivery is unique and requires different techniques, she combines the exercises and breathing methods of all other schools and introduces one of her own—**graduated breathing**. The main advantage of graduated breathing is that the mother gets large amounts of oxygen slowly, so that she does not experience the dizziness and tingling that sometimes occur with a rapid intake of large quantities of oxygen. Marilus stresses that exercises are preparation not only for birth but for the entire pregnancy and postpartum period.

Hypnosis and **acupuncture** also have been used to reduce pain in childbirth, and other techniques incorporate methods for inducing a light trance. They add education for childbirth, but all rely on relaxation, concentration, and self-suggestion. Acupuncture is used when local anesthesia is desired. Thus, the acupuncturist works with the obstetrician during delivery. As yet, few obstetricians have become interested in this method.

Parents may find themselves drawn to a specific method, but all share some common features: (1) factual information about the childbirth process, (2) physical exercises to tone the body for the work of childbirth, (3) breathing and relaxation exercises to remove tension and facilitate the birth process, and (4) inclusion of the husband or friend as coach. Many childbirth classes for women combine one or more of these methods. In selecting a childbirth class, the authors of *Our Bodies, Ourselves* recommend (1) a small class with ten or fewer couples if possible, (2) a class that lasts perhaps eight or ten weeks, so there is plenty of time to learn the exercises and practice them, (3) inclusion of father or friend, (4) discussions of feelings and attitudes about childbirth as well as about techniques, (5) a well-qualified instructor who provides references and describes personal and professional experiences with birth, (6) availability of psychological professionals with whom to discuss feelings, (7) a reasonable fee, and (8) a reputable sponsoring organization.[29]

Research findings suggest that preparation does not shorten the labor or reduce blood flow or tearing, but that it does heighten the mother's enjoyment of the experience of the childbirth.[30] Women who have taken childbirth classes report feeling in greater control of what was happening. They were excited and report feelings of greater closeness with the child. Thus, preparation heightens the mother's pleasure and satisfaction. Even when there has been little training, some effects are noticeable.

Alternative Birth Centers

Although most obstetricians recommend hospital deliveries, many suggest changes in hospital routines to create a more homelike atmosphere. Alternative birth centers in the hospital setting have advanced equipment and professional intervention quickly at hand. Yet the birthing room, usually used both for labor and delivery, resembles a bedroom and has a large double bed and the kind of furniture you would find in a home. Family members are present; music and food are available. Parents can bring pillows, pictures, and other personal possessions to make a home at the hospital.

Rooming-In

Giving mother and child an opportunity to get to know each other in the hospital greatly eases the transition of bringing a baby home. Rooming-in permits mother and child to stay in the same room for extended periods of time. Different hospitals have different arrangements, and often parents can decide how much time during the day the baby is with them. The mother cares for the child, nursing, changing diapers, bathing the baby. Nurses or other professionals are available to answer any questions she has. Some mothers prefer to have their infants with them during the day but in the nursery at night, so they can get as much rest as possible. Other mothers prefer to begin the routine of total care while they are in the hospital, and they want their babies with them 24 hours a day.

Stress

No matter how much a couple may want their new baby, no matter how carefully and completely they have planned for the infant's arrival, they will experience stress.

One way to anticipate the extent of stress is to examine an objective assessment, made by Thomas Holmes and Richard Rahe, of the amount of stress associated with various life events (see Table 5-1). They developed the *Social Readjustment Scale*, a list of stressful events weighted to indicate the demand each makes on an individual for adaptation.[31]

TABLE 5-1
THE STRESS OF ADJUSTING TO CHANGE

Event	Scale of Impact	Event	Scale of Impact
Death of spouse	100	* Change in responsibilities at work	29
Divorce	73	Son or daughter leaving home	29
Marital separation	65	Trouble with in-laws	29
Jail term	63	* Outstanding personal achievement	28
Death of close family member	63	* Wife begins or stops work	26
Personal injury or illness	53	Begin or end school	26
Marriage	50	* Change in living conditions	25
Fired at work	47	* Revision of personal habits	24
Marital reconciliation	45	Trouble with boss	23
Retirement	45	* Change in work hours or conditions	20
Change in health of family member	44	* Change in residence	20
* Pregnancy	40	Change in schools	20
* Sex difficulties	39	* Change in recreation	19
* Gain of new family member	39	Change in church activities	19
Business readjustment	39	* Change in social activities	18
* Change in financial status	38	Mortgage or loan less than $10,000	17
Death of close friend	37	* Change in sleeping habits	16
Change to different line of work	36	Change in number of family get-togethers	15
Change in number of arguments with spouse	35	* Change in eating habits	15
Mortgage over $10,000	31	Vacation	13
Foreclosure of mortgage or loan	30	Christmas	12
		Minor violations of the law	11

* Event associated with pregnancy.

Thomas H. Holmes and Richard H. Rahe, "The Social Readjustment Rating Scale," *Journal of Psychosomatic Research* 11 (1967): 216.

Holmes and Rahe found that, of the people they interviewed, 80 percent of those whose total scores were above 300 suffered heart attacks, depression, or some other serious illness within a year. A list, from the *Social Readjustment Scale,* of changes associated with pregnancy and birth (asterisked items in Table 5-1) totals 396—a score high enough to predict serious illness.

Parents who anticipate the changes they will be going through and who plan ways of coping with changes can reduce stress during the pregnancy and after birth. Remember, too, that the same stresses recur at the birth of each child, at least while adjustments are being made. There will always be lost sleep, irregular hours, and the adaptation required to include a new family member.

LABOR AND DELIVERY

The experience of being born is one of the most stressful in any individual's life. There is (1) a change from placental supply of oxygen to breathing with the lungs, (2) an extreme change in the environment, from a watery state to an oxygen atmosphere, (3) a temperature change from about 98°F in the uterus to about 70°F in the delivery room, (4) the appearance of strong light after months of darkness, and (5) the beginning of functioning of organs like the stomach, intestines, and hormonal system. The ability to survive these stresses depends on the health of the mother before and during pregnancy and on the health of the fetus at birth.

Labor is divided into three stages: (1) dilation or opening of the cervix, (2) expulsion of the infant, and (3) expulsion of the placenta. Labor may begin with contractions that come every 15 or 20 minutes and last about 25 to 35 seconds. In a small number of cases, however, it begins with the rupture of the amniotic sac, and a rush of fluid, with the contractions starting later. The uterus becomes narrow, thus straightening the baby's body and pressing the head or buttocks against the cervix. Muscles of the uterus contract and apply a force equal to about 55 pounds on the baby. The baby's head (or bottom) pushes against the cervix, flattens it, and forces it open. When the cervix is fully dilated to 10 centimeters (or five fingers) in width, the first stage of labor ends. The average length of the first stage varies; in first births it is about 8 hours, and in later births about 6 hours.

The second stage of labor begins when the child moves into the birth canal. The baby's head has soft places, and so the head can mold to go through the narrow passage. The mother pushes to move the baby down. As the baby's head reaches the vaginal opening, it stretches the skin. To prevent tearing of the skin from the vagina to the anus as the baby emerges, an incision, termed an **episiotomy**, is often made between the vagina and anus, and is stitched after birth.

The doctor helps the baby emerge from the canal and sucks out any fluid in the mouth. If the child does not cry spontaneously, the doctor can stroke the back or spank the bottom in order to stimulate a cry and the first breath. Frederick Leboyer, a French obstetrician, has urged that the birth process should be gentle and that the first minutes of the baby's life should occur in a soothing environment.[32] He recommends subdued lighting and a minimum amount of noise in the delivery room, skin contact with the mother, delaying the cutting of the umbilical cord for a few minutes after birth, and a warm, soothing bath, similar to the intrauterine environment, for the newborn. Although some of Leboyer's ideas—especially the warm bath—are controversial, many of his recommendations for a gentler birth have been adopted in modified forms.

When the infant emerges, he or she is placed on the mother's stomach and the umbilical cord is cut.

In the third stage of labor, uterine contractions separate the placenta from the lining of the uterus and the placenta is expelled. Further uterine contractions decrease the bleeding.

The amount of medication a mother receives during the birth process varies. With preparation, some women require little or none. Many women, however, experience moderate to severe discomfort at some time during the birth, especially if the infant

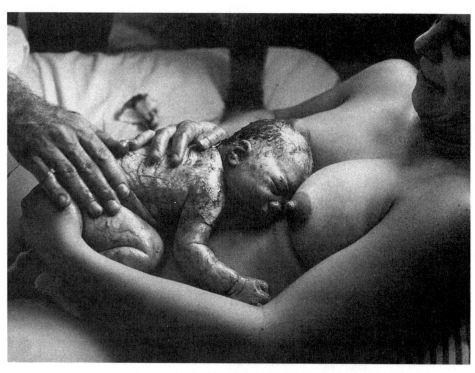

In the second stage of delivery, the emerged child is placed on the mother's stomach and the umbilical cord is cut. Leboyer believed that the birth process should be gentle and that the first few minutes of the baby's life should occur in a soothing environment.

is born buttocks first (a **breech birth**) or if the mother is delivering twins. Pain medication may be advised, and the major consideration in choosing medication is its effects on the child. Large doses of central nervous system drugs, such as general anesthesia, may interfere with the baby's breathing and have effects on the baby's functioning after birth. In cases where these powerful drugs were administered, sensorimotor functioning appeared disrupted in the first few days after birth, and even a year later some effects on cognitive functioning and gross motor abilities were still apparent.[33] Even local, epidural anesthesia (a pain relief technique that uses local anesthetic to block transmission of nerve impulses to and from the pelvic region), formerly thought to have few effects, has been related to poor state organization in the baby's first five days of life—patterns of waking, sleeping, eating, and crying seemed more labile than the patterns of babies without such anesthesia. When babies were one month old, these effects were not detectable by objective tests, but mothers of these babies continued to report that they were less adaptable, harder to care for, and less rewarding.[34] Mothers of nonmedicated babies reported that they were more social and responsive. Mothers' initial impressions of the babies, then, seemed to remain even after the babies themselves seemed more stable. The general rule is that the mildest sedation possible is the wisest choice.

Complications

Doctors and nurses assisting at labor are concerned not only with the survival and delivery of the child, but with survival of the child's capacity for normal life. Sometimes they must intervene in the natural process of labor and delivery to induce the birth, monitor the child's progress with electronic equipment, or perform a Caesarean section.

Several kinds of problems can produce complications. The contractions may be too weak or too strong. The child may be poorly positioned in the uterus, with the head at a poor angle or the buttocks facing the cervix. The mother's pelvis may be poorly shaped for delivering the size child she is carrying. The placenta may be poorly positioned and deliver first, depriving the child of oxygen. The mother may have chronic health problems that increase the risk for her and the child, or she may be delivering more than one baby.

Induction Labor may have to be started by artificial means because the child and the mother will be in danger if pregnancy continues. The mother's blood pressure may be too high, or the child may be postmature (may have been in the uterus more than 42 or 43 weeks) and have outlived the food supplies in the uterus and the mother's ability to supply oxygen.

Fetal Monitoring Although sometimes used in normal deliveries, electronic fetal monitoring is more often used when there are problems, to assess the baby's health during labor. Electronic monitors are of two kinds. First, ultrasonic sound echoes, which emanate from a small unit attached to the mother's abdomen, report fetal heartbeats without internal examination. This unit can be used before the rupture of the membranes and dilation of the cervix. A second unit is used to measure uterine contractions. Another method requires that the monitor be attached to the top of the baby's head; it is inserted in the uterus after the membranes are ruptured and contact with the head is possible. Fetal blood obtained from a sample from the scalp may also be used to check the amount of oxygen in the child's blood.

Caesarean Section The doctor may recommend that a baby be delivered by Caesarean section when any of the complications listed earlier occurs or if the mother had genital herpes simplex, which can infect the baby as it passes through the birth canal. Caesarean section is surgical removal of the child through an incision made in the uterus and abdominal cavity of the mother. With the use of nerve blocks, a mother can be given local anesthesia and still be conscious for the birth of her child. Once a mother has had Caesarean section, her subsequent children will probably be delivered this way to reduce the risk of uterine rupture at the point of the incision.

The Arrival

The arrival of the baby climaxes the birth process. Smiling and excited at the miracle of birth, parents eagerly look at the baby, often seeing resemblances between the child and other family members. Bradley describes the laughter that often bubbles up in parents when the birth has been a satisfying experience for both. Many parents are enthralled at the tininess of the child and the diminutiveness of the hands, feet, body. Other parents are surprised. We assume a newborn will look like a seven-month-old child, round, smiling, head held steadily. Instead, the baby, on average weighing 7 pounds and measuring 20 inches, is smaller and reddened, covered with a cheeselike substance (vernix caseosa) which protects the baby in the uterus from the effects of living in a fluid environment. Soon after birth the substance begins to disappear, leaving a velvety coating to the skin. The head is very large in relation to the body, and the baby cannot support it. The head may be misshapen and bruised from the delivery process, especially if forceps were used to pull the baby out of the birth canal.

An adult can hold a newborn easily on his or her forearm, cradling the head in one hand. Immediately following birth, at intervals of 1 and 5 minutes, and then again at one hour, the baby is rated on five dimensions of behavior by the pediatrician. The evaluation, devised by Virginia Apgar and named for her, rates five areas: (1) *appearance* or color of skin, (2) *pulse* as a measure of heart rate, (3) *grimace and gag reflexes* to measure reflex irritability, (4) *activity* to measure muscle tone, and (5) *respiration*. Each area is rated, 0, 1, or 2; if the child receives a total score of 8 to 10, he or she is healthy; if the total score is 0, 1, or 2, resuscitation is required.

BONDING

The first meeting between parents and child is an important occasion. In the first hour after birth, babies are more alert and visually attentive than they will be for the next 3 or 4 hours. And during that first hour they may be most responsive to contact with the parents. Pediatricians Marshall Klaus and John Kennell believe the first hour is a sensitive period during which parents need privacy and close physical contact with the infant.[35] This first chance to touch, hold, and explore the baby and to receive some response from the child in the form of eye or body movements is very important. Continuing contact with the baby, for at least 5 hours per day in the hospital, is also important. This close physical contact, thought to strengthen the attachment between parent and child, is termed **bonding**.

Recent research suggests that early intensive contact between mother and baby within the first hour after birth increases the mother's tender touching and cuddling behavior.[36] This effect, however, was only found with those mothers who planned their children. After 8 to 10 days, mothers without early contact touched their children as often as mothers with contact. When infants are separated from parents after birth because of prematurity or birth complications, the emotional attachment between mother and infant grows. At one year, attachment patterns were as strong in babies separated from mothers at birth as they were in infants who were not separated at birth.[37]

While early contact is pleasurable and starts the relationship between parent and child on a positive note, Michael Rutter is critical of the concept of bonding.[38] He points out that relationships are multifaceted and not dependent on a single sensory modality like skin contact. Relationships develop over time, and the sensitive period for parent-child attachment is the second half of the first year. Even older infants and children who lose an attachment figure can form strong new attachments to caretakers. So if it is not possible to have prolonged time with the infant at birth, parents can be assured that strong bonds still grow.

Parental involvement in the birth process, along with early and extended contact with the baby, strengthens the marriage when the couple view the experience positively.[39] The father feels included in the formation of the family. Marital closeness and family involvement, in turn, may further strengthen the father-infant tie. There is no evidence that a close father-infant relationship requires the father's attendance at birth or early and extended contact with the baby, so there is no need to feel guilty if this cannot occur. Most couples, however, want the father present, and fathers report powerful feelings that strengthen the couple's relationship and the family bond.

Besides forming a bond, the extra contact between parents and child in the hospital permits parents to learn how the baby reacts and how to care for the child's needs. When parents and baby go home, both parents feel more at ease when handling the infant.

Klaus and Kennell believe all hospitals can modify procedures to provide time for the bonding process. Even if a child is premature or needs special care, they believe it is often possible for the parents to hold the child briefly before the child goes to the intensive care nursery. And parents can go to the nursery and give as much physical care as possible during the child's stay there.

MAJOR POINTS OF CHAPTER 5

Parenting starts in pregnancy as parents:

- acquire information and work together to have healthiest pregnancy, labor, and delivery possible to minimize risk of long-term damage to child
- change lifestyle to protect child from harmful environmental agents
- experience effects of pregnancy on the couple relationship
- begin to make images of the baby and of themselves as parents
- experience pregnancy differently and may not be supportive of each other—mothers become engrossed with pregnancy more quickly and intensely, and fathers can feel left out

Prenatal development:

- first trimester (three-month period)—all the major organs and systems are laid down, so by twelve weeks, the baby has a well-formed body and is active—kicking, swallowing, turning head
- second trimester—baby's development continues and child is strong and active; parents can feel movements
- last trimester—baby gains weight and prepares for birth; practices reflexes of sucking, swallowing, breathing

Healthy lifestyle at conception and pregnancy includes:

- healthy, balanced diet
- regular exercise
- adequate rest
- minimal emotional stress
- healthy and safe work place and reasonable number of hours there
- abstaining from coffee, alcohol, cigarettes, prescription and nonprescription drugs
- avoiding external substances dangerous to babies in the uterus—radiation; infections such as syphilis, AIDS, genital herpes, cytomegalovirus, and toxoplasmosis

Guidelines for seeking obstetrical care include:

- getting information about doctor's qualifications and experience
- getting his views on delivery practices
- picking a doctor you can question and feel comfortable with

Techniques for assessing fetal health during pregnancy are:

- amniocentesis
- chorionic villi sampling
- ultrasound scanning

Parents' preparation includes:

- learning about childbirth
- practicing childbirth exercises
- selecting a pediatrician to care for baby
- creating space for baby, buying clothes and other items for baby care
- learning about care of baby after leaving hospital

Labor:

- three stages
- husband or friend acts as coach
- mildest form of sedation possible is the best as the effects of these drugs are detected in the baby for some time afterward

Delivery and arrival:

- birth is stressful experience involving many changes for baby—change in environment, temperature, functioning of his/her body for independent breathing, ingestion, and digestion of food

- complications of lack of oxygen in birth or prematurity occur even with careful medical attention
- if birth complications occur, parents play an important role in providing a supportive, nourishing environment that helps children overcome effects of birth complication

Bonding:

- occurs in the first hour after birth when parents and child have a time alone to get acquainted
- is exciting and highly pleasurable for both parents
- is not necessary for developing healthy, deep attachment should such a period together not be possible

Providing parental support at times of change includes:

- recognizing that many changes can be stressful to both parents
- seeking support from family and friends

ADDITIONAL READINGS

Barrett, Nina. *I Wish Someone Had Told Me.* New York: Simon & Schuster, 1990.

Eisenberg, Arlene; Murkoff, Heidi Eisenberg; and Hathaway, Sandee Eisenberg. *What to Expect When You're Expecting.* New York: Workman Publishing, 1988.

Hotchner, Tracy. *Pregnancy and Childbirth.* Rev. ed. New York: Avon, 1990.

Jones, Carl. *After The Baby Is Born.* New York: Henry Holt, 1986.

Kitzinger, Sheila. *Birth over Thirty.* New York: Viking Penguin, 1985.

Notes

1. R. J. McCorkel, "Husbands and Pregnancy: An Exploratory Study," M.A. thesis, University of North Carolina, 1964.

2. Ellen Galinsky, *Between Generations: The Six Stages of Parenthood* (New York: Times Books, 1981).

3. Myra Leifer, "Psychological Changes Accompanying Pregnancy and Motherhood," *Genetic Psychology Monographs* 95 (1977): 55–96.

4. Galinsky, *Between Generations.*

5. Leifer, "Psychological Changes Accompanying Pregnancy and Motherhood."

6. Galinsky, *Between Generations.*

7. Leah Yarrow, "Dreams During Pregnancy: Their Hidden Meanings," *Parents Magazine,* November 1979.

8. T. Berry Brazelton, *Doctor and Child* (New York: Dell, 1978).

9. Margaret Adams and Basil Lee, "Labor and Birth," in *A New Life: Pregnancy, Birth, and Your Child's First Year,* ed. John T. Queenan (New York: Van Nostrand and Reinhold, 1979), pp. 86–99.

10. David W. Smith, *Mothering Your Unborn Baby* (Philadelphia: W. B. Saunders, 1979).

11. Cyril Young, "The Mother in Pregnancy," in *A New Life: Pregnancy, Birth, and Your Child's First Year,* ed. John T. Queenan (New York: Van Nostrand and Reinhold, 1979), pp. 24–25.

12. Clark Gillespie, *Your Pregnancy Month by Month.* 3d ed. (New York: Harper & Row, 1985).

13. Carole S. McCauley, *Pregnancy After Thirty-Five* (New York: Pocket Books, 1978).

14. Judith Falloon, Janie Eddy, Lori Wiener, and Philip A. Pizzo, "Human Immunodeficiency Virus Infection in Children," *Pediatrics* 114 (1989): 1–30.

15. Ibid.

16. Edward Connor, Arlene Bardequez, and Joseph Apuzzio, "The Intrapartum Management of the HIV-infected Mother and Her Infant," *Clinics in Perinatology* 16 (1989): 899–908.

17. Ann P. Streissguth, Donald C. Martin, Helen M. Barr, Beth M. Sandman, Grace L. Kirchner, and Betty L. Darby, "Intrauterine Alcohol and Nicotine Exposure: Attention and Reaction Time in 4-Year-Old Children," *Developmental Psychology* 20 (1984): 533–541.

18. "Marijuana: What Are the Risks?" *The Harvard Medical School Health Letter* (June 1980), p. 2.

19. Bertis B. Little, Laura M. Snell, Victor R. Klein, and Larry C. Gilstrap III, "Cocaine Abuse during Pregnancy: Maternal and Fetal Implications," *Obstetrics and Gynecology* 73 (1989): 157–160.

20. Frances K. Graham et al., "Development Three Years After Perinatal Anoxia and Other Potentially Damaging Newborn Experiences," *Psychological Monographs* 76 (1962): whole number 3; Norman L. Corah et al., "Effects of Perinatal Anoxia After Seven Years," *Psychological Monographs* 79 (1965): whole number 3.

21. Cecil M. Drillien and Richard W. B. Ellis, *The Growth and Development of the Prematurely Born Infant* (Baltimore: Williams & Wilkins, 1964).

22. Emmy E. Werner and Ruth S. Smith, *Vulnerable but Invincible: A Study of Resilient Children* (New York: McGraw-Hill, 1982), p. 31.

23. Grantly Dick-Read, *Childbirth without Fear,* 2d ed. (New York: Harper & Row, 1959).

24. Robert A. Bradley, *Husband-Coached Childbirth,* rev. ed. (New York: Harper & Row, 1974).

25. Marjorie Karmel, *Thank You, Dr. Lamaze* (Philadelphia: J. P. Lippincott, 1959).

26. Elizabeth Bing, *Six Practical Lessons for an Easier Childbirth,* rev. ed. (New York: Bantam, 1977).

27. Sheila Kitzinger, *The Experience of Childbirth* (Baltimore: Penguin Books, 1967).

28. Esther Marilus, *Natural Childbirth the Swiss Way* (Englewood Cliffs, N.J.: Prentice-Hall, 1979).

29. The Boston Women's Health Book Collective, *Our Bodies, Ourselves* (New York: Simon & Schuster, 1973).

30. Allan G. Charles et al., "Obstetric and Psychological Effects of Psychoprophylactic Preparation for Childbirth," *American Journal of Obstetrics and Gynecology* 131 (1978): 44–52; Susan G. Doering and Doris R. Entwisle, "Preparation During Pregnancy and Ability to Cope with Labor and Delivery," *American Journal of Orthopsychiatry* 45 (1975): 825–837.

31. Thomas H. Holmes and Richard H. Rahe, "The Social Readjustment Rating Scale," *Journal of Psychosomatic Research* 11 (1967): 216.

32. Frederick Leboyer, *Birth without Violence* (New York: Alfred A. Knopf, 1975).

33. Yvonne Brackbill, "Obstetrical Medication and Infant Behavior," in *Handbook of Infant Development,* ed. Joy D. Osofsky (New York: John Wiley, 1979), pp. 76–124.

34. Anne D. Murray, Robyn M. Dolby, Roger L. Nation, and David B. Thomas, "Effects of Epidural Anesthesia on Newborns and Their Mothers," *Child Development* 52 (1981): 71–82.

35. Marshall H. Klaus and John H. Kennell, *Maternal-Infant Bonding* (St. Louis: C. V. Mosby, 1976).

36. Karin Grossman, Kerstin Thane, and Klaus E. Grossman, "Maternal Tactual Contact of the Newborn after Various Postpartum Conditions of Mother-Child Contact," *Developmental Psychology* 17 (1981): 158–169.

37. Sara S. Rode, Pi-Nian Chang, Robert O. Fisch, and L. Alan Sroufe, "Attachment Patterns of Infants Separated at Birth," *Developmental Psychology* 17 (1981): 195–202.

38. Michael Rutter, "Continuities and Discontinuities from Infancy," in *Handbook of Infant Development,* 2nd ed., ed. Joy Doniger Osofsky (New York: John Wiley, 1987): pp. 1256–1297.

39. Rob Palkovitz, "Father's Birth Attendance, Early Contact, and Extended Contact with Their Newborns: A Critical Review," *Child Development* 56 (1985): 392–406.

THE FIRST YEAR OF LIFE

CHAPTER 6

The first year of life is an exciting time of growth and development for both babies and their parents. Infants grow from little creatures who sleep much of the day and cannot hold up even their heads to little persons who are awake much of the day, mobile and curious, crawling or walking, speaking a few words. They grow from infants who are completely dependent on parents to feed them to children who sit in a high chair at the table and eat table food. From tiny babies who mostly sleep, eat, and cry, they develop into smiling, happy, curious persons who express excitement and surprise at the world around them. The rate of growth in this first year is truly amazing.

Parents grow, too. Adults who looked after their own needs now adjust to meet those of their child. As the child's needs change in the course of the year, so parents' ways of relating to the child change, too. This balancing of the child's needs with their own needs provides parents with a challenge. In this chapter we describe the mutual development of child and parents in this incorporation of a new life in the family.

THE NEWBORN

During the first days of life, the infant's states of consciousness are different from the clearly defined states of sleep or wakefulness exhibited by older children and adults. Peter Wolff has identified six stages of consciousness in infants: (1) *regular sleep,* in which the child is relaxed and still; (2) *irregular sleep,* in which the eyes are closed but the child is somewhat active; (3) *drowsiness,* in which the eyes flutter and the child has a glazed look; (4) *alert inactivity,* in which the eyes are open and the child is alert; (5) *waking activity,* in which the child is alert and physically active; and (6) *crying,* in which the child cries and moves about.[1]

Babies vary in how much time they spend in each activity. The average newborn spends 16 hours each day sleeping, though some sleep as little as 10 hours, and others sleep as much as 20 hours a day. Babies spend at least 50 percent of sleep time having **rapid eye movements** (REMs), a pattern of sleep that in adults is associated with dreaming. We do not know whether babies dream. Researchers speculate that the large percentage of rapid eye movement sleep serves as internal stimulation to promote development of higher brain centers.[2] Premature babies spend even more time than full-term infants in REM sleep. Percentages of REM sleep decrease during the first six months, but it is not until the child is in elementary school that the proportion of REM sleep drops to the adult average of 25 percent.

Newborns, and all human beings, have biological cycles of sleep, wakefulness, activity, hunger, fluctuations in body temperature and hormone secretions. These biological cycles, repeating about every 24 hours, are called **circadian rhythms.** It is important for the cycles to be in harmony—for example, to sleep as temperature descends and wake as temperature rises—if we are to feel and function at our best. Children and adults, if left to function as they please, would live in a 25-hour day. In caves or places of isolation with no indication of time of day, people operate on a 25-hour day, going to sleep an hour later each day, and sleeping an hour longer the following day. Scheduling regular meal, sleep, and wake times allows us to live happily in a 24-hour day.

During the newborn period, body rhythms are not organized. Neonates sleep, wake, and eat every few hours. Their systems are irregular, gradually settling into a more organized pattern in the first three months, with most achieving a stable pattern at about six months. As we will see, this unsettled initial period has implications for parenting.

Reflexes

The newborn is equipped with a variety of **reflexes,** defined as inborn responses triggered by specific stimuli. Some reflexes, like sucking, are present and well practiced before birth. All reflexes appear to help the newborn adapt to the new and different environment outside the mother for effective functioning during this critical period. The **tonic-neck reflex** (turning the head to the side), the **rooting reflex** (searching for breast), and the **sucking reflex** provide mechanisms for taking in nourishment. The **blinking, gagging,** and **withdrawal reflexes** protect the baby from external stimuli that are annoying or harmful.

The **righting reflex** maintains posture. The **Moro reflex** occurs whenever the baby loses support of head or body or is startled by a loud noise or some other surprise. The infant extends its arms and then throws them across its chest as though embracing someone or something for support. The **grasp reflex** enables the baby to close on an object.

Senses

For years psychologists thought newborn babies were incompetent creatures who were unable to comprehend the world around them. Because infants cannot tell us what they see, hear, taste, smell, and feel, our understanding of newborns' abilities was limited until complex equipment enabled us to detect babies' physiological

WHAT I WISH I HAD KNOWN ABOUT INFANCY

"I remember when we brought him home from the hospital, and we had him on the changing table for a minute, and I realized, 'I don't know how to keep the engine running.' I wondered how could they let him go home with us, this little package weighing seven or eight pounds. I had no idea of what to do. I kind of knew you fed him, and you cleaned him and kept him warm; but I didn't have any hands-on experience, anything practical. In a way I would have liked them to watch me for a day or two in the hospital while I changed him, to make sure I knew how to do it. It's kind of like giving me a car without seeing whether I could drive it around the block." FATHER

"I didn't have enough information about breastfeeding for two months. I almost gave up because it was so painful. I found a good breastfeeding nurse who showed me two things, and it changed the whole experience. It made such a difference, and breastfeeding became a joy." MOTHER

"I wish we had known a little more about establishing her first habits about sleeping. The way you set it up in the beginning is the way it is going to be. Having enough sleep is so important. We went too long before we decided to let her cry for five minutes. Then she got into good sleep habits." FATHER

"I had no idea how tired I would be. I'm not sure anyone can describe the level of tiredness you feel. I am getting eight hours of sleep now but I always sleep lightly and could wake up in an instant. When I wake up in the morning now, I don't feel refreshed. I'm still tired even though he is sleeping through the night." MOTHER

"I wish I had known how it would change things between me and my husband. The baby comes first, and by the time the day is over and he is in bed, we have two hours together, but I just want to curl up and take care of myself." MOTHER

responses to what they sense. As we learn about their abilities, we are more and more impressed with the competent behavior displayed by babies just a few hours old.

Newborns are sensitive to light and to changes in brightness immediately after birth. They can distinguish objects, although they see things in a hazy blur rather than as clear images. A newborn sees most clearly what is about 8 inches from his face, often the mother's or father's face. Babies are more interested in patterned objects—for example, faces or concentric circles—than in solid-colored circles. They tend to focus on the edges, however, perhaps because that is where contrast is sharpest. This may be disconcerting to the new mother, who wants her baby to look at her eyes, not at her forehead or chin. But within a few weeks the child will make eye contact. By the age of six months, the child's vision is similar to that of the adult.

Hearing is difficult to assess immediately after birth because there may be fluid in the ears. But tests done a few hours later suggest that babies can tell the difference between sounds of different pitch, loudness, and duration. Studies suggest that babies sleep and eat better when they hear rhythmic sounds reminiscent of the heart-

"I wish I had known about how much time babies take. It is like he needs twenty-four-hour attention. For an older parent who is used to having his own life and is very set in his ways, it is hard to make the changes and still have some time for your own life." FATHER

"I bottlefed him, and I wished I had had better information about bottlefeeding. I didn't know you weren't supposed to put nipples in the dishwasher because the holes get filled sometimes. I think it may have contributed to his waking up so much to eat the first several weeks, and it took him a long time to get full. I finally ran into a friend who said, 'Oh, get this kind of nipple because it is really the best.' I got it, and it really helped. Things like that were a problem. I think he was having a lot of trouble just getting milk, working too hard." MOTHER

"For me I had knowledge about feeding and what he would be like, and what the days would be like. I wish I had known what only experience can give you. I wish I had known how I would respond and how stressed I would be. I was sleep-deprived, and that was not easy for me. I wish I had had a mother who could be here and give me the benefit of her experience, to say, 'This is all normal, this is part of having a baby.' My mother died in the beginning of the pregnancy, and I had sisters and friends I called." MOTHER

"She had this periodic crying at night in the beginning, and you are caught in the raging hormones and somehow I thought if I just read Dr. Spock again or if I read more, I'd understand it better. And we joked about reading the same paragraph in the book over and over. We needed reassurance it would end, and at three months it ended. That was the hardest part." MOTHER

"I wish I had known enough to take advantage of the naps and sleep. You want to have some semblance of order, getting back to normal, and it's a big thing in the beginning to figure out that you can't do it all." MOTHER

beat—a metronome, for example.[3] Babies are most sensitive to the human voice and to sounds in the voice range.[4] Babies a few days old will respond differently to various odors, although it is not clear whether the odors are pleasant or unpleasant to the infants. It is difficult to assess accurately the baby's taste abilities

Not only are babies able to sense much that goes on around them, but they also quickly learn to use sensory stimuli to get rewards. For example, babies a few hours old learn to turn their head to the right for a sweet substance when a tone sounds, but turn it to the left for a reward when they hear a click. They can quickly learn to reverse these responses for rewards, thus demonstrating flexibility in learning.

Social Responses

The newborn is not as isolated and self-centered as so often described by psychologists.[5] A one-day-old infant cries empathetically in response to another baby's cry, but not to a synthetic cry. When less than a week old, a newborn can imitate an adult's facial expressions. After seeing an adult stick out her tongue, flutter her eyelids, or open and close her mouth, very young babies were observed imitating these movements. This suggests that (1) a newborn has a rudimentary sense of self as a human being capable of imitating a person, and (2) the baby has sufficient motor control to do it.

A fascinating study of the social capacities of newborns reveals that babies move their bodies in rhythm to the meaningful speech of adults.[6] Newborns between 12 hours and 24 days old were presented with tape recordings of spoken English, isolated vowel sounds, tapping noises, and spoken Chinese, along with an adult speaking in person. The babies moved in harmony with meaningful speech, both live and recorded, but not in response to the tapping or to the meaningless vowel sounds. This kind of adult-child interaction, in which the baby responds in a specific way to what the adult does, may be critical to development. If infants are not born with this ability to respond to what the mother does, the mother may become discouraged or depressed and eventually withdraw from the baby.

At six to ten days, the newborn can recognize the mother by her smell.[7] At about two weeks of age, babies will look at their own mothers more frequently than at strangers. When a voice that seems to come from the mother is that of a stranger, the baby will avert her gaze and refuse to look at the "mother" with a strange voice. Thus, very early in life babies have sensory knowledge of the mother.

Parents who are aware of these built-in behaviors and immediate capacity for learning that help the baby adapt and flourish in a variety of situations are less likely to be tense and worried about their new responsibility. They can relax and enjoy this new little person—babies are made of sturdy stuff.

Individual Differences

From the beginning babies are distinct individuals. Anneliese Korner, studying newborns before their mothers could influence their behavior significantly, noted differences among infants two to four days of age in: (1) frequency and duration of spontaneous crying, (2) ability to be soothed and comforted by the caretaker, (3) degree of postural adjustment (molding) to the person handling them, (4) amount of spontaneous oral activity, and (5) use of oral activity for comfort.[8] Rudolph Schaffer and Peggy Emerson also noted differences in how much newborns enjoy being held or cuddled.[9] These differences can influence how easily a mother can meet her baby's needs. A baby who cries frequently and will not be soothed or comforted, who stiffens and squirms when held, yet cannot comfort itself by sucking a finger, presents the new mother with problems not felt by the mother of an infant who rarely cries and is easily comforted when it does. The mother of the former infant may feel inadequate as she tries to meet her child's needs; the mother of the latter may develop great confidence in her parenting skills.

Newborns differ in their processing of external stimuli. Some are very sensitive and alert, quickly tracking a visual object or responding to a buzzer. The baby with a low threshold for stimulation can be easily overwhelmed or overstimulated. When responding to stimuli, some infants seem able to organize them, whereas other babies cannot and withdraw.

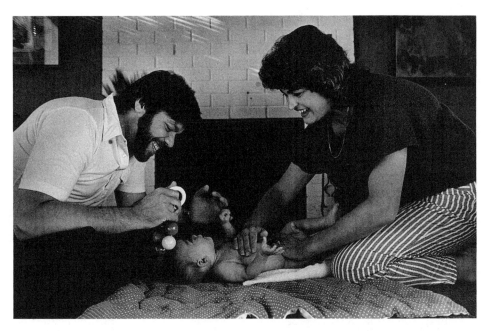

Newborns show a remarkable capacity for interactions, including moving their bodies in rhythm to the meaningful speech of adults. This kind of adult-child interaction may be crucial to development.

In their work with 136 children observed from infancy through adulthood, Alexander Thomas and Stella Chess found several dimensions of temperament.[10] Temperament is defined as constitutionally based biases towards certain moods and ways of reacting. The dimensions found by Thomas and Chess are: activity level, rhythmicity (regularity in eating and sleeping patterns), fussiness, distractibility, readiness to adapt to new situations, attention span, intensity of response, threshold of sensory stimulation (how quickly aware of outside stimuli), persistence in responding.

Thomas and Chess clustered the babies into three types: the easy child (about 75 percent), the difficult child (about 10 percent), and the slow-to-adapt child (about 15 percent). T. Berry Brazelton has formulated a similar typology of average baby, active baby, and quiet baby.[11] Easy babies, the largest single group, tend to be regular in behavior and to have predictable eating and sleeping schedules. They have a positive approach to new stimuli, new foods, new experiences; they adapt easily to changes and are in good humor much of the time. Difficult children, a much smaller group, have irregular eating and sleeping habits. They tend to respond negatively to, and sometimes to withdraw from, new stimuli. Their responses are usually intense, and they are often irritable and unhappy. Once they are able to adapt to a new situation, they often function happily. In infancy, however, they meet many new situations, and sensitive caretaking can be especially helpful in aiding them to adapt to the world. Babies who require a longer period of time to adapt to new situations are like difficult children who are slow to feel comfortable with new stimuli, but the slow-to-adapt group's responses are milder. They do not feel as negative about new stimuli as do the difficult infants, and instead of responding intensely they are more likely to withdraw. Although they are slow to warm up, in general parents have an easier time caring for them than for the difficult child.

Parents are curious to know how long and to what degree these early differences persist. Research has focused mostly on stability of activity level, irritability, fearfulness, and shyness. As we noted earlier, all babies are in an unsettled state for about the first three months. Differences noted very early in this period may disappear as babies' behavior becomes more organized. Nevertheless, research has found that a small cluster of this group seem to maintain early differences. For example, vigor of neonatal movements in the newborn nursery was related to children's daytime activity level when the children were between four and eight years of age. Active neonates were still perceived by parents at ages four to eight as outgoing and quick to approach new experiences.[12]

Early difficult temperament, measured at six months, predicted difficult temperament at thirteen and twenty-four months and behavior problems when the child was three years old.[13] While early crying and fussiness did not endure, irritability at age seven months tended to endure for the next year or two. Shyness appeared to be a temperamental quality that endures and is related both to genetic influences and to social experiences in the family. So shyness and low sociability appearing by the end of the first year seem to be enduring and are related to both genetic and environmental influences.[14]

Thus, differences among babies appear early. As the nervous system settles down in the first three to six months of life, some of these differences disappear. A small number of certain behaviors, however—such as vigorous response—will persist. Whether such differences persist will depend in part on the ways parents interact with their infants.

PHYSICAL DEVELOPMENT

On average, the baby grows from about 21 inches at birth to about 28 inches at the end of the year, and birth weight triples. Growth, however, involves more than an increase in size and weight—it includes increasing organization of behavior.

Growth proceeds according to three general principles. First, the direction of growth is from head to foot. Development occurs first in the head and neck area (see Figure 6-1). Sight and hearing continue to develop, and gradually the infant becomes able to control the head. Next, the baby is able to sit alone and to use arms and hands. And then the child becomes a toddler, learning to use the legs and to walk. Second, the direction of growth is from the center of the body to the extremities. Control of the neck and shoulders occurs before control of hands and fingers. The upper parts of the arms and legs develop before the forearms and forelegs. Third, the direction of growth is from gross activity to more differentiated and organized behaviors. For example, the ability to pick up an object develops in stages. First the child points to the object, then is able to reach for it with an awkward, clawlike, sweeping motion. Gradually the movements become more refined and better organized, so that by ten months a child can pick up a pellet with the thumb and forefinger.

FIGURE 6-1
MILESTONES OF LOCOMOTOR DEVELOPMENT. AS THE BABY'S BRAIN AND
MUSCLES MATURE, HER ACHIEVEMENTS CENTER ON PROGRESSIVELY LOWER
PARTS OF THE BODY, LEADING EVENTUALLY TO WALKING.

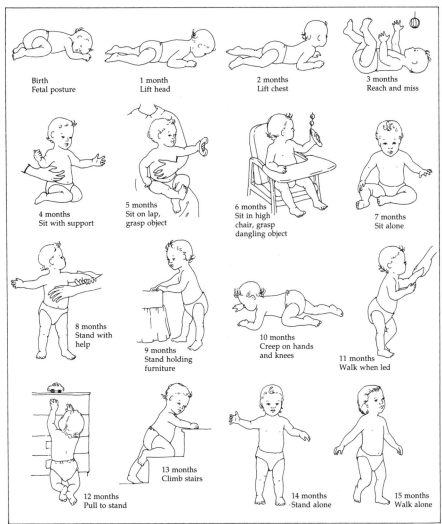

Birth
Fetal posture

1 month
Lift head

2 months
Lift chest

3 months
Reach and miss

4 months
Sit with support

5 months
Sit on lap,
grasp object

6 months
Sit in high
chair, grasp
dangling object

7 months
Sit alone

8 months
Stand with
help

9 months
Stand holding
furniture

10 months
Creep on hands
and knees

11 months
Walk when led

12 months
Pull to stand

13 months
Climb stairs

14 months
Stand alone

15 months
Walk alone

At about three months, changes occur in the nervous system. Increased myelination of nerves in cortical and subcortical neural pathways and an increase in the
number of neurons improve sensory abilities and bring greater stability and control
of behavior. The nervous system appears more integrated. Babies seem to settle
down with greater organization of bodily functioning. Voluntary, coordinated behaviors replace reflexes as the latter gradually disappear. Babies are more awake during
the day and at night drop into a quiet sleep before dreaming.

At about eight months there are a number of changes in physical development that underlie several changes in behavior. Increased myelination of neurons occurs in the motor area, in areas of the brain controlling coordination of movement, and in areas responsible for organization of behavior. At about this same time, most babies develop the capacity to sit alone. Next comes control of the trunk, which leads to creeping and crawling. Babies now can move rapidly in all directions.

Most babies stand and then walk while holding onto objects for support. This activity usually continues for some time before they can walk. Between twelve and eighteen months, walking replaces crawling. There are enormous individual differences in the ages at which children first walk. Some one-year-olds have been walking for weeks; others will be far from taking their first steps.

Locomotion has enormous impact on babies' exploratory and social behavior.[15] When babies crawl and move around their environment, they are able to look at, touch, and manipulate objects. Exploration triggers new social reactions to babies. When infants reach out for objects, mothers often begin to name what they are touching and to describe features of the objects, and so babies' language increases. Locomotion also brings social changes because babies can now initiate interactions with others more easily. Crawling babies often get close to adults, crawl in their laps, smile and vocalize more at them, and so locomotion is a reorganizer of babies' experiences.

INTELLECTUAL DEVELOPMENT

Physical and intellectual development are closely intertwined in the early months and years. To learn about the world, the child must be able to come in contact with it by getting around, exploring objects, and seeing how they work.

Jean Piaget, a Swiss psychologist, has deepened our understanding of how children's minds grow and develop. According to Piaget, the child *acts* on the world and builds up ideas from his or her own actions and the actions of others. Knowledge of the world is not a gradual accumulation of fact after fact. Rather, growth occurs in stages, and each stage is qualitatively different from the others. Thus, babies do not respond and organize the world in the same way that toddlers or older children do, and older children differ from adolescents and adults. Piaget's work has made fundamental contributions to our knowledge of children's intellectual growth and is a tremendous aid to parents in understanding their children's reasoning and intellectual abilities.

Piaget believes intelligence involves the individual's adaptation to the world in such a way that the person interacts effectively with the environment (Table 6-1).[16] Dividing early development into **periods** composed of various **stages**, Piaget terms both the first and second years the **sensorimotor period** to emphasize that the child perceives, then acts. Little mental thought intervenes between what is seen or heard and what is done. Within this period, the **reflexive stage** lasts from birth to the end of the first month. The infant repeats reflexive behaviors and becomes skilled at them. Sucking, for example, becomes smooth and efficient. The **primary circular reaction stage**, comprising the second and third months, involves repetition of sim-

TABLE 6-1
JEAN PIAGET'S PERIODS AND STAGES OF INTELLECTUAL DEVELOPMENT IN CHILDHOOD

	Ages	Behaviors
Sensorimotor period	0–2 years	Child perceives, then acts.
Reflexive stage	0–1 month	Baby practices built-in reflexes like sucking.
Primary circular reaction stage	1–4 months	Baby repeats acts like opening and closing hands. Baby often uses two senses at same time; e.g., seeing and hearing.
Secondary circular reaction stage	4–8 months	Baby repeats acts to see change in the environment; e.g., kicks mobile to make it go.
Coordination of secondary stage	8–12 months	Child uses responses to solve problem; e.g., child removes wrapping to get toy.
Tertiary circular reaction stage	12–18 months	Child is interested in properties of objects themselves, how they work. Can imitate more accurately.
Beginning of thought	18–24 months	Child begins to use language and symbolic mental representations.
Preoperational period	2–7 years	Child learns to represent objects, persons, and perceptions with symbols (e.g., language); can reason intuitively but not with a set of verbalized principles.
Preconceptual stage	2–4 years	Child can represent mentally what is seen or heard with language; child is more imaginative in play.
Intuitive stage	4–7 years	Child is able to reason intuitively, but pays attention to appearances of objects; e.g. believes taller, thinner glass holds more than short, fat glass.
Concrete operations period	7–11, 12 years	Child can think more logically and is not bound by appearances. Child can grasp relations between objects and easily arranges a series of sticks in terms of length.
Formal operations period	12 through adulthood	Child thinks logically and abstractly, thinks about possible alternative situations, imagines future.

Adapted from Herbert Ginsburg and Sylvia Opper, *Piaget's Theory of Intellectual Development* (Englewood Cliffs, N.J.: Prentice-Hall, 1969).

ple acts for their own sake—sucking, fingering a blanket, opening and closing of the hands. In this stage the infant coordinates an activity while using two senses—for example, vision and hearing; a baby who hears a loud noise turns to see what is causing it. During this time the infant begins to develop a concept of a coherent world.

In the first two stages, the child's own actions are the focus of his or her attention. The child acts—kicks legs, plays with fingers—for the sake of the activity, not to accomplish anything. In subsequent stages, activity is directed outward toward the

INTERVIEW
with Jacqueline Lerner and Richard Lerner

Richard M. Lerner is professor of child and adolescent development at The Pennsylvania State University, and Jacqueline V. Lerner is associate professor of human development at The Pennsylvania State University. They are co-principal investigators of the Replication and Extension of the Pennsylvania Early Adolescent Transitions Study.

Parents are interested in temperament and what this means for them as parents. What happens if they have a baby with a difficult temperament that is hard for them to deal with? Is this fixed? Will they have to keep coping with it?

R. Lerner: We don't believe temperament necessarily is fixed. We believe that temperament is a behavioral style and can, and typically does, show variation across a person's life. We're interested in the meaning of temperament for the person and the family in daily life.

J. Lerner: Although we know temperament is present at birth, we don't say that it is exclusively constitutionally derived. Temperament interacts with the environment. We find children who do seem to stay fairly difficult and children who stay fairly easy. Most children change, even from year to year. Given this, we can't possibly believe that temperament ever becomes fixed unless what happens in the family becomes fixed.

R. Lerner: What we are concerned with are individual differences. They are identifiable at birth, but they change and, we believe, in relation to the child's living situation. We find that what one parent might call difficult is well below the threshold of another parent's level of tolerance for difficulty. What some people find easy, others find quite annoying.

In fact, you can find in our case studies examples of how difficult children ended up developing in a particular context that reinterpreted their difficulty as artistic creativity. One girl picked up a musical instrument at age thirteen or fourteen and began playing. She had a gift for that. Prior to that, she had a difficult relation with her father who found her temperamental style totally abhorrent to him. As soon as she had this emerging talent, he said, "Oh, my daughter is an artist. This is an artistic temperament." They reinterpreted the first thirteen years of their relationship, believing they had always been close.

We believe the importance of temperament lies in what we call "goodness of fit" between the child's qualities and what the environment demands. The child brings characteristics to the parent-child relationship, but parents have to understand what they bring and how they create the meaning of the child's individuality by their own temperaments, and their demands, attitudes, and evaluations. Moreover, I think parents should understand that both they and the child have many other influences on them—friends, work, or school.

When you think about the fit with the environment, how do you think about the environment, what is it?

R. Lerner: We have divided demands from the environment into three broad categories: physical characteristics of the setting, the behavioral characteristics of the environment, and the behaviorial and psychological characteristics of the other important people in the child's life.

J. Lerner: The setting has physical characteristics, and the people have behavioral characteristics and demands, attitudes, and values.

R. Lerner: Parents need to understand the demands of the context (the living situation) they present to the child by means of their own values and behavioral style. Even the features of the physical environment the parents provide can affect the child's fit with the context. Parents need to understand there are numerous features of the context; and because of the child's individuality, a better or lesser fit will emerge. For example, if your child has a low threshold of reactivity and a high intensity of reactions, you don't want to put that child's bedroom next to a busy street. If you have a choice, you'll put that child's bedroom in the back of the house or won't let the child study in any part of the house where he or she will get distracted.

A poor fit also occurs if you have a child who is very arrhythmic and you demand regularity, not necessarily as a verbal demand but perhaps in the way you schedule your life. You begin to prepare breakfast every morning at 8:00, the bagel comes out at 8:05 and disappears at 8:15, and some days the child makes it and some days not. The parents have to see how they may be doing things that create poorness of fit. It's not just their verbal demands but also their behavioral demands and the physical set-up of the house.

J. Lerner: Some parents don't see what they are reinforcing and what they are teaching their child through their demands. There has to be consistency between the demands and the reinforcements. Sometimes you don't want to be too flexible. I learned this the hard way. My nine-year-old tells me about what I have done in the past. "But when I did this last week, it was okay and now it isn't."

In actively trying to get the child to behave or in trying to change a temperamental quality, parents need to focus themselves on what behaviors they want reinforced and what ones they don't. They need to be perceptive on both ends of the response—the demands they are setting up and what they are actually reinforcing. If you know a child is irregular in eating in the morning and you want to change the pattern because you know he'll get cranky and won't learn well if he doesn't have a full stomach, be consistent. "You don't walk out the door unless you have had at least three bites of cereal and a glass of juice." But if you let it go one morning, you can expect the child to say, "Well, yesterday you didn't make me do that."

From your research, do you see areas that can be supports for children as they are growing up?

R. Lerner: More and more children experience alternative-care settings, and this has to become a major support. The socialization of the child is moving out of the family more and more, and we are charging the schools with more of the socialization duties. Throughout infancy and childhood, the alternative caregiving setting is the day care, the preschool, and, obviously, the school. These settings have to be evaluated in terms of enhancing the child's fit and the ability to meet the demands of the context.

environment. In the third or **secondary circular reaction stage** (four to eight months), the child repeats an act to observe a change in the environment. The word **secondary** is used because reactions involve objects in the environment. The baby kicks a mobile to make it go or reaches to move an object. Each act is not organized with a purpose; rather, the goal is discovered accidentally in the process of activity. In the fourth **coordination of secondary reactions stage**, (eight to twelve months) the child uses responses to solve a problem and achieve some goal. For example, to reach a matchbox, the child brushes away the father's hand, which is an obstacle. The child knows what he or she wants and uses action to get it.

During the first year of life, the infant comes to understand the permanence of objects. This is a major occurrence and is essential to the development of the concept of a coherent world. A newborn's ability to remember is very limited; only gradually do infants become able to recall an object or person. It is easier for parents to empathize with the crying of a newborn baby when they remember that "Out of sight, out of mind" is almost literally true for infants. Gradually babies come to realize that objects and people exist even when they cannot be seen.

Piaget's theory emphasizes action in the development of thinking and reasoning powers. He believes babies and children have natural desires to approach the world and interact, to explore and learn. Research on early learning substantiates his theory. Babies enjoy learning for the sake of mastering a task—and as soon as they can do it, they lose interest.

Playing

Much of what infants learn about the world they learn through exploration and play. As a baby matures during its first year, parents find that the ways they play with the baby also change. In the early months parents play games with lots of touching to capture the child's attention and provide laughter. When babies are older, games like pat-a-cake and peek-a-boo include more physical activity and more interaction.

Beginning at about six months, babies are interested in the physical aspects of objects—the shape, feel, weight, and action of toys. The more things to investigate about an object, the longer a baby will interact with it. Once familiar with a toy, babies put it aside for awhile, and then return to it later with renewed enthusiasm. As babies mature, they spend less time putting things in their mouths and more time manipulating objects. If the object makes noise, wiggles or moves, the baby will elicit these responses over and over. If a toy is too simple, or too complex, the infant will lose interest in it quickly or ignore it altogether. By the end of the first year, children go beyond the sensory qualities of toys and try to figure out what they can do with objects. They try to dial a telephone and talk, or they try to stack a set of plastic donuts. They play more imaginatively with toys for longer periods of time.[17]

LANGUAGE DEVELOPMENT

Now let's look at language development. At birth babies can say nothing, but by the end of the first year they have a vocabulary of about three words; and by the end of the second year, they can put two words into a sentence. Language development is most rapid in the years between one and four, but experiences during the first year are crucial to the child's continuing acquisition of verbal skills.

At birth the baby is able to cry, and parents can distinguish a cry of anger from one of pain or hunger. Babies do not vocalize in the early weeks of life. They make noises that are related to eating and mouthing, and in the second month they begin cooing—making light, little noises when they are happy, usually after eating or while looking at smiling faces.

In the fourth or fifth month, babbling begins. Babies repeat syllables, often the same syllable over and over—*dadada, mamama*. During these months a baby can make all the sounds of all the languages in the world. As the baby grows and continues to vocalize, the sounds become more characteristic of the language he hears. A year or so later, the baby is unable to produce some of the sounds it could make easily at six months.

Babies appear preprogrammed to learn language. The fact that the timetable of vocal events is similar for babies around the world reinforces this notion. Babies in all cultures and countries babble at about four to six months, say their first words at about a year, and combine two words at about two years. The babbling of deaf children indicates that the start of this behavior does not depend on the ability to hear sound. Deaf babies, however, stop vocalizing after about six months. Evidently, babies need to hear sounds and receive vocal stimulation if verbal development is to continue.

In the earliest months, parents—especially mothers—treat babies as though they were competent speakers. In interactions with babies, mothers report events to them, request information from them, and give them directions even when they are only three months old. In these interactions, infants learn the rule of participating in conversation—one person speaks at a time, and each gets a turn. Babies learn to imitate the sounds of words long before they understand the meanings of the sounds. They also learn to get their parents' attention. First words are learned for themselves, then they are placed in the context of a social ritual.[18]

Even before babies begin to use words, the sounds they make have inflections that express happiness, requests, commands, and questions.[19] A baby who first begins to say words may use the same word as a statement, a command, or a request. "Mama," for example, can be a question, an order, an endearment, or a plea for help.

Language development in the first year depends on intellectual growth. Babies have to learn that objects and people exist whether they see them or not, that people, things, and events have names that they can use to communicate with others. Babies need to be able to remember words that go with objects, and they need to be able to recall the event they want to name.

The quality of interpersonal relations in the early weeks and months of an infant's life influences language development. Crying is a signal of discomfort and is thus a communication to the caretaker. When crying brings relief, then the baby learns communication is worthwhile. Ways of responding to crying are taken up later in this chapter. Some babies, as already noted, cry more than others. Those who cry a great deal do not respond as fully to the world and people in it.[20] Babies who do not cry a great deal develop words and gestures more rapidly than ones who cry often.[21]

EMOTIONAL DEVELOPMENT

Babies come into the world with feelings and emotions that are a basic part of what we mean by being human. L. Alan Sroufe writes, "The child grows not as a perceptive being, not as a cognitive being, but as a human being who expresses anxiety, joy, and anger, and who is connected to its world in an emotional way."[22]

Emotions are adaptive, regulatory processes. Emotional responses provide signals to others and give information as to what the individual wants or needs—for instance, babies' crying signals a need for help. Emotions also organize activity. For example, joy motivates the individual to continue certain kinds of behavior or inter-actions, sadness triggers behavior that might change the situation, fear motivates flight or a search for protection.

Psychologists agree that emotions are present at birth, but they debate the number of emotions and how specific or definite they are. Carroll Izard believes that at birth there are emotions of interest, rudimentary pleasure (seen in neonatal smiling, a sort of half smile that appears without cause and is the forerunner of pleasure), disgust, and the affect of pain.[23] Pain leads to the expression of physical distress and the accompanying cry for help. Joy, anger, and sadness are expressed at about two months of age, surprise at about four months of age, fear at about seven months of age, and shyness related to sense of self at about eight months of age. Since babies cannot talk, it is not clear just what feelings underlie the expression. Older children can verbalize that there is a specific feeling that accompanies each expression—joy accompanies smiling and laughter, anger accompanies an angry expression.

Other psychologists (such as Sroufe[24]) have a different timetable, but most agree that by the end of the first year there are emotions of pleasure, delight, joy, wariness, anger, fear, and anxiety.

Babies have a range of facial expressions that change rapidly—every 7 to 9 seconds in the first few months of life. Mothers respond quickly as well, but they do not mirror their babies' expressions. Instead, they tend to express only the positive emotions to very young infants.[25]

Babies have their own characteristic emotional responses that are detected as early as two days of life and persist for a period of two or more months. Babies' activity level, social responsiveness, and irritability persist from two weeks to two months, and irritability seems to persist to one year.[26] Infants' responses to pain at six months are similar to those at eighteen months.[27] These persistent emotional reactions are part of what we refer to as temperament, which becomes more stable in the last half of the first year.

The biological responses underlying some emotional responses are persistent as well. Heart variability accompanying social reactivity and restraint at five months was related to heart-rate variability at fourteen months.[28] Toward the end of the first year, babies who experience more stress in separating from mother in a laboratory situation have an increase in hormones related to stress.[29]

Infants and adults participate in a complex emotional communication system. In infancy it is babies' primary task to tell parents what they need. Babies will some-times repeat their emotional responses until they achieve their goals. They will cry until picked up or reach for an object with interest until the adult gets it.

Communication is not a one-way street. From the earliest days babies can detect emotions in other people and respond to them. One- to two-day-old infants discriminate and imitate expression of joy, sadness, and surprise when these are posed by a live model.[30] Infants as young as ten weeks mirror mothers' expressions and use them to modify their own moods. They respond with joy and interest to mothers' happy faces, with anger and with a forerunner of fear to mothers' angry faces, and with sadness to mothers' sad faces.[31]

Babies not only respond to mothers' emotions for a moment, but they also pattern their own moods after them on a more ongoing basis. Over time, mothers' positive feelings are related to an increase in babies' smiling and laughing.[32]

In addition to modifying their own moods, babies get information from others' feelings and change their behavior. For example, when ten-month-olds crawled to what looked like a visual cliff, they looked at mothers' expressions to guide their behavior. When mothers had angry or fearful expressions, babies did not continue. When mothers smiled, babies continued to crawl. When mothers presented toys to babies with a disgusted look, babies did not play with them. The negative reaction lasted; and even when the toys were presented later with a neutral expression, babies avoided them.[33]

Mothers begin to guide babies to control their emotional reactions in the first few months of life. They do this with both nonverbal and verbal techniques. They avoid negative facial expressions that the baby can copy; and, as mentioned, they emphasize the positive emotions. Verbally, they encourage positive emotions with such phrases as "Give me a smile," "Laugh for Mommy." At the same time they discourage negative reactions with such phrases as "Don't cry" and "Don't fuss now." In the second half of the first year, mothers discourage the overt expression of feelings. There is evidence that mothers of boys are more responsive to them and match their son's behavior more.[34]

While babies are clearly responsive to others' feelings, they are not totally dependent on caretakers. When confronted with negative stimulation, they can cope and soothe themselves.[35] In fact, Izard believes it is a basic task of infancy to begin to learn to regulate feelings.[36] When mothers of three-month-olds adopted depressed expressions for just 3 minutes, babies cried and fussed, then turned away and comforted themselves. Babies soothe themselves by sucking hands or fingers, manipulating themselves, finding a neutral scene to fix upon.[37]

Babies take an active role not only in soothing themselves but in giving themselves pleasure as well. Babies smile when they can make something happen.[38] Babies just a few months old get pleasure from making a mobile go or a rattle shake.

The greatest source of comfort and positive feelings in the world of babies is people, and so we turn to social and personal development.

PERSONAL AND SOCIAL DEVELOPMENT

The infant is introduced to the world of human beings by the quality of social experiences in the first year of life. From the beginning, the child lives in the social and emotional atmosphere created by the parents' marriage. The marital relation affects each parent, the way the parent relates to the baby, and how the baby grows and develops. It is not just that psychologically mature people make happy marriages and parent well. Recent research shows that a happy marriage improves parenting, even when psychological adjustment is controlled.[39]

When mothers and fathers feel support from each other, they are more competent parents and interact with the baby more effectively. Father-infant interactions and fathers' competence, particularly, is related to feeling support from mothers. Even basic activities are influenced by the quality of the marriage. Mothers feed babies more competently when their husbands are supportive and view them positively, whereas marital distress if related to inept feeding by the mother.[40]

Intimate emotional spousal support is related also to parents' satisfaction with themselves in the parental role and with the baby. When parents are happy with each other, they smile at the baby more and play with the baby. Babies profit from this atmosphere of positive regard, are more alert, and have more motor skills.

Warm, supportive relationships establish what Erikson describes as a sense of trust in the world that can generalize to other people and the world at large.[41] Direct physical care in these early months provides the basis for a growing social attachment. Recent research provides evidence that touching and close physical contact with infants serve to regulate their physiological functioning.[42] Small, premature babies who received stroking of their bodies and movement of their limbs for three 15-minute periods per day over a 10-day period, gained more weight per day; spent more time alert and active; and earned higher scores on developmental tests in the areas of orientation, motor, and range-of-state behaviors. It is thought that touching may stimulate the production of hormones that increase growth.[43]

At three months, when babies are awake more and so more available for interacting, they become more social. At about four months, their babbling increases the impression of sociability, and this has been termed the **awakening of sociability**;[44] babies send parents signals by means of facial expressions, vocalizations, motor activity. When babies seem happy, parents engage in play; when they seem interested, parents provide toys and objects; but when babies are distressed, parents simply soothe them. Four to six months has been termed the period of **reciprocal exchange**.[45] Babies are the initiators of activity and parents follow their leads. In face-to-face interactions, parents wait for babies to look at them before talking to their babies. Parents may talk, tickle, or physically stimulate the child, or play games like pat-a-cake. Parents often imitate babies' behavior—grimaces, frowns. Babies may enjoy the imitation, then imitate the parents' behavior in turn. Parents often **highlight** or interpret babies' activity, giving a running account of what is happening—"You were hungry. You had a nice, big bottle. Now you are ready for clean diapers."

In these first six or seven months, parents and babies engage in a social dialogue. The attachment of the child to the parent is developing, but is not fully complete until the child is about seven or eight months of age.

Attachment to Parents

Cultural lore, literature, and psychologists have long emphasized the warmth, comfort, security, and trust the child derives from the mother-child attachment. The baby's attachment to the mother begins in the early weeks of infancy and at about five months, it may give joyful kicks and gurgle and laugh to engage the mother in play. If the mother has been away, the baby will lift its arms or clasp its hands in greeting when the parent returns.

At four to five months, babies show signs of apprehension in the presence of strangers—freezing, lying or sitting still, and barely breathing. At seven to eight months, they show pronounced fear of strangers, sometimes crying as an unknown person approaches. This occurs at about the same time that babies develop an awareness that the mother exists even when she is not physically present, and this is followed by development of fear of separation from mother and other important persons.

Attachment is a strong psychological bond to a figure who is a source of security and emotional support. By seven or eight months, babies show such ties to parents. Some babies develop insecure attachments and show these in different ways. One group avoids the parent after separation. Another group resists the parent, alternatively clinging to the parent and pushing the parent away. When parents are accepting of the child, emotionally available, sensitive to the baby's needs, and cooperative in meshing activities with the tempo of the child, then a strong, secure attachment develops. When parents are intrusive and overstimulate the baby without regard for the baby's needs, the attachment is insecure and babies avoid the parent. When parents are uninvolved and unavailable, insecure attachment results, and babies resist the parent.[46] Infants with secure attachments explore more, are more persistent in tasks, and—as we shall see in later chapters—develop into socially and emotionally competent toddlers and preschoolers.

The baby uses the interactions with the attachment figure to form an internal model of the way people relate to each other in the world. The child comes to expect certain reactions on the part of adults and plans his or her own behavior accordingly. Further, the child develops a sense of personal value in the world. When attachment figures are accepting and available, then babies feel lovable and competent. Conversely, when figures are insensitive and rejecting, babies develop a sense of unworthiness.[47]

Until recently, the mother-child bond was considered the only attachment of importance in infancy. As researchers have observed parent-child interactions and attachments in nuclear families, however, they have found that babies become attached to both parents, although most will seek comfort from the mother if distressed. Mothers and fathers interact differently with babies. First, mothers spend more time with infants even though a high percentage are employed in the work force. Even in families with fathers' staying at home at least part of the time and mothers' going off to work, studies indicate that mothers were with children more than fathers.

There are differences not only in the quantity of time but also in the way parents spend time with babies.[48] Mothers, even when working, are significantly more engaging, responsive, stimulating, and affectionate. They are more likely to hold babies in caregiving activities and to verbalize more than fathers. Fathers, on the other hand, are more likely to be visually attentive and to be playful in physically active ways than mothers are. Though fathers spend less time than mothers with infants, they are sensitive caregivers and are as perceptive as mothers in adjusting their behavior to babies' needs. Fathers are most likely to be highly involved in caregiving and playing when the marital relationship is satisfying and wives are relaxed and outgoing. Both fathers and mothers give most care and physical affection in the first three months when babies are settling in. As babies become less fussy and more alert at three months, both parents in turn become more stimulating and reactive.[49]

Although mothers and fathers interact differently with babies, recent observations indicate parents do not treat their sons and daughters differently in routine caregiving activities at home. When mothers and fathers are observed at home interacting with their infants, they give sons and daughters equal amounts of affection, stimulation, care, and responsiveness. We cannot rule out possible differences in narrower measures of parent-child interaction (such as touching, frowning, physical closeness), but in these wide-ranging measures, including overall engagement with the child, modern parents treat their sons and daughters equally.[50]

Development of the Self

In the early months of life, the self is relatively undifferentiated. From birth to three months, the child learns there is a pattern to experience—simple action leads to an outcome. The action of the self is not separated from the actions of others. Learning is taking place all the while, however, and in the period from four to eight months a growing sense of self emerges. At six months, for example, infants can look at themselves in a mirror and enjoy their image, cooing and babbling in delight. At about this time, infants begin to imitate more actively. They get a sense that they can do things—grasp, mouth, make noise. As they interact with objects, they begin to form intentions about their activities. Out of their actions, children form a sense of themselves as separate from others, persons who can act and will. In the period from nine to twelve months, children develop a sense of self-permanence. The self is differentiated from others, and the child is able to maintain a sense of self independent of action and context. This permanent sense of self is consolidated in the second year of life.[51]

Development of Self-Regulation

Claire Kopp has described phases children go through as they develop the capacity for self-regulation and flexible self-control.[52] Self-control begins to develop in the earliest days of life. The period from birth to three months she terms the **neurophysiological modulation** phase. In this period, infants gain a form of control over their physiological functioning; they regulate arousal states of wake and sleep and the amount of stimulation they get. They also soothe themselves. The role of caregivers at this time is to help infants regularize their functioning by providing routines and social interactions.

From three to approximately nine months, infants are in the phase of **sensorimotor modulation**. They have gained some control over neurophysiological functioning, and now they modulate sensory and motor activities. They posses no conscious self-control yet, but they do use motor skills to gain parental attention and social interaction. As they reach out, form intentions, and develop a rudimentary sense of self, their capacity for control begins to emerge.

From nine to eighteen months, the **control** phase appears. Infants show awareness of social or task demands and begin to comply with their parents' requests. As infants act, investigate, explore, their sense of conscious awareness begins to appear. These trends continue in the second year.

Observing year-old babies' obedience to mothers' commands in the home, Donelda Stayton, Robert Hogan, and Mary Ainsworth found that babies obey their mothers' commands when the mothers are accepting and sensitive to babies' needs.[53] Mothers who establish harmonious relationships with their babies, who respect them as separate individuals and tailor the daily routines to harmonize with the children's needs, have babies who are affectionate and independent, able to play alone and, even at one year, are able to follow their mothers' requests. Thus, at this early age, a system of mutual cooperation between mother and child is established and maintained as each acts to meet the requests of the other.

Peers

Does an infant interact with other children? A recent study indicates babies are positively responsive to children ages three to four.[54] And infants are responsive to each other and initiate contact in play sessions in the first year of life. In one study, a researcher observed nine-month-old babies who played together once a week for ten weeks.[55] She found that the play of the babies became increasingly complex when they were in their own homes and presumably feeling more comfortable. When they played in another baby's home, the babies tended to be more interested in toys and objects. This lessened interest in peers when away from home may explain why, in the past, psychologists failed to note babies' interest in each other—because until recently psychologists have usually observed babies away from home, in laboratories.

PARENTING TASKS

Now that we have reviewed children's development in their first year, let us focus on parenting tasks, children's problems and behaviors, and finally parents' needs. In the first months, parents' main tasks are meeting their infants' needs for food, dry clothes, warmth, social contact, cuddling, and interaction. To meet these needs, parents become sensitive observers of their babies' behavior, responding to their babies' tempo and individual preferences. As they meet needs, parents encourage babies to settle into a routine by adjusting their own rhythm of activities to anticipate babies' needs. Responsive parenting contributes to a growing attachment between parent and child.

As children get older, parents reinforce reasonable sleep and eating times, though they do not tie babies to a rigid schedule. Parents reinforce the emerging schedule at four to six months by having a consistent routine that babies can adapt to. Parents

THE JOYS OF PARENTING INFANTS

"It's seeing the miracle of a growing person, growing from a little baby that can't move to a little person with ideas of her own, humor of her own." MOTHER

"The main thing was the joy of touch. She was so soft, so melting. I never touched so much as in the first year of infancy." MOTHER

"I don't know if it's a joy but there is this shift of priorities that happens when a baby is born. Feeding, changing, holding the baby become the center of your life. You can talk about diapers for a whole thirty minutes with another man as though that is the most important thing." FATHER

"I love babies. There is something about that bond between mother and baby. I love the way they look and smell and the way they hunker up to your neck. To me it's a magic time. I didn't like to babysit particularly growing up, and I wasn't wild about other people's babies, but there was something about having my own; I just love it. And every one, we used to wonder, how are we going to love another as much as the one before; and that is ridiculous, because you love every one." MOTHER

"There is joy in just watching her change, see her individualize. From the beginning it seemed she had her own personality—we see that this is not just a little blob of protoplasm here, this is a little individual already from the beginning. She has always had a real specialness about her. It was exciting to see her change." FATHER

"I think it's wonderful to have a baby in the house, to hear the baby laugh, sitting in the high chair, banging spoons, all the fun things babies do. They seem to me to light up a household. When there's a baby here, a lot of the aggravations in the household somehow disappear. Everyone looks at the baby, plays with the baby, and even if people are in a bad mood, they just light up when the baby comes in the room. I think there is something magical about having a baby in the house." MOTHER

"His ability to concentrate has always been amazing. I fed him when he was nine hours old in the hospital. The nurse showed me another way to burp him, by sitting him up and holding him under the chin at the jaw line, and rubbing his back, and letting him burp by sitting. So I did that, and at the first opportunity he had to look around the room, he was just staring with the most enormous alertness and concentration. At home he would stare at wall hangings in the house. When I took him home to see my family at four months he was so curious, just stared and looked around." MOTHER

"What I've discovered about parenting is there is a constant process of loss and gain. With every gain you give up something, so there is sadness and joy. The joy comes when he does something new, different. He crawls and that's great, but the loss is you no longer have to get him something or carry him there. Now I have to do less for him. My role shifts the less I do for him. So, it's a mixed thing. He's growing up too fast. I want to hold on to each phase; I like the new phase, but I want to hang on to each one too." MOTHER

"I don't mind getting up in the middle of the night like I thought I would. I check him two or three times to see if his blankets are covering him." FATHER

"When he was about three months old, we developed these little games when I was changing his diapers. He would take hold of my hands and push himself away from me or I would hold his feet, and he'd push away because the mat he was on would move. And he would take such delight in doing it, something he was in charge of, something he was doing himself. So, I got a sense even at this early age of his being a very active, curious little boy." MOTHER

"As he gets older, I relate more, play more. He is more of a joy. Some of the joys are so unexpected. I would stop myself and open up and think, 'Oh, this is my son, he's so joyful. He's smiling for no particular reason.' I am not that joyful, but he's joyful for no reason. He reminds me of joy." FATHER

"During the day, he giggles. Just hearing him laugh like that is so special. After his bottle at night, he would give me a big smile and a hug. I would look forward to that during the day—the smile and the hug." MOTHER

"For us, she's such a very, very good person. She's so marvelous. She likes the car, she likes the stroller. Everything is an adventure for her." MOTHER

"It's the first time in my life, I know what the term 'unconditional love' means. The wonder of this little girl and nature! I have never experienced anything like that. It is 'Yes,' without any 'Buts.'" FATHER

"I enjoy seeing her and her father together, hearing them talk, seeing him so happy with her all the time." MOTHER

"He does imitate us completely. I wonder why he does that, and I realize that is an expression I have. I enjoy learning about myself. My parents come, and they enjoy him and he enjoys them. I like seeing the three generations together. I like being a son to my parents, and then I am being a parent to my son." FATHER

"Crawling was just so wonderful for me, it just seemed to reveal something about his personality, his persistence. It was strenuous for him physically. I would be across the room, and he would start out across the room; and you could hear him, breathing, kind of panting, working and working and working to get himself across the room. There was something about that, so valiant. And his laughter; he loves to laugh, and he had such joy, such a sense of accomplishment he communicated when he got across the room." MOTHER

"I love the rocking and holding her close. It is hard to imagine her going to bed without having some time to hold her." FATHER

can use these ordinary routines of childcare as opportunities for learning and social interactions. Too often, a parent changes a diaper or feeds the child while doing something else—usually talking to another person. Emmi Pikler, a European pediatrician, recommends focusing attention on the infant, telling him or her exactly what is happening and what you are doing as you feed, diaper, dress, and bathe the child.[55]

Parents monitor the schedule to see that it keeps a 24-hour rhythm. Otherwise they would be running after the child around the clock as the child changes schedule an extra hour every day. Parents also monitor the amount of stimulation babies receive. Some babies need more; some need less. Escalona reports that active babies practice their skills against a background of normal family activity.[56] Less active babies need attention from one person who provides stimulation in direct interaction. Very active babies easily become overstimulated. Such children should have a calm atmosphere if they are to remain alert and responsive to the world rather than fretful and irritable.

As infants become more sociable, more skilled physically and intellectually, parents continue to stimulate their development in a variety of ways. From the earliest months and throughout development, children should be given opportunities to influence what happens to them. Infants experience joy, pleasure, and effectiveness when they have a chance to act upon the world. As babies gain control of the trunk and can sit alone and crawl about, they become capable of doing more for themselves. They can eat finger foods without help, suck oranges, eat toast, use a spoon.

Mobiles, attractive pictures on the bedroom walls, and good lighting all provide environmental stimulation. Objects that hang in the crib or the carriage are useful for encouraging exploration at the child's level of development. After the first few months, small objects that the baby can grasp and mouth but not swallow are attractive toys. Objects that have several potential uses are perhaps best—toys that can be grasped, banged, dropped, mouthed.

Why do psychologists suggest that you talk to your infant even before the baby can talk? Research indicates that vocalizing not only soothes the child, but also stimulates development. Both you and your baby will have fun if you respond to the baby's vocalizations with words, then wait for the baby to "answer" with increased attentiveness, physical activity, or babbling and cooing.

Psychologists have written little about the importance of music in the first year and do not often emphasize singing and crooning to babies. We know that the human voice soothes infants and brings them to an alert state in which they are more responsive to what is going on around them. Music with clear words may be especially useful, not only in soothing but also in facilitating language development.

During the last part of the first year, as children become more mobile, they need more opportunities to explore and move about. Freedom to explore in these months is associated with the ability to control behavior and follow parental commands. It is also related to later language development. Chapter 7 contains suggestions on babyproofing the home.

Parents are advised to purchase a bottle of ipecac to have immediately available as an antidote if a child swallows poison or any other internal irritant. They should also keep the telephone number of the local Poison Control Center on hand in case of emergency.

Many psychologists have described the egocentrism of babies in their first year. But observant mothers have long realized that babies can enjoy each other's company and the company of other children. Babies can learn things from older children they cannot learn from an adult. For example, one mother reported that her ten-month-old child learned how to crawl upstairs from a three-year-old brother after she had tried without success to teach the younger child to navigate the steps. Slightly older children may understand exactly what makes it difficult for the baby or may know exactly how to demonstrate what they are teaching because they are much closer to the infant in age and pattern of thinking than parents are. If there are no other children the same age as yours in the family or neighborhood, you may want to arrange a regular play group with the children of friends.

ROUTINES, PROBLEMS, AND STRATEGIES

We will discuss common routines and problems associated with the first year of life: feeding, sleeping, crying, dressing, and limit setting. The work of parenting strategists like Ginott, Gordon, and Briggs helps parents tune into their babies, become sensitive observers of their needs and responsive caretakers, whereas the theories of Dreikurs and the behaviorists are helpful in establishing regular routines and shaping behaviors.

Feeding

Experts have argued for years about which is better for the baby—nursing or bottle-feeding. Some experts felt that if the child did not have the satisfaction that comes only from nursing, he or she would suffer deprivation that might have lasting effects on the personality. A longitudinal study made over eighteen years compared the social and emotional characteristics of bottlefed children compared to breastfed children.[58] This study revealed that there were only a few significant differences between the two groups in personality characteristics and these could have occurred by chance. Thus, method of feeding, by itself, is not significant.

Today we realize that nursing has physical advantages for mother and child. Mothers' milk contains antibodies that protect the infant from disease while the baby's immunological system is becoming functional and efficient. And nursing is beneficial for the mother's physical condition. Nursing triggers the release of hormones that help the mother's uterus contract to its normal size.

The act of nursing provides all the kinds of stimulation that babies enjoy. Their mother holds and sometimes rocks them as they nurse. They can see their mother's face. Sometimes the mother talks or sings so that all senses are stimulated in a pleasurable way. The baby who is being bottlefed, however, can also be held and rocked and sung to.

Women's attitudes about nursing and their experience with it depend on many factors. If a woman's mother nursed, she is more likely to nurse. If the husband shows no jealousy of the nursing interaction, a mother tends to breastfeed. Mothers who have positive attitudes about nursing before the delivery generally obtain great satisfaction from nursing. Many choose to nurse because it offers them a way of continuing the close physical tie with their child. They feel they achieve a sense of emotional union with their child that is not equaled in any of the other caretaking activities. Mothers may decide not to nurse because they fear that the child may not get enough to eat, that they may not have enough patience. Some women are concerned that breastfeeding will decrease their attractiveness.

In addition to attitudes and previous experiences, events at birth influence breastfeeding. A mother who nurses her child just after delivery continues to do so for a longer time than a woman who must wait to have the first nursing. Thus, nursing can be encouraged by recent experiences as well as past ones. If a woman truly wants to nurse but has been discouraged from doing so by those around her (her doctor or family members), she can find useful information in *The Complete Book of Breastfeeding* by Marvin Eiger and Sally Olds.[59]

Self-demand (defined as feeding whenever the baby wishes) versus scheduled feedings is often an issue in the early months of life. While self-demand is generally encouraged, it can become oppressive for the mother if the infant prefers irregular, closely spaced feedings. If a mother finds that the baby's demands are excessive and that she is exhausted or needs time for herself, she can impose a schedule. The time between feedings can be lengthened by giving the baby a bottle of water to satisfy hunger and a pacifier to satisfy the urge to suck.

Gordon tells how he and his wife used mutual problem solving in a nonverbal way to solve a feeding problem.[60] When their daughter was five months old, the family went on a camping trip in northern Wisconsin. At home the baby had been sleeping through the night, from 11 p.m. until 7 a.m. The first night in this new physical environment, however, she woke up at 4 a.m. Not only did the parents want to sleep later, but the cabin was so cold at that hour that they had to get up and build a fire. This situation required mutual problem solving because there was a conflict of needs. The parents gave the baby her last bottle later than usual, and their daughter slept a little longer in the morning. The next night they gave more milk at the last feeding, and she slept through to her usual 7 a.m. feeding.

Dreikurs urges parents to establish a pattern so that the child learns regularity.[61] This pattern will depend on the age and characteristics of each child, but once the schedule is set it should not be deviated from unless changes in the child require changes in the schedule. Dreikurs also advises parents to remain quiet and calm during feeding, because parental anxiety can upset the child.

Behaviorists would agree with Dreikurs' approach. They place special importance on the feeding situation, which they believe is the foundation for learning. The main reward for an infant is a warm bottle or breast. Since the mother is present just before and as milk is given, the presence of the mother becomes reinforcing. Once the connection between mother and pleasure is made, her smiles and verbal statements of affection and praise become reinforcing as well. Later in life, acts associated with parental approval become reinforcing and facilitate learning.

Sleeping

We described the sleep patterns of newborns in an earlier section. Let us now take a quick look at the sleep patterns of older infants (Figure 6-2). After the first few months of life, the baby goes directly into a deep stage of sleep for 1½ to 3 or 4 hours, and then comes up to a light stage of REM sleep. At this point, the child may wake briefly and go back to sleep, fluctuating from light sleep and dreams to brief awakenings. The last two cycles of sleep may involve deep states of sleep. The average baby and child, as well as the average adult, wakes briefly several times in the night and all must be able to get back to sleep by themselves.

To ensure good sleep patterns, Dr. Richard Ferber, who directs the Center for Pediatric Sleep Disorders at Children's Hospital in Boston, recommends that parents develop a regular, enjoyable night-time ritual that prepares the child for going to bed—it may be songs, rocking for infants or a bath and story for older children.[62] Then they must put the child in the crib alone to fall asleep. By the time the child is five or six months old, he or she will sleep most of the night. If the child is not sleeping through the night, the source of the problem may lie in the way the child is put down. He or she has come to rely on rocking, sleeping, or nursing to sleep and cannot duplicate these conditions in the middle of the night. Parents must emphasize a pleasant bedtime ritual and going to bed alone. If crying persists, parents can use the behavioral methods detailed in Chapter 7 to help the child sleep through the night.

Other sleep problems include infants who sleep 6 hours during the day and then wake up for long periods during the night. Parents can handle this problem by waking the child earlier and earlier from the long day sleep so it gradually becomes a nap rather than a major sleeping period. Waking up earlier in the afternoon will help the child to go to sleep earlier and longer at night.

Other sleep problems can be related to intake of fluids. Ferber believes that once children are over three months of age, they do not need middle-of-the-night feeding unless the pediatrician specifically recommends it. Some children take one or more bottles at night, or nurse for varying lengths of time. If only 6 to 8 ounces is taken at night, awakening from sleep is probably related to the child's association of sucking with sleeping. If the child takes more than that amount, awakening may be related to too much fluid.

The awakening for milk can be eliminated using behavioral techniques of shaping behavior (Box 6-1). Every night the child gets 1 ounce less of milk at each feeding, or if the mother is nursing, 1 minute less time in nursing. At the same time, the interval between feedings is increased in half-hour segments, beginning with a minimum interval of 2 hours. Thus, parents are working on two aspects of the problem—decreasing amount and number of feedings. Parents then may have to help the child fall asleep without their presence. They may want to comfort the child with a pat while the child goes through the process of giving up the milk. When the amount of milk has been reduced to zero and awakenings still occur, then parents can use behavioral techniques to help the child fall asleep alone. These are described in detail in Chapter 7.

In the early months colic often disturbs sleep; babies cry and cannot be consoled.

FIGURE 6.2
TYPICAL SLEEP STAGE PROGRESSION

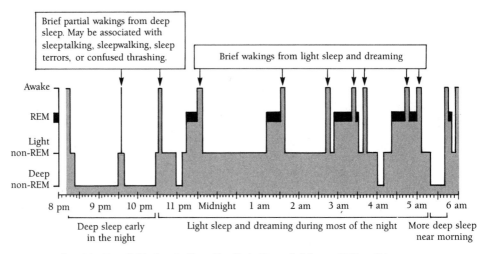

Brief partial wakings from deep sleep. May be associated with sleeptalking, sleepwalking, sleep terrors, or confused thrashing.

Brief wakings from light sleep and dreaming

Awake
REM
Light non-REM
Deep non-REM

8 pm   9 pm   10 pm   11 pm   Midnight   1 am   2 am   3 am   4 am   5 am   6 am

Deep sleep early in the night

Light sleep and dreaming during most of the night

More deep sleep near morning

(From R. Ferber, *Solve Your Child's Sleep Problems.* New York: Simon & Schuster, 1985, p. 31.)

Like Weissbluth,[63] Ferber recommends soothing strategies. If these fail, he recommends letting babies cry for 15 to 30 minutes and then trying again. By letting the child cry, he comments, parents are responding to the child's need to cry. Nevertheless, they must make the attempt to soothe the child first. Although colic disappears at about three months, colicky infants often develop chronic sleep problems. These may seem the same as in the colicky period, but they are not. Colicky babies who have been rocked, walked, or soothed to sleep may have learned to expect this treatment for every night wakening and come to expect it long after the colic is gone. Parents must wait until the colic has gone to stop these middle-of-the-night attentions, but this is not easy to determine because colic often clears up gradually. If the child does not seem in pain, however, if he or she is soothed when rocked, carried or patted on the back and falls back to sleep quickly, then colic is not the reason for the sleep problem. The problem is that the child has learned to fall asleep only with parental attention, and this pattern must be changed. Parents must teach their children to fall asleep alone, both for naps and for night sleep. Develop a pleasant ritual—but the child goes in the crib alone.

Crying

All babies cry and appear distressed some of the time. There are great individual differences, however. In newborn nurseries, babies cried from 1 to 11 minutes per hour. The average daily total per baby was about two hours of crying. When researchers attempted to classify reasons, they found hunger was a significant cause, as well as wet or dirty diapers. The largest single category, however, was "unknown reason." It may be that crying expressed a social need for cuddling, warmth, or rhythmic motion.[64]

BOX 6-1
ELIMINATING EXTRA FEEDINGS AT SLEEP TIMES

Day	Ounces in Each Bottle or Minutes Nursing	Minimum Hours between Feedings
1	7	2.0
2	6	2.5
3	5	3.0
4	4	3.5
5	3	4.0
6	2	4.5
7	1	5.0
8	No more bottles or nursing at sleep times	

Note: The ounces and times in this chart are general guidelines. You will want to alter them to fit your own routines.

Richard Ferber, *Solve Your Child's Sleep Problems* (New York: Simon & Schuster, 1985), p. 85.

Babies' crying increases to an average of about 3 hours at six weeks and decreases to an average of 1 hour per day at about three months. Though hunger seems a predominant reason, unknown causes remain the second highest category. As crying increases, it comes to be concentrated in the late afternoon or evening hours, with little during the day. By one year, babies have as many crying episodes as they had at three months, but spend much less time in each. Also, as children grow, the global negative reactions common to the first three months become more differentiated; crying becomes quieter, and the whole body is not involved.

Sylvia Bell and Mary Ainsworth conducted a thorough study of crying in the first year of life, obtaining surprising results confirmed in other studies.[65] Careful home observations were made. The timing and duration of the child's crying, the circumstances preceding crying, and the mother's responses were recorded and averaged for three-month periods, so the findings of this study describe change in the four quarters of the first year.

These researchers found that babies had as many crying episodes at the end of the year as at the beginning, but they spent much less time in each episode. Mothers tended to be consistent in how much they ignored the baby's crying, and there were marked differences among the mothers. One mother ignored only 4 percent of the cries, and one mother ignored 97 percent. Although each mother's behavior was consistent from quarter to quarter, the crying of each baby was not consistent until the last two quarters.

How does the baby's crying relate to the mother's behavior? In the first quarter, there was no relationship. In the second quarter, a trend appeared and was significant in the third and fourth quarters. Those mothers who responded immediately to the cries of the baby had babies who cried less! Conversely, ignoring a baby's cries seemed to increase the amount of crying as measured by frequency and duration. Those mothers who responded most at the beginning of the year had less to respond to at the end of the year.

What strategy is most effective in terminating crying? Picking up and holding the baby stopped the crying in 80 percent of the situations in which it occurred. Feeding, which involves physical contact, was almost as effective. The least effective method was to stand at a distance and talk to the child. By the end of the first year, any act that reduced the distance between mother and child stopped the crying. Although some maternal responses reduced crying more than others, the single most important factor in stopping the crying was the promptness with which the mother responded to the cry. If she came quickly, crying tended to decrease.

Judy Dunn reviews ways of providing comfort to crying babies and finds that caregivers around the world soothe by "rocking, patting, cuddling, swaddling, giving suck on breast or pacifier."[66] Effective techniques provide a background of continuous or rhythmic—as opposed to variable—sensations for the child. For example, constant temperatures, continuous sounds, and rhythmic rocking at a steady rate reduce the amount of time the infant cries. Effective soothing techniques also reduce the amount of stimulation the baby receives from his or her own movements. Thus, holding and swaddling reduce sensations from the child's flailing arms and legs and thus decrease crying.

Physicians Urs Hunziker and Ronald Barr recently speculated that American babies might be more content and cry less if they were carried more, as babies are in other cultures.[67] They studied two groups of mothers and babies—one group consisted of mothers who received infant carriers and carried babies three extra hours per day, when babies were not crying as well as when babies were crying; the other was a control group of mothers who carried their babies as usual. They monitored crying of the babies from three to twelve weeks and found that the supplemental carrying eliminated the peak of crying that usually occurs at six weeks, reduced crying overall, and modified the daily pattern of the crying so there was less in the evening hours. For example, at six weeks, those babies who received extra carrying cried 43 percent less overall than the control group, and 51 percent less than that group in the evening hours. At twelve weeks both groups decreased, but the carried babies still cried slightly less (23 percent less). Equally important, babies who were carried more were more content and more visually and aurally alert.

The researchers speculate that the supplemental carrying provides all the kinds of stimulation that we know soothes babies—rhythmic, repetitive movement with postural changes. Close physical contact with babies also gives mothers a better understanding of their infants' needs and reactions so that caretaking is more sensitive and responsive.

Another recent suggestion for soothing crying babies takes a different approach. In clinical and research training, pediatrician William Sammons observed many different kinds of babies and gradually developed the belief that babies have the ability to calm themselves, but they must be given the opportunity to develop this skill.[68] Babies suck on fingers, wrist, or arm; get into a certain body position; or focus on certain visual forms like walls or objects or light to soothe themselves. In his pediatric practice he has encouraged parents to engage in a mutual partnership with babies so that the infants can find their own ways of self-calming.

Parents help babies develop their skills by organizing a comfortable environment at home for the infant, attending to needs babies communicate, and learning the meanings of their babies' cries. When babies do cry and they are not clearly in need of food or some other specific intervention, parents intervene in a minimal way, talking to them, stroking them, giving them a chance to find their own particular way to calm themselves. The great advantage is that developing skills to do this enables babies to deal with a whole variety of unpredictable and unpleasant events like noise, heat, fatigue, and overstimulation. Babies become happier as do all family members.

Parents can combine these two latest solutions to the crying problem by increasing the amount of carrying they do and, at the same time, letting the infant find ways to calm themselves when they do cry and fuss without an identifiable cause.

Colic is a parent's nightmare. It is generally defined as "inconsolable crying for which no physical cause can be found, which lasts for more than three hours a day, occurs at least three days a week or more, and continues for at least three weeks."[69] Colic occurs in about 20 percent of babies. It begins at about two weeks of age; if the child is premature, it begins about two weeks following the due date, not the birth date. Colic disappears at about three to five months. Birth order, sex, allergy, parental social class, mother's intellectual ability and personality are not related to the condition.

Pediatrician Marc Weissbluth emphasizes that colic occurs in healthy babies who continue to thrive. It will pass; parents are not to blame—but there are ways to intervene. Weissbluth debunks what he considers are myths of colic. Colic is not a gastrointestinal problem caused by indigestion or the mother's diet; the gas that such babies experience is probably due to swallowing air during prolonged crying. Nor is colic caused by the mother's anxiety, inexperience, or personality.[70]

Weissbluth believes colic is an extreme form of normal crying behavior: Colic occurs at two to twelve weeks, just when the average baby is fussiest and disappears at about the same time that average crying decreases. Fussy, irritable babies with difficult temperaments appear most prone to colic. Colicky crying in the evening is possibly related to distorted or mixed-up biological rhythms; irregularities in the sleep-wake cycle, hormone secretions, temperatures, and breathing rhythm may cause the baby distress that results in inconsolable crying. Thus, more than one reason may underlie the distress. A physical cause is strongly suggested by the fact that premature babies develop colic about two weeks after their due date. If it were solely related to environmental causes, onset should occur two weeks after the birth date.[71]

There are many ways for parents to cope with colic. In addition to all the remedies already mentioned for crying, Weissbluth recommends that parents try to synchronize their actions with the baby's tempo.[72] If she is sobbing, rub her back in rhythm with her breathing. All remedies work for a while or at some times. When no remedy works, parents may want to put the child down in the crib for 15 or 30 minutes and then try a soothing activity again. Some experts believe the child may need to "cry it out"; if consolation were really wanted, the child would respond to the attempts to soothe.

All experts, and parents of formerly colicky babies, advise suffering parents not to lose hope. Babies grow out of it, and many turn into infants with wonderful dispositions. Weissbluth suggests loving babies whether they are crying or happy.

Dressing

In the very early weeks, children may fret while being changed. But they are still so small that they do not kick or flail their arms very much. And an infant's clothing is simple, so changing and dressing a baby can be done quickly. If the parent and infant both enjoy this activity, it can be prolonged. As children grow during the first year and become physically skilled, however, they are more active in their protest, kicking and wriggling and making it difficult to dress them. Gordon cites the example of how a mother handled her daughter's squirming behavior on the changing table with active listening.[73] The child cried when her diapers were changed because a bowel movement during her nap made her red and sore. Although the child was preverbal, the mother looked at the baby calmly and said that she knew how it hurt, but that the change would make her more comfortable. The child immediately calmed down, and although she whimpered with the pain, she did not fight the mother while the diaper was being changed.

Dreikurs gives a similar example of an eight-month-old baby who kicked and screamed when her mother changed her diapers.[74] In his example, however, there was no visible reason for the child to be upset, and Dreikurs interpreted the screaming as a method of seeking attention. The mother's task was to secure Lisa's cooperation by changing her own behavior. When Lisa was quiet, the mother was to talk to her with a warm smile, saying how quiet she was being. This was intended to reinforce Lisa's quiet, cooperative behavior. If Lisa started to scream, the mother was to put her hand quietly on the infant's body, with "loving firmness," until she stopped wiggling. As soon as she wiggled again, the mother was to hold her briefly until she stopped. Dreikurs does not consider this a form of reward or punishment, but a way of winning Lisa's cooperation. The intent is to teach Lisa that if she is quiet, the change goes faster than if she squirms. Behaviorists would follow a similar plan but would talk in terms of rewards for quiet behavior.

Both Gordon and Dreikurs advocate talking warmly to children and dressing the child quietly and calmly. They use different terms but suggest similar actions.

Setting Limits

Gordon urges parents to cooperate with children by listening to needs, responding to them, and modifying the environment so that children can explore safely.[75] See Chapter 7 for a discussion of babyproofing the environment. Parents remove things that are of value, e.g., fragile glassware, books. These changes create a safe environment in which the child is free to explore—one in which both parents and child can relax.

Even so, the child will inevitably want to play with something that is dangerous or that you want to preserve. When this happens, Gordon suggests that you "trade"—

find a different but safe activity to offer as a substitute. He uses the example of the child whose mother substituted a pair of stockings with runs for a new pair the child had found and wanted to play with. The child was still able to enjoy the texture and tug at the stockings, and the mother's needs were also met.

Trading and finding acceptable substitutes requires ingenuity. Gordon describes how one mother problem-solved in such a situation. This mother wanted her baby to stay in the playpen while she cleaned the house, and the baby wanted to be out, crawling around and exploring. The mother put the child in the playpen. She wrapped a trinket in a box with ribbons, then gave it to the baby. The package immediately caught the baby's attention. He stopped crying and spent half an hour undoing the box and playing with the trinket, and the mother was able to do her housework.

Dreikurs, talking about the same situation, sees the cause of the problem differently.[76] The baby has always been held and wants to be amused by the mother. Dreikurs says it is important for the baby to learn to play alone at least a portion of each day. Parents should provide toys and leave children to their own resources for definite periods each day. The tone sounds stern, but the main difference between Gordon and Dreikurs here is the amount of time the mother will spend searching for appealing toys to satisfy the child's need for novelty.

The behaviorists suggest another way of setting limits. Krumboltz and Krumboltz talk about developing an unpleasant association with a forbidden object or act to stop unacceptable behavior.[77] They give the example of a young child visiting a relative who builds model ships. The father sounded an old-fashioned automobile horn each time the child approached one of the fragile models. The child was startled, and after six sounds of the horn she stopped approaching the ships. If the parents had also said "no" just before sounding the horn, this experience would have helped the child learn the meaning of that important word.

Parents have to be careful not to create unpleasant associations with the wrong things. Krumboltz and Krumboltz tell of a baby who is sitting on the floor crying because she wants crackers. If the mother puts this child in her playpen every time she cries for crackers, the child may stop this behavior, but she will also begin to dislike the playpen.

PARENTS' EXPERIENCES

Ellen Galinsky describes the first year of an infant's life as the **nurturing stage**.[78] Parents focus on forming an attachment to the new baby, caring for the child, and accepting their new roles as parents. As they care for the child, they continue to question themselves: "Am I doing okay?" "Am I the kind of parent I want to be?" Though they devote most of their energy to the child during the first few months, gradually parents incorporate the other parts of their lives into caregiving activities. Relationships between mother and father and work activities are expanded to include the baby; relationships with other children and relatives are redefined. A great deal goes on during these early months.

It may be difficult, however, for parents to give each other the support that is so crucial in coping during this period. A significant number of new mothers report specific problems, including: (1) tiredness and exhaustion; (2) loss of sleep, especially in the first two months; (3) concern about ignoring husband's needs; (4) feeling inadequate as a mother; (5) inability to keep up with housework; and (6) feeling tied down.[79] Mothers did not anticipate the many changes that would occur in their lives when their babies arrived, in part because they did not realize how much work is involved in caring for an infant. Fathers had a similar ordering of complaints: (1) loss of sleep for up to six weeks; (2) need to adjust to new responsibilities and routines; (3) disruption of daily routines; (4) ignorance of the amount of work the baby requires; and (5) financial worries (62 percent of the wives were employed prior to the child and only 12 percent afterward). Husbands make such comments as, "My wife has less time for me" and "Getting used to being tied down is hard."

The new father may see the infant as a threat to his relationship with his wife and to their lifestyle. Concern about the amount of time and money and freedom that the baby will surely consume can obscure the joy he expects—and is expected—to feel. No more candlelit dinners, or even impromptu decisions to go to a movie or to make love, not for a while. The father has not had the physical experience of carrying the baby for nine months, nor is he as likely to be as involved as the mother in the care of the newborn. And for a while, at least, the needs of the baby will come before the wishes of the husband—and those needs will be frequent and unpredictable, delaying meals and interrupting sleep. But almost all fathers and mothers find that emotional attachment to their babies grows and deepens if they are patient and caring.

In the first few weeks after birth, obstetricians advise restraint from sexual intercourse. During this period the new mother is especially vulnerable to infection, her energy has been drained by pregnancy and birth, and her days and nights are devoted to care of the newborn. She is fulfilling the demands of an inarticulate and very dependent creature that she perform many unfamiliar tasks along with the usual household and personal routines. The fact that lovemaking, a source of pleasure in marriage, is interrupted adds to the feelings of stress felt by both parents after childbirth. During this early period of physical and emotional adjustment, the wife—particularly the working wife—needs time to regain her stamina and to establish new routines.

Couples who are prepared for the stresses that accompany the arrival of a new baby experience less anxiety and turmoil. Marriage and family courses in high school, family planning, childbirth courses, and satisfactory marital adjustment before the birth can alleviate stress after birth. The unknown is much more frightening and difficult to cope with than what we understand. The couple who have a realistic notion of how parenthood will change their lives will experience less stress from unanticipated problems. And they will be more open to experiencing joy in their new child and their new roles.

How can couples cope during this transition period? Social scientists emphasize the importance of communicating feelings and needs in open and nonjudgmental ways, of negotiating solutions when conflicts arise, and of sharing responsibilities for care of the infant and for household chores.

Gordon's active listening, I-message, and mutual problem-solving techniques are just as relevant to husband-wife interactions as they are to parent-child relations. Such techniques can help each partner to be aware of how the other is feeling and of what can be done to resolve problems.

There are pleasures in the reciprocal give-and-take between parent and child. Parents experience as much enjoyment as infants in playing games and often reexperience some of the joys they felt in their own childhood.

Parents interviewed about easing the transition to parenthood identify six basic ingredients in promoting parental well-being: (1) giving up the illusion of being a perfect parent, (2) looking for information you can apply to your child and your living situation rather than exact prescriptions of what to do, (3) learning the art of making decisions and setting goals (setting priorities on what is most important to do and following through on your priorities helps restore a sense of effectiveness), (4) considering parenthood as a series of tradeoffs and realizing that decisions to fill one member's needs may mean that someone else has to wait, (5) not trying to assume the role of parent without support from others, and (6) looking after yourself.[80]

Sometimes, even with looking after, mothers feel depressed. Physicians and nurses who work in hospitals report that 80 percent of new mothers have crying spells and postpartum blues at some time during their hospital stay.[81] In the weeks after the baby is born the mother may, from time to time, experience sadness, discouragement, and crying spells. These feelings are a natural part of the stress of incorporating a new baby into the family.

Awareness of the difficulties of the postpartum period and of specific ways of reducing stress have helped mothers deal with the emotional upset at this time. Husbands and friends can provide emotional support and can be available if the mother wants to talk about the worries, concerns, and frustrations she is feeling. The mother needs the kind of thoughtful care she gives her infant. She, too, must have enough rest. And she needs at least a little time she can spend alone or in a special, personal pursuit. A stable and serene environment helps to diminish stress. This is not the time to move or take on a new job if these events can be avoided.

If sadness persists and is accompanied by early morning awakening, loss of appetite and weight, apathy, or inability to concentrate and remember, then the new mother should seek both a thorough medical checkup and psychological counseling.

MAJOR POINTS OF CHAPTER 6

Newborns:

- are equipped with reflexes—such as sucking and gagging—that enable them to survive and flourish
- have six stages of consciousness ranging in level of arousal from regular sleep to crying
- are equipped with sensory, intellectual, and social abilities that enable them to make discriminations and learn new stimulus-response patterns
- are preprogrammed to respond to human beings
- are born with individual temperaments that influence parents' behavior

In the first year, babies

- gain control over their bodies and learn to sit alone, crawl, stand, and sometimes walk
- take a lively interest in the world around them, reaching out to explore objects within reach
- get pleasure from having effects on objects—kicking a mobile, rolling a ball

- develop language gradually from cooing and babbling in the early months to a few words at the end of the year
- develop a wide range of emotional reactions so that at the end of the year they express anger, fear, joy, pleasure, curiosity, and surprise and are learning to control their emotions

Attachment

- is a bond the baby forms with a caregiver
- is secure when parents are accepting and sensitive in meeting the baby's needs
- is insecure when parents are either unavailable and uninvolved or intrusive and controlling
- develops between babies and both parents
- is the basis for the baby's sense of being lovable and worthwhile

Mothers and fathers

- interact with babies in different ways, with mothers' holding babies more and doing more caregiving and fathers' being more playful and physically stimulating
- give infant sons and daughters equal amounts of attention, stimulation, care, and responsiveness

Babies

- begin to develop a sense of self in the last half of the first year
- begin to develop self-control, first over their physiological functioning, then over their motor activities, so that by the end of the first year, they can cooperate in following simple rules

Parents

- synchronize their behavior with the child's individual characteristics
- form enduring attachments with infants
- meet babies' physiological needs
- monitor amounts of stimulation
- reinforce regular schedules of eating, sleeping
- soothe babies when they cry by responding to them quickly, by giving additional carrying time, and by giving babies a chance to soothe themselves
- examine their own behavior to see how it creates a demand for adaptation on the part of the child
- stimulate babies' development when they play and converse with them

As they incorporate babies into family life, parents

- often do not anticipate the stress produced by all the changes
- are exhausted, unable to keep up with routine household chores, meals
- give up the illusion of being a perfect parent
- learn to set priorities and make decisions in terms of them
- seek support from each other and their social network
- seek expert help if mothers' postpartum depression continues without change
- experience many joys

Problems discussed center on:

- meeting babies' physiological needs
- beginning to set limits

Joys include:

- physical pleasures of babies
- playing with babies
- observing development of new skills
- joy and laughter of babies

ADDITIONAL READINGS

Brazelton, T. Berry. *Infants and Mothers.* Rev ed. New York: Dell, 1983.

Dorman, Marsha, and Klein, Diane. *How to Stay Two When Baby Makes Three.* New York: Ballantine, 1984.

Leach, Penelope. *Your Baby and Child.* Rev. ed. New York: Alfred A. Knopf, 1989.

Weissbluth, Marc. *Crybabies.* New York: Arbor House, 1984.

White, Burton L. *The First Three Years.* Rev. ed. New York: Prentice-Hall, 1985.

Notes

1. Peter H. Wolff, *The Causes, Controls, and Organization of Behavior in the Neonate* (New York: International Universities Press, 1966).
2. Howard P. Roffwarg, Joseph N. Muzio, and William C. Dement, "Ontogenetic Development of the Human Sleep–Dream Cycle," *Science* 152 (1966): 604–619.
3. Yvonne Brackbill et al., "Arousal Level in Neonates and Preschool Children under Continuous Stimulation," *Journal of Experimental Child Psychology* 4 (1966): 178–188.
4. Rudolph Schaffer, *Mothering* (Cambridge, Mass.: Harvard University Press, 1977).
5. Abraham Sagi and Martin Hoffman, "Empathic Distress in the Newborn," *Developmental Psychology* 12 (1976): 175–176. Andrew Meltzoff and M. Keith Moore, "Imitation of Facial and Manual Gestures by Human Neonates," *Science* 198 (1977): 75–78.

6. William S. Condon and Louis W. Sander, "Neonate Movement Is Synchronized with Adult Speech: Interactional Participation and Language Acquisition," *Science* 183 (1974): 99–101.

7. Aidan Macfarlane, *The Psychology of Childbirth* (Cambridge, Mass.: Harvard University Press, 1977), pp. 82–83.

8. Anneliese F. Korner, "Individual Differences at Birth: Implications for Early Experience and Later Development," *American Journal of Orthopsychiatry* 41 (1971): 608–619.

9. Rudolph Schaffer and Peggy E. Emerson, *The Development of Social Attachments in Infancy,* Monographs of the Society for Research in Child Development 29 (1964), whole number 94.

10. Alexander Thomas and Stella Chess, *Temperament and Development* (New York: Brunner/Mazel, 1977).

11. T. Berry Brazelton, *Infants and Mothers* (New York: Dell, 1969).

12. Anneliese F. Korner, Charles H. Zeanah, Janine Linden, Robert I. Berkowitz, Helena C. Kraemer, and W. Stewart Agras, "The Relation Between Neonatal and Later Activity and Temperament," *Child Development* 56 (1985): 38–42.

13. John E. Bates, Christine A. Maslin, and Karen H. Frankel, "Attachment Security, Mother-Child Interaction and Temperament as Predictors of Behavior Problem Ratings at Age Three Years," in *Growing Points of Attachment Theory and Research,* eds. Inge Bretherton and Everett Waters, Monographs of the Society for Research in Child Development 50 (1985), serial no. 109, pp. 167–193.

14. Denise Daniels and Robert Plomin, "Origins of Individual Differences in Infant Shyness," *Developmental Psychology* 21 (1985): 118–121.

15. Gwen E. Gustafson, "Effects of the Ability to Locomote on Infants' Social and Exploratory Behaviors: An Experimental Study," *Developmental Psychology* 20 (1984): 397–405.

16. Jean Piaget and Barbel Inhelder, *The Psychology of the Child* (New York: Basic Books, 1969); Herbert Ginsburg and Sylvia Opper, *Piaget's Theory of Intellectual Development* (Englewood Cliffs, N.J.: Prentice-Hall, 1969).

17. Robert McCall, *Exploratory Manipulation and Play in the Human Infant,* Monographs of the Society for Research in Child Development 39 (1974), whole number 155.

18. Mathilda Holzman, *The Language of Children* (Englewood Cliffs, N.J.: Prentice-Hall, 1983).

19. R. V. Tonkova-Yampol'skaya, "Development of Speech Intonation in Infants during the First Two Years of Live," in *Studies of Child Language Development,* eds. Charles A. Ferguson and Dan Isaac Slobin (New York: Holt, Rinehart & Winston, 1973), pp. 128–138.

20. Korner, "Individual Differences at Birth."

21. Sylvia M. Bell and Mary D. Salter Ainsworth, "Infant Crying and Maternal Responsiveness," *Child Development* 43 (1972): 1171–1190.

22. L. Alan Sroufe, "Socioemotional Development," in *Handbook of Infant Development,* ed. Joy D. Osofsky (New York: John Wiley, 1979), p. 462.

23. Carroll E. Izard and Carol Z. Malatesta, "Perspectives on Emotional Development I: Differential Emotions Theory of Early Emotional Development," in *Handbook of Infant Development,* 2nd ed., ed. Joy Doniger Osofsky (New York: John Wiley, 1987), p. 494–554.

24. Sroufe, "Socioemotional Development."

25. Carol Zander Malatesta and Jeannette M. Haviland, "Learning Display Rules: The Socialization of Emotion Expression in Infancy," *Child Development* 53 (1982): 991–1003.

26. John Worobey and Virginia M. Blajda, "Temperament Ratings at 2 Weeks, 2 Months and 1 Year: Differential Stability of Activity and Emotionality," *Developmental Psychology* 25 (1989): 257–263.

27. Carroll E. Izard, Elizabeth A. Hembree, and Robert Huebner, "Infants' Emotion Expressions to Acute Pain: Developmental Change and Stability of Individual Differences," *Developmental Psychology* 23 (1987): 105–113.

28. Nathan A. Fox, "Psychophysiological Correlations of Emotional Reactivity During the First Year of Life," *Developmental Psychology* 25 (1989): 364–372.

29. Megan R. Gunnar, Sarah Mangelsdorf, Mary Larson, and Louise Hertsgaard, "Attachment, Temperament, and Adrenocortical Activity in Infancy," *Developmental Psychology* 25 (1989): 355–363.

30. Charles A. Nelson, "The Recognition of Facial Expressions in the First Two Years of Life," *Child Development* 58 (1987): 889–909.

31. Jeannette M. Haviland and Mary Lelwica, "The Induced-Affect Response: 10-Week-Old Infants' Responses to Three Emotion Expressions," *Developmental Psychology* 23 (1987): 97–104.

32. Carol Z. Malatesta, Patricia Gregoryev, Catherine Lamb, Melanie Albin, and Clayton Culver, "Emotion Socialization and Expression Development in Preterm and Full Term Infants," *Child Development* 57 (1986): 316–330.

33. Robin Hornick, Nancy Risenhoover, and Megan Gunnar, "The Effects of Maternal Positive, Neutral, and Negative Affect Communication on Infant Responses to New Toys," *Child Development* 58 (1987): 936–944.

34. Malatesta and Haviland, "Learning Display Rules: The Socialization of Emotion Expression in Infancy."

35. Claire B. Kopp, "Regulation of Distress and Negative Emotions: A Developmental View," *Developmental Psychology* 25 (1989): 343–354; Edward Z. Tronick, "Emotions and Emotional Communication in Infants," *American Psychologist* 44 (1989): 112–119.

36. Izard and Malatesta, "Perspectives on Emotional Development I: Differential Emotions Theory of Early Emotional Development."

37. Tronick, "Emotions and Emotional Communication in Infants."

38. John S. Watson, "Smiling, Cooing and 'the Game,'" *Merrill-Palmer Quarterly* 18 (1972): 323–339.

39. Martha J. Cox, Margaret Tresch Owen, Jerry M. Lewis, and V. Kay Henderson, "Marriage, Adult Adjustment, and Early Parenting," *Child Development* 60 (1989): 1015–1024.

40. Ross D. Parke and Barbara J. Tinsley, "Family Interaction in Infancy," in *Handbook of Infant Development,* 2nd ed., ed. Joy Doniger Osofsky, (New York: John Wiley, 1987), pp. 579–641.

41. Erik H. Erikson, *Childhood and Society,* 2nd ed. (New York: W. W. Norton, 1963).

42. Myron A. Hofer, "Early Social Relationships: A Psychobiologist's View," *Child Development* 58 (1987): 633–647.

43. Saul M. Schanberg and Tiffany M. Field, "Sensory Deprivation Stress and Supplemental Stimulation in the Rat Pup and Preterm Neonate," *Child Development* 58 (1987): 1431–1447.

44. Robert Emde and James F. Sorce, "The Rewards of Infancy: Emotional Availability and Maternal Referencing," in *Frontiers of Infant Psychiatry,* eds. Justin D. Call, Eleanor Galenson, and Robert L. Tyson (New York: Basic Books, 1983), pp. 17–30.

45. Louis W. Sander, "Polarity, Paradox and the Organizing Process in Development," in *Frontiers of Infant Psychiatry,* ed. Justin D. Call, Eleanor Galenson, and Robert L. Tyson (New York: Basic Books, 1983), pp. 333–346.

46. Russell A. Isabella, Jay Belsky, and Alexander von Eye, "Origins of Infant-Mother Attachment: An Examination of Synchrony during the Infant's First Year," *Developmental Psychology* 25 (1989): 12–21.

47. Parke and Tinsley, "Family Interaction in Infancy."

48. Ross D. Parke, "Perspectives on Father-Infant Interaction," in *Handbook of Infant Development,* ed. Joy D. Osofsky, (New York: John Wiley, 1979), pp. 549–590.

49. Jay Belsky, Bonnie Gilstrap, and Michael Rovine, "The Pennsylvania Infant and Family Development Project, I: Stability and Change in Mother-Infant and Father-Infant Interaction in a Family Setting at One, Three and Nine Months," *Child Development* 55 (1984): 692–705.

50. Ibid.

51. Michael Lewis and Linda Michalson, *Children's Emotions and Moods: Developmental Theory and Measurement* (New York: Plenum, 1983).

52. Claire B. Kopp, "Antecedents of Self-Regulation: A Developmental Perspective," *Developmental Psychology* 18 (1982): 199–214.

53. Donelda J. Stayton, Robert Hogan, and Mary D. Salter Ainsworth, "Infant Obedience and Maternal Behavior: The Origins of Socialization Reconsidered," *Child Development* 42 (1971): 1057–1069.

54. Jeanne Brooks and Michael Lewis, "Infants' Responses to Strangers: Midget, Adult and Child," *Child Development* 47 (1976): 323–332.

55. Jacqueline M. T. Becker, "A Learning Analysis of the Development of Peer-Oriented Behavior in Nine-Month-Old Infants," *Developmental Psychology* 13 (1977): 481–491.

56. Phyllis LaFarge, "The Pikler Method: A New Way to Raise a Happier Baby," *Parents Magazine,* December 1979.

57. Sybil K. Escalona, *The Roots of Individuality* (Chicago: Aldine Press, 1968).

58. Martin I. Heinstein, *Behavioral Correlates of Breast-Bottle Regimes under Varying Parent-Infant Relationships*, Monographs of the Society for Research in Child Development 28 (1963), whole number 88.

59. Marvin S. Eiger and Sally W. Olds, *The Complete Book of Breastfeeding* (New York: Workman, 1976).

60. Thomas Gordon, *P.E.T. Parent Effectiveness Training* (New York: New American Library, 1975).

61. Rudolf Dreikurs, *The Challenge of Parenthood*, rev. ed. (New York: Hawthorn, 1958).

62. Richard Ferber, *Solve Your Child's Sleep Problems* (New York: Simon & Schuster, 1985).

63. Marc Weissbluth, *Crybabies* (New York: Arbor House, 1984).

64. Ibid.

65. Bell and Ainsworth, "Infant Crying and Maternal Responsiveness."

66. Judy Dunn, *Distress and Comfort* (Cambridge, Mass.: Harvard University Press, 1977), p. 23.

67. Urs A. Hunziker and Ronald G. Barr, "Increased Carrying Reduces Crying: A Randomized Controlled Trial," *Pediatrics* 77 (1986): 641-647.

68. William A. H. Sammons, *The Self-Calmed Baby* (Boston: Little, Brown, 1989).

69. Weissbluth, *Crybabies*, p. 13.

70. Ibid.

71. Ibid.

72. Ibid.

73. Thomas Gordon with Judith Gordon Sands, *P.E.T. in Action* (New York: Bantam Books, 1976).

74. Rudolf Dreikurs with Vicki Soltz, *Children: The Challenge* (New York: Hawthorn, 1964).

75. Gordon with Sands, *P.E.T. in Action.*

76. Dreikurs with Soltz, *Children: The Challenge*, p. 40.

77. John D. Krumboltz and Helen B. Krumboltz, *Changing Children's Behavior* (Englewood Cliffs, N.J.: Prentice-Hall, 1972).

78. Ellen Galinsky, *Between Generations: The Six Stages of Parenthood* (New York: Times Books, 1981).

79. Myra Leifer, "Psychological Changes Accompanying Motherhood and Pregnancy," *Genetic Psychology Monographs* 95 (1977): pp. 55–96.

80. Plutzik and Laghi, *The Private Life of Parents.*

81. Marshall Klaus and John Kennell, *Maternal-Infant Bonding* (St. Louis: C. V. Mosby, 1976).

TODDLERHOOD: THE YEARS FROM ONE TO THREE

C H A P T E R   7

The toddler period is of great importance for several reasons. Children from one to three years of age take their first steps, say their first sentence, run for the first time. As toddlers increase their physical and verbal skills, they become more independent of parents and are able to do more to care for themselves. They feed themselves, go to the toilet, partly dress themselves. The developing sense of self is frequently expressed in negativism; in refusing to do what others want, the toddler achieves a stronger sense of who he or she is. Happily, the child outgrows this negativism.

Life with toddlers is rarely dull. Their busyness, intensity, curiosity, independence, and increasing verbal skills make them both exciting and frustrating for parents. We are pleased by their achievements, intrigued by their verbal observations, and sometimes outraged by their stubbornness. Toddlers develop subtle skills of persuasion and distraction.

PHYSICAL DEVELOPMENT

By the end of the first year, the tiny newborn has become a little person who can probably stand alone and may even be able to walk. The average one-year-old is between 27 and 29 inches in height and weighs about 21 or 22 pounds. By the end of the third year, height has increased to about 36 inches and weight to about 35 pounds. Growth in the second and third years is slower than during infancy, but is still rapid—and about twice the rate of the years from three to five.

Growth in this period is related to such environmental factors as quality and amount of food, absence of chronic illness, medical care, and family socioeconomic status. Growth is also related to social and geographical conditions. For many years the average height and weight of people in industrialized countries have been increasing. Now this growth is thought to be leveling off. Studies suggest that chronic illness and deprivation of food may cause a temporary halt to growth but that when these stresses pass, catch-up growth occurs. The growth of an individual who has

WHAT I WISH I HAD KNOWN ABOUT TODDLERHOOD

"There are a couple of things. Most of the time he is okay about going to sleep, but sometimes he has a hard time; and reading a book gave me permission to put him in the crib while he was crying. He cried a little, made a few peeps, and went to sleep, but the book gave me permission to do that. Also being reminded to look at things from the child's perspective instead of the adult's is very helpful. You may know that it is not a great thing to pick up a toilet brush but he does not know or understand that. I have found myself yelling at him, and I have to remind myself to look at it from his point of view." MOTHER

"Someone said when you have a child, it's like two appointment books—his appointment book and yours. And first you do everything in the kid's appointment book; and then when you're done, you do everything in the kid's appointment book again. I wish I had known they weren't joking. I knew that it would be a challenge, and in some ways I wish I had known more. But in other ways I think if I had really known exactly how hard it would be sometimes, I might have been more reluctant or waited longer, and that I would really have regretted—not doing it." FATHER

"I wasn't prepared for all the decisions. Is it okay if he does this or not? He's trying to do something; shall I step in so he doesn't hurt himself or shall I let him go? It's making all those choices, making sure what I feel." MOTHER

"There is anxiety, a feeling of vulnerability I have never felt before. If he gets sick, what are we going to do? If he has a little sickness we just hope the doctor is doing the right thing. We went through a great deal in the past few weeks choosing a nursery school for him, and we hope we have done the right thing, but is this the one for him?" FATHER

"I wish I had known what to do about climbing. He climbs all over everything. I have the living room stripped bare, but I wonder if this is the right thing." MOTHER

"I wish we had—because he is our first child—more of a sense of the norms. What is okay versus what is a problem and what is really bad? Is this normal, is this just kids being kids? He pushed someone at school three times; is this par for the course or is this a problem? We don't know when we are reacting and when we are overreacting." FATHER

"I wish I had known how much time they needed between one and two. They are mobile, but they are clueless about judgment. I think it was one of the most difficult times. Even though she did not get into a lot of trouble, sticking her finger in light sockets, still she takes a lot of time and watching, so the transition to two was great." MOTHER

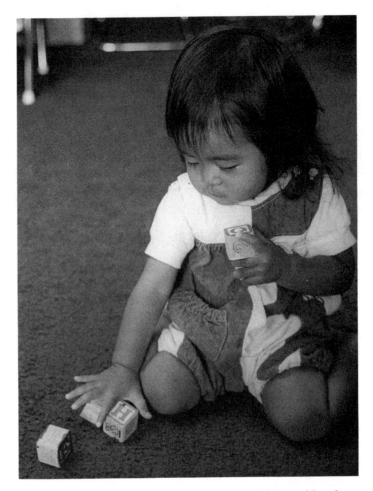

One basic caregiver function is to design the child's world and daily life, including the provision of appropriate toys. This fifteen-month-old is showing increased manual control. She can pick up blocks and put them down where she wants them. By age twenty-four months she will be able to build a tower of six blocks, and at thirty-six months a tower of ten blocks.

suffered from such illness or deprivation is not permanently stunted unless the stress occurs over a long period.

Now let's look at the development of motor abilities. By the time the child is two, the motor and sensory areas of the cortex are well developed, a circumstance reflected in increasingly complex motor behavior.

As babies gain experience as upright creatures, they modify their walk so that the steps are longer, the gait is smoother, and the width of the stepping gait is decreased. At about twenty-one months, the baby starts running. This activity, which requires the coordination of trunk and limbs, is more difficult to achieve than walking. By age three, walking and running are automatic activities for children, and they carry out other motor responses with confidence and verve. Children can jump from a height of 18 inches and descend a staircase, with support, while alternating footsteps. Most children of three can pedal a tricycle. The ability to throw also becomes refined. The baby of about eleven months can throw a ball from a sitting position, but is not yet able to send the ball in a specific direction. Not until about thirteen months can children repeatedly toss a ball to an adult on request.

Reaching and grasping develop rapidly in the first year of life. By eighteen months, reaching has become automatic, and the child focuses on the object to be reached rather than on the process itself. Manipulation of objects began during the first year; during toddlerhood the child develops the capacity to combine objects—to put several cubes in a cup, build a tower of three blocks, or place pellets in a bottle. The act of releasing an object is more difficult than reaching for and grasping it. In the second year, the letting-go process creates difficulties when children are building towers or releasing pellets into a bottle, for example. This is because control over finger extension occurs only after reaching and grasping are well developed. By age three, releasing has become a smoother process.

Motor development continues to bring the child into wider contact with the environment. Now toddlers can walk, run, and throw. They can move around more easily and cover more area. Children enjoy exercising and experimenting with the skills they are acquiring. Often they experiment with new ways of looking at the world—for example, bending over to watch the world upside down between their legs. As they get greater control of their bodies, toddlers begin to dance and twist about, imitating current dance steps. They improvise around their new skills. One toddler developed a baseball game that could be played in the kitchen with a wooden spoon and a tennis ball.

Children know no limits to their skills and will try to plunge into activities with older children, attempting to play ball or hide and seek with older siblings or children in the park. Even though they are just beginning to run, they try to be part of a group.

INTELLECTUAL DEVELOPMENT

Increased physical competence and the joy of exploration and exercise lead to activities that expand the child's understanding of the world. Let's look at how Jean Piaget describes development at this time (see Table 6-1).[1] Toddlers fall into the last two stages of Piaget's sensorimotor period and the first stage of the preoperational period.

In the stage of **tertiary circular reactions** (twelve to eighteen months), children's interest is directed beyond their bodies and beyond objects as tools to discovery of the properties of objects. The understanding that each object has an independent existence and permanence leads to exploration of these objects and how they work. Toddlers are curious about textures—they like to stroke a dog or cat and rub their cheeks against the fur. They are attracted to water and to toilets and will run again and again to play in the bathroom.

Toddlers are miniature scientists. They observe the world around them and develop ideas about what will happen if they perform certain acts and about how objects work. As they observe and have more experiences, their ideas increase in complexity. For example, children observe that when they drop an object, it falls. And before long they learn that some objects drop better than others and some objects break when dropped. Piaget calls these internal ideas about objects and events **schema**. Children's ideas, or schema, gradually modified by experience, serve to guide their actions.

In this period, children become capable of more accurate imitation. During the first year infants can imitate spontaneous movements that are much like their own actions—waving bye-bye, for example. Toddlers are more advanced. They can watch a model and imitate in a controlled fashion. The toddler pushing a teddy bear in a stroller or having a tea party for her dolls is imitating. Parents often delight in children's perception of behaviors—the toddler's imitation of his father going to work with exactly the posture and gestures of the father, or laughing in a conversational tone just as a parent does.

The sixth and last phase of the sensorimotor period is the **beginning of thought stage** (eighteen to twenty-four months), thought to serve as a transition from the sensorimotor period to the preoperational period. Up to this time, Piaget believes children are limited to immediate experiencing of objects, people, whatever is present at the moment. They act on what they see. As the child emerges from this period, however, we see the beginning of language use and of symbolic or mental representations. Piaget illustrates with the example of his sixteen-month-old daughter, who saw another toddler have a temper tantrum when he was put in his playpen. The next day she herself, when placed in the playpen, had an identical tantrum for the first time in her life. Clearly, the child remembered the tantrum in some symbolic form and imitated it after a period of delay.

At about two, children move into the **preoperational period**, which is divided into the **preconceptual stage** (years two to four) and the **intuitive stage** (four to seven). In the **preconceptual stage**, the child is able to represent mentally what is seen and observed in the environment. Recall the temper tantrum acted out by Piaget's daughter. Clearly the child had a memory for the event, but what was the mental representation? Children do not have the language needed to describe what they see, so this probably could not have been a verbal memory. Piaget suggests that children store the memory of those motor movements associated with the visual images. A child who saw a bicycle might store a memory of the bicycle moving back and forth. During this period language develops rapidly, and imaginative play and deferred imitation increase. Parents are often amazed at what children are able to remember and imitate later. One sixteen-month-old child startled his parents one day by nonchalantly taking the mother's key ring, walking over to the front door, and from many keys selecting the correct one.

Like Piaget, Burton White describes the toddler's increasing intellectual competence.[2] While he, too, notes children's curiosity, exploratory drive, and mastery of motor skills, he focuses on behaviors not referred to by others. He points to the "growth of learning-to-learn skills" during the period from eight to fourteen months.

Children at this age cannot build products or draw pictures, but they are learning the skills they will need to do these things later. They are learning how to put things together and take them apart. These skills are enjoyable in themselves, and they pave the way for more complex behaviors.

White emphasizes that parents should encourage children's various interests—in their caregivers, in exploring the world, and in mastering skills. Occasionally parents emphasize interest in exploration to the exclusion of interest in people or stress attachment to the neglect of exploring the world. At this period the child should be engaged in a variety of activities—developing language, noticing small details, planning and carrying out activities.

LANGUAGE DEVELOPMENT

You will recall that babies can discriminate among sounds in the first month of life. At about eight months they begin to comprehend words, and at about a year they begin to produce words. The year-old baby is able, by changing intonation, to use a single word to express statements, requests, questions, and commands. A two-year-old has a vocabulary of perhaps fifty words, which increases to about nine hundred words by the time the child is three and to about 14,000 when the child is six. This is an average of about nine new words a day.[3]

Characteristics of parents and home in the first two years contribute to children's language competence.[4] A strong, positive emotional tie with the mother—enhanced by the amount and quality of the time the mother spends with the newborn as well as by her talking to the child, asking questions and responding to what the child says—increases the child's verbal abilities. Homes that facilitate verbal skill provide many opportunities for exploration and play, and they are organized and structured in atmosphere. Language does not develop as rapidly when the home contains many people who reduce the amount of individual time that mothers speak directly to infants.[5]

How do children develop the ability to speak in such a brief period? Twenty years ago psychologists thought children learned language because parents reinforced a baby's babbling, rewarded the use of words by meeting the child's requests, and served as models. Although imitation and adults' shaping children's language surely play a role in language acquisition, current theories suggest that children have an inborn predisposition to learn language. Children have information-processing abilities or strategies for learning the structure of language—how words are put together. They learn formulas and rules for linking words to express experience. They also seem to develop "fast mapping" skills that enable them to form a quick, partially correct understanding of the word. They then refine their understanding with repeated exposures to the word. Exactly how they develop such rapid processing skills is not known.[6] Usually they learn the words that refer to meaningful aspects of their lives—*mama, dada, cookie.* Sometimes, however, they learn a word and then search for the experience it represents. Thus, words can expand a child's awareness as well as reflect it. Exploration and stimulating emotional relationships may be predictors of verbal competence, because they supply the essential ingredients for communication. Exploration leads to experiences the child wants to communicate about, and the emotional tie provides someone to receive the communication.

There are individual differences in the vocabularies of toddlers and in the complexity of their language. Some children have vocabularies of fifty words by the time they are fifteen months old, others by the time they are two years old. Toddlers' first words refer to people and objects important to them. They have names for parents, siblings, pets, and favorite toys, and they use words of action in relation to these important figures. They often have words for daily routines like eating and sleeping. When they put their first words together, toddlers continue to verbalize about who and what really matter in their everyday life.[7] When children are learning new words and sentence structures, a neutral emotional mood seems to help the learning.[8] It may be that too much emotional excitement distracts children and makes it hard for them to focus on words and their meaning.

Children use different strategies in learning words. Some say little, listening to words but not trying to produce them. When they understand enough words, they begin to talk freely and well. Others may use many words, seeming to try out words to see if they are appropriate. Children are motivated to learn to speak by the desire to communicate.

A review of the speech of two years olds around the world reveals that the two-word sentence, appearing between eighteen and twenty-four months, is a telegraphic communication that omits such words as *of, an, the* and emphasizes the actor-action-object dimensions.[9] Children communicate many different kinds of information and can specify: (1) identification ("see doggy"); (2) location ("coat there"); (3) recurrence ("more milk"); (4) nonexistence ("cookie all gone"); (5) negation ("no milk"); (6) possession ("Daddy car"); (7) agent-action ("I want") and (8) subject action ("Mommy throw"); (9) location ("Mama chair"); (10) action recipient ("bottle me"); (11) action instrument ("cut knife"); (12) attribution ("hat pretty"); and (13) questions ("Mama go").

Martin Braine has identified a **groping pattern**—the child's first uncertain attempt to convey a meaning, accompanied by repetition and hesitation.[10] A groping pattern occurs whenever a child is moving to a more advanced stage of speech—for example, from using one-word to two-word combinations. A parent may worry when a child seems to stutter or stammer, but this groping does not last very long. Toddlers can convey meanings with two words, changing inflection to change the meaning. "Mama go" may identify mother's leaving, the child's insistence that he or she be taken along, or a desire to leave a particular place.

Individual differences in language development occur not only in rate of development but also in the time and order in which patterns of speech emerge. For example, some two-year-olds learn actor-action sequences ("kitty meow") before identification patterns ("doggy there"); other children acquire the patterns in reverse order. Some emphasize possessives first; others refer to place. These individual differences in the order of emerging patterns of speech probably reflect differences in personality and orientation in the world. Parents can learn how their toddlers use words by keeping diaries of first words and early word combinations.

Children go through a process in which they overgeneralize rules. For example, a two-year-old who begins speaking may say "It broke," using the correct form of the past tense for *break*. As the child becomes sensitive to the rules for forming the past tense—adding *ed* to a verb—the child will go through a period in which he or she says "It breaked." Similarly, children may learn early such plurals as *feet, mice,* and *men*. But as the rule for forming plurals—adding *s* or *es*—is learned, the child may overgeneralize and say *foots, mouses, mans,* or add an *s* to the irregular form and say *feets, mices,* and *mens*.

Girls excel in verbal skills from the first year of life, and their ability is predictive of intellectual performance from age six well into the adult years. It is not clear whether parents provide early stimulation of girls' abilities or whether they have an innate advantage. Recent studies suggest that in the second year differences in verbal skills are evident in the average length of a child's remark rather than in the number of words known.[11]

EMOTIONAL DEVELOPMENT

As you recall, by the end of the first year, babies express interest, surprise, joy, anger, fear, and disgust. In the second year, feelings related to self-awareness are added to the emotional repertoire. Toddlers express embarrassment, shame, guilt, pride, and empathy.[12]

Language reflects the importance of emotions in our lives. As soon as toddlers can talk, they learn words referring to feelings and emotions. By the beginning of the third year toddlers talk about positive feelings such as being happy, having a good time, feeling good, and being proud. They talk about negative emotions as well— being sad, scared, angry. They talk about uncomfortable physical states—being hungry, hot, cold, sleepy, and in pain. Words play an important role in helping toddlers learn how to handle negative feelings by enabling them to communicate these states to parents, get feedback about how appropriate the feelings are, and think about how to manage them.[13]

Toddlers also use objects to handle negative feelings. They frequently have transitional objects like stuffed animals, blankets, pieces of cloth, and dolls to provide comfort in times of distress. The use of such objects reaches a peak in the middle of the second year when as many as 30 to 60 percent of children have them.[14]

Toddlers also enlist the help of parents and caregivers to resolve negative feelings and situations beyond them. They call or pull parents to what they want remedied. As they move beyond two, toddlers wait less time before getting a parent to move a barrier, get a prized possession, or in general "solve the problem." They seem to have a greater understanding of when they need the extra help and call for it more quickly.[15]

Toddlers are aware, too, of others' feelings, and they develop ideas about what actions cause feelings and what actions change feelings. Following are examples of comments from twenty-eight-month olds: "I give a big hug. Baby be happy." "Mommy exercise. Mommy having a good time." "I'm hurting your feelings 'cause I mean to you." "Grandma's mad. I wrote on wall." "You sad, Mommy. What Daddy do?" Toddlers also learn that one person's feelings can stimulate another person's actions. "I cry. Lady pick me up." "I scared of the shark. Close my eyes."[16]

Using their knowledge of emotions and what causes them, toddlers attempt to change others' behavior. They sometimes enact an emotion or feeling—sadness or tiredness—to get what they want. A psychiatrist described a two-year-old who spent 20 minutes acting in such a way in an airport that the mother finally bought a toy she had initially refused the child.[17] Toddlers respond not only to their own wishes, but they also reveal deep levels of sympathy with others as we shall see in the section on Empathy.

Children also use words about feelings to engage in new kinds of imaginative play.[18] They may play games with parents in which they pretend to have different emotions and wait for parents to react. A child may pretend to hit a parent lightly, the mother may pretend to cry, and the child comforts the parent. Children may also say they are "just pretending" when they act mad or sad in a game.

Autonomy

As toddlers become more exploratory, more independent, and more definite in their sense of who they are, they become more assertive in interaction with parents and peers. Toddlers are assertive in many ways. As they did in the first year of life, they assert themselves by refusing to do what parents want. "No" becomes a common word, and toddlers sometimes practice it, saying "no" as they play alone. They turn away from food, wriggle and squirm as parents try to help them dress. Even more frequent in this age period is the assertion seen in children's insistence that they can do something by themselves or in their own way. "Me do it" or "My way" are common refrains. Children also like to command parents, sometimes adopting an imperious tone as they say, "Come now!" or "Do that!"

Anger

Assertion turns to frustration and anger when toddlers cannot accomplish what they set out to do. In the toddler period, tantrums increase. The research of Florence Goodenough on anger and temper outbursts provides valuable information on how and why temper tantrums develop and on effective ways of handling anger.[19] She found that many factors influenced the occurrence of anger. Outbursts peak in the second year and are most likely to occur when children are hungry or tired (just before meals and at bedtime) or when they are ill. Thus, when reserves are down for physical reasons, tempers flare. Outbursts are usually short-lived—most last less than 5 minutes—and with young children under three the aftereffects were minimal. With increasing age, children tended to sulk and to have hard feelings. From one to three years, the immediate causes of anger seem to be conflict with authority, difficulties over the establishment of habits (eating, baths, bedtime), and problems with social relationships (wanting more attention, wanting a possession someone else has). With older children, social and particularly play relationships trigger more outbursts. After the second year, boys seem to have more outbursts than girls.

Goodenough found that the parents of children who had the fewest temper tantrums used the following methods: diverting the child's attention, reasoning, ignoring the outburst, isolating the child, and scolding. Parents of children who had the most frequent tantrums used the following methods: granting the child's desire, removing the source of the trouble, coaxing, soothing, and threatening. The children who had more outbursts tended to be angry for a much longer time afterward.

The parents of the children who had the fewest outbursts were more consistent, used preventive (rather than corrective) methods of control, used a daily schedule as a means to an end, and had a more tolerant, positive home atmosphere. Parents of children with few outbursts were consistent and fair in the rules they established. They had realistic expectations that children would be independent, curious, stubborn; they anticipated problems and found ways to prevent them. These parents had a schedule and a routine and tried to help children conform by preparing them for changes in activities. They announced mealtimes or bathtimes in advance so children had 10 minutes or so to get ready. In these homes, parents focused on the individuality of the child. When a real conflict arose, however, they were firm.

Parents of children with many outbursts were inconsistent and unpredictable, basing decisions on their own wants rather than the child's needs. These parents tended to ignore children's needs until a problem forced them to respond. In some of these families, parents imposed a routine regardless of the child's activity of the moment and forced the child to act quickly in terms of their own desire. Criticism and disapproval characterized the home atmosphere. In short, when children are tired, hungry or sick, they are likely to respond with anger. Parental behaviors that reinforce attachment—acceptance, sensitivity to children's needs, and cooperativeness—minimize temper outbursts.

Empathy

At the same time that anger is on the increase, expressions of affection and empathy increase as well. In the second year babies begin to give signs of affection—love pats and strokings—to parents, particularly the mother. They are also affectionate to animals and younger children.

Empathy develops in stages during the toddler period.[20] At ten to twelve months, babies respond to other children's distress by crying with agitation. In the second year, however, they take action, touching, cuddling, or rubbing the injured party. An eighteen-month-old girl, upset by her baby brother's crying, brought him a diaper to hold, because she liked to carry a diaper for comfort. Between eighteen months and two years, children begin to imitate the emotional reactions of the hurt individual, mimicking facial expressions of pain. Many go through a process of referring the pain to themselves. If a mother bumps her arm, the child rubs the mother's elbow, then his own. Compassionate action follows the self-referencing behavior. Investigators suggest that true kindness may depend on the ability to relate the other's distress to oneself.

What qualities in parents stimulate empathy in a toddler? Children who are kind and helpful in response to the suffering of others have mothers who are warm, caring individuals, concerned with the well-being of others. These mothers expect children to control aggression, and when they do not, mothers show disappointment—"Children are not for hitting," "Stop! You are hurting him." The researchers conclude that mothers of empathetic children model kindness to others, but they go beyond that to teach children how to do what is expected. They maintain high standards and continue a warm, caring relationship with children.

We noted that infants as young as three months react to the emotional expressions of mothers. Toddlers, too, are highly responsive to the emotional reactions of anger between parents. The most immediate response to anger was distress that increased with each exposure to the anger.[21] Children cried, frowned, seemed upset. When anger continued, children attempted to help parents—mediate or settle the argument, distract the parents by coming between them. When toddlers have witnessed aggression among adults, they tend to vent angry feelings on peers. They may be imitating parents' aggressive behavior, they may be so distressed by the anger that they have less frustration tolerance with peers, or they may be expressing anger intended for adults. Regardless of the reasons, children who witness anger tend to express it with peers even though they remain solicitous of the adults themselves.

Happiness

With age, the sources of pleasure expand. Parents are accustomed to seeing the pleasure infants take in being with people and in playing with parts of their body or with objects. What strikes parents forcefully now is the joy that comes with accomplishing what one sets out to. One mother describes the pleasure her toddler expressed as he manipulated a fork and finally was able to spear a strand of twirly spaghetti and get it into his mouth. His glowing smile after doing this expressed his feeling of triumph.

Harriet Rheingold, Kay Cook, and Vicki Kolowitz describe an unexpected source of pleasure for toddlers.[22] They studied toddlers' responses to a series of commands to perform certain tasks with toys. The toddlers had initially been playing in a mildly interested way with the toys. When asked to do easy and interesting tasks like arrange the toys in certain ways, they did so quickly and enthusiastically. Then when allowed to play freely with no adult involved, they happily repeated the tasks. The authors conclude that toddlers take enormous pleasure in matching their actions to the words of another, and the pleasure of accomplishing a goal is a powerful incentive for their obeying commands.

PERSONAL AND SOCIAL DEVELOPMENT

Erikson describes toddlerhood as the stage in which children develop a sense of autonomy or independent selfhood.[23] Children have matured physically and have learned to walk and climb. They begin to express their basic sense of self in their verbal "nos" and "Do it myself." Children's delight in independence is seen in the desire to do things by themselves—to go where they want, eat what they want, get what they want, and influence other people. If parents encourage this behavior and provide opportunities for self-direction, children gain control over their bodies and themselves. They develop a sense of autonomy, of being able to act independently. Failures occur, and parents are not always supportive and patient as children go at their own pace and do what they want. If failure and frustration occur often, children develop a sense of shame and doubt about themselves and their abilities. If most experiences are positive, children develop strength of will, the resolution to make free choices and to act with self-control.

Parent-Child Relations

Attachment, as we discussed in Chapter 6, is the emotional tie between child and parent (or other caregiver) and is reflected in the child's wanting to be with the parent, seeking him or her out, and being upset at separation from that person. The quality of the child's attachment to the parent influences the capacity to relate to others, to play with objects, and even to move around physically in the environment. For example, Jude Cassidy found that securely attached eighteen-month-olds have greater ability to maneuver physically in the world and, as a result, fall and stumble less.[24]

The benefits of attachment are seen not only in the present, but they extend into the future as well. Sroufe and his coworkers found that securely attached one-year-olds are more curious later in childhood; they attack a new problem vigorously and positively.[25] While they persist at a task, they are able to accept help from the mother and are not aggressive. Their mothers are supportive and helpful. Children whose attachment is tenuous are anxious, throw more tantrums when presented with problems, and are more negative in response to the mother, ignoring and opposing her in different ways. Securely attached toddlers are outgoing preschoolers who are well liked. They are sympathetic to others, suggest activities, and are able to be leaders. When involved in their own activities, they are self-directed, goal-oriented, eager to learn new skills and develop their abilities. The bond with the mother, then, increases the self-esteem and self-confidence that give the child a positive view of the world and permit exploration and satisfying interaction with others.

There are several important ingredients in the caretaker's behavior that solidify the attachment. First, the parent is available.[26] The mother's availability to the child, her readiness to respond to what the child does, creates an atmosphere that results in the child's enjoyment, curiosity, and greater exploration.

Second, the parent serves as a safe base that the child uses as a reference point in exploring the world. Toddlers note the emotional state of the parent as well as the words and gestures and pattern their behavior accordingly.[27] Third, synchronous relationships with toddlers enable parents to have maximum impact in giving information to the child. Children are more attentive to parents' concerns and wishes when they have experienced parents' respect for what they themselves are doing.[28]

A fourth important quality is the ability to balance support and guidance with increasing independence for the child. The effective parent observes the child's level of interaction in a situation and stays, in a sense, "one step ahead." When the child confronts a new barrier, the parent steps in to give just the amount of help that enables the child to solve the problem and move on. Jutta Heckhausen terms this behavior "balancing the child's weakness" in order to stimulate a new level of skill.[29] This behavior is sometimes referred to as "scaffolding," as parental help provides the structure to compensate for the child's lack of skill with the task.

INTERVIEW
with Claire Kopp

*Claire B. Kopp is professor of psychology at the University of California at Los Angeles. She has
followed two samples of children and observed their development of self-regulation and self-control.*

**I think encouraging the development of self-control and self-regulation are major goals
of parents in raising their children. What can they do or what are the best ways, in your
experience, to help children develop these capacities?**

Parents help children learn self-control in different ways depending on the age of the child.
Parents' activities will differ when the child is fifteen months of age compared to when the
child is three years of age. I shall start by discussing the developmental abilities of children
of different ages and then turn to what parents do with children of that age.

Early in the middle of the second year (fifteen months), children begin to understand daily
routines, such as mealtime routines, and bedtime routines. Although children are much more
active at this age, their expressive language is still limited. They are also beginning to show
signs of self-awareness. All of these factors have implications for what parents do.

In my view, the parent of a fifteen-month-old child should establish two or three important
rules and focus on them. The parent can then give a great deal of positive reinforcement for
following these rules and not make a fuss about other rules or behavior unless, of course, the
child is doing something unsafe—hurting someone or destroying something. A parent of a
fifteen-month-old might have such rules as, "You don't climb on a glass table," or "You don't
run away from me in a parking lot, you hold my hand instead."

Parents often have rules that protect the property of others. For example, "Don't go in your
brother's room when he has asked you not to as it upsets him," or "Don't touch the VCR when
I have told you it is forbidden." "No's" are kept to a minimum. When a parent has forbidden
an activity, he or she should try to move the child away from the temptation. So, at this age
parents have two or three rules, and they emphasize these rules by giving many rewards for
following them.

I think eighteen-month-olds have their own agendas. Although they have temper tantrums,
the tantrums are not extreme. I advise parents to handle such tantrums by distractions. Chil-

(continued)

A final essential quality in parenting at this age is the parent's ability to match his
or her behavior to the child's personality and particular needs. What is most helpful
for one child is not necessarily best for another. For example, highly active toddlers
will explore the environment most widely when parents give little stimulation or
direction and let the child control the activity. Less active toddlers require just the
opposite behavior and explore most widely when parents are more stimulating.[30]

As the child's independence increases, the mother's behavior shifts. There is less
physical contact, less caretaking, less specific help, more verbal stimulation, more
reasoning with the child, and more verbal feedback as to what is correct. The mother
serves as a mediator between the child and the environment. Her way of interacting
and playing with objects and toys serves as a model for the child.[31]

dren of this age are easily distracted, and a parent can pick them up, sing to them, introduce a new toy, and so forth.

It's enormously important that early in the second year, parents include structure and routine in the child's day. Children learn from this structure and from the environment their parents create for them. A few parents go to one of two extremes—either no structure so the child runs wild or too much structure so the child is limited physically.

Children love movement. Parents must consider this love of movement when making the rules. Children should have an opportunity to be active. For many eighteen-month-olds, just pushing their own strollers is a great activity.

Two-year-olds are vulnerable children, and their parents are vulnerable too. Two-year-olds need to assert themselves, and they are negativistic. Although the child needs structure, that structure must be tempered by what is happening with the child on that particular day. Thus parents need to be far more flexible with children of this age than with younger children.

Although parents never know what will set a two-year-old off, they are more effective as they become sensitive to the child's messages or signals. Clearly, safety rules and personal property rules remain no matter what, but parents can be flexible about routines. For example, a two-year-old may decide she has to wear a dress instead of overalls to day care. I don't think it is worth arguing with the child about this type of issue. We want to help the child to assume some responsibility. In choosing a dress, she is assuming responsibility for her behavior, so we should respect her choice.

With a two-year-old, on certain issues, like safety issues, a parent cannot be flexible and cannot give in. The parent must be firm and insist that the rule be followed. As a result, the child may lose emotional control. If the child has a tantrum, the child has a tantrum. A parent picks up the child and moves him or her to a safe spot. In a parking lot, the parent picks up the child. On a glass table, the parent removes the child. If that leads to six tantrums, the parent accepts that. When the parent is firm, the child gets the message.

I think parents become afraid of tantrums, particularly tantrums that occur in public. My advice is not to be afraid. The child will not die from a tantrum. It is most important that a parent exert control on safety issues. If it is not a safety issue, my advice is to be flexible.

Parents of children at this age seem to have certain things they find troublesome. I know mothers who do not care about sleep behavior—where or when the child sleeps. One mother said, "If he wants to go to bed at 11, that's okay. But meatime behavior is really important to

(continued)

As children spend more time in independent activity, parents intervene to stop them when their activity is not approved. In one study of two-year-olds, mothers intervened every 6 to 8 minutes to stop a behavior or give a command.[32] Mothers were more likely to interfere with the activities of boys.

In several studies concerning toddlers' compliance in avoiding certain objects and remaining in certain areas, researchers found that a preventive approach on the mother's part increased compliance. Suggesting new activities was a most effective way to prevent disapproved behavior. In grocery stores, mothers diverted children's attention away from disapproved objects, gave toddlers approved activities like helping pick out an object, and gave positive attention to the help toddlers gave. Physical punishment tended to produce the lowest level of compliance.[33]

INTERVIEW with Clair Kopp *continued*

me. I want him to sit down and eat with the family." Fine. That is structure. As I have said already, there has to be structure in a child's life so the child can learn self-control. First, structure comes from the outside. Then structure comes from the inside. And children need the structure of rules. What is important is that something in the child's life is repeated every day or every other day. Then the child learns there is a routine.

Organization comes not only from structure in what people do but also from structure in the child's inanimate world. For example, parents organize toys so they are not scattered all over the house. When mom says, "Clean up," or when dad says, "Time to put the toys away," they give children an important message about family values. It is not so important that the toys are put away, but it is important for children to learn that, in their family, things have a place. Thus, self-control is learned in structure in the inanimate world as well as in behavior and routines.

Although mothers are often inconsistent from day to day, parents should try for more consistency instead of less. It would take a robot to be perfectly consistent, so parents need not behave exactly the same way every time something comes up. I think parents have to recognize that sometimes a crisis occurs or sometimes they wake up feeling terrible. They cannot be tied to a rigid, inflexible schedule, but they do have to see that there is organization in the child's life.

Somewhere between the ages of two and three, children begin to understand that there are rules. Parents can make it easier for children to adopt the rules. When cleaning up, for example, parents can say, "Do it," or they can make a game of it, saying, "Pick up all the red toys first," or, "Pick up all the trucks first." Parents can think of strategies to help the child get through the task so the rules are fun, not albatrosses.

At around two and one-half to three years old, the use of reasons becomes very, very important. The reasons need not be elaborate. When the child puts toys away, parents can say, "We put them away so you will know where they are tomorrow when you want your doll," or "We put the toys away so someone doesn't fall on them." In the best of situations, the rules come before the act. With safety issues, however, parents sometimes have to act first and give explanations later.

So between ages two and three, it is most important for parents to make tasks more acceptable, and more fun, and to give reasons. Reasons are important because they provide clues for figuring out what to do in a new situation. In a year or two, the child may be able to reason independently, building on the clues parents have given.

This interview is continued in Chapter 8.

George Holden and Meredith West write:

Child compliance, though a highly attainable goal, requires not only parents to discipline their children but to be disciplined themselves in order to maintain the level of attention and involvement necessary for successful interactions. The more compliant behavior of the 3-year-old children indicates that the intense involvement mothers need for 2-year-olds lessens in only a year.[34]

Children's developing behaviors are not the only source of change in the quality of the mother-child relationship. Mothers' reactions to the children's changes as well as events in the mothers' own lives produce changes in the attachment relationship. In one study, a large percentage of infants who changed from secure attachments at twelve months to **anxious-resistant attachments** at eighteen months had single mothers who were not involved with men and were not getting emotional support in mothering, or were single mothers for the first six months of the infants' lives and then married.[35] Mothers may then have had less energy for the parent-child bond. Those infants who changed from secure attachments at twelve months to **anxious-avoidant attachments** at eighteen months generally had mothers who were aggressive, suspicious, tense, and irritable. They disliked motherhood and showed little interest or delight in their developing child though they were knowledgable about child development and were effective caregivers.

Those infants who had positive changes from anxious attachments at twelve months to secure attachments at eighteen months had mothers who initially lacked confidence and interest in being a mother. As babies grew and mothers gained experience and confidence in their effectiveness, their relationships with their children improved. Thus, we can see that a critical variable in the attachment relationship is the emotional involvement, interest, and delight the mother takes in the child. This diminishes when mothers lack confidence or interest.

When mothers perceive their six-month-old infant as difficult, they tend to persist in this view of the child into the toddler years.[36] Objective observers support the mother's impressions. Mothers and difficult children get into a vicious cycle in which children approach mild trouble—breaking a household rule or causing mild damage—about every 5 minutes. Mothers then react intensely even though the child has not actually carried out the act. Children then resist the mother's efforts at control, further irritating mothers. Easy or average toddlers are more responsive to mothers' efforts at control. Social support for mothers helps to counteract the effects of a difficult temperament in the child. The support increases the mother's feelings of self-esteem and protects against feelings of helplessness that the difficult temperament can create.

Like the infant, the toddler is attached to both parents, but the role of each parent may be different. Mothers are primarily nurturers and caregivers. Fathers tend to take the role of playmates who teach children how to get along with others. Through physical play, infants and toddlers learn how to interpret others' emotional signals and how others respond to theirs so that social competence grows.[37] As children grow, mothers spend less time in caregiving, and their interactions with children become similar to those of fathers.

The amount of time fathers spend with children and their involvement in caregiving activities are not so important for toddler development as the qualitative aspects of the relationship.[38] Fathers who are sensitive to their children's needs, who are not bothered by the childish behavior of their children or their own lack of knowledge about parenting, and who encourage toddlers, have children who are securely attached to them, positive in mood, and persistent at tasks. Thus, sensitive fathering, like sensitive mothering, has an important impact on toddler development.

Development of the Self

From age twelve months to eighteen months, toddlers develop a clearer sense of self-permanence than they previously had. They recognize themselves in pictures and videotapes, smiling, gazing, and pointing at their pictures when their names are called. Toddlers are most attuned to characteristics of sex and age and distinguish themselves from other babies on the bases of their physical features.[39]

From eighteen to twenty-four months of age, babies have a greater sense of self. Not only do they recognize themselves in mirrors, but they react to what they see. For example, if they see rouge on their noses, they immediately try to get it off. By twenty-four months, they will begin to use pronouns like "I," "Me," and "Mine" to reflect this increasing sense of self.[40] Self-descriptive statements like "I play" and "I run" increase at this age, reflecting a growing sense of self-awareness. The child is now aware of physical qualities ("I have blond hair") as well as action capabilities ("I play," "I go to sleep").[41]

Development of Self-Regulation

From nine to eighteen months of age, children are in the **control** phase.[42] They are integrating physical, motor, social, and cognitive functioning. As they become more active physically and explore the world as active performers, their sense of self becomes stronger. Although children first show control by following the requests of others, they soon begin to inhibit their activities on their own volition. For example, a toddler of fifteen or sixteen months may reach for an object, shake her head, and say, "No, no." Toddlers are most successful in avoiding forbidden activities when they direct their attention away from these objects or activities—looking elsewhere, playing with their hands, finding an acceptable substitute toy. A substantial number of two-year-olds can wait, alone, as long as 4 minutes, before receiving permission to touch.[43]

The child's development of control is influenced by other individual characteristics—for example, recall capacity, motor activity, language development. As children's enjoyment of motor activity increases, it is harder to inhibit behavior. Memory capacity is limited, making it harder for children to recall the rules to counteract the pleasure of movement. An increasing grasp of language allows the child to recall and apply the rules.

The capacity for control seems to develop from reciprocal interactions between parents and children. When parents and infants alternate behaviors, children learn to pay more attention to what parents do. This, in turn, makes children more aware of their participation in activity and perhaps better able to control their behavior, because they have had experience in taking turns and waiting.

The ages from twenty-four to thirty-six months make up the fourth or **self-control** phase.[44] The self is more firmly established now, and children show the capacity to comply with requests, to inhibit or delay activities. They can behave according to social expectations even when a parent is not physically present to monitor what is happening. The self-control phase differs from the control phase because it includes representational thinking. The child can remember sequences of action, can recall the mother's comments even when not looking at her. Conversely, the self-control phase differs from the **self-regulation** phase that begins at thirty-six months mainly in terms of flexibility. A two-year-old cannot wait or delay action well and is less flexible in adapting behavior to the social situation than a three-year-old. Even though children understand routines and rules, any strong stimulus can tempt them to forbidden behavior—a two-year-old, for example, may run into the street to pursue a prized ball.

As children grow and move through the control and self-control phases, their behavior shows increasing compliance with others' requests. Age brings not only compliance but also more sophisticated forms of noncompliance. Younger toddlers use avoidance as a way of escaping a task, whereas older ones focus on the task and use words to avoid what they are told to do. They filibuster so that the task is not done.[45]

Compliance is a complicated task in which the child has to have a clear concept of the exact outcome the adult wishes. Then the child has to focus on the outcome and direct his or her behavior toward achieving it, correcting any mistakes along the way. Merry Bullock and Paul Lutkenhaus observed the development of these abilities in toddlers fifteen to thirty-five months old.[46] They showed the children exactly how to stack blocks to make a tower, exactly how to wash a blackboard, and exactly how to arrange blocks in a square. They found that younger toddlers are activity-oriented and get lost in the process of what they are doing. Even if they achieve the correct solution, they do not stop but continue on with the activity itself.

As they get older, toddlers develop a clearer conception of the outcome or criteria. They are able to separate the achievement into several separate acts; and if they make a mistake, they go back and correct the one part. They know when they have met the standard and stop. Toddlers light up with pleasure when they examine their handi-work and see that they have accomplished what they set out to.

Parents and caregivers foster self-control and the development of self-regulation when they model appropriate behaviors, when they use language to explain what they want, when they state their expectations and the reasons for them as clearly as they can. Stressful events alter levels of control. When family functioning is disrupted and parents interact less with children, explaining less to them, children's self-control decreases.

We can see that development of self-control depends on the development of the child's abilities in motor, physical, language, and cognitive areas as well as on characteristics of the parents and the family environment.

Sexual Identity

Children are not born with a sense of sexual identity. The social environment, including parents, other adults, peers, and siblings, surround children with information about what it means to be a boy or a girl, a man or a woman in this particular culture. The child evolves a sense of sexual identity; and at about two to two and a half, proudly announces, "I am a boy" or "I am a girl." By the age of four, it is as difficult for a child to change gender identity as it is for an adult. John Money states that gender differentiation results from an interaction of physical, psychological, and social forces.[47]

Physical influences include genes, which in utero trigger hormones that lead to the development of both internal reproductive organs and external sex organs. Assignment of sex at birth is determined by the physical characteristics of the genitals. Societies and subcultures within societies have beliefs about what is appropriate for boys and girls. Once a child is designated a boy or girl, that child will be dressed, played with, and caressed in particular ways. Parents expect and approve specific behaviors from each sex.

A 1978 study found that children as young as three years of age agree on what is expected of boys and girls, both in the present and in the future.[48] Boys are active builders who help father and behave aggressively; girls are talkative, help mother, play quietly, never hit, but ask for help. Men are bosses, mow the grass, and can be doctors and pilots; women clean house, rear babies, and are nurses and teachers. Those who hope for less sex stereotyping of behavior in the future will be encouraged by the fact that boys and girls believe that both sexes have a common core of positive and negative traits—both sexes are described as strong, kind, fast runners, unafraid, messy, dirty, smart, and quiet. In addition, boys and girls have positive beliefs about their own sex, valuing traits associated with being a boy or a girl. Neither sex feels slighted; in fact, they tend to view the opposite sex as less favored than they are.

How do children use all the information provided to arrive at a sense of sexual identity? Beverly Fagot and Mary Leinbach believe that parents begin sex-typing behavior, perhaps without realizing it, by responding in an emotionally positive way to the child's appropriate sex-typed activities and appropriate object choices.[49] Parents encourage boys to manipulate objects and to learn about the world and discourage them from expressing feelings and asking for help. Parents encourage girls to ask for help and to help with tasks. Parents criticize girls for running, jumping, climbing, and manipulating objects.

Through parents' emotional responses toddlers learn that parents value certain behaviors, and children learn the appropriate gender labels for those behaviors. Sex role education begins with the parent's positive or negative emotional response. When the child learns the label, then he or she can organize behavior in terms of whether it is appropriate or not for that label.

Some parents begin sex-typing behavior early, and their toddlers are early (before twenty-seven months) to learn labels and are more sex-typed in their activities and choices of toys than are toddlers of parents who start later and learn labels later (after twenty-seven months). At age four the early labelers and the later labelers are similar in behavior and choice of toys, but the early labelers are more aware of sexual stereotypes.

Parents can help children build a firm, positive sexual identity by giving an emotionally positive response when both boys and girls show qualities of strength, kindness, emotional responsiveness, intelligence, confidence, and competence.

INTERVIEW
with Judy Dunn

Judy Dunn is professor of human development and director of the Center for the Study of Child and Adolescent Development at The Pennsylvania State University.

What are the most important ways to help children have satisfying relationships with brothers and sisters?

It is reassuring for parents to learn how common it is for brothers and sisters not to get on. They fight a great deal. The main variable is the children's personality. This child is one way and that child is another, and they don't get along. They don't have any choice about living together, and so it's easy to see why they don't get on. It is such a "No holds barred" relationship. There are no inhibitions, and both boys and girls can be very aggressive.

It is reassuring for parents to know that fights occur not just in their family. No one really knows what goes on in other families, and so you think it is just in your own. But children can fight a lot and still end up with a close relationship.

When there is the birth of a new sibling, keep the level of attention and affection as high as possible for the firstborn. I think it's almost impossible to give too much attention to the first child at this time.

Also, keep their life as similar as possible. Routine things matter a lot to little children. They like predictability. The mother structures their whole world, so that after a baby comes, they can be upset just by any changes mother makes in their routine.

In middle childhood, there is a strong association between sibling fights and feelings that the other child is favored by the parent or parents. It is important to be aware how early and how sensitive children are to what goes on between parents and children. It is never too early for parents to think about the effects of what they are doing on the other child. So always be aware of how sensitive children are and avoid favoritism.

Sibling Relationships

Growing up with brothers and sisters has long-lasting effects on children.[50] The relationships among siblings are emotional, intense, affectionate, but sometimes aggressive and full of conflict. Older siblings teach young siblings; they model activities for them. Sometimes they care for them and protect them; sometimes they fight.

How well siblings get along depends not only on the parent-child relationship, but also on the children's gender and temperament. Because most firstborns have mixed feelings about new brothers and sisters, arguing is not uncommon as they all grow up. Although psychologists have focused heavily on the feelings of jealousy, aggression, and rivalry among siblings, they are now turning to the many positive features of sibling relationships.

Older siblings, three and four, can act as substitute attachment figures for their toddler siblings in the absence of the mother.[51] Even young toddlers show positive feelings toward their older siblings, miss them when they are gone, and try to comfort them when they are in difficulty. We now know that youger toddler siblings engage in more advanced behavior with their older siblings than was previously thought possible for children of this age. They play in more complicated and imaginative ways. Toddlers are also capable of teasing older siblings in clever ways. They learn about family rules and are adept at getting mothers involved when the firstborn has violated a rule, but not when they themselves have. They learn to pay careful attention to the feelings and intentions of others. They learn to stand up for their own rights and argue persuasively with their siblings, and so their social reasoning and ability to protect their own interests increase. They also become skilled in giving sympathy and support to others.[52]

In this chapter we focus on the older child's reaction to the birth of a sibling since a toddler between one and three often experiences the arrival of a new brother or sister.[53] Most firstborn children under five show signs of upset after the baby's birth. The most common change, shown by 93 percent of children in one study, was an increase in misbehavior—refusing to follow rules and regular routines, being demanding when the mother was interacting with the baby. Over 50 percent of the children became more clinging and dependent. Many experienced changes in sleeping and toileting behavior. Most of these problems disappeared in eight or nine months.

Robert Stewart and his coworkers found there was some tendency for firstborns to imitate the newborn's behavior right after the birth—wanting bottles and seeking to eat, toilet, and play like a newborn—but these behaviors began to decrease after the first month or so.[54]

Positive changes occur as well. Eighty-two percent of two- to four-year-old firstborns had positive feelings about being a big brother or sister one month before the birth, and 80 percent remained positive in the first year. They most enjoyed cuddling and smiling with the baby. They reported being upset by the baby's crying, which decreased in the first twelve months and the infant's increasing interference with their toys and play.

Though upset at times, all firstborns reported helping with the baby, and 95 percent of mothers reported that they did. They got diapers, soothed the baby, and occupied the infant while the mother was busy. Most mothers (75 percent) reported that the two shared and played well by the end of the first year. The fact that 63 percent of firstborns wanted another sibling at the end of the first year suggests that overall it was a positive experience for them.

Many factors influence how firstborns will relate to the child. Children who are most likely to be upset at the birth of a sibling are those who are already irritable, sensitive, difficult to manage, and inclined to engage in many confrontations with their mothers. When mothers are unusually tired or depressed following the birth of the sibling, negative reactions are more common among firstborns. When fathers have close relationships with firstborns, the latter tend to have less conflict with their mothers following the birth of the sibling.

Family life with siblings is an intense experience in which children learn about emotions, both their own and others'. They are learning about rules, about what is approved and disapproved, and how to handle conflict with mothers and brothers and sisters. Their emotional range expands as they engage in teasing as well as in offering support and sympathy.

Peers

Though children at about ten months of age show curiosity and interest in each other, toddlers of thirteen months seem to go through a period of "stranger anxiety" with their peers.[55] When a strange peer and mother enter a playroom where the toddler and mother are playing, the toddler freezes, becomes inhibited, seeks close physical contact with mother. This reaction passes with time. When two-year-old toddlers with clear self-definition play, they appear to be wary of each other initially, but then go through a ritual of defining their own territory by claiming toys.[56] Once this is done with several exclamations of "Mine," positive interaction occurs. Claiming toys in this situation does not appear to be selfishness but rather a sign of progressive development. By the time peers are thirty months of age, they are more comfortable in each other's company.[57] They explore more of the environment together and increase their distance from mothers. Their play with objects is reality oriented—blocks are used for building, toy cars are used as cars. There is little fantasy in their play.

Carollee Howes studied social behavior of toddlers and preschoolers aged one to five years in a day care center. She found that in the early toddler period from thirteen to twenty-four months, children who engaged in complementary and reciprocal play, taking turns and interacting with others, were the children who, as cognitive abilities developed, engaged in social pretend play in the late toddler period from twenty-four to thirty-six months. Teachers described these children as sociable, and the children themselves entered into groups of other children easily. The social competence that these children showed early in toddlerhood persisted to the preschool period.

Howes observed that when given free access to children on a daily basis, toddlers form stable friendships that persist for as long as a year. Between 50 percent and 70 percent of reciprocated friendships lasted at least a year, and 10 percent lasted two years. Further, these friendships are important emotional attachments for the children. When children remained with the same group of friends or moved with their group of friends, their play remained reciprocal and interactive. When a change occurred without a friend or a friend moved, play became less interactive. It is important for parents to realize the depths of these relationships for some children.

The quality in relationships with peers is influenced by relationships in the family.[59] Toddlers who have secure attachments with their mothers are more sociable, more friendly and cooperative with their peers than those lacking strong attachments. Children who have anxious-resistance attachments to mothers are the most negative with peers, keeping a distance from them, not responding to them. "Only" children are more sociable and outgoing with peers than children who have siblings. Firstborn toddlers are next most sociable, and later borns are least outgoing. It may be that later-born children have had more negative social experiences with older siblings and are more wary with peers, uncertain of what they will do.[60] We see, though, that experience within the family creates ways of relating to others in the world outside.

Even young toddlers show positive feelings toward their older siblings, miss them when they are gone, and try to comfort them when they are in difficulty. How well siblings get along is partly determined by the parent-child relationship.

PARENTING TASKS

One of the caregiver's basic functions, according to Burton White, is to design the child's world and daily life (see Figure 7-1). Even before a baby begins to crawl, parents must babyproof the living area, both indoors and outside, removing all harmful objects and substances.[62] Medicines, cleaning substances, paints, and all other dangerous materials must be put far beyond the child's reach, perhaps even locked up. Electric outlets in use should be concealed behind heavy pieces of furniture, and those not in use should be babyproofed with plastic outlet covers. And remember, too, that even the loveliest plant may be poisonous—check to make sure that none of yours is. Babyproofing is essential because children must have freedom to explore. Toddlers can climb and reach further than you expect, so great care must be used. White recommends against the use of playpens, jumpseats, and gates that restrict exploration.

Carew, Chan, and Halfar find that optimal intellectual growth is fostered by parents who organize a daily schedule that enables the child to be involved in doing and learning much of the time. And these parents encourage children to help with

FIGURE 7-1
CHILDPROOFING THE HOUSE

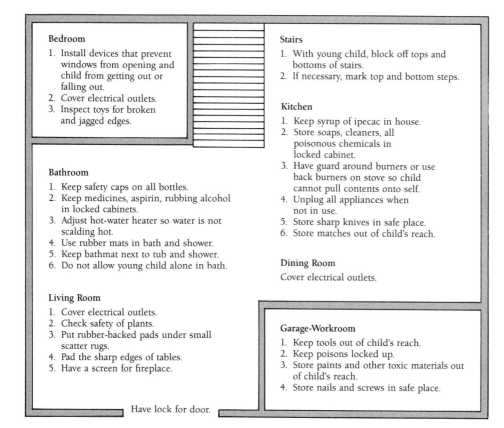

Bedroom
1. Install devices that prevent windows from opening and child from getting out or falling out.
2. Cover electrical outlets.
3. Inspect toys for broken and jagged edges.

Bathroom
1. Keep safety caps on all bottles.
2. Keep medicines, aspirin, rubbing alcohol in locked cabinets.
3. Adjust hot-water heater so water is not scalding hot.
4. Use rubber mats in bath and shower.
5. Keep bathmat next to tub and shower.
6. Do not allow young child alone in bath.

Living Room
1. Cover electrical outlets.
2. Check safety of plants.
3. Put rubber-backed pads under small scatter rugs.
4. Pad the sharp edges of tables.
5. Have a screen for fireplace.

Have lock for door.

Stairs
1. With young child, block off tops and bottoms of stairs.
2. If necessary, mark top and bottom steps.

Kitchen
1. Keep syrup of ipecac in house.
2. Store soaps, cleaners, all poisonous chemicals in locked cabinet.
3. Have guard around burners or use back burners on stove so child cannot pull contents onto self.
4. Unplug all appliances when not in use.
5. Store sharp knives in safe place.
6. Store matches out of child's reach.

Dining Room
Cover electrical outlets.

Garage-Workroom
1. Keep tools out of child's reach.
2. Keep poisons locked up.
3. Store paints and other toxic materials out of child's reach.
4. Store nails and screws in safe place.

General
1. Install smoke alarms in house.
2. Have fire extinguishers.
3. Plan fire escape routes.
4. Keep poison control, fire and police department numbers by the telephone.

Adapted from *Working Mother,* October 1985.

household activities.[63] Briggs suggests that parents permit children as much independence as possible in the daily routine—giving children time to move from one activity to another and letting them set timers that will ring when it is time to eat or to take a bath or when they must stop playing.[64] When routines must be done, she advises making positive suggestions in impersonal terms, "Time to wash hands," rather than giving orders, "Go wash your hands." Making a game of a routine can help it move smoothly, she believes. Instead of "Come in for lunch," a parent might say "Let's be birdies and fly in to lunch."

THE JOYS OF PARENTING TODDLERS

"I enjoy the way she enjoys nature. She hears everything—the wind, the birds, a squirrel high up in the trees." MOTHER

"I enjoy the way she connects so well to everyone. She respects each person. She's outgoing, she likes people. She has a talk with each one and brings them a present. I also enjoy seeing her and her father together. To hear them talk together, to see her father so happy with her all the time is a great joy." MOTHER

"I enjoy that she directs me more than I could sense. Before, there was a 'Yes' or 'No' response, but now there is more back and forth. If I dress her, she shows me she wants to sit or stand—'Do it this way' is what she seems to say. Before, she was tired or not tired, hungry or not hungry, okay or not okay. Now there is much more variation." FATHER

"There is the excitement of baby talk becoming real words." MOTHER

"What I appreciate about this age is that he is so into exploring everything about the world. He'll try everything. He has no preconceived ideas—he's so willing, so open, so excited. He loves his vitamin pill, and he gets so excited about it. When he can do something, he is so proud. The look on his face when he can feed himself pasta is so special." MOTHER

"I like sharing, teaching him. His attention span is limited now, but he does imitate us completely. I enjoy learning about myself as I see him with me and with my parents." FATHER

"It is wonderful now, he comes into a room and sees me, and he runs across the room and yells, 'Daddy,' and leaps on me. I like that. Or we had company, and I came down the stairs and he started to say over and over my whole name—'Michael_____. Michael_____.' I like that." FATHER

"To see him put ideas together, to see him remember something that happened one time four months ago and tell us about it—I am sure all children do these things, but they continue to be the miracle of this evolving person and who he is; it's such a thrill. The four-month thing came up yesterday because we were talking about his old day-care person. In the summer we went to visit her, and I took her fresh-ground coffee. Yesterday I told him we were going to see her, and he said, 'Oh, I want to take her ground coffee.' It just came out of the blue, and that was four or so months ago. There's a real person who remembers things that are important and significant to him." MOTHER

"I have these proud father moments every now and then when I think, 'That's my boy!' Those are wonderful. One happened a few months ago. We had some people here, and some were English-speaking and some were Spanish-speaking. I was speaking to one of the men in English, and Alexander came in. The man asked his age, and I said, 'He's two.' The man said hello to him and asked him if he could count, and Alexander said, 'Yes.' I asked him if he wanted to count, and Alexander said, 'Uno, dos, tres . . .' and rattled off one to ten in Spanish. We have this Spanish counting game. The man said, 'Bueno,' and I was very proud of him. 'That's my boy!' I was kind of amazed because I knew he could, but I never expected he would." FATHER

"He is kind of aggressive and wants what he wants; but a few weeks ago at a play group, there was another child who was looking for a particular piece for a toy he had, and he was crying because he could not find it. A woman said, 'Oh, I see you're upset because you can't find that. Maybe we can help you find it.' Meanwhile, Alexander heard the conversation and knew where the piece was and went and got it and gave it to the other boy, and I thought, 'oh, wonderful.'" MOTHER

"I've heard of this, and it's true; it's rediscovering the child in yourself. Sometimes, it's the joy that he and I hop around the couch like two frogs on our hands and knees. Or we're in the bathtub pretending we are submarines and alligators. Sometimes he likes to ride around on my shoulders, and I run and make noises like an airplane or a bird. And I am not just doing it for him, but we are doing it together, playing together." FATHER

"The joy comes from the things we do as a family, the three of us—going to see Santa Claus together or to see miniature trains and take a ride. Early in the morning we have a ritual. When he gets up, early, he has a bottle of milk and gets in bed with us; the lights are out, and we are lying in bed, and he tells us his dreams and we watch the light outside and see the trees and see the sun come up. We do that in the morning, and it is a quiet joy." FATHER

"When he began to learn words, he said the dog's name, but he called her 'Hotcha' for Sasha. And then he learned how to say it correctly, and he would say it all day long, 'Sasha.' I remember the first moment when I knew he understood language in that sense. One time we were in one room, and across the next room, outside on the deck, Sasha scratched at the door to come in; and he heard her. I heard her too, and he looked at me and said, 'Sasha,' as if to say 'Sasha wants to come in.' For the first time it was a definite, clear communication to do with Sasha, and that was wonderful." MOTHER

"I was just blown away by the way he tries to help other children. From a very young age, he has done this. Now, when a little girl he sees every day cries, he takes her one toy after another, and says, 'This is? This is?' meaning 'Is this what you want?' until he gets her to stop crying by giving her something she wants. He's very people-oriented, very affectionate, and seems so secure." MOTHER

"She is such a little girl, and she has a strong desire to be like me. She wants to put on my high heels, she wants to drape my clothes around her neck. She wants to do everything I do. If I am cooking, she wants to cook. She can do things boys do, like throw balls or garden with her father, but she does it the way I do. She wants me to be involved in what she does; she wants to show me everything she does, and she wants to be with me. If I or her father walk in the room, she drops everything and comes to us." MOTHER

continued

THE JOYS OF PARENTING TODDLERS *continued*

"The things that children do, you know they understand, but they haven't got the words to say what they want, so they tell you in the other things they do. They let you know they understand. It is so exciting to see her grow, and say, 'Yes, daddy.' At thirty-one months, they are so smart, they comprehend so much; but they cannot convey it in words. You see it in their actions." FATHER

"As a father of two boys, then a girl, it is really a joy the way she relates to me. I think of her at work, and when I come home, she sees me, and has a big smile, and runs and grabs me and says, 'Hi, daddy.' My boys did not do that; they were interested in their activities. If I'm sitting in a chair, she comes and climbs on me. It's very special." FATHER

"Watching her grow, seeing the different stages, I just take pleasure in every thing she does now, because I know she will be on to a new stage soon." MOTHER

Intellectual Growth

Parents can stimulate growth by sharing the toddler's enthusiasm and interest in what he or she is doing. When children express curiosity about an activity or object, parents can arrange time for exploration. Reading to the child gives the child information about the world by presenting new objects and activities. It is also a source of information about how people respond to challenges, difficulties, losses, pleasure, and fun. The sharing and close physical contact provide happy times for parents and children and contribute to warm emotional ties between them.

It is important for children to have games, toys, and books available. But White believes that during toddlerhood parents need not worry about providing elaborate educational toys or detailed explanations and/or discussions in response to questions. Carew, Chan, and Halfar note that an intellectually stimulating environment for children includes only educational television programs, like "Sesame Street" and "Mr. Rogers' Neighborhood." The child who spends time in passive activity has less time for active involvement with the world.

Language Growth

Mabel Rice describes ways parents can stimulate language.

The best way to encourage development of language is to provide many opportunities for a child to interact with objects and events and other children. Children's play is a primary source of language enrichment. Adult-directed teaching drills are not appropriate. In other words, most children do not need to be taught language, but they do need opportunities to develop language. The role of the adult in language facilitation is to follow the child's interests, paraphrase what the child says with simple elaborations, and interact in a conversational manner about objects and events on which the child's attention is focused. Also, children do not always need to respond in order to learn new language skills. They can benefit greatly by the opportunity to absorb conversations of others. At the same time, they do need opportunities to practice expressing words and sentences when they are ready to do so. An easy way to allow for opportunities is to provide pauses in conversations with children; in other words, for adults to refrain from doing all the talking.[65]

Social-Emotional Growth

As in infancy, parents are consistent caregivers who react promptly to toddlers and do not expect children to wait while parents satisfy their own needs first. White cautions parents, "Be careful as the child passes the first birthday not to let yourself become the child's all-purpose tool. Watch for subtle differences between (a) use of you when a child has determined he can't handle a task himself versus (b) use of you as the easiest way to achieve a goal, or (c) use of you simply to monopolize your attention: (a) is fine, but (b) and (c) lead to an overindulged child."[66] Parents establish a firm and consistent family routine and back up words with action when necessary.

Parents who expect the toddler's negativism and understand that this period will not last forever can weather the stage without being overwhelmed by the child's attempt at independence. While it is important to be firm on family limits, White believes that on less important issues it is useful to let children win some arguments so that they can see that their behavior has an effect on parents. Briggs suggests other ways parents can help toddlers to confirm their separateness as individuals. Parents can, for example, invent games that permit children to practice their negativism: "Do chickies go bow-wow?" Parents can also support children in their desires to have and protect their possessions. Children, she believes, must possess before they can share with others. White suggests, for example, that parents ask a child whether she wants to put her toys away when other children play in her room, so her rights are protected.

Play and positive feelings increase children's compliance. Though studies were carried out with preschoolers, the results appear applicable to toddlers as well. When mothers played with children 10 to 15 minutes per day in a nondirective, responsive manner, following the child's lead, when possible being a partner in the play, avoiding commands or questions, just being there, children's compliance in a laboratory task increased. To demonstrate that the positive feelings aroused in play were the important feature in the compliance, Keng-Ling Lay, Everett Waters, and Kathryn Park induced a positive, happy mood, telling children to recall an event that made them feel good or excited.[67] When feeling positive, children complied in a fraction of the time and picked up twice as many blocks as did children encouraged to have a negative mood. So playing with children brings benefits beyond the pleasures of the moment.

Toward the end of the toddler period, parents need to encourage children's social interactions with peers, if these have not developed already, and their emerging interests in creative, imaginative activities such as drawing and role playing.

White believes that as parents facilitate a child's development they need to achieve a balance among three areas—developing physical abilities, exploring the world, and attending to other people, particularly the caregiver.[68] None should be emphasized to the exclusion of the others. Parents must be alert to their own inclinations to encourage boys to excel in motor skills and exploration, and girls to excel in social interactions. Children of both sexes need both kinds of experiences.

ROUTINES, PROBLEMS, AND STRATEGIES

The main parenting tasks in this period are to continue to provide a safe emotional atmosphere for secure attachments with all family members and to provide secure limits within which the child is free to explore and develop skills and abilities independently. Those strategists who focus on feelings increase the child's feelings of selfhood and autonomy as they listen to the child's reactions and help the child label them. Dreikurs and the behaviorists are most helpful in their counsel on establishing fair and firm limits and helping children conform their behavior to the limits.

Eating

At about a year of age children are likely to grab the spoon from the parent who is trying to feed them—they want to try to feed themselves. The exact age at which a child has the physical skill to get food in her mouth varies. Benjamin Spock believes the most important determiner of self-feeding skill is the young child's opportunity to feed himself or herself.[69] If she gets finger food during the first year, she may be ready early to use a spoon for other foods. Spock encourages parents to let their children feed themselves at twelve to fifteen months. If parents wait, they may find that their two-year-olds expect to be fed.

Ilg and Ames encourage parents to let children have their own eating rituals and preferences.[70] During toddlerhood, children often want particular plates or glasses. They may think of some foods as appropriate only for breakfast and want other foods only at lunch or dinner. When parents permit the child to make such choices, the resulting sense of autonomy reinforces feelings of competence and self-esteem. Some parents worry when a child eats the same foods over and over. You do need to be sure that the child has a balanced diet, but there is always time to introduce variety later.

All methods suggest patience and understanding in helping children to learn how to eat. Most eating problems during toddlerhood are related to the mechanics of eating—the child is still developing the skills needed to get food to the mouth without dropping or spilling it and the control needed to sit quietly at the table. All schools encourage independence in eating. Even a two-year-old can be told how to get his or her own drink of water in the bathroom or to get a piece of fruit from the kitchen table. The parent's work is reduced and the child's self-esteem grows.

In conflicts, Gordon is more likely than other strategists to seek a solution that satisfies everyone's needs.[71] He gives the example of the toddler who left his bottle on a new rug in the living room. Milk leaked through the hole in the nipple and stained the rug. The mother made the hole in the nipple smaller, but still it leaked. She finally solved the problem by putting water in the bottles that he sucked in the living room, so that when they leaked no stain remained. She gave him milk in the bottles he drank elsewhere. Both mother and son were happy with the solution.

When a child begins to sit at the table and eat with the family, a few simple rules should be established. Gordon suggests that if a child breaks a rule, the parent should send an immediate I-message expressing displeasure and should use active listening to understand the child's response. If, for example, a child reaches over and takes food from the mother's plate, the mother can take the food back and give the child food from the serving bowl. There is no need for words. This simple, immediate, nonverbal I-message is adequate.

Dreikurs believes children of this age can eat meals with the family as soon as they can feed themselves and can obey the rules established by the parents.[72] If they cannot feed themselves, they are fed before the family mealtimes so that their feeding does not disrupt family relationships. Mealtimes are opportunities for the family to share conversation and humor. Children's preferences are considered, and children are given small portions. But children must eat everything on their plates so that they will have a balanced diet. And they must behave well. No scolding, threats, or punishments are given. If rules are broken, children are sent from the table and will be permitted to join the family at dinner the next evening. If children do not come when called for dinner, their food is served cold. If children dawdle, their plate is picked up when the table is cleared, whether they are finished or not. Dreikurs pays attention to individual needs in making the rules, and children are expected to follow the rules without being reprimanded.

Behaviorists emphasize breaking the act of eating into small steps and giving reinforcement as each step is accomplished.[73] Thus, as a child learns to eat with a spoon or to hold his own glass, behaviorists recommend praise or other reward for attempts at independence, even if food is spilled or help is required. As the child's skill increases, parents reward complete success. Parents must be careful not to reinforce disapproved behavior. For example, if a child whines and cries for a cookie and then receives it, whining is rewarded. Parents can request that the child stop whining before he or she gets the cookie.

Sleeping

As noted in Chapter 6, children sleep best when they learn to fall asleep alone in their own beds, in a quiet, darkened room. When they awaken in the night briefly, as we all do, they can drop off to sleep again on their own.

Older infants, toddlers, and preschoolers often develop sleep time routines that they cannot duplicate on their own. So, when they wake up in the night and cannot go back to sleep, they cry, wanting comfort; or, if they are older, they crawl in their parents' bed for the rest of the night. Parents can change children's sleep associations, but they must see this change as one that is helpful for the child, not a deprivation, and they must accept some crying in the process of change.

It is easier to institute change when parents imagine the difficulties they would have learning to sleep without a pillow. They might find it very difficult the first several nights. They would toss and turn, not able to get comfortable; they would awake several times in the night. But gradually they would become used to sleeping without a pillow; they would drop off easily and not awaken completely in the night. The situation is the same for children when parents change their sleep routines. Children will be very uncomfortable in the beginning but will gradually learn new associations. Parents feel better about the change when they see themselves not as cruel and depriving parents, but as people who are helping the child to fall asleep in healthy ways that permit a better night's sleep.

Dr. Richard Ferber describes a gradual method for changing sleep routines.[74] He pays attention to the child's feelings and needs for security, at the same time setting limits in ways that shape the child's behavior. Parents should start this method only when they have the time and commitment to carry it out for several nights. Since it means that they will also go without sleep in the beginning, it is best to start on a weekend when not many stresses are present. First, parents must be sure children fall asleep alone in their rooms at night and at nap time without the presence of a parent. The main thrust of the program is to let the child cry for increasingly long periods of time before going in briefly to reassure the child he or she is not being abandoned. Parents can speak to the child for a minute or two, pat the child, but must leave again within two to three minutes while the child is still awake. Parents enter *not* to stop the crying or get the child to sleep, but only to reassure the child there is no abandonment. If the child continues to cry for 10 minutes, parents return, reassure the child again, and again leave. If the child is still crying at the end of 15 minutes, parents return and repeat the intervention. After that, parents go in every 15 minutes if the child is still crying. Any awakenings in the middle of the night are treated in exactly the same way. The same procedure is followed at nap times, but a child who is still crying at the end of an hour is allowed to get up. On subsequent nights, 5 minutes is added to each interval so that the first entry on the second night occurs after 10 minutes of crying, the second after 15 minutes, an all other entries after 20 minutes. By the end of seven days, parents wait for 35 minutes of crying before making the first entry, 40 minutes for the second, and 45 minutes for all other occurrences. Nap time intervals are treated the same as the night ones for that day, with the child always allowed to get up after an hour of crying.

But suppose children don't stay in bed. Suppose they are older and can crawl out. Parents enter the room as soon as they suspect the child is out of bed. They put the child back in bed and say if the child does not stay in bed, the door will be closed. Parents do not threaten or spank the child. They offer support at the time of learning a new habit—perhaps reflecting the child's feelings of anger, frustration, isolation. If the child gets up again, parents close the door and hold it closed for 1 minute. If the child is still up at the end of that minute, parents reenter, put the child back in bed and say the door will be closed for 2 minutes if the child gets up again. The third and subsequent times, the interval is extended to 5 minutes. Parents make clear to the child that the open door is under the child's control. The second night, the interval of door closing starts at 2 minutes and increases to 8 minutes. Box 7-1 describes the number of minutes on subsequent nights. This method is used in the middle of the night as well and at nap times.

Parents can note that Ferber's approach takes account of the child's feelings and

◆
BOX 7-1
HOW LONG TO CLOSE THE DOOR
IF YOUR CHILD WILL NOT STAY IN BED

		If your child continues to get out of bed			
Day	First Closing	Second Closing	Third Closing	Fourth Closing	Subsequent Closings
1	1	2	3	5	5
2	2	4	6	8	8
3	3	5	7	10	10
4	5	7	10	15	15
5	7	10	15	20	20
6	10	15	20	25	25
7	15	20	25	30	30

Richard Ferber, *Solve Your Child's Sleep Problems* (New York: Simon & Schuster, 1985), p. 79.

provides emotional support to the child at the time of change. It also uses behavioral principles to shape the child's behavior. Parents must be consistent in their use of this method and willing to lose their own sleep to help children learn healthy sleep habits. They also must involve any daytime caregivers who will have to follow the same procedures at nap time.

Dressing

Dressing is an activity that children master slowly. By eighteen months of age, children will try to undress themselves, pulling off socks and shoes, and by about age two, they will be able to take off all their clothes. Dressing, however, requires skill, and it is not until age three that children can put on an easy item like a jacket. At about age four or five, they can completely dress themselves, including tying their shoelaces.

Dressing can be fun for both parent and child. Children can learn colors as parents name them; they learn to manipulate zippers and snaps; they play disappearing and reappearing games as they poke hands and arms through shirts and sweaters. The parent's task is to permit children as much independence as possible in the process of dressing, but to give help when needed. To encourage independence, parents can buy clothes that are easy to get on—pants with elasticized waists, loose pull-on shirts with big necks. They can encourage self-dressing by putting the item partly on and letting the child complete the act. For example, a mother can help children get their feet in pants legs, then let children pull on the pants themselves.

In the toddler years, dressing problems are likely to center on children's refusing to dress themselves as they can, refusing to hurry and be ready to go somewhere, wearing too few clothes outdoors. Each of the strategists focuses on different aspects of the possible problems. Ginott advises giving young children responsibility for choosing what to wear, as long as the choices are warm enough and loose enough for running and climbing.[75] Toddlers are not yet concerned about meeting their peers' dress standards, but they often have distinct likes and dislikes of their own. Having their choices respected increases self-esteem. Ginott recommends encouraging independence by buying clothing that is easy for them to put on by themselves.

Gordon suggests coping with dressing problems by setting limits with verbal or nonverbal I-messages.[76] If a child does not want to wear what is necessary, a parent can express concern about the child getting sick. If the child squirms and makes dressing difficult, Gordon again advises holding him and restraining his movements as a nonverbal I-message.

Dreikurs focuses on teaching children how to dress and undress themselves.[77] Even at an early age, children can learn if parents make the process a game. Children can play the game of pulling socks off or putting them on. As they get a little older, Dreikurs suggests "giving them permission" to dress themselves. Children may seek attention by asking for help even though they can dress themselves. Parents must refuse to help and wait while children complete the task. A child may take off a piece of clothing or put a piece on wrong. Sometimes parents can let them take the consequences, but not if the child then risks illness or injury.

Behaviorists take the same approach as Dreikurs, suggesting that parents teach the child to dress and ignore bids for attention by refusing any help when the child does not really need it.[78] However, they use social rewards for success in ways that Dreikurs would not. They suggest breaking the act of dressing into small steps that children can accomplish and giving praise after each step. "Your right hand in your coat sleeve. Good! Your left hand in your coat sleeve. Good! Now pull up the zipper and off you go!"

Toilet Training

Most experts suggest that sometime between eighteen and twenty-four months children are ready to learn approved toileting behavior. Nathan Azrin and Richard Foxx suggest three guidelines for determining the child's readiness: bladder control (the ability to stay dry for several hours, to anticipate urination, and to urinate a significant amount at one time); physical readiness (the ability to get to the toilet alone and the dexterity to get pants down); instructional readiness (the ability to understand an instruction and the ability to communicate a need).[79]

T. Berry Brazelton adds several other indicators of readiness: the child (1) has mastered running and walking and is able to sit and play quietly for a period of time; (2) shows an interest in the toilet; (3) wants to imitate adult behaviors, like brushing teeth and eating neatly; (4) knows when she has to go to the toilet and understands why it is desirable to wait until getting to an approved place; (5) shows an interest in neatness; and (6) is not highly negativistic.[80]

All methods of toilet training (1) take into account the child's physical readiness; (2) teach steps of the process through instruction or observation of others; (3) suggest that parents remain calm and unperturbed by accidents; (4) refuse to give punishments for accidents. The methods differ in the use of material rewards and praise. Ginott, Gordon, Dreikurs, and to some extent Brazelton recommend taking the accomplishments as indications of the child's natural capacities. The behaviorists and Azrin and Foxx use praise and rewards of candy or food, but they move in the direction of accepting the feat as a matter-of-fact event.

Ginott suggests that when the child is physically ready, the parents state clearly, "It was fun to mess when you were a little baby. You like the warm feeling inside your diapers, but we don't want that now anymore. Now we want to do it on the potty." The parents provide opportunities for messing with mud and clay or finger paints. They are careful not to associate any harsh physical treatments or punishments with the anal area.

Gordon reports a mother's account of how she trained her twenty-two-month-old boy. Since the mother relied on his older sister to help him, the exact method cannot be used by all families. But any parent of a child who is ready to be toilet trained can assume that the child can help train himself or herself. In Gordon's example, the mother told the toddler, when he asked to be changed, that she did not want to do that anymore, that he was big enough to go to the toilet like his older sister, who was four. A day later the mother found the older sister holding him on the toilet and telling him to go potty.

Dreikurs suggests a casual approach. The child learns by being put on the toilet at regular intervals, whether he needs to go or not. He is left there just a few minutes. This is continued until the child asks to go to the toilet. This method, like all others, requires time and patience. The parent does not get angry or irritated. Each day the parent puts pants on the child to see if the child can stay dry, but changes them if necessary. If the child wets after being trained, parents can look for a cause—a new baby, a move, change in friends—and can use diapers for one day, but they should return to the routine the following day.

Parents are advised not to give undue attention to toilet training. Do not talk about it much or give much praise, because then the child can use the achievement to frustrate parents if he is angry. The child can also gain power over the parents by going to the toilet when parents do not want him to.

Azrin and Foxx, the authors of *Toilet Training in One Day,* describe the most complete approach to toilet training, incorporating insights from many different schools. The method is very detailed, and only a brief summary can be reported here. The authors introduce the method with the statement, "No 'gimmick' or gadget caused the rapid learning. The child learns so fast because we have used so many factors to make learning pleasant, simple, and exciting."[81]

Before the day of actual training, children are prepared in a variety of ways. They are taught to put on their clothes and get them off. They observe other family members using the toilet. They are taught the words parents prefer for urination and bowel movement. The mother or any close adult can prepare the child.

Training occurs in several steps. The potty chair is put in a room with a washable floor. The child is dressed in loose training pants that can be pulled down easily, with no jeans or dress over them. The child drinks a large amount of beverages to encourage urinating. Dressed and full of liquids, the child watches the mother potty train a doll as a demonstration of what is expected of the child. As success occurs, the child is given enjoyable snacks for rewards.

This is one of the few methods that talks about what should be done if the child has a temper tantrum during the process. The parent must wait until the child's resistance dies down and then proceed with the training in a calm tone, giving approval for all correct actions. Because the process of toileting is broken down into simple steps that bring rewards, children learn that they are capable of doing what is asked. A couple of tantrums to test the parent's intentions are usually all that occur.

This method, which has been documented with successful results in research studies, draws heavily on behavioral techniques with rewards and vicarious learning through the doll. But the authors pay attention to individual differences in time of starting and in handling temper tantrums. It is, further, the only method that incorporates a doll.

Brazelton has designed a method to help children train themselves when they are ready. The method is similar to that of Azrin and Foxx, but the parent plays a less active role and children become trained at their own pace. Children become accustomed to a potty chair gradually, sitting on it while still dressed, being taken to use it once or twice a day, then having it close by and available to use during play. When children are used to the potty, they are told that now they are in charge of going to the bathroom. Parents undress the children from the waist down, so that they can use the potty chair easily and occasionally remind them, asking them if they need to use the potty. If children rebel or have accidents, parents put diapers on them and wait until they indicate that they are ready for training.

Before leaving this topic, let us note that even with the most successful techniques in the world, some parents will experience difficulty for reasons beyond their control. An extensive study by Mordecai Kaffman and Esther Elizur of the toilet training process revealed that many factors—physical, personality, and social—play a part in the child's ability to be trained.[82] Kaffman and Elizur developed a profile of a child at high risk for enuresis, or bed-wetting: (1) occurrence of enuresis among parents or siblings, (2) high level of motor activity and aggression, (3) poor adaptability to new situations, (4) low achievement motivation, (5) overdependent behavior, (6) lack of negative reactions to wetness and urine control, and (7) prematurity.

Parents who are having trouble toilet training a child need to remember that this is a new experience for them and for the child. And they need to accept that fact that, for reasons beyond the control of both children and parents, some children need more time than others to learn toilet habits.

Temper Tantrums

With Goodenough's study in mind, let us examine what Ginott, Gordon, Dreikurs, and the behaviorists suggest about parental managing of children's temper tantrums. Ginott recommends accepting all angry feelings, but directing children's behavior into acceptable channels. Parents can do this verbally by saying, "People are not for hitting; pillows are for hitting," or "Scribble on the paper, not on the wall." Neither parent nor child is permitted to hit. If children's tantrums are not ended by verbal statements, parents take action, even in public. In *Liberated Parents Liberated Children,* mothers report stopping the car until the fighting stopped in the back seat or returning home if a child has a tantrum in a store.[83] These methods require time, but the mothers report success and say they felt better as a result of taking action.

Gordon suggests finding substitute activities to head off trouble. If no jumping is permitted on the sofa, parents can allow children to jump on pillows on the floor. Once anger surfaces, Gordon suggests that parents listen actively and provide feedback about the frustration and irritation the child feels—sometimes a child needs nothing more than acceptance of what he is feeling.

Gordon recommends mutual problem solving to find a solution agreeable to both parent and child. But when a compromise is not possible and a child is still upset, active listening may again be useful. He cites the example of a child who was unable to go swimming because he had a cold. When the child's mother commented that it was hard for him to wait until the next day, he calmed down.

Dreikurs recommends many of the techniques that Goodenough found were used by parents whose children had few tantrums. In establishing routines, Dreikurs suggests being flexible with children, concerned with their needs and interests, but firm in enforcing the routines.[84] When tantrums occur, parents are urged to ignore them and leave the room. Ignoring a child is appropriate in public as well as at home.

The behaviorists use a similar method of ignoring. Krumboltz and Krumboltz tell of a little boy who learned that if he cried and had a tantrum, his parents would pick him up instead of paying attention to the new baby.[85] When they realized that their actions were creating the tantrums, they agreed to ignore the outbursts. When the boy learned that he gained nothing by banging his head and demanding what he wanted, the tantrums stopped. The behaviorists insist that parents must be firm and consistent. Otherwise tantrums will continue, and each time children will hold out longer because they have learned that they can win by outlasting the parents.

Strategists who emphasize communication of feelings to prevent tantrums suggest parental intervention by reflecting feelings. The parents of the boy who is jealous of a new baby might be advised to comment that if the boy wishes he could be held like a baby; only after attending to feelings would Ginott, for example, take action. The behaviorists and Dreikurs, in contrast, focus on handling tantrums once they have occurred.

Stanley Turecki and Leslie Tonner, whose work with difficult children is described in greater detail in Chapter 8, draw a distinction between the **manipulative tantrum** and the **temperamental tantrum**.[86] Children who want their way use the tantrum to manipulate the parents into getting them what they want. In the case of a manipulative outburst, Turecki recommends firm refusal to give into the tantrum. Distracting the child, ignoring the outburst, and sending children to their room are all techniques for handling that kind of tantrum.

In the more intense temperamental tantrum, children seem out of control. Some aspect of their temperament has been violated, and they are reacting to that. For example, the poorly adaptable child who is compelled to switch activities suddenly may have an outburst, or a child sensitive to material may do so when he or she has to wear a wool sweater. In these instances, Turecki advises a calm and sympathetic approach; parents can reflect the child's feelings of irritation or upset: "I know you don't like this, but it will be okay." Parents can then put their arms around the child, if permitted, or just be a physical presence near the child. No long discussion of what is upsetting the child takes place unless the child wants to talk. If the situation can be corrected, it should be. For example, if the wool sweater feels scratchy, let the child remove it and wear a soft sweatshirt. This is not giving in, but just correcting a mistake. All parents can do then is wait out the tantrum.

Throughout a display of the temperamental tantrum, parents convey the attitude that they will help the child deal with this situation. Though parents change their minds when good reasons are presented, they are generally consistent in waiting out the tantrum and insisting on behavior change when necessary. If parents believe that many of their toddler's tantrums are temperamental in nature, they should read the section on difficult children in Chapter 8 for further suggestions on ways of handling conflicts with toddlers.

Birth of a Sibling

Ginott says that the arrival of a new baby is a stressful event for an older child.[87] He tells parents that because no one likes to share center stage with another, a child is bound to feel some jealousy and hurt, no matter how well prepared for the event. Preparation does help, however. Parents can say that soon there will be a new baby in the family and that a baby is both fun and a nuisance. They should express, and permit the child to express, negative as well as positive feelings. Before the baby arrives parents can help the child to anticipate both the love and the left-out feelings that he or she will experience. After the child arrives, parents can be alert for signs of jealousy, which they can reflect, acknowledging the older child's jealousy, resentment, and hostility. Ginott suggests special attention and "extra loving" for the older child during these times of stress.

Gordon recommends active listening so that the child can express fear that the parent likes the other child better or anger at the intrusion. Active listening means listening to behavior as well as to words and realizing that when the child becomes irritable, aggressive, or immature, jealousy lies just under the surface. A parent can simply comment, "You are unhappy," "sad," or "lonely."

Dreikurs has a thorough discussion of sibling rivalry.[88] He shows how children's responses to the new baby depend on both their own feelings at the time and on the characteristics of the new arrival. Dreikurs recommends accepting any verbal statements of hostility, any talk about wanting to get rid of the baby. The main way to help older children cope is by making them your partner in caring for the baby. Point out the older children's advantages, how big they are, how well they bring a diaper for the baby or tell a parent the baby is crying, how smart they are to figure out that the baby wants company. If possible, the father can spend more time with the older child. When the older child makes unreasonable demands for attention, parents should overlook these. Parents can also try to plan special treats for the older child while the baby is asleep. To minimize difficulties as children grow, parents are urged not to compare them.

The behaviorists suggest that when a new baby arrives, the older child can learn to do special tasks that will increase self-esteem. Eimers and Aitchison cite the case of a child who was always asking her parents if they loved her.[89] At first they answered, but as the question became repetitive, behaviorists advised them to ignore the question and instead to build the child's self-esteem by giving positive attention for what she did well. They began playing games with her and spending more time talking and reading to her. The child felt valued and no longer needed to ask whether she was loved.

Briggs says preventing all jealousy is like trying to eliminate the common cold, but parents can learn to identify the signs of jealousy and can act to reduce it.[90] Jealous children may accuse parents of not loving them or of giving siblings more attention. They may become irritable and fight with parents, deliberately breaking rules and wanting to be punished—even punishment is a form of attention. Parents help children handle their feelings when they provide opportunities for verbal and creative expression. One mother gave her daughter a doll to hit to express the anger the child felt toward a younger sister. Coloring, drawing, and molding clay can also help to express feelings. Briggs also suggests building the older child's self-esteem by teaching new skills that increase the child's competence.

Again the strategists are in general agreement, although they focus on slightly different aspects of the problem. Ginott prepares the child for the birth. Gordon and Briggs elicit feelings through active listening. Briggs suggests ways to drain tension and, along with Dreikurs and the behaviorists, recommends building the child's self-esteem through attention and interest in positive behavior as well as through teaching new skills.

PARENTS' EXPERIENCES

Parents are in Galinsky's **authority stage**, which lasts from the child's second to fourth or fifth year.[91] Parents must deal with their own feelings about having power, setting rules, enforcing them. Parents have to decide what is reasonable when children mobilize all their energy to oppose them and gain their way. In the nurturing stage parents were primarily concerned with meeting babies' needs and coordinating their own with caregiving activities. Usually the appropriate childcare behavior was clear—the baby had to be fed, changed, bathed, put to bed. Although judgment was required in deciding about letting the child cry or timing sleep patterns, still the desired aim was clear.

In the authority stage parents must develop clear rules and have the confidence not only to enforce them, but also to deal with the tantrums that follow. Parents require self-assurance so they can act calmly and neutrally when they meet with opposition from their children. Many parents, bogged down in battle with their toddler, find themselves doing and saying things they vowed they never would—the very words they hated to hear from their own parents when they were children. Parents are shaken and upset as their ideal images of themselves as parents collide with the reality of rearing children.

Parents' images of themselves undergo revision in light of the way they actually behave. This can be a painful process because it involves change. Parents must change either their ideal image or their behavior to come closer to living up to their own standards. Parents' images of children are revised as well. They discover that children are not always nice, loving, cooperative, and affectionate. Children can be extremely aggressive, breaking things, hitting parents, pulling their hair.

One father described how he coped with these feelings by revising the kind of parent he wanted to be and by finding new ways to relate to children so that he met the images he wanted to keep of himself as parent.

Stanley and his wife have one son, eighteen months old. Stanley is a doctor. "In my family, growing up, when someone got angry at someone, they'd stop loving them—which made me feel abandoned as a child.

"When my son gets angry, the easiest thing for me to do would be the same—walk out and slam the door.

"But when you've suffered that yourself you don't want to see it repeated. What I do is to stay and let the rage go through my ears and try to think clearly about what's going on.

"I tell him that even though I've said no, I still love him. I hold him while he's having a temper tantrum, and I tell him it's okay for him to be angry with me.

"Being able to do this is recent, new, and learned, and it's hard work. In the past, I couldn't see beyond my own feelings. What I've now learned is that I have to see past them.

"Another thing I've learned is that if I've gotten angry at my son or if I've done something that I feel I shouldn't have, I'm not the Loch Ness monster or the worst person in the world. I learned the reparability of a mistake."[92]

Parents must also deal with each other as authorities. It is wonderful if both parents agree on how and when to enforce rules. But this is frequently not the case. One parent is often stricter or less consistent; one may dislike any physical punishment, and the other may believe it is the only technique to handle serious rule breaking. Communicating with each other, finding ways to handle differences, is important for parents. Parents sometimes agree to back each other up on all occasions. Other times, they agree to discuss in private any serious misgivings they have about the others' discipline; then the original rule setter is free to revise the rule. Still other times, one parent may decide to let the other handle discipline completely. This is a less desirable solution because it means one parent is withdrawn from interaction with the child. Parents need to find ways to resolve differences so they can give each other the support they need in childrearing. Mutual support is the most important source of strength in parenting.

Single parents and employed parents must work with other authorities, such as day caregivers or relatives who provide major care, to develop consistent ways of handling discipline. Again, communicating with other caregivers helps provide consistent solutions to problems. When authorities do not agree, children become confused and are less able to meet expectations.

As parents become aware of their personal feelings about being authorities and learn to deal with them, they can put these misgivings aside and deal as neutrally with rule enforcement as possible. As with handling infancy, a range of preparations such as reading books, gaining information from groups, parenting courses, and other parents helps parents handle the demands of conflicting feelings in the authority stage.

Sometimes parents are not able to contain the anger they feel at their children. They strike out at them physically in ways that bruise, injure, maim, or even kill the child. Exact figures on child abuse are difficult to determine, but we do know that child abuse occurs more frequently in families with husband-wife violence and sibling violence.[93] Abusive parents themselves were often the victims of abuse as children. Abusive parents are often under a high level of stress, with little support from others. Financial pressure is often present and parents are frequently young. Comparing poverty areas with high and low abuse rates, however, reveals that abuse is more likely to occur in those poor areas in which parents are experiencing much change with little help from family or neighbors.[94] There is much moving in and out of the home and the neighborhood; childcare is not easily available; families have little recreation time together.

Abused children are likely to have some qualities that make caregiving difficult. Such children may be highly active, have some physical problems, or be especially demanding. These children are unable to satisfy the high expectations parents have of them. Instead of being able to give to the parents, they demand more than the average child.[95]

Treatment for abuse includes individual counseling of the parents, children, and family as well as parent participation in groups for parents who have abused children. Group discussion helps parents build more realistic expectations of children so that anger does not flare up so easily. Learning about children's development also helps parents construct more realistic expectations. Parents in these groups learn to build networks of support so that they can get help when they feel under pressure.

Child abuse illustrates the many social and personal factors that influence parent-child relations. It highlights, as much research does, parents' need for social connections with family, friends, and neighbors who can be available not only at times of unusual stress, but also at times of frustration from daily caregiving.

MAJOR POINTS OF CHAPTER 7

Toddlers' increasing skills enable them to explore the world in more complex ways. Their:

- motor skills enable them to cover more area and manipulate objects more effectively
- cognitive skills enable them to focus on properties of objects and develop ideas about how objects work and what will happen if they perform certain acts
- capacity to form mental pictures of what they see increases memory and children's understanding of events
- ability to imitate others becomes more advanced, and so the behavior they copy is more complex
- language and ability to form sentences increases communication with others
- understanding of people's emotional reactions enable them to get parents' help as needed and to control others' emotional reactions more effectively

As their skills increase, toddlers:

- become more independent
- take pleasure and delight in their new accomplishments
- insist on doing as much as possible for themselves
- refuse to do what parents want if that conflicts with their goals
- have temper tantrums when they are frustrated

As their independence grows, toddlers also develop closer relationships with others, and they

- are more physically affectionate with family, friends, and pets
- become more concerned about others, imitating their distress when they are hurt
- are helpful and loving with newborn siblings
- are kinder and try to resolve angry interactions
- take delight in complying with some adult requests and meeting a standard of behavior

As they develop a greater sense of individuality, toddlers develop a sense of sexual identity that

- is proudly announced at about two to two and a half
- initially is based on parents' positive and negative emotional responses to sexually appropriate activities
- organizes activities so that boys manipulate objects and explore the world more and girls express feelings, ask for help, and give help more
- includes the belief that both boys and girls share common positive and negative traits—both sexes are strong, kind, fast runners, unafraid, messy, dirty, smart, and quiet
- views one's own sex as the more favored

Parents whose toddlers function well and have secure attachments:

- are available, attentive, and sensitive to the child's individual needs
- grant the child as much independence as possible within safety limits
- balance independence with support to overcome barriers the child may meet
- provide models of kind, caring, controlled behavior
- share the experiences of exploration and discovery with the child
- provide reasonable limits to give the child structure
- talk with the child to explain reasons for what is done, to understand the child's view of what is happening, and to let the child express himself or herself
- play with the child to increase the child's positive mood and desire to cooperate in routines and activities

Parents are learning to be fair authorities who:

- reason with children and explain the rules
- act to deal firmly with temper tantrums so children know their own intense feelings are controlled

- work together to settle their own conflicts about authority so children get a set of consistent limits
- do not abuse their power

Physical abuse of children is most likely to occur when parents:

- have experienced abuse themselves as children
- are under many stresses from financial problems, lack of social support from family or friends, and from children's difficult behavior
- do not get professional help at the time they experience intense anger and loss of control with children

Problems discussed center on:

- meeting physiological needs
- toilet training
- handling temper tantrums
- dealing with the birth of a sibling

Joys include:

- child's delight in personal achievements
- child's increasing abilities
- child's helping behaviors
- communication via verbal language
- playing with the child

ADDITIONAL READINGS

Arena, Jay, and Bachar, Miriam. *Child Safety Is No Accident.* New York: Hawthorn, 1978.

Brazelton, T. Berry. *Toddlers and Parents.* Rev. ed. New York: Dell, 1989.

Damon, William. *The Moral Child: Nurturing Children's Natural Moral Growth.* New York: Free Press, 1988.

Ferber, Richard. *Solve Your Child's Sleep Problems.* New York: Simon & Schuster, 1985.

Tomlinson-Keasey, Carol. *Child's Eye View.* New York: St. Martin's Press, 1980.

Notes

1. Jean Piaget and Barbel Inhelder, *The Psychology of the Child* (New York: Basic Books, 1969); Herbert Ginsburg and Sylvia Opper, *Piaget's Theory of Intellectual Development* (Englewood Cliffs, N.J.: Prentice-Hall, 1969).

2. Burton L. White, *The First Three Years of Life* (Englewood Cliffs, N.J.: Prentice-Hall, 1975).

3. Mabel L. Rice, "Children's Language Acquisition," *American Psychologist* 44 (1989): 149–156.

4. Richard Elardo, Robert Bradley, and Betty M. Caldwell, "A Longitudinal Study of the Relations of Infants' Home Environments to Language Development at Age Three," *Child Development* 48 (1977): 595–603.

5. Celeste Pappas Jones and Lauren B. Adamson, "Language Use in Mother-Child and Mother-Child-Sibling Interactions," *Child Development* 58 (1987): 356–366.

6. Mabel L. Rice, "Children's Language Acquisition."

7. Rice, "Children's Language Acquisition;" Michael Tomasello and Michael Jeffrey Farrar, "Joint Attention and Early Language," *Child Development* 57 (1986): 1454–1463.

8. Lois Bloom and Joanne Bitette Capatides, "Expression of Affect and the Emergence of Language," *Child Development* 58 (1987): 1513–1522.

9. N. a., *Developmental Psychology Today,* 2nd ed. (New York: Random House, 1975).

10. Martin D. S. Braine, *Children's First Word Combinations,* Monographs of the Society for Research in Child Development 41 (1976): whole number 164.

11. Eleanor E. Maccoby and Carol Nagy Jacklin, *The Psychology of Sex Differences* (Stanford: Stanford University Press, 1974).

12. L. Alan Sroufe, "Socioemotional Development," in *Handbook of Infant Development,* ed. Joy D. Osofsky (New York: John Wiley, 1979), pp. 462–506; Michael Lewis, Margaret W. Sullivan, Catherine Stanger, and Myra Weiss, "Self Development and Self-Conscious Emotions," *Child Development* 60 (1989): 146–156.

13. Inge Bretherton, Janet Fritz, Carolyn Zahn-Waxler, and Doreen Ridgeway, "Learning to Talk about Emotions: A Functionalist Perspective," *Child Development* 57 (1986): 529–548; Claire B. Kopp, "Regulation of Distress and Negative Emotions: A Developmental View," *Developmental Psychology* 25 (1989): 343–354.

14. Kopp, "Regulation of Distress and Negative Emotions."

15. Ibid.

16. Bretherton et al., "Learning to Talk about Emotions."

17. Milton H. Erickson, *Healing in Hypnosis* Vol. 1 (New York: Irvington, 1983).

18. Judy Dunn, Inge Bretherton, and Penny Munn, "Conversations about Feeling States between Mothers and Their Young Children," *Developmental Psychology* 23 (1987): 132–139.

19. Florence L. Goodenough, *Anger in Young Children* (Minneapolis: University of Minnesota Press, 1931).

20. Marion Radke-Yarrow et al., "Learning Concern for Others," *Developmental Psychology* 8 (1973): 240–260; Herbert Wray, *Emotions in the Lives of Young Children,* Department of Health, Education, and Welfare Publication no. 78-644 (Rockville, Md.: 1978).

21. E. Mark Cummings, Ronald J. Ianotti, and Carolyn Zahn-Waxler, "Influence of Conflict between Adults on the Emotions and Aggression of Young Children," *Developmental Psychology* 21 (1985): 495–507.

22. Harriet L. Rheingold, Kay V. Cook, Vicki Kolowitz, "Commands Cultivate the Behavioral Pleasure of 2-Year-Old Children," *Developmental Psychology* 23 (1987): 146–151.

23. Erik H. Erikson, *Childhood and Society,* 2nd ed. (New York: W. W. Norton, 1963).

24. Jude Cassidy, "The Ability to Negotiate the Environment: An Aspect of Infant Competence as Related to Quality of Attachment," *Child Development* 57 (1986): 331–337.

25. Everett Waters, Judith Wippman, and L. Alan Sroufe, "Attachment, Positive Affect, and Competence in the Peer Group: Two Studies in Construct Validation," *Child Development* 50 (1979): 821–829.

26. Robert N. Emde and James F. Sorce, "The Rewards of Infancy: Emotional Availability and Referencing," in *Frontiers of Infant Psychiatry,* ed. Justin D. Call, Eleanor Galenson, and Robert L. Tyson (New York: Basic Books, 1983), pp. 17–30.

27. Tedra A. Walden and Tamra A. Ogan, "The Development of Social Referencing," *Child Development* 59 (1988): 1230–1240.

28. Lorraine Rocissano, Arietta Slade, and Victoria Lynch, "Dyadic Synchrony and Toddler Compliance," *Developmental Psychology* 23 (1987): 698–704.

29. Jutta Heckhausen, "Balancing for Weaknesses and Challenging Developmental Potential: A Longitudinal Study of Mother-Infant Dyads in Apprenticeship Interactions," *Developmental Psychology* 23 (1987): 762–770.

30. Mary Jane Gandour, "Activity Level as a Dimension of Temperament in Toddlers: Its Relevance for the Organismic Specificity Hypothesis," *Child Development* 60 (1989): 1092–1098.

31. Arietta Slade, "A Longitudinal Study of

Maternal Involvement and Symbolic Play during the Toddler Period," *Child Development* 58 (1987): 367–375; K. Allison Clarke-Stewart, *Interactions Between Mothers and Their Young Children: Characteristics and Consequences,* Monographs of the Society for Research in Child Development 38 (1973): whole number 153.

32. Cheryl Minton, Jerome Kagan, and Janet A. Levine, "Maternal Control and Obedience in the Two-Year-Old," *Child Development* 42 (1971): 1873–1894.

33. George Holden, "Avoiding Conflicts: Mothers as Tacticians in the Supermarket," *Child Development* 54 (1983): 233–240; Thomas G. Power and M. Lynne Chapieski, "Childrearing and Impulsive Control in Toddlers: A Naturalistic Investigation," *Developmental Psychology* 22 (1986): 271–275.

34. George W. Holden and Meredith J. West, "Proximate Regulation by Mothers: A Demonstration of How Differing Styles Affect Young Children's Behavior," *Child Development* 60 (1989): p. 69.

35. Byron Egeland and Ellen A. Farber, "Infant-Mother Attachment: Factors Related to Its Development and Changes over Time," *Child Development* 55 (1984): 753–771.

36. Carolyn L. Lee and John E. Bates, "Mother-Child Interaction at Age Two Years and Perceived Difficult Temperament," *Child Development* 56 (1985): 1314–1325.

37. Lisa J. Bridges, James P. Connell, and Jay Belsky, "Similarities and Differences in Infant-Mother and Infant-Father Interaction in the Strange Situation: A Component Process Analysis," *Developmental Psychology* 24 (1988): 92–100.

38. M. Ann Easterbrooks and Wendy A. Goldberg, "Toddler Development in the Family: Impact of Father Involvement and Parenting Characteristics," *Child Development* 55 (1982): 841–864.

39. William Damon and Daniel Hart, "The Development of Self-Understanding from Infancy through Adolescence," *Child Development* 53 (1982): 841–864.

40. Michael Lewis and Linda Michalson, *Children's Emotions and Moods* (New York: Plenum, 1983).

41. Jerome Kagan, *The Second Year* (Cambridge, Mass.: Harvard University Press, 1981).

42. Claire B. Kopp, "Antecedents of Self-Regulation: A Developmental Perspective," *Developmental Psychology* 18 (1982): 199–214.

43. Brian E. Vaughn, Claire B. Kopp, Joanne B. Krakow, Kim Johnson, and Steven S. Schwartz, "Process Analyses of the Behavior of Very Young Children in Delay Tasks," *Developmental Psychology* 22 (1986): 752–759.

44. Kopp, "Antecedents of Self-Regulation."

45. Vaughn et al., "Process Analyses of the Behavior of Very Young Children in Delay Tasks."

46. Merry Bullock and Paul Lutkenhaus, "The Development of Volitional Behavior in the Toddler Years," *Child Development* 59 (1988): 664–674.

47. John Money, "Human Hermaphroditism," in *Human Sexuality in Four Perspectives,* ed. Frank A. Beach (Baltimore: Johns Hopkins University Press, 1976), pp. 62–86.

48. Deanna Kuhn, Sharon Churnin Nash, and Laura Brucken, "Sex Role Concepts of Two- and Three-Year-Olds," *Child Development* 49 (1978): 445–451.

49. Beverly I. Fagot and Mary D. Leinbach, "The Young Child's Gender Schema: Environmental Input, Internal Organization," *Child Development* 60 (1989): 663–672.

50. Judy Dunn, *Sisters and Brothers* (Cambridge, Mass.: Harvard University Press, 1985).

51. Robert B. Stewart, "Sibling Attachment Relationships: Child Infant Interactions in the Strange Situation," *Developmental Psychology* 19 (1983): 192–199.

52. Judy Dunn and Penny Munn, "Becoming a Family Member: Family Conflict and the Development of Social Understanding in the Second Year," *Child Development* 56 (1985): 480–492; Judy Dunn and Penny Munn, "Development of Justification in Disputes with Mother and Siblings," *Developmental Psychology* 23 (1987): 791–798.

53. Dunn, *Sisters and Brothers.*

54. Robert B. Stewart, Linda A. Mobley, Susan S. Van Tuyl, and Myron A. Salvador, "The Firstborn's Adjustment to the Birth of a Sibling: A Longitudinal Assessment," *Child Development* 58 (1987): 341–355.

55. Jerome Kagan, *The Second Year.*

56. Laura E. Levine, "Mine: Self-Definition in Two Year Old Boys," *Developmental Psychology* 19 (1983): 544–549.

57. Megan R. Gunner, Kathleen Senior, and Willard W. Hartup, "Peer Pressure and the Exploratory Behavior of Eighteen- and Thirty-Month-Old Children," *Child Development* 55 (1984): 1103–1109.

58. Carollee Howes, *Peer Interaction of Young Children,* with Commentary by Kenneth H. Rubin, Hildy S. Ross, and Doran C. French, Monographs of the Society for Research in Child Development 53 (1 Serial No. 217) (1987).

59. Donald L. Pastor, "The Quality of Mother-Infant Attachment and Its Relationship to Toddler's Initial Sociability with Peers," *Developmental Psychology* 17 (1981): 326–335.

60. Margaret Ellis Snow, Carol Nagy Jacklin, and Eleanor E. Maccoby, "Birth Order Differences in Peer Sociability at Thirty-Three Months," *Child Development* 52 (1981): 589–595.

61. White, *The First Three Years.*

62. Jay M. Arena and Miriam Bachar, *Child Safety Is No Accident* (New York: Hawthorn, 1978).

63. Jean V. Carew, Itty Chan, and Christine Halfar, *Observing Intelligence in Young Children* (Englewood Cliffs, N.J.: Prentice-Hall, 1976).

64. Dorothy C. Briggs, *Your Child's Self-Esteem* (Garden City, N.Y.: Doubleday, 1975).

65. Rice, "Children's Language Acquisition," p. 155.

66. White, *The First Three Years,* p. 139.

67. Keng-Ling Lay, Everett Waters, and Kathryn A. Park, "Maternal Responsiveness and Child Compliance: The Role of Mood as Mediator," *Child Development* 60 (1989): 1405–1411.

68. White, *The First Three Years.*

69. Benjamin Spock, *Baby and Child Care,* rev. ed. (New York: Pocket Books, 1976).

70. Frances L. Ilg and Louise Bates Ames, *Child Behavior* (New York: Harper & Row, 1955).

71. Thomas Gordon with Judith Gordon Sands, *P.E.T. in Action* (New York: Bantam, 1978).

72. Rudolf Dreikurs with Vicki Soltz, *Children: The Challenge* (New York: Hawthorn, 1964).

73. John D. Krumboltz and Helen B. Krumboltz, *Changing Children's Behavior* (Englewood Cliffs, N.J.: Prentice-Hall, 1972).

74. Richard Ferber, *Solve Your Child's Sleep Problems* (New York: Simon & Schuster, 1985).

75. Haim G. Ginott, *Between Parent and Child* (New York: Avon, 1969).

76. Thomas Gordon, *P.E.T. Parent Effectiveness Training* (New York: New American Library, 1975).

77. Rudolf Dreikurs, *The Challenge of Parenthood,* rev. ed. (New York: Hawthorn, 1958).

78. Wesley C. Becker, *Parents Are Teachers* (Champaign, Ill.: Research Press, 1971); Robert Eimers and Robert Aitchison, *Effective Parents/Responsible Children* (New York: McGraw-Hill, 1977).

79. Nathan H. Azrin and Richard M. Foxx, *Toilet Training in Less Than a Day* (New York: Pocket Books, 1974).

80. T. Berry Brazelton, *Doctor and Child* (New York: Dell, 1978).

81. Azrin and Foxx, *Toilet Training in Less Than a Day,* p. 12.

82. Mordecai Kaffman and Esther Elizur, *Infants Who Become Eneuretics: A Longitudinal Study of 161 Kibbutz Children,* Monographs of the Society for Research in Child Development 42 (1977): whole number 170.

83. Adele Faber and Elaine Mazlish, *Liberated Parents/Liberated Children* (New York: Avon, 1975).

84. Dreikurs with Soltz, *Children: The Challenge.*

85. Krumboltz and Krumboltz, *Changing Children's Behavior.*

86. Stanley Turecki and Leslie Tonner, *The Difficult Child* (New York: Bantam Books, 1985).

87. Ginnott, *Between Parent and Child.*

88. Dreikurs, *Challenge of Parenthood.*

89. Robert Eimers and Robert Aitchison, *Effective Parents/Responsible Children.*

90. Briggs, *Your Child's Self-Esteem.*

91. Ellen Galinsky, *Between Generations: The Six Stages of Parenthood* (New York: Times Books, 1981).

92. Ibid, pp. 136–137.

93. Ross D. Parke and Ronald G. Slaby, "The Development of Aggression," in *Handbook of Child Psychology,* eds. Paul H. Mussen and E. Mavis Hetherington, vol. 4, *Socialization, Personality and Social Development,* 4th ed. (New York: John Wiley, 1983), pp. 547–641.

94. James Garbarino and Deborah Sherman, "High-Risk Neighborhoods and High-Risk Families: The Human Ecology of Child Maltreatment," *Child Development* 51 (1980): 188–198.

95. Parke and Slaby, "The Development of Aggression."

THE PRESCHOOL YEARS

C H A P T E R 8

The **preschool** period from three to five is an exciting time. Children have control of their bodies and have mastered a variety of motor skills. They can communicate verbally and have a sense of personal identity. Now they are ready to turn to the outside world to initiate activities. Preschoolers strive to obtain goals, savor the pleasures of accomplishments, and enjoy competition with others. Their curiosity, refreshing observations on experience, and responsiveness to parents and others produce anecdotes that parents tell for years.

As children become more independent, they go farther from the house than they ventured as toddlers. If they have not already gone to day care, they may start nursery school or other group activities. Out of interactions with friends they begin to learn the art of negotiating, of settling arguments so that each person gets satisfaction. Their capabilities for sharing and giving to others increase.

As children grow, their capacities to think and reason about experience grow as well. Children become little philosophers, questioning all that happens to others as well as to themselves. Parents find they have to increase their own knowledge to keep up with the inquiring minds of their preschoolers, who want to know why the sky is blue and where rain comes from.

PHYSICAL DEVELOPMENT

Although their rate of physical growth has slowed, preschoolers still gain 2½ to 3 inches in height each year, and 3 to 5 pounds in weight. By age five, they are about 42 inches tall and 42 to 45 pounds in weight. The physical growth of the brain has been rapid since conception, but is now slowing. By age three, the brain has grown to 80 percent of adult size; by age five, to 90 percent. In this two-year period, growth increases in the connections between parts of the brain. This development facilitates control of voluntary movements and increases alertness, attention, and memory, which in turn underlie observable changes in motor and cognitive abilities.

**WHAT I WISH I HAD KNOWN
ABOUT THE PRESCHOOL YEARS**

"I wish I'd known how to react when they lied. You know kids lie, but it hurts me terribly. It was a very painful experience even though I know I did it." MOTHER

"I wish I had known how much frustration comes just because kids are kids and you have to be tolerant. They don't have the attention span for some things. They might want to do something with you, but they can only do it for about fifteen minutes. You have to go places prepared with all his things or with things to keep him entertained. In the car on a trip, we have a lot of things for him to do. When you plan ahead, you can still be spontaneous at times. You learn that if you are prepared, things really don't have to be a hassle." FATHER

"Everything. I wish I'd known more about communication, how to talk to your children, and the most effective way to help them grow with a strong ego, a good sense of self. We were raised with a lot of 'Do this and don't do that,' a lot of demanding and dictatorial things as opposed to trying to solicit participation in the process of decision making, trying to get in touch with your child's feelings so you really do understand how they feel about things. That's really hard to learn, and I don't know how you can learn it without the experience of actually having the child. But I'm continually learning how to understand her feelings about things." MOTHER

"I think it is incredible that we don't teach anything about being a parent. I have to learn it as I go along because I want things to be different for them than they were for me growing up. I can't use my own experiences as a guide." FATHER

"I wish I had known how to handle them so they could be spontaneous and feel good about the things they did. How to be spontaneous with them is one of the hardest things for me." FATHER

"I wish I had known how to handle things like believing in Santa Claus. I didn't know whether to encourage it or not or when to tell her there was none. She learned gradually, I think, but she doesn't want to tell her little brother yet." MOTHER

In the preschool period children gain greater control of their bodies. By age five, they have an easy gait and take longer steps when walking and running, and they have a grounded sense of balance. They can stand on their toes for several seconds, and they can stand on one foot with their eyes closed. They can skip with both feet off the ground, and many can make a broad jump of 28 to 35 inches. Fine motor coordination improves as well, and children can draw, use scissors, and begin to color. By age five they can draw a rudimentary person, mold figures out of clay or play dough, and paint with broad strokes. Thus, their increasing motor control opens the door to many creative activities.

INTELLECTUAL DEVELOPMENT

Physical maturation and motor development continue to prepare the way for intellectual development. Increased motor coordination leads the preschooler to more careful and detailed examination of objects and the environment in general. Maturation of the brain allows the child to interact with materials for a longer time because the attention span grows. Increased memory enables the child to recall sequences for longer. Children of three to four can sometimes recall events that occurred a year earlier.

Preschoolers are intellectually curious and actively seeking to learn as much about their world as possible. According to Piaget, the preschooler is in the **preoperational** period of development (see Table 6-1).[1] As children become more skilled in forming and using symbols, language becomes more complex. The increase in dreams and nightmares, increasing interest in symbolic play—"The two sticks will be my bow and arrow"—and the beginning of drawing and art are also indications of advances in intellectual abilities.

Questions begin in the preschool years, first about the names of objects and activities, then about why certain routines are necessary. David Elkind describes the child's excitement about the mysteries that wait to be explored:

> As one youngster expressed it, "Mommy, why is there such a lot of things in the world if no one knows all these things?" Here the child expresses not only his awe of all there is to be known in the world but also his belief that everything exists for the purpose of being labeled and understood.
>
> In this connection, it is well to remember that to young children parents are all-wise, all-knowing, and all-powerful. The child assumes that every question can be answered and that parents have all the answers. The discovery that parents are fallible can sometimes come as a shock to the child.[2]

During this period the child is also curious about the origins of life and death and about the purpose of various activities: "Where was I before I was born?" "Do I have to die?" "Why does it rain?" Elkind suggests that, when possible, parents phrase their answers in terms of purpose or function. One can say that the rain falls so trees and flowers grow. Because most phenomena have a purpose, it is not dishonest to answer in these terms.

Although children have enormous curiosity and interest, Piaget believes their concepts are limited because they pay attention to only a small number of characteristics, usually to sensory features. They do not observe a logical series of operations that can be reversed—hence the term *preoperational*. For example, if they see a liquid poured from a short, fat glass into a taller, thinner glass, children say there is more liquid even though they have seen that none has been added. Children in the preoperational stage seem to judge on the basis of their visual perception of changed shape rather than observing that the operations do not include added material.

Preschoolers cannot look at objects and group them into classes on the same logical basis as older children or adults. At this stage they cannot arrange objects according to a given quality, even though that quality may be very noticeable. For example,

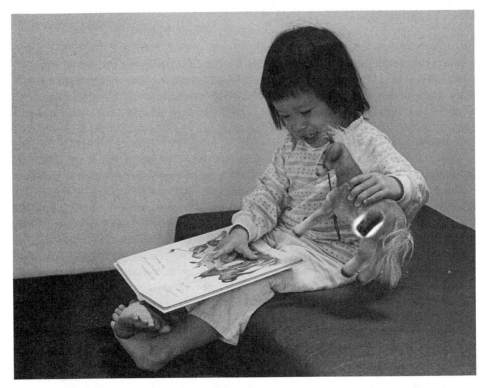

Parents need to keep differences in mind as they interact with their children. This four-year-old shares her book with "Horsey," without thinking about whether it can have experiences the way she can.

they cannot easily arrange several sticks according to the lengths of the sticks, although they can say which of two sticks is longer. They do not easily understand relational terms, such as "darker" or "lighter," unless the objects being compared are very different.

Piaget believes that children of this age do not make distinctions between mental and physical representations, and so it is hard for them to separate what is real from what is imagined and what is animate from what is inanimate. More recent studies of children's thinking, using questions phrased differently from those of Piaget, reveal that preschoolers struggle to make these distinctions.[3] While confusions occur, children are far more skilled than Piaget thought, in understanding, for example, the difference between a real dog and a dream of a dog. These investigators commented, "Our concern has been to establish the remarkable knowledge possessed by young children, even if this knowledge is incomplete."[4]

As parents interact with their children, they need to keep in mind that children's knowledge is incomplete. What is obvious and clear to parents as they look at an object or a series of events is not necessarily obvious to their preschool children. Thus, parents must be very specific in telling children how they see an object or event. Remember, too, that although children do not reason in the same logical way as adults, they are sometimes able to grasp intuitively the solution to a problem.

LANGUAGE DEVELOPMENT

During the preschool years children continue to enlarge their vocabularies, and their use of language becomes more complex. The child of three puts three or more words together and has a vocabulary of about 900 words. By age five, the child possesses strikingly well-developed language skills. Children generally speak clearly, but they may have some problems with pronunciation. Stuttering may occur at some point. This is usually temporary and a normal part of development. Vocabulary has increased to more than 2,000 words.

A recent study suggests that three is a pivotal year in language use.[5] At about three, children begin to direct an increasing amount of speech to peers. They express feelings and needs, and they begin to make boasting statements that enhance the ego—for example, they brag about new clothes or new toys. They express an interest in joining others in collaborative ventures. This shift in the function of speech occurs as children are learning to differentiate themselves from others. There is more talk about what "I" have and do. Between four and five, children pay more attention to their relations with peers, and they talk a lot about disagreements with peers and about resolving conflicts. Children progress from preoccupation with their own wants and desires (in the two- to three-year period) to focusing on the self as differentiated from others (at three and four), to focusing on relations with other people (at four and five).

EMOTIONAL DEVELOPMENT

Preschoolers' understanding and expression of feeling grow in breadth and complexity. Preschoolers become increasingly accurate in understanding the connections between feelings and the events and social interactions that produce them. While they at first believe that feelings are temporary, by the end of the preschool period, they recognize that feelings can persist and are influenced by what one thinks.[6]

Children are accurate in identifying what triggers emotions, especially when there is a social cause for the feelings. In one study, preschoolers agreed 91 percent of the time with adults in giving reasons for other preschoolers' feelings as they occurred in the course of everyday activity.[7] Preschoolers were most accurate in understanding anger and distress and less accurate in understanding happy and sad reactions.

While there are common areas of agreement between preschoolers and adults in understanding feelings, still there are differences; and parents are forewarned that they may well not understand their preschoolers' reactions. Preschoolers evaluate events by their outcome. If a wrongdoer is successful at getting what he or she wants, the preschooler assumes the child feels good about that. They may know an act is wrong, but not necessarily feel wrong or bad for doing it.[8] When adults were asked to predict how children of different ages would react emotionally in different situa-

INTERVIEW
with Claire Kopp

(Continued from Chapter 7)

What can parents do to help children learn self-control and self-regulation in the pre-school years? In Chapter 7 on Toddlerhood, we talked about the importance of parents' providing structure, simple rules, lots of rewards for following rules, and explantions for the rules. What can parents do when children are between three and five years of age?

Parents help children at ages three to four to develop strategies for doing things and strategies for emotional control. I think that it is around ages three and one-half to four that self-regulation and emotional control really come together. Society has rules for children's behavior and for their emotional outbursts and fears. We accept a child's fears and help the child to get control of the fears and learn to take responsibility for his or her behavior.

Of course, it is important for parents to expand the number of rules as children grow from two to four years old. As children are exposed to the larger social environment, more rules are appropriate for behavior with peers, with teachers, with parents, in stores, and in church. There may be a tendency to introduce many rules at one time, but parents are wise to introduce them gradually.

At this age, the issue of children's fantasy life comes up and whether or not these fantasies are lies. I do not think that four-year-olds lie with intent in the sense that an eight-year-old might lie. Rather, a four-year-old sometimes believes something happened when it did not. I do not think it is wise to argue with a child even though you have rules about not lying. The four-year-old fantasizes. Parents must accept that such fantasizing is his or her attempt to understand what is real and what isn't.

For example, a three-year-old boy was thrilled with a gift of several goldfish. Later, he came out of his room holding a dead goldfiish, its head hanging down one side and its tail on the other. Clearly the spine was severed. When asked what happened, the child said, "Oh, a man came in the house with a knife and hurt the goldfish." Obviously, the child had inadvertently crushed the goldfish. Because he felt remorse, he made up the story. The parent could become upset about the "lying." It would be better to explain that something happened to the goldfish but that a man was probably not involved. Then drop the subject. Parents can allow children to differentiate what is right from what is wrong without giving them a sense of guilt or shame. Parents' major task is to help children see right from wrong.

(continued)

tions, adults were not so skilled in understanding preschoolers as they were third- and sixth-graders.[9] Adults and all children agreed in predicting emotional outcomes to failure, nurturance, and justified punishment. Adults, however, did not anticipate how happy preschoolers would be to evade punishment while still getting what they want. Adults thought preschoolers would feel sad or mad, but the children reported they would feel happy. Preschoolers were highly sensitive to punishment, feeling angry or sad whether it was deserved or not.

Parents accept children's imaginary experiences as part of growing up without worrying too much about "lies." These imaginary tales occur because the child can't always tell reality from fantasy. When parents do not make too much of the imaginary story, children see that the rules can bend a little.

I see the years between the ages of one and four as a dance between parent and child. In the early stage, the parent is the leading partner in the dance. In the years two and one-half to four, the child leads sometimes, and the parent leads sometimes. The parent is always there, though, and able to lead if need be. In general, the child is the leader.

Let us turn to what really hurts the development of self-regulation in children. We can distinguish within-parent and within-child factors. Let us start with the parents. Parents who do not understand child development or parents who are under stress because of unemployment or divorce, may be too preoccupied to monitor children. Thus, they can not step in and take "the lead" when necessary.

The development of self-regulation can be a problem for children who are developmentally delayed, who have language delays, or who have sensory disorders. Children with such delays sometimes have trouble deriving principles about the rules. They need help in seeing the way in which the rules go together, and they need more structure in terms of explanations.

Both parents and children contribute to misunderstanding of the rules. Even if only one member misunderstands, eventually the dyad suffers. Sometimes there is just a terrible mismatch between parent and child. I am talking about the temperament disparity Thomas and Chess describe (see Chapter 6). For example, a very, very active child and parents who find it very difficult to deal with the high activity level. I think the child is vulnerable here. The child needs constraints without severe limits. He or she needs a way to control that activity. If the parent finds it hard because of the temperament mismatch, difficulty can arise. There is no definitive research on the matter because it is hard to identify what the mismatch is.

Where does self-control come from? It comes from a desire to be part of a social order, a desire to have love and affection. Children do not follow rules because they think the rules are wonderful. Children are not like that. They want love and affection, and they see that by following the rules, they get love and positive reinforcement. I am concerned about children being in a situation where they are not rewarded for following rules, where they are not given reasons for rules, and where they do not get techniques or strategies that help them develop cognitive understanding of the rules.

Parents must find a way to strike a balance between structure and flexibility. The fortunate thing is that somehow or other, most parents seem to strike that balance.

A recent study describes the most common form of upset as crying, and that accounts for 74 percent of the emotional upsets at home.[10] Anger represents about 23 percent of the upsets. Parent-child interactions are the main source (71 percent) of the upsets, with sibling conflicts accounting for only 13 percent and peer conflicts for 6 percent of the distress.

Parents' usual response to the distress is not to comfort but to give the child a practical, problem-solving response so that the child can deal with the situation.

Children appreciate the help. When parents give directives, children tend to get angry. Parents' ways of responding to emotional distress are related to children's competence in nursery school. When parents encourage children to take action with problems, children are better able to plan and are more effective in social activities and other areas as well.

Children not only express feelings, but can hide them as well. By age three, children are already beginning to hide anger, disappointment, and guilt.[11] In one study, preschoolers were given an opportunity to "peek" at a toy. Eighty-eight percent peeked, but only 38 percent admitted their peeking. Of great interest is the fact that adult observers of the children's responses could not tell when the children were lying. In another longitudinal study of problem behaviors 50 percent of four-year-old girls tried lying as a device to cope with parental demands. Boys followed this pattern about two years later.[12] Children not only hide their own wrongdoing, but also mask feelings of disappointment when others are present. Girls are more likely to hide negative feelings and give full expression to positive feelings.[13]

Children continue to be sensitive to anger outbursts whether they occur with family members or strangers, and their reactions to anger affect their social relationships with others. Preschoolers from families in which there is marital distress and resulting anger themselves become angry and noncompliant with parents and negative in their interactions with peers. These children appear under stress; they produce high levels of stress-related hormones. They play at a lower, less enthusiastic level with their friends, and when anger is aroused in these interactions, they have great difficulty dealing with it.[14]

Preschoolers who heard strangers arguing in the next room, showed heightened arousal during anger episodes and increased verbal aggressiveness in play following the anger exposure. Research found three emotional styles of responding to anger.[15] Concerned emotional responders (46 percent of children) showed negative feelings of upset during the episode and later said they felt sad and wanted to leave when they heard anger. Unresponsive children who showed no emotional reaction were only a small percentage of the group (15 percent). They were least likely to respond to aggressiveness in play with friends. Ambivalent responders (35 percent) showed both positive and negative feelings during the anger episode. They were upset, but later said they were happy during the episode. These children were most likely to become physically aggressive in play following the anger episode and were most responsive to aggressiveness in peers. Their behavior accounted for almost all the increased aggressiveness in play following the anger episode.

Preschoolers' emotional repertoire increases, and they have more diverse emotional reactions than toddlers.[16] They are more likely to share, more likely to give a positive response when anger is provoked; however, they express more distress than toddlers do. Different situations trigger a variety of feelings that are increasingly expressed in verbal form.

Anger

In the preschool years angry outbursts last about as long as they did in the toddler years, but preschoolers get angry over different things.[17] Toddlers are upset over routine habits, and preschoolers continue to battle with authority figures over bed-time routines, eating and table manners, control of anger. They resent restrictions and punishments, and they become angry when unable to accomplish what they want without help. In addition, children are increasingly frustrated and angry with playmates who take toys or who are unwilling to share. As children grow older, their outbursts feature less undirected physical energy and more organized activity directed to getting what is wanted.

In a study of problem behaviors, investigators found that direct expression of anger in temper outbursts decreased in the preschool years.[18] More subtle resistance took its place as children attempted instead to evade parental authority.

Fear

Fears are a natural part of life as children grow up. In the early years of infancy, fears of noise, of loss of support, and of strangers are most evident, but these anxieties gradually fade. In the preschool years children experience fears of animals, of the dark, of harm from imaginary creatures, and of natural disasters like fires and storms. Realistic concerns about dangers like falling out of a tree and hurting oneself can motivate the child to be cautious when that is appropriate. Fears can be harmful, however, if they are intense and prevent the child from exploring the world and inter-acting with other people. Research suggests further that intense fears at this time have long-term impact—preschool boys who experienced intense fears of bodily harm were, as adults, anxious about sexuality, uninvolved with traditional masculine activities, and concerned with intellectual performance.[19]

Empathy

Children grow in their ability to respond sensitively to others' needs. Preschoolers appear more able than toddlers to adopt the perspective of the other person and respond to him or her. Since they are better able to understand the sources of emotional reactions, their strategies for making things better go more directly to the source of the problem. When another child is angry, they are likely to give some material thing to the child, share with him or her.[20] When another child is sad or distressed, they are more likely to do something positive for the child, playing with the child, comforting the child.

Sharing and giving with friends occurs most frequently in an atmosphere of comfort and optimism. Best friends continue to share when happy, appreciative responses follow. When sharing does not occur, but the friend remains happy and smiling, the conflict does not escalate and sharing is resumed.[21]

In the last chapter, we discussed the family characteristics associated with empathy. By the preschool years, other sources of learning become important. Children learn empathic behavior from television programs like "Mister Rogers." They learn it from books and stories that have moral themes. Fairy tales, universal favorites of children, present models of kind, caring behavior that triumphs, often after many tribulations, over evil and cruelty.

Preschool children seem unable to think of themselves or others as having two distinct emotions at the same time.[22] They find it hard to understand that they can feel happy and sad all at once. Similarly, they feel if a person is nice, he is nice all the time. They find it difficult to comprehend a story in which a character is both nice and mean at the same time. In retelling the story, they separate the dissimilar emotions—first the person is nice; then, a long time later, the person is mean. In the school years, they come to understand and accept the reality of feeling two emotions simultaneously.

PERSONAL AND SOCIAL DEVELOPMENT

Erik Erikson believes that in the preschool years children have gained control over their bodies, have a good grasp of language, and are ready to plan and direct self-initiated activity.[23] They are active and curious. Their language skills are well developed, and they explore the world with questions.

This is the period of the Oedipal and Electra complexes. A boy experiences a romantic attachment to the mother, whom he wishes to marry, and a girl goes through a romantic attachment to the father, whom she wants to marry and have all to herself. Children give up these dreams of married life with the opposite-sex parent because of fear of punishment and abandonment by the parents. As children accept the commands of parents and society, the superego develops and becomes an integral part of the child's personality. If parents criticize children's activities, ridicule their fantasies, and refuse to answer questions, children develop guilt and feel that what they make and what they do is bad. If most experiences at this stage are positive, children develop strength of purpose, the ability to set goals and pursue them free of fears of failure, punishment, or criticism.

Development of the Self

In early childhood, children define themselves in terms of their physical characteristics—their size, hair color—and they differentiate themselves from others in terms of physical characteristics: "I am taller than Jimmy," "I have red hair." At the same time they continue to focus on their actions, what they can do, as ways of defining themselves: "I help Mommy," "I run fast." In one study, over half the responses describing the self related to actions. When given a choice between action and body statements to describe self, preschoolers overwhelmingly selected action statements. Though the active self predominates at this young level, a few children will refer to psychological qualities of the self—likes and dislikes.[24]

In this period children describe themselves in terms of skin color and facial features. Preschoolers identify themselves as black when asked. They, as well as American Indian preschoolers, when asked their preferences for pictures, choose those showing white figures. At the same time, however, these children have high self-esteem. Researchers speculate they are aware that white figures are preferred, feel good about themselves, and identify themselves with preferred status.[25]

As preschoolers approach tasks, they are optimistic.[26] They believe that when they want something, they will be able to achieve it, and they ignore any failures on

Preschool children handle four tasks: mastery of self, development of initiative, attachment to the parent of the opposite sex, and preference for the same sex. How many of these tasks are evident in this scene of a young girl helping her father with the family laundry? Is the parental modeling portrayed appropriate?

their way. The reason is not cognitive immaturity, for they can pay attention to others' failures and make realistic predictions about their chances for success. But when success is important, they believe they will be able to exert whatever effort is necessary to achieve their ends. As we shall see in later chapters, such optimism is an aid to accomplishment rather than an obstacle to it.

Sexual Identity

Preschool children have established their own sexual identity and know that this is an unchanging part of them. For example, 40 to 70 percent of preschoolers know that sexual identity does not change even if appearance or activities change.[27] They are also aware of sex role expectations; but they are flexible in accepting a variety of behaviors. Sex role expectations are seen as social conventions and are matters of personal choice for them. In general, they are more concerned about not looking like the opposite sex than about engaging in opposite-sex activities. They view boys' violations of sex role norms as more serious than girls'.[28] Although learning about sex roles appears universal, there are great individual differences in using that information to choose activities and toys.

Just as children are beginning to feel competent and effective, they experience an inevitable failure that may leave them with what Freud terms "a permanent injury to self-regard." This refers to the Oedipal complex or, as Dodson calls it, "the family romance," and its outcome of failure. Freud describes the child's desire to be romantically involved with the parent of the opposite sex—to marry that parent, to have children. The child's affection for that parent is mixed with tenderness, jealousy, and longing for intimate contact. Adults are often surprised by the flirtatiousness of a preschool girl who can be coy and charming, or by a boy that age who can be protective and seductive with his mother.

While this love flourishes, the preschoolers feel very competitive with the same-sex parent. These children want to surpass and outperform the adult, and they talk a lot about how grown-up they are. At the same time, children feel enormous rage and anger at this parent for standing in the way of their wishes for intimacy with the opposite-sex parent. When these impulses are at a peak, the child may cheerfully wish the parent dead and feel very guilty about this hostility. Later, the child may seek reassurances that the same-sex parent has not been a victim of his or her aggressive fantasies. If the parent gets ill or suffers some serious damage during this time in the child's life, the child may feel guilt that remains indefinitely.

Parents may be amazed at their own emotional reactions to a child's seductiveness. Instinctively, the parents may push the loving preschooler away and become cold and aloof, afraid to acknowledge their own feelings. When this happens, the child feels rejected and worries that he or she has done something wrong. These feelings of rejection, inadequacy, and guilt at having caused the rejection can last far into adulthood. Conversely, the parent may respond positively to these overtures and keep the child bound to him or her in a relationship that is too close and hampers the child's development.

Eventually the child deals with this anxiety by giving up the opposite-sex parent as love object and identifying with the same-sex parent as a model. As the child takes on the behaviors of the same-sex adult, the moral conscience and the commands of society become internalized in the form of what Freud calls the superego.

Development of Self-Regulation

Impulsivity decreases during the preschool years and children increase in their capacity to control behavior and follow rules even when no adult is present. There are great individual differences, however, in the rate at which they gain control. In studies of preschool children, we find a group who are identified as "uncontrolled."[29] These children are spontaneous, impulsive, emotionally expressive, nonconforming, and exploring. There is also an over-controlled group, who are conforming, inhibited, emotionally unexpressive, and narrow in interests. Finally, there is a highly resilient or adaptable group. These children can be controlled when necessary, and spontaneous and expressive when appropriate. Qualities of under-control persist so that those three-year-olds described as undercontrolled in nursery school will often be classed as undercontrolled one to four years later, when they attend elementary school. Qualities of resilience do not appear so persistent as qualities of undercontrol.

Children's capacity for control increases as they become able to use language to direct their behavior. In the preschool years, private speech directed to the self comes to have a guiding function for the child.[30] Initially, private speech follows actions and is a response to what has occurred: "I made that tower," "I got my shoes and socks." Gradually speech comes to precede the actions and helps the child plan appropriate behaviors: "I am going to get my shoes and socks," "I am going to get dressed." With increasing age, private speech changes from verbalizations to inner language and verbal thoughts.

As their attention span increases, children are able to concentrate more effectively and so control their behavior better. In one study, preschoolers were able to observe that noise and lack of interest in an activity interfered with attention and learning.[31] Preschoolers indicated that lack of interest was more important in decreasing learning than noise. Preschoolers' understanding of the effect of interest and noise in performance surprised investigators. But even though children are aware of the effects, they are not yet able to take steps to decrease the impact of these factors. That ability comes with age.

Parent-Child Relations

As in early years, parents have the closest relations with children and are most effective when they are sensitive, warm, understanding, and accepting. Acceptance-rejection is a major dimension underlying parent-child relations, but not the only one. A second is the dimension of control ranging from restrictiveness to permissiveness.

You may recall from Chapter 2 that Diana Baumrind identified three patterns of parenting preschoolers—authoritative, authoritarian, and permissive.[32] She found that competent, friendly, self-controlled children tended to come from authoritative families where parents balanced acceptance with control. Parents who were authoritarian—high on control and low on acceptance—tended to have children who were self-reliant but unhappy. This finding occurred mainly in the white families. Authoritarian parents of Afro-American girls had competent, outgoing daughters. Permissive parents, high on acceptance and low on control, had the least self-reliant and controlled children.

Parents' earlier ways of relating to children have an effect on children's behavior in their preschool years. Securely attached infants whose mothers continue to be sensitive and responsive to them have no behavior problems in the preschool period.[33] Even if mothers had anxious attachment relations with infants, these children show no behavior problems if mothers become more respectful of their autonomy, more sensitive and responsive to their needs, less intrusive. Children who had and continued to have anxious-avoidant attachments in infancy suffer many problems in the preschool years. They are dependent, noncompliant, hostile, impulsive, and withdrawn. Children with early and later anxious-resistant attachments lack confidence and assertiveness in their play, and they relate poorly to peers.

Parents may find it hard to change even when they want to because experiences with their own parents are shaping their behavior. Mothers who reported having secure attachments with their own parents were warm, helpful, and supportive with their own preschoolers. These children, in turn, were securely attached to them and received all the benefits of that close relationship. Mothers who reported remote, detached relationships with their own parents were cool, remote, and very directive with their own children. These children were insecurely attached to them, anxious, subdued, and suffering from behavior problems. A third group consisted of mothers who were also insecurely attached to their own parents but were preoccupied with these relationships. With their own children, these parents were confusing and controlling. They were sometimes warm and gentle, but then could be angry. Their children were negativistic and noncompliant.[34]

Mothers experiencing secure attachments reported as many negative events in their early lives as insecurely attached mothers, but they seemed to interpret them differently. They were able to focus on what was positive in the relationship and value that.

Though patterns of relationships can and do repeat themselves they need not. Even if parent-child relations get off to a shaky start in infancy, children can thrive if parents become more sensitive and responsive to them. In one study, mothers who become more reactive to children over time are women who have support from friends and are in a meaningful relationship with a man.[35] They feel more confident of their ability to deal with their children. Mothers who become less effective from infancy to the preschool years become gradually less supportive of children, less encouraging of them. They provide fewer toys and have less contact with children. These mothers are more confused and disorganized, less confident in childrearing techniques.

Direct control of children not only influences personal and social competence of the child, but also academic achievement. Children whose mothers were directly controlling—giving orders without explanation—performed less well on achievement tests in the early school years and at age twelve. So, when parents are attentive, warm, understanding, and authoritative, children are happier, more responsible, more enthusiastic, and cooperative, functioning well in intellectual as well as social situations. No matter how parents start out with children, they can always change; and children respond to the change.

Sibling Relationships

In the preschool years, children have close, intense relationships with brothers and sisters. When preschoolers are the older siblings, they often involve younger children in fantasy play, assigning them special roles that the younger ones are often happy to carry out. Preschoolers adapt their speech so that toddlers understand them better, speaking to them in short sentences, repeating phrases just as adults do. Preschoolers are helpful, soothing, comforting, sometimes entertaining the younger ones by joining with them in physical activities—rolling around on the floor, jumping.[36]

As in many close relationships, however, anger and frustration surface. In a Canadian study, 29 percent of the observed behavior between siblings was hostile.[37] Though the preschooler frustrates the younger child by taking advantage because of size, grabbing toys, or shoving, toddlers can be remarkably astute in irritating and distressing their older siblings. They, too, know how to tease in subtle ways, taking a toy they know the older one prefers, taking apart the older one's play creations. As toddlers get older, their aggression is expressed more directly in hitting, grabbing, and slapping. Sometimes one child in the interaction may be friendly and the other aggressive so that there is a mismatch in feeling tone. Children can learn to negotiate these differences.

Though many older siblings feel mothers favor younger siblings,[38] longitudinal studies of mothers' behavior with their two children at the same age—when each is one or two—reveal that mothers are quite consistent in the amount of affection and verbal responsiveness they direct to each child at that age.[39] Their behavior toward the child changes as the child grows, and so there is a difference in how they treat the two when they are different ages. Mothers are less consistent in their ways of controlling different children at a given age, probably because they have learned from experience.

Peers

In the preschool period, children engage in more cooperative play with each other than previously. Much of it continues to be reality-oriented, but there is an increase in fantasy play. As the sense of self becomes more secure, children are free to take on the roles of other people and pretend they are someone else. Boys' fantasy play involves using physical objects as pretend objects—a stick becomes a sword. Girls are more verbal, with their fantasy play oriented toward play acting.[40]

As noted in Chapter 7, children form stable friendships in these years. Friends have as many fights as casual acquaintances, but they handle them differently.[41] Whereas casual acquaintances stand up for their rights until someone wins, friends tend to disengage and find an equal solution that gives each partner something. Friends are then able to continue to play with each other while casual acquaintances drift away from each other after a fight.

Preschoolers like each other because they share the same activities and play together well. Preschoolers want to enjoy themselves and have fun with a minimum amount of friction. Those who disrupt play and cause trouble are disliked by other children.[42] Observations of children's nursery school behavior indicate that the majority of interactions between children are friendly.[43] Children spend a high percentage of time (81 percent in this study) in friendly encounters that include asking, suggesting, starting an activity with a smile or comment, saying, "Let's do . . ." Only a very small proportion of interactions (14 percent) are of a demanding, aggressive nature, and 5 percent involve whining, begging, and crying. Even when others are domineering, many preschoolers are mature enough to either ignore the response or agree with the other child and thus avoid a conflict. Preschoolers enjoy a friendly atmosphere and tend to return the positive overtures of others. Those children who reach out to others are sought out as companions.

Preschoolers demonstrate sensitivity to the needs and feelings of peers. Children who spontaneously help or comfort others—giving them their toys, assisting in a task—are sociable children who are not dependent on others. They seem to perceive a need and meet it. Other children respond positively to their behavior even though teachers rarely give praise or notice to such spontaneous behaviors. Another group of children who respond to others' requests for help meet with less positive responses from peers. These children are less sociable, more compliant and dependent, and less responsive to the social overtures of other children. Even when they engage in positive helping acts, they are not rewarded, and so many become even more socially unresponsive. The failure of such children to get rewards even when being giving seems due to other children's perception that they are forcing the helpful behavior; it is not spontaneous. A benign or vicious cycle of behavior is generated. Socially responsive, expressive children meet with success when they are helpful and sociable, reinforcing their social responses. Less expressive, less social children meet with less positive response even when they are helpful, and this may reinforce their maintaining of distance from others.[44]

Peer competence is related to family experience. Preschoolers who have had secure attachments with their mothers in infancy are warm, outgoing, socially mature children.[45] Children who have had anxious, resistant relationships with their mothers are lowest in peer status. This is especially true for girls.

Imaginary Companions

What do children do when they do not have access to other children? Many children invent imaginary companions to fill the void. Twenty or thirty years ago there was concern about the psychological stability of children who had such companions. But recent work indicates that children who have imaginary companions are bright, creative, verbal, and more cooperative and aggressive than children who do not.[46] They tend to be active self-initiators in play. These researchers found that only and firstborn children are most likely to have imaginary companions. Sometimes the companions are given up when a younger sibling is available for play or the child finds friends in kindergarten.

Children tend to play happily with their imaginary friends, sharing and talking with them. Such friends may increase the verbal development of children who have them. While about an equal percentage of boys and girls have imaginary companions, the companions tend to be males. Since companions rarely interfere in play with other children when this is possible, parents have little reason to discourage a child from having imaginary friends. The phenomenon of imaginary companions may possibly even be on the rise because families are now smaller and more only children are being raised. The existence of these companions suggests that children have the capacity to generate the kinds of experiences they need for their own development if the environment cannot provide them.

PARENTING TASKS

Children handle four tasks in this period: (1) mastery of the self, (2) development of initiative, (3) attachment to the parent of the opposite sex, and (4) preference for the same-sex parent. As in previous periods, sensitive, responsive parents help children meet and master challenges. Sensitive caregiving requires that parents help their children have successful experiences.

Intellectual development is enhanced by carefully chosen toys and new experiences. Interest in what children say and do, encouragement of exploration and play with toys—all these parenting behaviors enhance their children's skills in communication as well as intellectual growth. When parents listen and respond with positive interest and praise, when they avoid criticism and giving orders, children are encouraged to talk about their world as they see it.

In this period, a second task related to mastery is the development of initiative. Children must learn to begin a task with confidence that they can complete it as they wish. Encouragement when a child tries a new idea, even though the result is not completely successful, will ensure future attempts. A parent may find it hard to step aside, as all strategists recommend for so many problems in this period. But, as Freud and Erikson pointed out, the fate of a child's basic sense of initiative depends in part on the child's realization that he or she can act as an independent person and create something.

As children begin to initiate activities and to do more for themselves, parents may want to arrange for them to spend some time away from home in a play group or nursery school if they do not already spend time away from home. Many psychologists believe that the major value of nursery school is the opportunity children have to play with others their age in an environment equipped to meet their needs and interests. Children learn about themselves when they interact with same-sized peers who are preoccupied with the same questions about life. They learn to share and to settle disagreements that arise among equals. Frances Ilg and Louis Ames observe that time away from home pursuing satisfying activities often reduces tensions that arise as part of growing up.[47] Thus, children may have fewer behavior problems and become more cheerful and happy once they start preschool.

Maria Montessori, an Italian pediatrician in the early 1900s, believed that nursery schools can provide other benefits as well, if they are organized to do so; she demonstrated the effectiveness of nursery schools in stimulating the psychological growth of very poor children.[48] People came from around the world to see Montessori's schools. She advanced many ideas that Piaget later incorporated in his theories, stating that children learn by action and movement and are eager to learn as much as possible about the world; they readily absorb sensory stimuli that help to develop intellectual abilities. Montessori believed that children pass through a series of stages when it is easiest for them to learn different things—for example, colors at one stage, forms at another. To learn, children require both freedom and self-control. Adults impose broad limits to encourage self-discipline that protects the rights of everyone. Within these limits, however, each child learns at his or her own rate and develops a sense of worth by observing the products of this work. Montessori emphasized the pleasure children receive from participating in a large social group and contributing to group efforts.

Each child learns at his or her own rate and develops a sense of worth by observing the products of this work. A parent should encourage a child's exploration of new experiences, including attempts to "read," yet not expect results before the child is ready.

In deciding whether your child will have nursery school experience and if so, what kind, you need to keep in mind the individual needs of your child, the schools that are available, and the kinds of experiences possible without school. If you live in a place where there are many children who play together and your child is happy in this group, you may not want to send him or her to nursery school. If your child has no informal contact with peers, you can select a school that will meet the child's needs and will foster development. If a child is highly active, easily distracted, and isolated from other children, you may want to select a small school with a large outdoor area, many physical activities, and opportunities for interaction with others in small groups. A child who loves quiet activities, likes to pursue individual projects, and works independently might feel most at home in a Montessori school. The school should be selected on the basis of your knowledge of the child's needs and the school's staff, philosophy, and resources. Parents who decide not to send a child to nursery school will find suggestions for using Montessori principles at home in Joan Beck's *How to Raise a Brighter Child*.[49]

Mussen and Eisenberg-Berg summarize the ways that parents can help children develop helping and caring behaviors:

> Parents who want to raise prosocial children, or to increase the prosocial activities of their children, may be advised, with very little risk, to employ several time-honored practices: modeling helping and sharing behaviors clearly and frequently; reasoning with their children in disciplining them; encouraging the children to reflect on their own and others' feelings, emotions, and expectations; maintaining high standards for the child and being explicit about these; assigning responsibilities for others early.[50]

ROUTINES, PROBLEMS, AND STRATEGIES

Now let's turn to some of the behavioral problems that can arise and different strategies for handling them. We shall discuss problems related to physiological functioning—sleeping, eating, excessive masturbation, and high activity—and then problems related to interactions with others and the world at large—sibling rivalry, excessive dependency, aggressiveness, and fears.

Eating

We have all heard it said that "the way to a man's heart is through his stomach." Food is important. We enjoy it, are nourished by it, cannot live without it. Mealtime is doubly important—it is both a time when we eat and a time when family members are together and have a chance to talk and laugh and enjoy each other.

Yet rare is the child who does not, at some time, experience some eating problems. Most often children refuse to eat particular foods and then snack later on. Ginott encourages parents to use the eating situation to provide children with choices.[51] The child who is given choices—between scrambled eggs and boiled eggs, between milk or orange juice, between hot and cold cereal—has less reason to refuse to eat. This less authoritarian approach gives children some power over their lives and encourages them to take responsibility for themselves. Ginott suggests that most food problems occur when a mother tries to get her child to eat more than the child needs to be well nourished. Provide a reasonable amount of healthy food, and the child has the responsibility to eat.

Gordon suggests that parents use active listening and mutual problem solving when dealing with eating problems.[52] Sometimes a child who demands a food that

THE JOYS OF PARENTING PRESCHOOL CHILDREN

"When she was four, she was the only girl on an all-boy soccer team. Her mother thought she was signing her up for a coed team, but she was the only girl, and she enjoyed it and liked it even though she is not a natural athlete. She watches and learns and gets good at it, and we got a lot of joy out of watching her." FATHER

"Well, every night we have a bedtime ritual of telling a story and singing to her. This is probably beyond the time she needs it, but we need it." MOTHER

"He's very inventive, and it's fun for both of us when he tells stories or figures out ways to communicate something he's learned or heard. When his mother had morning sickness, he heard the baby was in her tummy so he figured out the baby is making the morning sickness, pushing the food out." FATHER

"It's fun to get home in the evening; he comes running out and jumps up which is really fun. It's a wonderful greeting." FATHER

"One of the delights that comes up is reading him stories, telling him the adventure of John Muir, at the four-year-old level. We were talking about places to go, and I said, 'Maybe we could go visit the home of John Muir.' He said, 'Oh, great, then I could go up there and have a cup of tea.' And I remembered I had told him a story about Muir's having tea in a blizzard, and he remembered that. He put that together, and it came out of nowhere. It knocked me over that he remembered that image." FATHER

"I enjoy her because I can talk to her; we have these wonderful conversations, and she can tell me about something that happened to her today at school that was really neat for her, and I just love to hear about it." MOTHER

"It's fun to hear him looking forward to doing things with us. He'll ask how many days until Saturday or Sunday because on those days I wait for him to get up before I have breakfast. Usually I'm up and gone before he gets up. He likes to come out and get up in my lap and share my breakfast, and it's a ritual. He looks forward to that and counts the days." FATHER

"She's really affectionate, always has been, but now out of nowhere, she'll tell you she loves you. She likes to do things with you, and when you give her special attention, one on one, she really likes it. We play games—Candy Land or Cinderella—or just one of us goes with her to the supermarket or to the park. We read stories every night and do some talking. Sometimes I put a record on and we dance." FATHER

parents cannot or will not give (for example, a piece of pie just before dinner) is really upset about something else. The request for food may be a request for attention or affection. If the parent senses this and can get the child to talk about it, what seemed like an unreasonable request may be forgotten as the child's real need is attended to. When a child refuses to eat necessary foods like vegetables, Gordon

"I miss this since the baby came, but we used to have special time together. We would go off and do things by ourselves. We would go driving in the car, go shopping, and have a lot of time to communicate, just the two of us. Four and a half is a really wonderful, talkative, growing stage. She would talk about the stuff going on in her life, questions she has: 'Why does it rain?' We would sing songs she learns in school." MOTHER

"I like sharing in their joy and pride in what they do. I think it's fun to decorate the refrigerator with their work." MOTHER

"The time I like best with her is hanging out together, and she loves doing projects with me. She likes to help me with a project when I am working in the garage, and I'll show her how to use tools, and its a special time with Dad." FATHER

"He's four, and he's so philosophical. He's always thinking about different things, and sometimes he'll tell me, and I am amazed. One day we were driving and he said, 'Can God see me riding here in the car?' Or one night at dinner, he was watching his little sister who's one, and he said, 'Do you think when she gets to be a big girl she'll remember what she did as a baby?'" MOTHER

"I like going for a walk with her, and we went skipping rocks at the reservoir. I was going to show her how to skip rocks because she had never seen that before. Of course, she wanted to try it, and I didn't think she was old enough to do it. I had found the best skipping rock; it was just perfect. I was going to hold her hand and do it with her. She said, 'No, I want to do it myself.' I thought, 'Oh, no!' The best skipping rock and it was just going to go plunk. No, I thought, it is more important to just let it go. So I said, 'Here let me show you how.' So I showed her, and she said, 'No, I can do it.' She threw it and it skipped three times! The first time she ever threw one! She wanted to stay till she did it again, and we did a little; but it will be a while before she does that again, I think." FATHER

"I love it when they come and get in our bed with us and cuddle. As they get older, they do it less, but they still do." MOTHER

"It's fun watching preschoolers interact with other kids too when your friends come over with their children. It's fun to see how they respond to new kids or kids who don't come over that often. It's neat watching them get to know each other. They'll stand and look at each other for a few minutes. They don't have any of those built-in dislikes that grown-ups might have. They might be shy with each other because they don't know each other, but they don't dislike each other." FATHER

advises that parent and child sit down and figure out how the problem can be resolved. One little boy agreed that if his mother gave him vegetables that he liked he would be happy to eat them. Then they made a list of the child's favorite vegetables, and both felt the problem had been solved.

Dreikurs, like Ginott, urges parents to be detached about children's eating.[53]

Children are presented with healthy amounts of food at meals and are permitted to eat what they like. At the end of dinner the plate is removed, and no other food is served until the next meal. If the meal is dinner and the child must wait until morning, that is acceptable. In a few days children learn that all the food they get is served at mealtime and the problem is solved.

Dreikurs recognizes that taking food away is difficult for parents to follow. Hunger pangs are thought to be painful. Dreikurs says he is always surprised that parents who would not hesitate to spank a child recoil in horror at the idea of allowing the child to go to bed hungry. He believes that parents are more concerned about power than about food. They want the child to do as they say, and that control is what the child fights. When parents do not exert power, children eat.

The behaviorists recommend rewards to encourage good eating habits. When children have difficulty finishing their meals, parents tell them they can have dessert after they have finished what is on their plates. If children do not drop food on the floor or on themselves, they are given rewards to encourage neat eating habits. Several behaviorists advise parents to use praise. If a child is eating very little but is praised for that, eating becomes pleasurable. Praise and attention for eating will reward, and so increase, eating.

Eating is the child's responsibility. Gordon is active in modifying the situation so that the child will want to eat. Ginott and Dreikurs take a detached view. Behaviorists use praise and rewards. Both Gordon and Ginott, and Dreikurs to some extent, offer the child choices.

Sleeping

Many children in the preschool years develop nighttime fears about sleep. They are afraid to go to bed, afraid of monsters and eerie creatures who will come in the night. Pediatrician Richard Ferber says such fears may be related to the fact that as children get into bed and begin to relax, they have less control of their thoughts.[54] Their minds run free, and children may feel out of control. Even children who are confident and assertive in the daytime may experience night fears.

Many children say they are afraid to go to bed and may seem afraid. Parents can reassure them that they are safe yet continue to follow the same bedtime routine, with the usual story and time for talk. Talking the fears over in the daytime can be helpful. Parents can practice active listening to understand the child's concerns. Ferber feels it is unwise to spend extended time checking the room to demonstrate that there are no monsters, for the child is basically anxious from trying to adapt to all that is required during the day and attaches this fear to the monsters.

> So, your child does not need protection from monsters, she needs a better understanding of her own feelings and urges. She needs to know that nothing bad will happen if she soils, has a temper tantrum, or feels anger toward her brother or sister. At these times, she can be most reassured if she knows that you are in complete control of yourself and of her and that you can and will protect her and keep her safe. If you can convince her that you will do this, then she will be able to relax. Your calm, firm, and loving assurance will do more to dispel goblins than will searches under the bed.[55]

If children indicate they are afraid to go to bed and go beyond fear to complete panic, clinging helplessly to parents, parents should try to determine what it is during the day that triggers such an intense affect. If the panic does not pass in a few weeks, parents are advised to seek counseling to determine the cause.

Sometimes children will awake in the night crying and upset from scary dreams. If they have had a nightmare, they will be awake and can often tell parents about the dream. Though these dreams occur at night, they are related to conflicts, feelings, stresses of the day. Children during this period may be worried about feelings of anger or jealousy or the sexual pleasure of masturbation. They need reassurance that parents are sympathetic to their concerns and will help them control these urges.

Nightmares are a part of growing up. They peak at about the time of school entry and again at ages nine through eleven. A child waking up from a nightmare is afraid and needs reassurance rather than logical arguments. A parent can remain with the child until he or she falls back to sleep, or perhaps can lie down with the child, but it is best not to make the latter practice a habit.

If nightmares occur frequently, parents can begin to examine what in the child's daylight hours is causing the trouble. There may be an adjustment to a new brother or sister, a change to a new preschool group. Helping the child cope with stress during the day is the surest way to prevent nightmares.

It is important not to confuse nightmares with night terrors. In both cases the child awakes in the night, appearing very frightened. The causes for these two behaviors, however, are different. Nightmares are scary dreams that occur during light REM sleep, and they result in full awakening, often with the child's having some memory of the dream. The child will call and want comfort. Night terrors, however, occur during a partial awakening after a very deep state of sleep. Night terrors happen during the first few hours of sleep at night—about 1½ to 3 or 4 hours after going to sleep—just as the child is entering a light stage of sleep. The child is not fully awake when he or she calls or cries. The cry may sound like a scream and so the parents assume the child has had a nightmare. In this case, however, if a parent tries to hold the child, the child pushes the parent away; comforting does not help. The child may drop back to sleep automatically and have no memory of the night terror the next day.

It may be hard to tell the difference between a nightmare and a night terror in very young children who cannot report dreams. As you try to wake the child from a night terror and the child struggles, you may assume the child is still dreaming. Children waking up from a night terror may also assume they have had a nightmare because their heart is racing and they have a feeling of dread. To make the distinction more difficult, children can seem dazed and confused waking up from either a nightmare or a night terror.

It is important to tell the difference between these two night occurrences because the treatment is different for each. For nightmares, reassurance and comfort are the effective parental response. For night terrors, parents should not attempt to wake the child or offer comfort. Avoid interacting with the child unless the child requests it, and let the child fall back to sleep. If you believe it was a night terror, it is best not to make too much of it with the child, who may be frightened to hear how terrified and out of control he or she felt. Night terrors disappear as children get older.

Nighttime Wetting

Nighttime wetting is more common among boys than girls, because the nervous system of boys matures more slowly. Gordon recommends I-messages and mutual problem solving; parents can present their reactions to the night wetting—saying that they don't like to get up and change sheets, that they don't like doing the extra laundry—and ask the child how he or she thinks they could help solve the problem. The child might volunteer not to drink liquids after dinner, go to the bathroom just before bed, and if he or she wets the bed, wait until morning to have clean sheets.

Dreikurs suggests a detached attitude toward such undesirable habits as thumb sucking, nail biting, and night wetting. Often the child who does these things believes he or she cannot control the unacceptable behavior. Parents must give encouragement yet remain unconcerned about the outcome. Scolding and punishment do not seem to help, and Dreikurs advises parents to turn the problem over to the child.

Behaviorists suggest that bed wetting can be controlled with rewards, a contracting system, and a learning program. Children may earn a gold star or a token for every dry night, and these can be exchanged for a privilege after so many are earned. At the time the contract goes into effect, however, parents must also encourage the child's overall responsibility, offering praise for other things done independently and making sure the child has age-appropriate chores that increase feelings of competence.

Various learning programs are available for dealing with bed wetting. Nathan Azrin and Victoria Besalel have developed a step-by-step program that actively involves the child. The child practices behavior that will enable him or her to become more sensitive to cues about bladder fullness and linking those cues with getting up and going to the bathroom. The procedure is described in their book, *A Parent's Guide to Bedwetting Control.*[56]

The methods just discussed rely on parents and children working together to solve the problem. Two other strategies are possible—medication and a pad-and-buzzer system. The latter is a system that can be used in conjunction with the Azrin and Besalel technique. A special pad is placed under the child's sheet; as soon as it becomes wet, a buzzer goes off. This wakes the child, who then goes to the bathroom. Mail-order companies sell the equipment for about $50. Even without any other practice in getting up, this technique has proven effective for about 90 percent of children in one study.[57] Many parents, however, object to the method for several reasons. The buzzer wakes other people in the family. Parents have to get up and reset the buzzer when it goes off (sometimes more than once a night), so they lose sleep, especially if the method takes several weeks to train the child. The cost also discourages parents. Finally, children may become irritated with the buzzer and attempt to disconnect it. Nevertheless, parents may wish to try this before seeking any medication.

When bed wetting has proved resistant to other techniques and children suffer psychologically from it, the medication imipramine is sometimes prescribed. This is effective only as long as the child takes it and in many instances is not completely effective in stopping wetting. Some medical authorities are concerned about prolonged use of the medication because of side effects. It can, however, provide a short-term solution for some children.

Excessive Masturbation

For many years parents discouraged masturbation with threats that it would lead to insanity, illness, and other dire consequences. Physicians and mental health professionals now consider masturbation a natural occurrence that has no harmful physical effects. However, the ways in which parents handle their child's masturbation can help either to prevent or to produce harmful psychological effects.

Frances Ilg and Louise Ames describe two possible responses.[58] First, parents can punish the child and prohibit the activity. Second, they can ignore the masturbation. If it is excessive, parents can try to find out whether the child is unhappy or tense and can help the child deal with any underlying source of anxiety. If parents punish and criticize the child, the child may come to feel he or she is evil for having sexual feelings. This can lead to difficulties at later ages, when the child may be unable to enjoy even approved sexual activity. In addition, children may feel so guilty that they cannot discuss any sexual activity or feelings with parents, even if they need help—for example, with infection or pregnancy.

Ginott is concerned only with prolonged masturbation, because it prevents children from seeking pleasure in other ways. Children who masturbate excessively may be reluctant to seek friends or to play in the neighborhood. Like Ilg and Ames, Ginott recommends looking for possible sources of tension in the child's life and correcting them. When children feel loved and have opportunities to explore the world and achieve their goals, sexual self-stimulation will not be the main source of satisfaction.

Dreikurs believes that excessive masturbation results from not being part of a social group. If parents try to force children to stop masturbating, however, children may only become more resistant. Dreikurs recommends providing many opportunities for activities and feelings of competence.

Benjamin Spock says he has no moral objection to masturbation, but he does not want the child to masturbate in public view.[59] He advises what he terms gentle inhibition. Spock suggests that the parent should not frighten the child, but should say that masturbation is not polite or approved in general company. Masturbation should be done privately. Like other professionals, Spock believes that encouraging other activities is enough to end the problem.

High Activity Levels

As the brain develops from birth to age three, the child's motor activity increases. From age three to nine, as the brain matures, the attention span increases, focusing improves, and motor activity decreases. The inability to inhibit motor behavior is, perhaps, the biggest single behavior problem in boys and often is identified as a problem in the preschool years. The child may always have been active; but when a great interest in activity continues after mastery is achieved in the toddler period and is accompanied by such other qualities as excessive restlessness, short attention span, and demanding behavior that permits no delay in gratification, problems arise. A child does not need to be classified hyperactive to experience these problems. Children with high levels of activity that are still within the normal range, though at the very high end, are perceived negatively by preschool teachers, parents, and peers.[60] High activity level in normal preschoolers is associated with poor impulse control, resistance to adult authority, and domineering behavior with peers. Highly active children are restless, fidgety, poorly controlled, and impulsive. They do not respond well to limits and are often seen as uncooperative, disobedient, and manipulative. With peers they are outgoing and self-assertive, aggressive, competitive, and dominant.

These qualities persist, and children described in this way at ages three and four are viewed in similar ways at ages seven and seven and a half. Not only is high activity related to poor impulse control, resistance to authority, and emotional excitability, but it is also linked to poor performance on intellectual tests at age seven and a half.[61] Inability to control motor behavior during the preschool period may make attention to cognitive tasks and involvement in them very difficult, thus paving the way for later school problems. Longitudinal data indicate that highly active preschool boys are likely to be competitive, sexually active men who lack intellectual interests.[62] High activity in girls was not as predictive of adult qualities.

Both mothers and fathers of highly active children possess qualities in common as well.[63] They tend to be directive, intrusive, and rather authoritarian with children. They get into power struggles and competition with children. Further, they appear hostile and unresponsive to the child's needs and interests. These qualities characterize mother-daughter, mother-son, father-daughter, and, to a lesser extent, father-son interactions. When fathers interact with highly active sons, they become more dramatic and seem to enjoy the challenge of their son's behavior, though they, too, get into power struggles.

Whether the behavior of highly active children produces these controlling qualities in parents or whether parents had these characteristics before the children became active is not known. Some evidence indicates that when hyperactive boys go on medication and their behavior changes, parents' behavior becomes less controlling.[64]

What can parents do? First, parents must get out of the vicious negative cycle that has been created. They must begin to spend some positive time with children, enjoying them. Russell Barkley, who has organized a program to train parents of hyperactive children, suggests that parents interrupt the cycle by spending at least 15 minutes per night doing whatever the child would like to do—playing a game, reading a story.[65] Parents are not to teach, direct, or criticize the child unless some extreme behavior occurs. Then parents may use discipline as usual. This 15 minutes is to be a pleasant time in which the parent observes the child and plays with him or her as the child likes. Positive comments on the child's behavior are permissible but not required. Both parents do this each day.

After this initial sharing of time, parents can then establish structure and daily routines in which the child can take an active role and can put to constructive use the high energy level that may otherwise be disrupting. The structure need not be rigid, but a general schedule of many daily activities will help a child be able to participate. If, for example, the child has a simple breakfast that he or she can help fix—cereal, juice, toast—confidence and independence are encouraged, energy is consumed, and structure is accepted. The old saying "a place for everything and everything in its place"—especially toys and clothes—can be used to help a child participate in creating order in his or her life while using up excess energy. Parents can provide a chest or boxes for toys and child-height hooks and shelves for clothes.

Donald Meichenbaum and Joseph Goodman have found that impulsive children can be taught to guide their behavior and achieve greater control by using a form of self-instruction.[66] Parents show the child what they want done and at the same time talk about what they are doing. The child then acts and talks out loud to describe the actions—"First I take off my pajamas, then I hang them up, then I put on my shirt and pants." In a third step, the child can internalize these instructions and repeat the words silently. Since highly active boys like to be busy much of the time, fathers can be especially important figures in modeling this sequence of "say, then do" as they spend time with their active sons.

Behaviorists Eimers and Aitchison advise parents to be alert and consistent in providing rewards for positive behaviors.[67] Highly active children often feel rewarded by the attention they receive for misdeeds. "Try to catch the child being good," they suggest and give rewards of praise and social approval. These seem to be more important to active children than material rewards.

Family rules should be simple, clear, and enforceable. When rules are broken, parents can use mild social disapproval delivered quickly. Each task the child is expected to perform should be broken down into simple easy steps that can be rewarded promptly. Putting toys away, dressing, helping to get meals—these can be divided into easy steps and rewarded with praise and social approval.

To increase attention span, Eimers and Aitchison recommend helping children with puzzles and other games that require concentration. They urge parents to praise the child for completion of the task rather than for correctness. Children should have a place where they can play without distractions. Gradually children are able to work at increasingly difficult games for longer periods of time.

Highly active children who are poorly coordinated benefit from opportunities to practice physical skills. Games that involve running, balancing, and gymnastic movements are helpful. Drawing and playing with Legos or other construction toys are activities that facilitate development of fine motor coordination. Parents can stimulate interest by giving genuine praise for what the child does and with material rewards of food or other treats.

Because the highly active child is more difficult to live with, more likely to get in trouble and receive social disapproval, parents must try to prevent the development of a poor self-concept—"I can't do anything right," "Nobody wants me around"— or a self-concept that reflects special privileges—"I am too much for anyone to handle," "I'm so active I don't have to go by the usual rules." Parents can point out to children that it is hard to have such a lot of energy without being able to control and enjoy it. When children harness their energy, they can accomplish a lot. The child who is rewarded for the things he or she does well and is given specific comments about behaviors that need changing can learn to deal with this high activity level.

Sibling Rivalry

In the last chapter, we examined problems that occur when a younger sibling is born. The older child feels jealousy and anger, as well as caring, warmth, and protectiveness. As children grow and become mobile and verbal, new kinds of problems arise.

Adele Faber and Elaine Mazlish apply Ginott's principles to sibling rivalry and suggest that parents consider themselves negotiators in these situations.[68] They can recognize that each child's feelings are unique and justified and can accept the feelings without necessarily approving them. Parents need not feel they must settle the differences as long as neither child is in danger. A parent can always interrupt and say, "Hitting doesn't solve problems." If that fails to stop physical aggression, parents can step in and calmly separate the children.

Gordon advocates use of active listening. This enables children to express their feelings and grants them freedom to resolve differences. When children listen actively to each other, a climate is created in which children can work out their own problems. One mother whose children were four, six, and eight found that the children, including the four-year-old, were able to devise rules that decreased fighting and name calling. The children were upset by verbal insults and decided they would try to send I-messages. If the situation became too heated, they would go to their rooms to cool off.

Dreikurs considers sibling rivalry in detail. He believes that parents can reduce the jealousy between children by making it clear to all that each child in the family is loved for his or her individual qualities and that it is not important whether one child does something better than another. Parents love each child. But a child's trust of that love can be diminished when parents use one sibling's behavior to humiliate another child—"Why can't you be more like Jimmy—he ate everything on his plate."

A fight is often an attempt to get a parent's attention and can be ignored. Parents may fear that a younger child will be hurt, but often children threaten violence to attact mother's attention. Dreikurs reported an incident in which a four-year-old girl seemed to be about to close the door on her little brother as he came through it. The mother was upset and dashed up to help the little boy. Dreikurs noted, however, that the little girl was very careful to shut the door without pinching her little brother's fingers. If the mother had been observant, she would have realized that the girl's desire was to get attention and the hug that would follow the scolding.

Dreikurs recommends treating all children the same when siblings bicker or fight. They are all sent to their rooms if play becomes noisy. If one child complains about another, parents can react so that children feel a responsibility to live in peace. Parents can point out that a child who acts up today may only be trying to retaliate for an incident that happened yesterday. Misbehavior involves all children in the family, and they can learn to take care of each other. Cooperation can be fostered by taking children on family expeditions and having all the children play together. When they see that life is more fun when they cooperate and get along with each other, children learn to settle their differences.

Behaviorists also suggest that parents withdraw from the sibling fights but substitute rewards for cooperation as a way to increase positive interactions. Children will blossom when they hear praise for their good points. Once a fight breaks out, however, parents are encouraged to say as little as possible and to offer a reward for good behavior.

All these techniques are important, and parents must decide just which ones are most needed in a particular situation: helping children become aware of each other's feelings, increasing verbal communication, ignoring fights or administering punishments yet making sure to reward positive interactions.

Aggression

Aggression has been defined as "an attitude of attack, as contrasted with passive withdrawal, which may or may not possess an element of hostility."[69] Children become aggressive for many reasons and express their feelings in several ways. If someone—an adult, a sibling, or a peer—interferes with a child's routine, takes a possession or toy, or forces an activity on a preschooler, the child may respond aggressively. The response may be physical—yanking the possession back, hitting the intruder—but a preschooler is most likely to respond with verbal insults, taunts, or threats.

Parents can accept aggressive feelings but not the hitting or hurting of others. Ginott suggests such comments as, "People are not for hitting; pillows are for hitting."

Gordon recommends active listening, as used in the following incident. Mary, a friend of four-year-old Tim, came to visit for an afternoon. Tim became angry and started a lot of fights with Mary. Tim's mother tried hard not to blame Tim or call him a bad boy. At first she responded to his anger by saying, "Mary doesn't like it when you hurt her," and then, "I can't have you hitting other children." Nothing worked until the mother tried active listening in an effort to understand her son's anger. She asked Tim whether he thought she was paying too much attention to Mary. He answered that he thought she loved Mary more.

Because Tim was young, his mother had to take an active role in supplying some of the possible feelings Tim might have. After Tim said he felt unloved, his mother explained that Tim was special to her and daddy, and Mary was special to her parents. Tim then began to settle down and talk about his special friends. If fighting continues after active listening, that approach has not worked. Parents should send I-messages saying they do not like the fighting and then withdraw if there is no danger to the children.

Dreikurs talks about the different meanings that aggression can have for children. One aggressive child may be motivated by a desire for attention, another may want power or revenge, a third may be feeling inadequate. If parents can get the child to talk about how he or she is feeling, the parent and child can work together to resolve the difficulty. Dreikurs urges parents to focus on the purpose of the behavior, on what it will get the child (attention, power, revenge), not on the causes (jealousy, lack of confidence, or a feeling of being neglected).

The behaviorists have a variety of responses to aggressiveness. If children talk about fighting with peers, parents can remind them of the consequences of such fights. Children may then try to avoid those consequences. If fighting is occurring, parents can separate children and perhaps send them to separate rooms for a while. And parents can reward children when they are playing happily and cooperatively with other children.

Dependency

Ginott describes dependency in children as the result of overprotective parents. Such parents feed and dress the child and hover over the child long after other children are encouraged to take care of themselves. Overprotected children do not have a chance to grow and get to a sense of who they are and what they want. They have had little experience caring for themselves and so they are afraid to try. As a result, they continue to be dependent on the parent who fosters dependency. A vicious cycle is set up, and parents need professional help if the dependency is too great.

There is no hard and fast rule for determining whether you, as a parent, are encouraging dependency. You must observe your own behavior to see whether you do things for the child that he or she could do alone. Do you rush to put on a sweater when the child could do it herself? Do you discourage the child from trying something new, like helping with the dishes, because you can do it faster?

It can be hard to know whether you are being appropriately careful or overprotective. Children mature at different rates, and there is no one age at which all children can do things independently. Look around at other children the same age. If they are all doing more for themselves than your child, perhaps you are delaying your child's independence.

If you decide you are overprotective, try to figure out why and change your behavior accordingly. Do you do it to save time? Are you fearful that something might happen if the child acts alone? Is your fear realistic? Are you worried because what the child does is not perfect? Sometimes parents are overprotective because the child's dependence gives them a sense of importance. If a parent cannot determine the reason and such dependency continues, professional counseling is desirable.

To cope with the usual problems that children have in mastering skills, Ginott recommends waiting patiently and making a calm comment that recognizes the difficulty—"It is hard to button your coat." Once such a comment is given, it makes no difference whether children succeed or fail. If they succeed, they know they have .accomplished a difficult task, and if they fail, they know the parent understands that it was hard.

Gordon states that when parents rely on solutions that draw on parental power to force children to conform, children in the early years become obedient, fearful, but also passive, and deny their own feelings. When adolescence comes and they feel they have more power, children frequently rebel with a vengeance, even though they are less mature than other children. When a family relies on mutual problem-solving techniques, children develop thinking skills and a sense of competence that carries over to other situations. With young children, parents may have to suggest many alternatives. But children can select acceptable answers, and gradually they learn to develop ideas.

Dreikurs describes varying degrees of dependent behavior. At one extreme is the child who seeks attention by asking repeatedly for help with skills already mastered. At the other is the child who has become so discouraged that he or she has mastered few skills and feels constantly inadequate and helpless. The remedy is to "never do for a child what he can do for himself." The parent's effort does not serve the child, who is handicapped by the parent's attention but instead serves the parent, who needs to demonstrate competence or is looking for meaning in his or her own life.

Behaviorists advocate reward for increasingly independent behaviors. Eimers and Aitchison describe the case of Randy, three and a half, who was so tied to his mother that he refused to be out of her sight for more than a few minutes at a time. Initially, his mother had been pleased that Randy was so attached to her and liked being her little helper. She soon realized, however, that Randy was not at all interested in playing with other children. And her concern turned to worry when no amount of encouragement would get him away from her for more than a few minutes.

The mother handled the problem by rewarding her son for increasing his distance from her. At first she rewarded him with praise and social approval for staying in the next room for 5 minutes, then for 10 minutes. She gradually increased the amount of time and the distance he was away. Soon she worked upstairs and he played downstairs. To get him out of the house and playing with others, she invited one child in to play, provided special food and games. She increased the number of children. One day, they invited him to play outside and he went along. At all stages, Randy's mother gave him praise, attention, and rewards. With time he found that playing with friends was more fun than being with his mother, and the play itself was the reward.

Strategists agree about the cause of dependency—it is the parent's desire to be too involved in the child's activities. Ginott, Gordon, and Dreikurs all urge parents to stand back and let children take care of themselves. The behaviorists recommend rewarding independent behaviors until these become self-perpetuating. Parents who use this approach are active initially, but they soon stand back as the children become independent.

Research by David Harrington, Jeanne Block, and Jack Block reveals that children who are dependent and indecisive as preschoolers may continue on this path into elementary school.[70] Timid, tense boys have greater difficulty with intellectual problems. Anxious, inhibited girls have difficulties in interpersonal relations and are likely to give in to others.

What can parents do to promote curiosity, creativity, and independence in their children? Give positive support of the child's exploratory behavior. Have and communicate confidence that what the child does or makes is valuable and worth attention, even if it is not perfect. Encourage the child's involvement in activities, and encourage the child to persist in an activity until he or she achieves the goal.

Fears

How can parents minimize the number of fears a child has? Some parents are sarcastic and critical, make fun of fears, or ridicule or punish children. These tactics do not decrease children's fears. They do diminish children's self-esteem and make them more vulnerable. A model of confident, nonfearful behavior helps children handle fears. The model can either be a parent or another child who is not fearful. Learning of nonfearful behavior occurs most easily in a happy atmosphere. An explanation of a frightening event—of a thunderstorm, for example—helps children understand what is happening and so helps to dispel their fears.

A newborn who is welcomed into a family that already includes a dog—even a Saint Bernard—will grow up unafraid of animals, which are an accepted part of the environment. If a child is afraid of animals, this fear can be overcome by exposing the child first to small, distant animals and gradually to closer, large animals. Visits to pet stores and later to a zoo can be fun and beneficial in dealing with fear. Eventually the child will be ready to play in a room where there is a small, friendly dog. And that experience will give the child a sense of control and confidence.

Many psychologists believe that children's greatest fear is fear of abandonment by parents. Parents should never threaten, even playfully, to leave the child. Parents are sometimes tempted, especially when out shopping, to tell the children that if they don't hurry they will be left behind. Ginott recommends against such statements because they "fan the flames" of the fantasy of being abandoned. If a parent must go away—for example, to the hospital or on a business trip—children should be prepared well in advance of the separation.

Doll play can be used very effectively to prepare a child for a parent's absence. Using dolls to take their roles, the child and the parent who is going away can enact the time of separation, the period of absence, and the parent's return. Tape-recorded messages from the parent for the child to listen to during the absence and pictures of the absent parent are also helpful.

The parent who makes careful preparation for even a short absence only to find that the child cries or is disconsolate anyway may find it wise to examine his or her feelings about being away from the child. Sometimes children seem to have built-in radar that makes them remarkably sensitive to even the unspoken feelings of those who are close to them. The child of an anxious parent may sense that anxiety and respond in kind.

Dreikurs considers separation anxiety the child's attempt to control the parent. He believes the best course is to ignore the fear. Parents must provide children with affection, love, and concern, but must not respond to fears. Because the fears often stem from feelings of helplessness, parents are encouraged to find opportunities for children to be more self-reliant and to win approval by cooperating with others.

Behaviorists handle separation fears and crying by finding ways of not reinforcing such behavior. They suggest that the mother should not stay home, because that rewards the crying. A parent should have a substitute caregiver whom she trusts. Then she should leave and let the child settle down. To help the child adjust to baby-sitters, Becker recommends that the mother leave for brief periods at first, gradually staying away for longer periods of time.[71]

To reduce and eliminate fears, the behaviorists Eimers and Aitchison recommend that parents remain calm when the child is afraid and handle one specific fear at a time. Select a specific fear, like fear of dogs, to work on, even if the child has many. As one fear decreases, others may also, and a child can usually only deal with one problem at a time. Make gradual progress in small steps; do not arrange dramatic encounters with the feared object.

Having the child observe other children, particularly friends, interacting with the feared object or situation also helps to reduce fears. Give praise and social approval for every approach to the feared object. Ignore statements about the fears, because that attention can be a reward. Instead, reward all positive statements the child makes that indicate ability to handle the situation.

As children grow and perceive and experience more in life, they become aware of the many possible dangers that exist. Fears are a result of increasing awareness that there are dangers that must be guarded against. Mild fears and caution in new situations are useful and protective for children so that they will not charge into potentially dangerous situations. When these fears occur, as they do in the preschool years, accept them as signs of the child's increasing maturity. Showing the child how to cope with fear and overcome it increases the child's competence and self-confidence.

The Difficult Child

Stanley Turecki, a New York psychiatrist, has developed a program for dealing with what he terms the "difficult child."[72] Chapter 6 describes the nine temperamental traits that Alexander Thomas and Stella Chess observed in young babies: activity level, distractibility, adaptability, negative mood, approach/withdrawal, intensity, regularity, sensory threshold, and persistence. On the basis of these traits, Thomas and Chess classified babies into three groups—easy babies (about 75 percent of the group), difficult babies (about 10 percent of the group), and slow-to-adapt babies (about 15 percent of the group). Other workers, too, especially John Bates and his coworkers, have identified infants with a difficult temperament.[73]

At the extreme, the difficult child is a highly active, distractible, intense child who finds it hard to adapt to change. This child generally has a negative mood and tends to withdraw from new situations. He or she tends to have a low sensory threshold and to be bothered by stimuli other children would not notice. The difficult child is also often irregular in schedule.

Though such a child is hard to raise, Turecki insists parents must accept that he or she is a normal child whose temperament creates the difficulty. Difficult children are not all alike. Some have few of the identifying characteristics; others have many in varying combinations. Although temperament is the problem, parents must nevertheless help the child live and function with it. Turecki's book *The Difficult Child,* written with Leslie Tonner, describes a program he developed at Beth Israel Medical Center in New York. Turecki became interested in the area when his third daughter proved to be a "difficult child." After he and his wife struggled to raise her, he could understand firsthand the problems that mothers especially—and also families—face when such a child comes to dominate family life. Turecki's program combines sensitive, responsive, feeling-oriented techniques with behavioral modification procedures.

The first step in the program is a ten-day study period in which the parents familiarize themselves with their child's behavior and temperament and the link between the two. Parents make lists of the child's problem behaviors and the situations in which they occur, then rate their child's behavior as either *very difficult, moderately difficult,* or *mildly difficult.* Parents then relate the child's problem behaviors to temperamental traits. For example, a four-year-old girl acts resistant and stubborn when she is getting dressed. She likes only certain clothes and refuses to wear others. This child is described as poorly adaptable, with a low sensory threshold for clothing. Parents also look at the whole family's reaction to the difficult child's behavior—for example, they may feel worn out, and siblings may wish the child had never been born, because the child fusses and cries so much over routine.

Having described the present situation in detail, parents work to regain adult authority in the various problem situations by changing their disciplinary techniques. Turecki insists parents put their frustrations and irritations aside and adopt a neutral attitude that emphasizes parents' thinking about the problem behavior episodes rather than simply expressing their feelings. Parents must first stand back and then react from a logical analysis that makes the child's behavior, not the child's or parent's mood or feelings, the focus of attention.

Parents question themselves when a problem arises: Is this behavior caused by temperament? Is it worth reacting to? Since parents of difficult children get into a vicious cycle with them, they tend to react to everything. Parents, however, must learn to set priorities. They work together to arrive at the three or four behaviors they will focus on. When they see that a certain misbehavior is related to temperament, parents openly label the behavior as a temperament problem: "I know you are sensitive to the feel of certain clothes," "I know you do not always feel ready for bed at this time," "I know it's hard to listen and pay attention sometimes." With such problems caused by temperament, parents must ask themselves whether it is worth intervening—Does it really matter whether the child wears the old or the new jeans? If an intervention is needed, Turecki prescribes many behavioral techniques: Intervene early; let the child cool off and calm down if necessary; prepare the child for changes; always get the child's attention when talking or giving directions. If punishment is needed, make it mild and quick.

A main thrust of Turecki's program is to help parents sympathize with the problems the difficult child experiences while still setting reasonable limits for the child. Many misbehaviors can be related to temperament; parents' neutral response helps both them and the child learn to live with the problem and eventually overcome it. Hostility is removed from disciplinary action, and both parents and child can focus on the behavior that needs controlling.

Turecki's approach helps parents understand their child and at the same time learn more effective ways to manage the child's behavior. Empathy with the child's problem does not produce lack of discipline but rather more effective discipline. This program deals with all the common problems of difficult children—temper tantrums, picky eating, sibling fighting—and is unusual in addressing the needs of all family members—parents, child, siblings. It includes parent group meetings that offer opportunities for parents to share their experiences and encourages ways of making the family stronger. Turecki summarizes:

> These vignettes illustrate how the principles of adult authority and the techniques of management go hand in hand with an education in temperament to enable you to handle your difficult child. Progress will occur gradually, interspersed with rougher periods for both the child and the parents. Be patient with yourselves; be loving with your child; learn to appreciate his good qualities and to enjoy him. In time, the vicious circle will be replaced by liking and respect between you and your child.[74]

PARENTS' EXPERIENCES

During this period of their children's lives, parents, according to Galinsky, are still in the authority stage, learning the wise use of power.[75] Family life, however, becomes smoother as preschoolers grow more accustomed to routines, become more interested in the outside world, and are able to enjoy more of the activities that parents enjoy, like trips to museums.

At this point, parents often consider having another child, if they have not already. Dual-career parents often wait until the older child is a preschooler, then wonder if they should start all over again with sleepless nights, tired days, infant's crying. Parents wonder how they will meet the needs of yet a fourth family member when everyone feels busy already, and many parents believe life is harder with two children. On the other hand, some parents feel they have already adapted to a child's schedule; to them, a second child does not seem twice the work. Changing day care arrangements sometimes helps because an in-home day care program is economically more reasonable with two children at home. Parents have to look at all their options and decide.

Whether they rear one or two children, it is clear that parents need each other's support as well as a social network in meeting the challenges of rearing children. In the rush of parenting, there is a tendency to put marriage low on the list of priorities. Yet studies describing factors that improve parenting point to the importance of parents' mutual support. Parents can only be supportive when they spend time with each other, when they can discuss what is happening in the family and how each person feels about it. Parents can create time for each other at home, but they must make the time to share the most important parts of their lives with each other.

Single parents must build a social network of friends to rely on and make time for them. Just as husbands and wives may be too busy for each other, single parents may feel they cannot take time out from their children to see their friends. Yet time with friends benefits the whole family. Parents feel recharged and more relaxed and thus can be more giving and understanding with their children.

MAJOR POINTS OF CHAPTER 8

Preschoolers have a greater sense of mastery. Their

- greater motor coordination enables them to explore the world and everything in it more thoroughly
- increased attention span enables them to interact with people and objects for a longer time
- increasing curiosity leads them to ask many questions about the nature of life and people
- increasing abilities to remember and think enable them to classify objects, often on the basis of appearance
- greater language skills enable them to express their own points of view and learn from others

Preschoolers' emotional reactions and understanding of emotions are more varied and advanced. They

- are increasingly accurate in understanding others' feelings and the situations leading to these feelings
- evaluate an event by its outcome—for example, if they obtain a forbidden goal without punishment, they are happy even when they know they broke a rule

- believe parent-child interactions cause most (71 percent) of their upsets at home
- learn to hide feelings of disappointment and anger
- feel upset, worried, and distressed when adults, even strange adults, express anger
- have fewer temper tantrums
- have more fears as they become aware the world can be dangerous
- share in a more sensitive way

Preschoolers have increased sense of themselves as:

- active agents
- different from others in physical ways like skin color
- having an unchanged sexual identity
- being able to choose opposite-sex activities if they wish
- being more in control of what they do

Acceptance of the child and control of behavior are two basic dimensions of parenting. When parents

- balance these two aspects and accept the child but control behavior, children are competent and controlled
- overemphasize control and do not give enough acceptance, children are self-reliant but unhappy
- overemphasize acceptance and permit any kind of behavior, children are least self-reliant and poorly controlled

Parenting in this period involves:

- balancing acceptance of the child and his/her individuality with control of individuality
- giving reasons for rules in terms the child can understand
- taking time to answer seriously as many of children's questions as possible
- helping children master challenges so they have successful experiences in making things and carrying out their plans
- looking for experiences that will expand the child's skills—appropriate toys, nursery school, contact with peers
- modeling controlled and sharing behaviors
- helping the child conform to rules outside the family circle—at church, nursery school
- playing with children and sharing their enjoyment of life

As children become more controlled, parents continue to be authorities who focus on helping children gain control in the areas they have not yet mastered:

- high activity
- excessive emotional reactions like aggressiveness, fearfulness, and over-dependence
- difficult temperaments

As parents become more comfortable as authorities, they

- sometimes think of having another child and have to balance everyone's needs as they make that decision
- are able to resolve differences with spouses about rules and enforcements

Problems discussed center on:

- meeting physiological needs
- getting control of bodily functions—masturbation activity level, bedwetting
- getting control of emotional reactions and behavior like fears and aggression

Joys include:

- children's reasoning
- increasing skills
- affection
- joint projects

ADDITIONAL READINGS

Eisenberg, Nancy, and Mussen, Paul H. *Roots of Prosocial Behavior in Children*. New York: Cambridge University Press, 1989.

Fraiberg, Selma. *The Magic Years*. New York: Charles Scribner's Sons, 1959.

Galinsky, Ellen, and David, Judy. *The Preschool Years*. New York: Times Books, 1988.

Schacter, Robert, and McCauley, Carole Spearin. *When Your Child Is Afraid*. New York: Simon & Schuster, 1988.

Turecki, Stanley, and Tonner, Leslie. *The Difficult Child*. New York: Bantam, 1985.

Notes

1. Jean Piaget and Barbel Inhelder, *The Psychology of the Child* (New York: Basic Books, 1969).
2. David Elkind, *Children and Adolescents*, 2nd ed. (New York: Oxford University Press, 1974). p. 32.
3. Henry M. Wellman and David Estes, "Early Understanding of Mental Entities: A Reexamination of Childhood Realism," *Child Development* 57 (1986): 910–923.
4. Ibid, p. 921.

5. Frances Fuchs Schacter et al., *Everyday Preschool Interpersonal Speech Usage: Methodological, Development, and Sociolinguistic Studies,* Monographs of the Society for Research in Child Development 39 (1974): whole number 156.

6. Sally K. Donaldson and Michael A. Westerman, "Development of Children's Understanding of Ambivalent and Causal Theories of Emotions," *Developmental Psychology* 22 (1986): 655–662.

7. Richard A. Fabes, Nancy Eisenberg, Sharon E. McCormick, and Michael S. Wilson, "Preschoolers' Attributions of the Situational Determinants of Others' Naturally Occurring Emotions," *Developmental Psychology* 24 (1988): 376–385.

8. Gertrude Nunner-Winkler and Beate Sodian, "Children's Understanding of Moral Emotions," *Child Development* 59 (1988): 1323–1338.

9. Frank A. Zelko, S. Wayne Duncan, R. Christopher Barden, Judy Garber, and John C. Masters, "Adult Expectancies about Children's Emotional Responsiveness: Implications for the Development of Implicit Theories of Affect," *Developmental Psychology* 22 (1986): 109–114.

10. William Roberts and Janet Strayer, "Parents' Responses to the Emotional Distress of Their Children: Relations with Children's Competence," *Developmental Psychology* 23 (1987): 415–422.

11. Michael Lewis, Catherine Stanger, and Margaret Sullivan, "Deception in 3-Year Olds," *Developmental Psychology* 25 (1989): 439–443.

12. Jean W. Macfarlane, Lucile Allen, and Marjorie P. Honzik, *A Developmental Study of the Behavior Problems of Normal Children between Twenty-One Months and Fourteen Years,* University of California Publications in Child Development, vol. 2 (Berkeley: University of California Press, 1954).

13. Pamela M. Cole, "Children's Spontaneous Control of Facial Expressions," *Child Development* 57 (1986): 1309–1321.

14. John M. Gottman and Lynn F. Katz, "Effects of Marital Discord on Young Children's Peer Interaction and Health," *Developmental Psychology* 25 (1989): 373–381.

15. E. Mark Cummings, "Coping with Background Anger in Early Childhood," *Child Development* 58 (1987): 976–984.

16. Ibid.

17. Florence L. Goodenough, *Anger in Young Children* (Minneapolis: University of Minnesota Press, 1931).

18. Macfarlane, Allen, and Honzik, *A Developmental Study of the Behavior Problems of Normal Children between Twenty-One Months and Fourteen Years.*

19. Jerome Kagan and Howard A. Moss, *From Birth to Maturity* (New York: John Wiley, 1962).

20. Fabes, Eisenberg, McCormick, and Wilson, "Preschoolers' Attributions of the Situational Determinants of Others' Naturally Occurring Emotions."

21. David Matsumoto, Norma Haan, Gary Yabrove, Paola Theodorou, and Caroline Cooke Carney, "Preschoolers' Moral Actions and Emotions in Prisoner's Dilemma," *Developmental Psychology* 22 (1986): 663–670.

22. Kurt W. Fischer and Daniel Bullock, "Cognitive Development in School Age Children: Conclusions and New Directions," in *Development during Middle Childhood: The Years from Six to Twelve,* ed. W. Andrew Collins (Washington, D.C.: National Academy Press, 1984).

23. Erik H. Erikson, *Childhood and Society,* 2nd ed. (New York: W. W. Norton, 1963).

24. William Damon and Daniel Hart, "The Development of Self-Understanding from Infancy through Adolescence," *Child Development* 53 (1982): 841–864.

25. Margaret Beale Spencer and Carol Markstrom-Adams, "Identity Processes among Racial and Ethnic Minority Children in America," *Child Development* 61 (1990): 290–310.

26. Deborah J. Stipek, Theresa A. Roberts, and Mary E. Sanborn, "Preschool-Age Children's Performance Expectations for Themselves and Another Child as a Function of the Incentive Value of Success and the Salience of Past Performance," *Child Development* 55 (1984): 1983–1989.

27. Sandra Lipsitz Bem, "Genital Knowledge and Gender Constancy in Preschool Children," *Child Development* 60 (1989): 649–662; Michael Siegal and Judith Robinson, "Order Effects in Children's Gender Constancy Responses," *Developmental Psychology* 23 (1987): 283–286.

28. Judith S. Smetana, "Preschool Children's Conceptions of Sex-Role Transgressions," *Child Development* 57 (1986): 862–871.

29. Jeanne H. Block and Jack Block, "The Role of Ego-Control and Ego Resiliency in the Organization of Behavior," in *Minnesota Symposia on Child Psychology,* vol. 13, ed. W. Andrew Collins (Hillsdale, N.J.: Erlbaum, 1980), pp. 29–101.

30. Marni H. Frauenglass and Rafael M. Diaz, "Self-Regulating Functions of Children's Private Speech: A Critical Analysis of Recent Challenges to Vygotsky's Theory," *Developmental Psychology* 21 (1985): 357–364.

31. Patricia Miller and Robert Zalenski, "Preschoolers' Knowledge About Attention," *Developmental Psychology* 18 (1982): 871–875.

32. Diana Baumrind, "The Development of Instrumental Competence through Socialization," in *Minnesota Symposia on Child Development,* vol. 7, ed. Ann D. Pick (Minneapolis: University of Minnesota Press, 1973), pp. 3–46.

33. Martha F. Erickson, L. Alan Sroufe, and Byron Egeland, "The Relationship Between Quality of Attachment and Behavior Problems in Preschool in a High Risk Sample," in *Growing Points of Attachment Theory and Research,* ed. Inge Bretherton and Everett Waters, Monographs of the Society for Research in Child Development 50 (1985), serial no. 109, pp. 147–166.

34. Judith A. Crowell and S. Shirley Feldman, "Mother's Internal Models of Relationships and Developmental Status: A Study of Mother-Child Interaction," *Child Development* 59 (1988): 1273–1285.

35. Erickson, Sroufe, and Egeland, "The Relationship between Quality of Attachment and Behavior Problems in Preschool in a High Risk Sample."

36. Judy Dunn, *Sisters and Brothers* (Cambridge, Mass.: Harvard University Press, 1985).

37. Ibid.

38. Gene H. Brody, Zolinda Stoneman, and Michelle Burke, "Child Temperaments, Maternal Differential Behavior, and Sibling Relationships," *Developmental Psychology* 23 (1987): 354–362; Robert B. Stewart, Linda A. Mobley, Susan S. Van Tuyl, and Myron A. Salvador, "The Firstborn's Adjustment to the Birth of a Sibling: A Longitudinal Assessment," *Child Development* 58 (1987): 341–355; Clare Stocker, Judy Dunn, and Robert Plomin, "Sibling Relationships: Links with Child Temperament, Maternal Behavior, and Family Structure," *Child Development* 60 (1989): 715–727.

39. Judith F. Dunn, Robert Plomin, and Denise Daniels, "Consistency and Change in Mothers' Behavior toward Young Siblings," *Child Development* 57 (1986): 348–356; Judith F. Dunn, Robert Plomin, and Margaret Nettles, "Consistency of Mothers' Behavior toward Infant Siblings," *Developmental Psychology* 21 (1985): 1188–1195.

40. Tiffany Field, Louis De Stefano, and John H. Koewler III, "Fantasy Play of Toddlers and Preschoolers," *Developmental Psychology* 18 (1982): 503–508.

41. Willard W. Hartup, Brett Laursen, Mark I. Stewart, and Amy Eastenson, "Conflict and the Friendship Relations of Young Children," *Child Development* 59 (1988): 1590–1600.

42. Donald S. Hayes, "Cognitive Bases for Liking and Disliking Among Preschool Children," *Child Development* 49 (1978): 906–909.

43. Michael P. Leiter, "A Study of Reciprocity in Preschool Play Groups," *Child Development* 48 (1977): 1288–1295.

44. Nancy Eisenberg, Ellen Cameron, Kelly Tryon, and Renee Dodez, "Socialization of Prosocial Behavior in the Preschool Classroom," *Developmental Psychology* 17 (1981): 773–782.

45. Peter J. LaFraniere and L. Alan Sroufe, "Profiles of Peer Competence in the Preschool: Interrelations between Measures, Influence of Social Ecology and Relation to Attachment History," *Developmental Psychology* 21 (1985): 56–69.

46. Martin Manosevitz, Norman M. Prentice, and Frances Wilson, "Individual and Family Correlates of Imaginary Companions in Preschool Children," *Developmental Psychology* 8 (1973): 72–79; Maya Pines, "Imaginary Playmates: A Revised Look," *Psychology Today,* September 1978.

47. Frances L. Ilg and Louise Bates Ames, *Child Behavior* (New York: Harper & Row, 1955).

48. Maria Montessori, *The Secret of Childhood* (New York: Ballantine, 1972); *The Discovery of the Child* (New York: Ballantine, 1967).

49. Joan Beck, *How to Raise a Brighter Child,* rev. ed. (New York: Pocket Books, 1975).

50. Paul Mussen and Nancy Eisenberg-Berg, *Roots of Caring, Sharing and Helping* (San Francisco: W. H. Freeman, 1977), p. 160.

51. Haim G. Ginott, *Between Parent and Child* (New York: Avon, 1969).

52. Thomas Gordon, *P.E.T.: Parent Effectiveness Training* (New York: New American Library,

1975); Thomas Gordon with Judith Gordon Sands, *P.E.T. in Action* (New York: Bantam, 1978).

53. Rudolf Dreikurs with Vicki Soltz, *Children: The Challenge* (New York: Hawthorn, 1964).

54. Richard Ferber, *Solve Your Child's Sleep Problems* (New York: Simon & Schuster, 1985).

55. Ibid., p. 49.

56. Nathan Azrin and Victoria Besalel, *A Parent's Guide to Bedwetting Control* (New York: Pocket Books, 1979).

57. Ibid.

58. Ilg and Ames, *Child Behavior.*

59. Benjamin Spock, *Baby and Child Care,* rev. ed. (New York: Pocket Books, 1976).

60. David M. Buss, Jeanne H. Block, and Jack Block, "Preschool Activity Level: Personality Correlates and Developmental Implications," *Child Development* 51 (1980): 401–408.

61. Charles H. Halverson and Mary Waldrop, "Relationship between Preschool Activity and Aspects of Intellectual and Social Behavior at Age Seven and a Half," *Developmental Psychology* 12 (1976): 107–112.

62. Kagan and Moss, *Birth to Maturity.*

63. David M. Buss, "Predicting Parent-Child Interactions from Children's Activity Level," *Developmental Psychology* 17 (1981): 59–65.

64. Russell A. Barkley, "The Use of Psychopharmacology to Study Reciprocal Influences in Parent-Child Interaction," *Journal of Abnormal Child Psychology* 9 (1981): 303–310.

65. Russell A. Barkley, *Hyperactive Children: A Handbook for Diagnosis and Treatment* (New York: Guilford, 1981).

66. Donald H. Meichenbaum and Joseph Goodman, "Training Impulsive Children to Talk to Themselves: A Means of Developing Self-Control," *Journal of Abnormal Psychology* 77 (1971): 115–126.

67. Robert Eimers and Robert Aitchison, *Effective Parents/Responsible Children* (New York: McGraw-Hill, 1977).

68. Adele Faber and Elaine Mazlish, *Liberated Parents/Liberated Children* (New York: Avon, 1975).

69. Dorothy Rogers, *Child Psychology* (Monterey, Calif.: Brooks/Cole, 1969), p. 453.

70. David M. Harrington, Jeanne Block, and Jack Block, "Intolerance of Ambiguity in Preschool Children," *Developmental Psychology* 14 (1978): 242–256.

71. Wesley C. Becker, *Parents Are Teachers* (Champaign, Ill.: Research Press, 1971).

72. Stanley Turecki and Leslie Tonner, *The Difficult Child* (New York: Bantam, 1985).

73. John E. Bates, Christine A. Maslin, and Karen H. Frankel, "Attachment Security, Mother-Child Interaction and Temperament as Predictors of Behavior Problem Ratings at Age Three Years," in *Growing Points of Attachment Theory and Research,* ed. Inge Bretherton and Everett Waters, Monographs of the Society for Research in Child Development 50 (1985), serial number 209, pp. 167–193; Carolyn L. Lee and John Bates, "Mother-Child Interaction at Age Two Years and Perceived Difficult Temperament," *Child Development* 56 (1985): 1314–1325.

74. Turecki and Tonner, *The Difficult Child,* p. 168.

75. Ellen Galinsky, *Between Generations: The Six Stages of Parenthood* (New York: Times Books, 1981).

THE ELEMENTARY
SCHOOL YEARS

C H A P T E R   9

These years, from five to eleven, are the golden age of childhood. Both parents and children enjoy the elementary years, when children have finally mastered eating, sleeping, dressing, and toileting. They have gained control of their physical behavior and language. They express themselves easily and can take care of many of their own needs. Their interest in the world continues to expand, and they are entertaining companions for parents and other adults. Children of this age do not have the responsibilities of adolescence, when they will need to make decisions and carry out activities that have lifelong impact. Yet they are building a sense of competence that will sustain them during adolescence, when so much changes and they often feel at odds with themselves, their parents, and their peers. Parents, too, build up a backlog of enjoyable experiences and a companionable relationship with children that will carry them through the crises that arise in the adolescent years.

PHYSICAL DEVELOPMENT

From ages five to ten, girls and boys have approximately the same height, weight, and general physical measurements. At five they are about 42 inches in height and about 40 to 45 pounds in weight. By age ten, they are about 52 inches in height and weigh about 75 to 80 pounds. Beginning at age ten, the growth patterns of boys and girls diverge, and these differences will be discussed in Chapter 10. By the elementary school years, children's coordination is well developed. They ride bikes, skate, swim, play team sports, draw, play musical instruments. Nearly all the basic skills in the area of gross (running, skipping) and fine (cutting with scissors, drawing) motor coordination are laid down by age seven, and further development consists basically of refining these skills.

WHAT I WISH I HAD KNOWN ABOUT THE ELEMENTARY SCHOOL YEARS

"I wish I'd known how much you need to be an advocate for your child with the school. When we grew up, our parents put us in public school and that was it. Then it was up to the teachers. Unless there was a discipline problem, parents did not get involved. Now, you have a lot more options, and the public schools aren't always great; so you realize how active you need to be in order to insure a good education for your children." MOTHER

"The main thing, I think, is how important temperament is. I knew about temperament, but I did not know how important it is to go with the child's temperament. My daughter was in one school that was very noncompetitive; that's a wonderful philosophy, but it wasn't right for her. She is very competitive, and in that atmosphere she did not do as well. So with the second child, we are going to be more careful to see that there is a good fit between her temperament and what she is doing." FATHER

"I was surprised that even though the children are older, they take as much time as when they were younger; but you spend the time in different ways. I thought when they started school, I would have a little more time. Instead of giving them baths at night and rocking them, I supervise homework and argue about taking baths. Instead of taking them on Saturday to play in the park, I take them on a Brownie event. Knowing that things were going to take as much time would have made me less impatient in the beginning, and I would have planned better." MOTHER

"I learned that especially from five to eight, say, children are not as competent as they look. They really can't do a lot of things that on the surface you think they can. They have language, and they look like they're reasoning, and they look like their motor skills are okay. So you say, 'When you get up in the morning, I want you to make your cereal,' and they can't do it consistently. And so because we didn't know that with the first child, I think we made excessive demands on her, which led to her being a little harsher on herself. Now with the second one, if she can't tie her shoes by herself today, even though she could two weeks ago, we're more likely to say, 'Okay,' instead of, 'Well, you can tie your shoes; go ahead and do it.' If you give them a little help, it doesn't mean you are making babies of them; it means they have room to take it from there." FATHER

"I wish I'd known more about their abilities and work readiness. My daughter had some special needs in school. In preschool, she did well, although I could see there were immaturities in her drawings and writing; but she got lots of happy faces. I was misled by the positive comments they always wanted to make to her, and I thought she was doing better than she was. When she got to school, it came as quite a shock that she was having problems. With my son, I have been more on top and I ask more questions abut how he is really doing, because I want to get any special needs he has addressed. My advice to any parent is that, if at all possible, volunteer in your child's school. I gave up half a day's pay, and in my financial situation that was a real hardship. It is very, very important to keep a handle on not just what is happening educationally, but also who the peers are and what is going on." MOTHER

INTELLECTUAL DEVELOPMENT

According to Piaget (see Table 6-1), intellectual growth takes two leaps during this period.[1] From four to seven, the intuitive stage of the preoperational period, the child is able to figure out problems intuitively and give reasons for what he or she thinks. These reasons are based on what is seen and observed at the moment rather than on a set of verbalized principles or operations. At about age seven, the child enters the period of **concrete operations**, and at about age twelve, the period of **formal operations**. Thus, a large share of mature reasoning capabilities emerge during the elementary years.

What does Piaget mean by concrete operations? He means that children can think more logically and are not so bound by the appearance of objects. They understand conservation of quantity—realizing, for example, that when a ball of clay is flattened into a long, round piece, the amount of clay remains the same. And gradually children come to understand conservation of weight and volume. They grasp relations among a series of objects and easily arrange a series of sticks in terms of length with little trial and error. Their thought moves quickly from a subset of elements to the whole picture. If given a box of brown wooden beads with a few white wooden ones mixed in and asked if a necklace made of wooden beads would be longer than one of brown beads, children at this stage quickly answer, "Yes," and explain "Because there are more wooden beads than brown beads."

In the period of concrete operations, children are able to think more logically, to form classes, and to count because they are increasingly **decentered**—that is, less focused on their own perceptions and more involved in the qualities and functional properties of what they observe. They are more objective in their observations, and they have a keen interest in understanding the mechanisms or principles by which objects operate. Children try to organize perceptions into operations for dealing with concrete objects in front of them.

Growth and maturation of the brain may underlie these perceptual and learning changes. Between four and seven, areas of the brain responsible for the coordination of sensory perception and additional association areas mature and yield information on the relations between objects that result in a higher level of intellectual functioning. Maturation in the prefrontal, cortical areas of the brain, responsible for planning and reasoning, may account for changes in children's abilities to reason at ages seven and twelve. Parents must recognize that shifts in the child's level of intellectual reasoning depend, in large part, on the growth and functioning of the brain. Children differ in the rate of maturation, with boys, on average, two years behind girls.

SCHOOL

Starting school is a great step forward in a child's life because the child is required to master new skills in a controlled setting, surrounded in many instances by strangers, and then is evaluated in terms of an external standard of excellence. But schools do more than teach cognitive skills. They are places to meet friends and have social relationships. They also introduce a whole new group of adults who come to

The most important event of these years is the child's entrance into school. Apart from the child's family, school is the most influential socializing force. School serves as a meeting place for peers and a setting for interpersonal interactions.

know children well but are outside the family circle. So, in addition to fostering intellectual development, at their best they help children to develop self-esteem, social competence, and community awareness. At their worst, when there is a mismatch between the child's qualities and the school's demands, the experience can be a nightmare for the child and the family.

As their children go off to school, parents may wonder about the effects of new ways of organized school experience. There are open classrooms in which children can move around freely, choose activities, work at their own pace, participate in small groups; the teacher becomes a facilitator in this teaching setting, helping children gather and organize material. There are also more traditional classrooms in which the teacher directs most of the learning activity. She explains, gives assignments, corrects papers. Children sit at their desks and follow routines. Research comparing the traditional and more open programs have found that academic achievement is about equal in the two kinds of classrooms. Children in open programs, however, appear more enthusiastic about school, more creative and independent in their work than children in closed programs. Further, peer relationships are more friendly and less competitive in these situations.

Recent studies of elementary and secondary schools suggest that smaller school units are better able to meet students' needs. When schools are large, restructuring them into "schools within schools" helps children to find their own particular niche and contributes to students' sense of identity so that they are less likely to drop out later.[2]

In the past, learning activities were customarily organized in competitive or individualistic ways. Children were encouraged to compete with each other to achieve rewards of praise or grades or special privileges, or they were taught to ignore other students and proceed on their own with learning. More recently, there have been attempts to rely on cooperation among students, to emphasize working together in small groups to organize and learn material. For example, if the task is to learn about George Washington, one person on the team might take Washington's growing-up years, another his early adult years as a surveyor and farmer, a third his years as a general, and a fourth his years as president. The students as a group would take some responsibility for sharing their specific information with everyone else on the team. Learning improves with this method, and children know and like their classmates better.

What characteristics of teachers relate to learning? How the teacher acts in the classroom has greater impact on learning than the teacher's particular personality characteristics.[3] When teachers are flexible, when they maintain a calm, friendly atmosphere in the classroom and use gentle disciplinary techniques, then students learn. When teachers give opportunities for active learning, when they have high, positive expectations for students, and are personally involved in supervision and monitoring of students, then students learn. So, active learning in a calm, controlled environment with high expectations for students predicts children's achievement.

Who most easily makes the transition to kindergarten from preschool? The child who gets along well with other children and can play and interact in a cooperative fashion adjusts most easily to kindergarten. Children who have had preschool experience are less anxious. Children who enter school with friends or who have a stable group of friends outside of school adjust more easily. The aggressive child who has negative peer contacts in preschool is seen as hostile and aggressive by teachers and is rejected by peers.[4]

Most children start school with positive self-evaluations of their abilities and high levels of confidence about their abilities to learn.[5] They are happy with their work and are not critical. Children in first grade believe all children can learn whatever is required, and it is just a matter of putting out effort—those who do well have worked harder. As children progress through school, they develop more differentiated views of intelligence and ability, and they have more experience of failure.[6] As this happens, they come to view their own abilities less positively. Girls are consistently more critical of their work and more complimentary of others' work.

Doris Entwisle and her co-workers studied how first-graders forge an academic self-image.[7] Young children ignore social categories and do not base their academic self-images on race, parent background, or family constellation. However, there are sex differences in academic self-image. From the very start of first grade, girls are eager to do what they believe parents and peers expect. They are very slow to form their own self-expectations about school performance. Boys, in contrast, are more oriented to their own self-evaluations and negatively value what parents want. They are competitive and want to learn quickly. Learning math is important to them, whereas it is unimportant to girls even though girls score as high on math tests and on math work as boys.

Academic self-image is initially independent of achievement. By the end of the first year a positive image is related to doing well in school. There is strong evidence that children base their self-image on their parents' beliefs about their abilities.[8] Debra Phillips found that about 20 percent of students in third and fifth grades, equal proportions of boys and girls, underestimate their abilities as measured by tests. They think they are incompetent. Because these students view their abilities poorly and expect less success, they are less persistent and less likely to succeed than more confident students. Their lack of success only reinforces their underestimations of their abilities.

Parents interpret children's performance in school and give them feedback that the children incorporate in their own self-image. How parents develop their own misperceptions of their children's abilities is not clear; but their views are passed along, and no degree of success seems to alter the children's feelings of incompetence.

Children's expectations of themselves in school gradually become related also to what teachers expect of them.[9] Even first-graders pick up the emotional atmosphere in a classroom, and when a teacher makes many distinctions between high- and low-ability students, first-graders begin to view their own abilities as the teacher does. Fifth-graders can clearly verbalize which teachers attend to differences in students' abilities, and students perform the way the teachers expect in those classrooms where large distinctions are made.

What do students consider is a fair way to handle the ability differences in a class? Students from first grade to college all felt that the fairest way was to let fast students complete their work and then help slower students to complete theirs.[10] This option was selected far more frequently than the traditional method of letting fast students go to other activities like reading or computers after work was completed. They selected this even though most had never experienced peer helping.

Schools are structured so that girls' abilities are most valued.[11] Girls tend to be less physical, more verbal, more responsive to auditory stimuli, and more able to concentrate on a task as early as the preschool years. Not all girls have these characteristics, but many do. Boys, on average, are active and curious. They are likely to learn from doing, manipulating, and seeing. They have greater difficulty concentrating for extended periods of time. Given these sex differences, it is not surprising that boys are described as hyperactive nine times as often as girls and that they are much more likely to experience reading problems. Until schools change to take greater account of the growth patterns of boys, parents can expect their sons may have more problems in school than their daughters.

School is often the place where minority group children get their first taste of discrimination. In the years before school, children are in environments that their parents select for them. If they experience and report an unhappy event, parents can change nursery schools or day care. But for many minority parents, there are no choices outside the public school because of lack of finances.

Just as school settings do not value boys' characteristics, they do not value the cultural traditions of many minority groups. The schools most often reward the majority culture's values of competition and independent achievement. Some minority groups, like the Chinese and Japanese, stress compatible values of hard work, individual effort, a strong drive for achievement, and respect for authority. Students from these groups do well and, in fact, often exceed the performance of majority group students.

Children from different cultural backgrounds, however, with different values, may feel at a loss to achieve in a foreign environment. Parents who are aware of the mismatch that can occur between the values of the child's culture and the values of the school or teacher will be able to help both teacher and child to modify behavior so that learning takes place. Here we can list only a few of the possible kinds of mismatches to help make parents aware of what to look for if their minority children experience difficulty.

Janice Hale-Benson describes several characteristics that influence Afro-American children's learning in schools.[12] Afro-American children enter school accustomed to a high level of noise, much activity, many people, and an abundance of stimulation. They are then expected to sit still, listen to one adult speak, and work by themselves when they would really rather be expressing themselves in activity with other children. The school stifles the enthusiasm of these children and labels many of them hyperactive, just as it does many boys.

Afro-Americans are feeling-oriented people who frequently express themselves in body language rather than words. Their use of words and their style of speech differ from that of the majority culture, so there is a mismatch between children and teacher.

A careful study carried out by S. Brice-Heath (cited in Diana Slaughter-Defoe et al.) illustrates how subtle this mismatch can be.[13] Brice-Heath observed that both parents of Afro-American students and their teachers complained of poor communication between teachers and pupils. Teachers said the children did not answer their verbal questions. The children complained the teachers asked stupid questions, didn't listen, and had their own set of rules.

Brice-Heath studied the use of questions by teachers and the Afro-American community. Teachers ask questions with obvious answers for several reasons—to start conversations with children, to draw their attention to an area they want them to think about, to direct their attention to behavior the teacher wants changed ("Are you finished talking to your friends now?" is a question we can all remember). In the Afro-American community, questions are asked to get new information, to make accusations ("Did you eat all the ice cream?"), and to get children to think.

Brice-Heath approached teachers, parents, and children to make them aware of the different uses of questions. Teachers took responsibility for making themselves clear to children.

Although minority students' achievement in school has improved in the last fifteen years, still there is a gap between their achievement and that of the majority students. Recent work suggests, however, that in certain areas (for example, math computation) skills are comparable at school entry, but achievement differences emerge as children move through the grades.[14]

For some years, experts thought achievement differences were related to minority students' low self-esteem and low level of aspiration or to lack of family interest and encouragement. New studies indicate these are not the source of achievement differences.[15] Now we find that Afro-American and Hispanic-American mothers of elementary school children place greater emphasis on their children's achievement than do Anglo-American mothers. Minority mothers want more homework, longer school days, and more competency testing of their children. Mothers have both high

INTERVIEW
with Barbara Keogh

Barbara K. Keogh is professor of educational psychology at the University of California at Los Angeles. Her research interests include the role of children's temperament in children's adjustment to school.

For many parents with children in the elementary school years, issues concerning school have a very great importance—how to get children ready for school on time, how to help them behave in school, how to get them to do school work. You have done a great deal of research on children's temperament and school, and I think temperament plays a role in many children's adjustment.

It intrigued me when I started work in this area, a long time ago, that most of the work with temperament had been done with interactions in families, and yet when you think of the number of interactions that teachers have with children per hour, per day, in a classroom and add that up over the school year, temperament is an enormous potential influence.

When we began our research, we found that teachers have a very clear picture of what teachable children are like. One of the very important contributors to teachability is the stylistic variables or temperament variables that characterize children. Some children are easy to teach. They settle down better, they are not as active, they are not as intense, their mood is good, they adapt well, they like novelty, they are curious. All those things make teachers think, "Gee, I am a great teacher," when they have a whole classroom full of children with those characteristics.

So we are really operating on the assumption that children's experiences in school are influenced by individual variations in temperament. We have tried to document and understand the kind of impact these variations have on the teachers. We have used the concept of "goodness of fit" in a loose way.

I am convinced, and this is not a new idea, that teachers do not operate at random. They make decisions based on how they attribute the reasons for the behavior. They may think that active, distractible children are mischievous and need to be restricted and punished, and that children who are very slow to warm up or are withdrawn are lazy and uninterested. When we work with teachers and make them aware of temperamental characteristics, we get a very consistent response: "Oh, I never thought of that." Making teachers sensitive to temperament variations helps them reframe the child's behavior, and it makes the behavior much less upsetting to teachers.

It also carries planning implications. If you know a youngster is very distractible, very

evaluations of their children's abilities and high expectations for their achievement in school and in later work. Minority mothers take an active part in seeing that homework gets done, though Hispanic mothers feel less capable of helping with the work of a foreign school system.

Minority children share their mothers' enthusiasm for education. They enjoy school, feel good about themselves and their achievements, and expect to do well in the future. They work hard and are self-disciplined.

While there are differences in minority students' level of achievement in the ele-

active, and very intense, then you can predict that every time you have a long wait in line, there's going to be a problem with him. It's predictable.

When teachers begin to think of the individual variations on a temperamental rather than motivational basis, they begin to manipulate the environment more effectively. Temperament helps teachers reframe the problem behavior so it is not viewed as purposeful. This is true for both temperamentally "difficult" and "slow to warm up" children.

Another example I like is that most of the youngsters in an elementary class are delighted by novelty. The teachers says, "Oh, we are going to have a wonderful surprise today. At ten o'clock the fire department is coming." Most of the kids are excited. There will be a few little "slow to warm up" youngsters who will say, "But at ten o'clock we are supposed to do our reading." They are upset because the usual routine is not followed. The teacher thinks, "What's the matter with that child? Why isn't he interested?" The child has a need for routine and a tendency to withdraw from newness or change. These children can profit from advance preparation. If they know a day in advance, they get a little forewarning.

Do you have any advice for parents as to how to help their children adjust to school?

Certainly parents have to be advocates for their child. That is absolutely necessary even if it means being confrontational, which is often not too productive. But certainly parents need to be aware when their child is unhappy at school, when their child is having problems, and address the problem with school people.

It has to be recognized that when we are working on a ratio of twenty-five youngsters to one teacher, there are going to be good matches and very poor matches in any class. In no sense does that demean the quality of the teacher or the nature of the child. But there are differences in style, and some styles match better than others.

One thing parents can do is to provide teachers with some recognition that their child might not be a good match for this classroom. It helps the teacher to know that the parents are aware of that. So they can direct their mutual efforts to modify the class so the demands are more reasonable, or they can give the child extra help in modifying his or her behavior so it is more compatible with what is going on in that class.

Do you feel most teachers are willing to change?

Yes, I do. We have worked with a lot of teachers in our research, and I think it helps them to think of ways that they can structure the situation so it is more compatible with the student without loss of educational goals. Yes, we have found teachers to be very open, and they were able to relate what we were saying to different children they have known: "Oh, yes, that's like Joey."

---

mentary years, these are minimal when social status is taken into account. Investigators do not understand why the high rates of failure and school dropout occur in the later years, when indicators at the fifth-grade level seem to predict future achievement for minority students. One speculation is that families may be so positive that they do not help children isolate those areas where they need improvement. Inappropriate curriculum content seems a factor in lowering minority children's reading level and also may play a role in their later decrease in achievement.

The important point here is that minority parents are currently as motivated, involved, and positive about their children's education as are majority parents of similar social class. Minority elementary school students are as motivated and excited about learning as their peers in the majority culture. So, we have to look at the curriculum and teaching strategies that maximize students' abilities because the present ones may interfere with learning.

Janice Hale-Benson believes minority parents must educate teachers about the differences and needs of Afro-American children.[16] They must also insist that efforts be made to give these children the help they need with language in the regular classroom—modeling standard English, allowing equal time for children's talking and teachers' talking. Encouraging group learning and a variety of activities for children will help channel energy and interest in people. Becoming an advocate for the child in school is discussed further in the Parenting Tasks section of this chapter.

EMOTIONAL DEVELOPMENT

Children's understanding of their feelings increases in this period. They realize feelings are not automatic responses to an event but depend, in part, on what led up to the event and how the event is interpreted.[17] For example, at ages six and seven, children are pleased with their success whether it comes from luck or effort. When they are nine and ten, children feel proud only if they believe their effort produced the success.

As children learn more about feelings, they realize they can have opposite feelings about a person or event.[18] Memories of a previous interaction with a person can trigger one set of feelings while the current interaction triggers a different set. Not until about age ten do children realize they can feel both love and anger toward a person.

Children also become increasingly skilled in understanding the difference between the appearance of emotions and the actual inner feeling of emotion.[19] By age six, they can talk about exactly how to hide feelings with words—most likely a result of parents having prompted many times, "Say you are sorry" or "Tell Grandma you like her new dress." Children have a much harder time changing facial expressions to hide their feelings.[20] Thus, a child's facial expression is probably a more accurate reflection of feelings than words.

Under what conditions are children most likely to express their inner feelings?[21] It happens when they are alone or when they believe their feelings will get a positive, understanding response from the other person. Unfortunately, as children—particularly boys—grow older, they anticipate a less positive response from others, even from parents. Thus, older boys are much less likely to express their feelings.

As understanding of others increases and helping and sharing become more developed, impulsivity and aggressiveness decrease.

Aggressiveness

Aggression not only decreases during this period, but it also takes different forms. In the younger years, aggression sometimes occurred as a means to achieve a specific goal—to get a desired toy, for example. Aggression in these years was more likely to be physical. In the elementary school period, aggression is more likely to be designed to hurt a person.

Although instances of aggressive behavior decrease, consistent individual differences emerge, and these are likely to persist over time. Further, those children who are aggressive tend to have other problems as well—poor peer relations, difficulty in acquiring academic skills. Boys are more frequently aggressive than girls, beginning in the toddler years. This sex difference in aggression is seen in animal species and in cultures around the world. The reasons for it are complex. Because sex differences appear early and consistently in so many cultures, there may well be a biological basis that is not specifically known at this time.

Gerald Patterson believes that family members train children to be aggressive by inconsistent rewards for positive and negative behaviors.[22] Parents may laugh at mischievous defiance or allow children to escape rules or requests when children ignore them, refuse, yell, or use other coercive measures. Thus, children are more likely to refuse in the future because they know if they persist in refusing, parents will give in. At the same time parents fail to train children for positive behaviors, so children are aggressive and also socially unskilled.

When aggressiveness continues into the elementary school years, children develop problems that do not disappear with time.[23] In a representative sample of children who were followed to adulthood, boys and girls who continued to have tantrums past preschool tended to have difficulties in many areas in adulthood. Men who had tantrums had problems at work and tended to be downwardly mobile in their occupations; they also had problems in marriages and were more frequently divorced. Women who had tantrums were perceived as very difficult by husbands and children and were more frequently divorced also.

Fearfulness

With age, children grow less fearful. Many of the fears of the preschool period—fears of animals, fear of the dark—decrease. Some specific ones remain, however—fear of snakes, fear of storms. These fears appear related to temperamental qualities involving general timidity.

Up to the age of five, fears are equally prevalent in boys and girls, but beginning with the school-age years sex differences increase. Fears and phobias are more prevalent in girls at all ages.

Unhappiness

Michael Rutter, Jack Tizard, and Kingsley Whitmore found that parents and teachers described 10 to 12 percent of a representative sample of ten-year-olds as often appearing miserable, unhappy, tearful, or distressed.[24] The children themselves reported similar depressive feelings. Boys and girls were equally as likely to report such feelings.

Some of the behaviors that parents consider problems occur so frequently that they are almost the norm for this age period. Throughout the years from five to eleven, boys and girls are active and restless as well as sensitive and fearful. Boys are more likely to have severe problems with overactivity and temper tantrums, and girls are more likely to hold their feelings in.[25]

Knowing that these behaviors occur frequently does not make them easy to live with, but it does help parents relax. When they realize that many children have these troubles, they are more understanding of their children and of themselves as parents.

What are the events and problems that children find stressful? Two samples of American children, ages nine to eleven, along with children from Egypt, Canada, Australia, Japan, and the Philippines have rated the twenty events listed in Table 9-1 on a seven-point scale from most upsetting (7) to least upsetting (1).[26] A common "culture of childhood" emerges. Children's responses from many different cultures resemble each other in terms of both the stressfulness of the ratings and the reported incidence of the events (not listed here). There is more rating agreement among children from different cultures than there is between adults and children in the same culture. Within each of the samples, there are few sex or age differences, and within

TABLE 9-1
SCALE VALUES OF CHILDREN'S RATINGS ON STRESSFULNESS OF LIFE EVENTS

Life Event	Egypt	Canada	Australia	Japan	Philippines	USA(a)	USA(b)
Losing parent	6.88	6.88	6.92	6.90	6.76	6.90	6.76
Going blind	6.83	6.75	6.83	6.68	6.70	6.86	6.58
Academic retainment	6.83	6.32	5.94	6.78	6.21	6.82	6.30
Wetting in class	6.73	6.17	6.58	6.73	5.43	6.74	5.78
Parental fights	6.83	5.57	6.16	6.23	6.32	6.71	6.54
Caught in theft	6.62	5.71	6.08	6.73	4.29	6.63	5.20
Suspected of lying	6.62	5.58	6.04	6.73	5.88	6.53	5.86
A poor report card	6.69	5.46	5.69	6.61	5.57	6.23	5.52
Sent to principal	6.63	4.45	5.11	6.63	3.22	5.75	4.68
Having an operation	6.55	4.35	4.58	5.82	4.28	5.51	4.80
Getting lost	6.52	4.22	5.22	5.01	3.90	5.49	4.52
Ridiculed in class	6.63	4.25	4.67	6.11	6.26	5.28	4.65
Move to a new school	6.52	3.41	4.17	5.21	2.55	4.60	4.09
Scary dream	6.59	3.69	4.63	5.07	4.80	4.08	4.06
Not making 100 on test	6.46	2.94	2.94	5.04	3.15	3.75	4.05
Picked last on team	4.73	3.94	2.40	5.92	3.45	3.30	3.30
Losing in game	5.68	2.79	2.23	4.48	3.33	3.16	2.75
Going to dentist	4.87	2.42	1.43	3.05	2.30	2.73	2.54
Giving class report	3.08	2.98	1.53	2.75	1.78	2.58	2.79
New baby sibling	1.20	1.42	1.18	1.43	1.25	1.27	1.46
N	296	283	191	248	156	367	273
Grade	3–6	7–9	3–8	4–6	5–6	4–6	4–6

From Kaoru Yamamoto, Abdalla Soliman, James Parsons, and O. L. Davies, Jr., "Voices in Unison: Stressful Events in the Lives of Children in Six Countries," *Journal of Child Psychology and Psychiatry* 28 (1987): p. 857.

the American samples, few ethnic differences. To the authors, these children are speaking "in unison" as they describe what upsets them.

Children around the world agree that loss of a parent is the most devastating, and the birth of a sibling, the least upsetting. Parental fights are highly stressful as well. Children reveal their sensitivity in their distress at embarrassing situations—wetting their pants, being caught in a theft, being ridiculed in class. Although many students like school, it is also a source or anxiety, frustration, and unhappiness with worry about grades, being retained, and making mistakes. Adults may be surprised at children's sensitivity to embarrassing situations and their concern about school. The data emphasize that children may have a different life perspective that may not be immediately apparent to parents.

When children ages six to twelve are asked how to handle stressful situations—like having a friend move away, going to the doctor's office for a shot, having a parent angry at them—their solutions generally attack the source of the problem to change the upsetting circumstances.[27] They are most likely to strike at the roots of the difficulty when the problem focuses on peers or school, where they feel they have more control.

Children are most likely to suggest adjusting to situations—like doctors' visits—that are seen as inevitable.[28] Younger children are the most active in changing the upsetting circumstances. As children grow older, they are more likely to adapt to circumstances, particularly when others are seen as having control.

When children are asked whom they seek for help and support for emotional, informational, instrumental, and companionship needs, "Children perceive their mothers as being the best multipurpose social provider available, in contrast to friends and teachers, who are relatively specialized in their social value."[29] Friends provide companionship and emotional support second only to parents. Teachers provide information but little companionship. Fathers are excellent providers of information, but are generally less available to give direct help. Social support, as well as skill in problem solving, is related to children's good adjustment during the stressful times of life.[30]

Empathy

We have described the parental behaviors—nurturing, modeling, reasoning, and explaining the benefits of prosocial behavior—that create sympathy and helping behavior in children.

Because children's awareness of others' feelings have increased, they are better helpers and are more likely to offer social strategies rather than material ones to change distress when they see it in other people. When asked how to help distressed four- and five-year-olds, older children suggested giving verbal reassurance that the situation will pass, giving suggestions on how to solve the problem (such as advice on how to retrieve a lost object), or providing social activity to compensate for the unhappiness (having someone over to play, staying with a crying child).[31]

Children are most likely to help others when they feel happy, competent, and effective themselves. They are most likely to help if they like the person and that person has helped them in the past. So positive feelings about oneself and others lead to generosity at this age.[32]

PERSONAL AND SOCIAL DEVELOPMENT

Erik Erikson describes the years from five to eleven or twelve as the period in which children develop a sense of industry, of being able to make things and accomplish tasks.[33] They are expanding their skills and abilities. They go off to school, learn to read and write, take up hobbies, start lessons, and join groups. They have an increasing number of adult models outside the home. They are busy and productive, and they experience pleasure in what they can do and produce. If children at this age have few experiences of success and accomplishment, they develop a sense of inferiority; they feel their efforts are doomed to failure and that they are useless. If the balance of experiences is positive, children develop a sense of competence—the feeling one can use one's skills and abilities to accomplish goals, free of feelings of inferiority.

Development of the Self

Children continue to define themselves in terms of their physical features, possessions, activities, and capabilities. Note this self-description by a nine-year-old boy: "My name is Bruce C. I have brown eyes. I have brown hair. I have brown eyebrows. I'm nine years old. I LOVE! Sports. I have seven people in my family. I have great! eyesight. I have lots! of friends. I live on 1923 Pinecrest Dr. I'm going on ten in September. I'm a boy. I have an uncle that is almost seven feet tall. My school is Pinecrest. My teacher is Mrs. V. I play Hockey! I'm almost the smartest boy in class. I LOVE! food. I love fresh air. I LOVE School."[34]

Abilities and actions are still prominent in self-descriptions, but now children begin to make comparisons between themselves and other children. We see this in Bruce's self-description as "almost the smartest boy in class." In older children we begin to see mention of social aspects of the self. Children mention membership in groups: "A Girl Scout," "a member of the soccer team." Psychological traits are also mentioned, as in Bruce's description of his intelligence.

As children develop a greater sense of themselves as individuals and become more aware of other children's qualities, they evaluate themselves and their own self-worth. Children from four to seven evaluate themselves in terms of two factors: (1) their overall level of competence and (2) their social acceptance. Just as children's conceptions of self become more differentiated with age, so the dimensions on which they evaluate themselves become more complex. Children of eight and older evaluate themselves on four dimensions: (1) their physical competence on sports, (2) their cognitive competence in school work, (3) their social competence with peers, and (4) their general self-worth. Children's general feeling of self-worth is most closely related to feelings of social competence and then to feelings of physical competence. Adults may not be aware of just how important physical competence is for their children. In children of this age, feelings of physical and social competence are closely related.[35]

In this period, minority group children are learning about their own ethnic identities and what it means to be part of that culture. By age ten, they know their identity and prefer their own group. Mary Jane Rotheram-Borus and Jean Phinney suggest children show ethnic differences on the four basic dimensions of behavior listed in Box 9-1.[36]

BOX 9-1
FOUR BASIC DIMENSIONS OF ETHNIC DIFFERENCES IN CHILDREN

1. An orientation toward group ties, interdependence, and sharing versus an orientation toward independence and competition
2. Active, achievement-oriented approach that changes a situation versus a passive, fatalistic approach that insists on self-change to remedy the situation
3. Acceptance of, respect for, and belief in powerful authorities versus an egalitarian view that allows questioning of authority
4. Overtly expressive, spontaneous style versus an inhibited, formal style

Adapted from Mary Jane Rotheram-Borus and Jean S. Phinney, "Patterns of Social Expectations among Black and Mexican-American Children," *Child Development* 61 (1990): 543.

Though there are variations within groups, many studies find that Mexican-American children tend to be more group-oriented, eager to share and cooperate, more adaptable to others' demands on them than either Anglo- or Afro-American children. They rely on adult figures for advice and are very respectful of them. If someone else is angry or aggressive toward them, be it child or adult, Mexican-American children feel sad and blame themselves. Compared to both Anglo- and Mexican-American children, Afro-American children are more emotionally expressive, action-oriented, assertive with peers. They too are respectful of adults but, if scolded, apologize and do not feel bad about themselves. Little is known about how Asian-American children differ.

As they progress through elementary school, minority students become more attached to their cultural traditions, and the children with the highest self-esteem are most identified with their cultural behavior pattern. Still, some children identify with the majority culture. How this occurs and what it means for the child's well-being are not known.

As children begin to make comparisons with other children, parents may want them to be accurate. However, evidence suggests that it is better to overrate your abilities and to see yourself more positively than objective tests or ratings might warrant. For example, children who overrate their abilities in school are more likely to respond to failure by getting help, finding out what they did wrong, and remedying the situation because it does not fit with their view of themselves.[37]

Albert Bandura, who has written on the importance of believing in one's own abilities to take effective action (self-efficacy), states that in hazardous situations, accuracy in self-perception of abilities is essential; for example, if you overestimate your ability to swim in heavy surf, you are in trouble and may not have a chance to correct the perception. In many nonhazardous situations, though, people are more effective when they overrate their abilities.[38]

Life is full of problems and, to overcome them, we have to persevere. People are most likely to persist when they believe in themselves. Optimistic views of the self, then, help people make the most of their talents. Young children appear naturally optimistic as they enter school and as they look ahead in life. Parents need to encourage and nurture this beneficial optimism.[39]

Development of Self-Regulation

To control behavior, children need to (1) monitor their own behavior, (2) compare their behavior with some standard or ideal, (3) then, when a discrepancy appears, modify their behavior to come as close to the standard as possible, and finally (4) develop new behaviors. We know most in this area about how children learn an internal standard to which they compare their behavior; we know least about how they monitor themselves and how they go about modifying their behavior on their own, before the involvement of an adult.[40]

Children begin to learn simple family rules when they are about one-year-old. It is in the elementary school period, however, that they *internalize* family and social values—that is, make them part of their own internal system of thinking. Freud used the term **superego** to describe the internalized values that direct an individual's behavior. The child adopts the same-sex parent's values and beliefs, which from then on govern the child's conduct. Freud believed that the superego arouses pleasure or anxiety or guilt about possible actions, and these feelings permit or prevent the anticipated behavior.

If parents are rigid and tyrannical, the child will adopt these values and become self-punishing and lacking in basic self-esteem. When parents use guilt and withdrawal of love to discipline children, the child's values tend to be rigid and rule-oriented. When parents use mild, indirect methods to obtain compliance, then children tend to be morally mature (see the interview with Paul Mussen in Chapter 4).

Learning theorists stress the importance of a model for self-control. A strong attachment to a principled, self-directed adult who not only describes approved behaviors but also practices them in everyday life is the most important factor in helping children to internalize and obey rules. Although the adult's own behavior is more important than the words, verbal statements about right and wrong help children to take the role of another and to link moral thoughts and attitudes with the rewards that follow approved behavior.

Children's moral development is also influenced by what they see happening to others. When a child observes that peers or adults break the rules and experience no consequences of their acts, that child is likely to break rules. When adults give harsh, unpredictable, and poorly explained punishments to decrease disapproved behaviors, children are least likely to develop a sense of self-control. When adults' responses are not predictable or fair, children learn to do whatever they want as long as they think they won't get caught.

Lawrence Kohlberg describes three levels of moral reasoning.[41] At the earliest (**premoral**) level, the individual acts to avoid punishments and gain pleasure or reward. There is little concern for the rights of others. At the second (**conventional**) level, the individual acts to conform to the rules or regulations laid down by powerful authorities like parents or the law. At the most advanced (**principled**) level, the individual acts to satisfy a set of internal standards of fairness and justice.

During the early elementary school years, until about age seven or eight, children reason at a premoral level and act to avoid punishments and gain rewards. By about the age of ten, conventional moral reasoning has developed, although premoral thinking still occurs. Very few children at this age display principled reasoning about moral problems. By the age of thirteen, a small percent rely on principled reasoning; conventional reasoning is still prevalent. Even at this age, however, many children still reason in terms of avoiding punishment and gaining rewards. And so it is important for parents of elementary school children to give praise and social recognition of approved acts and, at the very least, to give punishments by ignoring disapproved acts.

By the age of nine or ten, children can talk about how they use self-instructional plans to control anger, aggression, and other negative behavior and do what is correct. What works, though, varies with age. Younger boys, age six or seven, were most able to delay behavior when they simply verbalized not doing the forbidden act. Older boys were more successful when they verbalized directing their attention elsewhere.

In describing why they follow routines laid down by parents, routines they do not like—brushing teeth, going to bed on time, doing chores—children between six and twelve initially focus on external rewards of approval or disapproval and the importance of following a rule. As they get older, they focus on more internal reasons—cleaning their room to find things more easily, going to bed to feel better the next day. So there is a progression from external reasons for self-control to internal ones.[42]

By about eight, children become more self-critical and their sense of self-esteem becomes related to their ability to control verbal and physical aggression and other negative emotions. They feel ashamed when they violate a rule, and they take pride in being able to regulate their behavior and do what is approved. This is a good reason for parents' helping children to meet approved standards. Children do not feel good about themselves when they engage in behaviors they know others their age do not do.[43]

Parent-Child Relationships

As children come of school age, changes occur in parent-child relationships. Parents now spend half as much time with their children as they did when they were preschoolers. Concerns in the area of discipline change.[44] The most significant new issue is dealing with children's behavior in relation to school. Even when there are no specific difficulties, the parent generally oversees homework completion, decides acceptable levels of achievement, and helps children handle adjustments to new teachers and new peers.

In the elementary school period, differences continue to be seen in the ways mothers and fathers relate to children.[45] Mothers remain the caretakers who take major responsibility for managing family tasks—scheduling homework and baths, for example. Mothers interact more with children, and they are more directive with them. They are more positive in their reactions with children as well.

Fathers, though more generally neutral in affect, continue to engage in more physical play and give more affection to both boys and girls. When fathers have high-status jobs, they have less time to spend with their children, and so low job salience is related to men's playfulness and caregiving.[46] Men are most likely to be involved as fathers when mothers do not take on all the caregiving and managing and close fathers out. Nevertheless, the more skillful mothers are with children, the more skillful fathers become. Both parents are similar in being more demanding of boys and more disapproving of their misbehavior.[47]

Parents and children argue about a variety of everyday issues.[48] Issues that draw most conflicts have to do with children's interpersonal behavior with others (fighting, teasing); children's personality characteristics (stubbornness, irritability); and parents' regulating activities like TV, chores, bedtime, and curfews. These areas account for about two-thirds of the conflicts, which occur more with father than with mother, according to children. Appearance, regulating interpersonal activities like choice of friends, and homework account for another 25 percent of the fights. In arguing, children are more likely to justify what they want in terms of personal choice. Parents are more likely to justify their point of view in terms of convention and practical, health issues. Children are more likely to listen to parents' rules that prevent harm and psychological damage to other people.

The parent's role changes from almost exclusive control of the child and his or her environment during the preschool years to increased sharing of control with the child. Children make decisions and parents exercise a supervisory role, making a final decision on the matter. This sharing of control serves as a bridge to the preadolescent and adolescent years, when children will assume an ever greater share of control.

Even though parents become physically less demonstrative and affectionate with school-age children, acceptance remains an important positive variable. Diana Baumrind, describing parents' interactions with children eight and nine, found that for both boys and girls social responsibility (being cooperative, self-controlled) is related to parents' sensitivity and responsiveness to their needs. When parents make demands on the child, social responsibility increases in boys and self-assertiveness increases in girls. As Maccoby describes, Baumrind suggests that parents need to actively encourage characteristics outside the usual sex role stereotypes. Unless they exert a specific effort to encourage a broader range of characteristics, the natural tendencies for both mothers and fathers is to encourage assertiveness in boys and cooperation and a more dependent role in girls.[49]

Minority parents, in this period, direct more effort at socializing their children with regard to their racial or ethnic identity. Children reason more logically and better understand parents' statements about ethnic issues. Since children spend more time outside parents' direct control, in schools or other activities, they more likely experience prejudice or, at least, confusion at the different values other people hold. Children use this information to deal more effectively with negative experiences and to explore their ethnic heritage in the adolescent years when they achieve a sense of identity. This process is discussed in Chapter 10, but here we focus on how parents socialize children.

Parents serve as a buffer between children and the larger society. As in so many areas, they interpret social experiences for their children and help them deal with the situations. To socialize children with regard to racial and ethnic issues, parents first teach children (1) their own cultural values, (2) the values of the majority culture, and (3) the realities of being a member of their own group in the majority culture and how people cope with the realities.[50] Successful socialization goes beyond this to teach pride in one's ethnic group and the importance of one's own self-development.

◆

BOX 9-2
SOCIALIZATION MESSAGES
AFRO-AMERICAN PARENTS IMPART TO CHILDREN*

Message	% Parents
Achieving and working hard: *"Work hard and get a good education."*	22
Racial pride: *"Be proud of being black."*	17
Themes of black heritage: *"Taught what happened in the past and how people coped."*	9
Focus on intergroup relations: *Summary category of many responses—accommodate to whites,* *use collective action to help blacks*	9
Presence of racial restrictions and barriers: *"Blacks don't have the opportunities whites have."*	8
Good citizenship: *"Be honest, fair."*	7
Recognition and acceptance of racial background: *"Realize you are black."*	7
Fundamental equality of blacks and whites: *"Recognize all races as equal."*	6
Maintenance of a positive self-image: *Instruct children to stay away from whites.*	5 3**

* Information from the National Survey of Black Americans, a representative national sample
of 2,107 men and women. Statements tabulated from the answers to two questions: "In raising
children, have you told them things to help them know what it is to be black?" and "What are
the most important things you have said?"

** Remaining categories of 1 or 2 percent include a variety of responses having to do with
emphasizing religious principles, discussing personal traits, stressing general self-acceptance.

From Michael C. Thornton, Linda M. Chatters, Robert Joseph Taylor, and Walter R. Allen,
"Sociodemographic and Environmental Correlates of Racial Socialization by Black Parents,"
Child Development 61 (1990): 401–409.

Let us look at how Afro-American parents socialize children; more is known
about this group, and other groups may experience a similar process.[51] Afro-
American parents think teaching about their racial identity is important, but not *the*
most important information to pass on to children. To parents, being Afro-American
means children should learn how to deal with prejudice, feel pride and self-respect,

learn the value of a good education, and recognize that their fair and moral behavior is not always reciprocated.

Many parents do not discuss ethnic issues with their children. In a national sample, over one-third of parents reported making no statements, and few of the two-thirds who reported making a statement touched on more than one area. Which parents are most likely to talk to their children? Older parents who are married and who live in racially mixed neighborhoods where there is a sizeable white population are most likely to talk to children. Mothers are more likely to socialize children than fathers. Parents living in the Northeast are more likely to discuss racial matters, perhaps because, as in mixed neighborhoods, there is more contact between the two races.

What do parents say to children? Box 9-2 summarizes what parents say. Only about 22 percent teach racial pride and a positive self-image. Yet this is the area parents are most uniquely fitted to address. Both majority and minority children evaluate themselves as others close to them do, and so what parents convey strongly affects self-esteem. Since a minority child may get inaccurate and negative messages from other children, the media, and authority figures like coaches or teachers, it is even more important for minority parents to encourage a positive self-image and racial pride.

When parents emphasize awareness of social restrictions and barriers and at the same time encourage self-development and ethnic pride, children are happy and high in self-esteem and are successful in school.[52]

Sibling Relationships

The variety and intensity of feelings that marked sibling relationships in the preschool years continue through the elementary school years.[53] Some children like to play with brothers and sisters and report they hardly ever fight. Others—almost equal in number—report fighting all the time and rarely play together. One-third of children, when questioned, reported they would be happier without siblings, yet despite all the criticisms, almost 75 percent of the group would like another sibling perhaps because helpfulness and play occur more often than rivalry and hurt feelings.[54]

Brothers and sisters spend more time with each other than they spend with parents. At times they enjoy the same activities—coloring, reading. They help each other with the activities and, in fact, learn from each other's behavior, imitating what works best. There is continuity in the quality of relationships from the preschool years. Those preschoolers who had the most positive attitudes toward toddler siblings get along well with those same siblings now that they themselves are school-aged children.

Positive relationships between siblings are associated with mothers' reactions to the children. When mothers are responsive and meet their children's needs, children are more sharing, comforting, and helpful with each other. Having one's own needs met increases the ability to give to others. When mothers play favorites and respond to one child's needs but not the other's, hostility between siblings increases. So, as in the preschool years, parents can act to promote positive ties.[55]

Grandparents

As psychologists turn their attention to important people outside the child's nuclear family, they focus attention on grandparents. In a review article, Barbara Tinsley and Ross Parke summarize the limited work available and state that grandparents exert influence in direct and indirect ways.[56] They influence grandchildren directly when they serve as caregivers, playmates, and family historians who pass on information that solidifies a sense of generational continuity. They are a direct influence when they act as mentors to their grandchildren and when they negotiate between parent and child. They influence grandchildren indirectly when they provide both psychological and material support to parents, who then have more resources for parenting.

More information on the role of grandparents in minority families is available because these families are more often extended ones. For example, in 1984, 31 percent of Afro-American children lived in extended families with one or both parents.[57] The extended family often includes one or both grandparents. Grandmothers are resources that help families nurture and care for children in a less structured, more spontaneous way than is possible when there are only two generations. Grandparents' role depends on whether one or both parents live in the home. Grandmothers are less involved in parenting when both parents are present.[58]

There is limited current information on what percent of grandparents are involved with grandchildren and in what capacity they relate to them when they do not all live together. Research does suggest that family members in the home and in close proximity are positive forces in a variety of situations—at times of added parental responsibility with a sick child, at times of family transitions, at times of sudden individual crises for parents. No research as yet indicates that grandparents per se, as opposed to any positive support, are crucial. One can imagine, however, that there is something very special about a grandparent who combines the roles of playmate, caregiver, emotional confidant, family historian, and mentor for a child.

Peers

In the school-age period, children spend increasing amounts of time with their peers. At age four, 20 percent of children's time was spent with peers; between ages seven and eleven, slightly over 40 percent of children's time is spent with peers. Children and their friends usually live in the same neighborhood and are about the same age and the same sex. Children become friends as they participate in and enjoy the same things in a variety of areas. Physical aggression decreases in peer contacts, but abusive verbal exchanges, insults, and threats increase. Competition increases with age when rewards are given for it, but cooperation also increases if it is valued and rewarded. Prosocial behavior of support and help also increase.[59]

Children who are physically attractive, outgoing, and supportive of others are well liked. School achievement and athletic skill are also associated with being well liked. Children who are physically unattractive, immature, disruptive, and aggressive are rejected. Popular children tend to socialize with their own network of friends; rejected children find a small group of either younger children or unpopular children to associate with. A third group of children who often go unnoticed have been termed **neglected children**. Not enough is known about these children to describe them in any consistent way. They are neither well liked nor rejected. They do not engage in negative behaviors as rejected children do, but they do not have friends because they are so retiring.[60]

School-age children, on average, have about five friends, somewhat more than in preschool and adolescent years. About 90 percent of children report friendships and are selected by others as friends. Friends stress equality of treatment, mutuality, reciprocity in their relationships. The ability to sustain friendships is an important one and is related to later good adjustment. Conversely, when children are rejected in elementary school, especially as they get to be about ten years old, continuing rejection, along with difficulties in overall adjustment, are more likely.[61]

Peer sociability and its opposite, shyness, probably have a genetic component. Differences appear early and are persistent for long periods of time; further, there are resemblances among family members in ways that suggest a biological component. Life experiences contribute to these behaviors as well, however. Parental correlates of peer sociability and effectiveness include parents' affection, warmth, and acceptance of boys and girls, general parental satisfaction with children, and an absence of family tension. When fathers are both warm and dominant, boys seem more competent; when mothers are warm and dominant, girls are more competent. Thus, competence with peers is related to general family adjustment and warmth. There is some evidence that when the family is upset, peer relations change. In one study, peer relations suffered initially after a divorce but then improved. In another study, girls appeared reluctant to enter friendships following a divorce, whereas boys seemed to turn to friends to help them cope with family disorganization.[62]

Zimbardo and Radl list experiences that appear related to shy behavior: (1) specific failures in social settings like school, (2) loss of social supports, as may occur when a family makes many moves or becomes disorganized with separation or divorce, (3) poor parental role models, (4) lack of experience in social settings, and (5) feelings of shame.[63] These authors consider shyness the result of feelings of low self-worth and shame and of being so labeled by others.

Some argue that as peers become more important to children, their ties to parents and family lessen. This does not appear accurate. Children use both parents and peers as anchors for positive behavior, but they do detach from parents as anchors and misbehave in the preadolescent period. Peer standards of misconduct are increasingly important from third grade to eighth grade but do not increase beyond that point.[64]

Children at this age do engage in group activities, in sports and clubs like Girl Scouts or Boy Scouts. Leaders in groups are not necessarily aggressive, dominant, or popular. They are the ones who know how to help the group achieve its goal. The group is governed by norms, but it is not known how these norms emerge.

PARENTING TASKS

Parental tasks during this period include: (1) monitoring and guiding children from a distance when they are at school or with friends, (2) interacting effectively with children when they are present, (3) strengthening children's abilities to monitor their own behavior and function appropriately.[65]

Among the essential parenting tasks at any age is the need to interact effectively with children when they are present. Parents help children grow when they provide opportunities for children to learn new skills.

Parents help children grow when they provide opportunities for children to learn new skills, encourage them to try new activities, support their growing interest in peers, and accept their growing independence. A broad array of interests and activities for both boys and girls can have positive benefits. A wide range of interests is related to intellectual effectiveness and psychological stability in adulthood for men and women.[66]

Parents may become involved in children's activities as school aides or homeroom parents, team coaches, scout leaders. Such participation contributes to these activities and gives parents opportunities to be with other children the same ages as their own. In these groups, parents can get a better understanding of their children by observing them with their peers. Parents who are drawn into community activities serve as models for their children, who observe social and ethical attitudes in action.

In interacting with school personnel, parents have the role of the child's advocate. When there is a problem, parents work with the school to look for all the contribut-

THE JOYS OF PARENTING ELEMENTARY SCHOOL CHILDREN

"You enjoy seeing them learning to read. You take pride in their accomplishments, and you know they are accomplishing a lot on their own because you do not have a lot of time to spend with each one." FATHER

"It's the beginning of having friends over and seeing them go over to friends' houses, watching some of that." MOTHER

"I have a real memory of doing some of the same things my children are doing now. I remember kindergarten and first grade, and they are playing some of the same games I did. Jenny is jumping rope to the same rhymes and songs. That is a real joy." MOTHER

"I love watching them become little people who can take responsibility for chores, and also every now and then want to cook me dinner. Now they use the microwave; they can heat something up. They'll make tuna fish and raw vegetables." MOTHER

"Well, I take her to a dance lesson on Saturday morning, and this is one of our times together. We turn on the radio and we listen for certain songs." FATHER

"There is a lot of companionship. In the car now when we are driving any distance, Jenny stays awake, and we can have full conversations. Driving into San Francisco she's become a real companion in many ways. She is fun to go shopping with. She likes to talk about friends, what we've been doing, what we are going to be doing." MOTHER

"She's very interested in my childhood, what it was like when I was a little girl, what about my parents, what was it like where I grew up in New York. That is fairly new and fairly consistent. And that's a joy." MOTHER

ing factors in the situation. Parents do not assume the child is the problem, nor do they blame the school. Instead, they focus on solving the problem, sometimes asking the child to change and sometimes modifying the environment.

As advocates for their children, minority parents serve as translators of their culture for the teacher and the school. Many majority professionals have limited information on the great variety of different cultures represented in current school populations and are not often aware of how the cultures impact on the school experience. For example, before Brice-Heath made careful observations on the use of questions in the Afro-American culture, the teachers did not know that their questions made no sense to the children.

Parents themselves may not know all the subtle ways their culture affects their children's schooling. But they can explain their cultural traditions to teachers and how they think the culture makes schooling different. Further, they can encourage the teacher to point out clearly to the child exactly what is wanted in the areas where

"It's really fun learning more about girls. She is a lot like her mother in her interests and her understanding of people. I wasn't a reader; I was out on my bike, and I really like it that she is such a big reader and enjoys many of the books her mother had as a girl." FATHER

"This is the time when I can start instilling my values, why I do what I do, how people become homeless. When they were younger, you just had the rule, 'No play guns in the house,' and now you can talk about why you have the rule, and you are interacting on a whole new level." MOTHER

"Now they really are able to help. When it comes time to take snacks to school, they really can take a big part of the responsibility of doing much of the work. In terms of making cookies, they are really able to do a lot of the work." MOTHER

"I like to watch him draw and do projects. Once I came home with a paper eight feet square, and the three youngest ones got pencils, markers, and pens and crayons, and made up all these sketches and then colored them in and covered the whole paper. They started at about 7:30 one evening on the weekend and just kept going till I had to force them to bed. Then they hung it on one of their walls. Or they took all these cardboard boxes that I brought large amounts of food home in, and they cut them up, and pasted them, sometimes with wood, to make these fancy guitars. They painted them all up with magic markers, and they had a stack of twenty cardboard instruments at one time." FATHER

"Even taking them places like the zoo or the aquarium is different now. Their interest or attention span level used to be minimal, but now their interest level is higher." MOTHER

"I love to teach French, and I do it at the school, so I have had both my children as students. It is really fun to do what I like doing and do it with them." MOTHER

continued

the child is confused. Parents can also help teachers see how children are adjusting and becoming bicultural. At the same time, parents serve as coaches for their children. Parents point out where the child has to change traditional behavior to meet social expectations.

Minority parents also reinforce children's feelings of self-worth when they become discouraged by their school experience. They encourage children to question when they do not understand what the teacher wants. In order to help teachers and children understand their culture, they can offer to teach the class about special cultural aspects not covered in the curriculum.

Parents are interpreters of the outside world and of life in general for their children. They pass on the values of their ethnic traditions and socialize their children to be members of their group. Also, parents interpret different social expectations that other children may have and show the child how to deal with the social situation.

THE JOYS OF PARENTING
ELEMENTARY SCHOOL CHILDREN *continued*

"He's nine, and for the last several months, maybe because I'm the Dad, he's come and said, 'Now there's this girl who's written me a note, what do I do?' Or, 'I have an interest here, how do I act?' I never heard any of this from my daughters. Then he says, 'What were you doing in the third grade? How would you deal with this when you were in the third grade?'" FATHER

"One of the joys is you are learning or relearning through your children, whether it's actual subject matter or reexperiencing things and seeing the way they handle something versus the way you did. It gives me insight into their independence that they think of different solutions for things. There's always another way besides 'Mom's way.'" MOTHER

"Every night we have a talking time just before he goes to bed, either he and his Dad or he and I. He's a real deep thinker and he likes to get advice or get a response, and he just needs that verbal connection. So a few years ago when he was five, he was talking about being afraid of death and that he might not be married and he might not have children and that would be the worst. I can hear parts of what he might hear at church or other places like school, and he takes it all very seriously; when it collides, he wants to know what the answer is. They are always things we don't know the answer to either." MOTHER

"I enjoy the rituals we have developed. I don't know how it started but every night we eat by candlelight. One lights the candles, and one turns down the dimmer, and it's a very nice touch after a day at work." MOTHER

"I can say as a father of two girls between five and ten that to be a father to girls is delightful. It's nice being looked on as a combination of God and Robert Redford. They have a little glow in their eyes when they look at Dad, and it's great. The younger one said, 'When I'm ticklish, you know why? Because I love you so much.'" FATHER

"It's wonderful to have a conversation with them that isn't about some nursery rhyme. You can sit down and have an extended conversation." MOTHER

"He does well in school because he's willing to put in time on things. It is fun to work with him on projects. He wanted a Nintendo, and we said no because it is addictive and you spend too much time on it. He had a science fair project at school, and he decided to make up a questionnaire on how kids used their Nintendo, which he handed out to everyone. I helped him analyze the answers; and he proved the longer kids had it, the less they used it, and so it wasn't addictive. When his birthday came, we got it for him. He proved he was right." FATHER

"I enjoy having them jump into bed with us. I like the way they look and feel, knowing they are my children and I can claim some of the credit." MOTHER

"One of the things that's most fun is to see my daughter sit down and read a book that I read as a child, to see her eyes light up over certain parts, and to have a conversation with her about what part was special for her." MOTHER

During the elementary years, many parents contemplate providing formal religious education. These are the years when children internalize family and social values. If parents are identified with a church, they can include the children in family church activities. If parents have no religious affiliation, however, they may wonder what to do.

One such father of a young child wrote to Joan Beck, author of *Effective Parenting*, to ask for her advice.[67] He could not pretend a belief he did not have in God, but he wanted his daughter to have the freedom to make her own decision as she matured.

Beck's response is summarized as follows. First, each family must find its own answer. Parents have three alternatives: (1) ignore the whole question, (2) send children for religious instruction without their participation, and (3) develop an inquiring attitude about religion that can be shared with the children as they grow.

Church attendance is relatively low, and so it is increasingly easy to raise a child without religious training. Children, however, will then have many questions that remain unanswered: Who is God? What happens when we die? Will God punish me? As children see the involvement of grandparents and of other families with religion, as they encounter religious references in reading, they may feel a void in their own experiences. This void may be intensified if they lack a source of comfort or solace when a painful loss occurs.

Sending a child for instruction without parental participation, however, seems hypocritical. The most reasonable alternative for some parents is to develop an individual belief system that they share with children as they grow. Parents can explore different conceptions of God, convey to children what they accept and do not accept in each conception, discuss the meanings of rituals and symbols, and why others may find them important. In investigating the ideas of different churches, parents may discover a group they can join wholeheartedly. They may rediscover the religion of their parents. Or they may find they want to join a group that is devoted to social action rather than worship. The process of searching for an agreed-upon code can enrich the entire family.

Work, too, can be a family affair that results in fun and family cohesiveness. Parents and children play more complex games together. Board games and card games are interesting for children and appealing to adults during the elementary school years. When family members work and play together, communication increases and improves. Dreikurs writes, "What people enjoy together brings them together. Through games and projects in which all enjoy the fun, a feeling of group solidarity develops. Solidarity is essential for the equality it promotes and for the relaxed and harmonious atmosphere that can become a part of family living."[68]

In all their interactions with children at home and in the community, it is important for parents to encourage children, to support their enthusiasm, optimism, and active efforts to enjoy their activities and life in general.

ROUTINES, PROBLEMS, AND STRATEGIES

School is clearly a source of worry to children, and school work is a source of concern to parents. Let's look at three problems related to school—getting to school on time, homework, and grades.

Getting to School on Time

The child who is always—or even frequently—late for school needs help. Such behavior, if not dealt with, can become a habit that will be difficult to change.

Ginott, Gordon, and the behaviorists all encourage independence in children.[69] They all recommend that parents purchase an alarm clock for the child, help the child set the alarm to allow plenty of time to get ready in the morning, and then let the child take the consequences of being late. A child who misses the school bus and must walk will be late. And the child who is frequently late to school will be subjected to ridicule by peers and to discipline by the teacher.

Gordon suggests active listening. What is the source of the problem? When you learn that, you can take appropriate action. Gordon tells of a mother who learned, by talking with her son, that he liked school but disliked the morning routine—he always had to rush because she waited until the last minute to get him up. She told him he could pick out his clothes the night before, and she gave him an alarm clock so he could get himself up. After that, he had enough time to feed the dog and help with breakfast, and he went off to school each morning feeling cheerful. The solution was simple, once the parent and child thought about it.

Dreikurs believes parents should prepare children for school by helping them to care for themselves—washing, dressing, getting to school alone, taking care of their toys.[70] The child should walk or go to school independently, and the mother should let the child take the natural and logical consequences of being late. Behavioral strategists use the same techniques as well as rewards and punishments.

One of the mothers in Ginott's group had a creative solution to the problem of her young son's dawdling.[71] He was eight and had to catch a school bus to go to school. He frequently missed it, and so his mother ended up driving him to school because it was too far to walk. She talked to him about the problem, his behavior improved briefly, and then he missed the bus again on several days. She decided she was not going to drive him. If he missed the bus, she would call a taxi, and after the first ride he would pay for it out of his allowance. She explained the consequences to him and could see he did not take it seriously. The next day when he missed the bus, she called a cab. He was very upset, but he went. He did not miss the school bus again because he did not like going alone in the cab.

Homework

We see the same emphasis on independence when it comes to homework. Both Ginott and Gordon believe that the child owns the homework problem. Parents can help by actively listening to the child's problems and making clear statements about their concern and their desire to see the child complete the homework. But parents must let the children experience the consequences of not doing homework. This is similar to what Dreikurs recommends. Some parents will have difficulty standing back and seeing their child suffer the consequences, but it is precisely that experience that will motivate the child in the future.

Is this all that parents can do to encourage effective performance at school? No. Although strategists advise against direct help with homework, all advise organizing the environment around homework. We tend to think of homework as a simple matter of getting it done or not getting it done. There are several steps to doing homework, however, and several points at which the child can experience problems. Helping the child identify the source of the difficulty can help him or her correct the problem. First, children have to listen in class and hear the assignment. Distractible, talkative children may genuinely believe they have no work because they did not hear the assignment given. They have to learn to check with the teacher or with some written assignment log. Second, children have to get the assignment and the books home together. If books do not come home when needed, parents can send the child back to get them or insist that all books come home each night. Third, children have to do the homework. Fourth, they have to get the work out of the house and back to school. Sometimes the work gets lost in the house or on the way back to school. Having a special place the child puts and keeps the work—for example, in a backpack placed in a certain location at home—helps. Once at school, the child has a fifth and final step: turning the homework in. Many children actually do assignments but get no credit because they stuff them in their desks and never hand them in to the teacher.

In encouraging homework, parents can suggest children have a special place for books and put them there as soon as they get home, eliminating the necessity of hunting around for them later. Children must also have a special time for doing homework. Some parents and children agree it is best to do homework right after school. Play follows work and serves as motivation to complete the work. Other parents and professionals believe that playtime after school is important. Children run off accumulated tension and are ready to settle down after dinner. Regardless of when it is, children should have a specific time when they always do their homework. Parents provide a desk or a special work area in the dining room. As soon as the work is completed, books go back to their special places and are ready to be picked up in the morning.

Grades

As noted earlier, children worry about school and their performance there. Though few children are made to repeat a grade, many worry about it. Parents need to know their children well to establish reasonable expectations about school. A highly active child may be doing well to get only one "Needs Improvement" when he or she enters first grade and stays in school five straight hours for the first time. For other children, such a grade would not be acceptable. It is difficult for parents to establish reasonable expectations of their children's academic work without the teacher's comments. Some children have difficulties where parents least expect it.

So, any time a grade or teacher's comment distresses a parent or a child, parents need to talk with their child and the teacher to figure out the nature and source of the problem. Parents have to answer the following questions: (1) What is the exact problem? Is it academic or behavioral? and (2) What needs to be done about it? A drop in grade may occur because a child has been moved to sit near a friend and now talks instead of doing classwork. Failure to progress in an area like reading or math may signal a learning disability, discussed in Chapter 15. Or the child may be doing poorly because of dislike for a teacher who is considered unfair. In this case the parent must initiate active listening both with the child and with the teacher.

In interacting with school personnel, the parent has the role of the child's advocate. The parent does not assume the child is the problem but looks for all the contributing factors in the situation. Equally, the parent does not assume the teacher is the problem. Instead, the parent must focus on solving the difficulty so the child can do his or her best in the school situation.

Once the parent has understood the problem, then he or she must describe to the child specific actions to be taken. For example, the child must talk less in class; the child must improve grades on spelling tests; the child must complete classwork that day. Then parents can arrange contracts with their children to improve performance in these areas. Improvements are expected to be gradual, not immediate and total. To earn a reward, for example, spelling tests must improve from Ds to Cs or daily work in five or six subjects must be completed. If perfection must be achieved for rewards, children become discouraged.

With young children with behavioral difficulties or with older children with many problems, daily reports from the teacher on acceptable behavior can earn TV time, extra game time with parents, or staying up 15 minutes later that night. For older children who are improving a single academic area, weekly reports and rewards are sufficient. Children decide which rewards will be most motivating to them.

The Isolated Child

If a child shows little interest in other people but has many activities that absorb attention and seems happy, parents may not want to intervene because the child has interests and seems content. Activities, however, are sometimes used as substitutes for friends, and many children who do not have friends wish they did. There are two major reasons for not having friends, and they require somewhat different actions on the part of parents.

First, there are shy children who are hesitant to reach out, uncertain what to say to other children, uncertain how to join in games, worried about rejection. They are the neglected children mentioned earlier in the section on peer relations. Other children do not dislike them, but rather overlook them. These children have to learn to be more friendly, outgoing, and confident with others. A second group of children are isolated because they are actively rejected. They are often demanding of attention, aggressive, disruptive with other children, wanting to direct the games, accusing others of being unfair to them. Others dislike these children and actively reject them. Underneath their outgoing, aggressive behavior they may have the same feelings and worries as shy children, but they handle them differently. They must learn to curb their aggressiveness, however, and also learn friendly behaviors.

As noted earlier, shy behavior has several causes. To help children deal with shyness requires several actions, as seen in the example of a mother who used Ginott's method. She took action to help her son make friends by discussing the problem with his teacher, who said she would involve him in more group activities.[72] The teacher also gave the mother a list of boys' names, so the mother could organize a group activity. After talking it over with her son, the mother started a bowling club. The club lasted only a week—at the first meeting her son had the lowest score, and he refused to try again. A few days later, however, one of the boys invited him over to play, and a friendship began to grow.

As the mother observed her own and her son's behavior, she realized she had encouraged the boy to depend on her for companionship and had protected him from the rougher and more critical companionship of his older brother and father. She decided to give up her role as protector and to encourage a closer relationship between father and son. Thus, the mother modified her own behavior and at the same time increased the child's skills, just as a behaviorist would.

Gordon considers the child owns the problem with friends. Parents can encourage children to talk about this problem and can listen actively. As children talk about what is bothering them, they may find ways of solving their problems. But until then, or until the child asks for help, parents must accept isolation as the child's problem.

Dreikurs also stresses the child's need to learn how to get along and to accommodate his or her interests and activities to those of peers. He believes that bashfulness and timidity may stem from overindulgence by parents. The child seeks attention and regard from others by doing nothing rather than by taking an active role. Parents can encourage positive interaction and ignore demands for attention. Although it sounds like Dreikurs recommends doing very little, nevertheless he does advise paying appropriate attention to children, playing games and working on projects with them, and encouraging them to participate in activities with other children.

More than other strategists, behaviorists have focused on strategies for helping children to make friends. Oden and Asher have devised a system of coaching children in interpersonal skills.[73] They give children verbal instructions about effective ways of interacting and provide opportunities to apply the rules in play sessions. Instructions cover four topics: (1) participating in group activities (getting started, paying attention to the game), (2) cooperating in play (sharing, taking turns), (3) communicating with partner (talking or listening), and (4) validating and supporting the peer (giving attention and help). Benefits persisted and were measurable a year later.

Parents can try to do this coaching as they observe their children's interactions with others. When parents comment later, in a calm way, on troubles that interfered with the child's having optimal fun and ask how such problems might have been avoided, they help to increase the child's social competence. The parents should not sound critical and interfering when making these remarks.

Zimbardo and Radl offer many suggestions for the parent of the school-aged shy child (Box 9-3).[74] All these actions are designed to increase self-esteem, confidence, and socially outgoing behavior.

Parents of rejected children can adopt all these methods, too, in addition to helping their children curb aggressiveness. First, parents must have a detached attitude about tales of being picked on or discriminated against by peers, because rejected children often feel justified in being aggressive. Parents must talk to teachers and principals to determine what really does happen at school. If children fail to see their part in provoking others' rejection, parents can go over events with them, after the children have cooled down, and present the other child's point of view. If children

◆

BOX 9-3
THINGS TO DO WITH YOUR SHY CHILD

1. Actively listen to your child and try to see the social situation from the child's point of view.
2. Talk about what you have done or thought during the day while the child was at school and encourage the child to share his or her day.
3. When you ask a question, wait and listen for the answer. Do not jump in to answer it yourself. Shy persons take a while to answer, but the answer will come.
4. Enroll the child in drama or dance lessons if he or she might like that.
5. Encourage physical skills that can be used in a team sport.
6. Help the shy child step out of that role in fantasy play at home—with puppets, dolls—and in activities like shouting for a brief period or dressing up in crazy costumes.
7. Share some of your own difficult childhood experiences with your child; describe how you overcame them.
8. Pretend you are the child's grandparent for the weekend and see how your view of the child changes.
9. Help the child make eye contact while speaking.
10. Notice how often your child smiles and do all you can to increase the smiles.
11. Encourage laughter and a sense of humor.
12. Teach and display listening skills—paying attention to what others say, reflecting back at times what the person says to be sure you are clear on it.
13. Encourage children to speak for themselves—order their own meals in restaurants, get information by telephone.
14. Teach them to identify themselves and take accurate phone messages.
15. Teach friends and relatives to talk to children on matters of interest to both.
16. Give compliments to all family members and make it clear you enjoy receiving them in return.
17. Teach the child to interrupt politely to make a parent give more information if needed—"Excuse me, I have a question," "Excuse me, I didn't understand what you wanted me to do."
18. Watch your child play with other children and note any inappropriate behavior that needs changing. Discuss it later.
19. Have slightly younger playmates over occasionally so the child has a chance to practice skills with children who may be a little less dominant.
20. Involve other children in car rides to school or invite them along to the movies.

Adapted from Philip Zimbardo and Shirley Radl, *The Shy Child* (Garden City, N.Y.: Doubleday, 1982), pp. 152–155.

get in many fights at school or are very disruptive of others' play, a reward system can be set up with the teacher so that children get a reward each day a positive report comes home. The teacher is involved and sends home a card with checks for all acceptable behavior in class, at recess, and at lunch. If children do not bring home the report at all, there are no TV or other privileges for that day. This procedure is followed every day.

At the same time that they discourage disruptive, aggressive behaviors, parents must help rejected children learn more social skills just as they would with shy children. Parents can invite other children over and encourage positive interactions, help children obtain skills so they can participate in activities as equals.

The Aggressive Child

Aggressiveness can take many forms. Children may physically hit or hurt others; they may be verbally assaultive, taunting, teasing, humiliating, threatening, or demanding. Many children are aggressive at home, at school, and with friends, but a sizeable number are aggressive in only one setting. For handling occasional aggressive outbursts, the methods of Ginott, Gordon, and Dreikurs are useful.

Ginott suggests that parents accept the child's anger with sympathy and understanding, although physical and verbal abuse must be controlled. When nine-year-old Eric came home furious because rain had canceled a class picnic, his mother's impulse was to say, "There will be other days," or to criticize him for complaining. Instead, she commented that he seemed disappointed and frustrated. She was astounded when Eric's anger vanished—often his rages upset the entire household.

Gordon suggests sending I-messages when children act aggressively. This permits the child to resolve the problem. When safety is involved, however, parents must send the message in a forceful tone and, if necessary, must take action so the child will respond.

Dreikurs believes that fighting among children is best ignored by parents. If siblings are involved, let them settle the differences themselves. If a child fights with neighborhood children, parents are advised to stand back and let the other children teach the natural and logical consequences of fighting. Peers will either fight back or refuse to play with the child. Parents can talk about the difficulties later, raising questions about consequences of other ways of relating. But parents do not intervene actively.

For the child who has developed many aggressive behaviors—hitting, yelling, teasing—and uses these negative behaviors in response to the parent's discipline, Gerald Patterson and his co-workers have developed an effective program parents can use.[75] Patterson describes the coercive, or forcing, process the child uses to try to get family members to do what he or she wants. To change these behaviors in the child, all family members must change. The program, developed at the Oregon Research Institute, involves an intake interview with the whole family. At this time, parents specify behaviors they wish to change. A trained team observes the family at home for two weeks to record and understand patterns of interaction in the family.

Parents then read either *Families*[76] or *Living with Children,*[77] books that introduce them to behavior modification techniques. After they pass a brief test on the ideas in the book, parents come in and pinpoint exactly the behaviors they wish to change. They are then trained in procedures for recording the behavior. Parents record the occurrence of negative and positive behaviors before making any changes in order to get an idea of exactly what is happening before interventions are made.

The parents and child draw up a contract. It is important that the child gets points or tokens daily for behavior. For example, a child could accumulate 2 points for bed-making, 2 points for making a school lunch, 3 points for completing homework by a specific time, 2 points for picking up the bedroom, 1 point for brushing teeth without being reminded. The child could use the points for an extra 30 minutes of TV (5 points), extra story (2 points), extra 30 minutes up in the evening (3 points). A child loses points for sibling fighting (2 points), yelling at parents (2 points). Parents deduct points without nagging, criticizing, or scolding. The number of points are added up daily, and rewards are given each evening. Psychologists from the institute contact families at certain times to note progress in changing behavior.

The Oregon Research Institute treatment has the following effects: (1) significant and persistent changes in the child's behavior, (2) modest decrease in coercive behavior of all family members, (3) increased positive perception of the child by parents, (4) no further unconscious parental rewards for negative behavior, (5) more effective punishments, (6) a more active role by fathers in controlling children's behavior, (7) mothers' perception of their whole family as happier.

Lying and Stealing

Ginott makes several basic points about lying. First, lying may represent the child's basic hopes and fears and, in that sense, is an accurate statement of feelings although not an accurate statement of fact. This is particularly true of preschool children. When a parent knows a young child is lying, the parent can reflect the child's feelings: "You wish you owned a horse," or "You wish you were going to the zoo." Second, parents sometimes encourage lying about feelings. They punish a child who says she hates her sister or tells a relative she is ugly. The child learns it is best to lie about how she really feels. Parents are wiser to accept the child's feelings. They can also explain that polite refusal to comment is a way of being both kind and honest. There really are times when "if you can't say something nice, you shouldn't say anything at all."

Third, parents must avoid provoking a lie by asking an embarrassing question to which they already have the answer. For example, if a parent finds an overdue library book that the child has said he returned, the parent should not ask, "Did you return that book to the library?"

Dreikurs takes an understanding attitude toward lying and urges parents not to view it as a terrible act. If parents are not severe when children commit a misdeed, children will not be afraid and will not feel that they must always present themselves in the best possible light. When parents are truthful in their everyday lives, children are more likely to be truthful. When lying does occur, Dreikurs suggests parents remain unimpressed. Children may be lying to get attention or to win a power struggle and make the parents feel helpless.

If a child lies and a parent does not know what to do, Dreikurs suggests thinking of what you should not do, and doing anything else. You might point out how easy it is to fool a parent, and add that if the child needs to lie to feel important you can take it. If this approach does not work, Dreikurs advises a game in which the parent demonstrates how important truthfulness in the family is. In the game, everybody is free to say whatever they like, whether it is true or not. Mother may call a child for a meal that is not there or promise a movie and then say she did not mean it. A child may come to prefer the truth after such a game. When lying stems from a need to boost confidence, parents need to show approval and appreciation for positive behavior, so that lying is not the only route to attention.

Like Dreikurs, the behaviorists urge parents to make telling the truth worthwhile. They illustrate how lying is rewarded in the following episode.[78] A young boy knocked over his mother's highly valued vase and broke it. Although he initially denied any knowledge about what had happened to the vase, a few days later he admitted he had broken it. His mother immediately restricted him to the house for the rest of the month, saying that would certainly teach him a lesson. From this incident, the boy learned he could avoid punishment if he lied and that if he told the truth he could get into trouble. The mother could have said that she was glad the boy had told the truth and asked him to contribute chore money to help pay for a new vase. If she had done that, her son would have learned that honesty is rewarded with respect and that he would have to help replace things he broke.

Like lying, stealing is not that uncommon among children. Ginott urges parents to remain calm and to insist that the child return the object or make restitution. If, as often happens, the child steals from the parent, the parent asks for return of the object or deducts the cost from the child's allowance. Children are expected to discuss their needs for money or possessions with parents. When stealing occurs, however, parents do not get angry. They express disappointment and hurt. As with lying, if parents know that a child has broken a rule, it is unwise to try to trap the child with questions like, "And where did you get this new whistle?" Once a parent has expressed frustration and upset, it is the child's responsibility to change his or her behavior.

Gordon recommends mutual problem solving, as in the following example. A father discovered that his five-year-old son was stealing loose change from the dresser. Father and son held a mutual problem-solving session. The father agreed to give the boy a small allowance, and the boy agreed to save for the special things he wanted.

Dreikurs recommends taking a calm approach in which the child is not criticized or blamed but helped to be honest.

Stealing results from a variety of motives. Often the child hopes "to put something over" on the adult and to get attention, power, or revenge. Often children do not know precisely why they steal. Calm insistence that articles be returned usually teaches the child not to steal again.

Sibling Rivalry

As children grow more skilled and competent in action and language, sibling rivalry takes on new dimensions. Preschoolers cannot have the long-winded verbal, teasing, and haranguing arguments that school-age children have, because their language is not sophisticated enough. Also, parents are able to remember their own elementary school years, when they argued with siblings. When this happens, parents may react to their children's fights and take sides on the basis of their feelings toward their own brothers and sisters. This happened to a couple who have been using Ginott's system.[79] The mother said she could not help taking the side of her younger son because she could recall how her older brother had dominated her. Her husband, however, was able to remain detached. He reflected the anger between the two boys and suggested they go to their rooms and write down how the conflict started and what could be done to avoid similar arguments.

Gordon suggests using mutual problem solving to eliminate the conflict. In the following example, a boy (John) took his brother's (Bob's) baseball cards to show to his friends at school. Bob was upset, sure that his brother would lose or damage the cards. The father, with his arms around both boys, reflected that both boys were upset. He described how worried Bob was and asked for suggestions. And the boys worked out a solution. John purchased some of the cards from Bob. Then John had some cards of his own, and Bob had money to buy more cards. Mutual problem solving can eliminate conflicts between brothers and sisters, and it also helps to strengthen relationships. When parents use Gordon's active listening and mutual problem-solving techniques, children get similar amounts of attention and neither is favored.

Dreikurs believes that much sibling rivalry occurs because children want attention from parents. When they realize that fighting doesn't work, they are likely to give it up. Dreikurs' unique contribution is his suggestion that when one child disrupts the family, all children should receive the same treatment. Charles, age eight, was a middle child between an achieving, older brother and a well-behaved younger sister. He lied, stole, ruined furniture, and crayoned the walls. Dreikurs advised the mother to treat the children as a unit and make them all responsible for what Charles did.

The next time Charles crayoned on the walls, the mother asked all the children to clean the walls. Charles did not help, but he did not mark the walls again. He said it was no fun if the other children cleaned it up and his mother wasn't angry. When misbehavior no longer resulted in attention, the misbehavior stopped.

Behaviorists use rewards to promote acceptable behavior. In an illustrative incident, a mother offered her older son a trip to the store for an ice cream cone if he could get along with his sister all afternoon.[80] When the children began quarreling, the mother reminded the boy of their agreement. He was unhappy, but he didn't say anything. The mother maintained the calm, detached attitude that Dreikurs recommends.

Chores

In every home there are chores that must be done. Children who help with chores contribute to the well-being of the whole family. Simultaneously, these responsibilities contribute to the psychological development of children—their competence and feelings of independence increase as they participate in activities that are necessary and useful to all. Children who help with family chores learn what is required to run a household, and they learn skills they will need as independent adults. When families share in planning and executing household tasks, they learn about each other's special strengths as workers, and they come to rely on each other. Thus, working together brings a special closeness not achieved in other activities.

Gordon recommends that when a parent needs help from a child, the parent should send I-messages that state the need clearly, and then parent and child should engage in mutual problem solving to decide exactly how the chores can be completed. Behaviorists establish a more formal system. They suggest listing all the jobs that need completing, parceling them out among family members, and writing a formal contract, and posting a chart of everyone's jobs. It is difficult to establish a general timetable for including children in family chores. Dreikurs believes they can be included very early, as young as eighteen months to two years. Some families wait until children are older, between five and eight.

Television

Television is a powerful teaching tool not only because children spend more time watching it than any other activity they engage in, but also because the visual medium has a powerful impact on children. Children begin to watch and respond to television in infancy. Infants of six months become distressed when the audio or visual part of the program is changed. Preschool and elementary school children watch increasing amounts of TV, with the peak coming just before adolescence. In adolescence, interest turns to music and movies for entertainment.[81]

Children can absorb many different kinds of information from TV, depending on what they watch. Children learn cognitive skills by watching educational programs like "Sesame Street" and "The Electric Company." Children from both middle-income and low-income families learn when they watch such programs. Children also absorb social stereotypes about the roles of men and women, minority groups, and disabled persons. The impact of programs is greatest in areas where children have the least information because they are unable to evaluate what they see. So, majority group members may be highly influenced by programs about minority group individuals because they have little contact with these people, and vice versa. Low-income viewers may be most influenced by programs concerning majority group members.

The positive side of television's impact is that it can be used to teach in dramatic form what many parents want their children to learn. Although TV can increase social stereotypes, it can also break them down. Children who saw a series of programs called "Freestyle" developed more nontraditional views of work roles and activities for both boys and girls. Increased interest in people in other countries was fostered by a series called "The Big Blue Marble." Although these were educational programs designed to change attitudes, even a single positive activity inserted in a regular comedy had an effect on young viewers. The day after Fonzie got a library card on "Happy Days," there was a fivefold increase in the number of children who took out library cards.

Not only does television affect attitudes, but it changes feelings as well. Children about to have surgery were shown a presurgery film describing what happens and how people might feel. Compared to a presurgery group who did not see the film, children from four to twelve who saw it were less fearful before and after the operations and had fewer postoperative problems. Television's ability to stimulate emotional reactions can present problems, however. Violence and aggression depicted repeatedly can harden individuals. One eleven-year-old commented, "You see so much violence that it's meaningless. If I saw someone really get killed, it wouldn't be a big deal. I guess I'm turning into a hard rock."[82] Equally, seeing too much of adults' problems may upset and worry young children about the difficulties they may face as adults.

Evidence on the effects of TV come from a comparison of three Canadian cities—"Notel," which had no television initially; "Unitel," which had one channel; and "Multitel," which had three channels. Increase in children's aggressive behavior and sexual stereotyping was measured in the three cities. Initially, there was no difference among children in the three cities, but when Notel got TV two years later, that city had an increase in aggressive behavior on playgrounds and in sexual stereotyping. The change, however, may have been temporary and a response to the novelty of TV.[83]

Commercials have an impact on children. In the preschool and early elementary years, children have a difficult time evaluating them. They believe the commercials are statements of fact. One four-year-old was reported very unhappy when he bought a new pair of sneakers and could not leap high in the air in slow motion as he had seen in the commercial; he assumed he would be able to achieve this feat with the new shoes of that brand. By the end of elementary school years, children's ability to evaluate commercials is greatest.

There is almost no research on how parents can counteract what their children see on TV. However, when adults discuss with children what they are watching, when adults ask questions and stimulate thinking, children become more questioning of what they see. Parents can then spend time watching programs with children, talking about their reactions, what parents liked and disliked. This provides children with guidelines for thinking about what they have seen.

Television is here to stay. It will not go away just because we see its negative aspects. Parents can help children make the wisest use of this powerful medium by limiting the amount of time children watch, encouraging selective viewing so they learn material that is compatible with family values, and discussing programs. Television then becomes a social and enriching experience for children and parents.

Keeping Children Safe

As children spend more time away from home and parents, going to and from school or to friends' homes, parents become concerned about their safety. They want to help children be independent and safe in the world, yet they do not want to frighten them and make them afraid of strangers and new experiences. Grace Hechinger, an educational consultant, has interviewed police officials, school safety officials, individuals involved in neighborhood safety programs, and people who have been victims of crime and assaults.[84] From this research she has organized information to help parents prepare their children to be safe as they spend more time on their own.

Fostering children's awareness of danger, caution, and preparedness for unsafe situations does not mean making children live in fear. Children can learn that even though most people in the world are good and helpful and most situations are safe, some small number of people and experiences are not, and everyone must learn to protect himself or herself from dangers that arise. It is helpful if parents can put this knowledge in some kind of perspective for children. Life has always involved danger of some sort, and many objects or experiences that are positive also have dangerous

BOX 9-4
SOME "WHAT IF" QUESTIONS FOR YOUNG CHILDREN

Parents ask children what they would do if the following situations happened. If children give the wrong answers, parents can calmly tell them more practical alternative responses.

1. We are separated in a shopping center, in the movies, at the beach?
2. You are lost in a department store, in the park, at a parade?
3. A stranger offered you candy or presents to leave the playground?
4. A stranger wanted you to get into his car?
5. A stranger started fussing with your clothing?
6. Your friends wanted to play with matches?
7. Someone you did not know asked your name and phone number?

Grace Hechinger, *How to Raise a Street-Smart Child* (New York: Ballantine, 1984), p. 59.

aspects. Cars are useful—they get us to work, to stores, to hospitals. We need them, but they can be dangerous if they hit us while we are crossing the street. The answer lies not in eliminating cars, because before we had cars, there were dangers from horses and horse-drawn vehicles. The solution is to take precautions to minimize dangers and enjoy the benefits.

Families need to develop a set of instructions for major dangerous situations, to be discussed and revised as necessary. A one-time discussion is not enough; periodically, parents must review instructions with children. Children can learn these safety rules gradually—for example, at what hours and where they may go alone, what to do if bothered by someone on the street or in a store, even when parents are nearby. Learning safety rules becomes as natural as learning to brush teeth. The emphasis in teaching is that children are learning skills to master the environment, to make them competent and independent.

Although parents worry that talk of possible fearful events will damage the child, the risks that come with ignorance are much greater. Parents can begin with simple discussions of traffic safety—where, when, how to cross the street. They can move from that topic to others of importance for the child. Television may start a discussion. Mrs. Hechinger suggests a game, "What If?" Parents ask a variety of questions and give children chances to develop solutions to difficult situations (Box 9-4). Parents should not be upset if their children's initial answers are impractical because children can then learn more reasonable responses.

Parents should have clear safety rules on: (1) behavior for a fire at home, (2) traffic behavior, whether on foot or on a bicycle, (3) boundaries within which the child can come and go freely and outside of which an adult or parent must be present, (4) behavior in public with strangers, (5) behavior at home if strangers telephone or come to the house, (6) behavior when a victim or witness of muggings by peers or adults, (7) behavior when sexual misconduct occurs (Box 9-5).

◆

BOX 9-5
STREET SAFETY RULES

1. Walk to and from school with a group of friends.
2. Don't linger in the schoolyard when the rest of your friends have left.
3. Know your school route.
4. If you have any problem after school, go back to find a teacher when there is no one at home.
5. Walk in the middle of the sidewalk; avoid bushes and doorways.
6. Know your neighborhood. Remember safe places to go if you need immediate help—storekeepers, gas stations, a nearby friend, local fire and police stations, the post office.
7. Know the location of public phone booths in your area.
8. Never flash money, bus passes, transistor radios, cameras, or other possessions. Don't tell your classmates you don't know well about the things you have in your locker or at home.

Grace Hechinger, *How to Raise a Street-Smart Child* (New York: Ballantine, 1984), p. 68.

If children are victimized—a bike is stolen, money taken, a stranger approaches them—parents' reactions can help speed a healing process. When parents listen to children's reactions and help children take any possible action, such as notifying the police, they help children cope. When parents' responses are exaggerated—"This is horrible!"—or detached—"I cannot deal with this"—children get no help in coping with their feelings. If they cannot talk about how they feel, they will find it difficult to work out their feelings. Active listening, sending simple I-messages—"If that happened to me, I'd be really upset"—give children a chance to say what the experience meant to them. Sometimes children need to describe the event several times. Each time more details emerge as well as more feeling. Gradually, after the incident, children will regain self-confidence. If a child's eating, sleeping, or play habits change or there are marked changes in schoolwork or personality that continue for some time, professional help should be sought.

An important step in promoting children's safety is working with people in the community. Developing community awareness and community programs gives everyone a positive feeling of working together that does much to banish fear. Promoting public safety programs with school and police officials, organizing block-watch programs to help children in the neighborhood are useful steps. In Block-Parent Programs, one house in the neighborhood is designated as a house where children may come if they need help or reassurance when no one is home.

Family members grow stronger when they face problems and work together to deal with them. Sense of community is strengthened when families and agencies cooperate to make the environment safe for children.

PARENTS' EXPERIENCES

Children's entrance into school marks a new stage in parenthood. Children spend more time away from parents, in school and with peers. They are absorbing new information and are exposed to new values. Ellen Galinsky describes this parental stage as the **interpretive stage**.[85] Parents share facts and information about the world, teach values, and guide children's behavior in certain directions. They decide how they will handle the child's greater independence and involvement with people who may not share similar values.

At this point, parents have a more realistic view of themselves as parents and a greater understanding of their children as individuals. Parents have been through sleepless nights, the crying of infancy, the temper tantrums of the toddler, and the instruction of their children in basic routines and habits. They have a sense of how they and their child will react in any given situation. Though some parents have a very negative view of themselves as parents, most have developed a sense of their strengths and difficulties and a confidence that, by and large, they and their children are okay. Children, however, leave their control and enter a structured environment with rules and regulations. Children are evaluated in terms of their ability to control their behavior and learn skills that have reference to the adult world. For the first time there are external standards, grades, which compare children to each other. Parents must deal with, and help their children deal with, these external evaluations, which may be different from those parents have formed at home.

For parents, bridging the gap between the way they treat their children and the way their children are treated by teachers, group leaders, and peers may be a constant struggle. Parents will develop strategies for dealing with teachers who may not see the child as they do, with doctors, and with principals. An attitude that stresses cooperation among adults seems most effective. When parents seek information about the child and offer observations from home, if the focus is on eliminating the problem or settling the difference, adults can work together to make the child's experience in that environment an optimal one.

In the process of explaining the world and people's behavior, parents refine beliefs and values. They may discard some beliefs and add others. Children often prompt changes when they discover inconsistencies and hypocrisies in what parents say. If lying is bad, why do parents tell relatives they are busy when they are not? If parents care about the world and want to make it a safer place, why are they not doing something to make it safe? In the process of answering these questions, parents grow as well as children.

MAJOR POINTS OF CHAPTER 9

Children's competence increases, and by the end of this period, they have

- acquired all the basic skills in gross and fine motor coordination
- developed concrete logical thinking abilities so that they can grasp the relations between objects

- learned greater understanding of their own and others' emotional reactions
- gained greater control of their aggressiveness
- become less fearful
- learned to remedy situations they control and adjust to situations others control
- become more sensitive helpers

Children's growing independence is seen in their being away from home and

- spending several hours per day in school learning new skills
- joining formal groups like Scouts, Brownies, and athletic teams
- spending more time in peer play with minimal adult supervision

Socializing forces outside the family include:

- schools
- TV
- organized groups like athletic teams, Scouts
- church

Schools:

- are the major socializing force outside the family
- provide more effective learning settings when class or school units are small and students' cooperation on learning tasks is encouraged
- are structured so that verbal and listening skills are valued in students and physical skills are devalued
- create stress in children's lives because children worry about making mistakes, being ridiculed, and failing
- promote learning when they provide a calm, controlled environment and teachers are gentle disciplinarians with high expectations for students
- often do not reward the values of ethnic groups that emphasize cooperation and sharing among its members
- often make learning more difficult for children who use different styles of speech and communication patterns
- are highly valued by many ethnic group members who wish their children to spend more time there, do more homework, and have more proficiency tests

Children value themselves on four dimensions:

- physical competence
- intellectual competence
- social competence with peers
- general self-worth

Children interact with peers:

- in an egalitarian, give-and-take fashion
- and prefer those who are outgoing and supportive of other children
- and become friends when they enjoy the same activities
- more effectively when parents have been affectionate, warm, and accepting with them
- less effectively when there is stress in the family

Parenting tasks in this period include:

- monitoring and guiding children from a distance as children move into new activities on their own
- interacting in a warm, accepting, yet firm manner when children are present
- strengthening children's abilities to monitor their own behavior
- providing opportunities for children to develop new skills
- structuring the home environment so the child is able to meet school responsibilities
- serving as an advocate for the child in activities outside the home—for example, with schools, with sports teams, in organized activities

Parents are in Galinsky's interpretive stage, in which they

- have achieved greater understanding of both themselves as parents and their children
- help children meet external evaluations that may be different from those at home
- develop strategies for helping children cope with new authorities like teachers, coaches

Problems discussed center on:

- helping children meet school responsibilities
- dealing with social problems such as social isolation
- changing rule-breaking behavior such as lying
- ensuring safety behaviors

Joys include:

- observing increasing motor, cognitive, and social skills
- reexperiencing one's own childhood pleasures through child's experience
- sharing mutually enjoyable experiences and companionship
- sharing or experiencing emotional closeness

ADDITIONAL READINGS

Armstrong, Thomas. *In Their Own Way.* Los Angeles: Jeremy P. Tarcher, 1987.

Dunn, Judy. *Sisters and Brothers.* Cambridge, Mass.: Harvard University Press, 1985.

Hechinger, Grace. *How to Raise a Street-Smart Child.* New York: Ballantine, 1984.

Oppenheim, Joanne. *The Elementary School Handbook.* New York: Random House, 1989.

Winn, Marie. *The Plug-In Drug.* Rev. ed. New York: Viking Penguin, 1985.

Zimbardo, Philip G., and Radl, Shirley L. *The Shy Child.* Garden City, N.Y.: Doubleday, 1982.

Notes

1. Jean Piaget and Barbel Inhelder, *The Psychology of the Child* (New York: Basic Books, 1969); Herbert Ginsburg and Sylvia Opper, *Piaget's Theory of Intellectual Development* (Englewood Cliffs, N.J.: Prentice-Hall, 1969); David Elkind, *Children and Adolescents,* 2nd. ed. (New York: Oxford University Press, 1974).

2. Jean Ann Linney and Edward Seidman, "The Future of Schooling," *American Psychologist* 44 (1989): 336–340.

3. Ibid.

4. Gary W. Ladd and Joseph M. Price, "Predicting Children's Social and School Adjustment following the Transition from Preschool to Kindergarten," *Child Development* 58 (1987): 1168–1189.

5. Karin S. Frey and Diane N. Ruble, "What Children Say about Classroom Performance: Sex and Grade Differences in Perceived Competence," *Child Development* 58 (1987): 1066–1078.

6. John G. Nicholls, Michael Patashnick, and Gwendolyn Mettetal, "Conceptions of Ability and Intelligence," *Child Development* 57 (1986): 636–645.

7. Doris R. Entwisle, Karl L. Alexander, Aaron M. Pallas, and Doris Cadigan, "The Emergent Academic Self-Image of First Graders: Its Response to Social Structure," *Child Development* 58 (1987): 1190–1206.

8. Deborah Phillips, "The Illusion of Incompetence among Academically Competent Children," *Child Development* 55 (1984): 2000–2016; Deborah A. Phillips, "Socialization of Perceived Academic Competence among Highly Competent Children," *Child Development* 58 (1987): 1308–1320..

9. Rhona S. Weinstein, Hermine H. Marshall, Lee Sharp, and Meryl Botken, "Pygmalion and the Student: Age and Classroom Differences in Children's Awareness of Teacher Expectations," *Child Development* 58 (1987): 1079–1093.

10. Theresa A. Thorkildsen, "Justice in the Classroom: The Student's View," *Child Development* 60 (1989): 323–334.

11. Diane McGuiness, "How Schools Discriminate against Boys," *Human Nature,* February 1979.

12. Janice E. Hale-Benson, *Black Children: Their Roots, Culture, and Learning Styles,* rev. ed. (Baltimore: Johns Hopkins University Press, 1986).

13. Diana T. Slaughter-Defoe, Kathryn Nakagawa, Ruby Takanishi, and Deborah J. Johnson, "Toward Cultural/Ecological Perspectives on Schooling and Achievement in African- and Asian-American Children," *Child Development* 61 (1990): 363–383.

14. Doris R. Entwisle and Karl L. Alexander, "Beginning Math Competence: Minority and Majority Comparisons," *Child Development* 61 (1990): 454–471.

15. Harold W. Stevenson, Chuansheng Chen, and David H. Uttal, "Beliefs and Achievement: A Study of Black, White, and Hispanic Children," *Child Development* 61 (1990): 508–523.

16. Hale-Benson, *Black Children: Their Roots, Culture, and Learning Styles.*

17. Deborah J. Stipek and Karen M. DeCotis, "Children's Understanding of the Implications of Causal Attributions for Emotional Experiences," *Child Development* 59 (1988): 1601–1616.

18. Sally K. Donaldson and Michael A. Westerman, "Development of Children's Understanding of Ambivalence and Causal Theories of Emotions," *Developmental Psychology* 22 (1986): 655–662.

19. Paul L. Harris, Kara Donnelly, Gabriella R. Guz, and Rosemary Pitt-Watson, "Children's Understanding of the Distinction between Real and Apparent Emotion," *Child Development* 57 (1986): 895–909.

20. Jackie Gnepp and Debra L. R. Hess, "Children's Understanding of Verbal and Facial Display Rules," *Developmental Psychology* 22 (1986): 103–108.

21. Dayna Fuchs and Mark H. Thelen, "Children's Expected Interpersonal Consequences of Communicating Their Affective State and Reported Likelihood of Expression," *Child Development* 59 (1988): 1314–1322.

22. G. R. Patterson, Barbara D. DeBaryshe, and Elizabeth Ramsey, "A Developmental Perspective on Antisocial Behavior," *American Psychologist* 44 (1989): 329–335.

23. Avshalom Caspi, Glen H. Elder, Jr., and Daryl J. Bem, "Moving Against the World: Life Course Patterns of Explosive Children," *Developmental Psychology* 23 (1987): 308–313.

24. Michael Rutter, Jack Tizard, and Kingsley Whitmore, eds., *Education, Health and Behavior* (Huntington, N.Y.: Kruger, 1981).

25. Jean W. Macfarlane, Lucile Allen, and Marjorie P. Honzik, *A Developmental Study of the Behavior Problems of Normal Children between Twenty-One Months and Fourteen Years,* University of California Publications in Child Development, vol. 2 (Berkeley, Calif.: University of California Press, 1954); Read D. Tuddenham, Jane B. Brooks, and Lucille Milkovich, "Mothers' Reports of Behavior of Ten-Year-Olds: Relationships with Sex, Ethnicity, and Mother's Education," *Developmental Psychology* 10 (1974): 959–995.

26. Kaoru Yamamoto, Abdalla Soliman, James Parsons, and O. L. Davies, Jr., "Voices in Unison: Stressful Events in the Lives of Children in Six Countries," *Journal of Child Psychology and Psychiatry* 28 (1987): 855–864.

27. Eve Brotman-Band and John R. Weisz, "How to Feel Better When It Feels Bad," *Developmental Psychology* 24 (1988): 247–253.

28. Jennifer L. Altshuler and Diane N. Ruble, "Developmental Changes in Children's Awareness of Strategies for Coping with Uncontrollable Stress," *Child Development* 60 (1989): 1337–1349.

29. Molly Reid, Sharm Landesman, Robert Treder, and James Jaccard, "'My Family and Friends': Six- to Twelve-Year-Old Children's Perceptions of Social Support," *Child Development* 60 (1989): 907.

30. Eric F. Dubow and John Tisak, "The Relation between Stressful Life Events and Adjustment in Elementary School Children: The Role of Social Support and Social Problem-Solving Skills," *Child Development* 60 (1989): 1412–1423.

31. Charles L. McCoy and John C. Masters, "The Development of Children's Strategies for the Social Control of Emotion," *Child Development* 56 (1985): 1214–1222.

32. Nancy Eisenberg and Paul H. Mussen, *The Roots of Prosocial Behavior in Children* (Cambridge: Cambridge University Press, 1989).

33. Erik H. Erikson, *Childhood and Society,* 2nd ed. (New York: W. W. Norton, 1963).

34. Raymond Montemayor and Marvin Eisen, "The Development of Self-Conceptions from Childhood to Adolescence," *Developmental Psychology* 13 (1977): 317.

35. Susan Harter, "Developmental Perspectives on the Self-System," in *Handbook of Child Psychology,* eds. Paul H. Mussen and E. Mavis Hetherington, vol. 4, *Socialization, Personality and Social Development* (New York: John Wiley, 1983), pp. 275–385.

36. Mary Jane Rotheram-Borus and Jean S. Phinney, "Patterns of Social Expectations among Black and Mexican-American Children," *Child Development* 61 (1990): 542–556.

37. James P. Connell and Barbara C. Ilardi, "Self System Concomitants of Discrepancies between Children's and Teacher's Evaluations of Academic Competence," *Child Development* 58 (1987): 1297–1307.

38. Albert Bandura, "Regulation of Cognitive Processes through Perceived Self-Efficacy," *Developmental Psychology* 25 (1989): pp. 729–735.

39. Mariellen Fischer and Harold Leitenberg, "Optimism and Pessimism in Elementary School-Aged Children," *Child Development* 57 (1986): 241–248.

40. Hazel J. Markus and Paula S. Nurius, "Self-Understanding and Self-Regulation in Middle Childhood," in *Development During Middle Childhood,* ed. W. Andrew Collins (Washington, D.C.: National Academy Press, 1984), pp. 147–183.

41. Lawrence Kohlberg, "The Development of Children's Orientations Toward a Moral Order: I Sequence in the Development of Moral Thought," *Vita Humana* 6 (1963): 11–33.

42. Markus and Nurius, "Self-Understanding and Self-Regulation in Middle Childhood."

43. Harter, "Developmental Perspectives in the Self-System."

44. Eleanor E. Maccoby, "Middle Childhood in the Context of the Family," in *Development During Middle Childhood,* ed. Collins, pp. 184–239.

45. Graeme Russell and Alan Russell, "Mother-Child and Father-Child in Middle Childhood," *Child Development* 58 (1987): 1573–1585.

46. Frances K. Grossman, William S. Pollack, and Ellen Golding, "Fathers and Children: Predicting the Quality and Quantity of Fathering," *Developmental Psychology* 24 (1988): 822–891.

47. Russell and Russell, "Mother-Child and Father-Child in Middle Childhood."

48. Judith G. Smetana, "Adolescents' and Parents' Reasoning about Actual Family Conflict," *Child Development* 60 (1989): 1052–1067.

49. Maccoby, "Middle Childhood in the Context of the Family."

50. Michael C. Thornton, Linda M. Chatters, Robert Joseph Taylor, and Walter R. Allen, "Sociodemographic and Environmental Correlates of Racial Socialization by Black Parents," *Child Development* 61 (1990): 401–409.

51. Ibid.

52. Algea O. Harrison, Melvin N. Wilson, Charles J. Pine, Samuel Q. Chan, and Raymond Buriel, "Family Ecologies of Ethnic Minority Children," *Child Development* 61 (1990): 347–362; Margaret Beale Spencer and Carol Markstrom-Adams, "Identity Processes among Racial and Ethnic Minority Children in America," *Child Development* 61 (1990): 290–310.

53. Judy Dunn, *Sisters and Brothers* (Cambridge, Mass.: Harvard University Press, 1985).

54. Rona Abramovitch, Carl Corter, Debra J. Pepler, and Linda Stanhope, "Sibling and Peer Interaction: A Final Follow-up and a Comparison," *Child Development* 57 (1986): 217–229.

55. Brenda K. Bryant and Susan Crockenberg, "Correlates and Dimensions of Prosocial Behavior: A Study of Female Siblings with Their Mothers," *Child Development* 51 (1980): 529–544.

56. Barbara R. Tinsley and Ross D. Parke, "Grandparents as Support and Socialization Agents," in *Beyond The Dyad,* ed. Michael Lewis (New York: Plenum, 1984), pp. 161–194.

57. Timothy F. J. Tolson and Melvin N. Wilson, "The Impact of Two- and Three-Generational Family Structure on Perceived Family Style," *Child Development* 61 (1990): 416–428.

58. Jane L. Pearson, Andrea G. Hunter, Margaret E. Ensminger, and Sheppard G. Killam, "Black Grandmothers in Multigenerational Households: Diversity in Family Structures on Parenting in the Woodlawn Community," *Child Development* 61 (1990): 434–442.

59. Willard W. Hartup, "The Peer Context in Middle Childhood," in *Development During Middle Childhood,* ed. Collins, pp. 240–282.

60. John D. Coie, Kenneth A. Dodge, and Heidi Coppotelli, "Dimensions and Types of Social Status: A Cross-Age Perspective," *Developmental Psychology* 18 (1982): 557–570.

61. Hartup, "Peer Context in Middle Childhood."

62. Ibid.

63. Philip G. Zimbardo and Shirley Radl, *The Shy Child* (Garden City, N.Y.: Doubleday, 1982).

64. Hartup, "Peer Context in Middle Childhood."

65. Maccoby, "Middle Childhood in the Context of the Family."

66. Jane B. Brooks and Doris M. Elliott, "Prediction of Psychological Adjustment at Age Thirty from Leisure Time Activities and Satisfactions in Childhood," *Human Development* 14 (1971): 61–71.

67. Joan Beck, *Effective Parenting* (New York: Simon & Schuster, 1976).

68. Rudolf Dreikurs with Vicki Soltz, *Children: The Challenge* (New York: Hawthorn, 1964), p. 285.

69. Haim G. Ginott, *Between Parent and Child* (New York: Avon, 1969); Thomas Gordon, *P.E.T.: Parent Effectiveness Training* (New York: New American Library, 1975); Thomas Gordon with Judith Gordon Sands, *P.E.T. in Action* (New York: Bantam Books, 1978); Wesley C. Becker, *Parents Are Teachers* (Champaign, Ill.: Research Press, 1971).

70. Rudolf Dreikurs, *The Challenge of Parenthood,* rev. ed. (New York: Hawthorn, 1958); Dreikurs with Soltz, *Children: The Challenge.*

71. Adele Faber and Elaine Mazlish, *Liberated Parents/Liberated Children* (New York: Avon, 1974).

72. Ibid.

73. Sherri Oden and Steven R. Asher, "Coaching Children in Social Skills for Friendship Making," *Child Development* 48 (1977): 495–506.

74. Zimbardo and Radl, *The Shy Child*.

75. Gerald R. Patterson, John B. Reid, Richard R. Jones, and Robert E. Conger, *A Social Learning Approach to Family Intervention,* vol. 1, *Families with Aggressive Children* (Eugene, Ore.: Castalia, 1975).

76. Gerald R. Patterson, *Families: Applications of Social Learning to Family Life,* rev. ed. (Champaign, Ill.: Research Press, 1975).

77. Gerald R. Patterson, *Living with Children,* rev. ed. (Champaign, Ill.: Research Press, 1976).

78. John D. Krumboltz and Helen B. Krumboltz, *Changing Children's Behavior* (Englewood Cliffs, N.J.: Prentice-Hall, 1972).

79. Faber and Mazlish, *Liberated Parents/Liberated Children.*

80. Krumboltz and Krumboltz, *Changing Children's Behavior.*

81. Patricia Marks Greenfield, *Mind and Media: The Effects of Television, Video Games and Computers* (Cambridge, Mass.: Harvard University Press, 1984).

82. Ibid., p. 51.

83. Ibid.

84. Grace Hechinger, *How to Raise a Street-Smart Child* (New York: Ballantine Books, 1984).

85. Ellen Galinsky, *Between Generations: The Six Stages of Parenthood* (New York: Time Books, 1981).

EARLY ADOLESCENCE: THE YEARS FROM ELEVEN TO FIFTEEN

The early adolescent years are a turning point for children, who leave the childhood years of stable and steady growth and experience all the stresses of rapid physical growth, a changing hormonal system, and physical development that results in sexual and reproductive maturity. As their bodies and hormones change, children's emotions often become more intense and harder to control. Their thinking changes; they become more aware of possibilities; they think more abstractly. At the same time that children undergo these physical and cognitive changes, they are reaching out socially to peers, becoming independent of their parents. They are beginning to search for their own identity—who they are, what they like, and what goals they will set for themselves.

As early adolescents begin to seek a sense of who they are, they question parents' authority, rebel against restrictions, and argue their own point of view for long hours. Early adolescents are no longer young children to be guided carefully. They are in middle schools or junior highs, wanting more independence. Parents must encourage the growth of their children's independence and self-esteem, helping them become more competent. Yet parents must not permit so much freedom that children get into trouble they cannot handle. Though it is taxing for parents, this is an exciting time to watch children blossoming as they take their first steps out of childhood into a new life.

PHYSICAL DEVELOPMENT

Adolescence begins with biological change. The term **puberty** refers to that stage of development occurring in early adolescence in which the individual reaches sexual maturity and becomes capable of sexual reproduction. Puberty begins with hormonal changes that are not themselves observable but produce dramatic long-term physical changes. The pituitary gland at the base of the brain receives signals from the brain to send stimulating hormones to different parts of the body—to the adrenal

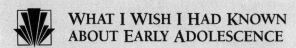 **WHAT I WISH I HAD KNOWN
ABOUT EARLY ADOLESCENCE**

"They seem to get caught up in fads in junior high. They do certain things to the max to be part of the crowd. I wish I'd known how to handle that. At what point are these fads okay, because it's important to identify with your peer group, and at what point do you say no? If they are really dangerous, then it's easy; but with a lot of them, it's a gray area, and I wish I'd known what to do better." FATHER

"I wish I had realized that she needed more structure and control. Because she had always been a good student and done her work, I thought I could trust her to manage the school tasks without my checking. But she lost interest in school, and I learned only very gradually that I had to be more of a monitor with her work than I had been in the past." MOTHER

"I wish I had known more about the mood swings. When the girls became thirteen, they each got moody for a while, and I stopped taking it personally. I just relaxed. The youngest one said, 'Do I have to go through that? Can't I just skip that?' Sure enough, when she became thirteen, she was moody too." MOTHER

"I wish I'd known how to help the boys get along a little better. They have real fights at times, and while they have a lot of fun together and help each other out, I wish I knew how to cut down on the fighting." FATHER

"I wish I knew what to expect. They are all so different, and they don't necessarily do what the books say. Sometimes, I'm waiting for a stage; now I'm waiting for adolescent rebellion, and there is none." MOTHER

"I wish I had known about their indecisiveness. He wants to do this; no, he doesn't. He gets pressure from peers and from what we think is right, and sometimes he goes back and forth. I am more patient about that now." MOTHER

"I wish I had known that if we had dealt with some behaviors when they were younger, we would not have had a problem from eleven to fourteen. He was always a little stubborn and hardheaded, wanting to do what he wanted. But right now, I wish we had done something about the stubbornness because it is a problem. He does not take responsibility, and it gets him into trouble at school. Looking back it has always been a problem, but we did not deal with it." MOTHER

glands, the ovaries, the testes. These glands and organs, in turn, release hormones that stimulate physical development (see Table 10-1 and Figure 10-1). Boys and girls both produce **estrogens**, the female hormone, and **androgens**, the male hormone. It is the ratio between these two kinds of hormones that differentiates male from female—boys produce more androgens, girls produce more estrogens. Exactly when all these changes take place depends on many factors—genetic influence, metabolism, diet. Conditions of starvation, for example, prevent the onset or continuation of menstruation in girls.

312

CHAPTER 10
Early
Adolescence:
The Years
from Eleven
to Fifteen

TABLE 10-1
SUMMARY OF THE CHANGES OF PUBERTY AND THEIR SEQUENCE

GIRLS

Characteristic	Age of First Appearance (Years)	Major Hormonal Influence
1. Growth of breasts	8–13	Pituitary growth hormone, estrogen, progesterone, thyroxine
2. Growth of pubic hair	8–14	Adrenal androgen
3. Body growth	9.5–14.5	Pituitary growth hormone, adrenal androgen, estrogen
4. Menarche	10–16.5	Hypothalamic releasing factors, FSH, LH, estrogen, progesterone
5. Underarm hair	About two years after pubic hair	Adrenal androgens
6. Oil- and sweat-producing glands (acne occurs when glands are clogged)	About the same time as underarm hair	Adrenal androgens

BOYS

Characteristic	Age of First Appearance (Years)	Major Hormonal Influence
1. Growth of testes, scrotal sac	10–13.5	Pituitary growth hormone, testosterone
2. Growth of pubic hair	10–15	Testosterone
3. Body growth	10.5–16	Pituitary growth hormone, testosterone
4. Growth of penis	11–14.5	Testosterone
5. Change in voice (growth of larynx)	About the same time as penis growth	Testosterone
6. Facial and underarm hair	About two years after pubic hair appears	Testosterone
7. Oil- and sweat-producing glands, acne	About the same time as underarm hair	Testosterone

Bernard Goldstein, *Introduction to Human Sexuality* (Belmont, CA: Star, 1976), pp. 80–81.

FIGURE 10-1
PHYSICAL CHANGES AS A RESULT OF HORMONES

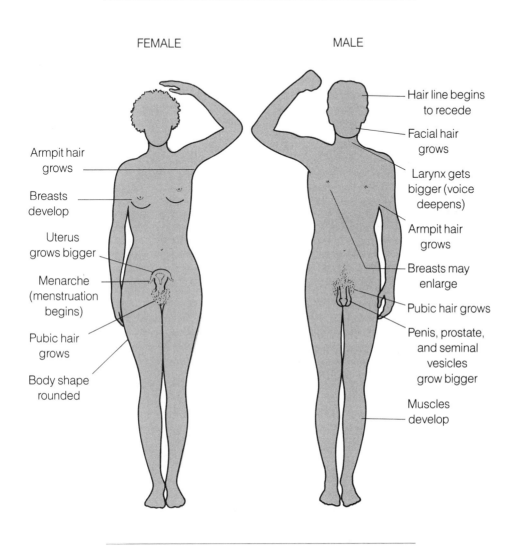

FEMALE MALE

Armpit hair
grows

Breasts
develop

Uterus
grows bigger

Menarche
(menstruation
begins)

Pubic hair
grows

Body shape
rounded

Hair line begins
to recede

Facial hair
grows

Larynx gets
bigger (voice
deepens)

Armpit hair
grows

Breasts may
enlarge

Pubic hair grows

Penis, prostate,
and seminal
vesicles
grow bigger

Muscles
develop

From Paul Insel and Walton T. Roth, *Core Concepts in Health* (Mountain View, Calif.: Mayfield, 1988), p. 87.

A more observable feature of puberty, which occurs after the hormonal changes
have started, is a growth spurt that lasts about four years. From ages five to ten, girls
and boys have been approximately the same height and weight and have had the
same general physical measurements. Beginning in the tenth year, however, most

CHAPTER 10
Early
Adolescence:
The Years
from Eleven
to Fifteen

girls begin their adolescent growth spurt, reaching their peak growth period at about age eleven, and finishing around thirteen to fourteen. Boys, on average, begin their growth spurt about two years later at age eleven, peak at about age thirteen, and level off at age fifteen.

Body parts do not all grow at the same time. Heads, hands, and feet are first to reach adult proportions. Arms and legs grow before body width, and the trunk grows last though it has the greatest proportion of increase in height. Because of these uneven rates of growth, teenagers may go through a thin and gawky period, unable to control their gangly arms and legs.

The sexes differ in how parts of the body grow in relation to each other. Beginning at about age nine, girls' hip bones become wider than those of boys. Average shoulder measurements remain the same for the two sexes until about thirteen, when boys' shoulders broaden and increase in strength. We tend to think that mature women have broader hips than men, but in fact the main difference between men's and women's outlines is produced by the broader shoulders of men.

In addition to increasing height and changing body shape, there are changes in muscle and fat tissue. Muscle tissue increases in both boys and girls, but boys have a more rapid increase than girls. Throughout their adult years, they maintain their advantage, which leads to greater physical strength in men. Fat tissue declines in rate of development in both boys and girls. The rate of decline is so marked in boys that they lose fat at their peak velocity of growth. Although the rate declines in girls, they still manage to gain some fat tissue. Internal organs are growing as well. The heart and lungs increase in size and capacity. Sex differences become marked. Boys' heart and lung capacities are greater than girls' following puberty. This, along with the increase in muscle, gives them an advantage in physical activities.

Sexual maturation accompanies the growth spurt (Table 10-1). As mentioned, hormonal stimulation of the sex glands begins first in girls. Then at about age nine or ten, downy, light pubic hair appears and is most often the first sign of sexual maturity. Breast changes occur at the same time that downy, unpigmented body hair appears. In the near year, the sex organs themselves grow—the uterus and vagina, the labia and clitoris. Pubic hair continues to grow and vaginal secretions appear. By the time **menarche** or menstruation begins at about age twelve and a half, the breast is well formed, and pubic and body hair are well developed. Although girls begin to menstruate at twelve and a half, they do not ovulate—send an egg to the uterus—with each period. Thus, conception is more difficult, though not impossible, in the period immediately following the onset of menstruation.

As with girls, boys' hormonal secretions of the sex glands first begin at about age eleven and a half, but the first visible sign of impending puberty is growth of the testes and the scrotum, the baglike structure that holds them. Pubic hair may appear as well. About a year later, as the physical growth spurt starts, the penis grows in size. Body and facial hair appear about two years after the pubic hair. Genetic factors determine how much body hair there will be.

Boys' voices change later in puberty. The larynx or Adam's apple grows significantly, and vocal cords double in length so their voices become lower. It takes many months, in some cases a year or two, for boys to control their voices.

Psychological Reactions to Growth and Development

We have seen that at earlier ages, particularly in the elementary school years, physical qualities play an important role in how children evaluate themselves. Among adolescents, physical characteristics are mentioned most often as things teenagers do not like about themselves. Areas of concern are skin problems, height, weight, overall figure. Early adolescents are most dissatisfied with their bodies, whereas older adolescents feel better about their bodies, and college students best of all. With time, adolescents adjust to all the changes that have taken place and eventually feel good about themselves.

The timing of all these changes influences how adolescents react to them. There are marked individual differences in the onset of puberty. Two boys or two girls who will have the same adult height may be seven or eight inches apart in height at age twelve. Such differences can cause problems for two groups—the early-maturing girls and the late-maturing boys. Harold Jones[1] found that early-maturing girls were less popular, less sociable, less cheerful, less poised, and less expressive. Classmates considered them submissive and withdrawn. Because early maturation intensified girls' interests in boys and dating at a time when other girls and boys were not interested, the withdrawal from peers is understandable. These girls often sought older friends who had the same interests, but they were not as socially mature as older friends and so were often rejected by this group, too.

More recent research continues to suggest that early-maturing girls are susceptible to social problems with peers.[2] They tend to get involved with older peers who break rules. Parental support acts as a buffer against the problems of early maturing and protects adolescent girls from rule-breaking tendencies. Because late-maturing girls are more like the boys in their classes in rate of development and general interests, and because they have a longer period to grow and adapt to all the physical changes, late-maturing girls seem to be above average in social poise, expressiveness, sociability, and attractiveness. Other work suggests that girls who are on time with respect to maturation enjoy the same advantages as late-maturing girls.[3]

Menarche is an important milestone in a girl's life. Initially girls have feelings of ambivalence, confusion, frustration at the inconvenience; these feelings are particularly strong in early-maturing girls and girls who are poorly prepared for the experience.[4] Girls who have begun to menstruate report less distress (less pain, less fluid retention, less negative emotion) than premenstrual girls anticipate. Expectations, however, are related to later experience. Those girls who anticipate distress later experience it. When girls get preparation for both physical and psychological aspects of the experience, when they feel menstruation is a normal part of life, then they are able to accept it as a more positive experience.[5]

The early-maturing boy has the advantage of increased height, weight, and strength for games and sports.[6] Elementary school children value athletic skills and the qualities of a "real boy." And so the early-maturing boy is likely to be popular, outgoing, happy, self-confident, and a leader among peers. Peers consider late maturers childish because of their physical appearance. Because they cannot get attention in more approved ways, late maturers may seek attention through restless,

316

CHAPTER 10
Early
Adolescence:
The Years
from Eleven
to Fifteen

Menarche is an important milestone in a girl's life. Initially girls have feelings of ambivalence, confusion, and frustration. These feelings are particularly strong in early-maturing girls who are poorly prepared for the experience. Parents of effective, well-adjusted early adolescents exhibit such qualities as acceptance, love, warmth, and consistent, fair limit-setting.

childlike behavior such as clowning. However, other strengths or other sources of security may counterbalance the stress of temporary physical inadequacies, and so it is impossible to predict the effects of rate of development on any given child.

Ejaculation in boys usually comes within a year of the beginning of the growth spurt—at about age fourteen. At this point, boys are sterile, and it takes from one to three years before the ejaculate contains sperm. The first ejaculation may come during masturbation or in dreams at night. Boys who have had no preparation for ejaculation may experience as much surprise and worry as girls who are unprepared for first menstruation. They may worry that they are sick or have some disease, because they have had erections since birth and this is the first time that a substance has come from the penis. Thus, boys need as much preparation for this event as girls do for menstruation.

Boys may also worry about breast changes that can take place in them at puberty. In all boys, the area around the nipple enlarges and the nipple is elevated. About 20 to 30 percent of boys have some breast enlargement at some point during adolescence. This passes away, but boys may become very concerned that they are not masculine. They may also worry about disease or hormonal abnormality. Information from parents about these changes helps reduce anxiety.

Though information and preparation about puberty and all the changes that can and will take place help reduce anxiety and worry, many parents do not feel comfortable talking to their children on this subject. Children, too, feel uncomfortable asking questions. Over half of adolescents feel they cannot talk to their parents about sexual matters and over half feel they do not get the information they want in sex education courses—either the teacher is too embarrassed or the information is not touched on.[7]

Adolescents do not know as much about sex as the mass media have suggested and parents may believe.[8] Sometimes they have fanciful notions—for example, if you do not want to get pregnant, you will not, no matter how often you have sex without contraceptives; you won't get pregnant if you have intercourse standing up. Even though parents may feel truly uncomfortable talking about sex, early adolescents need this information.

INTELLECTUAL DEVELOPMENT

Piaget (Table 6-1) describes the years from twelve to fourteen as the period when adolescents begin to think like adults.[9] They enter the **formal operations period**, during which they come to think more abstractly than previously. Although children can reason logically when confronted with tangible objects and changes during the period of concrete operations, Piaget believes they still cannot reason logically about verbal propositions or hypothetical situations. In the formal operations period, adolescents can freely speculate and arrive at solutions without having the objects or people directly at hand. They can analyze a problem in their heads. Further, they are able to enumerate all possible combinations of events and take action to see what possibilities actually exist.

318

CHAPTER 10
Early
Adolescence:
The Years
from Eleven
to Fifteen

Early adolescents' ability to think more abstractly than children enables them to think about their own thoughts and reason about them. They become introspective, analyzing themselves and their reactions. They are also able to think about other people's reactions and anticipate them. They think of the future. They can imagine what they might be doing as adults, what might be happening in the world. They can think of ideal situations or ideal solutions and become impatient with the present because it does not meet the ideal they have pictured.

Their introspectiveness, concern about the future, idealism, and impatience with the present all affect parent-child relationships, as we will see.

School

A great deal of research exists on children in elementary school and adolescents in high school, but much less work has been done on the schooling of younger adolescents. In part, this gap exists because there are so many different school experiences possible for children eleven through fourteen. Joan Lipsitz has described thirty-four different kinds of school settings for young adolescents.[10] Some adolescents are in kindergarten through eighth grade schools; others are in some form of junior high (seventh to ninth or seventh to eighth grades); still others may be in some form of middle school (fifth through eighth or sixth through ninth grades).

The age range of students is a crucial factor of every school setting. In one study students in all seventh to ninth grades were studied before and after a new school was added in the community.[11] All the students had been in junior high when a new secondary school was added for ninth and tenth graders. So seventh and eighth graders had their school, ninth and tenth graders had their school, and eleventh and twelfth graders remained at high school. Boys and girls were affected by the presence of older students, who seemed to push the younger ones in the direction of greater sophistication. For example, substance abuse increased for ninth graders in the new school and decreased for eighth graders in the junior high. Seventh-grade girls dated more, had higher self-esteem, and had a lower incidence of intercourse after ninth graders left the school. In both junior high and high schools, younger students were victimized by older ones, who solicited them for drugs and stole their money.

A recent study of students making the transition to junior high school finds a dramatic drop in the quality of school life for boys and girls when they enter junior high.[12] Students are less satisfied with school, less pleased with their teachers, and much less committed to their classwork. Both achieving and nonachieving adolescents experience the decline in satisfaction with school.

The National Institute of Education is aware of the problems younger adolescents face in school and has urged that successful middle schools be identified and studied to understand how they foster the healthy social and intellectual development of students.[13] When the NIE identified four middle schools that met the needs of students and communities, these schools and their principals proved to have many of the qualities of effective parents and families. The principals were strong leaders with a clear vision of what the school could accomplish. They had effective leadership skills that enabled them to interact well with teachers and people in the community and bring their ideas into reality. In interacting with others, they emphasized reasons for what they were doing and reasons for the plans they made. The schools rewarded students' involvement and participation in several areas—sports, academic activity, the arts. Teachers received rewards as well as students. All four schools were responsive to community needs and provided services desired in the community. They fostered a very positive atmosphere of clear and well-understood goals, reasons for planned actions, rewards for all. This kind of school atmosphere is desirable at all levels, not just in middle schools.

EMOTIONAL DEVELOPMENT

Early adolescents describe their overall mood as a favorable one 75 percent of the time.[14] Psychologists gave early and late adolescents pagers for one week; every time the pagers were beeped, they described what they were doing and how they felt. These adolescents reported feeling more positive than adults did in a similar study. Though they were happier than adults, however, they were not generally as involved or committed to their activities nor did they concentrate as well as adults.

When the moods of early adolescents are compared to those of preadolescents, however, early adolescents' moods were less favorable than those of younger children.[15] There is a gradual move downward in self-descriptions of cheerfulness, happiness, and friendliness. Even so, early adolescents report more positive than negative moods, but early adolescents are no more variable than younger children.

Early adolescents are most active and interested in settings where they have control—with friends, away from home in parks, at the school lunchroom.[16] They are least involved and motivated in adult-controlled activities—classrooms at school, church, jobs, school library. But even though they feel least involved in adult-controlled activities like classroom studying and working, these activities bring feelings of challenge and satisfaction, of being alive. Teens do not seek out these activities; but when they accomplish them, they feel good.

Teens most enjoy doing things with friends. Anything is more fun when done with a companion—shopping for school supplies, an errand, studying. Talking, jokes, and excitement enliven the occasions. Early adolescents most enjoy activities like arts and hobbies, sports and games, and listening to music. There is a sex difference here, with girls preferring arts and hobbies, and boys preferring sports and games. Teens also enjoy eating and resting. Reading and watching TV are low on the list of enjoyable things to do. Most activities that make teenagers happy are leisure activities, not activities like work that prepare them for the adult world.

Although these are generally happy times, the transition into junior high produces a drop in self-esteem for white girls, but not for black girls or white and black boys.[17] In general, several changes coming quickly are required to produce stress for early adolescents. In a large study in Milwaukee, Roberta Simmons and her co-workers found that several changes (entry into junior high, pubertal changes, dating, a move, family change) in a short time put early adolescents at risk.[18] If too much changes, then a young person lacks an "arena of comfort," some area of life where he or she can just relax and feel comfortable, where there is no demand for adaptation.

What are the "down" times for early adolescents? Teens are most upset when

320

CHAPTER 10
Early
Adolescence:
The Years
from Eleven
to Fifteen

alone in their room, studying, because they are deprived of company and made to do work they do not enjoy. What worries and upsets most thirteen- to fifteen-year-olds? Tables 10-2 and 10-3 illustrate major concerns expressed in a large-scale study and compares them to concerns of older adolescents.[19] For early adolescents, school is the greatest concern. Parents are not as upsetting to them as brothers and sisters and friends. Interestingly, parents' greatest concern for their children—usually drugs, alcohol, and sexual experiences—are not what bother teens.

What do teens fear? Here information is not broken down by age because children between the ages of thirteen and eighteen show few differences. Far and away the big-

TABLE 10-2
ADOLESCENT WORRIES

What Bothers You the Most? 13–15-Year-Olds		What Bothers You the Most? 16–18-Year-Olds	
School	30%	School	29%
Brothers and sisters	30%	Parents	28%
Friends	26%	Money	24%
Parents	23%	Friends	22%
Money	13%	Brothers and sisters	21%
Drinking and drugs	10%	Drinking and drugs	9%
Sex	9%	Sex	7%

Jane Norman and Myron Harris, *The Private Life of the American Teenager* (New York: Rawson Wade, 1981), p. 177.

TABLE 10-3
ADOLESCENT FEARS

What Are Your Greatest Fears?*	
Losing your parents	58%
Dying	28%
Not getting a good job or being successful	21%
Not doing well in school	18%
Nuclear war	14%
People not liking you	12%
Getting cancer	10%
Not getting married	6%
Getting attacked or mugged	6%

* The participants chose more than one response in some cases.

Jane Norman and Myron Harris, *The Private Life of the American Teenager* (New York: Rawson Wade, 1981), pp. 184–185.

gest fear of teens is that something may happen to their parents. They also fear many things that parents would agree are sources of concern: dying, not getting a good job. As in earlier years, they worry about school. As one would expect in times of expanding social contacts, social fears are important as well.

There is increasing evidence that hormonal changes contribute to negative affect and aggressiveness as well in this period.[20] Nevertheless, teenagers' depressed moods and nervousness are primarily related to social interactions and life events.[21] Adolescents who reported many negative events were more likely to suffer poor physical health and depressed negative mood following the event. The experience of positive events seems to protect against the effects of these negative events when they did occur.

PERSONAL AND SOCIAL DEVELOPMENT

Adolescence is the time when individuals gain what Erik Erikson calls a sense of identity, a feeling of who they are, what they can do, what they want to do.[22] The word *identity* refers to a sense of sameness and continuity of the self—the real inner me who thinks, perceives, feels and experiences life in an active, vital way. From the earliest days of infancy, children have been developing a sense of an individual, unique self.

Development of the Self

Children must now incorporate sexuality into their evolving sense of self. This is the task of the adolescent years—to integrate all previous experiences with a blossoming sexuality and increased intellectual competence, to form a psychosocial identity that will permit the individual to meet the tasks of adulthood. In addition to sexual and intellectual influences, Erikson emphasizes, we incorporate social values in our individual identities. For example, we all incorporate, in our individual ways, society's views of what men are, what women are, what members of our race and religion are.

Individuals need to have their identities validated and confirmed by their parents and the society. If teenagers are unable to integrate previous life experiences with their emerging capacities and obtain confirmation from others that they are who they think they are, role confusion results. They remain uncertain of who they are and where they are heading. Lack of identity hampers future development, for there is neither a sense of direction nor a push for productive action. All teenagers experience doubts about who they are and where they are going. These doubts usually pass, however, and gradually adolescents integrate their past experiences with present feelings and abilities to establish a stable sense of identity.

When life events and family members have not been supportive, individuals may develop negative identities. They may become delinquents, dropouts, persons who feel unable to do anything positive. This is a risk for minority adolescents who experience negative stereotyping. When the balance of the experiences is on the positive side and a sense of identity is formed, the virtue that develops is **fidelity**—what Erikson describes as faithfulness and loyalty to one's choices, whether they are persons, goals, or ideals.

322

CHAPTER 10
Early
Adolescence:
The Years
from Eleven
to Fifteen

Adolescents explore life and their feelings about themselves and others. They develop new interests and deepen already existing ones. Their social life with friends takes on a new importance. James Marcia believes that following a period of exploration, adolescents make a commitment to values, goals, and behavior and, in doing so, achieve a **sense of identity**.[23]

The process of achieving this identity is a gradual one, lasting over several years; and it is the usual path for most adolescents. It is not, however, the only path to identity. Some adolescents make a commitment to traditional values without even considering for themselves what they want to do with their lives. There is no crisis or conflict because these adolescents do not want to deal with issues. Marcia terms commitment without exploration **identity foreclosure** to indicate that possibilities have been closed off prematurely.

A different path is taken by adolescents who experience a **moratorium**. They experience a crisis about what they want to do. They have ideas they explore, but they have not yet made a commitment. So a moratorium is exploration without commitment. Finally, some adolescents experience **identity diffusion** in which they can make no choices at all. They drift without direction.

Achieving a sense of identity is a more complicated task for minority youth. They have two cultures to explore, understand, and integrate in their quest for identity. They begin with a diffused view of their ethnic background. They talk to parents, family friends, and other adults about ethnic issues. They read books and share experiences with friends. They are aware of prejudice and think about its effects on work and life goals. In the eighth grade, about a third of Afro-American students are actively involved in the exploration. By age fifteen, about half of minority students are actively exploring their cultural roots and traditions and an additional one-fourth percent have already achieved a sense of identity.[24]

Two difficulties arise.[25] First, many minority parents do not talk with their children about their cultural background, and they do not share their own experiences with the majority culture. Perhaps because they do not want to burden their children with experiences that no longer occur or perhaps because they are uncomfortable with issues of culture and race, many parents remain silent and offer no models for children. Children have to seek information elsewhere and cannot consciously pattern themselves after their parents.

Second, minority adolescents have to explore and integrate two cultures. Integrating one set of cultural traditions with the realities of everyday life is difficult enough. When there are two cultures that sometimes conflict with each other, the task becomes very complicated.

Which values does one select? Children and adolescents ideally should be permitted a bicultural identification that includes both cultures. Minority youth who combine, for example, emphasis on both cooperation and sharing found in many ethnic cultures with the assertive independence of the majority culture are effective in a wider range of situations than are those attached to just one set of values. A bicultural orientation is not easy to achieve because peers or family may pressure the adolescent to adopt only the traditional cultural values.

The process of achieving identity is even more difficult when the minority culture is devalued and adolescents experience negative stereotyping. Youth may then refuse to explore their ethnic roots and seek a foreclosed identity. There is some evidence that this happens more frequently among minority adolescents.[26] Other adolescents internalize the negative images, feel deficient and worthless, and develop what Erikson calls a **negative identity**. Currently, more minority youth develop a positive cultural identity and feel high self-esteem. A positive ethnic identity enables youth to replace tension and defensiveness with self-confidence about the future.

In the process of self-reflection, adolescents of all groups come to have an increased respect for what they can accomplish and do, a greater sense of the "I" who wills and acts. It may be this basic self-respect that accounts for the general positive view of the self-concept in these times of change. When self-esteem is measured yearly from the ages of twelve to eighteen, we find that most adolescents are stable in their overall view of themselves.[27] Seven out of ten report they like themselves and there is much to like.[28] Through the period from early to late adolescence, they mature, become more independent, more perceptive of others, and more communicative. By fifteen or sixteen, they are psychologically strong individuals. A small group of adolescents, about 20 percent, appear to experience the tumult and turbulence clinicians often associate with this period. They suffer intense anxiety and extreme mood swings. Still a third group is generally stable and has difficulty only when some unexpected stress occurs.[29] So, though there are occasional times of uncertainty and self-doubt, of loneliness and concern about the future, most adolescents also experience self-confidence, a zest for life, an excitement about the future, a sense of challenge and competence in meeting new situations.

Development of Self-Regulation

Although early adolescence is a time of increasing physical and intellectual change, nevertheless ways of handling impulses and degree of impulse control have become characteristic features by this age period. Longitudinal studies of early adolescents that have followed them into adulthood through their thirties and forties find adult impulse control is well predicted from behavior during this period.[30] Early adolescents who are responsible, self-controlled, warm, and cooperative tend to behave that way in adulthood thirty years later. Good impulse control at this period is accompanied by self-esteem, independence, and freedom to develop some of the qualities associated with the opposite sex. For example, well-controlled early adolescent girls are also more independent and assertive, and well-controlled early adolescent boys are warm, sympathetic, and considerate.

Jack Block looked at family characteristics associated with under- and overcontrol.[31] He finds that poorly controlled men and women come from families who, in the early adolescent years, are unable to give children models of effective control. The parents are not able to put aside their own concerns and interests and provide the necessary consistency in discipline. They do not reward and punish children's behavior in a logical way that teaches children how to control themselves. Instead, they use discipline only when they themselves are extremely angry. The child, fearful and panicked by the rage, cannot absorb the lesson and thus has not received the teaching necessary to achieve good control of impulses.

Overcontrol in men seems to come when parents are authoritarian and highly

324

CHAPTER 10
Early
Adolescence:
The Years
from Eleven
to Fifteen

controlling of boys this age. The dominant mother who sets high standards and arouses guilt to punish the child for misdeeds is a powerful figure in establishing overcontrol. Fathers in these families withdraw from the parenting role and support their wives' domination. Together, the parents so overcontrol the son that he remains fearful of impulse expression, even of pleasure, as an adult. The average girl is so well controlled that Block found it difficult to isolate any one group of overcontrolled girls to study the qualities of the family.

Although enduring modes of impulse control appear by the early adolescent years, not every impulsive act is a sign of a future life of impulsivity. Even the most responsible, dependable young teenager will engage in forbidden acts—partly to test the limits, partly to savor the experience, partly to impress friends. Such acts include drinking, smoking, driving the car, cutting school.

How to distinguish an isolated forbidden act from a more serious problem with impulse control is a skill parents must develop. This is discussed in the section on parenting tasks.

Parent-Child Relationships

Adolescents' fears of losing a parent highlight in a dramatic way how important parents are to their children. Having heard much about the generation gap and how distant children have grown from their families, parents may be surprised at their teenagers' concerns for them. After reviewing a substantial body of research, John Conger and Anne Petersen reinforce the importance of the parent by concluding:

> The single most important external influence in aiding or hindering the average adolescent (particularly the younger one) in the accomplishment of the developmental tasks of adolescence—at least in today's relatively isolated nuclear family—is his or her parents. The real question is not whether parental models are any longer important; rather, it is what kinds of parental models are necessary and appropriate in preparing contemporary adolescents to cope with the largely unpredictable world of tomorrow.[32]

Parents who are helpful, available to the teenager, concerned about what is happening in his or her life, have the most influence with the child. A guiding code of ethics, as noted by Block, is an important ingredient of effective parenting at this time.[33] Diana Baumrind states that parents of adolescents high in social responsibility have a "consistent adherence to a code of ethics or conventions and benevolent regard for their children and other persons."[34] Parents of children low in responsibility lack consistent adherence to a code of values; they are either overly strict or too permissive.

Family lifestyles are changing, she writes, and parents, especially mothers, are no longer content to define themselves by their traditional roles as providers or procreators. Still, parents must recognize that the family is the basic unit in which children are socialized. If parents reject traditional roles, they must provide other satisfying role models that youths can use as a guideline. If adolescents see no positive adult models, then they run the risk of rejecting all adult models and remaining childlike.

How can parents be models for early adolescents? They can be available, listen to children's concerns, and give information adolescents want to have. One study finds that adults spend relatively little time with their adolescents. Though early adolescents spend 25 percent of their time with their family, they spend as little as 5 percent exclusively with parents.[35] Eight out of ten teens feel they can talk to their parents, but only six out of ten feel parents really listen to them.[36] Adolescents wants parents' advice on important issues like getting a job, choosing a college, handling a school problem, and trouble with brothers and sisters—just the issues parents want them to be concerned about. They are less interested in advice about drugs and trouble with friends. When they ask for advice, they want information. Half the time, though, early adolescents feel like they do not get a reasonable answer. They get parents' insistence that teens do things their way. Both boys and girls feel it is generally easier to talk with mothers. Fathers are frequently described as distant and unavailable for conversation.[37]

In the preadolescent years children begin to gain decision-making power in certain areas of their lives—clothes and use of money, for example. How quickly and in how many areas they gain this power are often sources of dispute between parents and children.

The early adolescent years see an increase in the disagreements between parents and teens as teens want to take control of many areas and make their own decisions. Early adolescents report more fights with parents than parents report with them, but both agree that it is the mundane, routine behaviors that cause conflicts. School work and grades become more a frequent topic as early adolescents move into junior high school. As they move into high school, chores become a focus and remain a major topic during later adolescence.[38]

As was noted with preadolescents, early adolescents understand parents' insistence on following conventions. Teens simply do not agree with them. Early adolescents insist that many of these issues should be matters under their personal control. Parents are aware of their children's point of view but will not accept it as valid. Early adolescents recognize that certain behaviors have important effects on other people; and they, like parents, consider these moral issues that they will not challenge—for example, hitting others, not sharing.

Parents and children agree that most of the time conflicts end because children follow parents' wishes. In only eighteen percent of conflicts do parents follow children's requests, and joint discussion and decision settle just thirteen percent of the disagreements. So although there are conflicts, children acquiesce.[39] The basic relationship between parents and children remains solid.

Mothers, however, bear the burden of the increasing disagreements.[40] It may be that since mothers are more involved in routine household management and scheduling, children argue with them about everyday events. It also may be that mothers are more emotionally reactive with adolescents, so both boys and girls argue with them more. When fathers are present as a third party in disagreements, boys are more respectful and mother-son relations improve. Father-adolescent relations are more open and interactive when mothers are not present as a third party.[41] Mothers seem to dominate the relationship, and fathers withdraw.

Recent research indicates that physical development influences the changes in social behavior.[42] As physical maturation occurs at puberty, both boys and girls report increasing conflicts with parents and feelings of distance from them. Boys and girls, as already noted, report more arguments with mothers. Girls also report a

326

CHAPTER 10
Early
Adolescence:
The Years
from Eleven
to Fifteen

INTERVIEW
with Anne Petersen

Anne C. Petersen is Dean of the College of Health and Human Development, Professor of Health and Human Development and Women's Studies at The Pennsylvania State University. Her research interests center on adolescence; and with John Janeway Conger, she is the author of Adolescence and Youth: Psychological Development in a Changing World.

What is important for parents of adolescents to know?

The societal view of adolescents is negative. I collect cartoons, and they portray an extreme view of adolescents as having hormone attacks, being difficult, impossible.

This belief in our country that adolescents are difficult and want to be independent is one of the biggest pitfalls for parents. We know that though adolescents want to be autonomous, they need parents. We know that young adolescents are argumentative, sometimes obnoxious. Parents throw in the towel and that is the worst thing they can do. Adolescents need to know that parental support is there. There have been historical changes in the family, increasing the possibility for kids to be independent with cars and to have more time away from home; all these changes have exacerbated the trend toward independence and separation. Too much freedom is detrimental to adolescents' development.

Parents need to know that when you ask adolescents, especially young adolescents, who is most important to them, they say the parents, even if the parents are reporting conflict. We find, then, that parents are less positive about their adolescents than their adolescents are about them. Adolescents' off-putting behavior—telling parents to get lost because the adolescents are mature—is not really the message they want to send. They are asking for a little more space; they are asking for help in becoming autonomous and interdependent rather than independent.

Research shows that conflicts are about little things, not big things. The conflicts are not about values, but largely about doing dishes, taking out the garbage. They are a way of relieving tensions. Parents ought to be a safe source for venting tensions. If they cease to be a safe source, then young adolescents are really lost; they have no one.

Parents sometimes believe that they need to be their child's buddy, but that's not true. They need to be parents. They need to provide unconditional love, firm guidelines, and strong expectations.

---

decrease in calm discussions with fathers, and boys report less father-son cohesiveness. Hormone changes may play a role in the rise of conflicts. Increases in certain hormones have been found with increasing amounts of anger boys and particularly girls show in recorded family disputes.[43]

Though parents and adolescents have intense emotional interactions in these conflicts, each is preoccupied as well with his or her own life events. When a family member develops psychological symptoms as a result of these events and daily hassles in the home increase, then other family members are affected. When family members are able to deal with their individual problems without developing symptoms or becoming overly stressed, then other family members are not drawn in and

Puberty and all the change that accompanies it is a difficult time for boys and girls, especially when they have to change schools. It seems to work slightly differently for boys and girls. In general, boys seem less influenced by what is going on with parents, but basic support is pretty important. If parental support is not there, it is very bad for girls. Those girls who have a lot of family conflict or lack support are the ones who become the most depressed.

How would you say your own research has influenced the way you rear your children?

I think it has changed a lot of things. That my daughter rebelled was a big shock. I remember vividly the day she refused to do something. There was no door banging, but she said she would not do something I had just assumed she would do. I immediately had the stereotypic reaction, "Oh my heavens, what is going on here?" All of a sudden I realized that this was what I had been talking about for a long time. Knowing all the data, why should I be surprised that my kid goes through this too?

It helped a lot to know what could be effective in dealing with this. We had a family conference. What she was saying was, "How about taking my needs into account?" She was upset that we just assumed she would be a part of some activity. It is enlightening to realize that we don't treat an adult, a colleague, or a friend like that. It makes sense to change your behavior toward young adolescents. Well we worked it out. There are still occasional lapses of communication, and that's where the problems really are. Somebody assumes that somebody else is going to do something, and there is either a conflict of schedules or wishes. But at least saying, "Yes, you are right, you ought to have an increasing role in family decision making" and have a forum within which to do it made a lot of difference to her. She did not have to explode. She could put her two cents in.

When there is a good reason, we change our plans to meet her needs. It is important for us to show that we do not need to be controlling things, that we do respect her views, that she does have a voice. I am sure if you were to ask both our children, they would say they do not have as much say as they would like. That is because we still do believe that we are the parents and there are some things that we need to decide.

We believe that it is important to let them see how we are thinking about things and to understand decision-making processes. So, we talk in the family about money and about vacation plans, and we really try to include them—not just out of respect for them to increasingly become a part, but also to let them see how we think about things so they have the benefit of knowing how adults make decisions. That seems to work pretty well.

upset. It is not the occurrence of a major life event that disrupts the family; it is how the individual involved copes with it. Both parents and children respond to the distress they see in those close to them.[44]

There are suggestions that adolescents are more reactive to fathers' symptoms. Mothers in general are more expressive of negative feelings such as anxiety and depression, so children may be more accustomed to their upset and become alarmed only when fathers reveal marked distress. However, when mothers show major symptoms of depression, and parent-child relationships are disrupted, then poor grades and behavioral problems at school follow.[45]

So, though there are intense conflicts about everyday life activities and teens tend

328

CHAPTER 10
Early
Adolescence:
The Years
from Eleven
to Fifteen

to draw away from parents, still all family members want the best for each other and react negatively when another family member is distressed.

Happy family times are important because they provide a reservoir of good feeling that sustains all family members through times of conflict and crisis. Family life focuses so heavily on routine chores that it is mainly when the family leaves home for an outing that members can be together to share fun. Happy experiences, however, need not be limited to excursions. Family card games, family rituals of certain meals, watching certain TV programs together all provide a sense of sharing and solidarity that adolescents report as highly meaningful to them. Making time for fun and games in a busy schedule may save time in the long run as conflicts and arguing decrease.

Sibling Relationships

As in previous age periods, there is a great deal of ambivalence toward siblings. Ninety-seven percent of a large group of teens say they sometimes, or usually, do like their brothers and sisters, and only 3 percent say they do not like them. However, they rank brothers and sisters as one of the biggest problems, more of a problem than parents or peers.[46]

What do siblings do that is so upsetting? Primarily they invade the early adolescent's privacy. They go into their rooms, take their possessions, try to be part of their activities. A second major complaint is that younger brothers and sisters get privileges older ones did not get at that age. Adolescents feel their brothers and sisters are getting away with something. Teasing is a third source of complaint. Sometimes teasing is not meant to be cruel, but it is a way of having a kind of conversation. A fourth reason for resentment is that parents favor another child. Sometimes early teens feel that older siblings get more respect and trust, and younger ones get more attention. Sibling conflict may be fueled by tensions from other areas. For example, if a teen has had a hard day with teachers and a fight with friends, he or she cannot come home and yell at parents, but can yell at a bratty brother or sister who made a face at them.[47]

Siblings can become close during these years for the same reasons that peers are close—they can understand the emotional ups and downs, the problems that early adolescents are feeling, in ways that parents may not, and they may become allies in asking parents for privileges or rule changes. Sibling relationships usually improve as older siblings become more independent and are no longer competing for parental attention or resources.

Peers

Adolescents increasingly seek out and enjoy time with age mates. Peers are engaged in the same process of separating from parents and becoming more independent. They can talk to each other, exchange painful and exciting feelings, share doubts and triumphs, get support. As in earlier years, peers have the advantage of being equals and understanding what the other is experiencing in ways parents often do not. It is also with peers that early adolescents sharpen their definition of themselves. They learn their social qualities, their intellectual skills. Sometimes it is possible to reverse earlier negative experiences in the family. A girl whose family had little time for her gained affection and support from a boyfriend and his family. "I never would have grown up to be an adult without him and his family," she remarked as a college student.

Parents worry about the influence of peer groups in these years. They sometimes fear they have lost their children to their age mates. This is not so. Friends tend to share the same values and backgrounds; they are not that different from each other. Second, peers defer to each other on matters of music and entertainment, clothing and language. But they rely much more on parents in regard to moral and social values, vocational suggestions—just the areas where parents want to have the most influence. Teenagers want input from their parents on the important issues.

The healthiest teenagers strike a balance between acceptance of peer values and parental values. Adolescents who are peer-oriented rather than adult-oriented may be turning to age mates because they lack closeness with adults.[48] Their parents seem to be uninterested in them, neither giving them guidance nor establishing limits. These teenagers are likely to have low self-esteem, a dimmer view of the future, less interest in making and doing things, and less competence in academic work than adolescents who are also adult-oriented. They do not appear to find in their peer attachments the emotional warmth and closeness they require to be productive and effective.

Both boys and girls engage in more active pursuits when they are with their friends than when they are alone. Girls go through stages in forming friendships. Though shared activities are an initial start to a friendship, the personality of the other person becomes more important in time. Loyalty and genuineness, the ability to talk and share experiences, are qualities valued in friendships. In these years, too, girls form **cliques**, a small group of five to nine girls. A major activity is talking and sharing impressions. Girls at this age especially enjoy talking on the phone as long as possible.

Boys also tend to congregate in same-sex groups. While girls are involved with cliques, however, boys are involved with their gangs. Playing sports accounts for 45 percent of their time spent with friends.[49] Boys' relationships with peers are less intimate than girls; they are less revealing of themselves, how they think and feel.

Girls, and to some extent boys, seem to go through three stages as they begin to date. In the preadolescent years, they are anxious about the prospect of dating, although they may still be emotionally uninterested in the opposite sex. In early adolescence, focus of the anxiety changes as dating begins and teenagers feel nervous about measuring up to standards of masculinity and femininity. As they gain more experience, they relax. By the end of adolescence, they feel more comfortable and able to be natural in relationships.

Research suggests that becoming highly involved in dating either too early or too late can reflect problems.[50] Girls eleven to fourteen who were going steady were outgoing and confident but were superficial in their relationships with boys. Because they had not had a chance to develop themselves, they had less to share. Those who were not dating by late adolescence seemed to be immature, socially isolated, and preoccupied with themselves. Conger and Petersen summarized studies on dating

330

CHAPTER 10
Early
Adolescence:
The Years
from Eleven
to Fifteen

 THE JOYS OF PARENTING EARLY ADOLESCENTS

"Seeing him care for younger children and babies is a great pleasure. He's a great nurturer with small children. He has endless patience." MOTHER

"He is a talented athlete, and his soccer team got to a championship game. He scored the winning goal, and when he took off with the ball down the field, I was very proud of him. It was a unique feeling of being proud that someone I had helped to create was doing that. He had felt a lot of pressure in the game, so to see how incredibly pleased he was gave me great joy." FATHER

"Now that they are older, they bring new skills into our lives. I did not learn algebra in school, but to help him with problems now and then, I learned algebra from the book. I am very pleased to be able to help." MOTHER

"It is gratifying to me to see him learn the rules. He makes sure his homework is done, and he does it on his own steam." MOTHER

"I like that he does things I did, like play the trumpet. He started at the same age I did and since he took it up, it has rekindled my interest and I started practicing again. This last weekend, we played together. He also brings new interests too. Because he likes sailing I have started that and really like it." FATHER

"She is in that dreamy preteen state where she writes things. She wrote a poem about the difference between being alone and loneliness. She has a real appreciation of time on her own and how nice being alone can be. I like that because I had that at her age." MOTHER

"It's nice just being able to help them, feeling good because they are being helped out and benefited." FATHER

"It's nice to see her being able to analyze situations with friends or with her teachers and come to conclusions. She said about one of her teachers, "Well, she gets

and concluded that teenagers who are best prepared for the adult roles of worker and partner have had opportunities in adolescence to experience many different social and personal roles.[51] Optimally they will have had close relationships with same-sex and opposite-sex peers.

Let us now look briefly at the special parenting tasks associated with the teenage years.

PARENTING TASKS

At all age periods, the tasks of parenting are to maintain positive relationships with children as well as setting and enforcing limits. These limits, however, become broader in early adolescence. Parents still have a supervisory role in controlling their children's behavior, but they will begin to give even more power to children in mat-

excited and she never follows through with what she says, so you know you don't have to take her seriously." MOTHER

"I really enjoy being in the scouts with the boys. Once a month we go on a camping weekend, and I really look forward to that." FATHER

"I was so impressed and pleased that after the earthquake, he and a friend decided to go door to door and offer to sell drawings they made of Teenage Mutant Ninja Turtles. He raised $150 that he gave for earthquake relief. I was very proud that he thought this up all by himself." FATHER

"I was very happy one day when I found this note she left on my desk. It said, 'Hello!!! Have a happy day! Don't worry about home, everyone's fine! Do your work the very best you can. But most important, have a fruitful life!!!' I saved that note because it made me feel so good." MOTHER

"He enjoys life. He has a sense of humor. He's like a butterfly enjoying everything; eventually he'll settle in." MOTHER

"He's very sensitive, and his cousins two years older than he ask his advice about boys. They may not take it, but they ask him even though he's younger." FATHER

"It's very rewarding to see them in their school activities. My daughter sings in the school chorus, and I enjoy that, and my son is in school plays." FATHER

"I am very pleased that she is less moody now than she used to be. We used to refer to her lows as 'Puddles of Frustration,' but she has got past that now." MOTHER

"Well, they have their friends over, and we have Ping Pong, pool, cards, and we stressed having these things available. I enjoy playing all these games with them." FATHER

ters of friendship, clothes, music, and general appearance. A major task of parenting is to be available to teenagers. Just as toddlers idled around the house, parents need to idle around to be free for conversation on the spur of the moment. Parents may want to jump in with solutions when they see their children unhappy, but active listening, which enables the children to clarify thoughts and reactions and reach an independent solution, is a more effective tactic.

As in all age periods, parents continue to provide models of effective behavior and the behavior they want in their children. They set standards for sibling relationships by equal and fair treatment. Especially in this period, parents can be helpful models of mature thinking processes that children are just beginning to master. As children reason out problems, parents can encourage them to enumerate all their options, consider carefully all the consequences of each option, and then make a decision. A helpful suggestion is to have them consider what they would tell a friend who presented that problem.

332

CHAPTER 10
Early
Adolescence:
The Years
from Eleven
to Fifteen

A parental task is to provide children with information they need on a variety of topics—sexuality, alcohol, drugs, and ways of maintaining a healthy lifestyle. All too often parents fail to provide their children with information about sex. One survey of college students showed that the students received only 15.5 percent of their information about sex from their parents.[52]

In addition to supplying factual information about the physiology of sex, parents help children form values. Parents need to discuss their own values with their teenage children, not dictating attitudes but presenting points of view that their children may not have considered. Parents need not worry about presenting a conservative view—many teenagers want to hear just that. If you are concerned about seeming old-fashioned, remember that about 25 percent of boys and 40 percent of girls wish, in retrospect, that they had waited longer before being sexually active.

If you find sexual matters too difficult to discuss with teenage children, it is best to say that to them honestly and then suggest that they talk to a counselor or a doctor. For example, you might say, "I'd like to answer your questions about sex without getting all flustered, but frankly I can't. As I grew up, this subject wasn't discussed and I feel uncomfortable with it. I'll answer the questions I can, even if I flounder, and I'll get books for fuller details. I only hope you'll be more relaxed talking about this subject when you're a parent."[53]

Just as most parents avoid talking about sex, they also avoid talking about the use of mind-altering substances and tobacco. In one survey, 55 percent of the teens said their parents did not discuss drugs with them.[54] Yet a significant number (42 percent) of younger teens thirteen to fifteen were experimenting with marijuana.[55] So parents are well-advised to become knowledgable about the physical effects of alcohol, tobacco, and drugs like marijuana and cocaine and discuss the information with their adolescent children. This information should be reliable and well documented. Parents do more harm than good when they present exaggerated reports of drug effects because teens then dismiss everything that is said to them.

Parents also serve as models and sources of information for minority adolescents who are exploring their ethnic culture and achieving a sense of identity. Psychiatrist James P. Comer states that the entire Afro-American community has to act together "to help each child establish a personal and group identity . . . that allows each young person to feel, 'I am an individual, an Afro-American with a tradition of sacrifice, struggle, and excellence; and it is my job to restore and carry on the tradition for my own sake, for the good of the Afro-American community, and for the good of America.'"[56] These are appropriate feelings for all children to have about their ethnic tradition. Margaret Spencer and Carol Markstrom-Adams make nine recommendations, listed in Box 10-1, to promote positive identity formation of minority youth.[57]

Parents must not hurry their children through the early adolescent period. Sometimes children will retreat a bit when they need time to think or deal with a conflict. David Elkind has described the stress children experience when parents are eager for them to grow up and take on adult characteristics. In *The Hurried Child* he writes that parents who experience extreme pressure in their own lives wish their children to grow up quickly, eliminating that source of stress.[58] Children are pressured to achieve, to take on more chores and responsibilities, without too much participation

AN EXAMPLE OF HOW AFRO-AMERICAN PARENTS SOCIALIZE CHILDREN
by Robert C. Maynard

When strangers stop me on the street or at airports, often it is to comment on the essays I write about my family. Those about life in our old home in Brooklyn provoke the most response. "It is obvious," a nun in a brown habit said one day, "that yours was a house of joy." I loved the phrase, but it troubled me.

It was not, I started to say to her, always so joyful. In fact, there were times that were painful, as there might be in any family. Some of our dinner-table discussions touched sensitive subjects. For example, our parents often struggled to help us understand and battle racial rejection. It was not always easy for them, proud immigrants in a new land.

One of the heroes of our family in the late 1940s was Dr. Ralph J. Bunche. He was then this nation's highest-ranking black diplomat. He was also a leading academic. His field at Harvard had been international organization, a subject of special interest to our family. It was at the time of the formation of the United Nations. There must have been a dozen pictures of Dr. Bunche around our home. We owned at least one copy of everything published under his name.

The difficult time came the night of Dr. Bunche's public humiliation. He was denied entry to the Forest Hills Tennis Club, then the scene of the most prestigious matches in the world of tennis. Dr. Bunche's rejection became our own. . . .

The idea that it would reject the hero of our family meant it had rejected each of us. . . .

As one of my three sisters, a tennis player, began to put her troubled thoughts into words, tears welled up in her eyes, and she stopped talking. My mother's eyes met my father's. I could tell they had been discussing this between themselves.

"I want you children to understand what you are seeing here." He pointed across to a side table where the *New York Daily News* lay. The story of Dr. Bunche's rejection was prominently displayed. "I know you feel sorry about Dr. Bunche, but I tell you my prayers tonight are for those men who have humiliated them. . . .

"People who create special rules of exclusiveness think they are showing the rest of us what great status they have achieved. In fact they are telling us the very opposite. . . . "

"The very opposite." My mother repeated my father's last phrase for special emphasis. They often reinforced each other's points by repeating a few of the exact words.

"In fact," my father continued, "when people need racial exclusiveness in their social lives, it is usually to prove to others they have 'arrived.' But that's not how I read such men. I read them as socially insecure. Have you ever noticed that truly confident people walk and work among all with ease? The strong do not need that sort of status; the wealthy but weak do."

"Dr. Bunche," my mother said with a wry smile, "is fortunate he will not have to associate with such people." At last we laughed.

Reprinted from *The Oakland Tribune*, August 5, 1990.

on the parents' part. The push to turn children quickly into adults can be very detrimental at this age, because many early adolescents seem to like the greater freedom but are not yet able to handle it. Elkind regrets this pressure on children, because it robs them of the childhood they need to grow, learn, and develop fully.

334

CHAPTER 10
Early
Adolescence:
The Years
from Eleven
to Fifteen

BOX 10-1
METHODS TO ENHANCE IDENTITY FORMATION
OF ETHNIC MINORITY YOUTH

1. Methods should be proposed to keep minority youth in school and academically oriented since lack of education increases the risk of poverty and disadvantage.
2. Efforts are required to heighten health consciousness, because poor health interferes with identity processes. The physical health of many minority youth lags behind that of majority youth.
3. Importance of social networks should be affirmed. Churches and extended families are important resources for minority families as they socialize children.
4. Methods should be proposed to support parents as cultural transmitters. Many ethnic group parents do not discuss their distinctive values and experiences, and parents must receive support as they begin to do this.
5. Proposals are needed to offer a media-focused, cultural emphasis that affirms positive group identity for all youth to combat the negative stereotyping that occurs.
6. Methods are needed to promote teaching of native languages and cultures, particularly for American Indians who are at risk for losing their cultural heritage. Creativity is required to encourage biculturalism at the same time one preserves cultural traditions.
7. Programs are required for the special training of teachers so that they will be sensitive to cultural traditions, communicative patterns, and sometimes the language of minority students.
8. Childrearing support by way of teaching parenting skills is required to promote parents' sense of ethnic pride and enhance the home-school partnership.
9. Improved training is required for mental health workers serving ethnic minority populations.

Adapted from Margaret Beale Spencer and Carol Markstrom-Adams, "Identity Processes among Racial and Ethnic Minority Children in America," *Child Development* 61 (1990): 305–306.

ROUTINES, PROBLEMS, AND STRATEGIES

In the early years, we focused on routine behaviors like eating and sleeping. It seems strange to consider them again with early adolescents, yet problems in eating and sleeping occur in the adolescent years and require attention.

Eating

With changes brought by physical maturation and increases in peer sociability, eating patterns may change in adolescence. Parents grow concerned that teenagers do not get the proper nutrition necessary for healthy growth. Parents, of course, have no control over what children eat when they are not at home; they do, however, control the food purchased and served in the home.

Using behavioral techniques, parents can encourage healthy eating habits. Having regular family meals consisting of well-balanced foods can be difficult when family members have so many different activities. But eating together is an important social as well as nutritional event, and well worth the effort required to cook a meal and get everyone together for it. When good food is served well, teenagers will most likely eat even if they have been snacking beforehand. Though it is easier to get people together for dinner during the week, large breakfasts or brunches may be most feasible on weekends.

At the same time that parents provide and eat healthy foods, they can occasionally discuss the importance of healthy diets. They need not preach or expect a dramatic response from teens. Discussions can be initiated by newspaper articles or television programs that highlight the value of healthy food for feeling good and preventing serious disease. Teens learn that good nutrition is an essential ingredient of a healthy, vital life, especially at times of rapid physical growth.

Sleeping

The average eleven- to fifteen-year-old needs between 9 and 10 hours sleep every night, says Richard Ferber, head of the Children's Hospital Sleep Disorder Clinic.[59] Most, however, get only about 8 hours of sleep, with the result that they may continually be sleep deprived and be forced to make up for it on weekends. To get the best night's sleep possible, even early adolescents need a pleasant bedtime routine, time to unwind.

Adolescents, too, can have sleep problems. Problems of late sleeping can occur when they stay up late on weekends and sleep until noon or 1 o'clock the next day. Then they also have a late sleep phase during the week when they most need to be alert. Ferber describes the case of a fifteen-year-old boy who went to bed at 11:30 p.m. but could not fall asleep until 4 or 5 a.m. His parents could not arouse him to go to school at 7:30. On weekends he watched television until 4 or 5 a.m. and slept until 1:00 the next afternoon. Ferber put the boy in charge of his own waking and sleeping. The boy bought an alarm clock to get himself up; he was motivated to change because he wanted to go to school so he could graduate. The desired sleeping schedule was 11:00 p.m. to 6:30 a.m. Ferber made two suggestions: First, there was to be no radio at sleep time because it was distracting and making sleep harder. Second, the boy was to go to sleep 3 hours later each day and wake 3 hours later that day until he reached his schedule of 11:00 p.m. to 6:30 a.m. For example, because he was naturally sleeping from 4 a.m. to 12 p.m., the first day he slept from 7 a.m. to 3 p.m. and the next day, from 10 a.m. to 6 p.m. By the end of one week, he had reached his desired schedule.

Teenagers also sometimes have night terrors and partial awakening in which they may yell and scream, thrash about, and even get up and walk. Although there is no magic age to determine if awakening is a problem, the general rule is that beyond seven, the awakenings are psychological in origin. Psychological difficulties may not be severe, but they do require attention. The child may be under special stress or have few outlets for emotional expression and so may be discharging feelings in that way. Parents can talk to children, listen to feelings, suggest actions to take to remedy any stresses. The parents can also try to be sure that the child gets sufficient sleep because these awakenings are more likely to occur when the child is tired.

336

CHAPTER 10
Early
Adolescence:
The Years
from Eleven
to Fifteen

Temper Tantrums

During periods of typical moodiness, early adolescents often lose their tempers and go storming off. Parents can no longer practice time out with adolescents, but they can do active listening.

Ginott gives the example of a thirteen-year-old girl who wanted to play the violin in the kitchen while her mother cooked dinner.[60] The mother repeated the rule, "No practicing in the kitchen at 6:00." The girl left the kitchen, but when her sister began practicing the piano, she ran screaming to her mother, demanding to know why the sister could practice and she couldn't. Her mother replied that she knew why. The next day the girl was furious because she felt her mother was not giving her answers. She wrote her a note, expressing her rage. Her mother wrote back and repeated the household rule—no violin playing in the kitchen between 5 and 7 p.m. The mother accepted her daughter's feelings but repeated the rule.

Gordon describes the family in which the thirteen-year-old was used to getting her way. Her parents were trying to solve the problem when she charged out of the room and ran off in tears. Instead of consoling or ignoring her, her father ran to the bedroom door and sent an I-message about how upset both parents were that she would not try to find a solution in which they all could win. He made strong statements: "I'm darned angry at you right now. Here we bring up something that is bothering your mother and me and you run away. That really feels like you don't give a darn about our needs. I don't like that. I think it's unfair. We want this problem solved now. We don't want you to lose, but we sure are not going to be the ones to lose while you win. I think we can find a solution so we'll both win, but we can't for sure unless you come back to talk." Her father did not give in to the tantrum but expressed his views strongly.[61]

Don Dinkmeyer and Gary McKay use Dreikurs' approach.[62] Adolescents, they say, can use their emotions to try to have their own way. Crying and shouting invite parents to retreat or to get into a battle that either obscures the issue or makes them feel sorry for the child. Crying and shouting can be used to obtain attention, power, and revenge or to display inadequacy. Dinkmeyer and McKay recommend that parents let adolescents be responsible for their emotions. Parents may listen, try to understand or to help find a solution, but basically the feelings belong to the teen, and the parent remains detached. Thus, when a daughter had a tantrum, her father went for a walk.

The behaviorists Eimers and Aitchison recommend techniques very similar to those of Ginott and Gordon.[63] When a teen explodes, they advise parents to be good listeners; don't blame but state your own feelings. Deal with specific behaviors and not character traits, and praise the child for communicating.

All experts advise parents not to give in, but to listen to the child's feelings and express their own. In general, parents need to maintain a detached attitude toward the child's intense feelings and an interested attitude toward working to find a solution to what is causing the child's problem.

Dirty Room

Ginott says a child's room is a private place.[64] Parents should maintain distance and let the chid do as he or she pleases about dirt. If the room becomes too smelly or unsanitary, however, then we assume he would advise the parent to take action.

Gordon[65] and Eimers and Aitchison[66] recommend problem solving and contracting to reach an agreement acceptable to parents and teenager alike. Gordon described a situation in which mother and daughter discussed what to do about the daughter's dirty room. She did not mind it, but her mother did, so they arrived at an agreement. The daughter liked to cook and agreed to cook two evenings a week in exchange for her mother's cleaning her room.

Eimers and Aitchison described a contracting session in which a boy and his parents wrote up a contract so that each could get what was wanted. The boy wanted certain privileges about going out, freedom to wear longer hair, and freedom to be alone in his room when he chose to be. Parents wanted no more profanity and help around the house, including cleaning his room. They made an agreement by which both the boy and his parents got what they wanted.

Dinkmeyer and McKay describe an approach based on Dreikurs' strategy.[67] The daughter's room stays as she likes it until it offends the mother. When the mother becomes concerned because of the smell and disarray, a new limit is set: The daughter has to clean the room before she leaves the house that day.

All approaches involve a form of problem solving, contracting, or negotiating. The child's privacy is respected up to the point it infringes on parents' sensitivities, and then parents and teenager negotiate a new solution.

The Noncommunicative Early Adolescent

This is a common problem for parents though it is not so viewed by the child. Parents complain that children come home, go to their rooms, and shut the door. When they emerge for meals or snacks, they say little, answer any question with only a word or two. They don't talk about what they are doing, thinking, or feeling. Children don't seem unhappy, but parents feel they don't know them anymore. Parents may feel hurt when children say little to them but talk for hours on the phone to their friends.

Parents can, however, interact with children to promote conversation. Don Dinkmeyer and Gary McKay advise three strategies: (1) comment on nonverbal behavior, (2) ask for comments, (3) be a model of conversing.[68] For example, parents can try commenting on facial expressions or body language: "Looks like you had a good day today," or "You look happy." Teens may not follow up with any comments, but parents have made an effort.

Parents can ask for comments, saying, "How's school going?" or "What are you and Jenny doing tonight?" If the child answers with one word or two, parents drop the conversation and wait for another time. Parents can remain good models of communication, however, talking about their day, their friends, their plans.

Once teens begin to talk, parents listen and communicate feelings. If parents jump in with criticism, judgments of the child or others, blame, or sarcasm, all children clam up. Reflecting feelings helps teens to continue to talk. If teens talk about problems they are trying to work out and want to discuss them, parents can encourage them to list options, explore the advantages of each, and then act.

There are many *don'ts* to the process of encouraging conversation. Don't force the child to reveal feelings. Don't give advice once the teen has begun to talk. Don't rush to find the solution. Don't hurry to answer questions; delaying an answer can stimulate thinking. Adele Faber and Elaine Mazlish give the example of a girl who asked

338

CHAPTER 10
Early
Adolescence:
The Years
from Eleven
to Fifteen

Many parents dread the onset of adolescence in their children, assuming that their children are going to go through a phase of isolation and noncommunication in the home. This adolescent has defied the stereotype. His parents taught him to be secure and to communicate openly in his home environment, key elements for successful development into adulthood.

her mother, "Why don't we ever go to any place good on vacation like Bermuda or Florida?" The mother answered, "Why don't we?"

The girl replied, "I know, I know. Because it's too expensive. . . . Well, at least can we go to the zoo?"[69]

Faber and Mazlish describe useful techniques when teens begin to talk about discouragement or frustration. They suggest showing respect for the child's struggle with comments like "That can be hard," "It's not easy," or "Sometimes it helps when . . ." and then parents give a piece of information: "It helps when you're rushed to concentrate on the most important item." Teens are free to use the information or not. Parents have to watch their tone of voice or the information can sound like advice.

Faber and Mazlish also present interesting alternative responses to saying "no." Since teens are very sensitive to control and may not like to ask if they hear a lot of "nos" in response, having other ways to respond is useful and will encourage greater talkativeness. Suppose a teen wants you to take him to the store at 5:30 while you are cooking dinner. Instead of giving a flat "no," a parent can say, "I'll take you after dinner." If you are completely unable to do it, you can say, "I'd like to be able to help you out, but I have to get dinner on the table and get to that meeting at 7:00." A parent can leave out the "no" and just give information. For example, if a teen asks for an extra, expensive piece of clothing, the parent can say, "The budget just won't take it this month." If there are ways the teen can get the item, the parent can pass that information on. "If you want that as a birthday present at the end of the month, that would be fine."

All strategies recommend fostering self-esteem and autonomy by focusing on the positive things teens do. When children feel good about themselves, they talk more. Dinkmeyer and McKay describe how parents use encouragement to foster self-esteem at times of frustration. Encouragement focuses on effort, improvement, and interest and is reflected in phrases like, "You really worked hard on that," or "I can see a lot of progress," or "You were really a big help to your brother in cleaning his room."

Using all these different strategies does not guarantee a talkative teenager in the home, but it increases the likelihood of conversation.

Forbidden Acts

A major task for parents is to learn when to take firm action about impulsive acts and when to be understanding. If problems occur with drinking or violating a major rule more than once or twice and seem to be developing into a serious problem, parents take several actions. Dinkmeyer and McKay state parents must change their attitudes toward the teen and the abusive behavior. It is pointless to criticize, blame the teen or themselves. Alcohol and other substances are available for use when teens are discouraged or frustrated. Rather than blaming, the focus must be on finding resources for meeting the problem. Since low self-esteem and lack of confidence often underlie such behavior, communicating respect for the child and looking for resources initiate positive movements. It is wise to seek family counseling at least for an evaluation of the problem. Sometimes parents have a tendency to want to deny a problem, and more objective observers may be able to see the extent of any problem that exists.

The Isolated Child

In this chapter we will focus on the silent child, the isolated child. Although the socially outgoing child presents some problems to parents, these can usually be worked out with contracting sessions or mutual problem solving. The aggressive child often has the same problems as the isolated child with an extra layer of aggressiveness that can be controlled with rewards and negative consequences. The isolated child, however, requires action on a variety of fronts as described in Chapter 9. We raise the issue again here, however, because adolescence gives a special poignancy to such a problem. Because the emphasis in these years is on getting along with others, isolation is especially frustrating.

Philip Zimbardo, a psychologist who has studied shyness in all age groups and has established a Shyness Clinic at Stanford, and Shirley Radl recommend several actions.[70] Theirs are the only suggestions specifically geared for the adolescent years of twelve to seventeen. Because appearance is so important in the early and late adolescent years, Zimbardo and Radl suggest working from the outside in, concen-

340

CHAPTER 10
Early
Adolescence:
The Years
from Eleven
to Fifteen

trating first on appearance so that a teenager looks as well as possible from their point of view. Skin problems should be attended to immediately. Acne, which can create real misery, comes from many causes. Medicines likes creams, lotions, and antibiotics can be used on severe cases. Parents must consult a dermatologist if skin problems present any problem to teens. Weight, too, can be a problem. They recommend first seeing a pediatrician who can discuss weight and put the child on a diet. Parents then have suitable foods available and serve as models of good eating patterns.

Teeth sometimes need attention. Since most children and many adults wear braces, they are not the source of embarrassment they once were. Parents may be concerned about expense, but many dentists have a no-interest payment plan. Grooming and clothes also aid appearance. Most early adolescents will take lengthy showers and shampoo their hair daily. At age eleven, however, there may be a reluctance to bathe, and parents may have to encourage bath taking. When it comes to clothing, parents should provide the current fashion so far as the budget allows. When clothes are more expensive than parents can afford, possible solutions include buying, for example, one or two pairs of expensive pants rather than four or five cheaper ones. Or teens can earn money to make up the difference between what the parents can afford and what the clothes cost.

At home, parents do all the things that increase children's sense of security and importance. Respecting privacy, treating the child with respect, keeping lines of communication open, giving responsibility, giving appropriate praise, not prying into the child's thoughts and feelings, having rules and structure all contribute to a sense of security that enables the child to reach out to others in these sensitive years.

School Problems

Experts are divided on the handling of school problems. Some give all the responsibility to the early adolescent to handle the problem; others encourage the parent to take an active role.

Ginott cites the example of a thirteen-year-old boy who brought home a note from the teacher about his poor behavior.[71] His mother said, "You must have felt terrible to have to bring home a note like that." He agreed he did. His mother wrote the school that she was sure he would handle the problem. (In the past she would have yelled and screamed.) The next day she met the principal, but her son had already begun to improve his behavior.

Gordon, as well as Dinkmeyer and McKay, consider that the child has the problem. This is an issue he or she must deal with. A parent can be a model of effective work habits, can be interested in the child's feelings about school, but essentially schoolwork is up to the child.

Not so with the behaviorists. Eimers and Aitchison describe recommendations to help an eleven-year-old boy who was failing school.[72] Testing revealed he was bright and had no special learning problem. He just misbehaved in class and did not do homework. Eimers and Aitchison described the problem as the boy's not getting sufficient rewards for doing work. Parents found a suitable work place in the dining room, and the boy was given a choice of rewards for spending so much time on his homework. Initially, the amount of time he put in was brief, but gradually it was increased so that he could obtain the reward.

But as the boy's homework improved, his classroom behavior still required changing. He was given points for working predetermined amounts of time at his desk. When he clowned in class, he was put in time out for a brief period. The teacher also praised the boy for on-task behavior. We can see here that parents and teachers can do many things to change school behavior—organizing the environment, giving praise and rewards for appropriate behavior, and giving punishment for inappropriate behavior.

Exactly which method—giving the child the problem to handle or setting up a behavioral regime—will work in individual cases depends on the parents' values and the seriousness of the problem. Given the age of early adolescents, mutual problem-solving sessions and sending strong I-statements of concern might be appropriate tactics. If this does not lead to an effective plan for change, then parents can try the behavioral system. If children fall behind in school because they aren't doing the work, they can find it very hard to catch up when they finally decide to take action. For that reason the more active approach of the behaviorists has merit.

PARENTS' EXPERIENCES

Parents report they do not feel ready to have teenage children. The childhood years have gone so fast, it seems too soon to have a daughter with a mature figure and sons with bulging muscles and low voices. Parents find their children's sexual maturity disconcerting. They are surprised to see sons with *Playboy* magazines and hear girls talking about the sexual attractiveness of boys.

Their adolescents' mood swings and desires for greater freedom throw parents back to some of the same conflicts of the early toddler and preschool years. The elementary school years were stable because parents could talk and reason with children, but now they are back to dealing with screaming, crying, moody creatures who sometimes act younger but at the same time want more freedom. Parents may have felt they themselves have grown and matured as parents, able to handle crises, only to find themselves back at square 1, yelling and feeling uncontrolled with their children.

It is difficult to give up images, but that is what parents must do. Children are no longer children; they are physically and sexually mature. They are not psychologically mature, however, and they still need the guidance parents can give. Parents often have to give up images of themselves as the perfect parent of an adolescent. We all recall our own adolescence, the ways our parents handled us, and in many cases we want to improve on that. Sometimes we find we are not doing as well as we want and have to step back and see where we are going off the track.

Early adolescents are maturing and gain the physical glow and psychological vitality that comes from feeling the world is a magical place while parents are marching to or through middle age. Parents often do not feel vibrant and alert, and it is hard to live with offspring who may present such a physical contrast to how parents themselves feel. Further, the world is opening up to adolescents just as parents may feel

342

CHAPTER 10
Early
Adolescence:
The Years
from Eleven
to Fifteen

it is weighing them down. Parents have heavy work responsibilities, often duties of taking care of aging parents as well as growing children. Parents feel they have little time and money at their own disposal, yet they live with young people who seem to have a great deal of both.

Thus, parents have to be careful not to let resentment of the freedom and excitement of their teenagers get in the way of being effective parents. As parents develop reasonable expectations of the amount of freedom and responsibilities their children are to have, they must be careful not to overrestrict or overcriticize out of envy.

Ellen Galinsky calls this the **interdependent stage** of parenting to highlight the greater freedom and control children have.[73] Parents have several years to work through these issues before their children are launched. When parents can become more separate from their children, be available to help them grow yet not stifle them in the process, then parents' and children's relationships take on a new dimension and richness.

MAJOR POINTS OF CHAPTER 10

In this period, sexual development begins:

- for most boys and girls
- on different timetables for the two sexes, with girls starting approximately two years earlier than boys
- with internal hormonal changes that are not visible; as a result, neither the early adolescent nor others know changes have begun
- and the process takes years to complete
- and influences mood swings
- and is related to increases in family conflicts
- and triggers psychological reactions in early adolescents
- but many youth receive little preparation for it

Early adolescents:

- begin to think more abstractly and analyze themselves and other people
- think of future possibilities for themselves
- flourish in a school atmosphere of clear positive goals for students, reasons for planned actions, rewards for participation in extracurricular and community activities
- are active and interested in settings where they have control and are least motivated in adult-controlled settings
- continue to worry about losing a parent and school-related matters
- experience stress when many changes occur at the same time
- by and large have high self-esteem

Sense of identity:

- develops gradually over a period of time
- depends on exploring a variety of alternatives and making a commitment to values, goals, and behavior
- can be foreclosed if youth make a commitment without exploring their options
- is diffused if adolescents drift and take no action at all
- is not achieved when early adolescents experience a moratorium and explore without making a commitment
- is achieved in a more complicated way by youth of different ethnic groups

Early adolescents of different ethnic groups:

- must integrate two cultures
- must consider prejudice and its effects on their lives
- must engage adults in their culture in talking about their roots and their experiences in integrating two cultures

Peers:

- are models for clothes, language, taste in music and entertainment
- are sought as primary attachment figures when parents are uninterested and give little guidance
- are sought for different kinds of relationships by boys and girls—with girls wanting to talk and express their feelings and boys wanting to engage in group activities with little self-revelation

In this period, parents

- continue to be the single most important influence in aiding or hindering the adolescents' development
- provide role models of ethical, principled behavior
- must be available and listen to children
- provide accurate information on topics such as sexual behavior and substance use/abuse
- give more decision-making power to adolescents
- are likely to get their way in conflicts with children most of the time
- add to children's stress when they cannot deal with problems in their own lives
- must not pressure adolescents to hurry and grow up

Problems discussed center on:

- maintaining regular routines at times of change

344

CHAPTER 10
Early
Adolescence:
The Years
from Eleven
to Fifteen

- controlling emotional reactions
- dealing with social difficulties
- failures in communication

Joys include:

- observing accomplishments in physical, artistic, intellectual endeavors
- feeing good because the parent has helped the child in a specific way
- observing child's capacity to take responsibility for self
- emotional closeness
- seeing child concerned about others

ADDITIONAL READINGS

Csikszentmihalyi, Mihaly. *Being Adolescent*. New York: Basic Books, 1984.

Dinkmeyer, Don, and McKay, Gary D. *STEP/TEEN Systematic Training for Effective Parenting of Teens*. Circle Pines, Minn.: American Guidance Service, 1983.

Elkind, David. *The Hurried Child*. Reading, Mass.: Addison-Wesley, 1981.

Gordon, Sol, and Gordon, Judith. *Raising a Child Conservatively in a Sexually Permissive World*. Rev. ed. New York: Simon & Schuster, 1983.

Norman, Jane, and Harris, Myron. *The Private Life of the American Teenager*. New York: Rawson Wade, 1981.

Notes

1. Harold E. Jones, "Physical Maturing Among Girls as Related to Behavior," in *The Course of Human Development,* ed. Mary C. Jones et al. (Waltham, Mass.: Xerox, 1971), pp. 257–259.
2. Rainer K. Silbereisen, Anne C. Petersen, Helfried T. Albrecht, and Barbel Kracke, "Maturational Timing and the Development of Problem Behavior: Longitudinal Studies in Adolescence," *Journal of Early Adolescence* 9 (1989): 247–268.
3. John Janeway Conger and Anne C. Petersen, *Adolescence and Youth,* 3rd ed. (New York: Harper & Row, 1984).
4. Diane N. Ruble and Jeanne Brooks-Gunn, "The Experience of Menarche," *Child Development* 53 (1982): 1557–1566.
5. Jeanne Brooks-Gunn and Diane N. Ruble, "The Development of Menstrual-Related Beliefs and Behaviors during Early Adolescence," *Child Development* 53 (1982): 1567–1577.
6. Mary C. Jones and Nancy Bayley, "Physical Maturing among Boys as Related to Behavior," *Journal of Educational Psychology* 41 (1950): 129–148.
7. Jane Norman and Myron Harris, *The Private Life of the American Teenager* (New York: Rawson Wade, 1981).
8. Ibid.
9. Jean Piaget and Barbel Inhelder, *The Psychology of the Child* (New York: Basic Books, 1969); Herbert Ginsburg and Sylvia Opper, *Piaget's Theory of Intellectual Development* (Englewood Cliffs, N.J.: Prentice-Hall, 1969).
10. Conger and Petersen, *Adolescence and Youth.*
11. Ibid.
12. Barton J. Hirsch and Bruce D. Rapkin, "The Transition to Junior High School: A Longitudinal Study of Self-Esteem, Psychological Symptomatology, School Life, and Social Support," *Child Development* 58 (1987): 1235–1243.
13. Conger and Petersen, *Adolescence and Youth.*

14. Mihaly Csikszentmihalyi and Reed Larson, *Being Adolescent* (New York: Basic Books, 1984).

15. Reid Larson and Claudia Lampman-Petraitis, "Daily Emotional States as Reported by Children and Adolescents," *Child Development* 60 (1989): 1250–1260.

16. Csikszentmihalyi and Larson, *Being Adolescent.*

17. Hirsch and Rapkin, "The Transition to Junior High School."

18. Roberta G. Simmons, Richard Burgeson, Steven Carlton-Ford, and Dale A. Blyth, "The Impact of Cumulative Changes in Early Adolescence," *Child Development* 58 (1987): 1220–1234.

19. Norman and Harris, *Private Life of the American Teenager.*

20. J. Brooks-Gunn and Michelle P. Warren, "Biological and Social Contributions to Negative Affect in Young Adolescent Girls," *Child Development* 60 (1989): 40–55.

21. Judith M. Siegel and Jonathan D. Brown, "A Prospective Study of Stressful Circumstances, Illness Symptoms, and Depressed Mood among Adolescents," *Developmental Psychology* 24 (1988): 715–721.

22. Erik H. Erikson, *Childhood and Society,* 2d ed. (New York: W. W. Norton, 1963).

23. James E. Marcia, "Identity in Adolescence," in *The Handbook of Adolescent Psychology,* ed. Joseph Adelson (New York: John Wiley, 1980), pp. 159–187.

24. Jean S. Phinney, "Stages of Ethnic Identity Development in Minority Group Adolescents," *Journal of Early Adolescence* 9 (1989): 34–49.

25. Margaret Beale Spencer and Carol Markstrom-Adams, "Identity Processes among Racial and Ethnic Minority Children in America," *Child Development* 61 (1990): 290–310; Michael C. Thornton, Linda M. Chatters, Robert Joseph Taylor, and Walter R. Allen, "Sociodemographic and Environmental Correlates of Racial Socialization by Black Parents," *Child Development* 61 (1990): 401–409.

26. Phinney, "Stages of Ethnic Identity Development in Minority Group Adolescents."

27. Conger and Petersen, *Adolescence and Youth.*

28. Norman and Harris, *Private Life of the American Teenager.*

29. Daniel Offer and Judith Offer, *From Teenage to Young Manhood: A Psychological Study* (New York: Basic Books, 1975).

30. Jane B. Brooks, "Social Maturity in Middle Age and Its Developmental Antecedents," in *Present and Past in Middle Life,* ed. Dorothy H. Eichorn et al. (New York: Academic Press, 1981), pp. 243–265.

31. Jack Block with Norma Haan, *Lives Through Time* (Berkeley, Calif.: Bancroft Books, 1971).

32. Conger and Petersen, *Adolescence and Youth,* p. 231.

33. Block with Haan, *Lives Through Time.*

34. Diana Baumrind, "Early Socialization and Adolescent Competence," in *Adolescence in the Life Cycle,* ed. Sigmund Dragastin and Glen H. Elder (New York: John Wiley, 1975), p. 137.

35. Csikszentmihalyi and Larson, *Being Adolescent.*

36. Norman and Harris, *Private Life of the American Teenager.*

37. Csikszentmihalyi and Larson, *Being Adolescent.*

38. Judith G. Smetana, "Concepts of Self and Social Convention: Adolescents' and Parents' Reasoning about Hypothetical and Actual Family Conflicts," in *Development during the Transition to Adolescence: Minnesota Symposia on Child Psychology,* vol. 21, ed. Megan R. Gunnar and W. Andrew Collins (Hillsdale, N.J.: Erlbaum, 1988), pp. 79–122; Judith G. Smetana, "Adolescents' and Parents' Reasoning about Actual Family Conflict," *Child Development* 60 (1989): 1052–1067.

39. Smetana, "Concepts of Self and Social Convention."

40. Laurence Steinberg, "Impact of Puberty on Family Relations: Effects of Pubertal Status and Pubertal Timing," *Developmental Psychology* 23 (1987): 451–460.

41. Per F. Gjerde, "The Interpersonal Structure of Family Interaction Settings: Parent-Adolescent Relations in Dyads and Triads," *Developmental Psychology* 22 (1986): 297–304.

42. Laurence Steinberg, "Reciprocal Relation between Parent-Child Distance and Pubertal Maturation," *Developmental Psychology* 24 (1988): 122–128.

43. Gale Inoff-Germain, Gina Snyder Arnold, Editha D. Nottlemann, Elizabeth J. Susman, Gordon B. Cutler, Jr., and George P. Chrousos, "Relations between Hormone Levels and Observational Measures of Aggressive Behavior of Young Adolescents in Family Interactions," *Developmental Psychology* 24 (1988): 129–139.

CHAPTER 10
Early
Adolescence:
The Years
from Eleven
to Fifteen

44. Bruce E. Compas, David C. Howell, Vicky Phares, Rebecca Williams, and Normal Ledoux, "Parents and Child Stress Symptoms: An Integrative Analysis," *Developmental Psychology* 25 (1989): 550–559.

45. Rex Forehand, Nicholas Long, Gene H. Brody, and Robert Fauber, "Home Predictors of Young Adolescents' School Behavior and Academic Performance," *Child Development* 57 (1986): 1528–1533.

46. Norman and Harris, *Private Life of the American Teenager.*

47. Ibid.

48. John Condry and Michael L. Siman, "Characteristics of Peer- and Adult-Oriented Children," *Journal of Marriage and the Family* 36 (1974): 543–554.

49. Csikszentmihalyi and Larson, *Being Adolescent.*

50. Elizabeth Douvan and Joseph Adelson, *The Adolescent Experience* (New York: John Wiley, 1966).

51. Conger and Petersen, *Adolescence and Youth.*

52. H. D. Thornberg, *Development in Adolescence* (Monterey, Calif.: Brooks/Cole, 1975).

53. Dorothy C. Briggs, *Your Child's Self-Esteem* (Garden City, N.Y.: Doubleday, 1970), p. 302.

54. Norman and Harris, *Private Life of an American Teenager.*

55. Ibid.

56. James P. Comer, "What Makes the New Generation Tick?" *Ebony* August 1990, p. 38.

57. Spencer and Markstrom-Adams, "Identity Processes among Racial and Ethnic Minority Children in America."

58. David Elkind, *The Hurried Child* (Reading, Mass.: Addison-Wesley, 1981).

59. Richard Ferber, *Solve Your Child's Sleep Problems* (New York: Simon & Schuster, 1985).

60. Haim G. Ginott, *Between Parent and Teenager* (New York: Avon, 1969).

61. Thomas Gordon, *P.E.T.: Parent Effectiveness Training* (New York: New American Library, 1975), p. 252.

62. Don Dinkmeyer and Gary D. McKay, *STEP/TEEN Systematic Training for Effective Parenting of Teens* (Circle Pines, Minn.: American Guidance Service, 1983).

63. Robert Eimers and Robert Aitchison, *Effective Parents/Responsible Children* (New York: McGraw-Hill, 1977).

64. Ginott, *Between Parent and Teenager.*

65. Gordon, *P.E.T.*

66. Eimers and Aitchison, *Effective Parents/ Responsible Children.*

67. Dinkmeyer and McKay, *STEP/TEEN Systematic Training for Effective Parenting of Teens.*

68. Ibid.

69. Adele Faber and Elaine Mazlish, *How to Talk So Kids Will Listen and Listen So Kids Will Talk* (New York: Rawson Wade, 1980), p. 165.

70. Philip Zimbardo and Shirley Radl, *The Shy Child* (Garden City, N.Y.: Doubleday, 1982).

71. Ginott, *Between Parent and Teenager.*

72. Eimers and Aitchison, *Effective Parents/ Responsible Children.*

73. Ellen Galinsky, *Between Generations: The Six Stages of Parenthood* (New York: Time Books, 1981).

LATE ADOLESCENCE: THE YEARS FROM FIFTEEN TO NINETEEN

Late adolescents have matured physically and sexually. They have adjusted to bodies with new silhouettes and new capacities. They have adapted to their new ways of thinking and grown accustomed to the idea of a world that does not exist in an ideal state, that has imperfections. They have become used to their moods, more moderate in their self-criticisms.

Having accommodated themselves to these many changes, late adolescents are ready to look to the future. They begin to envision careers, future lifestyles. They spend increasing amounts of time away from home and away from parents. Sexual relationships become important to them; they make choices about sexual activity, deciding how far to go and with whom. At the same time, they are balancing pleasure with work at school or in jobs.

Parents, too, are in a process of adjusting to the many changes their children experience. As adolescents make choices, parents stand by to provide information and to help if problems develop. Parents in this stage sense their children's impending departure from home and what life may be like for them as mature adults.

PHYSICAL DEVELOPMENT

Adolescents in this age period are reaching physical and sexual maturity. Although both boys and girls have increased sexual interest and activity, boys on average show greater interest than girls. Although hormones influence sexual drive and interest, learning also plays an important role. Cross-cultural studies of sexual behavior in many different settings indicate marked differences in the amount and kind of sexual activity occurring at different ages.[1]

In our own society, we have seen marked changes in sexual attitudes and behavior in the last twenty-five years. Clearly, our physiology has not changed in that time, but our thinking about sexual matters has. Currently, young people are more open and honest about sex than previously and show a willingness to base decisions about sexual behavior on their own personal beliefs rather than on a rigid social code of appropriate sexual behavior.

348

CHAPTER 11
Late
Adolescence:
The Years
from Fifteen
to Nineteen

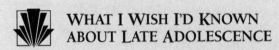

WHAT I WISH I'D KNOWN ABOUT LATE ADOLESCENCE

"I wish that I had got my children involved in more family activities. When they were mostly through adolescence I heard a talk by a child psychiatrist who said that often when teenagers say they don't want to do something with the family, at times you have to insist because they do go along and enjoy the event. I wish I had known that sooner, because I accepted their first 'No,' when I perhaps should have pushed more." MOTHER

"This may begin earlier, but it goes through adolescence. I had always heard they look for their own independence, their own things to participate in; but until you really experience it with your own, it's hard to deal with it. When you read about independence, it sounds like it's carefully planned out. When it actually happens, all of a sudden they want to do something that they have never done before and which you firmly believe they have no idea how to do. It can be driving for the first time or suddenly announcing they want to go somewhere with friends. I knew it was going to happen; but exactly how to handle it myself and handle it with them so they got a chance to do something new without its being dangerous has been a challenge to me." FATHER

"I wish that I had known that I had to listen more to them in order to understand what they were experiencing. I sort of assumed that I knew what adolescence was about from my own experience, but things had a different meaning to them. What was important to me was not that important to them, and I wish I had realized that in the beginning." MOTHER

"I wish I knew how to raise children in adolescence when you have traditional values and many of the people around you do not. It's very hard to do here in California compared to the South, where we came from. There, everyone reinforces the same values, and it is a lot easier for parents." MOTHER

"I wish I had known to be more attentive, to really listen, because kids have a lot of worthwhile things to say and you come to find out they hold a lot of your viewpoints." FATHER

"I wish I had known it was important to spend time with the children individually. We did things as a family, but the children are so different, and I think I would have understood them better if I had spent time with them alone." MOTHER

Given these attitude changes, what are teenagers actually doing? For boys, the number who masturbate—about 85 to 90 percent—has remained the same in the last forty years, but boys begin masturbating at an earlier age.[2] For girls, there have been greater changes in behavior. In the late 1930s and 1940s, only about 15 percent of women masturbated by age thirteen and 30 percent by age twenty. Comparable recent figures are 33 percent by age thirteen and 60 percent by age twenty.[3] Girls still do not approach boys' level of sexual activity. Not as many girls masturbate, and even when they do, they do not do it as frequently. Petting too has increased and involves greater physical intimacy. Both masturbation and petting to orgasm may aid girls' later sexual adjustment following marriage. There is evidence that those girls who masturbate and pet to orgasm are more likely to experience orgasm in the first year after marriage.

There have been increases, too, in the numbers reporting sexual intercourse during adolescence. The increases are especially large for girls and boys of higher educational and socioeconomic levels. This trend began in the 1960s, has continued through the 1970s, but patterns of sexual behavior are thought to have been stable since 1979.[4] In 1979, 38 percent of unmarried sixteen-year-old girls and 69 percent of unmarried nineteen-year-old girls had engaged in intercourse. This sample, however, included a small number of married women. In 1979, 56 percent of seventeen-year-old boys and 77 percent of nineteen-year-old boys had engaged in intercourse. Thus, between two-thirds and three-quarters of adolescent boys and girls have experienced premarital sexual relations by the age of nineteen.[5]

Sexually transmitted diseases (STDs) are a major risk for adolescents because of early age of intercourse and a lack of regular contraceptive use. Next to homosexual men and prostitutes, adolescent females have the highest rates of gonorrhea, cytomegalovirus, and pelvic inflammatory disease of any age group. And now there is the specter of AIDS (acquired immunodeficiency disease syndrome).[6]

The precise risk that AIDS presents to teenagers is not known because of the disease's long incubation period. Many people coming down with it in their twenties presumably contracted it as teenagers. However, adolescents may be at high risk because the number of teen cases is increasing and because teens often do not use contraceptives. Unprotected sex with drug-using individuals is a major form of transmission in the heterosexual population. Further, teens are more susceptible to all STDs, so they may be vulnerable to AIDS as well.[7]

INTELLECTUAL DEVELOPMENT

Early adolescents have begun to move into Piaget's formal operations period (see Table 6-1) and think more abstractly. This trend is continued in later adolescence and on into the early twenties, where an increasing number use formal thought.[8]

Abstract thought processes focus on concerns about other people and about society at large. Adolescents begin to think about justice and equality, and they try to apply these concepts to their everyday lives. Some become involved in social action groups or volunteer activities. Adelson describes the shift in thought processes from preadolescence to adolescence:

> At the onset of adolescence, the child's mind is all fierce, retributory moralism on the one hand, and deficient competence on the other. How does one treat the thief? Clap him in jail, and if he will not learn his lesson, double or triple his sentence, or put him in solitary confinement or torture him. How would you keep people from breaking a law against cigarette smoking? Spies and informers and secret surveillance. . . . Later in adolescence, the child pondering crime and justice speaks altogether differently. He tells us that we must

350

CHAPTER 11
Late
Adolescence:
The Years
from Fifteen
to Nineteen

try to understand the sources of crime and that these are likely to be found in the criminal's motives and these in turn are rooted in past and present milieus, in family and companions. He argues that we ought to think beyond punishment to rehabilitation and that jailing someone merely puts him in bad company and reinforces bad habits. A few ... may feel that the roots of crime run so deep as to require psychotherapy ... one sometimes senses that the child confessing these sentiments is merely showing off his acquisition of liberal cliches. Nevertheless, these ideas, even if superficial, or superficially felt, reflect a remarkable advance over what went before.[9]

Compared with younger children, then, adolescents are able to take a more tolerant, more understanding view of people and issues. They are able to stand back and examine their own thought processes and the relationship between abstract ideas they ponder.

SCHOOL

Adolescents spend one-third of their daily life in school. How do they feel about it? A survey of 160,000 teenagers ages thirteen to eighteen gave the responses in Table 11-1.[10] Four out of ten students found school necessary, but only two out of ten found it interesting or challenging. This view of school is supported by students' reports of how they were feeling when they were paged. Time in class is associated with lower than average feeling states.[11] Students feel bored, confused, trapped. They are most excited and alive at school when permitted to be active participants—discussing, experimenting, doing. They enjoy classes with concrete goals like physical education, industrial arts, music. They least enjoy strictly academic classes.

What teachers do students like? Students cite fairness as the most important quality of a good teacher.[12] Well-liked teachers grade fairly, do not pick favorite students. They have knowledge of the subject and enthusiasm for it. Students are drawn to teachers who are involved in what they teach. Students also stress personal aspects of the teacher—likes kids, will help kids with school or other problems. Students feel that teachers, like parents, tend to disregard their ideas and opinions and put them down.

Students report that the high points of school life come from contacts with friends. Lunch times, time between classes or after school are times of positive feeling because adolescents are free of the classroom restraints and are able to talk and joke with their friends. Friends revitalize adolescents and increase their ability to concentrate on schoolwork.

Parents' qualities are related to students' achievement in high school. Parents of high-achieving boys are more democratic than parents of low-achieving boys. There is sharing of ideas and recreation. Parents approve of and trust the boys, encouraging them to achieve but not insisting on it. Overall family morale is high. Parents of underachieving boys are domineering, more severe in discipline, and more critical of boys. As one researcher reports, "Strong and positive parent-child relationships are more likely in the case of achieving than of underachieving children and adolescents."[13]

TABLE 11-1
HOW ADOLESCENTS FEEL ABOUT SCHOOL

Do you feel that school is...?*	
Necessary	42%
Boring	27%
Puts too much pressure on kids	22%
Interesting	21%
Challenging	19%
Frustrating	15%
A waste of time	9%

* Some respondents checked more than one answer.

Jane Norman and Myron Harris, *The Private Life of the American Teenager* (New York: Rawson Wade, 1981), p. 184–146.

Parental expectations play a role in achievement and students' goals, too. When parents', especially mothers', expectations are high, students' aspiration levels increase. Though parents worry that their children will be led astray from school achievement by friends, in fact peers have less influence than parents on future goals. Further, most adolescents pick friends who share similar goals with the adolescents' parents.

Some students find school so frustrating and unsatisfying that they drop out. Dropouts usually have a long history of school problems and many have repeated grades. Though most are of average intelligence, they are two years behind in reading and arithmetic achievement by the seventh grade, and most of their grades are below average. Further, they appear to have difficulties in many areas. For example, 90 percent of future dropouts are lower-status adolescents who feel they do not fit in with middle class adolescents socially as well as academically.[14]

Family characteristics associated with dropping out are lack of understanding and acceptance of the adolescent, poor communication, and a generally unhappy home atmosphere. These families have weaker ties with friends and are generally less stable than families of students who graduate from high school, who tend to come from the same kinds of homes as high-achieving boys—homes where parents share recreation with children, are understanding and accepting of teens. These families are more stable, more involved in a network of friends with whom they share mutual support and reciprocity.

Students who drop out share certain psychological characteristics. They are less happy, less confident, less sure of themselves and where they are going than students who finish school. They feel frustrated at school and see leaving it as the only solution. They are rebellious and angry at others, wanting to resist adult authority. When parents talk to dropouts and stress the importance of staying in school, dropping out is less likely.

What are the results of dropping out? The main negative consequences are fear of unemployment and actual higher rates of unemployment. If they can get work,

352

CHAPTER 11
Late
Adolescence:
The Years
from Fifteen
to Nineteen

however, high school dropouts do not, when compared to high school graduates, have worse, unsatisfying jobs. They can be good employees.[15]

To prevent dropping out, school interventions must occur early in students' careers so that their frustration and low self-esteem do not accumulate. Students do not drop out at the first hint of trouble; they usually have been having difficulties for a long time and see little hope of reversing the process. Early interventions can enable them in some small measure to experience success and pleasure at school.

WORKING

A significant number of adolescents have part-time jobs during high school. Most are employed in retail sales, food services, and general unskilled work. In the Chicago study of adolescents, 41 percent were employed an average of 18 hours a week.[16] Thus, some adolescents spend a substantial amount of time at work.

In the Chicago study, students who were paged at work often wished they were doing something else. When they reported their moods at work, however, they nevertheless often felt active and happy. Adolescents derive decided benefits from work. They gain in understanding of other people as a result of their work experience. They come to understand the dynamics underlying conflicts between co-workers, between supervisors and workers, and between workers and customers. In addition, working students feel more self-reliant and independent following employment.[17]

There are few changes in the relationships between parents and working adolescents. Parents tend to control the money students earn and determine the amount they save. There is some evidence that working girls feel more distant from their families, whereas working boys were more likely to talk about problems with fathers. Work causes few changes in peer relationships. Employed students spend as much time with friends as nonworking students; they keep their friends with no tendency to substitute co-workers for friends.

There appear to be costs to adolescents' working, however. First, they show less interest and enjoyment of school. This attitude seems to follow getting a job, because those who seek jobs do not dislike school before starting to work. Second, adolescents show effects from stress in the job itself.[18] Stresses on the jobs include such features as poor work environment (heat, noise, dirt, time pressures); meaningless tasks that are routine and boring; conflict with other roles (interfering with school activities); domineering supervisors; impersonal organizations; and low wage structure. When job stress scores are related to measures of physical or psychological distress, we find that adolescents with high-stress jobs are more likely to be absent from school, to use alcohol, cigarettes, and marijuana more. Thus, a stressful job puts strain on the adaptation reserves of adolescents just as it does on adults. So, the value of a job for adolescents depends in part on the nature of the work. If the job will be stressful, the teenager may be well advised to wait until a less stressful job is available.

Ellen Greenberger and Laurence Steinberg, who conducted a large study of teenage work experience, are concerned that the current pattern of adolescent employment—spending many hours in unrewarding work—not only creates the stress just detailed, but also prevents adolescents from developing fully as individuals.[19] Teenagers who work many hours do not have leisure to explore and develop interests, do not have solitude to think about their lives and fantasize about the future, and do not have time for deepening friendships with peers. The cynicism that develops from poor work experience and the poor habits of alcohol and drug use may be costly effects of adolescent work. Their guidelines for teen work experience are discussed in the section on parenting tasks.

To do the kind of work they want is very important to adolescents. The process of selecting some kind of vocational goal—college, work—begins during childhood, so that by adolescence many children already have some ideas about what interests they may want to pursue. Let's look at the steps in this process.[20]

Childhood is a fantasy period in which children explore many occupations—firefighter, policeman or policewoman, pilot, president. As children move through elementary school, they begin to develop interests and skills that are related to work. At home, they take on many roles. When caring for their clothes and cleaning their rooms, they take on hotel roles; when preparing food and cleaning up after meals, restaurant roles; when helping siblings with homework or chores, teaching roles. In school, sports, and scouting activities children develop discipline and establish habits of meeting standards—qualities that are valued in the world of work.

During the adolescent years, as individuals acquire a sense of who they are and what they might like to do, they begin to test and taste various careers. An adolescent may study physics, Russian, and weaving in school and may have an afterschool job in a florist shop or a television repair store. In all of these activities he or she is exploring new fields and learning what he or she does and does not enjoy. From this information and from other experiences decisions emerge about whether to go on for additional education or training and what kind of job to look for.

As individuals move from school to work in their late teens or early twenties, they go through a **transition period** and then an **establishment period**. It is during the latter time that men and women make serious commitments to work. There are, of course, wide variations among individuals—some adolescents know, while still in their early teens, what they want to do in their work lives, whereas other young people choose an occupation later on, after having some work experience.

What is the parent's role in helping a child traverse these different stages? First, the parent who works provides a model. We know that a high percentage of sons follow in their fathers' professional footsteps. A son may be most likely to enter the father's occupation if it is one the child observes while growing up—if, for example, the father is a veterinarian or has a small business. Studies show a relationship between the example of a father who is happy and satisfied in his work and a son's occupational adjustment and success in adulthood.[21] Girls, too, model their work commitments on their mother's examples.[22] Daughters of working women are more likely to plan to work when they are married than are girls whose mothers do not work. The parent does not need to have a job to serve as a work model. If a mother or father has stimulating interests, such as hobbies and community activities, children have the example of a disciplined and accomplished person to copy. Fathers who do not earn much money or achieve high status can still be excellent models because of their interests and their commitment to what they enjoy.

354

CHAPTER 11
Late
Adolescence:
The Years
from Fifteen
to Nineteen

EMOTIONAL DEVELOPMENT

In Chapter 10 we reviewed findings concerning the happy and unhappy times of the Chicago students who wore pagers for a week. Describing overall mood changes, the authors write:

Is there a pattern in the ways in which things go wrong?

The most frequent scenarios seem to involve becoming overwhelmed. Again and again, adolescents are overpowered by situations: the demands of school, the intransigence of a parent, high expectations they impose of themselves. The result is anxiety, worry, agitation, panic, anger, and fear. A girl described sitting in chemistry, "Listening to Mr. Molitor and going 'insane'; I just don't understand why H+ is +." A boy described "going out of my mind" because he couldn't solve an algebra equation. A major paper required in English classes made many students distraught long before it was even assigned.[23]

Teenagers feel overwhelmed by the expectations of school, family, and peers. However, they are most often overwhelmed by their own expectations, which they must learn to refine so that they become more realistic. As noted earlier, adolescents are very idealistic, hopeful that what they want will work out perfectly. They do not have an accurate sense of their own abilities to achieve what they want. They do not always plan well and as a result become overworked, overcommitted, and overtired.

The opposite of feeling overwhelmed is feeling bored, uninterested in what is happening. This is most likely to occur when teens feel others are in control of what is happening—for example, at school. Boredom comes, too, when adolescents do not have worthwhile goals that challenge them.

Teens' feelings about themselves and their lives tend to be stable from early to late adolescence.[24] Those who were happy as freshmen in high school are happy as juniors. They show more stability in their feelings about friends and school, however, than they do in their feelings about family and solitude, which change. Feelings about family improve—52 percent say they are happier with family as juniors, 12 percent say less happy, and 36 percent report no change. This greater happiness appears to derive from late adolescents' broader perspective. They interpret experiences in a new light and as a result become more accepting both of family and of solitude.

As in the early adolescent years, teens continue to enjoy friends, sports, hobbies, art. These activities and experiences make them feel alive. A definite pattern appears in enjoyable activities. First, enjoyable activities require concentration on some aspect of the environment. Teens have to learn rules of interaction, whether it be music or a game like football. As they learn an activity and really participate in it, they get feedback about their performance and are able to improve. As they continue with the activity, teenagers feel less self-conscious and experience a feeling of self-transcendence. There is great involvement in the activity itself and a feeling of effortlessness. To achieve these positive feelings, there has to be a good match between the teen's skills and the activity's challenges.

PERSONAL AND SOCIAL DEVELOPMENT

Adolescents are consolidating a sense of who they are, where they are going, what they want to do. They continue to spend more time with friends, less time at home with family. Peer relationships now include more active dating and settling into a relationship with a person of the opposite sex. Adolescents will begin to make vocational plans, even if it is simply to pursue their education in another school setting.

Development of the Self

Adolescents think of themselves in terms of psychological qualities. They describe how they relate to other people, their social style, and begin to see patterns in their behavior. They reflect on their own characteristics, see themselves as fitting certain categories, and have a greater sense of their abilities to do things. Note this self-description of a seventeen-year-old girl.

> I am a human being. I am a girl. I am an individual. I don't know who I am. I am a Pisces. I am a moody person. I am an indecisive person. I am an ambitious person. I am a very curious person. I am not an individual. I am a loner. I am an American (God help me). I am a Democrat. I am a liberal person. I am a radical. I am a conservative. I am a pseudo-liberal. I am an atheist. I am not a classifiable person (i.e., I don't want to be).[25]

When asked what they like best about themselves, adolescents described their social characteristics—their friendliness. When asked about the traits they would like to have, 70 percent of the adolescent respondents cited interpersonal traits. Though they believed social characteristics were very important to develop, they described themselves as most ashamed when they lost control.[26]

Self-perceptions continue to change over the adolescent years. At age eighteen, boys see themselves as more attuned to interpersonal relations than they were at age eleven—more affectionate, sympathetic, considerate and assertive; more masculine and less free-spirited, but less conforming as well. Girls at age eighteen see themselves as more mature and involved with others (being affectionate and sympathetic with them), perhaps at the cost of their own desires, as they see themselves as less playful, ambitious, and generous.[27]

Sex differences in self-descriptions at age eighteen reveal that boys see themselves as more daring, rebellious, and playful in life than girls and, at the same time, more logical, curious, and calm. Girls see themselves as more attuned to people than boys are—more sympathetic, social, considerate, and affectionate—and more emotionally reactive—more worrisome, more easily upset, more needing of approval.[28]

So adolescents continue to define their own identities, and they do this, in part, by means of the activities they engage in. Figures 11-1, 11-2, and 11-3 describe where, with whom, and how adolescents spend their time. Teenagers spend over a quarter of their time alone, usually at home in the bedroom. They study, watch TV, do chores, and think about life and the future. What do teens want out of life? Their responses are presented in Table 11-2.

356

CHAPTER 11
Late
Adolescence:
The Years
from Fifteen
to Nineteen

INTERVIEW
with Jack Block

Jack Block is professor of psychology at the University of California at Berkeley. In 1968, he and his late wife, Jeanne H. Block, initiated the Block and Block Longitudinal Study, which followed a sample of children for twenty-three years.

You have followed a sample of children from age three into their twenties and have studied their growth and development with a variety of different measures.

We are seeing the subjects again now at age twenty-three. We have seen them before at ages three, four, five, seven, eleven, fourteen, and eighteen. The current assessment involves six sessions, each about 2½ hours long. No group has been as extensively studied psychologically as this sample.

Our primary conceptual dimensions were ego control and ego resilience, but we also were interested in self-concept and the way it develops over the years, sex role development and its influencing factors, and some of the theoretical issues in personality.

Many more people talk about resilience now, but you selected that word over twenty years ago.

We selected that word very carefully, about forty years ago. We thought that the psychoanalytic concept of ego strength had two components—what we chose to call *resiliency* and what we chose to call *control*. Resiliency is dynamic resourcefulness, not just static competence.

You can be overly controlled, so can you be overly resilient?

No, no. You can't be overly resilient. Resiliency is defined in terms of the ability to modulate ego control. In resilient individuals, ego control can vary in ways that are responsive to environmental demands and pressures. Think for a minute about the ordinarily highly planful engineer who can, when necessary, brainstorm and think broadly. That's resiliency. Ordinarily, he's uptight, rigid, obsessive, but when he needs to, he can associate freely to solve a problem. Or think of the generally diffuse, chaotic, impulsive graduate student who has to study for oral examinations and becomes highly obsessive-compulsive for 6 months in order to prepare effectively. After he passes his orals, he becomes a laid-back, diffuse, impulsive person again. Well, that is resiliency going the other way. Some people cannot change in response to situational demands, and they are not resilient.

Do you think ego control and resiliency are temperamental qualities?

Well, like many psychologists, I have moved away from being primarily an environmentalist toward giving weight to inborn temperamental qualities that influence people to develop in certain ways. I think ego control and resiliency are likely to be temperamentally influenced.

From age three one can certainly distinguish children with respect to the ego control dimension, and these consistencies extend through age eighteen. The ordering of boys and also girls with respect to ego control at age three correlates .4 or .45 with ego control at age eighteen. *(continued)*

Ego-resiliency shows good ordering correspondence for boys between three and eighteen, but not for girls. For boys, it is again about .45. For girls, early resiliency (ages three and four) correlates .00 with resiliency at fourteen and eighteen. Girls appear to psychologically restructure when they are preadolescent. Something profound and so far mysterious happens to girls about this age.

Do you have any idea what that is?

I think they reference themselves against different personal criterion. They start to think of themselves in terms of the social value of being attractive. They adopt a different frame of reference, and they are no longer their own selves.

These are girls born in the mid-1960s living in Berkeley, and they are orienting toward their sexual role?

These girls have experienced the perhaps special world of the Bay Area environment where feminism is emphasized. These are not girls from a sheltered area such as Utah.

Somewhat simplistically, it seems to me that the developmental problem for girls is to move away from overcontrol while boys have to move away from undercontrol. This finding seems to come up in our study in so many ways. Undercontrol gets boys into trouble and resiliency gets them out of it by providing them the control they need. For girls, the problem is to move away from overcontrol; resiliency provides the spontaneity needed for self-realization.

Did you read the Chicago adolescent study that used beepers?

Yes, we replicated that in our eighteen-year-old assessment, but we had additional information on the adolescents. We have only partially worked up these data with respect just to depression. Girls who report depressive tendencies feel less in control of their daily life situations, as evaluated by the beeper, than girls who do not report depression or than boys.

Do you find much depression in boys?

When our subjects were age eighteen, we studied depression using standard measures. Boys and girls manifest depression in different ways. Girls interiorize, are inner-directed, blame themselves, have low self-esteem, and ruminate. Boys with depressive tendencies are angry with the world, undercontrolled, hostile. They don't have low self-esteem, but they are depressed by the world in which they find themselves.

We can trace the antecedents of depression in our study back to age eleven, and perhaps seven. For boys stretching limits and undercontrol foretell depression later. For girls, being reserved, shy, oversocialized—being considerate of others instead of self-assertive—are the forerunners of later depressive tendencies.

We have a lot to do in our study. At this stage of the game we have interesting outcome, and we can look back fifteen and soon twenty years to see what led up to them. We have interesting early variables and we can look ahead twenty years and see their implications. It is a lot of fun now.

358

CHAPTER 11
Late
Adolescence:
The Years
from Fifteen
to Nineteen

FIGURE 11-1
WHERE ADOLESCENTS SPEND THEIR TIME

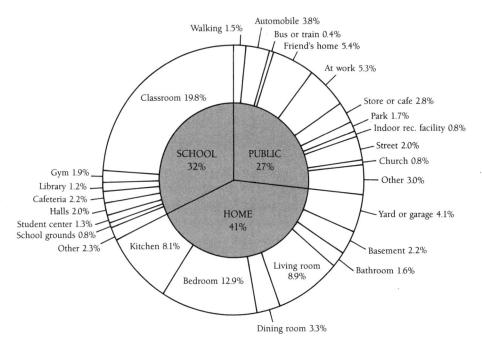

From M. Csikszentmihalyi and R. Larson, *Being Adolescent* (New York: Basic Books, 1984), p. 59.

Development of Self-Regulation

Ways of controlling impulses tend to remain stable from early to late adolescence. Young teens who are dependable, responsible, sympathetic, and considerate continue that behavior through late adolescence.[29] They come from families in which parents initiate a positive cycle of behavior. Parents are self-confident, reliable persons whom children trust and respect. The world is a reliable place, and children become self-confident, trusting persons who are responsible, well-controlled, and involved with peers in satisfying relationships. Both parents and children appear high in self-esteem.

A rather different set of family qualities is related to delinquent activities. Gerald Patterson and Magda Stouthamer-Loeber summarize the four kinds of family interaction associated with delinquency: (1) lack of family routine and structure so that there are no clear-cut rules of what children may or may not do, (2) lack of personal supervision and monitoring so that parents do not know what children are doing, (3) lack of effective consequences for behavior—parents may yell and threaten but do not follow through—and (4) inability to deal with tension and crises so that conflicts linger and are not solved.[30]

FIGURE 11-2
WHAT ADOLESCENTS SPEND THEIR TIME DOING

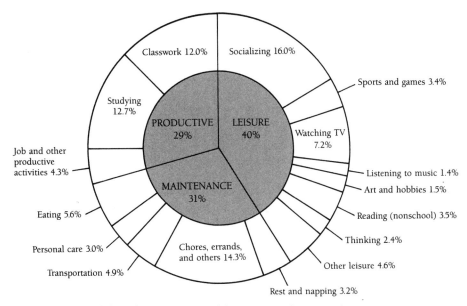

From M. Csikszentmihalyi and R. Larson, *Being Adolescent* (New York: Basic Books, 1984), p. 63.

John Conger and Anne Petersen survey evidence on the relationship between adolescent delinquency and adult criminality.[31] Most adolescents who engage in occasional delinquent acts will not progress to criminal careers in adulthood. The younger the age at which the act was committed, however, the more repetitions of delinquent acts, the more serious the offenses committed, and the more a delinquent peer group is involved, the more likely it is that delinquency will continue into adulthood.

Parent-Child Relations

Late adolescents are spending even less time with families than early adolescents. As freshmen in high school, they spent 25 percent of their time with families, but that drops to 15 percent by the time they are seniors, and much less of that 15 percent is spent exclusively with parents.[32]

What kinds of activities do adolescents share with their families? About half the time is spent in routine activities—eating, chores, personal care, studying—and the other half in leisure activities—socializing, watching TV, reading. The family appears to be the place where teens come to rest and recuperate; leisure activities and eating are the preferred activities. Adolescents who spend much time with their families appear more self-controlled and more successful in the school situation than those who do not.[33]

360

CHAPTER 11
Late
Adolescence:
The Years
from Fifteen
to Nineteen

FIGURE 11-3
WHO ADOLESCENTS SPEND THEIR TIME WITH

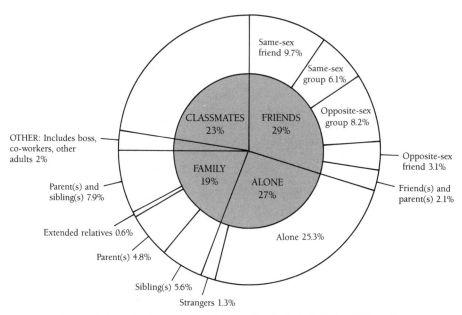

From M. Csikszentmihalyi and R. Larson, *Being Adolescent* (New York: Basic Books, 1984), p. 71.

Though later adolescents may be spending less time in the family, they appear more likely to understand that some activities are done because they benefit the whole family. While conflicts about everyday issues continue, late teens accept and respect their parents' conventional views on situations, and so parents are pleased. Teens do not necessarily give in, but parents are more likely to grant their requests now perhaps because teens seem to understand their reasoning.[34]

When adolescents struggle less over power with their parents, they are able to become more self-governing and independent without giving up warm family relationships. So late teenagers report a greater sense of well-being in the process of separation from parents. When separation occurs in the context of family misunderstandings and emotional distance from the parents, then teens report greater loneliness and feelings of dejection.[35]

When issues of power are settled, then about half the respondents in a large survey report positive relationships with parents, and they want these close relationships to continue as they move through later adolescence.[36]

What makes for positive relationships?[37] Adolescents want parents to trust and accept them, to be warm, to help but not overprotect, to have fun with them. They do not want orders without explanations, parents' just adding, "Because I said so." They do not want nagging, and a "Do it now!" approach. They do not enjoy the "When I was young . . . " lecture. They also do not like parents who are too busy for

TABLE 11-2
WHAT ADOLESCENTS WANT MOST IN LIFE

To be loved	41%
To be healthy	38%
To do the kind of work you really like	29%
To be successful in your work	25%
To be rich	22%
To be married	13%
To do something worthwhile for the world	9%

Jane Norman and Myron Harris, *The Private Life of the American Teenager* (New York: Rawson Wade, 1981), p. 289.

them. Further, they do not approve of parents' bad habits—heavy drinking, lying, hypocrisy.

Diana Baumrind, following families from the child's preschool years through adolescence, examined parental qualities that predict both adolescent competence and absence of substance abuse.[38] She defines competence as the capacity for independent, self-reliant behavior and the capacity for meaningful relationships with other people.

Like Jay Belsky, Elliot Robins, and Wendy Gamble, Baumrind cites parental commitment to children as one of three factors in predicting competence in children. Commitment, along with the balance between demandingness (establishing rules, monitoring compliance, and enforcing the rules) and responsiveness (being supportive of the child and paying attention to the child's needs and interests) are the three main parental influences on children's development. Baumrind finds too that current parenting practices are more important in determining adolescent competence than earlier parenting techniques.

Baumrind describes six different parenting patterns. *Authoritative* parents have strong commitments to children and balance demands with responsiveness to children's needs: "Unlike any other pattern, Authoritative upbringing *consistently* generated competence and deterred problem behavior in both boys and girls, at *all* stages."[39] *Democratic* parents who have strong commitment to children and are highly responsive to their needs are only average in demandingness. Their children are highly competent as well, but are freer to explore drugs.

Nonauthoritarian Directive parents who are high on conventional control and value conformity have children with the least drug use, but this is accomplished by strict obedience to rules so that children are conforming and dependent upon adult approval. *Authoritarian-Directive* parents are even more restrictive and less supportive and have less competent children. Parents of both types are moderately committed to their children.

Unengaged parents are neither demanding nor responsive nor committed to children. They either actively reject or neglect parenting responsibilities. Children from these families are free of adult authority, but they have little direction and so are described as immature. These adolescents have had problems dating back to the pre-

362

CHAPTER 11
Late
Adolescence:
The Years
from Fifteen
to Nineteen

Late teens may spend more time in their bedrooms than in any other setting in the home. Parents are expected to respect the teen's privacy, including phone conversations, mail, and personal effects, but they are also expected to include them in leisure time activities and family events.

school years, and they lack competence in many areas of adolescent functioning. The *Good Enough* parent is about average on the different dimensions, and their children are about average in competence.

Baumrind was surprised that the dimensions of parenting predicting preschool competence continue to predict adolescent functioning. She had expected that the greater freedom of the Democratic families would have been helpful to children in the adolescent years. Baumrind concludes that we live in a society where there is marked instability, and so greater parental protection and supervision are needed.

Adolescents are affected not only by parents' behavior, but also by events in parents' lives that affect their behavior with teens. A study of the effects of economic hardship in the Midwest found that when financial difficulties occur, then parents become less nurturant and less consistent in discipline. Teenagers then become lonely and depressed, and boys sometimes develop acting-out behavior and can become involved in drugs.[40]

The authors of *Being Adolescent* summarize the parents' roles:

> What can an adult do for an adolescent? Perhaps the best thing we can offer is examples—examples of how to choose among goals, how to persevere, how to have patience, how to recognize the challenges of life and enjoy meeting them. We can help adolescents by letting them share our hard-won habits of skill and discipline. We can help by letting them see that achieving control over experience can bring serenity and enjoyment in its wake.[41]

Sibling Relationships

Sibling relationships may improve in later adolescence. As teens become more independent, less competitive, they report that their brothers and sisters are less of a problem. Siblings at this age often help each other through the experiences of adolescence—romances, getting a job, making vocational plans. Interaction seems enjoyable in family gatherings and with extended relatives.

Peers

Peers play many important roles in the psychological development of adolescents. As in previous age periods, they provide opportunities for developing social skills, but peers are also sources of support and understanding in the process of separating from parents. In Japan and the Soviet Union, adolescents spend 2 or 3 hours per week with peers. In the United States, adolescents spend about 20 hours a week with peers, with high school seniors spending almost 25 hours a week.[42] Peers are important not only in terms of time spent with them, but also in terms of the sheer pleasure that comes with these encounters.

Time with friends is spent primarily in leisure—joking, talking, fooling around. From friends, adolescents get a clearer view of themselves. They also get positive feedback and encouragement. If they are depressed, peers help them feel better:

> Close friends can be relaxed with each other and don't need to be aware of their actions. Each can talk freely about emotions and show them. With each other, the two friends have a chance to see themselves wide open; they are not afraid of talking too much about themselves. One can say he likes or dislikes someone, and he knows the other won't tell. One can be in a sour mood one day and know that the other will understand. Best friends can complain to each other, and most important, they can act stupid or silly, loud or crazy with one another and understand that there is no need to feel that the silliness endangers the friendship.[43]

Adolescents who are well liked by others share many characteristics. They like other people and are sympathetic and understanding of their problems. They are cheerful, lively, and fun to be around. They like to plan events, and their enthusiasm arouses others. Thus, they make others feel comfortable and accepted by promoting positive social interactions or by planning enjoyable events. Other adolescents are less well liked for a variety of reasons. Some are ignored or neglected because they are social isolates who retreat in nervous shyness. Others arouse antagonisms because they are aggressive, demand attention, are critical and complaining.

Adolescents feel very loyal to their friends. Not only are they loyal in continuing friendship, despite parental disapproval, but they are also loyal in not revealing details of the relationship to others. Although overall 56 percent would report that a friend was considering suicide, far fewer (17–20 percent) would break a confidence about drugs and alcohol, and almost none (6 percent) would tell if a friend was shoplifting.[44]

Though intimacy and support are important positive elements in individual friendships, group situations provide different experiences. Teens become boisterous, loud, expressive; they "let go" in these situations. They seem to feel free to be carried along in group activities. They yield control to the group and, in a sense, practice giving up control. Teens have to learn to leave the group, however, if lack of control exceeds a reasonable limit. Otherwise, they can be carried too far and do things they personally do not approve of.

364

CHAPTER 11
Late
Adolescence:
The Years
from Fifteen
to Nineteen

Dating

Dating serves many important functions in adolescence. It is a way to learn how to relate to people of the opposite sex; it provides a structure for meeting people, exploring compatibility, and terminating a relationship with a minimum of embarrassment. Finally, dating gives practice in developing feelings of trust and enjoyment with the opposite sex.

Although the sexual revolution has brought many changes, still the concerns of adolescents who date are much the same as those of their parents. "Will he like me?" "Will she go out with me?" "What do I say on a date?" Girls still wait for boys to call, and almost two-thirds of a national sample of girls say they have never asked a boy out. Boys rather enjoy being asked out, and only 13 percent said it would "turn them off."[45]

What qualities do boys and girls seek in each other? Over 90 percent of girls ages sixteen to twenty-one said the important qualities in boys are good personality, kindness, good manners, a sense of humor. Over 70 percent said compassion, good looks, and charm are important. The least popular qualities are heavy drinking, inability to communicate, drug use, and profanity, followed by indecisiveness, being a "super jock" and not being affectionate. Boys said they are initially attracted by a good figure and good looks, but for them, too, the most important qualities are personality and a good sense of humor—then beauty, intelligence, and psychological warmth. So even though boys place an initial emphasis on physical qualities, they are basically seeking the same qualities in girls that girls seek in them.[46]

Most girls begin dating at about fourteen and boys between fourteen and fifteen. By their senior year in high school, about half of adolescents date more than once a week, and one-third between two and three times a week. It is widely held that boys are oriented toward sexual activity more than girls. But even though adolescent boys desire physical intimacy early in the dating relationship, they, too, want increasing affection and intimacy as the relationship progresses, just as girls do.[47]

About one-quarter of boys and one-third of girls say they are going steady. Going steady occurs most frequently among older adolescents sixteen to eighteen; 30 percent of boys and 40 percent of girls of this age say they are going steady. Over half the adolescents say they have been in love, with girls reporting this more frequently than boys. The intensity of these feelings and the pain that comes when the relationship ends rival anything any adult feels in such a situation. Some love relationships of adolescence develop into more committed relationships, but frequently the feelings fade.[48]

Adolescents who have definite educational and vocational plans and who wish for marriages like those of their parents go steady less often and report being in love less often during adolescence. When girls have high self-esteem, they date more often but go steady less often. Those who are most likely to be going steady do not want marriages like their parents. As noted in Chapter 10, involvement in dating that is too early and too intense may block opportunities for same-sex relationships or more casual opposite-sex relationships that develop the capacity for intimacy and closeness at later ages.

Adolescents believe that the quality of the relationship between people, the way they treat each other, is the most important factor in making the decision about sexual activity. About three-quarters of adolescents today believe it is all right for people to have sex before marriage if they love each other, and about two-thirds believe that what two people want to do sexually is moral if they both want to do it and it doesn't hurt anyone. Over two-thirds believe that two people should not have to get married in order to live together.[49]

Although both boys and girls are more liberal than before, girls still tie sexual relations to feelings of love, and 75 percent say they would have sexual relations only if they loved the person. An almost equal number of boys insist that they must like the person, but only 47 percent tie having sexual intercourse to feelings of love for the other person.[50]

Several different patterns of sexual activity emerge during adolescence, however. Most adolescents have one partner with whom they have close emotional ties. Partners care about each other and are open and honest with each other. Though there is no definite commitment to each other, more than half believe they will marry the person they have intercourse with. These people are termed **serial monogamists** because they have only one partner at a time and find another when that relationship ends.[51] A very small group of both boys and girls—about 8 percent—are **sexual adventurers**.[52] They have many partners and little involvement with each one. They enjoy the experience of sexual activity but feel love does not need to be part of the relationship for them to experience pleasure. Sexual adventurers, as a group, report more difficulty with parents, do not like to be around them, and do not respect them as much as monogamists respect their parents. Though adventurers want many partners, girls who fall in this category do not experience orgasm as often as girls who are serial monogamists.

Increases in premarital intercourse for girls may cause observers to overlook the conservative views many adolescent girls hold. Girls are usually going steady with their first sexual partner, and a large number plan on marrying the partner. Girls are more likely to feel anxious and fearful after their first intercourse, and about 40 percent wish they had waited. In contrast, boys usually feel positive and optimistic about their first intercourse, even though in nearly half the instances the girl was not someone they knew well.[53]

Even though adolescents are more active sexually today than previously, they are not using contraceptives on a widespread basis. Only about one-third of sexually active women aged fifteen to nineteen always use contraceptives. About 27 percent never use contraceptives, and still another third do only sometimes.[54] Girls with high self-esteem who are confident and happy with their lives and on good terms with their parents are most likely to use contraceptives. Boys who are older, more responsible, and have parents who approve of sexual activity are most likely to use contraceptives. When used, the most popular methods are condoms, withdrawal, and the pill.[55]

Those sexually active adolescents not using contraceptives seem to have more psychological difficulties. Girls tend to be passive, fatalistic individuals who feel helpless in controlling their lives. Boys tend to be either naive or exploitive, believing

366

CHAPTER 11
Late
Adolescence:
The Years
from Fifteen
to Nineteen

it is the girl's responsibility.[56] Unfortunately, failure to use contraceptives leads to an increasing number of adolescent pregnancies. Those adolescents who get pregnant are precisely those with psychological characteristics that make early parenthood very difficult. About 1 million girls between ages fifteen and nineteen become pregnant each year. In 1976, 16 percent of sexually active fifteen-year-olds and 35 percent of sexually active nineteen-year-olds experienced premarital conception.[57]

We have seen that with changing attitudes about sexuality in our society, sexual activity has increased. Girls and upper-socioeconomic status boys have experienced greater increases in sexual activity than boys in general. Even with all the changes, however, we must keep in mind that many girls—about 25 percent—do not have premarital sexual experience and many wish they had waited.

PARENTING TASKS

Parents serve as communicators, models, consultants, and limit-setters for late adolescents. They can be most helpful by providing objective information and being available for questions as children apply this information in their lives. Teenagers want their parents' opinions and insights, but they also want to make up their own minds. To accomplish these tasks, parents must set aside the time to be with adolescents—time to talk to them, time to listen to them, time to have fun with them, and time to work together. Teenagers value the contact, and it has positive benefits for all family members. As noted earlier, enjoying pleasurable times together fosters close relationships.

Serving as a Consultant

Parents frequently serve as their children's consultants on sexual behavior. What can parents do to help adolescents make informed choices? First, parents make sure that adolescents have accurate information about reproduction, fertility control, and the use of contraceptives for protected sex. Many parents may not want to discuss the possibility of having sexual relations, fearing that such discussion may appear to give permission for such activity. Nevertheless, having accurate information is a major safeguard against early sexual activity.

Another major safeguard against the risks of sexual activity is postponing the activity until teens are better able to handle the responsibilities.[58] Parental communication with adolescents is associated with postponement. Equally important, parents encourage teens to have interests and sources of gratification that absorb time and attention so that sexual activity can be postponed more easily.

Adolescents must see the relevance of factual information to their personal lives. Many teens believe that pregnancy could not happen to them, and parents need to help them see that pregnancy can happen. Adolescents also must have the social skills to use the information. Are they able to withstand the pressure for sexual activity? Are they able to seek out information that they need? Are they able to use contraceptives or insist that their partner use contraceptives as well? Parents can discuss in general terms how hard it is to be assertive, yet how important for personal well-being.

In addition to providing information, establishing open communication, encouraging interests and the development of assertive social skills, parents also provide supervision. As far as possible, they do not permit teens to be in situations that can lead to spontaneous sexual activity. For example, since first intercourse most often happens at home, parents do not go away for the weekend and leave teenagers alone at home. Teenagers need to stay with friends. Parental supervision is related to delay in sexual activity.[59]

Briggs reminds us that good insurance for healthy sexual behavior is high self-esteem:

> A sense of personal values insulates a youngster from selling himself short and lessens interest in irresponsible sexual behavior. The youngster who likes himself seeks wholesome relationships that nourish self-esteem rather than meaningless ones that tear it apart. Belief in himself makes a youngster less wary of commitment—he knows he can handle it. And he is freer to take a firm stand on moral issues. And his self-respect makes him seek others who handle their lives similarly.[60]

Parents also serve as consultants when teenagers want to enter the world of work. Ellen Greenberger and Laurence Steinberg suggest parents play an active role in discussing the pros and cons of work in the light of the child's needs and other demands on the child's time.[61] If work is an option, then parents can help teens decide the kind of job that would meet their needs—how many hours, how far from home, the exact time of day for working, ways to handle the money. Parents then monitor the child's work experience after the job has started to be sure it is not too stressful and does not have negative effects on school work, friendships, and social behavior like drinking. If it does, then parents can discuss changing the job or the hours.

The ways that parents can help teenagers make long-term vocational plans are similar to the ways they help them make choices about sexual activity. Parents can provide factual information about expanding fields and possible careers, about the personal qualities and interests needed to do various kinds of work, and about how teenagers can get more information and test their interests. Parents can also provide information about possible occupations based on their observation of children's skills and interests. Ginott has an excellent section on the importance of parental appreciation of those very special acts and traits that can only be seen at home and about the need to tell children about their special talents.

Parents also can help children develop the interpersonal skills and the self-confidence that will enable them to pursue vocational goals. They can talk about how to prepare for interviews, how to present abilities and special qualifications for a job, how to remain at ease in an interview. At times of failure and frustration, parents can offer encouragement and suggest alternative actions. As children make choices, however, parents must stand back and keep silent.

In the past, parents have encouraged a commitment to work for boys but not for girls. Because work is now a more important part of a woman's life across the life span, parents encourage their daughters as well as their sons to search for meaningful work that they can enjoy.

368

CHAPTER 11
Late
Adolescence:
The Years
from Fifteen
to Nineteen

 THE JOYS OF PARENTING LATE ADOLESCENTS

"I think it's really fun to watch them grow up and mature. It's fun to see them discover things about themselves and their lives. The older ones have boyfriends, and I'm seeing them interact with the boyfriends." MOTHER

"Sometimes the kids have friends over, and they all start to talk about things. It's nice to see them get along with their siblings as well as their friends. It gives you a good feeling to see them enjoying themselves." FATHER

"I felt very pleased when my son at sixteen could get a summer job in the city and commute and be responsible for getting there and doing a good job." MOTHER

"I like it when they sit around and reminisce about the things they or the family have done in the past. They sit around the table and talk about an outing or a trip we took, saying 'Remember this?' It's always interesting what they remember. This last summer we took a long sightseeing trip, and what stands out in their minds about it is funny. They remember Filene's basement in Boston or a chicken ranch where we stopped to see friends. One father took the scouts on a ski trip. They got stuck in the snow on the highway for hours, and the car almost slid off the road. He said, 'Never again.' I said, 'Don't you realize that because of those things, the boys will probably remember that trip forever. You have given them wonderful memories.'" MOTHER

"I really enjoy her happiness. She always sees the positive side to a situation. Things might bother her from time to time, but she has a good perspective on things." FATHER

"I really like to see them taking responsibility. Yesterday they had a school holiday, and I was donating some time at an open house fundraiser. They got all dressed up and came along and helped too. The older one coaches a soccer team of four-year-olds, and the younger is a patrol leader in the Scouts, so they both have responsibility for children. They complain sometimes that it's hard to get the little kids' attention to show them things, but I think they like it." MOTHER

General Guidelines

The strategists whose work is discussed in this book, including the behaviorists Eimers and Aitchison,[62] agree that parents need to provide many opportunities for meaningful communication of feelings between parent and child, and for self-direction by teenagers. And parents must provide models of responsible behavior.

Briggs emphasizes that parents must not give children reasons to feel guilty about wanting to separate from parents.[63] Parents need to recognize when it is time for teenagers to rely as much on peers as on themselves. She stresses the usefulness of a sense of humor in easing the ups and downs of life with adolescents. A good laugh about the funny side of a frustrating incident can restore a cheerful family atmosphere. And that increases the likelihood of finding a reasonable solution.

"I enjoy that she is following in the family tradition of rowing. I rowed in college, and my brothers did, my father and grandfather did, and she saw a city team and signed up. She does it all on her own and has made a nice group of friends through it." FATHER

"I can't believe that she has had her first boyfriend and it worked out so well. They met at a competition; and he lives some distance away, so they talk on the phone. He has a friend who lives here, and he comes for a visit sometime and does lots of things with the family. We all like him, and it is nice for her to have a boyfriend like that." MOTHER

"The joys are seeing them go from a totally disorganized state to a partially motivated, organized state. You can see their adult characteristics emerging." FATHER

"I enjoy seeing my daughter develop musical ability, seeing her progression from beginning flute to an accomplished player who performs, and seeing how much pleasure she takes in her accomplishment." MOTHER

"It really gives me a lot of pleasure to see the two of them help each other. They seem to have respect for each other. She is the brain and helps him with school, and he helps her too at times." FATHER

"I enjoy his maturity. He's so responsible. He tests us, but when we're firm, he accepts that. I'm real proud of him because he looks at the consequences of what he does." FATHER

"I enjoy his honesty and the relationship he has with his friends. He is real open with his feelings, and his friends look up to him. He's a leader." MOTHER

"He's not prejudiced. His best friends are of different ethnic groups. People trust him and like him because he's real concerned about people." FATHER

"I feel really pleased about the way the boys get along together. There is rivalry, but there is a lot of love. The older one takes the younger one under his wing, and the younger one looks up to him." FATHER

Shirley Gould, who applies the theories of Rudolf Dreikurs to the adolescent years, emphasizes the importance of parents' accepting their own imperfections.[64] When parents do not accept themselves, they become overly upset by any problems children experience. When a child has trouble, these parents experience guilt, a mixture of failure, shame, blame, and depression. If these feelings are intense, they can trigger a variety of responses. Parents may become defensive and offer excuses for why the child is having trouble or why they themselves are worried. They may verbally attack others, often children, hoping to stimulate guilt in them. Parents may withdraw and say nothing, holding the guilt in, or they may cry long and hard, giving up any chance to control what is happening.

If parents understand the purpose of guilt feelings, they may be better able to

CHAPTER 11
Late
Adolescence:
The Years
from Fifteen
to Nineteen

handle them. Gould believes parental guilt feelings are attempts to: (1) control others and force them to do what we want, (2) demonstrate suffering in order to get appreciation from others, (3) punish ourselves, (4) get sympathy, and (5) prove our own worth. Guilt, she believes, is mainly a sign of good intentions that we wanted to succeed but were unable to accomplish our goals. Accepting that we will fall short of our goals, and dealing with guilt as outlined in Chapter 2, enables individuals to get on with the business of living in a confident, constructive, productive manner.

Many parents find it difficult to accept a limited role during the teen years, when children's decisions can have serious consequences. Yet the agreement among all strategists is impressive. At no other age period is there such uniformity of opinion about the appropriate path for parents. Parents of teenagers are advised to be models for their children, stimulators of communication, and consultants.

We have relied on research and experts to tell us what children need. But in this age period children's opinions are at least as objective and insightful. What do they think? A bright, perceptive teenage girl, Tina deVaron, has described the parents' role in the teenage years:

> Now that I'm sixteen, and can look back on my growing up, I see parents as valuable in two ways. I am learning to live with others and myself at the same time, and if I have difficulties, they will not walk out on me if I get a little hard to live with. They are also my blood relations, they have known me longer and better than anyone else. Because of this, I can be sure that they, above all others, will stand behind me if I get in a bind. The love they gave me as a child has helped me to reinforce this feeling, and helped me to feel how important we are to each other.[65]

The usual problems of adolescence are intensified by behavioral problems of childhood. If parents have been overprotective or neglecting, children will have greater difficulty making and carrying out independent decisions. If teenagers have never had satisfying friendships with important emotional interchanges, they will be poorly prepared to handle the difficulties of achieving peer acceptance, and they may acquiesce easily to peer pressure. When control of impulses and physical activity has always been hard, teenagers will find it hard to cope with the excessive push to action that many feel during these years.

David Elkind has pointed out that adolescents may try to pay parents back for treatment they felt was unfair when they were younger.[66] As young people achieve increasing capacity to earn their own money, physical equality with parents, and freedom to drive and do things for themselves, many feel that they are, at last, on somewhat equal footing with parents. If they have felt mistreated, now they are capable of redressing the imbalance between what parents have demanded and what they have given. Nevertheless, most teenagers *do* want good relationships, and family ties can be strengthened during these years.

ROUTINES, PROBLEMS, AND STRATEGIES

The problems encountered during adolescence relate to physical and intellectual functioning, social behavior, and family interactions. Among the most prevalent and difficult are those associated with family, school, friends, and social behavior—shyness, dress, sexual activity, and limit-setting that involves curfew and the use of alcohol and drugs.

Eating Problems

As physical growth stabilizes during the adolescent years, most teenagers attain a desirable weight and maintain it with only occasional departures that are corrected with diet. A minority of adolescents, however, develop problems in eating that result in obesity (gross overweight), **anorexia nervosa** (severe underweight), or **bulimia nervosa** (binge eating followed by self-induced vomiting or purging with laxatives). In contrast to obesity and anorexia, which are observable because they change physical appearance, bulimia may be difficult to detect because the bulimic frequently maintains average weight.

These three eating problems are not entirely distinct from each other. About 50 percent of anorexics are also bulimics who use vomiting and purging to lose their weight. Anorexics and bulimics may, at one point, have been obese or become obese as they grow older. It is difficult to know the exact numbers of adolescents suffering from these eating disorders. Though anorexia and bulimia are rare, they do appear to be increasing in the population. These two disorders are more commonly seen in girls than boys, most probably because physical attractiveness, defined as thinness, is so valued for girls in our society.

Although the three eating problems have different outcomes in terms of physical appearance, they share several features in common. Each condition may be caused by a variety of factors: hereditary factors play a role in weight gain; physical factors such as metabolism or feedback control mechanisms may be related to anorexia nervosa; family patterns of eating and interacting influence eating behavior. Though physical and biological factors play a role, psychological and social factors are thought to be the major contributors to these disorders.

Many kinds of psychological factors can predispose individuals to gain or lose excessive weight. In the case of obesity, families may equate love with food; adolescents may then use food to buffer them in times of disappointment. In the case of all three eating disorders, problems in identity formation may underlie the behavior. Teenagers who have found it difficult to establish separate identities for themselves as worthwhile, valued individuals may overeat, starve, or purge themselves. Anorexics often have outstanding successes in many areas but still do not feel competent and independent even though others believe they are. Underlying concerns about sexuality and interactions with opposite-sex peers can spur eating problems that prevent appropriate dating and sexual behavior because appearance is so deviant.

Eating problems in turn create difficulties. People with eating disorders often feel self-conscious, depressed, and discouraged about their pattern of eating. Bulimics often fear being discovered in their purging, anorexics fear their weight loss will be noted. (Most adolescents, in fact, feel others are critical of them for their eating behaviors.) Not only do psychological problems result, but serious medical conditions can follow as well. Bulimia can lead to metabolic changes, electrolyte imbalances, ulcers, bowel problems. Severe overweight can result in heart and blood

372

CHAPTER 11
Late
Adolescence:
The Years
from Fifteen
to Nineteen

pressure problems, diabetes. Anorexia can result in electrolyte imbalances, malnutrition, cessation of menstruation, and even death in between 5 and 15 percent of cases.

Parents whose children develop these problems can first consult physicians for medical confirmation of the problem and for help in planning treatment. Parents play a role in modifying eating behavior by having appropriate foods at home and establishing regular mealtimes that are enjoyable occasions for all family members. Parents are also advised to seek psychological counseling for children with these difficulties. In some instances, family counseling that includes all members of the family is the treatment of choice. Salvador Minuchin and his associates,[67] for example, report very good treatment results for anorexics when they and their families are seen together. In some cases, individual or group therapy may be most useful. Individual therapy is most helpful in getting at conflicts that underlie the eating disorder. Group therapy can enable adolescents to share their feelings about the psychological factors that cause and follow the eating disorder. Adolescents often get strong feelings of support for themselves in these groups. Parents also help children with their eating problems when they act to increase their children's self-esteem and self-confidence.

Dress and Physical Appearance

In matters of dress and physical appearance, all strategists agree that the choices belong to the teenager except under special circumstances. Accepting such an approach is not easy for many parents. One father wanted his children to dress to please his peer group, not theirs. When he thought about the problem, he realized that his children were individuals who were also trying to please their peer group. He accepted their desire to be like their friends and said no more about the issue.

Special circumstances will permit parents a greater say in the matter. For example, if teenagers are going to attend a function made up of parents' friends, then the young people will dress to be more acceptable in that group. If they feel they cannot, parents might ask them to stay home. When adolescents see that what they do has a specific effect on the parents, they often will change, as seen in an example cited by Gordon. The father, a school principal, felt his son's long hair jeopardized his job in a conservative city. When he explained the tangible effect of his son's appearance on him, the boy cut his hair.

Alcohol and Drugs

Since parents often serve as consultants on these topics, general information on adolescent substance use is valuable so parents can form a realistic assessment of their child's behavior. In their discussion of adolescents and drugs, John Conger and Anne Petersen make several important general points.[68] First, as a society we have been developing into a "drug culture" for years. The most widely used drug in the country is the tranquilizer Valium, and over one-third of all prescriptions written are for diet and pep pills. In their use of mind-altering substances, adolescents follow in adults' footsteps. The actual choice of drugs is different, but reliance on mind-altering drugs is characteristic of our society as a whole. Second, while some adolescents are serious substance abusers, the vast majority are not. Third, the use of substances seemed to plateau between 1979 and 1981; since then, there has been a slight decrease. For example, in 1978, 10.7 percent of high school students were regular users of marijuana, but by 1981 only 7 percent were. Adolescent substance abuse is still a matter for concern, however.

Cigarettes In 1979, about 12 percent of adolescents between twelve and eighteen smoked cigarettes at least weekly. Though this represents an overall decrease in boys' smoking from a high of 31 percent in 1968, it does represent a general increase in girls' smoking.[69]

Though adolescents know the health risks of smoking, they continue to do it. Adolescents with parents and older siblings who smoke, as well as early adolescents with peers who smoke, are the most likely to develop the habit.

Alcohol Alcohol is the mind-altering substance most widely used and abused by teenagers. By the end of adolescence almost all teenagers have at least tried alcohol. In 1981, 93 percent of high school seniors said they had tried it, and 71 percent said they had had a drink in the last 30 days. Not only is alcohol used more widespread than it was in the 1960s, it begins at earlier ages and involves more serious drinking.[70]

In 1975, 6 percent of high school seniors reported daily use of alcohol, and 12 percent reported drinking heavily (more than five drinks at one sitting) three to five times in the previous 2 weeks. In another national study, 21 percent of tenth and twelfth grade boys and 9 percent of girls were categorized as heavy drinkers—drinking more than 2.7 ounces of absolute alcohol at least once a week. Further, 4.3 percent of thirteen-year-olds and 10 percent of fourteen-year-olds were classified as heavy drinkers.[71]

Who does the heavy drinking? In general, those who drink are gregarious, social, impulsive adolescents who break many kinds of rules—cutting school, cheating, speeding in cars, using other drugs. Many times they report feeling bored, unable to get going. Girls report feeling lonely, irritable, depressed, and agitated. At all ages, heavy drinkers report more problems with their parents.

Marijuana Apart from alcohol, marijuana is the most widely used drug in North America. Surveys reveal that 25 percent of all adults and 40 percent of teenagers have had some experience with marijuana. Like alcohol use, marijuana use may be declining slightly. Most recent figures indicate that 59 percent of seniors have used it at some point, 32 percent have used it in the last 30 days, 7 percent are daily users, and 5 percent use marijuana more than forty times a month.[72] Only 5 percent go on to other drugs.

Marijuana's effects depend on the strength of the dose, the personality characteristics of the user, and the social setting in which it is used. People who are anticipating a good time, who are with people they like and trust, and who are fairly stable individuals report feelings of pleasure, warmth, relaxation. People who are distrustful and are in an unsupportive environment may find their feelings of anxiety and suspicion enhanced by the drug.

374

CHAPTER 11
Late
Adolescence:
The Years
from Fifteen
to Nineteen

Though marijuana produces positive feelings, it has several negative effects as well. Cognitive and motor functioning change. At low dosages and with simple tasks the effects are minimal, but with more complicated tasks or with higher dosages comes impairment in learning tasks, especially in tasks involving long-term memory. The 4 to 10 percent who are heavy users show failure in developing skills, interests, and effective ways of coping with stress.

At present, we do not know the long-term effects of marijuana use. There is no definitive evidence that it causes permanent damage to the brain, changes to reproductive functioning, or leads to a **burnout** syndrome in which the person is passive, has a shortened attention span, and appears confused and lacking in motivation. Burnout may be related to the use of marijuana with harder drugs.

Cocaine Since 1981 small, steady declines have been found in the use of most drugs, with the exception of cocaine. There were increases of up to 40 percent in lifetime use reported in samples of young adults. However, there is now more appreciation of the risk that cocaine represents; and in 1987, a decline in interest in cocaine was observed. Still, a study reported in 1987 that 15 percent of seniors in high school had tried cocaine and 6 percent had tried crack.[73]

Other Drugs Very small percentages of adolescents use other drugs such as amphetamines, barbiturates, heroin, and hallucinogens like LSD. Many of these drugs are available at high schools, so adolescents have choices about using them. Adolescents are at an age when they are more likely to feel invulnerable to negative effects, and they are curious about what the drugs are like. Though experimentation with drugs carries risks, clinicians are most concerned about that small percentage who become regular heavy users as a way of coping with problems.

As with other substances, family patterns associated with drug use are poor communication between parents and children, parents who blame children for all family problems, and parents who ignore the child's opinions, ideas, and preferences—in brief, a family environment in which the child is treated as a nonentity.

Two longitudinal studies provide information on the antecedents and implications of substance use and abuse in the high school years.[74] Both samples were followed from the preschool years with careful assessments of both parents and children. Children's substance use was determined in interviews in the 1980s.

Though investigators categorized substance use slightly differently, both found that the most serious use of alcohol and drugs in their samples was related to serious psychological problems both in adolescence and in early and middle childhood. In both studies, adolescents with the most serious alcohol and drug use lack general competence, have poor impulse control, and experience emotional distress. In Diana Baumrind's study, these problems date back to preschool years; and in Jonathan Shedler and Jack Block's study, frequent users have different personality characteristics from experimenters and abstainers as early as age seven, when they relate poorly to other children and feel generally insecure.

Both studies find that adolescents who experiment casually with drugs do not have serious psychological problems and, in fact, are competent, outgoing adolescents. These studies find, too, that many abstainers are anxious, conforming individuals who are fearful of taking risks. Baumrind divided abstainers into two groups—risk-avoidant nonusers and rational nonusers who justify their choice for realistic reasons—"I don't like my mood changed chemically." Risk-avoidant nonusers are less explorative, less resilient, and less competent than rational nonusers who are more socially and intellectually confident.

Several family variables are identified as antecedents. Baumrind found that adolescent substance use parallels parent use. Abstainers come from families where parents do not use substances, and abusers come from families where parents abuse substances. Adolescents with the lowest substance use come from nonauthoritarian-directive and authoritative homes (see the Parent-Child section for descriptions of these parenting patterns), and the abusers from unengaged families where they lack direction and encouragement. Findings from the Shedler and Block study reinforce the view that abusers come from disorganized, unprotective families. Abstainers, as in Baumrind's study, come from homes where parents exert control over children, but these homes are not as supportive and encouraging as are the families of nonusers in the Baumrind sample.

The agreement in the findings of the two studies is noteworthy. Both indicate casual or experimental use occurs in the context of competent, outgoing social behavior in adolescents. The most serious use of substances is associated with lack of competence and psychological problems dating back to early and middle childhood. Shedler and Block point out the importance of recognizing the long-standing nature of the substance abuser's problems and the need for extensive help if the problem is to be dealt with.

Although some parents may be alert to their child's relationship to drugs, many parents overlook indicators of possible drug use because the idea is painful to them. They ignore their children's grade changes, lack of energy, lack of interest in usual activities, changes in friends, and changes in aggressive behavior. They engage in what writer Beth Polson and psychologist Miller Newton term **parent denial**, refusing to look at the problem and pretending it is not there.[75] Parents find many excuses for their teen's altered behavior, and most teens who are using drugs are happy to accept the excuses put forth by parents.

Newton's experience with his son provides an illuminating example. Newton served as the executive director of the state association of alcohol treatment in Florida, and his wife was a supervising counselor at a treatment agency. Both parents were knowledgable about the use of at least one drug. Their two older children, nineteen and twenty, were both happy and competent people. The first time their fifteen-year-old son Mark came home drunk, the family rallied around him, gave him information about alcoholism in the family, and began to monitor his behavior more closely. He was a bright, curious boy with many interests and a passion for healthy living, so the family was unprepared for the next drunk episode two months later. Mark was violent and threatening with his father and brother. At that time he admitted he was using some pot as well.

Close family supervision followed, and Mark was allowed to go only certain places and had to be home at certain times. His parents said that if there were recurrences, Mark would go into a treatment program. When a fight erupted a few months later, the parents found evidence of much drug use. Mark entered a residential treatment program and has been free of drugs for four years.

376

CHAPTER 11
Late
Adolescence:
The Years
from Fifteen
to Nineteen

In their book *Not My Kid: A Parent's Guide to Kids and Drugs*, Polson and Newton outline actions parents can take to promote a healthy, drug-free adolescence.[76] They insist that how families live day by day is the most important factor. Parents need to be involved family members who know what their children are doing and who their friends are. Then they make it clear to adolescents that theirs is a drug-free family in which (1) no one uses an illegal drug or misuses any legal drugs or prescriptions; (2) there is no routine use of alcohol by parents; (3) no intoxication by adults; (4) no alcohol use by underage children; (5) no use of drugs to lose weight, sleep, relax, or wake up. Every family member agrees to this contract. If a child is found to be using some drugs, parents call the parents of all the child's friends to discuss ways of promoting organized student activities.

If a child tries drugs, the family contract is repeated. If the behavior continues, the child is taken to some additional form of counseling that deals with the child and the family. Since family members can help drug-oriented children, it is important for there to be family counseling in addition to any individual therapy prescribed. As in many other areas, the family joins together with other families to provide support and activity to promote a healthier, safer adolescence.

School Problems

Teenagers cut classes; they ignore homework assignments; they fail to complete courses; they pick courses that will not prepare them for what they say they want to do; they drop out of school. All strategists advise parents to move cautiously. School work and college and vocational choices fall in the areas where children make choices. Parents, however, can be helpful consultants. Parents can place responsibility on children, question the source of the problem, seek remedies, and support children's coping techniques by reminding them of earlier successes. They can also communicate their feelings about the seriousness of the situation and the importance of dealing with it. This approach takes more time than criticism or advice on how to improve.

Gould reports a school problem handled in a similar way even though the consequences were serious. Peter, fourteen and a freshman in high school, began to cut classes. His parents, both college graduates with advanced degrees, emphasized education. But when Peter reached the age where he could drop out of school, he asked them to sign the required form and they did so. They realized they could not make him study or enjoy school. Peter got a job and supported himself while he continued to live at home. Eventually, he decided he needed more education and returned to school at night to get his high school diploma. Then Peter asked his parents to support him while he went to college full time. His parents insisted that he show some signs of determination, and he completed two semesters, paying for half his expenses himself. Then they paid for the rest of his college education.

Fitzhugh Dodson cites an example of how parents can be consultants in helping children with courses of study. He received the following letter:

My son is sixteen and he just despises the academic aspects of school (and 90 percent of it is academic). The only things he likes are wood shop, metal shop, auto mechanics, and P.E.

He does poorly in all of his academic subjects. But he is very good with his hands. He loves to take his car apart and work on it, and he's terrific when it comes to fixing our TV set or tinkering with radios or CBs. But college is coming up soon, and I don't know what to do.[77]

Dodson advises getting information on community colleges or trade schools nearby since the son seems to be suited for a skilled trade. Show the young man the variety of skilled trades and how to get some training in whatever one appeals to him. Dodson concludes with this comment: "Some parents have a snobbish resistance to the idea of their son or daughter learning a skilled trade instead of going to an academic college. I think this is a mistake. Better a good auto mechanic, happy at his job, than an unhappy and inept teacher or insurance salesman."[78]

Curfews

Once children have friends, they want to stay out. When adolescents come home after the agreed-upon time, parents worry. Ginott and Gordon both recommend expressing the fear and worry that underlie the anger parents often express when children are late. One parent who had been following Ginott varied the curfew with the occasion and encouraged her daughter to call if she were to be late. The mother told the girl that she would like a worry-free evening; the girl accepted her parent's concern and called.

Krumboltz and Krumboltz describe an active way to handle lateness.[79] Parents can set an alarm clock for 15 minutes after the curfew. If the child is home, then he or she turns off the alarm before it goes off. If the child is still out, the alarm alerts the parents. Dodson, using behavioral principles, suggests overlooking lateness of 15 or 20 minutes. He says if children come home 45 minutes or an hour late, parents are entitled to make a ruckus.

A more unusual curfew problem was cited by Briggs. A teenager asked her mother to come downstairs five minutes after she came home from a dance with her boyfriend and insist that she come to bed. When the mother asked why, the daughter said the boy liked to "make out," and she was not interested. The mother came down as instructed and delivered her message. As she went upstairs, she heard her daughter whisper, "She's a drag, isn't she?" Briggs explains that the daughter needed a scapegoat, so that her denial seemed not to be what she wanted but what she was forced to do. Briggs advises parents to help children be assertive, clear about what they want, and able to communicate their own wishes in a gentle but firm way.

Express your concern about the child's welfare. Adjust curfews if they are unreasonable. If lateness is habitual, this should be discussed in a family session.

Choice of Friends

By the time children reach their teens, they are aware of the qualities that their parents value in people. They are also, more than ever before in their lives, subject to pressures from their peers. And they are experiencing for the first time the strong and unfamiliar stirrings of sexual feelings. Small wonder, then, that our teens—pushed and pulled by these many influences—often seem to pick friends we find less than desirable.

378

CHAPTER 11
Late
Adolescence:
The Years
from Fifteen
to Nineteen

Sometimes they are wiser and more discerning than we are. The quiet girl who dresses in dull colors turns out, on closer acquaintance, to be bright and kind and gentle, and interesting too. The very tall, fidgety boy with all those freckles and a strange laugh, we learn after a few weeks, is good with cars and even better with pets—and not afraid to express his affection for animals or people, or food.

But what should parents do when a teenager loses her good sense over a Robert Redford look-alike who is inconsiderate and insensitive, or when an adolescent son can suddenly think and talk about nothing but what the parent sees as an empty-headed cheerleader?

All the strategies discussed in this book agree that parents should not intervene directly to forbid or end a relationship. Instead, they should do what behaviorists call "letting the behavior run its course." The child's choice is respected, and the child respects the parents' feelings. The strategies differ on how parents should express their reservations. The possibilities include waiting to comment, refusing to encourage or facilitate the relationship, and arranging situations in which the child can see the problem as the parents do.

When teens pick same-sex friends with different values, parents may worry that their children will be led into situations they cannot handle—heavy drinking, speeding in cars, cutting school. Parents should first examine their own reactions. Is the friend really likely to create trouble for your child? Or are you objecting to less important characteristics, such as appearance and manners? If the friend really is a problem, does your child have some underlying conflict or need that attracts him or her to such a friend? Does your child feel insecure and seek out a daredevil to mask the insecurity? If so, it is best for parents to deal with the underlying problem and try to find ways of bolstering confidence.

If you are objecting because the friend has a terrible driving record, cuts school frequently, or is failing courses, sit down and share your concerns with your teenager. Respect the child's right to have this friend, but point out the possible consequences to your child. If not pressured, the child will be able to understand what you are saying and may begin to spend less time with the friend. If the two continue to spend time together, it is possible that the friend may change. It is also possible that, as you get to know the friend, you may begin to understand why your child values this friendship. If the friendship continues and trouble does result for your child or seems about to occur, you may want to take action to end the relationship by forbidding it. This is difficult to enforce if the teen is determined to see the friend. In some situations, however, this firm action may be what your child wants.

Ginott tells of a situation in which parents gave their teenager freedom of choice yet exerted influence by raising questions for her to consider. Their eighteen-year-old daughter felt she had met the boy of her dreams. Her mother worried she was being swept away in a world of fantasy and physical attraction, and was not asking practical questions about how compatible they might be in a permanent relationship. The mother, however, did not raise these issues while her daughter was up in the clouds. Empathizing with her daughter's feelings, she waited for the best time to suggest realistic considerations.

Gould cites the example of a boy in his late teens who became interested in a girl his parents disapproved of. Gould advises being pleasant to the girl, but says the parents do not need to lend the car for dates nor entertain her in their home.

In another example, described by Krumboltz and Krumboltz, a couple found that their sixteen-year-old daughter was serious about an older boy they disliked, and they feared an early marriage would occur.[80] They disliked the boy and were worried because their daughter wanted to go steady. Instead of forbidding the relationship, they invited the boy to eat all weekday dinners with them and to spend time on weekends going on family excursions. The parents came to like certain qualities in the boy, but after three months their daughter ended the relationship and started dating other boys.

Sexual Behavior

Parents can provide as much information as they feel comfortable with, and they refer teenagers to physicians or other professionals who can answer questions. Parents discuss their values. Experts disagree on whether the parent should go with the adolescent to get contraceptive devices. Dodson recommends this active approach, but Ginott does not. In the light of Diana Baumrind's comments and the deadly risk of AIDS, parents might want to take an active role.

One million teenage girls get pregnant each year. Katherine Oettinger discusses teenage pregnancy and how to handle it in *Not My Daughter.*[81] Parents and daughter must consider the circumstances, the maturity of the partners, and the emotional and financial supports available. Professionals emphasize that once a teenage girl is pregnant, there are no simple, easy alternatives. It is important that everyone communicate feelings openly, consider all the alternatives, and keep a clear focus on handling the problem without making accusations or placing blame. In making plans for the future, it is very important to keep in mind the adolescent's continuing education. When adolescents continue in school, their future, with or without children, can be very like that of women who get pregnant at older ages.

Sexually transmitted diseases are another problem being experienced by an increasing number of teenagers. Ginott describes the case of a mother who was horrified when confronted with the possibility that her daughter might have gonorrhea. The mother did not blame or criticize the child, however. She remained calm and talked about what they would do—see the doctor, get the diagnosis, and obtain treatment if necessary. Of primary importance from any perspective is dealing with the infection. Then the girl must decide whether and how she will protect herself in the future. If this is a divisive issue for family members, then family counseling is in order.

Delinquency or Responsibility?

As teenagers become more independent, they want more privileges but often also fewer responsibilities. The average teenager does not hesitate to ask to use the family car, but is also likely to have a disorderly room and no interest in washing the dinner dishes. More and more teenagers are going beyond the kinds of behavior your parents may have thought appropriate when you were in your teens—like staying out late and having a beer after bowling—and are drinking or using drugs, or both. And many are leaving home at an age when that can still be considered running away.

CHAPTER 11
Late
Adolescence:
The Years
from Fifteen
to Nineteen

All the strategists discussed in this book agree on some principles to be kept in mind when coping with the problems that result from the growing independence of teenagers. Parents need to grant freedom of choice, particularly in clothes, entertainment, and friends. They must also set limits by stating their views and what they want and insisting that those limits and values be incorporated in solutions. Communication and sensitivity continue to be essential ingredients in the relationships between parents and children.

Conflicts arise around work. Ginott gives the example of a woman whose son was offered a job as art director of a camp. She thought it was an ideal job for him, but he was reluctant to take it. She had a hard time not urging him to take the job. But she realized that he had to make his own choice, that her task was to observe silently from the sidelines unless he asked for her opinion.

Gould tells of a nineteen-year-old who wanted to stay at college during the summer and earn money there, although his parents wanted him to work in the family business. They felt he owed it to them to do that, because they had been paying his college expenses and providing spending money. After discussing the matter with Gould, the parents decided to give their son his college expenses and a limited amount of spending money, with no strings attached. The boy learned that he could not have everything he wanted from his parents, but he was free to spend his time as he pleased. His respect for his parents and himself grew as he became more independent and relied less on his parents.

Often the needs of parent and child conflict. Ginott tells of the problem one mother had with her teenage daughter, who charged an expensive dress to the mother's account. The daughter was excited and pleased with the choice, but the mother was upset at the expense. She calmly insisted that the girl take the dress back. The mother reflected the daughter's feelings about not wanting to return the dress but was firm, and the girl took it back. In this case Gordon might have problem-solved the situation to see if there were some way that the daughter could have earned the money for the dress so that she could have kept it but the mother would not have paid for it.

Gordon cites many examples in which problem solving is used to meet the needs of all family members. And he tells of a situation that occurred in his own family. When his daughter was fifteen, she told her parents she wanted to spend Easter vacation at a beach with friends her own age. Her parents were afraid of what might go on during an unsupervised vacation with boys and liquor, but their daughter discounted their worries. Through active listening, they discovered she wanted (1) to spend the vacation with a particular friend, (2) to be near a beach so she could have a tan when she returned to school, and (3) possibly to meet boys. She suggested that her parents take her and the girlfriend to an area where the parents could enjoy golf, and she and her friends could go to the beach each day. Because the parents had not had a vacation, they were delighted—and everyone had a good time. Note that parents do not automatically go along with a child's request when they think it could involve danger. Instead, parents and children all work together to find an acceptable alternative.

Briggs makes a unique suggestion. She advises talking to children who are about to be teenagers, as well as to their brothers and sisters, about the difficulties of adolescence. With advance coaching, siblings may be more understanding and less provocative and teasing with teenagers. The adolescents are forewarned and not so surprised when they have mood swings and feel a need to explode or to go off by themselves.

Role playing can help teenagers rehearse new and possibly fearful situations. Krumboltz and Krumboltz tell of a father who helped his adolescent daughter prepare for pressure from her friends to smoke marijuana. She did not want to, nor did she want to seem square. The father took the role of pressuring friend. The daughter stood her ground and came up with answers that suited her.

Many parents are afraid that if fighting escalates in the family, teenagers will run away. Both Gordon and Krumboltz and Krumboltz give examples of how such problems can be handled. Gordon tells of a family in which two teenagers, both on drugs, ran away from home after months of fighting with their parents about friends, cutting school, and drug use.[82] The parents had tried psychiatric counseling for one boy and psychiatric hospitalization for the other after a drug overdose. The teens found that being independent at fourteen and sixteen was extremely difficult, and before long they returned home. The parents began to use Gordon's parent effectiveness principles. Although they were awkward in active listening, they tried expressing feelings, and gradually the family atmosphere changed. Initially, laughter and teasing followed the active listening, but parents continued to tell the children their reactions to what was going on. I-messages were difficult to send, but gradually everyone learned to state their feelings and concerns clearly. The mother felt the problems of the two older children could have been avoided if she and her husband had learned these skills earlier.

Krumboltz and Krumboltz cite the case of Frank, a sixteen-year-old boy who had been a quiet but somewhat surly teenager. He ran away with a friend, leaving no explanation, no address. Three weeks later the police found the two boys working in another city and contacted their parents. Frank's parents conferred with the police, the high school principal, and a swimming coach of the boy's team, and then decided to let Frank stay where he was. The police kept an eye on the boys but did not talk with them. A week later Frank returned home and his parents welcomed him warmly. He said he realized he needed an education to get a decent job and had decided to finish school. The cooperation of the police, who watched out for the boys' welfare but did not interfere, enabled the parents to let the boy's behavior run its course.

ToughLove is an organization started by parents to help themselves and other parents cope with rebellious, out-of-control adolescents. Parents form support groups with other parents, developing communication with agencies and individuals to promote community responses to truancy, drug abuse, running away, and vandalism. Parents seek real consequences for this behavior so adolescents will learn to avoid the disapproved behaviors.

The founders of ToughLove, Phyllis and David York, are professional people who had difficulty with their impulsive, acting-out adolescents.[83] They found it hard to set firm, fair limits that they could enforce. Meeting and talking with other parents gave them feelings of support as they set limits and carried them out. In fact, when parents in the group find limit-setting difficult, other parents will meet with the

382

CHAPTER 11
Late
Adolescence:
The Years
from Fifteen
to Nineteen

family or the teenager and back up the rules. Others offer to go to court hearings or other official meetings. The group provides many sets of adults to help parents help children. It becomes a community effort to establish and maintain a safe environment for all children.

The founders of ToughLove see the roots of the problem as cultural and social. Too much emphasis, they believe, is placed on psychological explanations for impulsive behavior, with too little awareness of all the social changes that have occurred since the 1960s. These changes encourage freedom and less responsibility for teenagers. With all these freedoms granted to children, we have not valued enough the firm, fair limits that they require for healthy growth. Parents alone, however, are not always able to establish limits, especially in the middle of a crisis situation. ToughLove helps parents by giving them the support they need to provide limits and reasonable guidelines for adolescents.

Many parents may believe the general principles discussed in this chapter are fine as long as serious acting out is not involved. But they think that when teenagers break the law and get in serious trouble, other approaches—including severe punishment—are required. Research suggests, however, that the techniques discussed here are equally valuable with delinquent teenagers. One convict, when asked about advice for parents of delinquent adolescents, said, "The job of a parent is not to be a cop, preacher, judge, or even a perfect parent; but that of a loving, concerned guide, to provide direction that will allow your kids to be whole, stable, mature adults."

PARENTS' EXPERIENCES

As their new identities are forming, teenagers need confirmation from parents and the society at large that these identities are valued. Such confirmation comes from respectful treatment, but it also comes from work and activities that reinforce the teenagers' feelings of competence. At the very time when changes are rapid and children's needs are great, many parents experience mid-life crises. Men may be dissatisfied with their occupational achievements and style of life. As children leave home and women have more time, they may wish they had broader horizons. Both husbands and wives may have gnawing feelings that life has not given them what they want and perhaps never will. On the other hand, many parents find that their children's growing independence leaves them free to explore possibilities in their own lives—to travel, to take new jobs, to develop new interests. Parents, then, may have varying reactions to their teenagers, who are young and ready to embark on all kinds of adventures. If they are unhappy in their own lives, they may feel envious of their children and find it hard to accept the increasing freedom teenagers have. If parents feel a corresponding freedom and sense of choice in their own lives, they may be especially understanding of their adolescents' dilemmas. Parents' reactions to their teenagers' behavior stimulates their own personal growth. George Vaillant writes, "In his discovery of his adolescent children, the adult remembers, rediscovers, and often defensively reworks parts of himself. Like the character disorder and infant, the adolescent has the capacity to get under our skin, rekindle old flames, and to stimulate parents in parts of their innermost selves that they had forgotten existed. These fresh identifications act as catalysts for change within adult personalities and allow for further growth."[84]

Parents can be a great strength to each other as they rear teenagers. Single parents can find a friend or friends who supply the support given by a second parent. Parents balance each other; when one is weary and tired, the other takes over. Combining two parents' views of a situation often results in a more accurate, reliable picture. For example, a parent who always encourages independence may overlook possible dangers for a teenage son. When independence is tempered by the other parent's more cautious view, more realistic guidelines for the adolescent emerge. Parents may learn greater understanding of each other in the process. They may get a clearer view of each other's strengths and a greater respect for each other's judgment. Parents become closer as they share doubts about their decisions, doubts about how teenagers will handle more freedom, worries about what may be happening to children when they are late coming home at night. There are also the joys to share— vicarious enjoyment of special dances or parties; the thrills of achievements that come after long hours of work on the adolescent's part; the warm delight that comes when teenagers show kindness and thoughtfulness to others or good judgment when parents thought they could not look beyond tomorrow. All these experiences bring parents closer and enrich their lives together, as they feel they have contributed to the child's growth and development.

MAJOR POINTS OF CHAPTER 11

In this period late adolescents:

- reach sexual maturity
- in large numbers—about two-thirds of girls and three-quarters of boys—have their first experience of sexual intercourse
- think more abstractly and focus on social concerns of justice and equality
- most often find school boring and uninteresting
- get excited at school when permitted active participation in discussing or organizing experiments
- are stable in their feelings about friends and school but become more positive in their feelings about their parents
- want parents to really listen to them

Work experience:

- is gained by a sizeable number who work an average of 18 hours a week
- benefits adolescents as they understand people better, feel more self-reliant, earn money
- seems to result in decreased interest in school
- can create stress for teens who have demanding jobs and domineering supervisors

384

CHAPTER 11
Late
Adolescence:
The Years
from Fifteen
to Nineteen

- exposes adolescents to poor habits of drug and alcohol use
- takes away from time to explore and develop interests and plans for the future

When late adolescents consider themselves, they:

- describe themselves in psychological terms and through introspection begin to see patterns to their behavior
- like their social qualities like friendliness best and want to develop them further
- reveal sex differences in their self-descriptions, with boys seeing themselves as both more daring, logical, and calm than girls, and girls seeing themselves as more attuned to people and more emotionally reactive than boys

Peers:

- are major sources of support and pleasure in life
- spend about 20 hours per week together
- seek friends who are sympathetic, understanding, lively, and interested in mutually enjoyable activities
- begin dating at about age fourteen and go steady more frequently in the sixteen- to eighteen-year-old period
- seek personal characteristics of good humor and responsibility in opposite-sex relationships, though boys do place an initial emphasis on good looks
- usually seek only one sexual partner at a time and are only very rarely sexual adventurers with each other

Parents:

- continue their commitment to children by monitoring, supervising, and enforcing rules, yet at the same time supporting and accepting children's individuality
- serve as consultants and provide factual information on topics of importance to teens
- share more power in decision making with teens so they can be more self-governing in the context of warm family relationships
- encourage children to separate with a sense of well-being when they share power

Parents' reactions to their children's growth:

- stimulate their own growth, as parents often rediscover and rework feelings and conflicts from their own childhoods
- often stimulate parents to find new possibilities in their own lives
- may bring parents closer to each other

Problems discussed center on:

- dating issues
- substance use/abuse
- failure to take responsibility for sexual behavior
- delinquent behaviors
- school problems

Joys include:

- observing increasing social maturity and closeness with friends
- seeing children follow family traditions
- seeing altruistic behavior
- watching adult traits emerge

ADDITIONAL READINGS

Davitz, Lois, and Davitz, Joel R. *How to Live Almost Happily with a Teenager.* Minneapolis: Winston, 1982.

Greenberger, Ellen, and Steinberg, Laurence. *When Teenagers Work.* New York: Basic Books, 1986.

Polson, Beth, and Newton, Miller. *Not My Kid: A Parent's Guide to Kids and Drugs.* New York: Avon, 1985.

Rinzler, Jane. *Teens Speak Out.* New York: Donald I. Fine, 1985.

York, Phyllis, York, David, and Wachtel, Ted. *ToughLove Solutions.* New York: Bantam, 1984.

Notes

1. Clellan Ford and Frank A. Beach, *Patterns of Sexual Behavior* (New York: Harper & Row, 1951).
2. John Janeway Conger and Anne C. Petersen, *Adolescence and Youth,* 3d ed. (New York: Harper & Row, 1984).
3. Ibid.
4. Jeanne Brooks-Gunn and Frank J. Furstenberg, Jr., "Adolescent Sexual Behavior," *American Psychologist* 44, (1989): 249–257.
5. Melvin Zelnick and John F. Kantner, "Sexual Activity, Contraceptive Use, and Pregnancy Among Metropolitan-Area Teenagers: 1971–1979," *Family Planning Perspectives* 12 (1980): 230–237.
6. Brooks-Gunn and Furstenberg, "Adolescent Sexual Behavior."
7. Ibid.
8. Deanna Kuhn et al., "The Development of Formal Operations in Logical and Moral Thought," *Genetic Psychology Monographs* 95 (1977): 97–188.
9. Joseph Adelson, "The Development of Ideology in Adolescence," in *Adolescence in the Life Cycle,* ed. Sigmund E. Dragastin and Glen H. Elder (New York: John Wiley, 1975), pp. 66–67.
10. Jane Norman and Myron Harris, *The Private Life of the American Teenager* (New York: Rawson Wade, 1981).
11. Mihaly Csikszentmihalyi and Reed Larson, *Being Adolescent* (New York: Basic Books, 1984).
12. Norman and Harris, *Private Life of the American Teenager.*
13. Conger and Petersen, *Adolescence and Youth,* p. 408.
14. Conger and Petersen, *Adolescence and Youth.*

CHAPTER 11
Late
Adolescence:
The Years
from Fifteen
to Nineteen

15. Ibid.

16. Csikszentmihalyi and Larson, *Being Adolescent.*

17. Ellen Greenberger and Laurence D. Steinberg, "The Workplace as a Contest for the Socialization of Youth," *Journal of Youth and Adolescence* 10 (1981): 185–210; Laurence Steinberg and Ellen Greenberger, "The Part-Time Employment of High School Students: A Research Agenda," *Children and Youth Services Review* 2 (1980): 161–185.

18. Ellen Greenberger, Laurence D. Steinberg, and Alan Vaux, "Adolescents Who Work: Health and Behavioral Consequences of Job Stress," *Developmental Psychology* 17 (1981): 691–703.

19. Ellen Greenberger and Laurence Steinberg, *When Teenagers Work* (New York: Basic Books, 1986).

20. Eli Ginzberg, "Jobs, Drop-Outs, and Automation," in *Profile of the School Drop-Out*, ed. D. Schreiber (New York: Vintage Books, 1968), pp. 236–246; Robert P. O'Hara and David V. Tiedeman, "Vocational Self-Concept in Adolescence," *Journal of Counseling Psychology* 6 (1959): 292–301; Donald E. Super, *The Psychology of Careers* (New York: Harper & Row, 1957).

21. Alan P. Bell, "Role Modeling of Fathers in Adolescence and Young Adulthood," *Journal of Counseling Psychology* 16 (1969): 30–35.

22. Lois Wladis Hoffman, "Maternal Employment: 1979," *American Psychologist* 34 (1979): 859–865.

23. Csikszentmihalyi and Larson, *Being Adolescent*, p. 234.

24. Csikszentmihalyi and Larson, *Being Adolescent.*

25. Raymond Montemayor and Marvin Eisen, "The Development of Self-Conceptions from Childhood to Adolescence," *Developmental Psychology* 13 (1977): 318.

26. William Damon and Daniel Hart, "The Development of Self-Understanding from Infancy through Adolescence," *Child Development* 53 (1982): 841–864.

27. Jack Block, "Some Relationships Regarding the Self from the Block and Block Longitudinal Study." Paper presented at the Social Science Research Council Conference on Selfhood, October 1985, Stanford, Calif.

28. Ibid.

29. Jane B. Brooks, "Social Maturity in Middle Age and Its Developmental Antecedents," in *Present and Past in Middle Life*, ed. Dorothy H. Eichorn et al. (New York: Academic Press, 1981), pp. 243–265.

30. Gerald R. Patterson and Magda Stouthamer-Loeber, "The Correlation of Family Management Practices and Delinquency," *Child Development* 55 (1984): 1299–1307.

31. Conger and Petersen, *Adolescence and Youth.*

32. Norman and Harris, *Private Life of the American Teenager.*

33. Csikszentmihalyi and Larson, *Being Adolescent.*

34. Judith G. Smetana, "Concepts of Self and Social Convention: Adolescents' and Parents' Reasoning about Hypothetical and Actual Family Conflicts," in *Development During Transition to Adolescence: Minnesota Symposia on Child Psychology*, vol. 21, ed. Megan R. Gunnar and W. Andrew Collins (Hillsdale, N.J.: Erlbaum, 1988), pp. 79–122.

35. DeWayne Moore, "Parent-Adolescent Separation: The Construction of Adulthood by Late Adolescents," *Developmental Psychology* 23 (1987): 298–307.

36. S. Shirley Feldman and Thomas M. Gehring, "Changing Perceptions of Family Cohesion and Power across Adolescence," *Child Development* 59 (1988): 1034–1045.

37. Norman and Harris, *Life of the American Teenager.*

38. Diana Baumrind, "The Influence of Parenting Style on Adolescent Competence and Problem Behavior." Paper presented at the American Psychological Association Meetings, August 1989, New Orleans.

39. Ibid., p. 16.

40. Jacques D. Lempers, Dania Clark-Lempers, and Ronald L. Simons, "Economic Hardship, Parenting, and Distress in Adolescence," *Child Development* 60 (1989): 25–39.

41. Csikszentmihalyi and Larson, *Being Adolescent*, p. 284.

42. Csikszentmihalyi and Larson, *Being Adolescent.*

43. Tina deVaron, "Growing Up," in *Twelve to Sixteen: Early Adolescence*, ed. Jerome Kagan and Robert Coles (New York: W. W. Norton, 1972), pp. 340–341.

44. Norman and Harris, *Private Life of the American Teenager.*

45. Conger and Petersen, *Adolescence and Youth.*

46. Ibid.

47. Ibid.

48. Ibid.

49. Robert C. Sorenson, *Adolescent Sexuality in Contemporary America: Personal Values and*

Sexual Behavior Ages 13–19 (New York: Harry N. Abrams, 1973).

50. Vance Packard, *The Sexual Wilderness: The Contemporary Upheaval in Male-Female Relationships* (New York: Pocket Books, 1970).

51. Sorenson, *Adolescent Sexuality in Contemporary America.*

52. Ibid.

53. Judith Stevens-Long and Nancy J. Cobb, *Adolescence and Early Adulthood* (Palo Alto, CA: Mayfield, 1983).

54. Zelnick and Kantner, "Sexual Activity, Contraceptive Use, and Pregnancy Among Metropolitan-Area Teenagers."

55. Conger and Petersen, *Adolescence and Youth.*

56. Catherine S. Chilman, *Adolescent Sexuality in a Changing American Society: Social and Psychological Perspectives* (Washington, D.C.: U.S. Government Printing Office, 1978).

57. Zelnick and Kantner, "Sexual Activity, Contraceptive Use, and Pregnancy Among Metropolitan-Area Teenagers."

58. Brooks-Gunn and Furstenberg, "Adolescent Sexual Behavior."

59. Ibid.

60. Dorothy C. Briggs, *Your Child's Self-Esteem* (Garden City, N.Y.: Doubleday, 1970), p. 302.

61. Greenberger and Steinberg, *When Teenagers Work.*

62. Robert Eimers and Robert Aitchison, *Effective Parents/Responsible Children* (New York: McGraw-Hill, 1977).

63. Briggs, *Your Child's Self-Esteem.*

64. Shirley Gould, *Teenagers: The Continuing Challenge* (New York: Hawthorn, 1977).

65. deVaron, "Growing Up," pp. 344–345.

66. David Elkind, "Growing Up Faster," *Psychology Today,* February 1979.

67. Salvador Minuchin, Bernice L. Rossman, and Lester Baker, *Psychosomatic Families: Anorexia Nervosa in Context* (Cambridge, Mass.: Harvard University Press, 1978).

68. Conger and Petersen, *Adolescence and Youth.*

69. Ibid.

70. Ibid.

71. Ibid.

72. Ibid.

73. Michael D. Newcomb and Peter M. Bentler, "Substance Use and Abuse among Children and Teenagers," *American Psychologist* 44 (1989): 242–248.

74. Baumrind, "The Influence of Parenting Style on Adolescent Competence and Problem Behavior;" Jonathan Shedler and Jack Block, "Adolescent Drug Use and Psychological Health: A Longitudinal Inquiry," *American Psychologist* 45 (1990): 612–630.

75. Beth Polson and Miller Newton, *Not My Kid: A Parent's Guide to Kids and Drugs* (New York: Avon, 1985).

76. Ibid.

77. Fitzhugh Dodson, *How to Discipline with Love* (New York: Rawson, 1977).

78. Ibid., pp. 410–411.

79. John D. Krumboltz and Helen B. Krumboltz, *Changing Children's Behavior* (Englewood Cliffs, N.J.: Prentice-Hall, 1972).

80. Ibid.

81. Katherine B. Oettinger, *Not My Daughter* (Englewood Cliffs, N.J.: Prentice-Hall, 1979).

82. Gordon with Sands, *P.E.T. in Action.*

83. Phyllis York, David York, and Ted Wachtel, *ToughLove* (Garden City, N.Y.: Doubleday, 1982).

84. George E. Vaillant, *Adaptation to Life* (Boston: Little, Brown, 1977), p. 225.

PARENTING/WORKING

C H A P T E R   12

Combining working and parenting is a challenge for men and women in the 1990s. As more mothers are committed to the role of worker and more fathers are involved in childcare and the family, they face the demands of a combined 80-hour work week on family life. And they are feeling pressure. A 1990 survey of a thousand men and women reveals that 40 percent of men and 80 percent of women said they would stay at home and care for their children if they could. Further, 57 percent of men and 55 percent of women report feeling guilty that they do not spend as much time with their children as they should, and they neglect important rituals like having dinner together as a family.[1]

Although both men and women feel pressure, women take primary responsibility for the home and family. It is they who feel the effects of these responsibilities on their work. Only 2 percent of men in the survey report that their family responsibilities have hurt their careers while 41 percent of women feel family demands have negatively affected their careers.[2] While many want to see working and parenting as "a women's issue," it is not. It is a family and societal concern and requires widespread changes so that both men and women can enjoy the pleasures and challenges of working and parenting.[3]

In this chapter we examine how parents' work influences parenting behaviors and, in turn, children. We look first at men and work, then at women and work. We look at how parents provide childcare in their absence and present guidelines for selecting the care most appropriate for children of different ages. Finally, we examine common problems in integrating work and family lives as well as parents' solutions to them.

MEN AND WORK

Men's work has rarely been examined in terms of its impact on family life and children. The few studies available do indicate, however, that the nature of fathers' work influences not only their values in childrearing, but their wives' values as well. Children are raised to develop characteristics that fit their fathers' work. Amount of time and degree of satisfaction or frustration associated with their fathers' work have a further impact on children. Most important, the fact of the fathers' employment influences the family. When fathers are not employed, everyone is affected. Let us look at the findings in greater detail.

Fathers' unemployment can have enormous impact on their families. This effect was most carefully studied in families before it became commonplace for mothers to work outside the home. When fathers did not have jobs, their families had no money at all. Today the impact of a father's unemployment may not be as great because so many families have two incomes. The most exhaustive and detailed study on this topic is Glen Elder's series of longitudinal studies of children who grew up in the 1930s during the Depression.[4] Elder looked at children whose families maintained an income during the Depression and compared them with children whose families had lost more than a third of their income during those years. When children were adolescents at the time of their fathers' unemployment, there was a stimulating effect. Families pulled together; everyone did his or her share. Boys got jobs and worked outside the home, as did mothers; girls stayed home and did housework. Boys developed initiative, did better in school, and as adults were more competent and satisfied than boys whose fathers continued to work. Women from families that suffered economic loss tended to marry highly successful men and to remain family-oriented, happy with their roles as wives and mothers, whether they were adolescents or preschoolers during the Depression. These women continued, and enjoyed very much, their traditional interest in the home and family.

When boys were preschoolers at the time of their fathers' unemployment, however, the effects appeared more depressing. Compared to those whose fathers remained at work, these boys did less well in school and were less stable and mature as adults. The link between economic hardship and children's functioning is parental behavior toward children. Fathers who lost income became more hostile, more rejecting of children, less supportive. Mothers' behavior did not change. Fathers had less impact on adolescent boys, who were out of the home much of the time, than on their preschool sons. They did affect adolescent girls who stayed in the home, and consequently many of these girls had less self-esteem than their age mates, whose employed fathers were more accepting. For reasons not known, preschool girls seemed to escape this negative influence.[5]

When men do work, the nature of their job influences—indirectly and directly—many aspects of family life. The indirect effects of fathers' work are seen, for example, in a recent study comparing family activities and childrearing attitudes in father-absent and father-present homes.[6] Father-absent homes were those in which fathers were gone for periods of time because of work in remote areas or because of unusual shifts; as a result, fathers were not home during the child's waking hours. When fathers are absent, mothers engage in fewer community and social activities—they see fewer friends and participate in fewer organized activities. Mothers then lose support from the social network that nurtures them, and they, in turn, are less playful and stimulating with their children. So, when fathers do not participate in family life, it is less social and stimulating.

Fathers' work directly influences the social status or social class of their family, which in turn affects childrearing and children. Fathers' job classification—professional, business, skilled or unskilled labor—is the major determinant of the family's social status. The family's social status in turn influences social attitudes and childrearing practices. Middle-class parents value self-reliance and independence in children. To encourage these qualities, parents are more likely to give explanations for what they want, to motivate the child to do what is necessary on his or her own. Working-class parents value obedience and conformity in children and are more likely to use power-assertive techniques to force compliance. They use physical punishment more than middle-class parents; they refuse to give explanations, simply stating, "Because I said so." They are less interested in explanations, saying, "Do it now."[7]

These childrearing attitudes are thought to result from the fathers' experiences in the work world. Middle-class work often requires independent, assertive, self-motivated behavior to achieve success. Parents then train children in this direction. Because blue-collar workers are required to be submissive, controlled, and responsive to the directions of others, working-class parents train their children accordingly. Working-class parents may also be more power assertive at home because it is the one place they can be directive and controlling.

Even when fathers are of the same social class but have different kinds of jobs, they value different qualities in their children.[8] For example, when fathers work in bureaucratic organizations with secure positions, regular hours and pay, and insurance benefits, getting along with others in the bureaucracy is most important. Such parents are more permissive and place greater emphasis on children's developing interpersonal skills, being able to fit in with other people. When fathers work in entrepreneurial jobs—in their own small businesses, for example, they must be more assertive, more competitive, more willing to take risks. These parents stress achievement and striving in their childrearing and are less indulgent.

When fathers have lower-status jobs, the family has less money, fewer resources, and greater vulnerability to any additional stress, like a car's breaking down or a child's having trouble in school. The higher stress level in these families may in turn affect children. It is possible that families with less money use more force in childrearing, omit explanations, and demand obedience because they do not have the time or energy to give detailed reasons or to motivate children to do what is required. High stress makes these parents less understanding when brothers and sisters fight or when there are problems at school because they have fewer material and psychological resources to draw on.[9] (See Vonnie McLoyd's model in Chapter 2.)

Although the number of hours fathers spend at work has an influence on family life, it is difficult to find clear-cut relationships between the number of hours they spend at work and outcomes in the family. Middle-class and working-class men alike spend many hours at work. Working-class fathers often hold two jobs to make ends meet, whereas professional and business men often work long hours at a single job. There are some indications that fathers who spend a great deal of time away from the family report more conflict between work and family, and their wives have similar conflicts about their husbands' work. Studies of men who are absent from home for work reasons—going to sea, for example—find that sons are often more dependent, less active and stereotypically masculine than sons whose fathers are home on a regular basis. Those men who work the swing shift and do not see their children during the week are in a sense absent from their families, and this appears to cause a great strain on the marital relationship when wives work during the day.[10]

Levels of satisfaction and stress at work affect men's family lives, but the exact effects are not clear-cut. When their occupations are highly stressful, men may return home emotionally drained and highly frustrated, with little to give family members—policemen, for example, are known to have high rates of family problems. Conversely, when men have satisfying work, they may be more giving fathers. But it happens also that satisfying work can so absorb a father that he is not present at home. This is especially true of men in higher-status occupations. In a recent national sample, over half of college-educated men said work interfered with life at home, whereas only 21 percent of grade-school–educated men reported their work as interfering with family life.[11] Men who have less important jobs and few satisfactions at work may invest their energy and time in family members.

So, the nature and extent of fathers' work has a wide-ranging influence on family life and children. When fathers find their work highly absorbing and satisfying, they feel conflict between work and family commitments. When their work is highly stressful, they find it difficult to have the energy to establish stable, happy homes.

WOMEN AND WORK

As we noted in Chapter 1, when Western society was industrialized in the early nineteenth century and the work place became separated from the family, men, when economically possible, went off to work and left women at home to be caregivers of children. Women lost their role as joint economic providers and became primarily wives and mothers. When women began in recent times to return to work in increasing numbers, the focus of interest on women and work was on the effects of maternal absence on children, the effects of early day care, the effects of stress on mothers. However, women's increasing participation in the labor force is now a fact of life that is unlikely to change in the near future. Questions about women and work now center on how fathers' caregiving and mothers' interactions with children change when mothers work.

Before we turn to specific findings, several cautions are in order. First, of the studies we are reviewing, some were done over a period of years. Though the emphasis is on the most recent work available, it still takes time to carry out and publish research. The existence and acceptance of the two-wage family has increased so much in the last five years that research already published no longer mirrors what is happening in families today; documented descriptions of how much women work, their satisfactions, and their changing family life may already be slightly dated. Second, it is difficult to study employment in isolation; the factors are interrelated and make simple conclusions impossible. For example, a mother's education, amount of family income, age of children, number of hours worked all influence employment patterns, and conclusions about women's work must take all these factors into account. In this section we look at amount of time worked, mother's satisfaction and morale, and ways children change when their mother has paid employment.

Amount of Work

Though more women are working now, there is great variation in how much time they work. Of a random Boston sample of women with children ages five to fourteen, 56 percent were employed but only 15 percent were working more than 30 hours a week; 21 percent worked 20 to 29 hours during the time their children were in school. Many did not work during school vacations. Taking full-time work as 35 hours per week or more, when mothers' employment was categorized as full-time, part-time, and none, studies from 1974

> found part-time employment an unusually successful adaptation to the conflict between the difficulties of being a full-time housewife and the strain of combining this role with full-time employment. These mothers seemed to be physically and psychologically healthy, positive toward their maternal roles, and active in recreational and community activities. Their children compare favorably to the other groups with respect to self-esteem, social adjustment, and attitudes toward their parents; scattered findings suggest that the marital satisfaction is the highest of the three groups.[12]

Part-time employment, however, has the disadvantages of being lower paid, more difficult to find, and less useful in advancing a career than full-time employment. It may be most beneficial for mothers of very young children. Urie Bronfenbrenner and his colleagues recently found that mothers of three-year-olds are most satisfied with themselves, their work, and most especially their children when they are employed part-time. They have positive views of both sons and daughters. Because mothers' positive attitudes influence fathers' views in turn, the whole family system is affected.[13]

We have little systematic information about the effects of their mothers' long-term employment on children. Does it matter if mothers start work early and continue through the child's growing years? We do not know because no longitudinal studies have followed the same sample of children for a long period of time.

Mothers' Satisfaction and Morale

Numerous studies indicate that the important factor is not whether the mother works or not, but whether she is satisfied with what she is doing. A mother who is satisfied with her decision is a more effective caregiver and her children flourish. For example, in a recent study of kindergartners' academic and social performance, those children who scored least well came from homes in which mothers stayed home even though they thought having a job would benefit the child.[14] Next lowest were children from homes in which mothers worked but felt children would be better off if they stayed home. Higher scores were earned by children from homes where mothers worked and thought they were better mothers because of it. Highest scores were obtained by those from homes where mothers stayed home and thought that was best. So, their mothers' satisfaction with what they are doing is the critical factor in understanding the impact of mothers' employment on children. From existing research it is impossible to say whether children do well because their mothers are satisfied with their own activities or whether their mothers' overall satisfaction comes from the fact their children are doing well; longitudinal research is required to determine cause and effect.

There are indications that being unemployed when they want to work produces strain in mothers. According to several studies, women who wish to get out of the house are the most frustrated and depressed. This is especially true of women who are well educated and have skills. They feel less competent, less attractive, more lonely and uncertain about who they are when they do not work.[15]

Changes in Mothers' Home Activities

How does a mother's behavior at home change when she returns to work? This is not entirely clear. Much depends on the time when the mother returns to work, the ages of her children, and how many hours she works. Large-scale studies of mothers' time use summarized by Sandra Scarr indicate minimal differences between activities with children of employed and nonemployed mothers.[16] One study found that non-working mothers spend more time watching TV (21 minutes per day) than playing or reading to children (10 minutes). Nonworking mothers tend to do household chores and their children spend only 5 percent of their waking time in direct interaction with them (4 percent is spent in direct interaction with fathers). These time studies show that employed mothers spend as much time in direct interaction with children as nonemployed mothers do.

Lois Hoffman, however, concludes after reviewing several studies that employed mothers generally spend less time with each child, regardless of the child's age, than nonemployed mothers.[17] There is minimal difference between educated employed mothers and educated nonemployed mothers because they give up their personal time to spend with their children. The differences may be greatest when children are youngest. Recent work indicates that when mothers of infants work an average of 12 hours a week, they are less involved in the direct care of their babies than nonworking mothers. Even when they are home, working mothers spend less time alone with their babies than nonworking mothers because the father is usually there at the same time.[18]

Effects of Working Mothers on Children

All research thus far indicates that

> taken by itself, the fact that the mother works outside the home has no universally predict-
> able effects on the child. Maternal employment does appear to exert influence, however,
> under certain conditions defined by the age and sex of the child, the family's position in
> society, and the nature of the mother's work.[19]

Let us look at what is known about the effects of working mothers on children of different ages. With infants, a major area of research has centered on the attachment relationship between mother and child when the mother is employed. Jay Belsky and Michael Rovine, reviewing five studies of non-risk working- and middle-class families, state that there is a growing body of evidence that, in this country, at this time,

INTERVIEW
with Susan McHale

Susan McHale is associate professor of human development at The Pennsylvania State University and co-director of the Pennsylvania State University Family Relations Project.

From your experience in studying dual-earner families, what kinds of things make it easiest for parents when both work?

We are looking at how the whole family system changes when mothers work, and we found very interesting changes in how fathers relate to children when their wives are employed. The children in our study are between nine and twelve years old. We collect a measure of "exclusive" or dyadic time that fathers spend with children. This is a measure of how much time the father spends alone with the child doing some fun activity like attending a concert or school activity. In single-earner families, fathers spend about 90 minutes a week with boys in "exclusive" (dyadic) and about 30 minutes with girls, so there is quite a sex distinction in these families. In dual-earner families, fathers spend equal amounts of "exclusive" time with boys and girls—about 60 minutes per week.

Past research tends to look at changes in children's behavior when mothers work as being the result of changes in the *mother's* behavior. For example, girls are thought to do well because they have a role model of a competent woman, and middle class boys are thought to do less well, for example, in cognitive achievements because of the absence of the mother. However, these changes also may occur because the mother's working enhances the relationship between *father* and daughter and decreases involvement between father and son. Changes in father's behavior may be powerful influences on changes in children's behavior when mothers are employed. The point is that instead of treating "maternal employment" as a problem for mothers, we must recognize that families are systems in which the activities of one family member affect and are affected by all members.

We do not get any straightforward sex differences in the effects of mother's working—that is, boys do not necessarily do less well—unless these are mediated by some other process. For example, we have just finished a paper on parental monitoring of children's activities. To collect data on monitoring, we telephone both the parent and the child and ask specific questions about what has happened that day: Did the child do his homework? Did he have a special success at school that day? Did she have a fight at school that day? These are the things parents could really know about only if they had communicated with the child that day. We separately ask the child the same questions. Our measure of monitoring is the discrepancy between the

(continued)

extensive nonmaternal care in the first year of life is "associated with patterns of attachment that are commonly regarded as evidence of insecurity."[20] When there are more than 20 hours a week of nonmaternal care, then infants seem more likely to avoid the mother. These same studies find, however, that though there is risk, 50 percent of infants have secure attachments with their mothers, and 50 percent of sons have secure attachments with fathers, so about two-thirds of boys experiencing extensive nonmaternal care have secure attachments with at least one parent.

Belsky and Rovine describe six factors that seem, in thirty-six comparisons, to

children's report and the parent's report. (We presume the children are right.) We thought that monitoring might be related to children's adjustment. We do find that in families where the child is less well monitored, boys are a little bit more at risk for problems in conduct and school achievement. This is independent of who does the monitoring; as long as you have at least one parent who is a good monitor, you do not get these effects.

When we look at what helps families function well when parents work, on the level of their interpersonal relationships we find that one factor pertains to the importance of agreement between values and attitudes on the one hand and the actual roles family members assume in daily life. This finding applies to adults and children. I am talking about sex-role attitudes. When parents have young children, we found that incongruencies between sex-role attitudes and behavior are related to problems in the marital relation. Specifically, when husbands and wives have traditional sex-role attitudes but the organization of daily life is egalitarian, couples were much more likely to fight, to have lower scores on a measure of love, and to find the relationship less satisfying.

When we looked at children's involvement in household chores, we found additional evidence of the importance of congruence between attitudes and family roles. For example, the more chores boys in dual-earner families perform, the better their adjustment; the reverse was true for boys in single-earner families, however. The mediating factor seems to be the father's sex-role attitudes. In single-earner families, fathers are more traditional and less involved in tasks themselves. Therefore, when sons do a lot of housework, their behavior is out of concordance with their fathers' values. In both kinds of families, dual and single earners, boys whose roles are incongruent with their fathers' values feel less competent and more stressed, and they report less positive relationships with their parents.

The congruence between values and beliefs and the kinds of family roles children and adults assume is what predicts better adjustment. Whether you can change people's attitudes and beliefs or whether it is easier to change family roles is hard to say. Part of the problem is that the work demands in dual-earner families require that family roles change before people feel really comfortable with that.

One of our former students, Maureen Perry-Jenkins, looked at men's "gut" reactions about their sex-roles and compared those with men's actual family roles. In her dissertation research Maureen found that dual-earner men who feel they are *coproducers* in the family perform more housework. When men feel they are the sole provider (even though their wives are working), they are less inclined to help out. This partly explains why many men do not pitch in at home even when women are working full time—at a gut level, they really do not feel the wife is sharing the breadwinner role. When men do feel the wife is a coproducer, they help out, and their sons will too.

identify those infants (of mothers working more than 20 hours per week) who are more likely to develop insecure attachments. The six factors are (1) being boys, (2) having a difficult, fussy temperament, (3) having mothers with limited interpersonal sensitivity, (4) having mothers who are less satisfied with their marriages, (5) having mothers who are highly career-oriented, and (6) not having the father as alternative caregiver. In their study, all infants who were cared for by fathers, in the absence of the mother, had secure attachments to the mother.

These risk factors seem important only when mothers work more than 20 hours per week. Even then, as noted, a significant proportion of infants develop secure attachments because, one suspects, they are in the care of sensitive, involved, child-oriented individuals who find satisfaction in caregiving.

Beyond the infancy period, there are a growing number of studies indicating that high-quality day care—reflected in experienced directors, well-trained staff, and a good staff-child ratio—is related to a variety of positive outcomes: language development,[21] toddlers' ability to self-regulate in a laboratory situation,[22] social development[23] and participation,[24] and later performance in school.[25]

It appears that highly motivated parents seek out high-quality care for their children, and so development is promoted at home and at school by sensitive caregivers. Of concern, however, is the fact that a vicious cycle may develop for those children in low-quality day care. Their families are often highly stressed, so children receive little attention at home and then go to day care where there are fewer adults with whom to interact.[26] So these children have less contact with adults and get less stimulation. This is not a necessary consequence of mothers' employment; it is possible to establish more high-quality day care programs.

Preschool children in day care are both more outgoing and empathic and more pushy and aggressive than children reared at home. They appear more skilled in the social world, better able to get what they want from other children and adults outside the home.[27] There are indications that full-time working mothers regard their preschool children differently than part-time and nonworking mothers. Bronfenbrenner and his co-workers found that educated full-time working mothers regard their daughters very positively and their sons very negatively.[28] Less-educated full-time working mothers regard both their sons and daughters negatively. Mothers who work only part-time, regardless of their level of education, regard both their sons and daughters positively. There are suggestions that because boys may be so active, requiring more supervision and monitoring than girls, full-time working mothers are frustrated by them. Less-educated mothers may have so many demands on them that both sons and daughters are a strain.

In the elementary school years, daughters of working mothers appear more self-confident and more independent than daughters of nonworking mothers. They make better grades at school and are more likely to think about careers for themselves. Here it seems likely that their mothers become role models of competence and independence. Both boys and girls see men and women as contributing equally to the family and so they become less stereotyped in their views of men's and women's roles. They also become more independent themselves as they do chores around the house and take responsibility for household activities.[29]

As in the preschool years, there are indications that elementary school–age boys may suffer more than girls from their mothers' employment. Middle-class sons of working mothers do not appear to do as well in school as middle-class sons of nonworking mothers. Whether this is a temporary finding (it is not found among adolescent boys) or whether it reflects a real deficit in experience is not known. Bronfenbrenner and colleagues speculate that sons need more parental supervision and contact than girls for optimal behavior.[30] Working-class mothers usually give their children the same amount of supervision regardless of whether or not they are employed. Middle-class mothers traditionally provide more supervision, and when they are employed and absent, their boys' functioning tends to decrease. Hoffman offers a similar possible explanation.[31] Boys are generally allowed more independence than girls. When they are allowed more independence than they can handle, as in the middle-class homes of working mothers, boys' intellectual performance decreases. As Susan McHale noted, it may be that boys do less well because they do not have as much individual attention from fathers.

There are suggestions that working-class sons admire their fathers less and see them as less competent if their mothers feel burdened by work or the social context is disapproving. When their mothers feel comfortable and their fathers support their mothers' activities, sons' perceptions of their fathers' competence do not change.[32]

Most studies of children in the adolescent years have found mainly positive effects from working mothers. The benefits appear pronounced for daughters of employed mothers, who are more active, independent, and competent in both social and intellectual activities than daughters of mothers who are not employed. Boys, too, show social and personal effectiveness when their mothers are employed.

Knowing what research says about possible negative effects of mothers' employment allows parents to compensate for these problems. As all researchers note, working mothers are here to stay. The evidence suggests that close contact with a caregiver is important in infancy, and, as we shall see, appropriate monitoring of the child is important as that child grows.

Timing of Working

Urie Bronfenbrenner and Ann Crouter conclude there is some indication that boys' intellectual performance was inhibited when their mothers began work before they were three.[33] Effects were confined to intellectual functioning for boys; girls showed no negative effects.

One study of divorcing families suggests that when mothers were working before the divorce, the work had no negative effect on the children.[34] When mothers started to work immediately following the divorce, then children seemed to develop behavior problems. They experienced the loss of two parents, and the disruption resulted in problems. Again, not the fact of employment but the number of stresses contributes to problems of this nature.

In this section we have looked at amount of time worked, mothers' attitudes about work, how mothers' behavior at home changes, the effects of employment on children's behavior, and the timing of working. There is no information available, as there is for men, on the effects of different kinds of women's work on family values or childrearing behaviors. Let us turn now to looking at what happens in the family as men and women adapt to two wage earners in the family.

MEN AND WOMEN AT WORK

There is much less information on the impact of two working parents on children than we would wish. We do know that men become more involved in childcare and

INTERVIEW
with Arlie Hochschild

Arlie Hochschild is a professor of sociology at the University of California at Berkeley. She is the author of The Second Shift: Working Parents and the Revolution at Home. *It describes how couples combine work, children, and marriage.*

How can couples negotiate so they work out issues around family and work? How can people know how they will react and what they want before they marry and have children?

I think this is something young people can become more self-conscious about. I think it is especially important to talk with one another about the division of labor before a child arrives. This kind of problem has both private and public solutions. I think we have to look at both equally, simultaneously.

I was sitting next to a young woman who is a metallurgist at a manufacturing company, where I was giving a talk on issues of corporate reform—getting part-time work and parental phases of work. This woman was 8 months pregnant; she was a manager at this company, and she said to me, "My husband and I work all the time. Just yesterday I got up at 5:15 with him; he was out the door at 5:45, and I was out the door at 6:00 A.M. and returned at 6:00 P.M." She described this tremendously loaded day. She said to herself, "If I can't get all the things I have to do done now, what am I going to do when the baby comes?"

This is what we ought to be avoiding. She hadn't sat down and talked this over with her husband. He was not planning to make any modifications in his schedule when the baby arrived, and she was only going to take the 6-week maternity leave and then hop right back on the horse. She was involved in a highly workaholic culture, and her entire community was based at work; I could already foresee that in that 6 weeks she would feel guilty that she was not at work.

What is the solution for such a woman's problems? I think it is not simply negotiating things with her husband, but also getting working couples together in neighborhoods to discuss making time for childhood and parenthood. It requires corporations making revolutionary changes in the very social structure of work.

I don't even use the word *part-time* because it sounds like it is part of something whole. I talk about having parental phases in every regular job so that when you have a child, you would automatically go on 60 percent time or 80 percent time with a cut in pay. Perhaps the company can pay you for full-time and you can pay them back later. There are arrangements that could be made financially as well. This would last through the child's preschool years, after which a parent could go back to full-time work.

I would like to see every parent get job relief for the period of parenthood. This could be done, and it wouldn't be a loss of productivity for the company. It takes some creative thinking and coordinating of work schedules, but I think we need something that profound to really address the problems of modern parents.

Modern parents are workers. Today you have women joining men in a basically male culture of work that was initially premised on a provider husband who had a full-time wife at home. It just won't do to put two parents in that structure of work. I don't think that only focusing on day care (I hear talk of weekend day care) is the answer. We have to do other things to restructure work, creating an alternative to the "Mommy track," because I don't envision a change that creates a track or that is confined to women. This is the crucial issue, really, giving children a piece of their parents back.

So the solution to the problems of a young parent like the one I sat next to is both a public and a private one. I would like to see her get together with other young parents, male and female, to pressure their employers to make these accommodations.

Do you feel it is usually the woman who takes the initiative in establishing a more equal division of family responsibilities?

Usually it is, because by tradition the second shift falls to her.

Will women have to be socialized differently to insist on this negotiation?

Women have to feel empowered, have to feel that what they want will matter.

In your book, when men were interested in being equal partners, it was not clear exactly how they arrived at this point.

Most of the men in *The Second Shift* had a father whom they were critical of. Men in their teens and 20s now may not be similar.

Were there characteristics of women who wanted equal relationships?

Yes, they tended to have high educations and to be invested in their careers, and that's about where my work stopped. In *The Third Sex*, Patricia McBrum finds that women who feel empowered generally identify with their mother, regardless of whether she was a housewife or career woman. It didn't matter. The girl experienced the mother as efficacious, and that had a positive effect on her.

We have a whole new generation of young people coming up who want to avoid the pitfalls of their parents. Yet at the moment they are not thinking of the big picture. They are living with a Reaganesque presumption that they can live the private lives they want to live without structural changes. I don't believe they can.

To live the happy, stable lives they aspire to, we need changes in the work place, new governmental supports for families, and a new cultural emphasis on the needs of children. Sometimes you have to look out before you look in. The larger structural changes make it easier to make the private ones you want.

If we don't make these larger structural arrangements children will suffer. All the trends in the family point away from investing in our children; I don't yet see the reforms at work, and I don't see the government doing anything. President Bush offers rhetoric of morality and nurturance without the policies that would make it a reality. The struggle is asked of us to organize locally and nationally for progressive programs to ease the strain on two-job families. It is a matter of urgency.

housework when women work. This is especially true of young fathers who partici-pate actively in childbirth classes and learn caregiving skills. The more hours moth-ers work, the more caregiving fathers do. Interestingly, when fathers are involved in physical caregiving, the whole family spends more leisure time together.

When fathers become primary caregivers (while mothers go off to work) or equal caregivers, they manage the routine and care for children much as mothers do. The tasks of running a household and caring for children demand the same behaviors whether one is a man or woman. Children fare well under this system. There are sug-gestions that homes are more enriched, and parents are less punitive with children, when fathers are equal or primary caregivers.[35]

In most families, however, fathers help out, but not on an equal basis. When wives are employed, fathers of preschoolers work around the house about 12.8 hours per week—20 minutes more than fathers with nonworking wives. Because both parents are home with their children in the evenings, fathers with employed wives spend somewhat less time with their children in the evenings than fathers with nonworking wives. Nonworking wives, who have been with their children much of the day, reserve evening time for fathers. Mothers who have worked all day have only eve-nings and weekends as their main time to spend with children, and thus they get some of the time that children usually spend with their fathers.

Sociologist Arlie Hochschild has interviewed men and women, day-care workers and sitters, observed them in their homes, and followed them in their activities with their families to understand how men and women combine work and families in what she terms the "stalled revolution."[36] Although women have paid employment in increasing numbers, society has made few changes to accommodate the fact that family needs must be met in new ways. There is little subsidized day care, few sick leave policies that include absence because of child illness, no paternity leave, little job sharing, and only sporadic plans for flexible hours.

Until society as a whole provides more assistance, then men and women will struggle to meet the goals of meaningful family relationships in the context of satisfy-ing work. Because women have been traditional child caregivers and home main-tainers, in most instances they continue this role while they work. Although many men's attitudes have changed, and many men care for children in addition to work, it is rare that the husband and father feels equal responsibility for seeing that the family's needs are met. In one study, 113 of 160 fathers reported they were responsi-ble for no childcare tasks, and 150 of the 160 fathers said they did no traditionally feminine household chores.[37] As a result, women put in what Hochschild calls a "second shift" of work before and after paid employment and, in the course of a year, have an extra month of 24-hour-a-day work beyond what men do.

Hochschild believes that both men and women develop a gender strategy for meshing personal desires for work and family with societal options. Women make decisions about where to concentrate their energy (work or home), what kinds of help they want and need, what kinds of help they will insist upon, and what priority they will give to their work and what to their husband's work. Men, too, decide how much responsibility they want to shoulder for providing economic resources for the family and what family needs they will meet.

In traditional strategies, men and women agree that the wife/mother takes responsibility for home and children, even when working, and the husband's/father's work comes first. Men may share family responsibilities when and if they want. In egalitarian strategies, there is equal sharing of work and family tasks. There are also transitional strategies that are blends of these two. Each couple will work out daily activities based on their gender strategies, and harmony will depend on their working out compromises where differences exist. Where differences in values exist, even positive behavior may meet with a negative response because it does not fit the gender strategy. For example, traditional women sometimes resent the help husbands give because they are not meeting their own standards of doing it all themselves.

Ann Crouter, Ted Huston, Susan McHale, and their co-workers have carried out longitudinal research illustrating that the couple's satisfaction with the solution is a crucial ingredient in determining how successful a solution will be for that family.[38] For example, dual-earner fathers who share in childcare and feel this is what they want to do increase in love for their wives, whereas dual-earner fathers who resent the same amount of time in childcare feel more negatively towards their wives and marriage, perhaps blaming them for the extra work.[39]

Hochschild believes society must establish a stronger family policy (outlined in Box 12-1) that will make it easier for men to enjoy the enriching experience of caring for children and will relieve women of the extra work that creates resentment between men and women. She concludes:

> But as the government and society shape a new gender strategy, as the young learn from example, many more women and men will be able to enjoy the leisurely bodily rhythms and freer laughter that arise when family life is family life and not a second shift.[40]

HANDLING GUILT AND FRUSTRATION

Parents need to establish priorities so that they accomplish what they consider most important and are comfortable neglecting the unessentials. Each parent must figure out how much time he or she needs to spend each day on essential activities—including eating and sleeping. And then they must decide how to allocate the remaining hours of each day. When children are very young, the mother may decide to work part-time, so that more hours are available for the family. Or she may choose full-time employment that can be done at home. One mother who wanted to work at home set up a small business making fancy desserts. Another did bookkeeping at home. When children start school, the mother who works at a job with a flexible schedule can arrange her work day so that she is at home during most of the hours when the children are not in school.

Many parents eliminate some household chores and reduce social commitments. They change the beds less frequently, cook simpler meals, and buy clothes that are easy to care for. Instead of having friends over for dinner, they invite them for dessert and coffee. Many two-career families reduce strain and minimize guilt by socializing with other two-career families, who share their values and have the same problems of limited time.

BOX 12-1
A PROFAMILY POLICY

An honestly profamily policy in the United States would give tax breaks to companies that encourage "family leave" for new fathers, job sharing, part-time work, and flex time. Through comparable worth, it would pull up wages in "women's" jobs. It would go beyond half-time work (which makes it sound like a person is only doing "half" of something else that is "whole") by instituting lower-hour, more flexible "family phases" for all regular jobs filled by parents of young children.

The government would give tax credits to developers who build affordable housing near places of work and shopping centers, with nearby meal-preparation facilities, as Delores Hayden describes in her book *Redesigning the American Dream*. It would create warm and creative daycare centers. If the best daycare comes from elderly neighbors, students, grandparents, they could be paid to care for children. Traveling vans for daycare enrichment could roam the neighborhoods as the ice-cream man did in my childhood.

In these ways, the American government could create a "safer environment" for the two-job family. It could draw men into children's lives, reduce the number of children in "self-care," and make marriages happier.

From Arlie Hochschild, *The Second Shift* (New York: Viking, 1989), p. 268.

Gloria Norris and JoAnn Miller, in *The Working Mother's Complete Handbook*, give two rules for handling guilt that apply equally to mothers and fathers:

Rule 1. If you are doing something you know is wrong, stop doing it. If you feel guilty about yelling at your children a lot when you are at home, learn to stop by behavior modification techniques. Count the times you break your own rule about yelling; reward yourself every day you decrease your yelling average of the previous week. The reward need not be large—an extra five minutes of reading a magazine, for example. With time the yelling should decrease. At the same time, substitute an acceptable response for the yelling—that is, waiting five minutes and talking about the issue. If you feel guilty because children are unhappy in child care, look for new arrangements or consider working part time.

Rule 2. Do not quickly blame all family problems on a parent's work schedule. If a child is unhappy, listen to what is said to determine what is really going on. Loss of a friend, failure to make a team, a fight with friends may be the source of unhappiness. The average child has problems growing up, and a child will experience difficulties that have nothing to do with a working parent.[41]

As both parents become engrossed with their children and strongly bonded to them, they may resent having to leave the children to become immersed in the work world. Both parents, but especially mothers, may feel cheated that they are deprived of daylong contact because they are not present when important milestones occur. They are not there when their children begin to crawl, walk, talk, or peddle a tricycle for the first time.

Parents who want as much contact as possible yet must work often alter their young children's schedules so that they have long afternoon naps at day care and thus stay alert and awake for play with parents until 9 or 9:30 p.m. When children are in school, a portion of afternoon time at day care can be used for homework so that their evening time becomes family time. All members clean up after dinner and then share pleasurable activities, talking over daily events, playing games, watching TV together.

CHILDCARE

Several kinds of childcare are available when both parents work outside the home. Parents can select the kind that best suits their and their children's needs. Recent data concerning childcare for children under five reveal that 28 percent are cared for by a nonrelative at home or in another home, 24 percent are in day care or nursery school, 15 percent are cared for by father, 9 percent by mother at her work, 21 percent by another relative, and 1 percent in some other form of care.[42]

Parents and relatives have the advantage that children know them and special ties already exist. If, however, this is not possible, then parents may seek other substitute care.

Substitute care at home or in a family day care situation can provide warmth, consistency, and the caring attention young children need. As Belsky noted, the quality of the caregiver-child relationship, its stability, and the relationship between caregiver and parent are three basic criteria in selecting a caregiver. If financial considerations are not foremost, parents may wish to hire someone to care for the child in the home. Employment agencies can provide names, but parents are wise always to check references thoroughly. Box 12-2 presents guidelines for interviewing a caregiver.

Once a caregiver is hired, a period of overlap when parent and caregiver are both present gives the caregiver an opportunity to observe family routine and the specific qualities of the children. When parents are specific and clear about values and about their preferences for certain routines—demonstrating what they like done and how they like it to be done—caregivers can be more effective substitutes. A trial period is recommended in which parents, caregiver, and children can see how the arrangement will work out. A checklist of cautions and precautions to provide for caregivers is presented in Box 12-3.

Once a caregiver is hired and comfortable on the job, parents can check on the quality of the care by coming home unannounced or having some friend or relative drop by—a sitter in your home is totally unsupervised, and even though many are fine, distressing incidents can occur. At-home care does provide children with a specific substitute caregiver, familiar surroundings, and uninterrupted care in the event of the child's illness. Back-up arrangements are always needed, however, because caregivers can get sick or have emergencies.

Family day care—that is, care in the home of another family with other children—is cheaper than home care and has some advantages. Provence, Naylor, and Patterson believe that the family day care setting provides a more varied environment for chil-

INTERVIEW
with Jay Belsky

Jay Belsky is Professor of Human Development at The Pennsylvania State University in College Park. He is the initiator and director of the Pennsylvania Infant and Family Development Project, an ongoing study of 250 firstborn children whose parents were enrolled for study when the mothers were pregnant in 1981. He has done systematic research on the effects of day care.

What are your thoughts on what to look for in day care?

I think you have to consider a number of parameters. The first is America. The fact is we have a country in which (1) we have no parental leave; (2) no viable part-time jobs—that is, full-time jobs that turn into part-time jobs when you have a baby, maintaining all the benefits, and revert to full-time jobs thereafter; and (3) you don't have much support for quality care. I think those contextual considerations have to be in the forefront before I go further.

Having said that, there are clear indications that children who are in care for more than 20 hours per week in the first year of life, and certainly more than 30 hours per week, are at increased risk for having an insecure attachment relationship with their mothers, and boys with their fathers as well, and at three- to eight-years old, being more aggressive and noncompliant. I don't think we are talking about psychopathology. Some people argue that the differences in the development of children with and without extensive nonparental care in the first year are not big enough to be meaningful. They argue that these kids with extensive infant care who look more disobedient are simply more assertive. I think that's precarious because some studies show these children are more likely than other children to hit, kick, and punch and to have difficulty extricating themselves from potential trouble.

It is because of such research evidence that I stand by the conclusion I came to in 1986 that caused controversy, namely, that extensive nonparental care initiated in the first year of life, *as we know it in this country,* is a risk factor for child development. That does not mean that every child succumbs to the risk. What it does mean is that like all other risk factors, when this risk occurs in concert with other risks, the probability of deleterious outcomes increases.

Someone needs to know the baby well, and the baby needs to get to know the caregiver well. It's challenging and difficult, though some people can get to know the baby well and to read his or her cues well when both parents are gone 30 or 40 hours per week and (most importantly) come home from work tired. Couple this stressful situation with inconsistent care arrangements, even if they are of high quality while they last (to say nothing about if they are not of high quality), and it is hard to imagine how that parent and infant are supposed to get off to a good start.

I wonder when a child has attachment and insecurity in the first year and then aggression and noncompliance thereafter at three to eight years, if the intermediary process involves what may be going on in the family during the so-called "terrible twos." In these families, parents are coping even more than most parents cope, because of two working parents and changing childcare arrangements. They enter their child's second and third years of life with even less expertise than people in other families have. Then the child starts throwing curve balls—autonomy-seeking tantrums, "no," "by myself." If parents don't have the knowledge and the expertise and if he or she is worn out from work, these "curve balls" turn into unnecessarily complicated exchanges.

(continued)

Perhaps then during the second and third year you begin to get the kind of processes that Gerry Patterson calls "coercive." The child starts to throw a tantrum, and instead of finding a way to ease him out of it or giving him time-out, all of a sudden the parent gets angry, and an escalating conflict develops. This process may be the breeding ground of later aggression and noncompliance. Thus, such disconcerting patterns of behavior are only indirectly influenced by day care through the family processes that day care may engender.

The ecology of infant day care in this country, as opposed to that in Sweden where we don't see these effects, really poses risks for society. Some people say, "Oh, these children are only a little more aggressive" and want to call them "assertive." What happens in the third grade classroom when we have seven or eight of these children instead of two or three? They conspire to engender classroom processes that are greater than the effect of any of them individually. So, the teacher has less time to teach and spends more time managing the class.

What advice would you give to parents in the first two years about day care?

The most important thing, as Urie Bronfenbrenner used to say, is that parents have some biological advantages in caring for young kids. They are theirs; they have an investment in them that other people simply don't have. So I tell parents that if they can and want to (and when I say can, I mean are we talking about food on the table or are we talking about two-week vacations or wardrobes?), certainly stay home part of the time. I find it hard to believe that most American women who want to have a baby also want to be back at work in six weeks. I think most women—economics and personal aspirations being what they are—would say, "I'd like to be home with my baby for the first year, or part of that year, and return to work gradually." From a company policy perspective that would mean parental leaves without pay at first, and then part-time work with pay that reverts to full-time work after one year. For people who can't take leaves, quality care arrangements would be a part of the policy.

For working parents I say again and again that nothing matters as much as the person who cares for your baby. All too often parents don't look "under the hood" of the childcare situation. They walk in, the walls are painted nicely, the toys are bright, the lunches are nutritious. Especially with a baby, once the minimal safety standards are met, what matters more than anything else psychologically is to find out about this person who'll care for the baby. So, who is this person, and what is his or her capacity to give individualized care? Because babies need individualized care, this issue matters above all else.

The second thing to consider is whether the caregiver and parent can talk together easily. Each person spends less than full time with the baby. The time factor is not necessarily handicapping them, but it can if information is not being communicated back and forth. So the trick then is, "If the caregiver gets to know my baby during the day, what can she tell me in the afternoon, and if I have the baby in the evening and the morning, what can I tell her when I drop the baby off?" There has to be an effective two-way flow of information.

The third thing to consider in selecting care is that the arrangement has to last a decent interval of time. That doesn't mean that you must take the child to the same center for a year's time, it means that the same *person*, or *persons*, takes care of him or her for a year or so. If you find a great person who treats the child as an individual and communicates well with the parent, but stays for only a few months, you are not buying yourself a lot. In a baby's life, changing caregivers more than once a year will be stressful. If a baby goes through three or four changes in a year, it may not matter what kind of caregiver he or she gets. Even though the caregivers may get to know the child, the child won't know them. Each has to know the other.

◆
BOX 12-2
GUIDELINES FOR INTERVIEWING YOUR CHILD'S CAREGIVER

1. Before you set up an interview, give the individual basic information about the job (live-in/day position, number of hours, driver's license required) to be sure the person has the basic qualifications.
2. Before the interview, obtain the names of references and check them. Be sure to ask why the person left each position. Information obtained from previous employers can provide background for the interview and can help you make your choice.
3. During the interview, describe all the details of the job, both pleasant and unpleasant. Be specific about what you want and about the salary and benefits of the job—vacation, sick pay, holidays, possible time off.
4. Have the children meet the individual and observe the children's reactions. Often children respond immediately in a positive or negative way, and you will want to consider their reactions.
5. To understand the applicant's way of interacting with children, ask specific rather than general questions. Questions such as, "What would you do if Jennifer refused to take her nap or eat her food?" or "What will you do if Amy hits her little brother?" will elicit more revealing answers than "How do you discipline children?"
6. Try to make the applicant comfortable enough so that he or she will feel free to ask questions and reveal personal qualities like humor, adaptability, and curiosity. A general question such as, "What things did you like best and least about your previous job?" may elicit important information that reveals a lot about the person.
7. Do not set impossible standards for the person. You are looking for someone who will care for your children in your absence, not an individual who will take over their complete upbringing. The individual must be someone who will follow your guidelines and be supportive of both your needs and your children's needs.

Adapted from Gloria Norris and JoAnn Miller, *The Working Mother's Complete Handbook* (New York: E. P. Dutton, 1979), pp. 42–44.

dren in the toddler years than a day care center.[43] There are kitchens, laundry areas, bedrooms, and a wealth of activities that cannot be duplicated in a center. In family day care, children can engage in many of the same activities they would if they were at home with their mothers.

Family day care is also more flexible in meeting children's individual needs, because there are fewer children. Some single parents choose family day care because it provides a family atmosphere that may be missing after a death or divorce. Family day care homes are licensed; some are part of a larger umbrella organization that supplies toys and training to home caregivers. Day caregivers who are part of such a network can give higher quality care than untrained caregivers. Box 12-4 contains guidelines for making a choice. It is wise to make one visit with the child and one visit alone.

BOX 12-3
RULES AND INFORMATION FOR YOUR CHILD'S CAREGIVER

1. Post all important phone numbers (parents' work numbers, doctor's number, general emergency number or police and fire department numbers, poison control center number, numbers of two relatives or close friends who can be reached if parents are not available in an emergency, children's school numbers). This list should be kept next to the telephone.
2. Clearly list the safety rules. Children as well as caregiver must understand restrictions on leaving the home or yard, visiting friends, riding bikes, using appliances.
3. The caregiver must become familiar with the children's and family's routines. He or she must know where to find clothes, what foods the family prefers, nap times.
4. Caregiver and children must know the children's rules about having friends over, watching television, doing chores.
5. The caregiver must know any specific rules that govern his or her behavior— for example, making or receiving telephone calls, watching television, using appliances.
6. Parents and caregivers should have specific agreements about what happens if parents are late getting home or if caregiver is late to work.

Adapted from Gloria Norris and JoAnn Miller, *The Working Mother's Complete Handbook* (New York: E. P. Dutton, 1979), p. 52.

Day care centers provide care for children from infancy, and many provide after-school care for children in the elementary grades. In most states such centers must meet specific standards intended to assure the health and safety of the children. The parent whose child goes to a day care center is sure of having childcare available every day, at some centers from seven in the morning until seven in the evening. Many centers have credentialed personnel who have been trained to work with children, and many centers have play equipment and supplies not found in most home care situations. All centers provide opportunities for contact with children of the same age.

However, day care is more expensive than family care, the child receives less individualized attention because each caretaker is responsible for more children, and changes in the staff may be frequent. Other mothers are likely to have firsthand knowledge of various day care centers. And some social service departments have lists of licensed centers. Plan at least two visits to each center you are considering, and observe the responsiveness and competence of the caregivers. Perhaps most important, pay attention to your gut reactions—to the director, to the staff, to the physical environment, and to the children being cared for.

Some years ago, a group of child development advisors drew up the Federal Interagency Day Care Requirements. Congressional approval was sought but not obtained. These represent minimal requirements for what is considered adequate day care:

◆

BOX 12-4
CHOOSING A FAMILY DAY CARE HOME

1. Physical characteristics: Are the physical surroundings safe (fenced outdoor area, protected stairs), clean, spacious enough for the number of children enrolled? Are lunches and snacks nutritious? Is the home licensed? If not, why not? Remember that licensing regulations are intended to protect the children but may not be rigidly enforced.
2. Do toys and equipment provide a variety of activities for children? Are they appropriate for the ages of the children? What happens on rainy or snowy days?
3. Do children have special areas apart from family living quarters? Children need some small area to hang coats, keep belongings. Where do they rest?
4. Does the day care mother plan small excursions to the store, post office, library?
5. Does the day care mother seem to be a competent person? Can she cope, physically and psychologically, with the demands of the children? How does she respond when a child cries or several demands are made of her at the same time?
6. Are any other family members available—husband, children, grandparents? If so, do they enjoy and interact with the children?

Adapted from Gloria Norris and JoAnn Miller, *The Working Mother's Complete Handbook* (New York: E. P. Dutton, 1979), pp. 66–68.

---

1. A daily planned program of age-appropriate activities to stimulate physical, intellectual, social, and emotional development.
2. Trained care providers who have had courses in childcare, health, safety, and programming for the center.
3. Healthy meals.
4. Information to give to parents about health services in the community and records of immunizations.
5. Opportunities for parents to become familiar with the day care center and how it is run, and to have access to any evaluations of the center.
6. Group sizes and staff to child ratios were recommended as given in Table 12-1.[44]

When children start elementary school, they receive care there for 3 to 6 hours per day and require special provisions only before or after school and on vacations. Some school systems provide afterschool activities. When these are not available, babysitters and family day care continue to be reasonable alternatives. A recent sampling of child care arrangements in Minnesota and Virginia in 1981–82 found that 27 percent of school children in Minnesota and 25 percent in Virginia care for themselves on a regular basis.[45] Although many are children of single parents, a sizeable proportion come from two-parent households. Many parents consider that a child of

TABLE 12-1
RECOMMENDED DAY CARE GROUP SIZES AND STAFF : CHILD RATIOS

	Age of Child	Staff : Child Ratio	Maximum Size
Day care center	birth–2 years	1 : 3	6
	2–3	1 : 4	12
	3–6	1 : 8	16
Family day care home	birth–2 years	1 : 5	10
	2–6	1 : 6	12

Sandra Scarr, *Mother Care/Other Care* (New York: Warner, 1985), p. 186.

eight is able to stay alone. They have a key to let themselves into the house or apartment and are termed "latchkey children." A more recent term is "self-care" children. Most frequently, they come straight home from school, call their parents to say they have arrived, and then stay indoors, doing homework, chores, or watching TV until parents come home.

There are many drawbacks to leaving children unsupervised. First, it can be dangerous—if children have accidents or injuries or a fire occurs, no adult is there to help. Children alone can become lonely and frightened, isolated from friends and activities. Siblings may argue and fight without supervision.

Parents sometimes choose this form of care because they cannot afford better care. Other parents choose it because childcare arrangements have collapsed. A relative may have moved out of the house, a day care family may have moved, or the family itself may have moved. Sometimes no other arrangements are readily available or parents have had bad experiences with them. Once the child has begun to stay alone, the arrangement continues because it is easier for parents. There is no dropoff or pickup at a babysitter's, no financial cost, and household chores get done.[46]

Parents, however, may pay for this care in other ways—in anxiety about their children's safety and emotional needs. Parents worry that their children are lonely and isolated from their friends. If siblings fight, parents worry that one may get hurt. Some parents feel guilty leaving the children alone; others feel angry at being forced to do it because of circumstances. Still others find they cannot concentrate on work because of worry about the children. A major cost of the arrangement may be that parents and children communicate much less with each other. Some children feel parents are too busy, too tired. Children do not want to burden them further with their own fears and worries, recognizing that parents feel guilty enough already.

Research on self-care as opposed to adult-care children is preliminary. Two studies of elementary school children[47] and adolescents[48] find no statistically significant differences between these two groups of children. However, there are many forms of self-care, and there are suggestions that adolescents who "hang out" with unsupervised peers while parents are working are more susceptible to peer pressures.[49]

Even though numerous problems can occur in the "latchkey" arrangement many children enjoy self-care and describe the benefits of the arrangement. Lynette and Thomas Long, who interviewed latchkey children, their parents, and adults who had been latchkey children, found that the positive aspects of the latchkey experience are feelings of increased independence, freedom, and responsibility; learning practical skills; having time to think and reflect on the day's events; having time to develop a hobby or skill.[50] Many adults felt being latchkey children helped them to learn to be alone and enjoy their own company.

In part, some children flourish in the independence because of their own personalities. Either they entertain themselves well, or often children have friends and are permitted to visit or have friends over. Boys are involved in sports in the neighborhood and play outside much of the time, exactly as they would do if a parent were home. Often children have a support person or resource nearby to make them feel safe; there may be a neighbor they can seek if necessary, or a relative a few blocks away. These children, then, are not completely alone.

A recurrent theme in the accounts of successful latchkey experiences is that the relationship between parents and children is already a sound one. Children feel they understand their parents' situation and parents are supportive of children; they talk to each other. Parents encourage activities and pursuits during their absence, and they encourage contact with other children.

The experience of latchkey children highlights the need for more readily available and affordable day care for working parents. The United States is one of the few major Western countries that does not provide childcare support for working parents. The federal government gives a small amount of tax relief for childcare, but this is of little benefit to the poor, who need it most. Groups in some communities have established switchboards to serve as day care referral sources for parents. Other communities have established switchboards to answer the questions of latchkey children who need advice or someone to talk to and cannot contact a parent.

When children reach adolescence, they should be able to take care of themselves, and they are likely to resent an outsider's presence. Some parents, worried about adolescent sexual activity (first sexual intercourse most often occurs in the teen's home when parents are away), are reluctant to leave teenagers alone at home. When teens in the family do not get along and fight when alone, there is additional cause for concern. Fitzhugh Dodson recommends that parents tell children that if fighting does not stop, a college student will be hired to stay with them after school.[51]

A particularly difficult problem occurs when the child becomes sick. Caregivers at day care centers and in family day care settings may insist that the child stay home so that the other children are not at risk. Most parents have a list of alternative arrangements, with backup care provided by a relative or a paid sitter. Many mothers feel very guilty at leaving a sick child with a minor ailment, but one mother reported: "I handle it exactly the way my mother did. I remember it was extremely disappointing, but I also remember surviving it. The general message is 'You're sick, but I'm not and I'm going to work, and you stay home and I will call you twice during the day, and you can have ice cream for your throat. And you'll be much happier and much less bored when you're back in school.'"[52] This mother finds that her children have very few illnesses and that they recover very quickly, just as she did.

RETURNING TO WORK

Following the birth of a baby, many parents wonder about the best time for mothers to return to work. Some professionals have been quoted as saying the best time is before seven or eight months, "when stranger anxiety" hits, or before twelve to fourteen months, when children begin saying "no" frequently. Sidney Greenspan, director of the Clinical Infant Program at the National Institute of Mental Health, says there is no best time, but there is a best process, for returning to work.[53] Ideally, the mother should have a prolonged time to get to know her baby and form an intimate relationship. But parents, other children, and businesses have needs, too, so mothers must sometimes return to work sooner than they would like. This means finding a suitable caregiver.

When a caregiver is selected—either at home, at family day care, or at a day care center—the child is eased gradually into the relationship with the person, first going for short visits, then for longer ones. When mothers actually return to work, it is best if mother and caregivers can overlap by 30 minutes so each can catch up on what has happened during the day or the preceding night. When mothers are optimistic about caregivers, babies often are, too.

Greenspan says it is especially important for infants to have special play or quiet time with their mother when she gets home so that their relationship can be reestablished after the day's absence. Mothers are not to be concerned if their babies are sometimes negative after an absence and turn away from them. Accepting the baby's annoyance and going on to share a more rewarding time are helpful ways to respond.

MAINTAINING TIES TO CHILDREN

When both parents are at work all day and the children are home, with a caregiver when young or unattended when older, parents and children want to keep in touch during these hours of separation. When the child is old enough to use the phone, a regular call at a time convenient for both—during the parent's midmorning or midafternoon break, just after the child's nap, or when the child gets home from school—provides contact and gives them a chance to share news, to talk about an incident on the playground or what is planned for supper. Some parents leave messages where the child will find them. Others send postcards, to the delight of the child who doesn't receive much mail.

Dodson suggests using a tape cassette. The imaginative parent can use time during lunch hour or after the children are in bed to tape a "letter" or a story, perhaps chapters from a child's favorite book. These are for the child to listen to during the parent's absence. Older children can use the tape recorder to tell parents about important events at school, make suggestions for meals or family activities, and leave messages if they are going to be away when the parents get home. Tapes should be used to enhance communication, not as a substitute for communication between parent and child. Tapes should not be prepared during time that parent and child could be spending together.

Working parents find it helpful to meet with children's teachers at the beginning of each school year. During these conferences parents can describe their work schedules, and they can talk about how each parent would like to be involved in school projects. Usually, communicating the interest and willingness of both parents to help is sufficient to prompt the teacher to include both. Meetings between parents and teachers also give parents opportunities to demonstrate their interest in the child's work and behavior in school. The teacher who knows that parents are interested is most likely to keep them informed about the child's problems and progress.

Parents can strengthen ties with children by including them in their work lives whenever possible, just as parents participate in school events and observe classes whenever they can. The child who visits the parent's office, shop, or factory and even helps there on a vacation day learns a little about what the parent does all day and something about a particular vocation. When parents discuss their jobs with each other, consulting with each other and sharing the problems as well as the successes, children begin to get some sense of what is involved in working with other people, of what it means to have a job with responsibilities and opportunities and frustrations and satisfactions.

Similarly, the parent who attends events that are important to the child learns about the child's life—the environment and the people who are contributing to the child's development and perception of the world. The working parent may find it difficult to take the time to go even to PTA meetings that are held after working hours. Events during the day—school plays, games, class days when parents can observe teachers and children—are at least as important. But rare is the working parent who has not had to miss these opportunities. When your child comes home with an announcement of an event you cannot possibly attend, how can you respond? Be clear in expressing your disappointment, and explain why you cannot be present. The child will be at least somewhat comforted by the knowledge that you would like to attend. And you can set aside some special time to spend only with that child, as another, different way to be together.

This is the kind of conflict that makes working outside the home so difficult for many women. Each parent must decide how often and when children take precedence over work and when work comes first. Effective parents take care of themselves as well as of their families. They learn when to say no as well as when to say yes. How do you balance the desire to share your child's world with the demands of your job and your need for time for yourself? There are no easy answers, but certainly it helps to be clear about what you want and flexible in how you respond to each day.

Separation Anxieties

Separation anxiety is not a phenomenon experienced solely by children. Working parents—both mothers and fathers—often feel guilt about leaving children with a caretaker, and their separation anxiety is as traumatic for them as it is for young children.

Looking at mothers' anxiety in the first year of the baby's life reveals that mothers' anxiety about separation from the infant, particularly separation related to employ-

◆

Box 12-5
MINIMIZING SEPARATION ANXIETY AT DAY CARE CENTERS

1. Ease entry into the day care center by remaining with the child for a significant amount of time each day for the first few weeks and by having extra time to stay a few minutes when the child first arrives.
2. Give the director and staff information about the child's home life—brothers and sisters, pets, daily routines—so that caregivers can talk about home during the day.
3. Give the child something from home—a favorite toy, a pillow, or blanket—to keep at the school to remind the child of home during the day.
4. Give the child pictures of family members to keep at school; a child sometimes finds it reassuring to go to her locker and look at the pictures.
5. Telephone children over two years old to maintain contact during the day.
6. Exchange information with caregivers at the end of the day so that you can talk about what has happened in school and be aware of any special experiences the child may have had.
7. Caregivers can ease separations by helping children wave hello or goodbye and by encouraging the child to talk about home.
8. Caregivers can help children build skills and competencies, increasing a sense of self-esteem and mastery that can help children deal with separation. When children feel more in control and less helpless, they are better able to cope with stress.
9. Caregivers can help children cope with feelings of separation by encouraging games of coming and going, hiding and rediscovering, losing and finding. Even though these games have nothing to do with the parents, the theme of separation and reunion helps handle feelings.

Adapted from Sally Provence, Audrey Naylor, and June Patterson, *The Challenge of Day Care* (New Haven: Yale University Press, 1977), pp. 65–67.

ment, changes with time.[54] Educated, older career women, for the first two months of the infant's life, have strong feelings of anxiety about separation from their infant, seeing the child as vulnerable and in need of nurturance. In the course of the first year, such anxiety decreases; and it decreases most rapidly in those women who want to return to work. Among women who do not want to return but do, there is an increase in anxiety about their ability to balance work and family needs; but the anxiety too decreases with time. Women who continue to stay home as their infant grows continue to have strong concerns about their ability to be both mothers and workers, and no doubt these concerns keep them at home.

In another longitudinal study, Susan McBride and Jay Belsky find that anxiety about balancing home and work commitments is a distinguishing feature for those mothers who have secure attachments with their infants, regardless of whether they work or not.[55] This anxiety again may be what keeps mothers at home, but even employed mothers who had strong concerns in this area had infants with secure attachments to them. It is possible that the anxiety motivates employed mothers to find the best nonmaternal care.

A parent who believes that it is reasonable for him or her to work and that doing so does not deprive the child of anything essential can handle crying or pouting at separation calmly. The child's feelings are recognized and accepted—he or she is entitled to feel disappointed that the parent will not be available for several hours. But the parent's behavior is not changed to suit the child's wishes. Children learn to find satisfaction in other activities as they come to understand and accept the parent's absence. Box 12-5 gives some strategies for coping with separation anxiety.

Many parents set aside a time for the child each evening. During these hours, parent and child can read stories, take a walk together, work on homework or hobbies. The parent's undivided attention is focused on the child and the activity for a given period. No interruptions are permitted—phone calls and chores must wait. Often the child's knowledge that he or she will have that half hour in the evening eases the morning departure.

Norris and Miller use the term **reentry frenzies** to describe the bedlam that breaks loose when a mother opens the front door at the end of her working day or picks the children up at the sitter's or a center. The children may have been playing happily, absorbed in an activity. When their mother appears, they leap at her with pieces of news or demands, a detailed description of an event or a game, expressing feelings and thoughts they have saved all day. One couple complained that their four-year-old son refused to let anybody else talk in the car on the way home from the day care center. When the parents realized that this was the child's way of saying that he has missed his parents, they were able to be more patient and accepting of this nonstop chatter.

This may be the most difficult hour of the day for both parents and children. This is a time when feelings run close to the surface. Young children especially are hungry and easily frustrated, and tantrums are not unusual at this hour. Some parents spend the first half hour at home listening to children's conversations, settling arguments, and talking over the day. This is a good strategy with young children, who may not be able to wait for an hour until after dinner. A second strategy is for parents to devote the first half hour to relaxing from the day. This time can be spent resting, taking a shower, reading the mail. Then the parent seeks out the children and listens to their news while preparing dinner.

Quality Time

The parent who works spends less time with children than the parent who is home and available to the children all day. And the working parent must, during nonworking hours, manage to do chores and errands and eat and sleep and play. Time is precious. And the *quality* of the time shared by parent and child is important.

Dorothy Briggs's definition of a genuine encounter provides a good definition of **quality time**: "focused attention [on the child]. . . . attention with a special intensity born of direct, personal involvement. . . . being intimately open to the particular, unique qualities of your child."[56] Having a genuine encounter means being "all there" with the child. The quality of the relationship, not the nature of the specific activity, is the crucial factor.

Genuine encounters differ according to the age of the child. In infancy, quality time may be active play with the baby, expanding his or her world by introducing new objects or toys or by taking time with routine care, smiling and talking. In the toddler years, quality time may be watching as your child explores an area, waiting for the child to bring you the latest discovery. It is resisting the urge to help the child who tries to climb the stairs or sweep the kitchen floor. In the preschool years, quality time may be arranging a special experience—a trip to a dairy farm or fruit orchard or a special occasion at home with his friends. It may be getting a puppy or kitten and taking the time to show the preschooler how to play with and care for the animal. In the elementary school years, it is helping the child create a work area and a routine for school work. It is going on excursions with a group, like the Cub Scouts or Brownies, or listening as the child practices a musical instrument. In the adolescent years, it is listening to long discussions on the merits of different kinds of jeans or the advantages of a particular kind of sports equipment.

We easily understand that quality time can incorporate play, but we think less often of shared experiences doing household work as quality time. Yet in the course of working together, parents and children learn about each other's special strengths and weaknesses as they can in no other situation. The teenager who keeps her room a mess may reveal unexpected competence as she devises shortcuts while working in the yard with her mother. Working together also provides time for conversations that might never occur otherwise. With the activity as a common focus, children may talk about their friends and their opinions in ways they would not if they sat down with parents to "have a talk." One full-time mother described several years ago how her relationships with both her teenage daughters improved when she started doing dishes with each of them separately. In the course of that routine activity, the girls discussed their friends, their hopes and worries without her asking a single question.

Quality time is work and play with children, but it is also attention focused on the needs of the child even when that child is not present. Quality time is spent planning some special event for him, thinking about the wisdom of getting her into a sport, encouraging him to take on a volunteer activity, searching the stores on a lunch hour for special jeans or shorts. Although no direct interaction with the child occurs, this time is devoted to actions that convey to the child that he or she is special and worthy of attention. The parent who spends a Saturday afternoon helping to paint playground equipment, or a Tuesday evening baking cookies for a school bake sale, demonstrates that the child's activities are important and worthy of support. It may be precisely this kind of quality time that is most likely to be lost when mothers return to work. The working parent who is aware of the importance of thought and time devoted to the child's needs will make time available for this.

How is quality time related to quantity of time? Quality time is time spent with children when parents have the energy and interest to focus on the children. Other concerns and worries must be put aside, which may be difficult when so much must be done. Spending large amounts of time in the general vicinity of the child does not guarantee quality time. The parent who can arrange quality time will have a different kind of communication with the child. The working parent who is able to set aside a few hours for himself or herself will have a chance to mull over the child's needs in a more relaxed way, and will be rested and calmer with the child. It is harder for a mother to give quality time when she works, but not impossible. Many women believe that their work makes them more alert and interested companions for children, able to give a kind of attention that they could not before.

SETTING APPROPRIATE LIMITS

As in all families, reasonable limits are required. Ellen Greenberger and Wendy Goldberg find in a study of parents of preschoolers that having high investment in work does not mean parents must drastically change their standards for behavior or their disciplinary methods.[57] In fact, parents can have high investments in both areas; and when this is the case for mothers, they are most likely to rely on authoritative disciplinary techniques that have been found successful with children of all ages. Parents using these techniques are more likely to view their children's behavior positively and see them as having fewer behavior problems.

It is of course important to set and enforce appropriate limits. The line between being too lenient and being too demanding is very fine. Parents may be inclined to indulge children to compensate for being gone all day. Some mothers ask little from their children in the way of household help because the housekeeper does the work during the day or the babysitter picks up, or because they are reluctant to ask children to do chores they consider "mother's work." The working parent needs to remember that chores are not an imposition but a shared responsibility in the home. Children who have regular chores learn valuable habits and a sense of responsibility and participation in the family.

Parents who permit immature and emotional behavior are also being indulgent. Working parents sometimes feel children are justified in being angry at their absence. When a four-year-old has a temper tantrum because both parents are leaving the house and he cannot go, the parents are sometimes apologetic and comforting, giving the child the impression that a tantrum is a realistic response. Susan, the mother of a three-year-old, found that when she was clear in her own mind that her working was acceptable, she was able to explain to Billy that she was leaving three mornings a week for work. After exploring his feelings that he wanted her to be home, she said she understood his wish to have her home, but she was going to work. If Billy wanted to continue the tantrums, she was going to ignore them. Billy looked at her for a few minutes and went off to play with the housekeeper. The tantrums did not stop instantly, but they gradually disappeared.

Parents may find that when both work outside the home, they demand too much from children. They may ask them to do chores that are too difficult. They may ask them to care for younger children when they are just able to care for themselves. They may ask energetic children to be quiet while a parent sleeps in the daytime so he or she can work at night. As parents set limits and establish structure, they must check their expectations of children: Is the child able to do the task? If the child is able to, is the amount of work or responsibility so great that the child is robbed of childhood pleasures? There is no easy way to decide just how much to ask of a child.

Don't allow yourself to become so overwhelmed by the demands on you that you, in turn, make demands on your children they are not ready for. Often children can do far more than we expect. However, if children begin to develop behavior problems as described in Chapter 16, then parents can decide to change the responsibilities.

THE COOPERATING FAMILY

Although power is shared and the division of labor in the family changes somewhat when women work, women still retain primary responsibility for household management. Though infrequent, men's participation in feminine household chores serves as a positive example for boys and girls. Boys and girls do less stereotyping when fathers do such chores.[58] In dual-earner families, boys who do feminine chores feel competent and less stressed about them because their behavior is congruent with parents' behavior. In single-earner families with a more traditional division of work, boys who do feminine household chores feel less competent and more stressed about them.[59]

Though women may have traditionally borne the major responsibility for meeting the household needs, they may want to shift the burden to the family as a whole and establish a cooperating family. When children are young, a cooperating couple will share *all* the tasks. As children grow into the toddler years, they can begin to help. Very young children take pride and pleasure in doing things for and like adults. Parents should capitalize on this natural desire to help and should encourage young children to do chores. The child's room can be arranged so there are shelves and boxes for toys, clothes pegs and rods low enough for the child to reach, a place for shoes, and a stool so the child can get to dresser drawers. At eighteen months a child can, with help, put away toys and clothes.

As children get older, they can be given household chores—for example, emptying wastebaskets and putting away plastic dishes. Children of four and five can dust and polish furniture, clean counters, and scrub pots and pans. Children of eight to ten can learn to prepare simple meals, put away groceries, and do the laundry.

Household chores can be organized at weekly family meetings. In the beginning, a list is made of all household jobs. Each family member picks the chores he or she is willing to do for a one- or two-week period. The chores that no one wants can be rotated. Family members may want to work in pairs, particularly when children are young and when chores are time-consuming. When all chores have been distributed, a chart can be made, with the list of chores, the name of the family member responsible for each chore, and spaces for check marks to be made as the chores are completed. Family members will have the satisfaction of helping. And parents will be able to tell from a glance at the chart whether chores are being done on time.

Several steps need to be taken to ensure the success of this method. First, the parents must show the children how to do chores they are not already familiar with. Second, and very important, parents must not apply their standards to the child's work. In the beginning work is bound to be less perfect and to take longer. Appreciation of the effort and praise for what is done correctly will improve performance. Third, children may not always complete their chores on schedule. Parents should

For dual-career couples, quality time with their children is especially important. Dorothy Briggs defines a genuine encounter as "focused attention (on the child)...attention with a special intensity born of direct, personal involvement...being intimately open to the particular, unique qualities of your child."

be patient and understanding, and they should not take over the job. If children select their own chores, they are more likely to get to them. Even if children choose difficult chores, let them try. They may learn about their own limits—and they may surprise you with their skills.

Family meetings should be held weekly—or more often if necessary in the beginning—to talk about how this arrangement is working. A family may need several meetings to design a workable schedule that all members can meet. Don't expect this system to be an instant success. Do be generous with encouragement, appreciation, and praise. One family rewards itself as a group by going out to dinner when everyone completes chores on time. This encourages children to help each other, so everyone can have fun.

The family needs to discuss how to handle neglected chores, and everyone should agree on the method. Some families impose restrictions—no dinner out with the rest of the family, loss of a week's allowance, loss of a privilege. One mother demonstrated what would happen if she didn't do her work—for one week she didn't shop, cook, or do laundry. After just a few days the children had learned the importance of everyone's doing their share.

The family will be most successful when they set priorities and recognize there are only 24 hours in a day. Organization will be a key factor in accomplishing all the tasks. Values may change as well. It may be more important for the family to go on a picnic at the beach than to rake leaves or scrub the kitchen floor. Priorities shift to focus on relationships and satisfying family time.

THE MARRIAGE

In the excitement and busyness of working, parents forget that the family started with the primacy of the couple. Further, the satisfaction that the couple have with each other and their ways of doing things make solutions effective. The continuance of a strong, loving bond between parents is a primary factor in the success of combining working and parenting. So parents must plan time for each other as they plan time for children. Husband and wife need time together, regularly and as frequently as possible, to talk about things other than household or childcare matters. Some couples reserve one evening a week for dinner out, even if it's just hamburgers and a cup of coffee. Others get away for a weekend. Marjorie Shaevitz and Morton Shaevitz, who counsel two-career couples, suggest the following methods of strengthening the tie:[60]

1. Include your partner in professional relationships when possible.
2. Devote time to individual interests that express your uniqueness, so you have information and enthusiasm to share.
3. Accept your partner as he or she really is and enjoy the positive traits; realize that the positive traits will also have negative features—the conscientious, responsible parent may want children to be superresponsible and may nag to improve behavior.
4. Applaud and appreciate your partner's accomplishments.
5. Please the partner by buying an occasional extravagance or doing a special favor.
6. Develop closeness by touching and sexual expression; because there is less time for sexual encounters, you need to plan to ensure that both partners have time and are in the mood.
7. Take time to plan the future together.

TAKING CARE OF YOURSELF

Working parents who take care of themselves can take better care of their children and of each other. To reduce tension and fatigue associated with the dual roles of worker and parent, you should each set aside some time in the day for rest and relaxation. Such activities may initially seem self-indulgent, but they will increase your ability to manage both roles.

Working parents who take care of their own needs—exercise regularly, eat a balanced diet, and make sure they have private time for thinking and pursuing interests—are less likely to be tense and tired and more likely to enjoy their job and family. Norris and Miller suggest the following ways for parents to be good to themselves:[61]

1. Keep up your own friendships—exercising with a friend several times a week is ideal.

2. Develop ways of easing the transition from office to home—walk the last block or two, take a quick shower before dinner, rest for ten minutes after arriving home.

3. Learn your own personal signs of stress and do not ignore them; get rest and spend time relaxing.

4. Discover the most stressful times of the day and find ways of relieving tension. You may need a different morning or evening routine. Get up an hour earlier to reduce stress—the loss of sleep is worth feeling more relaxed.

5. Develop a quick tension reliever, like yoga exercises, deep breathing, or meditation.

The life of the working parent is challenging and demanding. As mothers, especially, learn to value what they accomplish, they relax and are more efficient and happier. Most working parents find the challenges worth the efforts required, as life becomes richer and more exciting for the whole family.

MAJOR POINTS OF CHAPTER 12

Men's work

- influences social status of the family
- affects not only family's financial well-being but also its psychological well-being
- influences values in childrearing
- can absorb fathers so they have little time for families

Women's work

- may be most satisfying on a part-time basis for mothers of young children
- results in fathers' having more exclusive time with daughters
- changes home activities as they spend less individualized time with children
- by itself has no universally predictable effects on children

Working mothers of infant children are more at risk for insecure attachments with children if:

- they work more than 20 hours a week
- their infants are boys

- their infants have difficult, fussy temperaments
- they have unhappy marriages
- the father does not provide alternative care

Beyond infancy, high quality day care is related to such positive outcomes as increased:

- language development
- self-regulation, self-control
- social development
- participation in school

When mothers of preschoolers work:

- full-time and are well-educated, they regard daughters positively and sons negatively
- full-time and are less well-educated, they regard both daughters and sons negatively
- part-time, they, regardless of educational level, view sons and daughters positively

When children are in elementary school, mothers' working may influence:

- girls positively and boys negatively
- amount of child monitoring a parent does
- children differently depending on the social class of the family
- sons' attitudes toward father

When fathers are active caregivers:

- the family spends more leisure time together
- they manage routine care as mothers do
- homes are more enriched and less punitive

Societal supports required to help parents combine work and parenting are:

- job sharing
- part-time work
- flex time
- family phases for jobs filled by parents of young children
- family leave for fathers
- warm, creative, high-quality, easily accessible day care centers

Each form of day care has some advantages:

- at-home care provides a specific caregiver in familiar surroundings
- family day care involves smaller numbers of children in a homelike atmosphere that can provide more individualized attention at a lower cost
- day care centers have trained personnel, greater variety of educational and play equipment, reliable care providing contact with children of the same age
- self-care for older children can increase children's sense of responsibility, freedom, independence; give a child time for hobbies and an opportunity to develop practical skills

Self-care is most likely to work well when:

- parents and children have a good relationship and talk to each other
- parents encourage children to develop interests
- parents encourage contact with other children

Working parents maintain quality relationships with children by:

- including children in their work when possible
- spending time alone with the child
- staying involved in child's school activities
- leaving notes, taped messages for child
- telephoning to touch base

Parents deal with any guilt by:

- setting priorities as to what is most important
- reducing household tasks that are unnecessary burdens
- changing what is possible and necessary to improve
- refusing to blame all problems on parents' work

Quality time is time:

- spent focused on child
- working together as well as playing together

Effectively combining working and parenting requires parents to:

- find time for marriage
- find time to attend to their own individualized needs

ADDITIONAL READINGS

Brazelton, T. Berry. *Working and Caring.* Reading, Mass.: Addison-Wesley, 1985.

Hochschild, Arlie. *The Second Shift.* New York: Viking, 1989.

Miller, Angela Browne. *The Day Care Dilemma: Critical Concerns for American Families.* New York: Plenum, 1990.

Olds, Sally Wendkos. *The Working Parents' Survival Guide.* Rocklin, Calif.: Prima, 1989.

Scarr, Sandra. *Mother Care/Other Care.* New York: Warner, 1985.

Notes

1. Lynn Smith and Bob Sipchen, "Workers Crave Time With Kids," *San Francisco Chronicle,* August 13, 1990.

2. Ibid.

3. Arlie Hochschild, *The Second Shift* (New York: Viking Press, 1989).

4. Glen H. Elder, *Children of the Great Depression* (Chicago: University of Chicago Press, 1974); Glen H. Elder, "Families, Kin and the Life Course: A Sociological Perspective," in *A Review of Child Development Research,* vol. 7, ed. Ross D. Parke (Chicago: University of Chicago Press, 1984), pp. 80–136; Glen H. Elder, Tri Van Nguyen, and Avshalom Caspi, "Linking Family Hardship to Children's Lives," *Child Development* 56 (1985): 361–375.

5. Elder, Nguyen, and Caspi, "Linking Family Hardship to Children's Lives."

6. John L. Cotterell, "Work and Community Influences on the Quality of Child Rearing," *Child Development* 57 (1986): 362–374.

7. Melvin L. Kohn, *Class and Conformity: A Study in Values* (Homewood, Ill.: Dorsey, 1969).

8. Daniel R. Miller and Guy E. Swanson, *The Changing American Parent: A Study in the Detroit Area* (New York: John Wiley, 1959).

9. Lois Wladis Hoffman, "Work, Family, and the Socialization of the Child," in *A Review of Child Development Research,* vol. 7, ed. Parke, pp. 223–282.

10. Ibid.

11. Joseph Veroff, Elizabeth Douvan, and Richard Kulka, *The Inner American: A Self-Portrait from 1957 to 1976* (New York: Basic Books, 1981).

12. Lois Wladis Hoffman and F. Ivan Nye, *Working Mothers* (San Francisco: Jossey-Bass, 1974), p. 228.

13. Urie Bronfenbrenner, William F. Alvarez, and Charles R. Henderson, "Working and Watching: Maternal Employment Status and Parents' Perceptions of Their Three-Year-Old Children," *Child Development* 55 (1984): 1362–1378.

14. Anita M. Farel, "Effects of Preferred Maternal Roles, Maternal Employment and Sociodemographic Status on School Adjustment and Competence," *Child Development* 50 (1980): 1179–1186.

15. Hoffman, "Work, Family, and the Socialization of the Child."

16. Sandra Scarr, *Mother Care/Other Care* (New York: Warner, 1985).

17. Hoffman, "Work, Family, and the Socialization of the Child."

18. Susan M. McHale and Ted L. Huston, "Men and Women as Parents: Sex Role Orientations, Employment, and Parental Roles with Infants," *Child Development* 55 (1984): 1349–1361.

19. Urie Bronfenbrenner and Ann C. Crouter, "Work and Family Through Time and Space," in *Families That Work: Children in a Changing World,* eds. Sheila B. Kamerman and Cheryl D. Hayes (Washington, D.C.: National Academy Press, 1982), p. 51.

20. Jay Belsky and Michael J. Rovine, "Non-maternal Care in the First Year of Life and the Security of Infant-Parent Attachment," *Child Development* 59 (1988): 164.

21. Kathleen McCartney, "Effect of Quality of Day Care Environment on Children's Language Development," *Developmental Psychology* 20 (1984): 244–260.

22. Carollee Howes and Michael Olenick, "Family and Child Care Influences on Toddler's Compliance," *Child Development* 57 (1986): 202–216.

23. Deborah Phillips, Kathleen McCartney, and Sandra Scarr, "Child-Care Quality and Children's Social Development," *Developmental Psychology* 23 (1987): 537–543; Deborah Lowe Vandell, V. Kay Henderson, and Kathy Shores Wilson, "A Longitudinal Study of Children with Day-Care Experiences of Varying Quality," *Child Development* 59 (1988): 1286–1292.

24. Patricia J. Schindler, Barbara E. Moely, and Alyssa L. Frank, "Time in Day Care and Social Participation of Young Children," *Developmental Psychology* 23 (1987): 255–261.

25. Carollee Howes, "Early Child Care and Schooling," *Developmental Psychology* 24 (1988): 53–57.

26. Carollee Howes and Phyllis Stewart, "Child's Play with Adults, Toys, and Peers: An Examination of Family and Child-Care Influences," *Developmental Psychology* 23 (1987): 423–430.

27. Jay Belsky, "Daycare Policy and Research: Infant Day Care and Child Development," *Newsletter of Division of Developmental Psychology* (Fall 1984): 46–47.

28. Bronfenbrenner, Alvarez, and Henderson, "Working and Watching."

29. Lois Wladis Hoffman, "Effects on Children," in *Working Mothers,* eds. Hoffman and Nye, pp. 126–166; Lois Wladis Hoffman, "Maternal Employment: 1979," *American Psychologist* 34 (1979): 859–865.

30. Bronfenbrenner and Crouter, "Work and Family Through Time and Space."

31. Hoffman, "Work, Family, and the Socialization of the Child."

32. Hoffman, "Effects on Children."

33. Bronfenbrenner and Crouter, "Work and Family Through Time and Space."

34. E. Mavis Hetherington, "Divorce: A Child's Perspective," *American Psychologist* 34 (1979): 851–858.

35. Scarr, *Mother Care/Other Care.*

36. Arlie Hochschild, *The Second Shift* (New York: Viking, 1989).

37. Grace K. Baruch and Rosalind C. Barnett, "Fathers' Participation in Family Work and Children's Sex-Role Attitudes," *Child Development* 57 (1986): 1210–1223.

38. Ann C. Crouter, Maureen Perry-Jenkins, Ted L. Huston, and Susan M. McHale, "Processes Underlying Father-Involvement

in Dual-Earner and Single-Earner Families," *Developmental Psychology* 23 (1987): 431–440; Susan M. McHale, W. Todd Bartko, Ann C. Crouter, and Maureen Perry-Jenkins, "Children's Housework and Psychosocial Functioning: The Mediating Effect of Parents' Sex Role Behaviors and Attitudes," *Child Development,* in press.

39. Crouter et al., "Processes Underlying Father Involvement in Dual-Earner and Single-Earner Families."

40. Hochschild, *The Second Shift,* p. 270.

41. Gloria Norris and JoAnn Miller, *The Working Mother's Complete Handbook* (New York: E. P. Dutton, 1979).

42. Ramon G. McLeod, "U.S. Study Finds Big Shift in Child Care," *San Francisco Chronicle,* August 15, 1990.

43. Sally Provence, Audrey Naylor, and June Patterson, *The Challenge of Daycare* (New Haven: Yale University Press, 1977).

44. Scarr, *Mother Care/Other Care.*

45. Lynette Long and Thomas Long, *The Handbook for Latchkey Children and Their Parents* (New York: Arbor House, 1983).

46. Ibid.

47. Hyman Rodman, David J. Pratto, and Rosemary Smith Nelson, "Child Care Arrangements and Children's Functioning: A Comparison of Self-Care and Adult-Care Children," *Developmental Psychology* 21 (1985): 413–418.

48. Laurence Steinberg, "Latchkey Children and Susceptibility to Peer Pressure: An Ecological Analysis," *Developmental Psychology* 22 (1986): 433–439.

49. Ibid.

50. Long and Long, *The Handbook for Latchkey Children and Their Parents.*

51. Fitzhugh Dodson, *How to Discipline with Love* (New York: Rawson, 1977).

52. Norris and Miller, *Working Mother's Complete Handbook,* pp. 141–143.

53. Sidney Greenspan, "After the Baby: The Best Time to Go to Work," *Working Mother,* November 1982.

54. Debra K. DeMeis, Ellen Hock, and Susan L. McBride, "The Balance of Employment and Motherhood: Longitudinal Study of Mothers' Feelings About Separation From Their First-Born Infants," *Developmental Psychology* 22 (1986): 627–632.

55. Susan McBride and Jay Belsky, "Characteristics, Determinants, and Consequences of Maternal Separation Anxiety," *Developmental Psychology* 24 (1988): 407–414.

56. Dorothy C. Briggs, *Your Child's Self-Esteem* (Garden City, N.Y.: Doubleday, 1975), p. 64.

57. Ellen Greenberger and Wendy Goldberg, "Work, Parenting, and the Socialization of Children," *Developmental Psychology* 25 (1989): 22–35.

58. Baruch and Barnett, "Fathers' Participation in Family Work and Children's Sex Role Attitudes."

59. McHale et al., "Children's Housework and Psychosocial Functioning."

60. Marjorie H. Shaevitz and Morton H. Shaevitz, *Making It Together* (Boston: Houghton Mifflin, 1980).

61. Norris and Miller, *Working Mother's Complete Handbook.*

SINGLE PARENTING

CHAPTER 13

When two people marry and have children, they hope to live together in harmony for the rest of their lives, but in this country such long-term marriages occur less frequently. When parents live together and fight, that situation has consequences for children's development. In many cases, parents live together, fight, and decide to divorce. The divorce rate rose dramatically from 1965 to 1979 and has leveled off. Nevertheless, in 1987, 27 percent of children lived in a single-parent household—24 percent headed by a mother and 3 percent headed by a father—while 73 percent of children lived in two-parent families.[1] The vast majority of single households result from separation and divorce.

It is estimated that 40–50 percent of children born in the 1980s will experience divorce. Many will go on to live in stepfamilies and may experience another divorce, for about 50 percent of these marriages fail.[2] Before discussing divorce, we look at the effects of marital disharmony on children's development; parental conflict is the forerunner of divorce and may well continue to exert strong effects after the divorce.

MARITAL DISHARMONY

In recent years we have become more aware of the devastating effects that anger has on people. In Chapter 3, we described how immobilized children become when they hear unknown adults arguing. When the arguing adults are their parents, then the effects are profound. John Gottman and Lynn Katz found that when children live with parents who are maritally distressed, they themselves have high levels of stress hormones, are less able to deal with feelings, and play with their friends in unenthusiastic and halfhearted ways.[3]

How does marital disharmony have such widespread effects? When parents are unhappily married, they are often less effective parents. As we noted in Chapter 6, parents are less sensitive caretakers of infants when they are unhappy with their mates. When parents of toddlers are unhappily married, parents experience more negative emotions in their everyday lives—more anger, guilt, sadness—and they express these emotions in the family, so there is less positive feeling between mother and father and between parent and child.[4] Fathers who are unhappily married are more negative with children and consider them a bother. Both parents tend to see children as difficult in temperament and as interfering with their lifestyle. Unhappily married fathers of school-age children are also more negative and intrusive with children, and mothers seem to try to compensate for this by being more positive and less intrusive.[5]

Children in a negative atmosphere begin to develop behavior problems. Boys, in particular, become more restless, more impulsive, and more resistant; they also manipulate the rules more.[6] These problems persist; and in adolescence, both boys and girls who experienced parental disagreements in the preschool years are poorly controlled and interpersonally less skilled.[7] Boys also show some difficulties with intellectual functioning. So boys whose parents later divorce are already impulsive and poorly controlled ten years before the divorce.[8]

Long before divorce occurs, the anger and conflict between parents affect children negatively and result in their having behavior problems, most likely because of the negative childrearing practices and the spillover of angry feelings. When parental conflicts persist and become intolerable, then parents decide to separate.

Mavis Hetherington and Kathleen Camara emphasize that divorce is a parental solution to parental problems.[9] Conversely, children often view divorce as the cause of all their problems. For both parent and child, however, divorce is a stress. It forces people to change their relationships to those who have been most important to them. And divorce is a stress that brings many other stresses with it. Financial problems arise; there is no way two families can live as cheaply as one. Often mothers must go to work or increase their hours at work, so children may see much less of their father, who is no longer living with them, and less of their mother, who must work more. Reduced income means many families must move, so the child has a new neighborhood, new school, and new friends to deal with. As resources grow more limited, parents may become more irritable, discouraged, impatient with children.

As the divorce rate has risen, society has begun to make accommodations to the needs of divorcing families. The legal system has changed, making it easier for both parents to continue to be involved in the care of children. With joint legal custody, mothers and fathers, though divorced, continue to make decisions about children, with each parent taking an equal part. In some cases there is joint physical custody, in which children spend significant amounts of time with both parents. When parents have difficulty coming to agreement about custody issues, many states now provide court mediation services. Professional counselors help parents explore children's and parents' needs and reach agreement on reasonable living arrangements.

Further, laws have been passed to make it easier for single mothers to obtain child support payments decreed by the court. This is imperative because mothers who are single heads of household have an income far below that of other family units. Two-parent families with children under 18 have a median family income of $36,365 in 1987 dollars—significantly higher because the wife often works. Single-parent families headed by a man have an average income of $20,967—lower because there is a single wage earner. The average income of a household headed by a woman, however, is $10,551,[10] dramatically below the income of other family units. Indeed, the feminization of poverty—the poverty of single mothers and their children—is a major social concern.

A divorce is a series of changes within the family, leading to a reorganization of the family unit. Constance Ahrons uses the term **binuclear** to refer to the form of family organization that emerges following a divorce—children have two biological parents living in two different homes.[11] Divorced parents take equal care of the children and are termed **coparents**. The family is not dead, fractured, or broken, and one parent does not take sole responsibility and become the single parent. The family is still a family, but a binuclear one. If and when remarriages occur, stepparents, stepbrothers, and stepsisters become part of the binuclear family. This sequence represents an optimal resolution to the changes taking place in our society.

In this chapter, we focus on how families change in organization when one adult leaves. Since divorce is the most common reason for the reorganization, we dwell most heavily on changes that occur in that process, but we will also touch on changes that result from a parent's death. We look at the process of family reorganization, common difficulties in the course of change, and resources and supports that promote coping and effective functioning. Because most divorcing families have a single custodial parent and coparenting is not always part of the agreement, we touch on the special needs of single parents. This chapter and Chapter 14, on stepparenting, form a unit, as Chapter 14 describes the changes that occur as families move on to incorporate new members.

THE PROCESS OF RESTRUCTURING THE FAMILY

Constance Ahrons has described five transitions in the divorce process, as parents change in relation to each other and gradually form a new family identity.[12]

The first transition, which she calls **individual cognition**, refers to the period in which one of the two parents becomes aware that something is wrong in the marriage. Wives are most likely to focus on the issues of infidelity and lack of communication, affection, and shared interests as reason for divorce. Husbands rate in-laws and sexual difficulties as causes. They may seek solutions to the problem, and when these do not produce positive changes, they begin to consider separation and divorce. It is during this period that parents often blame each other for their problems or scapegoat a child. Parents often keep their discussions to themselves and try not to involve children, and so children may or may not be aware of the tension, unhappiness, seriousness of the situation. Many children of divorcing parents say they felt very comfortable in the marriages.[13]

In the second transition, **family metacognition**, the family becomes aware of the problem and begins to discuss a separation openly. Parents' roles are fading, the future seems uncertain, and everyone is anxious. In the third transition, **separation**, there is an actual separation in which one parent moves out, occasionally accompanied by one or more children. Sometimes this period of separation is an extended one. The separation may be a trial one; parents still have strong feelings of attachment for each other even when they argue, and they are ambivalent about severing the relationship and moving into the unknown world of the divorced. So parents hesitate and frequently reconcile even when they thought their separation was permanent. If a decision is made to separate for the final time, they seek a legal divorce. Sometime during this period, parents go through the painful process of telling friends, relatives, and co-workers of the impending divorce. They also often encounter problems in the legal system that makes them adversaries as they prepare to go to court.

In the fourth transition, **family reorganization**, parents dissolve their spousal ties and spousal roles and redefine their parenting roles. Parents are no longer husbands and wives, but they remain mothers and fathers. They develop a set of rules within the family about how they are going to interact with their children on various issues—visiting, discipline. If parents do not agree, they can discuss how they will handle the differences.

In the fifth transition, **family redefinition**, the family regroups. In the past, one parent was often identified as the problem parent and was consequently excluded from the family. The remaining parent, usually the mother, encouraged little contact because of previous problems. Today, all professionals encourage joint parent involvement with children except in very rare instances of severe family violence.

Children's Reactions

Judith Wallerstein and Joan Kelly have found that, although some emotional reactions are common to children of all ages—sadness, fear, depression, anger, confusion, and sometimes relief—the predominant emotions vary with age and require somewhat different reactions from parents.[14] In the preschool years, children often feel abandoned and overwhelmed by the events. They worry that they may have caused the divorce. Although usually they try hard to handle their feelings with denial, they need parents who will talk to them and explain what is happening, not once but many times. Children may regress, begin wetting the bed, have temper tantrums, and develop fears. Parents can help most by providing emotional support. Wallerstein and Kelly believe that outside interventions are not as useful as interventions by parents. They urge that parents (1) communicate with the child about the divorce and the new adjustments, explaining in simple language the reasons for each change that occurs, and (2) reduce the child's suffering, where possible, by giving reassurance that the child's needs will be met and by doing concrete things such as arranging visits with the absent parent.

Preschool children are often protected initially by their ability to deny what is happening. Five- to seven-year-olds are vulnerable because they understand more but do not have the maturity to cope with what they see and hear. The most outstanding reaction of a child this age is sadness and grief. Children may deny that the parents are really divorcing, rationalize that the divorce is between the parents and will not affect them, or pretend that parents will reunite someday. But these often-used defenses do not make the pain go away, and the child is not yet old enough or independent enough to arrange activities that will bring pleasure and some relief from the worry. The divorce dominates the thoughts of a child this age. One little girl, whose parents had just divorced, was asked what she would like if she could have just three wishes. Her reply: "First, that my daddy would come home. Second, that my parents would get back together. And third, that they would never, ever divorce again."[15]

Fear is another frequent response. Children worry that no one will love them or care for them. The world has fallen apart and there is no safe place. Many children feel that only a father can maintain discipline in the family.

Preschoolers and children in the early elementary years have difficulty with counseling because talking about the situation is so painful. A monologue from a therapist who talks about the divorce and describes the fears, the sadness, the worries the child is experiencing can be helpful.[16] For example, one therapist worked with an eight-year-old boy who wouldn't talk because he was afraid he would cry. She told him that she talked to many other children whose parents were divorced and they often felt very sad about the family breakup and sometimes mad at the parents because they would not stay together. She sympathized and said that it was hard for the boy to know how to act because he did not want to hurt his parents. The boy eagerly nodded his head, indicating that was how he felt. Most parents cannot start by saying they have talked to many children about divorce, but they can start by saying they have read an article or seen a television show on divorce that says children sometimes have whatever feelings the child seems to be showing. Then the child has an opportunity to express reactions.

Children nine or ten and older may find outside intervention useful, and three to four weeks of counseling may help them sort out their feelings and begin to decide how they feel about issues of custody and visitation. Counseling provides a neutral third party to validate the child's feelings. When children are depressed, angry, and worried, it is reassuring for them to hear a professional person say, "Yes, this is a very difficult time, and it is understandable that you feel upset and sad." Children can then accept their feelings more easily.

In helping older children handle divorce, parents need to keep in mind that children may feel responsible—they may believe they have done something that has brought about the divorce. Parents need to say clearly and often, when opportunities occur, that the divorce was *not* caused by the children, but it *was* caused by difficulties between the parents. In addition, parents need to remember that children worry about them and how they are doing. It is not always possible to confine grief and distress to times when the children are not there, but you can help the children by trying to wait until you are alone to express your sadness or anger.

The children of a divorcing or divorced couple need, perhaps more than anything else, to be able to talk with their parents about what is happening. Parents can encourage children to ask questions and to express their feelings. And they should respond to questions with clear statements. Children need to know what the practical arrangements for their lives are—where they will be living and with whom. And they need to know that their parents continue to care about their welfare and about their feelings.

Thus far we have described the reactions of children who regret their parents' divorce. There are some children, about 10 percent, who feel relieved at their parents' divorce.[17] Often they are older children who have witnessed violence or severe

I N T E R V I E W
with Judith Wallerstein

Judith S. Wallerstein is Senior Lecturer in the Department of Social Welfare at the University of California, Berkeley, and founder and director of the Center for the Family in Transition. She is the senior author with Joan B. Kelly of Surviving the Breakup *and senior author with Sandra Blakeslee of* Second Chances.

Your book, Second Chances, *describes in very readable form your findings from your fifteen-year follow-up. Although you have written articles and in* Surviving the Breakup *discuss the usefulness of counseling at the time of the divorce, in* Second Chances *you do not say much about the role of counseling at the time of the divorce. I wonder if you have some comments on that?*

My findings show that how the child reacts at the time of the divorce does not predict how he or she will react later on. If children can get help at the time, it can enormously reduce suffering. It does not necessarily set them on a course that is going to work out better for them psychologically, socially, or educationally, but it can enormously reduce suffering.

If the child has been a continual witness to chronic marital violence, then I think the child should have treatment. Treatment is needed because one is dealing with the very critical issues of helping the child to break out of identifications with the parent either as victim or as aggressor, and that requires more than counseling.

My work shows that, if possible, people, and children especially, should have counseling at the time of the divorce. Additionally, the third decade of life is of critical importance to the young person whose parents divorced when he or she was a child. This is a good time to address the common fear of commitment, fear of being abandoned, fear of being betrayed—all those issues are the ghosts that rise from the past to haunt a person at this critical time of trying to establish intimacy, love, relationships, and a family. It is a second time to get help.

The problem is that many people cannot afford treatment, and insurance generally does not provide adequate coverage for psychological treatment. Also, training for work with children and adults in the divorced population is often insufficient. We really need to revise our educational curricula for the professions. Knowledge about divorce is building very fast, but there are serious gaps in what we know. Right now in our law schools, in our preparation of judges, our teaching of psychiatrists and psychologists or social workers, relatively little of this information is included, yet many patients that people see come in many instances from nonintact families.

---

psychological suffering on the part of a parent or other family member. These children feel that dissolution of the marriage is the best solution, and progressing from a conflict-ridden home to a more stable environment with one parent helps these children's overall level of adjustment and functioning.

From a follow-up of children fifteen years after the divorce, Judith Wallerstein concludes that it is very difficult to determine the long-term adjustment of the child from the child's reactions at the time of the divorce.[18] Some children who seemed to have very strong, disorganizing reactions were, nevertheless, doing well many years later while others who seemed to make a good initial adjustment had long-standing problems.

Parents' Reactions

Parents' reactions are many and varied, but almost all are intense. Parents often suffer many symptoms—headaches, rapid heartbeats, fatigue, dizziness.[19] Their moods and behavior change at the time of the divorce and these mood changes may be one of the most upsetting aspects of the divorce process for their children. Each parent may respond differently at different times, and both may show similar behavior only when they are angry with each other. Children are helpless in the face of their parents' extreme moods. One parent may be sad, depressed, lacking in energy; the other may be busy, agitated, preoccupied with his or her concerns. Both often lack self-esteem and seek out people or experiences to make them feel good again.

Divorced men and women both start dating again, though men date in larger numbers and older women tend to remain isolated and alone. Heterosexual relationships now become a source of anxiety and tension. Women wonder how to respond to sexual advances, and men worry about sexual performance. Nevertheless, new intimate relationships after divorce tend to boost parents' self-esteem.

Parents must deal with the intense feelings that arise during the divorce process, even if they were not there in the beginning: They feel sad at the ending of their marriage, even if it was necessary. They feel pain as the divorce becomes real—material possessions are divided, money is dispersed, and custody and visiting rights are arranged. Anger keeps the relationship alive for a time, but gradually detachment and distance mean the marital relationship is truly ended. The loss is real.

Factors Affecting Adjustment to Divorce

Several factors influence how well a family adapts to divorce:[20] (1) the amount of conflict among family members, (2) the availability of both parents to their children, (3) the nature of the relationship changes in the family, (4) the responsibilities family members take, and (5) the defensibility of the divorce from the child's point of view.[21]

Most divorces involve conflict at certain points. When parents have hostile battles in front of children, boys are more likely to react with undercontrolled behavior and girls with overcontrolled behaviors.[22] There are indications that moving from a household with two parents always in conflict to a stable household with one parent can lead to better adjustment for children.[23] Parents often continue the fighting when they live separately, however, and this is harmful to children. It is likely that the increased conflict children witness during divorce leads to their poorer adjustment, not the divorce itself. Increased conflicts can also occur between parents and children in a one-parent household where the second parent is not available as a buffering agent. In addition, a parent may find the child a convenient target for feelings aroused by the other parent. In the midst of this raging conflict, the child feels very alone. Minimizing the fighting in all arenas aids everyone's adjustment.

BOX 13-1
OUT OF HARM'S WAY:
PROTECTING CHILDREN FROM PARENTAL CONFLICT

Children can continue to grow and thrive even through a divorce if their parents insulate them from intense or prolonged hostilities. Parents who accomplish this share some important qualities:

1. They make it clear that they value their child's relationship and time both with them *and* with the other parent.
2. They work out a fair and practical timesharing schedule, either temporary or long-term, as soon as possible.
3. Once that agreement is reached, they make every effort to live up to its terms.
4. They tell each other in advance about necessary changes in plans.
5. They are reasonably flexible in "trading off" to accommodate the other parent's needs.
6. They prepare the child, in a positive way, for each upcoming stay with the other parent.
7. They *do not* conduct adult business when they meet to transfer the child.
8. They refrain from using the child as a confidant, messenger, bill collector, or spy.
9. They listen caringly but encourage their child to work out problems with the other parent directly.
10. They work on their problems with each other in private.

From Robert Adler, *Sharing the Children* (New York: Adler and Adler, 1988).

When children have continuing relationships with both parents, they can adjust well following the divorce process.[24] It is impossible to predict how fathers, who are usually the ones to move out of the home, will respond after the divorce. Some previously devoted fathers find not living with their children so painful that they withdraw and see less of the children. Other fathers, previously uninvolved, discover that caring for children alone on visits deepens their attachment, and thus they increase their contact with their children. Fathers are more likely to maintain relationships with their sons than with their daughters. In fact, many mothers relinquish custody of older sons to fathers because they feel sons need a role model.

Not only do children need relationships with both parents, but they also need to be able to relate to each parent separately as a parent.[25] Parents often find it difficult to direct their energy to parenting. At this time of great need in the first year following divorce, when they actually need *more* attention, children receive less attention from their parents. Frequently children's behavior goes unmonitored, and rules are not enforced. The parent outside the home often becomes highly indulgent and permissive with children; seeing so little of them, he or she hates to spend precious time in discipline. But children function most effectively when both parents take time to monitor their behavior and enforce the usual rules, as in the past.

In the binuclear family, with two households and both parents working, there is greater need for children to take on more responsibilities.[26] When demands are not excessive and are tailored to the abilities of children, then children may feel pleased with their contribution to the family and the new competence they are developing. When the demands are too great, however—when they are given too much responsibility for caring for younger children or doing chores—then children become resentful, feeling they have been robbed of their childhood. Realistic demands for responsibility can help children grow in this situation.

Children seem better able to cope with divorce and its aftermath when the divorce is a carefully thought out, reasonable response to a specific problem.[27] When the problem improves after the divorce, children are better able to accept it. They are less able to deal with divorce that is an impulsive act, that may have had little to do with the marriage but was related to other problems in the parent's life. For example, one woman divorced her husband following the death of her mother. She later regretted the decision, but could not undo what had hurt four people.

Protective Factors

Based on research following families for six years after divorce, Mavis Hetherington identifies several protective factors for children as they adjust to the divorce— qualities in the child, supportive aspects of the family system, and external social supports.[28]

Qualities of the child such as age, sex, and intelligence serve as protection. Intelligence can be a resource in coping with all the stress. Children who are younger appear less affected than those who are school-aged or early adolescent at the time of the divorce or remarriage. Later adolescents seem less affected than younger children because they are becoming increasingly independent of the family. Boys appear to suffer more difficulties at the time of the divorce, and girls appear to have more problems at the time of the mother's remarriage.

The child's temperamental qualities also influence the process of divorce. Having an easy, adaptable temperament helps. Children with a difficult temperament are more sensitive to change and less adaptable to it, and so they can become a center for parental anger. In part, they elicit the anger with their reactive behavior; and, in part, they provide a convenient target for parental anger that may belong elsewhere.

When mothers are not overwhelmed with stress or experiencing personal problems themselves, they are able to treat easy and difficult children in similar ways. However, if stress increases or mothers' coping techniques decrease, then there is a tendency to focus on the difficult child. Social supports in the situation minimize this tendency when stress is at a moderate level. Social supports cannot counteract this tendency when stress is at a high level or when mothers' personality problems increase.

When there is high stress and little support, both easy and difficult children have problems adapting. For difficult children, the more stress, the more problems. For easy children, the relationship is different. With moderate amounts of stress, easy children actually develop increased coping skills and become more competent than when stress is either low or high.

We have already touched on some of the forms of family interaction that are protective—reduced conflict between the parents, structure and organization in daily life, reasonable assignment of responsibilities within the family. Mothers must be especially firm and fair in establishing limits with boys as there is a tendency to develop a vicious repetitive cycle of complaining and fighting.

Both Hetherington and Wallerstein point to siblings and grandparents as potential family supports.[29] When family life is harmonious after divorce, then sibling relationships are similar to what they are in intact families.[30] When there is conflict between parents, siblings fight, with the greatest difficulty occurring between older brothers and younger sisters.

Grandparents can support grandchildren directly with time, attention, and special outings and privileges that help to ease the pain of the divorce. One girl told Judy Wallerstein, "If it weren't for my grandparents, I don't think I could have made it past sixteen."[31]

Grandparents provide support indirectly by helping one of the parents. In fact, returning to live in the home of one's parents is a solution that many young parents choose when they do not have the resources to be on their own. Grandparents can be loving, stable babysitters who enrich children's lives in ways that no one else can. The mother can work and carry on a social life, knowing that her child is well cared for in her absence. And this arrangement usually reduces living expenses. When mother and grandparents agree on childrearing techniques and the mother is respected in the household as a mature adult, this solution may be attractive.

Such an arrangement, however, can reflect neurotic needs of both the mother and the grandparents—and when this is true, it is likely to create additional problems for the child. If the grandmother was a protective mother who refused to allow the daughter to become independent, that relationship may continue. The daughter may have tried to escape into a marriage that did not last. If the daughter returns to her parents' home, she may have to start again to develop her independence. She will have to establish new supports that will enable her to become more independent and to continue her growth as an individual.

School is a major source of support for children. Authoritative, kindly teachers and peer friendship give pleasure and a sense of esteem to children. School and athletic accomplishments contribute to feelings of competence that stimulate resilience in children.

Some of the protective factors are beyond a parent's control—age, sex, temperament of the child—but many are within a parent's control—setting aside anger, establishing structure, monitoring behavior, and seeking out external supports for children.

PARENTING TASKS

The main tasks of parents are (1) to establish effective channels of communication so that emotions are expressed and important information is clearly exchanged, (2) to establish a stable family structure in the home of each parent, (3) to establish reasonable visiting arrangements for the child, (4) to help children cope with the process of divorce, and (5) to establish meaningful lives so all participants in the divorce process have an opportunity for what Wallerstein calls "second chances."

Effective Channels of Communication

Open communication begins with telling children about the divorce. Wallerstein makes several specific recommendations about how to explain the situation in a way that is helpful to children.[32] First, if possible, both parents together should tell all the children at the same time before one parent leaves. The children get the news at the same time, see that parents are together in the decision, and are prepared, not suddenly shocked that one parent is absent. Wallerstein suggests wording like this, "We married fully hoping and expecting to love each other forever, but we have discovered that one (or both) of us is unhappy. One (or both) does not love the other anymore. We fight with each other. The divorce is going to stop the fighting and restore peace."[33]

Parents present the decision as a rational, sad one: "The goal is to present the child with models of parents who admit they made a serious mistake, tried to rectify the mistake, and are now embarking on a moral, socially acceptable remedy. The parents are responsible people who remain committed to the family and to the children even though they have decided to go their separate ways."[34] When parents express their sadness at the solution, then children have permission to mourn without hiding their feelings from adults.

It is also important to express reluctance at the solution because children need to hear that parents know how upsetting this will be for them: "Put simply, parents should tell the children they are sorry for all the hurt they are causing."[35]

There are many things divorcing parents should *not* say. Do not burden your children with your own negative views of the other parent. Do not blame the other parent for all the problems. And do not ask children to take sides—they usually need and want to be loyal to both parents. Parents may be surprised at the loyalty that children feel to both parents, to the marriage, and to the family. Even when one parent has abused the other or the children, children often want the abusive parent present in the family. Even when children are willing to accept a parent's absence, they often do not want anything negative said about him or her.

Wallerstein comments on how little support most children get as they go through the initial turmoil of divorce. Often no one talks to them, no one listens to them talk about their feelings or answers their questions, and few relatives give added help and support. Children are often left on their own to maneuver as best they can.

To keep communication going as the family goes through the process of restructuring, each parent permits the child to express his or her feelings and guides the child into acceptable forms of behavior that remedy what can be changed. Parents need to hear that children may be angry at them or the other parent. Active listening and sending I-messages are appropriate ways to keep channels of communication open.

There will be times when children complain about the other parent. A parent can acknowledge the feelings and encourage the child to communicate directly with the other parent, who can take action. One parent is unwise to take responsibility for remedying what the other parent does unless there is some form of extreme abuse or neglect.

Stable Family Structure

As we have noted, children adjust best when each parent establishes and enforces stable family routines. The parent who feels, even unrealistically, responsible for having deprived the children of the other parent may try to compensate for the absence of the other by giving gifts and privileges and being flexible about rules and limits. Parents who respond in this way help neither the children nor themselves. The parent who is inclined to feel guilty may find support in the words of Ilg and Ames:

> Not having a father is a serious lack, but there are a great many handicaps equally severe— serious mental or physical difficulties, being members of a minority group in an excessively intolerant community, living in an "unbroken" home where quarreling and hateful discord is the order of the day.
>
> Nearly all children have to learn to face some adverse circumstances, to accept them, and to go on from there.
>
> If, as a divorced mother (or father), you allow yourself to feel too sorry for your poor son or daughter who is having to grow up without a father's close companionship, your oversolicitude may well do him more harm than the absence of his father.[36]

When two single parents share the care of their children, the children may, at times, try to play one parent off against the other with such statements as, "I don't have to do that when I am at Daddy's" or "Mommy lets me stay up much later than you do." Even when parents are living in the same household, they do not always agree on discipline, so single parents should not feel apologetic about wanting different behaviors from children. Gordon recognizes that parents are different people and that such differences, if openly discussed and handled with children, can be respected by the children.

Parents must help children to develop increased competencies. A single parent who works and cares for children must rely on the children to help keep the family unit functioning. Children may have more chores and greater independence than their peers. Increased responsibility can lead to increased self-esteem, if neither parent nor child perceives it as an unfair burden. One mother of a son, seven, and a daughter, eleven, described the process the three went through to work together to complete all the chores, and the advantages that came to the family unit as a result.[37] They held a family meeting, listed all the chores that had to be done in the household, and each took some chores. A list was signed as an indication of willingness to carry out the work. When the children found the chores conflicted with after-school activities, the family had another meeting. The children spontaneously suggesting getting up earlier in the morning to finish their work before school. Also, the three decided to impose consequences if the jobs were not completed. As the children did their chores, their mother praised all the work even though it may not have been done exactly as she would have done it. Then her son and daughter

When children have continuing relationships with both parents, they can adjust well following the divorce process. Not only do children need relationships with both parents, but they also need to be able to relate to each parent separately as a parent.

decided that they wanted more variety in their work, and again the family sat down as a unit. They listed all the chores and made a huge daily chart, indicating exactly what each person did on each day. This system worked well for the family for five years.

Having established stable routines within the family, single parents must begin to find people outside the family to serve as substitutes for the missing parent. The brothers and cousins of single mothers can serve as male models for their sons, as can athletic coaches or Scout leaders. Time spent with men who can help guide their development is also important for girls, and mothers will have to make special efforts to find male coaches, male music teachers, or male school teachers who will interact with girls as fathers, brothers, or uncles would. It is unwise to have the mother's male friends fill this role. The child needs to feel that the man is interested in him or her and that the relationship is not dependent on the man's attachment to the mother.

Establishing Reasonable Visiting Arrangements

Parents are strongly encouraged to arrange visiting that meets children's needs for contact with both parents and is not stressful to the child. In the past, most children of divorce lived with the mother, who had full custody, and most of what we know about divorce is divorce under these circumstances. Mavis Hetherington reports there is some evidence that a child does best in the custody of the same-sex parent.[38] Joint physical custody in which children spend about equal amounts of time with both parents has become more popular.

A recent study following families for two years after divorce finds that children's adjustment is no better under voluntary joint custody than under single-parent custody.[39] There are indications that when joint custody is imposed by the courts, children's adjustment is worse.[40]

Custody arrangements may change as the child grows up. Sometimes when boys are adolescents they go to live with fathers. Teenagers, for example, are more likely to want to spend most of their time at one residence so that all their social life is centered there.

At all ages, it is most important that contact be ongoing, even if it is at irregular intervals as children mature, and that arrangements focus primarily on the children's needs while they are still in the process of developing.

Helping Children Cope with Divorce

Judith Wallerstein describes several tasks children face.[41] They must mourn the loss of the family as they have known it. To do this, they need to understand, at whatever level they can, the reasons for the divorce and its permanence. While most children fantasize that parents will be back together again, they must come to recognize that they are maintaining a fantasy that in all likelihood will not come true.

They need to deal with their anger at the loss and give up any guilt they may feel. Children may overhear parents arguing about their behavior and feel they are the cause. As we have seen, noncompliance is more likely a result of marital distress than the cause. Even if it is the cause, parents committed to each other find ways to change the child's behavior rather than end the marriage.

As children deal with their feelings, they are able to turn their energy to their own lives and get on with them. Of concern is the possibility that children will become so bogged down in the divorce that it will prevent their making meaningful commitments to work or to loving relationships of their own. Wallerstein noted in the ten- and fifteen-year follow-ups what she termed a "sleeper" effect. Girls seemed to be doing well until it was time for them to become involved in satisfying love relationships. Then fears of intimacy and commitment, uncertainties about the kind of man they wished to be with, all surfaced. This long-term problem that girls experience may balance the behavior problems that boys manifest at the time of divorce and change our view that boys suffer more.

Parents help when they listen to children's feelings and when they foster children's activities at school and with peers. Parents can seek out situations where children can exercise their abilities and feel good about their accomplishments.

Parents also help children when they do not rely on them as confidants, allies, or major sources of support in their own handling of divorce. Children are then much freer to live their own lives.

What are the enduring effects of divorce on children? After two decades of research comparing the behavior of children in intact, single, and remarried families, Mavis Hetherington concludes:

> Depending on the characteristics of the child, particularly age and gender of the child, available resources, subsequent life experiences, and especially interpersonal relationships, children in the long run may be survivors, losers, or winners of their parents' divorce or remarriage.[42]

Establishing New Lives

Divorce is a time of upheaval. For some, divorce brings an end to unhappy family experiences; for everyone, it is the beginning of a period of difficulty, challenge, and as Judith Wallerstein describes, a second chance to build a new life. Accompanying the second chance are the added responsibilities of children and the necessity to work, but it is an opportunity to create a more meaningful life with new relationships. Certainly everyone does not prosper in the situation, and many adults remain unhappy and unfulfilled for decades following the divorce.

Parents who can adjust to the standard of living necessary, who can set new goals for themselves, and reorganize their behavior to maximize their resources fare best.[43] When parents focus on the essential decisions that must be made and then look ahead to what they want to achieve and work toward it, they feel better. When mothers with low-paying jobs go back to school or get extra training to improve their work situation, they report better morale. When women have nontraditional attitudes about sexual roles and are more flexible in behavior, they have increased self-esteem and a greater sense of competence. Those women who had these qualities before the divorce are better able to navigate this turbulent time, but many people find that a crisis helps them to develop the very qualities they need if they can stay focused on their goal.[44]

It is harder to see that it is a second chance for children. Wallerstein writes that though their childhood has been drastically changed, they too have second chances as they enter adulthood. They can find better and different solutions from those of their parents.

WHEN A PARENT DIES

Much of what has been written about changes in the family at the time of divorce applies to the family that experiences the death of a parent: One parent assumes all the responsibility; there may be financial changes; and certainly there will be role changes as the surviving parent takes on both roles without relief. A widower describes all his new responsibilities:

> Someone had to get a meal. That someone was me, a kitchen novice who, literally, had difficulty operating an electric can opener on his first several assaults. Someone also had to see about laundry, do the shopping, balance the checkbook, make three sets of school lunches, drive two younger children to school, pay the insurance, the real estate and income taxes, the mortgage, take the cat to the vet's, have the lawn mower fixed, argue with the roofer, attend the PTA meetings, sign the report cards, see about winter coats and boots,

dental and doctor checkups, urge letters to grandmothers, and bedevil three children who weren't so confused or grief-stricken that they didn't know their own minds when it came to making beds, hanging up pajamas and clothes, and eating green vegetables. Given the opportunity, they would vote negative every time.

I clearly recall the satisfaction and shameless, inordinate pride that came with the accomplishment of small household tasks. Once I had managed to get the supper served and eaten, the dishes done, the garbage carried out, the homework secured, and the lunches made, I felt in a rank with Caesar Augustus.[45]

As parents go about the business of taking on new responsibilities after a spouse's death, they must deal with grief and help their children deal with it.

Grief

Death of a spouse ranks as the most stressful problem encountered in adult life. Books dealing with death suggest three or four possible stages of grief and sorrow. First, there is a period of shock. The loss is sometimes denied—perhaps accepted intellectually but not emotionally. There is a feeling of numbness, as though the loss cannot possibly have happened or is happening to someone else. Second, there is a stage of anger, bitterness, resentment at the world or the person lost. Even when the person has died and had no choice in the leaving, the surviving parent may be angry at being left. Third, there is a stage of depression in which the person experiences the sadness and sense of loss. Memories of the person are gone over, and the loss becomes real. Last comes a period of acceptance of what has happened.

Not everyone goes through mourning in this way. And those who *do* progress through the stages at varying rates. But everyone who experiences a deep loss must, finally, accept the loss and begin to build a new life. This process may take far longer than has been estimated. In the past, psychiatrists considered that about a year after the death of a spouse the mature adult was ready to take up life again in the usual fashion. Depression lasting beyond a year was considered a sign of more than average difficulty in coping with the loss. More recent studies suggest that about two years may be the more usual period of mourning.

If prolonged illness and pain precede death of a parent, the surviving parent comes to the mourning period with a long history of stress and coping that will make the experience different from one in which the loss resulted from an accident. Regardless of the circumstances surrounding the loss, the grief work must be done. The bereaved individual needs to talk about his or her feelings and reactions to friends, relatives, or a counselor. If the grief work is not done, the feelings that are repressed will be expressed in physical symptoms, long-lasting depression, extreme fears, and phobias. If you know that there are stages of grief, that it is customary to be numb for awhile, and that the depression you feel some time—perhaps months—after a loss can usher in acceptance, that knowledge can help you to cope. Lynn Caine, a widow, wrote, "I am convinced that if I had known the facts of grief before I had to experience them, it would not have made my grief less intense, not have lessened my misery, minimized my loss or quietened my anger. No, none of these things. But it would have allowed me to hope. It would have given me courage. I would have known that once my grief was worked through, I would be joyful again."[46]

Coping with the Death of a Parent

Earl Grollman writes, "One of the greatest crises in the life of a child is the death of a parent. Never again will the world be as secure a place as it was before. The familiar design of family life is completely disrupted. The child suffers not only the loss of the parent, but is deprived of the attention he needs at a time when he craves that extra reassurance that he is cared for."[47]

Telling Children How can one tell a child a parent has died? Just exactly what is said depends on the age of the child and the family's view of death. Very young children below the age of five have a limited conception of death and may consider it a reversible condition; one dies but comes back to life again at a later time. Between six and eight or nine, children recognize that death happens and is irreversible, but they believe it happens mainly to other people. Because logical thinking is not yet established, children may associate unrelated events with death. One boy had heard that Abraham Lincoln was shot to death. When told of his grandfather's death, the boy asked, "Who shot him?" Sometimes a child associates death with the place that it occurred and refuses to go there. For example, a child who thinks that hospitals cause death may be afraid to go to a hospital. Children from three to nine can be both very cautious and emotional about death. As children move into the preadolescent years, they begin to understand death about as well as adults do.

In giving explanations about death, parents should be truthful and should phrase the information in a way that makes sense to the child. The child's questions will indicate the need for more information, which the parent can then give. It is not always possible to be both truthful and helpful. In telling her daughter about the death of the child's brother, one mother found herself telling a lie to help the child understand the reason for the death.[48] Robby had died of a chronic heart condition after years of illness and treatment. When the mother told her daughter that he had died because he was sick, her daughter answered that he had been sick many times, but he always got well. In desperation, the mother finally said Robby had died because he had been in pain, although, in fact, he had not been. The child could understand this. Years later she said that that statement, although false, was the only one that made sense to her. She was grateful that her mother, who was usually very honest, had told a lie. Remember, though, that in most situations it is possible to be both honest and helpful.

Because each situation is unique and needs to be handled with sensitivity, it is impossible to determine exactly what a parent should say. Grollman does list explanations to avoid. Do not describe heaven and tell the child that the dead parent is happy for eternity, if you do not believe this yourself. A child will sense the discrepancy between what a parent says and how the parent feels and will become more confused. It is unwise to say that a parent has gone on a long journey, because the child may focus on the return or feel angry at being abandoned. One child, told that his mother had gone on a journey, cursed every time he heard her name, until he was told she had died and was shown her grave. When he understood his mother's absence, the boy was sad but no longer felt abandoned or rejected by her. It is also unwise to say that the parent died "because God loves good people and wants them in heaven." If goodness is rewarded with death, the child may shun good behavior or assume that those who live long lives are, in some undetectable way, bad. When death is equated with sleep, some children begin to fear sleep and are unwilling to go to bed.

Children's Reactions   Once the information is given, how can we expect the child will experience the grief? John Bowlby of the Tavistock Clinic in London describes three phases similar to those experienced by adults: (1) protest when the child cannot accept the death and tries to regain the parent, (2) pain and despair as the child gradually accepts the death, and (3) acceptance and hope that life goes on.[49]

After the child has been told of the parent's death, experts agree it is wise to include the child in as much of the funeral and formal mourning process as seems comfortable to parent and child. Experts agree that, unless children protest, they should view the body to understand that the parent is truly gone. This is not a rigid rule, however, and if either parent or child feels too upset, or if the body of the dead parent has been devastated by disease or injury, then this is not wise. During the mourning period surrounding the funeral and burial, family members may be surprised when young children, although devastated with grief, may scamper away to play, only to cry bitter tears an hour later. Parents should not hold back their own tears and they should not discourage children from crying. Tears are a healthy release of emotion, and many books on grief and mourning recognize the healing quality of tears. Also, do not encourage children to "Be brave!" or "Be a little man!" Rather, say realistically, "Yes, this is a hard time for you. Life is very sad now." Such statements acknowledge grief without minimizing it. Parents, however, should not insist on a display of grief.

Grollman lists a variety of children's reactions to death; many adults have similar responses.[50]

1. Denial: "I dreamt it! Mommy is coming home tomorrow." The child cannot accept the death because it is too painful.

2. Anxiety expressed in bodily symptoms: The child develops symptoms the dead parent had or symptoms expressing tension and sadness. "I can't eat," "I have stomach pains."

3. Hostile reactions: "Why did Mommy leave me like this?" These reactions may be very upsetting to the surviving parent.

4. Guilt reactions: "Daddy died because I didn't wash the dishes right. I killed him."

5. Hostile reactions: Anger at doctors, nurses, or the surviving parent, who did not do what they should have to save the parent.

6. Panic: "Who will love me now?" The child anticipates being abandoned by the remaining parent through death or remarriage.

7. Replacement: The child looks for a family member or friend who will move in and take the parent's place.

8. Taking on mannerisms or habits of deceased parent: The child tries to be like the dead person in interests, activities, and personal traits, as a way of replacing the person who had died.

9. Idealization: "No one can say anything against Mommy. She was wonderful."

Healthy mourning may include some or all of these reactions. Mourning becomes unhealthy when such reactions persist without stopping many months after the death and interfere with a return to satisfying activities. It is important to note that the reactions of some children and adults may be so marked during the grieving period that they hallucinate about the dead person. This is one of the few situations in life in which hallucinations can occur in the course of a healthy adaptation to a crisis.

A frequent reaction in a serious crisis, and one that has to be handled carefully, is guilt. Young children, particularly, often assume they are personally responsible for what happens even though they are in no way involved. The surviving parent must be very alert to pick up on statements suggesting guilt and should introduce the possibility that the child feels guilt, even if the child has not mentioned it. For example: "Sometimes when a person dies, those close to her wonder if something they did was related to the death. I sometimes think, 'Would things have been different if I had called the doctor sooner?' But I know everything was done that could be done. Do you ever wonder or have thoughts like that?"

Gordon gives the example of a mother who actively listened as her three-year-old asked such painful questions as, "When is Daddy coming home?" and "Where did they put him?"[51] One night, two months after the father's death, the boy awoke and began crying and saying that his daddy was dead. As the mother reflected his upset, the boy was able to talk about how much he missed his father and wanted him back. The mother thought that after this expression of feeling her son seemed less anxious about the death. This three-and-a-half-year-old child asked many questions that were hard for the mother to answer. But she responded as well as she could, without criticism or complaint.

When you understand and accept your child's feelings and respond with empathy and love, you help the child move through the grief process. As memories of the parent are recalled and relived, the death gradually becomes real. At times the child may want to express unbearable pain or anger by striking at pillows or engaging in some physical activity. This can be encouraged. The child's individual reaction to death always should be respected. Grollman sums up the most helpful parental responses:

Demonstrate in word and touch how much he [the child] is truly loved. A stable and emotionally mature adult who accepts the fact of death with courage and wisdom will bring the truth to the youngster that the business of life is life. Emotional energy formerly directed toward the absent person must now be directed toward the living. This does not mean wiping out the memories of the deceased. Even in death, the absent member can and should remain a constructive force in family life and be remembered in love without constant bitterness or morbidity.[52]

EFFECTS OF FATHER ABSENCE

We discuss here the effects of father absence. Because some fathers die and a small percentage of children living in a single-parent household are the children of single mothers who were not married, some children have no ongoing relationship of any kind with their father. Further, fathers, when they are not the custodial parent, may become less and less involved after the first two postdivorce years, which means that children of divorce can also live without a father present in their lives.

It is difficult to disentangle the effects of father absence from the effects of the financial problems that almost always accompany such an absence. Preschool boys separated from their fathers at an early age are most affected by the absence. In comparison to age mates, they tend to be less aggressive, more dependent, more feminine in their interests and self-concept. As these children go off to school and interact with other boys, their dependency decreases and their aggressiveness increases. If boys are six or older at the time of separation, there is less effect on the child's masculinity. The presence of older male models increases appropriate sex-typing.

Both boys and girls from father-absent homes have difficulties with some intellectual tasks.[53] In particular, they have been found to score lower on math and science tests. However, such difficulties may result not from poorer abilities, but from personal qualities that fail to develop when a family is disrupted. Children may not develop the persistence and attention to detail that are particularly required for math and science. Adolescent girls from father-absent homes show two kinds of problems:[54] Either they are very anxious, shy, and inhibited, or they are too assertive, provocative, and somewhat promiscuous. Girls from widowed homes tend to be shy, and girls from divorced homes tend to be assertive. Similar behavior is found in their interactions with peers and adults, and this pattern persists into the adult years. Daughters of divorced women are likely to marry at younger ages and tend to be pregnant at the time of marriage, whereas daughters of widows may avoid men and marry later.

The critical factor may not be the absence of the father, but the mother's attitude toward the father. Divorced mothers, while they love their daughters and use the same parenting techniques as other parents, are more likely than widows to be unhappy women with low self-concepts and an angry attitude toward their ex-husbands. They may view their marriages negatively and may feel they got little support from others after the divorce. Nevertheless, a happy marriage is important to them and they are likely to feel deprived. In contrast, widows have a positive view of their husbands and their marriages and feel they received support from other people at the time of the death. Girls from father-absent homes are likely to be anxious around men. In young adulthood, they are more likely to select men who are similar to their fathers than are girls from intact families. At least two factors seem to affect girls from father-absent homes. The first is lack of contact and experience with men. The second is the mother's attitude toward herself. If she feels unloved and unwanted without a man, her daughter may marry early to create the happiness that has eluded the mother.

Many single mothers do rear children successfully. How do they compensate for the absence of the father? Primarily by providing contact with men—relatives, friends, stepfathers, grandfathers—who love and care for children. If possible, this should include continuing relationships in which these men play with the children, teaching and guiding their behavior, recognizing achievements, and helping to correct mistakes.

COMMUNITY SUPPORTS

Single parents, as we have already noted, mobilize social support in their individual lives from friends, relatives, children's schools, and community activities. They can also seek out or organize informal social networks as outlined in Box 13-2.

When money is a problem, as it so often is, Fitzhugh Dodson recommends bartering services.[55] He tells of a woman who exchanged her typing skills for the gardening talents of a writer. *Momma: The Sourcebook for Single Mothers* contains ideas for pooling resources and is as useful for single fathers as mothers.[56] Dodson's suggestions include sharing a home or apartment with another single-parent family, exchanging childcare services with a mother who does not work the same hours, and combining resources to increase purchasing power. All these things take time, a precious commodity, but all of them can help the single parent enhance the family's lifestyle, and they all include the bonus of being ways to meet new people (see Box 13-2).

This is especially important for women, whose social lives, more than those of men, are likely to be minimal after divorce or widowhood. To some extent this is the result of limited resources, which restrict the amount of money available for babysitters and appropriate clothes. To some extent, it is also the result of the social discomfort married couples feel toward the single person. But another factor, and one that the single mother can more easily deal with, is the guilt many women feel about spending any of their precious free time away from the children, or about thinking of becoming involved in another relationship after the death of a beloved spouse. To combat such guilt, Dodson suggests that single parents should contemplate the absurdity of total devotion to their children. The fuller and happier the life of the single parent, the fuller and happier the life of the children.

But beyond informal networks of support, Judith Wallerstein points to the need for expanded social services.[57] Divorcing families need legal services, psychological counseling, and mediation services that extend many years. These services help parents to make realistic psychological and economic provisions for their children during the whole course of development. She believes this is a responsibility of the whole society. Since we are quick to accept the needs for divorce, we must be equally quick to see that children do not bear the major burden of this widespread social change.

AN OPTIMISTIC VIEW

Optimism has been identified as a key factor in adapting well under stress.[58] Single parents may wonder how they can be optimistic when confronted with so much stress. An optimistic view does not deny the reality of the difficulties but rather sees

---

BOX 13-2
SUGGESTIONS FOR SINGLE PARENTS

1. Take classes with your children and work on a joint project together as equals. Developing new skills together brings a new dimension to the relationship between parent and child.
2. Use sleeping bags for bedding. They are comfortable and even young children can make their beds in the morning.
3. Form a cooperative group with friends and clean each other's houses as a team. It not only saves time, but it is an enjoyable social occasion.
4. Spend twenty or thirty minutes each day with each child. The child feels cared for and is less likely to nag at other times.
5. Form cooperative babysitting groups and trade off weekends as well as evenings.
6. Arrange door latches and hooks for clothes and mirrors so small children can use them easily.
7. Form a food cooperative with several families so that you can buy in bulk and save money.
8. Pool money for living expenses with another single parent and find a bigger and perhaps more enjoyable place for the two families. Babysitting will be easier, and there will be two adults to manage the household.

Adapted from Karol Hope and Nancy Young, eds., *Momma: The Sourcebook for Single Mothers* (New York: New American Library, 1976), pp. 314–321.

---

the difficulties as challenges to be met and managed. Optimistic parents can choose their goals and work toward them, setting priorities for what must be done and then doing it. Optimistic parents are confident that either they have the abilities or resources to do what is required or they can mobilize the necessary help from those around them. Fear decreases, and they function well.

Divorcing parents may wonder how they can be optimistic when they read of the turmoil and turbulent feelings everyone in the family experiences and the disruptions and difficulties children have. These stresses usually decrease by the end of the second year as divorced parents and children settle into a new style of life. By the end of three or four years, there is increased well-being for both parents.[59]

Diana Baumrind found in her study of parenting behaviors and adolescent competence that teens of divorced parents indeed had more problems and were less competent than peers in intact homes.[60] She concluded, however, that such problems were not an inevitable result of separation and divorce, but rather occurred because divorced parents were nondirective or disengaged in their parenting behaviors. Adolescents from single, authoritative homes were as competent as adolescents from intact authoritative homes. Conversely, adolescents from intact disengaged homes were as incompetent as youth from single disengaged homes. The parenting behavior, not the structure of the family, is the critical variable.

Mihaly Csikszentmihalyi and Reed Larson, in their study of teenagers in Chicago (reported in Chapters 10 and 11), compared the 20 percent of their sample from single-parent households with the 80 percent from two-parent households.[61] There were no differences between the two groups in academic achievement or number of friendships. What differences existed favored the adolescents from single-parent households, all but one headed by a mother. Children from single-parent households rated themselves as stronger, freer, more skilled; their goals were in agreement with those around them. Children from these families feel more mature and independent than children from two-parent families and seem to show no ill effects of the divorce. The length of time since divorce was not stated in these cases, so it is not clear how long the teenagers had had to adjust to the divorce. It is possible that later in adulthood some of these people may feel they had too much independence; but while they remain adolescents in the process of achieving independence, these children function well and are happy.

As they turn to the future, there is no formula that parents can use to create a satisfactory lifestyle. Instead, they must carefully examine the needs and personalities of all family members and search creatively for ways to satisfy these needs. In the process of solving problems, parents and children will find the pleasures and satisfactions that come from working together to accomplish difficult tasks. Dodson sums up the process of single parenting this way:

> You have a lot going for you as a single parent, which you may tend to overlook when things get rough. First, your children's love for you is a great psychological reservoir to draw upon. Second, the psychological methods for raising children effectively are the same in a single-parent family as in a two-parent family. Third, if you are well-informed . . . you will know far more about raising children than most parents in two-parent families do. All these factors put together mean that you can do a better job of raising children in your single-parent family than most parents in a two-parent family can. So take heart, and feel confident that you will succeed.[62]

MAJOR POINTS OF CHAPTER 13

When parents are unhappily married,

- fathers are frequently more negative with children
- parents view children as being difficult and interfering with their lives
- children frequently develop behavior problems
- children have a rise in hormones reflecting stress, are less able to deal with their feelings, and play with friends less enthusiastically
- many boys are impulsive and poorly controlled years before the divorce

The process of restructuring the family includes these stages:

- individual cognition
- family metacognition
- separation
- family reorganization
- family redefinition

Society has begun to make accommodations to the needs of divorcing families by:

- making it easier for both parents to stay involved with children
- providing court mediation services to aid families in making decisions in the child's best interests
- making it easier for mothers to get financial support from ex-husbands

Children's emotional reactions at the time of divorce:

- include feelings common to children regardless of age, like sadness, anger, fear, confusion, sometimes relief
- do not predict long-term adjustment to divorce

Children's emotional reactions also vary by age:

- preschoolers feel overwhelmed, abandoned, and worried they caused it; they need parents' acceptance of feelings and support
- children five to seven are vulnerable, try to deny intense feelings of sadness and grief; but divorce dominates their thoughts, and they need to talk about feelings
- children nine and older may feel responsible for helping parents and may get benefit from counseling

Parents' emotional reactions:

- are intense and include many of the feelings children feel—anger, sadness, anxiety, depression
- can interfere with their providing care and support for children

Factors affecting adjustment to divorce include:

- amount of conflict among family members
- availability of both parents to children
- nature of relationships in the family
- responsibilities family members take
- defensibility of divorce from child's point of view

Factors that protect children at time of divorce include:

- child's age, sex, intelligence
- child's easygoing temperament
- manageable amounts of stress
- appropriate supports in help from grandparents, other relatives
- child's getting positive feelings from own achievements

Parenting tasks include establishing:

- effective channels of communication
- stable family structure in each parent's home
- reasonable visiting arrangements
- support for children in coping with divorce
- meaningful lives so everyone can get on with life

In telling children of divorce, it is best if parents:

- do it together
- do it before a parent moves out
- tell all the children together
- refuse to ask the child to take sides
- refuse to burden child with either parents' negative view of the other

Establishing reasonable visiting arrangements involve:

- working out fair, practical timesharing schedule
- making effort to live up to agreements
- being flexible in trading times
- preparing child calmly to stay with other parent
- not doing business with other parent at time of transfer
- encouraging child to work out problems directly with other parent

When a parent dies, children go through stages of grief:

- protest against death
- pain and despair as child accepts death
- acceptance

Parent's role in helping children is to:

- be truthful in telling child about parent's death
- include child as active participant in funeral/memorial
- offer child many opportunities to express feelings
- accept child's feelings
- provide model of adult who grieves and goes on with life

Effects of father absence depend on:

- child's age—young boys and older girls appear most affected
- mother's attitude about father and men in general

An optimistic view of divorce points out:

- when parents remain authoritative, children do well
- when parents provide effective models, children do well

ADDITIONAL READINGS

Adler, Robert E. *Sharing the Children*. Bethesda: Adler & Adler, 1988.

Ahrons, Constance R., and Rodgers, Roy H. *Divorced Families*. New York: W. W. Norton, 1987.

Gardner, Richard. *The Parents' Book about Divorce*. New York: Bantam, 1979.

Wallerstein, Judith S., and Kelly, Joan B. *Surviving the Breakup*. New York: Basic Books, 1980.

Wallerstein, Judith S., and Blakeslee, Sandra. *Second Chances*. New York: Ticknor & Fields, 1989.

Notes

1. United States Bureau of the Census, *Statistical Abstract of the United States: 1989*. 109th ed. (Washington, D.C.: U.S. Government Printing Office, 1989).

2. E. Mavis Hetherington and Kathleen A. Camara, "Families in Transition: The Process of Dissolution and Reconstruction," in *A Review of Child Development Research,* vol. 7, ed. Ross D. Parke (Chicago: University of Chicago Press, 1984), pp. 398–439.

3. John M. Gottman and Lynn Fainsilber Katz, "Effects of Marital Discord on Young Children's Peer Interaction and Health," *Developmental Psychology* 25 (1989): 373–381.

4. M. Ann Easterbrooks and Robert N. Emde, "Marital and Parent-Child Relationships: The Role of Affect in the Family," in *Relationships within Families: Mutual Influences,* ed. Robert A. Hinde and Joan Stevenson-Hinde (Oxford: Clarendon Press, 1988), pp. 83–103.

5. Gene H. Brody, Anthony D. Pellegrini, and Irving E. Sigel, "Marital Quality and Mother-Child and Father-Child Interactions with School-Aged Children," *Developmental Psychology* 22 (1986): 291–296.

6. Jeanne H. Block, Jack Block, and Andrea Morrison, "Parental Disagreement on Child-rearing Orientations and Gender-related Personality Correlates in Children," *Child Development* 52 (1981): 965–974.

7. Brian E. Vaughn, Jeanne H. Block, and Jack Block, "Parental Agreement on Child Rearing during Early Childhood and the Psychological Characteristics of Adolescents," *Child Development* 59 (1988): 1020–1033.

8. Jeanne H. Block, Jack Block, and Per F. Gjerde, "The Personality of Children prior to Divorce: A Prospective Study," *Child Development* 57 (1986): 827–840.

9. Hetherington and Camara, "Families in Transition."

10. U.S. Bureau of the Census: *Statistical Abstract: 1989*.

11. Constance Ahrons, "Divorce: Before, During and After," in *Stress and the Family,* vol. 1, *Coping with Normative Transitions,* ed. Hamilton I. McCubbin and Charles R. Figley (New York: Brunner/Mazel, 1983), pp. 102–115.

12. Ibid.

13. Judith S. Wallerstein and Joan B. Kelly, *Surviving the Breakup* (New York: Basic Books, 1980).

14. Ibid.

15. Ibid, p. 66.

16. Joan B. Kelly and Judith S. Wallerstein, "Brief Interventions with Children in Divorcing Families," *American Journal of Orthopsychiatry* 47 (1977): 23–39.

17. Wallerstein and Kelly, *Surviving the Breakup*.

18. Judith S. Wallerstein and Sandra Blakeslee, *Second Chances* (New York: Ticknor & Fields, 1989).

19. M. Janice Hogan, Cheryl Buehler, and Beatrice Robinson, "Single Parenting: Transitioning Alone," in *Stress and the Family,* vol. 1, *Coping with Normative Transitions,* pp. 116–132.

20. Hetherington and Camara, "Families in Transition."
21. Wallerstein and Kelly, *Surviving the Breakup.*
22. Hetherington and Camara, "Families in Transition."
23. Ibid.
24. Hetherington and Camara, "Families in Transition"; Wallerstein and Kelly, *Surviving the Breakup.*
25. Ibid.
26. Ibid.
27. Wallerstein and Kelly, *Surviving the Breakup.*
28. E. Mavis Hetherington, "Coping with Family Transitions: Winners, Losers, and Survivors," *Child Development* 60 (1989): 1–14.
29. Wallerstein and Blakeslee, *Second Chances.*
30. Carol E. MacKinnon, "An Observational Investigation of Sibling Interactions in Married and Divorced Families," *Developmental Psychology* 25 (1989): 36–44.
31. Wallerstein and Blakeslee, *Second Chances,* p. 110.
32. Wallerstein and Blakeslee, *Second Chances.*
33. Ibid., p. 286.
34. Ibid.
35. Wallerstein and Blakeslee, *Second Chances,* p. 287.
36. Frances L. Ilg and Louise Bates Ames, *Child Behavior* (New York: Harper & Row, 1955), pp. 334–335.
37. Conni Rust, "Who Gets to Clean the Toilets in Your House?" in *Momma: The Sourcebook for Single Mothers,* ed. Karol Hope and Nancy Young (New American Library, 1976) pp. 272–277.
38. Hetherington, "Coping with Family Transitions."
39. Marsha Klein, Jeanne M. Tschann, Janet R. Johnston, and Judith S. Wallerstein, "Children's Adjustment in Joint and Sole Physical Custody Families," *Developmental Psychology* 25 (1989): 430–438.
40. Wallerstein and Blakeslee, *Second Chances.*
41. Ibid.
42. Hetherington, "Coping with Family Transitions," p. 13.
43. Hogan, Buehler, and Robinson, "Single Parenting."

44. Hetherington and Camara, "Families in Transition."
45. Bard Lindeman, "Widower, Heal Thyself," in *Human Adaptation,* ed. Rudolf H. Moos (Lexington, Mass.: D. C. Heath, 1976), p. 280.
46. Lynn Caine, *Widow* (New York: Bantam, 1975), p. 69.
47. Earl Grollman, "Prologue," in *Explaining Death to Children,* ed. Earl A. Grollman (Boston: Beacon Press, 1967), p. 15.
48. Harriet Schiff Sarnoff, *The Bereaved Parent* (New York: Penguin, 1978).
49. John Bowlby, "Childhood Mourning and Its Implications for Psychiatry," *American Journal of Psychiatry* 118 (1961): 481–498.
50. Grollman, "Prologue."
51. Thomas Gordon with Judith Gordon Sands, *P.E.T. in Action* (New York: Bantam, 1978).
52. Grollman, "Prologue," p. 27.
53. E. Mavis Hetherington and Ross D. Parke, *Child Psychology: A Contemporary Viewpoint* (New York: McGraw-Hill, 1975).
54. E. Mavis Hetherington, "Effects of Father-Absence on Personality Development in Adolescent Daughters," *Developmental Psychology* 7 (1972): 313–326.
55. Fitzhugh Dodson, *How to Discipline with Love* (New York: Rawson, 1977).
56. Karol Hope and Nancy Young, eds., *Momma: The Sourcebook for Single Mothers* (New York: New American Library, 1976).
57. Wallerstein and Blakeslee, *Second Chances.*
58. Hamilton I. McCubbin and Charles R. Rigley, "Introduction," in *Stress and the Family,* vol. 1, *Coping with Normative Transitions.*
59. Hetherington and Camara, "Families in Transition."
60. Diana Baumrind, "The Influence of Parenting Style on Adolescent Competence and Problem Behavior," American Psychological Association Meetings, New Orleans, August 12–13, 1989.
61. Mihaly Csikszentmihalyi and Reed Larson, *Being Adolescent* (New York: Basic Books, 1984).
62. Dodson, *How to Discipline with Love,* pp. 200–201.

STEPPARENTING

C H A P T E R   14

We have focused on the process of divorce and single parenting. Between 70 and 80 percent of single parents remarry—slightly more men than women remarry and more parents under forty than over forty at the time of divorce remarry.[1] In our current society it is estimated that as many as 35 percent of children, 54 percent of women, and 60 percent of men live in second marriages.[2]

This chapter talks about the special bond that can grow between an adult and child who initially are strangers but come to know each other because the child's parent married the adult. In this chapter we focus on children who live or visit regularly with the parent and stepparent. Stepfamilies face many challenges in establishing a home that will be nurturing and satisfying for all members. Stepfamilies encounter many special problems; but when individuals who are not biologically related form a caring family, they also experience closeness and rewards.

Traditionally we have used the term **stepfamilies** to refer to second marriages in which one or both parents have children by a previous spouse, but a great diversity of terms currently exists. Monica McGoldrick and Betty Carter prefer the term **remarried families**.[3] They believe that the term **blended** implies a closer integration than usually occurs, the term **stepfamily** implies it is not a real family, and the term **restructured** implies that it is just a matter of rearranging the parts. Since the Stepfamily Association of America, the largest support group for stepfamilies, still uses that term, we use it as well as the other terms in this chapter.

EFFECTS OF REMARRIAGE ON PARENTS

Remarriage provides many benefits to parents. First, it provides emotional closeness, intimacy, and sexual satisfaction for parents. In caring relationships, parents feel greater self-esteem, greater contentment and happiness. Second, parents have someone with whom they can share both the financial and the caregiving responsibilities. Judith Wallerstein[4] finds that many parents do not repeat mistakes of the first marriage again, and she and Joan Kelly[5] find that even though extra work and responsibility may follow remarriage, parents are energetic and happy because of the positive emotional experiences.

Remarriages also bring problems because there are more people to consider and few guidelines for how to integrate everyone: "Newly remarried parents report experiencing levels of both positive and negative stress twice that of nondivorced parents."[6] The divorce rate here is thought to be only slightly higher than in first marriages; but in second marriages, parents are quicker to decide that divorce is necessary.

EFFECTS OF REMARRIAGE ON CHILDREN

When two divorced parents postpone remarriage, they are more likely to continue sharing parenting equally. Noncustodial fathers are more likely to remain active and involved parents if they do not remarry. When parents do remarry, this means children must share them with a widening circle of people—stepparents and step-siblings.

Custodial mothers' behavior changes after remarriage. Mothers report that they are less emotionally responsive to children and that there is poorer communication between them. They are less consistent in the rules, supervise and monitor children less, and are more authoritarian in matters of discipline. So, it is not surprising that both boys and girls are more resistant and rebellious in the first two years of the remarriage. This is particularly true if the children are adolescents at the time.[7]

Boys seem to have less difficulty making the transition to the new family. Perhaps because many boys have had a poor relationship with a single mother, they respond to a stepfather who is warm and involved and spends time with them. So after the first two years, they tend to be accepting of such a stepfather.[8]

Girls, however, are not so accepting. Perhaps because they have had a very good relationship with the mother during the period of single parenting, they seem to resent the new husband as a rival for the mother's time and attention, which are now more limited. No matter how supportively the stepfather behaves, girls tend to remain aloof even after two years.[9]

When children live with custodial fathers and stepmothers, it is again girls who have greater difficulty. Frequent contact with their biological mothers seems to increase the difficulty, but this unusual finding may be the result of the mothers' having special problems that argued against their having custody. However, the longer girls live in such families, the more positive the relationship grows between the daughter and stepmother.[10]

Judith Wallerstein and Joan Kelly found that about one-quarter of children in stepfamilies, mostly those children ten and older, had needs that differed from those of their parents.[11] These children often felt ignored and isolated in the new family. Parents seemed to have less time for them, and they felt lonely. This was particularly true when the noncustodial father faded from the picture. Just as during the divorce process, the continuing involvement with both biological parents is an important factor in adapting well to the new stepfamily.

THE SPECIAL PROBLEMS OF STEPFAMILIES

What makes stepparenting even more difficult than parenting? After all, the biological parents of a newborn are not likely to have much more training for their new roles than does a stepparent—and they may have even less, if the stepparent has children of his own. Fitzhugh Dodson presents six reasons.[12] First, in families of biological parents and children, the parents' mistakes are overcome by longstanding emotional bonds. When a stepfamily is formed, such ties do not exist but are created over time. Second, these blended families are more complex than biological families and often include more people. When the wife and husband both have children, the family includes two sets of stepchildren. If each of the former spouses has remarried, the two sets of children will have two stepparents plus various stepbrothers and stepsisters, and perhaps half-brothers and half-sisters. The number of grandparents also increases. Each of these people from all of these families has needs and interests that must be considered.

Third, members of blended families may have deep feelings of jealousy and ambivalence. Because so many more people are involved and have to be consulted about decisions and the newly married parents want to devote time to their relationship, stepparents may have less time to give to individual children. Children may feel that the new marriage is depriving them of the parent. Parents must accept those feelings as realistic—there is less time for each child. Conversely, the parents may feel that the children are intruding on the marriage. Because living intimately with new people causes some stress, both parents and children may develop mixed feelings toward family members. A child's hostility may be directed at the new stepparent or stepsiblings, or at her or his own parent and brothers and sisters.

Fourth, both parents and children are haunted by the earlier marriage. Stepparents may feel insecure as they live with children who are constant proof that the spouse loved another person. Furthermore, the biological parent continues to have contact with the former spouse because of the children. When the stepparent enters the family, children must recognize that the other biological parent is no longer part of the family. If the absent biological parent has died, children may have created an idealized image of this parent that no flesh-and-blood person can measure up to. It is not surprising, then, that research suggests that it is harder for a stepparent to enter a family in which the absent parent has died.

Fifth, former spouses may use the children and their needs to attack the biological parent and the stepparent. One father and stepmother reported that the mother never bought the children clothes, and when the father did this in addition to the monthly payment, the mother did not wash or care for them. She let the children come for visits looking like beggars and told them the father did not care to provide enough money so she could buy clothes. Conversely, one mother reported that the father and stepmother, rather than providing money for clothes for the children, instead bought the children fancy clothes that were appropriate for the father and stepmother's lifestyle, but not for the children's needs at school and play.

Sixth, there are no clear guidelines for being a stepparent. There are few enough for biological parents, but the role of stepparent remains even more vague. The stepparent must create this role depending on his or her individual personality, the ages and sexes of the children, and their living arrangements. When a biological parent is dead or absent and children live with the stepparent, that stepparent has a larger role. When children live with the biological parent and come only for short visits, the stepparent has a more limited role. Whatever the circumstances, stepparents can create meaningful, caring relationships with children with time, patience, and interest.

Stepparents who are forewarned about the problems of stepparenting and who think and talk, in advance, about how to cope with these problems, can find their new roles rewarding and exciting. We can usefully adopt Alice Rossi's stages of transition to marriage, work, and parenting roles to understand the process of becoming a stepparent.[13] You will recall from Chapter 2 that Rossi describes (1) the anticipatory period, (2) the honeymoon, (3) the plateau, and (4) discontinuation or termination. Only the fourth stage does not apply here.

THE ANTICIPATORY PERIOD

The anticipatory stage for a parent includes mourning the loss of the previous family, dating, finding a prospective partner, and planning the remarriage. Parents must complete the process of grieving, described in the previous chapter, and experience the range of emotions connected with the loss of the marriage. When the loss is not accepted or the remarriage occurs so quickly that individuals do not have time to accept the loss, problems may arise in stepparenting. For example, one fourteen-year-old boy got in a series of fights with his stepfather, who married the mother one year after the divorce. He was close to his father and had not accepted the divorce. The boy resented his stepfather and, particularly after a visit with his father, got into fights with the stepfather. Counseling for the boy and the family helped him to accept his feelings of loss.

Dating

As single parents begin to date again, they may lack confidence in themselves and may fear they will repeat mistakes they made in the past. Parents may be on the alert for signs they are failing in the new relationship. A hardworking father may find again that his work habits interfere with a new relationship. A working mother may fear that her independence—which upset her first husband—will drive away the man she is beginning to feel attached to. Just as children grow when their feelings are accepted as valid, parents will grow if they can accept their own doubts, fears, and worries. When feelings are recognized and accepted, individuals can find ways to handle them.

Children react in various ways when their parents begin dating. Some children are eager to have a single mother remarry, so they will have a father. Such children are likely to continually question the mother about how well she likes the men she meets and about the progress of the relationships. If a mother does not find men to date, children—particularly young children—may try to seek them out. Sometimes children hope a father will remarry because he seems lonely, and the children think they may not be affected by a stepmother they do not expect to see frequently.

Children may be resentful of a possible remarriage. They have little enough time with the parents as it is, and they resent having to share the parent's free time with a stranger. Often the bond between parent and child in single-parent families is intense, and the child wishes that to continue without the interference of outside people. Still other children have both positive and negative feelings. Whatever the reactions to dating, parents can accept them without feeling they have to do what their children want.

Primacy of the Couple Bond

As a dating relationship continues and is a source of pleasure to both individuals, they begin to think about making commitments to each other. Here, parenting experts and stepparents agree in insisting that parents consider the attachment to the partner the primary bond in the stepfamily. Parents are advised not to marry to give Johnny a father or Suzy a mother. The two partners must care about each other and the marriage must come first if it is to be a success.

Psychiatrist L. Eugene Arnold, writing guidelines for stepparents, uses the term "reasonable primacy of the husband-wife bond."[14] This can be interpreted to mean that, in ordinary circumstances, the importance of the marital tie will be emphasized so children do not feel they can force the stepparent out. However, under extreme circumstances—for example, if a stepparent physically or sexually abuses a stepchild—the parent would consider the parent-child bond to be primary and would consider ending the marriage. In that situation it is the responsibility of the parent to protect the child, who is unable to protect herself or himself, from the destructive actions of the stepparent.

Prospective partners need to look at each other not only as possible mates, but also as parents to their children. In planning a first marriage, couples can fantasize and guess what they will be like as parents. If they have had extended contact with children, their fantasies may be quite realistic. When approaching remarriage, parents already have experience. They know whether they tend to use physical punishments, permit back talk, run a tight or a loose ship. Expectations and attitudes can be and must be examined. The successful merging of a group of people will depend on how well both the partners can work together to satisfy each others' needs while parenting children.

Getting to Know Each Other

As adults consider commitments to each other, they must get to know each other's children as individuals. Going on outings without the biological parent along and spending time in projects provide useful opportunities for adults and children to become better acquainted and to form a special relationship between them. If a child is reserved at first, you must not assume you are failing. Give the child time to get to know you and to warm up.

One of the prime difficulties in many stepfamilies is that the parents have high expectations for themselves and for their relationships with the children. Because partners love each other, they assume that they will love the children and that the love will be returned immediately. Even when stepparents have known other stepparents who had difficulties in forming relationships, they believe "those people" had special problems and were coping poorly.

Unrealistic expectations are often coupled with a tendency to idealize what occurs in biological families. When this is true, comparisons always reflect badly on the stepfamily and create problems. For example, sometimes stepparents feel unappreciated. A stepmother feels that she cooks and cleans, washes and shops for children who are not her own. A stepfather earns money and provides a home for children who may consider him an intruder in the family. Stepparents may feel that in biological families children love and appreciate their parents, and in comparison they feel cheated. Certainly there is a long history of caring between parents and children in biological families. But many biological parents believe their children do not appreciate all their efforts or value their virtues, taking them for granted.

It is possible that prospective stepparents may not especially enjoy contact with children. But it should be at least tolerable and perhaps potentially satisfying. Stepparents must be honest with themselves. In the blush of romance, it may be tempting to think everything will work out, that the children are part of the package and adjustments will be made. But too often the problems do not get resolved and the second marriage ends.

What if you don't really like your prospective stepchildren? Does this mean that the marriage should be called off? First, if you truly care for the other person, get professional help in evaluating the situation. It is possible that both partners are overlooking some facet of the situation that can be clarified with counseling. Second, recognize that though honesty is a requirement of relationships, in the anticipatory period enthusiasm and warmth for the children are not initial requirements for a good relationship. Often relationships build with time and increased contact, if stepparents can be honest about their initial feelings and realistic about the length of time it takes to establish closeness.

As partners and children get to know each other, the adults should discuss the specifics of discipline—for example, the use of punishments, the number of chores expected, the amount of back talk allowed—as well as the amount of time parents will spend with children and the ways money will be allocated. They will not be in exact agreement. If opinions diverge sharply, the couple can work out differences, getting counseling if necessary. When at least some differences are worked out before the marriage, problems that surface later will be easier to handle. If, for example, parents know that they tend to disagree about how much time should be spent with children, they will be prepared to compromise.

During this anticipatory period, as concrete plans for the remarriage are discussed, children may have fears about the effects of the blended family on their lives. Some children have worried that they will be automatically adopted, or that they will no longer be permitted to visit the other biological parent. Such fears can result in distant or withdrawn behavior. Prospective stepparents will have to listen carefully to what children say and try to understand their feelings. Active listening, feedback of feelings, and communication of wishes and thoughts are helpful. Dodson describes one prospective stepfather who could not seem to get along with his partner's son. This man felt that if the relationship with the boy could not be improved, he could not marry the mother. Dodson suggested that this man should try to get to know the boy by taking him off on an outing. The man got expensive football tickets, bought food, and tried very hard to relate to the boy. Although it was hard for him, the man accepted the boy's hostility calmly and let him talk. Gradually the boy's fears that he would no longer be able to relate to his own father emerged. Active listening enabled the boy to express these fears, and the prospective stepfather reassured him that the fears were unrealistic.

Concrete Plans

During the anticipatory period, very practical problems need to be handled. The solutions found for them can tell something very important about how the group will function as a family. For example, careful consideration should be given to where the family will live. Experts agree that, if possible, new living quarters should be found. Otherwise, the members moving into the home of the other partner may feel like invaders. Sometimes this is not possible—a move might be too costly or might require the children to change schools. If so, it is wise to see if the present home can be rearranged so that each person feels he belongs there. Even if children come only for weekends, they need to feel they have their own space. Having special drawers and closet space, having individual sets of sheets and towels will help children feel at home, even if they cannot have a whole room to themselves.

Suppose you have gone through the process of mourning the previous marriage, have dated, committed yourself to a new relationship, exchanged ideas about parenting and found yourself in general agreement, and decided to remarry. How do you tell the children? When possible, children should have an extended opportunity to know the prospective stepparent, and they should be told about the decision as soon as it is reached. Children report great bitterness over being told just before or after the wedding. In some situations, children refuse to hear the news, and occasionally they deny they were told. Once informed, they should be included in the wedding if possible. Many children have reported feeling rejected and angry that parents did not want them present—and those feelings made it difficult for them to begin to adjust to the new family and especially to the stepparent.

Parents may be surprised that the wedding itself may change children's attitudes toward their new stepparents. Some stepparents have reported that, although the children liked them before the wedding, after the remarriage the children were rejecting, hostile, or withdrawn. If the adult who seemed to be a friend suddenly becomes a disciplinarian as well, the children may be surprised. Remember that the realities of day-to-day living are quite different from the atmosphere of visits and outings. Try to get to know as much as you can about each other before the wedding. And then it may be wise to assume gradually some of the facets of the new role.

Practical questions must be answered. What will the stepparents be called? "Mom" and "Dad" may be inappropriate when the biological parent is alive and involved with the child. Most stepparents, in this period, are called by their first names. As intimacy develops, children may start to use "Mom" and "Dad." But this should be the child's choice. Remember that the name does not create the relationship. If and when a child feels that a stepparent has become a mother or father, then the use of the more intimate term will come naturally and will have the desired meaning.

THE HONEYMOON PERIOD

In marriage, this is a period of extended pleasure and freedom from intense pressures of day-to-day life. In parenting it is a period of increased pressure—there is so much to do for the newborn, and the child is a mystery. In stepparenting, the children are known before the wedding, but all relationships change with the wedding and the daily presence and interaction among new family members.

Emotional Rapport

Children, and parents, are most likely to thrive in an emotional environment that is nurturing and fosters each person's growth and independence. This is as true of stepfamilies as it is of biological families, but such an environment may be more difficult for stepparents to create. Many have found that active listening, communicating feelings, and sharing activities all contribute to such an environment. See Box 14-1 for some suggestions.

In a discussion of how relationships are developed in a stepfamily, Shirley Gould advises parents to keep in mind three factors that influence this process.[15] First, children have strong loyalty to the biological parent not living with them and to the previous marriage. Even when the biological parent has been absent or unresponsive to the child's needs, the child is likely to be reluctant to do anything that he or she thinks might endanger whatever relationship exists. Second, trust is not quickly established. This is ordinarily true in a relationship between two mature adults. And it is especially true in a relationship between a child who has gone through an emotional trauma (the divorce) and an adult who has entered that child's life uninvited by the child. Third, respect between stepparent and stepchild does not occur immediately or automatically. Respect, like trust, is the product of time and sharing and intimacy.

Parents have to accept that both they and their children have illusions about what the relationship will be like—some overly positive and some overly negative illusions. It may have been easy to maintain illusions prior to marriage, to assume that remarriage itself would change what is negative for the better and give an opportunity for all the positive aspects to come forth. For example, some stepparents believe they will make up for all the negative things that have happened to the child in the past, that they will be such a wonderful parent the child will have no more problems. Or, conversely, the child expects the ideal, all-giving parent, and an imperfect adult appears. Both parents and children have to relinquish illusions and find the satisfactions that are truly there.

◆
Box 14-1
EIGHT-STEP PROGRAM FOR STEPPING AHEAD

Step 1: Nurturing Couple Relationship

    a. Plan something you like away from home once a week

    b. Arrange 20 minutes of relaxed time alone each day

    c. Talk together about the running of the household at least 30 minutes each week

Step 2: Finding Personal Space and Time

    a. Take time to make a special "private" place for each adult and child in the house

    b. Each person takes at least 2 hours a week to do something special for that person—reading, TV, hobby, sport

Step 3: Nourishing Family Relationships

    a. Share with one another something you appreciate each day—perhaps at dinner, where each person shares, or in less formal settings

    b. Do not link discussion of problems with what is liked

Step 4: Maintaining Close Parent/Child Relationships

    a. Do something fun together for at least 20 minutes once or twice a week

    b. These times are given no matter what and do not depend on good behavior

Step 5: Developing Stepparent/Stepchild Relationship

    a. Do something fun together 15 or 20 minutes a week—if child only comes occasionally, make this a longer time, less often

    b. If child refuses, accept that and offer to do something at a later time

Step 6: Building Family Trust

    a. Schedule a family event once a month and give each person a chance to choose what you do

    b. Begin special traditions in your remarried family

    c. Do not always schedule events when nonresident children are there because resident children may believe they are less important

Step 7: Strengthen Stepfamily Ties with Regular Family Meeting

Step 8: Work with Child's Other Household

    a. Give adults in the other household positive feedback once a month

    b. Give positive message without expectation of return

Adapted from: Emily Visher, "The Stepping Ahead Program," in *Stepfamilies Stepping Ahead,*
ed. Mala Burt (Baltimore: Stepfamilies Press, 1989), pp. 57–89.

To create emotional rapport, learn as much as you can about your stepchildren—about their lives before you knew them, about what is important to them, about what makes each unique. Be observant when you are with them and sensitive to their feelings and needs. Find activities you can share that will give pleasure to them and to you—perhaps special hobbies of interest to all, but also the simpler pleasures of picnics, games, and reading. Share yourself with them as you would like them to share with you. And gradually, as in any human relationship, bonds and closeness will be created.

Stepparents need to recognize that children continue psychological ties with the absent biological parent, whether the earlier marriage was ended by death or divorce. The parent needs to confirm that indeed the stepparent has intruded in the child's life by taking some of the spouse's time and energy, but that the stepparent is within his or her rights when doing this. No apologies need to be made, nor should the child be chastised for having trouble adjusting. Stepparents and spouses must accept that becoming a marital partner and parent at the same time creates stress. With learning and practice, however, stress decreases.

As parents recognize there are real problems, they can accept negative feelings in themselves and in their children. Negative reactions in children do not mean that a stepparent has failed or that a child has rejected him or her. A child may like a stepparent and want to be close, but not feel ready. Members of stepfamilies need to remember that in biological families children get angry at parents for many reasons, and that this is particularly true during adolescence. Rejection by the child may be the result of the child's longing for the biological parent, not the result of anything the stepparent has or has not done.

A stepparent may find that he or she is not interested in the stepchildren and does not really want close relationships with them. Perhaps the stepparent is involved in work or other interests or grew up in a family in which emotional distance was maintained. When a woman who has married a man whose children come to visit finds she cannot have children of her own, she may resent his children, taking her pain and frustration out on them without realizing why.

If a man has shown little interest in the children and the mother has married him anyhow, Richard Gardner recommends honest discussion of the matter. A mother might say to her children, "Look, Joe is a nice guy, and I love him very much. I wish he were the kind of man who is really interested in children, but he isn't. Not all men are. I would like you to know that I wish he'd be more affectionate with you, but he isn't likely to be. You have Daddy and Uncle John, and you have me."[16] This approach helps the children to realize they are not responsible for the stepfather's lack of affection, and it may prevent them from having unrealistic expectations.

Honesty in relationships and feelings about others is important at all stages in stepparenting. Openly admitting to yourself that you do not like your stepchildren or are upset about some particular aspect of their behavior can pave the way to solutions to the problems. At the very least, such honesty allows you to express to your spouse your anger, confusion, and guilt about the problems. Many of the difficult feelings may result from unrealistic expectations of what you or the children can do in the situation. Not until each of you shares your feelings can you begin to help each other resolve problems. Instant closeness between stepparent and child does not occur any more frequently than instant closeness between any two individuals. As you make the adjustments of creating a new family, there will be conflicts. If all members of the stepfamily try to examine the situation realistically and to be honest with each other, the period of adjustment may be more emotionally chaotic but it is also likely to be more fun and to be shorter.

Stepfathers' Problems

A stepfather whose biological children live with their mother may experience painful feelings as he goes about establishing relationships with his stepchildren. He may regret the time he gives to another man's children when his own children do not get his attention. As a stepfather engages in new activities with stepchildren—playing ball, bike riding, roughhousing—he may yearn to have his children with him. If his former wife has remarried, he may resent the man who is now parenting his children. Relationships are further complicated if the stepfather sees his own children for only brief visits. He may find himself seeking their favor, fearful of disciplining them because he does not want to alienate them, to spoil the little time they have together. In this situation, a stepfather may want to spend some time with his own children in activities away from the blended family so that he can maintain close relationships with his children.

Discipline

Discipline is probably the single biggest issue in stepparenting and accounts for the research findings that stepparents are best accepted when children are very young (and stepparents can help to establish discipline from the very beginning), or are young adults (presumably no longer in need of discipline). Adolescents are least able to accept a new parent because they are having difficulty coming to terms with any authority and are often already at loggerheads with their biological parents.

The techniques for handling discipline problems in stepfamilies are the same as those used in biological families. The main differences are that in stepfamilies there are more sources of problems. Biological parents do not always feel comfortable when dealing with discipline, and they have long and strong relationships with their children. So it is easy to understand that discipline may be even more difficult in stepfamilies, especially in the beginning.

The Role of the Stepparent Effective discipline depends on children wanting the approval and acceptance of adults. Thus, experts advise stepparents to wait until emotional rapport is established before beginning to discipline. Once a friendly bond is formed, stepparents can begin to play a role. When children are young and eager to have a stepparent, the stepparent will assume an active role sooner than in stepfamilies where children are older or have been disciplined by a single biological parent for many years.

In biological families, a set of rules for living develops over a period of time. In stepfamilies such rules must be established quickly. Stepparents can most easily take an active role in forming rules in family councils. There all members of the family over the age of three or four contribute their opinion on issues. Dodson recommends that all decisions be made by unanimous vote, so that everyone feels the rules are what they want to live with. Parents may have to explain to young children the need for rules and limits in certain areas. But even young children can suggest rules and have their feelings considered. If unanimous agreement cannot be reached, issues can be brought up again until the family finds solutions acceptable to all. When the blended family is just beginning to function as a unit, it is important to have everyone's support and cooperation.

Forming a Parenting Coalition

Parents in remarried families can seek to form an alliance with all the parenting figures in the children's lives. This can include biological parent and stepparent in the other household, and it can also include grandparents and stepgrandparents who may play a role in caring for children. When adults can share information about what the rules are in each house and describe the parenting strategies that seem to work best for each child, everyone has at least a greater understanding of what the child is experiencing in each household, even if no greater agreement occurs. Other adults in the child's life may have come up with a particularly good way of doing something that is well worth carrying over to other households.

Handling Conflicts Children in a blended family are likely to go through a period of testing the parent or stepparent to see if the agreed-upon rules really hold firm. Will they get in trouble for violating the rules? Parents should not set rules unless they are prepared to enforce them—taking action, sending I-messages, looking for resolutions of the problems, or using some form of punishment.

A common retort when rules are laid down is, "You are not my real parent!" Patricia Papernow suggests that parents respond, "You are absolutely right. And it's going to take time for us to get to know each other, and it's really hard for both of us. And then we may still not like each other. Meanwhile, we do have to find a better way to live."[17]

A stepparent can use active listening and reflect the child's wishes that the adult was not making these decisions. "You're not my real parent" is the stepfamily equivalent of "I hate you." The child is most likely to say this when feeling threatened, upset, or hurt and wanting to hurt back. It is wise to try to explore the feelings underneath and to respond in a way that is appropriate for those feelings and the circumstances that provoked the feelings.

When conflicts occur, some stepparents want to fight their own battles with stepchildren, and parents are advised to let them do it. Stepparents can send I-messages to convey concern about rule violations. Specific statements describing the upsetting behavior and why it bothers the stepparent can prevent the anger and bitterness that accusations, criticisms, and sarcasm can provoke. However, the stepparent must have the emotional support of the spouse. The spouse should communicate a sense of trust and respect for the stepparent's judgment. Support can be expressed in appreciative I-messages that bolster the stepparent and are heard by the child being disciplined.

INTERVIEW
with Emily Visher and John Visher

Emily Visher is a clinical psychologist and John Visher is a psychiatrist. They are founders of the Stepfamily Association and authors of such books as Stepfamilies: Myths and Realities *and* Old Loyalties, New Ties: Therapeutic Strategies with Stepfamilies.

You have worked with stepparents and stepfamilies for many years, so I want to talk to you about what you feel are the important things for parents to do in order to ease the difficulties that can arise in stepfamilies.

E. Visher: We feel very strongly that we are talking about not just stepparents (adults who are parents to the spouse's child or children by a previous marriage) but also remarried parents (parents who have had children, been divorced or widowed, and are now married again). They are both in the family. We know many couples where one parent is a stepparent and the other is a remarried parent because just one has children.

What happens in our opinion is that so much of the functioning in a stepfamily gets related to the stepparent, but we feel that the remarried parent brings a lot to the marriage. Being a remarried parent is a lot different from being in a first marriage. People don't recognize the contribution of the remarried parent in the stepfamily.

J. Visher: We like the term *stepfamily* because it puts everyone together in one unit and that is where they belong. They are all in it together, trying to work out integration and a more successful family.

E. Visher: We talk about a parenting coalition that is the coalition between all the adults in the child's life. For example, you see, there could be three or four parenting adults—if both parents have remarried, there will be four. If those adults can somehow develop a working relationship around raising the children, the loyalty conflicts of the children will be much less. The adults will get a lot out of it, too, because there is less tension, and better relationships develop between stepparent and stepchild.

We chose the word *coalition* because it means a temporary alliance of separate entities for accomplishing a task. The households and couples are separate, and it is a temporary alliance between all the adults. The task they are working on together is raising the children.

Families can flounder on the basis of the stepparent's trying to be a parent, and the children say basically, "I've got a mother or a father." We have moderated panels of teenagers in stepfamilies, and we always ask them, "What do you want your stepparents to be? What is their role?" I don't think we have ever heard anyone say anything other than "a friend." The difficulty is that, by "friend," they mean something very different. They don't mean a pal; it's closer than that.

They are able to talk to the stepparent in a meaningful way that is different from the way they would talk to a parent. They are freer to talk to a stepparent because they are not so involved. One teenager on a panel said she wanted her stepfather to be her friend, and then later she said, "I love my stepfather, and I've never told him." She's saying she wants a friend, but she has very deep feelings for him. He was in the back of the room and heard her.

It is important to take a role that is satisfying to the adult and to the child, and that may be different for children living in the same household and for children in different house-

continued

INTERVIEW

with Emily Visher and John Visher *continued*

holds. The relationship is different depending on the age of the child—a six-year-old needs something different than a sixteen-year-old. For the young child, the stepparent may well become a parent.

J. Visher: The only power the stepparent has as a parent is delegated from the remarried parent.

E. Visher: The adults need to be supportive of one another. Together they need to decide what the house rules are, and the parent of the children takes care of enforcing the rules until a relationship is set up.

J. Visher: Another major tip is to develop realistic expectations about what it is going to take to make everything work. So many people feel they have failed after a few weeks or months, that the remarriage has faltered because things are chaotic. It takes four or five years for things to settle down and for people really to get satisfaction out of the whole family relationship.

One of the keys is for people to inform themselves by reading or talking to other people who also are in stepfamilies. They learn that making the stepfamily work takes time and you shouldn't expect close family relationships quickly.

The most common pattern now is for children to move back and forth and feel part of two households. If all the adults form a parenting coalition, then children are most likely to feel they belong in both places.

Working out the parenting coalition so that it is at least civil makes an enormous difference to everybody. The children can go through the remarriage smoothly if there is not constant warfare. Sometimes parents who divorce or separate are tied together in bonds of anger. The anger can reflect an inadequate separation between the biological parents. They keep together by fighting.

E. Visher: Truman Capote said, "It's easy to lose a good friend, but it's hard to lose a good enemy." The anger ties you together. Hostility eats you up and you are not free to go on.

J. Visher: Most people don't understand how much damage they are doing to themselves and to the children. Sometimes people say, "How can I work with that S.O.B. when I couldn't even stay married to him?" We say maybe you can split off the part that does not want to be married to him and share the parenting experience.

E. Visher: What the children need from that parent is different from what the spouse needed.

What can you do to decrease the hostility?

J. Visher: One thing is to trade assurances between the households that you are not trying to take the child away from them or trying to get the child to like you better. Often, in a single-parent household, the parent is afraid of further loss, afraid that the ex-spouse and his or her new spouse will encourage the child to stay there and the child will want to because it is a more attractive place or there is more money. This fear fuels the anger and makes the parent cling to the child more and try to influence the child to turn against the other parent.

E. Visher: So we think that sometimes the anger is not left over from the former marriage, but has to do with the fear that builds up between the two households, the fear of more loss. The other household becomes a threat, and the ex-spouses become like enemies rather than like people trying to raise a child. The parents are afraid of each other, and they are not aware that the anger substitutes for fear. If they are more aware of it, they can deal with it.

Also important is the guilt the remarried parent feels. He or she feels guilty that the children have been unhappy through the death or divorce and then the remarriage. That parent has a real investment in its being a big, happy family right away. Yet they have difficulty setting limits for the children who live there or visit there. The stepparent goes up the wall.

Sometimes they feel that to form a good couple relationship and make that primary is a betrayal of their relationship with their child. The parent-child relationship is different from the relationship with the spouse.

J. Visher: There may be an unusually strong bond between parent and child; perhaps it has lasted for many years, and the new spouse is a rival. It becomes a power struggle between spouse and child for the loyalty of the biological parent. The child is sometimes suddenly out of a job as confidant.

E. Visher: I don't think people realize the change for the children, that now they have to share. One mother described that she and her daughter had lived together for five years. When she came home from work, she talked to her daughter. Now that she is remarried, she talks to her husband. That one little thing is not so little, as the daughter has to share her mother.

If people are aware of the losses for the children in the new structure, they can acknowledge those changes with the children and do things differently—sit down with the children alone and talk. When children sense their feelings are accepted, they will talk about them. One stepmother commented to her stepson that when the father talked to the son, she felt left out, and she wondered if he felt left out when the father talked to her. He agreed he did, and they talked about it. There was not a lot they could change, but after they had the talk, they got along better.

J. Visher: We hope that as people are more informed, they will be able to deal more effectively with the situation.

E. Visher: Society needs to make changes to ease the interface between stepfamilies and society. For example, one mother baked birthday cupcakes for her son to have at his school on his birthday, but the school would not let her deliver them because he lived with the father and stepmother. The school sometimes gets caught in the middle between warring households, but the school could have accepted the cupcakes.

Our institutions do not make it easy for parents. The schools could make adjustments. For example, many school notes go home on Fridays, but many children visit the noncustodial parent on Fridays, so the note does not get where it needs to be. Notes could go home on Thursdays. It is a little thing, but it could help. Another problem is that stepparents, no matter how involved they may have been in the child's life, have absolutely no legal relationship. If the biological parent dies or there is a divorce, the stepparent has no right to continue the relationship even though it may have existed since shortly after birth and be every bit as important as that between biological parent and child. They have responsibilities but no rights, and that needs to be changed.

J. Visher: In our workshops and talks, we always emphasize that with all the problems, there are so many satisfactions. For example, children have an opportunity to see a positive working relationship between two adults, giving them models for their own lives and their own marriages. They would not have had that model growing up in a fighting household.

continued

INTERVIEW
with Emily Visher and John Visher *continued*

*In many of the chapters I have included parents' descriptions of the joys of that age.
Perhaps you would like to describe the joys of stepparenting.*

E. Visher: Because there are more adults in the household, they have more models to choose
from, more diversity for everyone.

J. Visher: There is an opportunity for the child to experience different points of view,
different orientations, different skills than they would have had otherwise.

E. Visher: Adults learn to be creative and flexible. One man, when asked what he liked
about being a stepparent, said, "I used to be a pretty rigid guy, but I have had to become more
flexible. This helps at home, but also in my work." We have wonderful quotes from children.
One seventeen-year-old girl said, "I think I understand people better, and I am a better friend."
It goes beyond the family because you become aware of what it takes to form relationships and
what it takes to maintain them. This is important. Relationships are not taken for granted.

The couple has a real chance for happiness. If they had it before and lost it through death,
it is nice to have it again. If they did not have it in a first marriage, they now have a second
chance to have it.

J. Visher: Another joy is the joy of being able to be in a parenting position with children
you would never have known and to make a real contribution to their growth and development. From the point of view of the adult, you have children and grandchildren who come
to mean a great deal.

E. Visher: Stepbrothers and stepsisters have relationships they would not have. One of our
boys commented about a stepbrother, "This is someone I would never have had as a friend
because we are so different. I was glad I had the opportunity. We wanted the relationship to
work out so we worked on it." Many other stepchildren say they were not so lonely because
they had stepbrothers and stepsisters. A younger child may use an older stepsib as a model.
So there are more relationships to enjoy and learn from.

Does this mean that a biological parent can never disagree with the stepparent?
No. There will be instances when the two parents will disagree and will want to discuss the difference between themselves. In a small number of situations the biological parent may feel the child has been disciplined too severely—perhaps restricted
more drastically than ever before with little advance warning. When this happens,
the biological parent will voice disagreement in the child's presence—"The penalty
seems too severe. The behavior doesn't seem that bad. Let's talk about it." Some
experts believe children need to hear, in such a situation, that the biological parent
is not abandoning them.

Parents may want to resolve some problems by changing their expectations of
children. Particularly when the stepparent has not had children of his or her own,
expectations may be too high. In some situations parents must back off, look at their
own standards, talk to children, and perhaps revise the rules.

Special Problems When stepchildren visit the home of the parent who does not have custody, children's needs for discipline, consistency, and love do not change. But the relationships are different from those in the home in which they live. Should they be required to abide by the rules of the family they are visiting? Or should they, because time is short and the emotional ties are fragile, be treated like guests? In most situations, visiting children should abide by the house rules (see Box 14-2). Responsibilities for chores, table manners, general respect for the others' property and needs should be expected. Children often feel most comfortable when they are treated like members of the family. A few exceptions to the rules may be made in the beginning, particularly if the rules are very different from those in the child's other home. Parents can say, "It may take a little time to get used to our rules, but this is how we do it here." Parents need not apologize, and often children will accept the differences, as they do when they visit grandparents or other relatives.

In Chapter 13 we talked about the single parent who moves back to the parents' home to live in a three-generation family. When these women marry again, they are especially likely to have difficulties with discipline in the new family. If the child has been indulged by grandparents, he or she may resent the discipline of the new stepfather more than the average child. The stepfather may consider it unwise to give the child everything he or she has had in the past. He may then be seen as cruel and depriving, and the child may become bitter and even aggressive. With all the changes going on in the family, the child may count on being indulged. When the children are sons, the stepfather often has great difficulty, because the boy who has lacked a male model is sometimes more passive as well as more indulged. A stepfather finds it hard to come between mother and child. But he must, if he is to establish his place in the family. Also, differences in style of discipline may set mother against stepfather.

As we noted, the aims, purposes and techniques of discipline are the same in stepfamilies as in biological families. Discipline problems are likely to be most complicated and numerous during the first few months. Time, patience, and involvement can help solve these problems.

THE PLATEAU PERIOD

As new family members come to know each other more intimately and family life is organized and structured with rules that are agreeable to all, the role of the stepparent increases and both parents are able to contribute to the growth of the independence and ego mastery skills of their children. As stepparents love and care for children, we see that adults and children need not be biologically related for adults to be central figures in their lives. Stepparents make a valuable contribution to children's growth because they can sometimes be more objective about stepchildren than the biological parent. Precisely because they lack long-term relationships with children and are less invested in what the child does, stepparents may be able to look at the child's current behavior with unbiased eyes. Many a biological parent feels grateful for the new insights or the calm, controlled approach of the stepparent.

One stepparent described what happened when her husband's teenage son came

BOX 14-2
GUIDELINES FOR STEPFAMILIES

1. Try to start out in a new apartment or house to minimize feelings of territoriality.
2. A primary couple relationship is critical for the continuing existence of the stepfamily. Adults often need time alone.
3. Activities among family members can help foster new relationships— undertaking a family project, going shopping together.
4. Preserving original relationships between parent and biological offspring may require special times away from the blended family.
5. Do not expect instant love—relationships build over time.
6. Accept that a stepfamily, whose members have experienced loss, is a different kind of family. Nevertheless, it can bring pleasure and satisfaction to all members.
7. Divided loyalties make it hard for children to relate to new stepparents. As parents permit children to care for new adults, children will respond.
8. Courteous relationships between current family and the former family require time to work out and can be especially beneficial to all because hostility is reduced.
9. Accept that all members of the new family have a history of different values, styles of preference, ways of life. Parents must be supportive and helpful to children.
10. Stepparenting is more effective "if stepparents carve out a role for themselves that is different from and does not compete with the natural parents."
11. Integrating teenagers can be particularly difficult.
12. Include stepchildren who are just visiting in family routine work and other activities.
13. Affection is important, but stepparents need to be careful not to allow that to lead to incest.
14. Understanding there will be many stresses and strains can help prepare family members for the realities of being a stepfamily.
15. Even occasional contacts with adult stepchildren can lead to strong ties among family members in later years.

Adapted from Emily B. Visher and John S. Visher, *Stepfamilies: A Guide to Working with Stepparents and Stepchildren* (New York: Brunner/Mazel, 1979), pp. 261–265.

to live with the couple after living with his mother for five years following the divorce.[18] Father and son began to bicker and fight. The father saw his tall son as a rival, and the son resented his father's discipline. At first the stepmother intervened in the fights. When she found that she did not help, she changed her tactics and became a mediator. She took her husband aside and explained how hard it was for the son, during adolescence, suddenly to be living with his father and disciplined by him. And she took the son aside and explained the adjustments the father was having to make to this new situation. With the stepmother's help, father and son were able to back off and arrive at a better relationship.

Stepparents can add to children's feelings of uniqueness and specialness. As step-parents get to know children, they spend time in joint activities, enjoy their humor, and appreciate each child's individuality and sense of self. The children's feelings of self-esteem grow as they find another person who regards them positively. For exam-ple, another stepmother described how she incorporated her two stepsons in the blended family when she was pregnant with her own child.[19] This woman asked her husband about what the boys had been like as babies and young children and about especially memorable moments and events in their lives. Then she was able to enhance the sense of individuality of each of the boys by telling them stories about themselves. As her own children arrived and grew up, she was able to talk to her step-sons about their behavior at the same ages, and they enjoyed the descriptions immensely and also felt closer to their halfsiblings. This stepmother's warmth and concern for her stepsons gave them each a feeling of specialness that contributed to feelings of competence. This woman dealt with one of the biggest drawbacks in stepparenting—not having long-term relationships with the children she was parenting—by learning about the boys from their father.

A Child of Your Own

Parents in a blended family may wonder whether they should have a child of their own. Dodson advises parents to make this decision the same way anyone else does—on the basis of their own needs and wishes. Although children of a second marriage can create problems and children of previous marriages may feel left out, they often help to unify the family and strengthen family ties. Everyone feels attached to the new baby. The stepmother who found out about her stepsons' baby-hoods was able to use her pregnancy to draw the family closer together. The Nobles described a mother who included her stepchildren, fourteen and sixteen, as impor-tant figures for her son in that marriage. The teenage children played with the baby and took him places, and the mother felt that their attentions helped to stimulate the child's growth. She was warm in her praise of the two older children and shared with them her feelings about how important they were to the young child.

The desirability of adoption depends on the particular circumstances of the fam-ily. In some situations, children have not known the biological father and are eager to be adopted by a caring stepfather they love. They cannot wait to change their names and to be truly able to call their stepfather "Dad." In other situations, when the absent biological parent plays a role, even a limited one, adoption is not advised unless all parties are in hearty agreement. Children may feel deprived of their rela-tionship with their biological parent and resent being included in the new family in this way. Conversely, stepparents may not feel comfortable with adoption for various reasons—financial obligations, lack of closeness, and fear of responsibilities if the marriage is not going well. Thus, adoption should be carefully considered.

Incest

The taboo on incest in the nuclear family is nearly universal. Experts advance many reasons for the prohibition against incest—it decreases jealousy and rivalry within the family, it helps to ensure that parents will meet the children's dependency needs rather than seeking sexual favors from them, it increases contact between families and other groups as they seek sexual partners, and it reduces the possibility of an inbred population. But despite the taboo, incest does occur in both biological and stepfamilies. Between 10 and 20 percent of women report at least one childhood episode, with the youngest women reporting more. Between 1 and 3 percent of prepubescent boys are thought to have experienced abuse.[20]

Sexuality is a greater source of tension in stepfamilies than in biological families. Stepbrothers and stepsisters living close together during adolescence may develop sexual feelings for each other. This leads to tension and often to fighting that is an expression of these feelings. The sexual activities of newly married stepparents are likely to be more frequent and ardent than those that precede divorce and are likely to stimulate children's interest in sex. Stepparents may be attracted to stepchildren or vice versa. According to Emily and John Visher, a clinic specializing in the treatment of problems related to incest reports that 50 percent of the clients are stepfathers and stepdaughters.[21] This suggests that incest is higher in stepfamilies than in biological families, because most families—certainly more than 50 percent—are biological families. It is possible, however, that there is less reluctance to report incest in stepfamilies, rather than a lower incidence of incest in biological families.

To minimize the possibility of incest between a stepbrother and stepsister, parents are advised by Frank Strange, a psychologist, to establish rules.[22] For example, all family members are to dress modestly, only one person is to use the bathroom at a time, no one is to enter anyone else's bedroom without knocking and being given permission to enter. When the parents are away from home and teenage stepchildren are there, an adult should be present. Parents would not leave unrelated boys and girls alone together and should not leave adolescent siblings unattended.

These precautions are necessary. Since brothers and sisters are available and stimulating to each other, teenagers who would not engage in such activities with peers outside the family may be overwhelmed by their intense and persistent sexual feelings. They require protection from too much stimulation and limits for their actions. They should be treated as parents would treat any other boys and girls. Sexual activity, if it does occur, can give children strong feelings of guilt and shame about their sexuality; and the guilt, particularly, may have long-lasting effects.

Not only does sexual stimulation occur between teenage children, but their parents' active sexual life is also an influence and can trigger children's fantasies. Teenage children are aware that parents are active sexually—going to their bedroom early in the evening, going there during the day. It is not surprising, then, that teenage children, who are just becoming aware of their own sexual feelings, may find themselves attracted to stepparents of the opposite sex. In physical contacts with preadolescent and adolescent children, parents must draw a line between the desire for affection and the expression of erotic feelings. Stepparents can respond warmly to requests for affection but must be careful not to provide gratification for erotic feelings.

A more difficult problem occurs when a parent is attracted to a child in the family. Arnold emphasizes the difference between feelings and behavior.[23] Many individuals experience fleeting feelings of attraction but never act on such feelings. Other adults do act, and the results are certainly even more destructive than the emotional trauma of sibling incest. The most often reported incest is between men and their stepdaughters, usually young girls. And these are likely to be their first sexual experiences—traumatic, guilt-laden, premature, and physically painful. Such experiences are likely to shape and distort, perhaps permanently, the attitudes of these girls toward sex and toward men.

Meiselman identifies high-risk families as having one or more of the following components: (1) an alcoholic and violent father; (2) a mother who is away from home, physically ill, depressed, or passive; (3) an older daughter who has had the responsibility of a mother; (4) parents who have failed to establish a satisfying sexual relationship; (5) fathers and daughters who spend too much time alone with each other; (6) any condition, such as psychosis or below-average intelligence, that reduces an individual's capacity for self-control; (7) previous incest in a parent's family; and (8) a romantic attachment with unusual amounts of physical affection between adult and child. Family members can observe when a too-close attachment is developing and step in to advise professional counseling.

If incest takes place, it is unlikely to be reported to an adult or to an outside authority. Often children remain quiet for years, feeling guilty and dirty, believing they somehow caused the behavior. When a family member becomes aware of incest within the family, he or she must take steps immediately to protect the child. After making an extensive review of the literature on incest and carrying out a study of her own, Meiselman writes:

> When a current or recent case of incest has been reported, the incest victim should be assured that he or she will be protected against any further incestuous incidents, and the responsible authority should take whatever steps are necessary to guarantee the security of the child. Peters, who has dealt with a large number of cases of sexual assaults on children, has emphasized that this basic assurance of protection is the cornerstone of treatment, which often dictates what kinds of therapeutic interventions will be employed. In father-daughter incest cases where a younger daughter is also present in the home, this principle of protection should be extended to her, since there is abundant evidence that such daughters are at high risk for incest should the elder daughter be removed from the home.[24]

Meiselman advises that a report of incest should be accepted as true. Research indicates such acts have taken place in the vast majority of cases reported—the victims are not fantasizing. When authorities are called in, the family often protects the adult because of fear and shame about incest, because of loss of the stepfather's income, and because of fear of retaliation from the accused family member. Members may also worry about public knowledge of such an event if there is a trial or other legal proceedings. The family may hesitate to bring on the adult the condemnation and incarceration that may result.

What should be done when incest has occurred and has been reported? First, the security of the child should immediately be arranged. Meiselman asserts that incest is a negative life experience that continues to damage people after it is stopped. The father or the child can be removed from the home; it is not sufficient to state that the parent and child will not be permitted in the house alone. Incest can occur during the night, when everyone else is asleep yet all are at home. Second, the child should have the opportunity to vent feelings of anger, fear, guilt, and shame about the act with a therapist. Although some children may be initially hesitant to talk, the experienced therapist can encourage the child to talk and can offer reassurances that help the child deal with the feelings created by incest. Family members may have suggested that the child is somehow permanently tainted or damaged, and the therapist should reassure the child that this is not true.

Self-help groups have arisen to help adolescents deal with the experience of incest, and participation in such a group may do even more than a therapist to help the child talk and handle what has occurred and what she is feeling. When a young girl hears that others have had the same experience, when she realizes that she has not been singled out for some inexplicable reason and hears that others also were victims, it may be easier for her to accept this interpretation for herself.

Some form of therapy for all family members should be started once the situation is arranged so that any further incest is impossible. Therapists have had difficulty in keeping the sexually abusing parent, usually the father or stepfather, in treatment. Couple therapy that focuses on sexual problems in the marriage and improves sexual satisfaction is sometimes helpful. If the father has left the home and is no longer an active part of the family, the mother may need to be helped to deal with her passivity, which is often a factor prolonging the situation. If family meetings include all individuals, it is important that in the process of looking at the dynamics of the family the child does not get the feeling that he or she is responsible.

Money

In any family, money can be a major source of problems, and it is a factor in the failure of many marriages. The flow of money to and from a household can be complicated and complicating, especially if both the wife and the husband have been married before and both have children from the earlier marriages. Who has how many children of what ages in which household? Which wives are working? Which husbands? Which children need childcare, special medical care, special education? How far must each set of children travel to visit the other biological parent? Is one parent, or set of parents, more responsible than another about making the agreed payments for child support?

Money, itself a symbol of the labor required to earn it, is often used to represent feelings. The wife who complains about the amount of child support her husband is providing for his children who live with their mother may, in reality, be expressing resentment about the amount of attention and concern her husband continues to give to his former wife. The father who is late in making child support payments to his former wife may be expressing anger that he is not permitted to spend more time with his biological children. Children, too, become involved in money battles. For example, a child may—silently or aloud–accuse his father and stepmother of having more than enough money, while the mother with whom he lives works long hours and both he and she do without necessities. In reality he may also be expressing feelings of being rejected by the father.

In an ideal world, divorce settlements and arrangements for child support would be equitable for all involved. But such is not always the case, even at the time of divorce. And as one partner or the other remarries, moves, changes jobs, has additional children, sustains a costly illness, or finds it necessary to care for an aging parent, circumstances and financial abilities change and all are caught in the flux of events. How can these problems be dealt with so that they are not destructive?

First, prospective spouses should discuss money in detail before they get married. And they should talk not only about amounts—which are certain to change as circumstances change—but also about attitudes, as should any couple before they marry. Is there a specific expense, or kind of expense, that one or the other objects to—for example, supporting a teenager in college? Does one want a new car every year while the other believes in regular savings? A dislike of stinginess or extravagance is as important a factor in a marriage as a dislike of sharing chores.

Even a thorough and specific discussion about money and clearly stated arrangements about the dispersement of child support and about expectations of the way money is to be spent cannot eliminate all money problems. When disagreements occur after marriage, these can best be handled in family councils, especially if the children are past the preschool years. Family members can state their priorities and can share ways to get the most for the money available. Children, as well as adults, often have useful ideas about how to achieve goals while spending the fewest possible dollars.

Family councils are also opportunities for all family members to discuss and listen to each other's feelings. Remember that talk about money is often talk about feelings as well. Active listening can elicit feelings that children may be reluctant or fearful about expressing directly—frustration, anger, sadness. Children need to know that parents and stepparents are interested in their feelings and are truly hearing what is behind talk that sounds as if it is about money but that is really about feelings. Jealousy of a sibling or stepsibling or concern about being accepted as the new child in a new school in a new town may be expressed as a demand for a higher allowance or new clothes. Both the money problem and the underlying problem are closer to resolution when children and parents are able to express feelings, needs, and limits openly.

Stepgrandparents

Just as parents need not be biologically related to children to be central figures in their lives, grandparents need not be biologically related to grandchildren to fill the grandparent role. Stepparents enlarge the family, provide other adults who both love and appreciate children's special qualities. There is the fun of large family gatherings, the sharing of a lifetime of experiences that teach children about the past.

Not all stepgrandparents enjoy this role. Some older people have rigid notions that only biological children and grandchildren are really family members. Sometimes grandparents are fond of the earlier spouse or do not approve of the marriage that gave them stepgrandchildren. Some refuse to accept stepgrandchildren and sometimes adopted grandchildren as well. Many stepparents have been deeply hurt when their parents have refused to accept stepgrandchildren. A stepfather cannot force his parents to accept and love his stepchildren as their own. But he can sit down and talk with his parents, sending I-messages about how important this is to him.

Just as it takes time for stepparents and stepchildren to get to know each other, so too is this true for stepgrandparents and stepgrandchildren. And there are even more obstacles here. First, many older people have difficulty accepting divorce, anyone's divorce. Affection and loyalty to the earlier spouse may make it difficult to accept the new spouse, and that in turn can get in the way of acceptance of the stepgrandchildren. Remember, too, that grandparents spend less time with the children, often in the relatively strained circumstances of visits or family gatherings where relationships must be explained and other people need attention or are more congenial companions.

But remember, also, that children, and especially young children, are not consciously aware of all these undercurrents of feelings. They are most aware of whether they are accepted and treated as members of the family or as intruders. If your parents have difficulty accepting your stepchildren, try talking with them, telling them how you feel and how your spouse and stepchildren feel. Ask your parents about their feelings and reactions and about what they suggest can be done. If, over time, their attitudes do not change and they are unable or unwilling to be more accepting of their stepgrandchildren, visits and time spent together can be decreased. Then the members of all three generations are less often upset by disturbing encounters. As always, when family contact is diminished, all members suffer and all lose the enrichment of their lives that only family can contribute. In this situation it is often the stepgrandparents who lose the most, for they are usually at the period in their lives when they have time to enjoy grandchildren, when they have the most to give of themselves, and when they need the support and company of children and grandchildren. So it is, for everyone, worth the time and emotional effort to try to bring about mutual acceptance that can lead to pleasure for all.

In a sense there is no termination of the stepparent role, certainly as long as the marriage lasts and often even if it does not. Just as biological parents parent their adult children, so stepparents are involved with adult stepchildren and with stepgrandchildren. Stepparents can help at times of emergency—illness, accidents—and be supportive of both the adult stepchild and the spouse. The experience of many members of stepfamilies is that living together closely, being concerned with the needs of all, forges bonds that last a lifetime.

Ex-spouses

Blended families include not only the husband and wife along with his, hers, and their children, but also include the ex-spouse or ex-spouses as important influences. In Chapter 13 we described the binuclear family in which biological parents divorce yet strive equally for a goal of active involvement with their children. Such ongoing involvement bodes well for children's development. Yet incorporating the other parent with whom the remaining parent could not live happily is a challenge for all involved.

Relationships go most smoothly when biological parents have accepted the end of their marriage and focus on how best to meet the needs of their children. When parents do not have unfinished business with each other, do not wish to make the other parent the villain or the uncaring figure in their child's life, they will have the energy and flexibility to handle the problems that arise. Here we discuss problems of visiting, using children to bear messages, and finding ways to cooperate.

Children may refuse to visit the noncustodial parent or refuse to return to the custodial parent's home, saying perhaps that they do not like the new stepparent. Such resistance most frequently occurs when one parent expresses, covertly or overtly, negative feelings about the other parent and his or her home. When both biological parents have clear agreements with each other about regular visiting privileges, children are likely to accept these arrangements. This does not mean that parents must be rigid about the arrangement. Both parents need to be flexible, especially as children move into the adolescent years, so that a child does not miss a friend's birthday party or some important school event. Consistent protest accompanied by real distress at going to one of the homes indicates a problem that both parents can discuss with each other and then with children. Some special circumstances in need of change may justify the protest, such as sleeping arrangements or discrepancy in discipline between the two homes. Whatever it is, parents need to work it out together.

Fitzhugh Dodson uses the term *shuttle children* to refer to those who go back and forth between two households.[25] Often these shuttle children are used to bear messages from one biological parent to the other. These messages may concern a new spouse, child support, or the general lifestyle of the parent, and may be direct and verbal—"Tell your father the child support is not enough"—or indirect and nonverbal—packing only tattered clothes for the child to wear. These messages, however, burden children and cast a shadow on their visits with the other parent. Often children return with a new set of directives. Any concerns biological parents have with arrangements should be worked out between the two of them.

Occasionally one parent may cancel visits or outings with children because he or she does not like something the other person has done. When child support does not arrive or when it is changed, when one parent marries or when the other parent is living with an "undesirable" person—the reasons are many and varied. Children's contact with the noncustodial parent, however, should not be at the whim of the custodial parent. Such contact is a child's right as long as the environment is a safe one. If it is not, parents address this concern by consulting their lawyers, not by canceling visits.

Noncustodial parents are most easily and beneficially incorporated into their children's lives when they are permitted to be themselves and contribute to their children's welfare in whatever way they see fit as long as reasonable standards of health and safety are preserved. Often biological parents battle with each other about the manner in which the other parent relates to children or spends time with them. Claire Berman cites a father who was jealous of the lavish home and expensive trips a stepfather could provide and so made it difficult for his children to enjoy them.[26] Another father in a similar position, however, was happy that his son was able to enjoy such advantages with his stepfather. That father felt confident he was offering his son positive experiences of a different sort and so was not threatened with his son's enjoyment of new countries and new customs.

More frequently it is the noncustodial parent, often the father, who provides more entertainment, more physical signs of love and caring, and fewer restrictions to make up for the many absent hours. Custodial parents dread the return of the "royal" children after a visit because discipline must be reestablished and is greeted with protest. Discussions between parents, and the passage of time, may reduce great discrepancies between the two households in terms of rules and entertainment.

Again, the touchstone of positive relationships here is parents' abilities to work with each other for the benefit of children. This happens when parents give up rigid expectations of each other, give up demands they want to insist upon, and focus energy instead on meeting children's needs in the most reasonable and effective manner.

NEW RELATIONSHIPS

Everything written about stepparenting attests to it complexity, its intensity, and its challenge. We do not often enough emphasize the rewards. Brenda Maddox sums up the strengths of the stepfamily and the joys of participation in it:

> There are a few plain truths about stepparenthood that I learned writing this book. I was blind not to have recognized them when I got married. Stepfamilies can be happy, even happier than families in which there has never been more than one mother or father but it takes more work. The tensions of the stepfamily are special and real. A stepparent cannot be the same as a real parent. There are no new Mommies and new Daddies. Yet there are compensations for the strains. My own particular reward has been to help two young people who are nothing like me to be more like themselves and to watch the bond grow between the two sets of children. Stepfamilies in general do have positive advantages. When a stranger has to be taken into the family circle, when children have a parent who lives somewhere else, the family has an extra dimension. There is not that claustrophobia that led the anthropologist Dr. Edmund Leach to describe the ordinary family "with its narrow privacy and tawdry secrets" as "the source of all our discontents." The stepfamily is open and tough. It is not a bad place to live for those who can accept the uncomfortable fact that many of the tensions between stepparents and stepchildren will be inevitable as long as spouses are replaceable and parents are not.[27]

Though life in stepfamilies is tough, there are special pleasures in seeing children biologically unrelated to you flourish and grow and in taking part in that growth. Such close and warm and sometimes conflictful relationships can serve as an example that people do not need to be either biologically related or romantically connected to produce profound and positive effects on each other's lives. The essential ingredients for both biological parents and stepparents are to feel comfortable with themselves and free of inflexible views of the other parents, so all can help children become "more like themselves." When adults relate to their own or other people's children in this way, there is no distinction between a biological parent and a stepparent.

MAJOR POINTS OF CHAPTER 14

When parents remarry, they:

- experience many emotional benefits like closeness, intimacy, and sexual satisfaction
- do not necessarily repeat the mistakes of the first marriage
- experience stress as they integrate everyone into a new family

When parents remarry, children:

- receive less attention from parents, have less communication with them
- have less consistent rules at home
- differ in their reactions with girls' having more difficulty and the difficulty lasting a longer time than with boys

Stepparenting is more difficult than biological parenting because:

- long-standing emotional ties do not exist among family members
- the family is more complex with more people
- members of the stepfamily may have deep feelings of jealousy and ambivalence
- members have memories of other marriage
- former spouses may use children to attack parent and stepparent
- there are no clear guidelines for stepparenting

In the anticipation period before the marriage, parents:

- mourn the loss of the previous marriage
- date and get to know each other
- establish a primary couple bond and exchange ideas about parenting
- introduce all family members to each other and begin to get acquainted
- make concrete plans for the marriage and living afterwards

In the honeymoon period following the marriage, family members:

- begin to build emotional bonds to each other
- handle issues of discipline with biological parent initially handling most of the discipline
- form a parenting coalition among all parents involved
- handle conflicts about discipline

In the plateau period, parents:

- and stepparents more often share parenting responsibilities equally
- and stepparents decide about having children of their own
- establish agreed-upon ways to spend money
- do not use children to deal with ex-spouse

Close emotional relationships are built when stepparents and parents:

- allow time for relationships to develop and do not become impatient
- respect individuality of each child
- arrange to spend time with each child regularly in mutually enjoyable activities
- arrange family activities
- express positive appreciation to each person
- begin to establish special rituals and traditions of stepfamily

When incest is reported, children:

- are most likely to be telling the truth
- must be protected so there is no more contact with abuser
- can benefit from individual counseling to handle feelings and group therapy as well
- and other members of the family need some family counseling to deal with everyone's feelings

Joys of stepparenting include:

- presenting new models for children to relate to
- giving children opportunity to see positive working relationship between two adults
- establishing close relationships in which children learn more about people and how to get along in intimate relations

ADDITIONAL READINGS

Adler, Robert E. *Sharing the Children*. Bethesda: Adler & Adler, 1988.

Berman, Claire. *Making It as a Stepparent*. New York: Harper & Row, 1986.

Bernstein, Anne C. *Yours, Mine, and Ours*. New York: W. W. Norton, 1989.

Visher, Emily B., and Visher, John S. *Stepfamilies: Myths and Realities*. New York: Citadel, 1979.

Wallerstein, Judith S., and Blakeslee, Sandra. *Second Chances*. New York: Ticknor & Fields, 1989.

Notes

1. Judith S. Wallerstein and Sandra Blakeslee, *Second Chances* (New York: Ticknor & Fields, 1989).

2. Monica McGoldrick and Betty Carter, "Forming a Remarried Family," in *The Changing Family Life Cycle* 2d ed., ed. Betty Carter and Monica McGoldrick (New York: Gardner Press, 1988), pp. 399–409.

3. Ibid.

4. Wallerstein and Blakeslee, *Second Chances.*

5. Judith Wallerstein and Joan B. Kelly, *Surviving the Breakup* (New York: Basic Books, 1980).

6. E. Mavis Hetherington, Margaret Stanley Hagan, and Edward R. Anderson, "Marital Transitions: A Child's Perspective," *American Psychologist* 44 (1989): 309.

7. Hetherington, Hagan, and Anderson, "Marital Transitions."

8. Ibid.

9. Ibid.

10. W. Glenn Clingempeel and Sion Segal, "Stepparent-Stepchild Relationships and the Psychological Adjustment of Children in Stepmother and Stepfather Families," *Child Development* 57 (1986): 474–484.

11. Wallerstein and Kelly, *Surviving the Breakup.*

12. Fitzhugh Dodson, *How to Discipline with Love* (New York: Rawson Associates, 1977).

13. Alice S. Rossi, "Transition to Parenthood," *Journal of Marriage and Family* 30 (1968): 26–39.

14. L. Eugene Arnold, "A Summary of Guidance Implications," in *Helping Parents Help Their Children,* ed. L. Eugene Arnold (New York: Brunner/Mazel, 1978), pp. 301–303.

15. Shirley Gould, *Teen-agers: The Continuing Challenge* (New York: Hawthorn Books, 1977).

16. Ruth Roosevelt and Jeanette Lofas, *Living in Step* (New York: McGraw-Hill, 1976), p. 180.

17. Patricia Papernow, "Stages in Becoming a Stepfamily," in *Stepfamilies Stepping Ahead,* ed. Mala Burt (Baltimore: Stepfamilies Press, 1989), pp. 27–48.

18. June Noble and William Noble, *How to Live with Other People's Children* (New York: Hawthorn, 1977).

19. Ibid.

20. Karin C. Meiselman, *Resolving the Trama of Incest* (San Francisco: Jossey-Bass, 1990).

21. Emily B. Visher and John S. Visher, *Stepfamilies: A Guide to Working with Stepparents and Stepchildren* (New York: Brunner/Mazel, 1979).

22. Noble and Noble, *How to Live with Other People's Children.*

23. Arnold, "A Summary of Guidance Implications."

24. Meiselman, *Incest* (San Francisco: Jossey-Bass, 1978), p. 337.

25. Dodson, *How to Discipline with Love.*

26. Claire Berman, *Making It as a Stepparent* (New York: Harper & Row, 1986).

27. Brenda Maddox, *The Half-Parent* (New York: New American Library, 1975), p. 167.

PARENTING CHILDREN WITH SPECIAL NEEDS

C H A P T E R 15

In this chapter we look at a sampling of children who have special needs as they develop—children who are premature, children who are adopted, children who have physical illnesses, children who are depressed, children who have attention-deficit hyperactivity disorder (in the past termed hyperactivity), children with learning disabilities, and children who are gifted. We do not attempt to discuss children with serious lifelong needs posed by such conditions as Downs' syndrome and cerebral palsy. A large section of the chapter is devoted to children who are physically ill, because all children experience illness at some time in their growing-up period. The focus here is on how the special needs of illness change the parenting process and how parents with such children adapt to the special circumstances of the family; detailed descriptions of the causes and medical treatments of children with special problems are not presented. There are many other children with special needs that could be discussed—for example, children who are twins or triplets, children of artificial insemination—but those presented in this chapter represent the main categories of special need.

CHILDREN WHO ARE PREMATURE

Approximately 10 percent of children are born prematurely; that is, before the thirty-seventh week of pregnancy (a full-term pregnancy is forty weeks).[1] The term **premature** covers a wide variety of newborns—from the child born three months early in need of intensive care to the thirty-five-week gestation child who weighs 5 pounds or more and is able to go home within a few days. Premature babies are divided into two groups—low-birth-weight babies who weigh between 3 pounds, 5 ounces and 5 pounds, 8 ounces, and very-low–birth-weight babies who are under 3 pounds, 5 ounces. Babies in the first category do very well, with 95 percent surviving and 90 percent showing no scars from their prematurity. Babies in the second category are being successfully treated as well, with the vast majority surviving and 75 percent of these with no scars from prematurity. Even when problems arise, they are mild and include such things as nearsightedness and learning disabilities. A minority of these children have serious impairments such as cerebral palsy or mental retardation.[2] This section is written for those parents with very-low–birth-weight babies who require extensive care. It covers the grieving process, the bonding process, and relating to the child when he or she comes home from the hospital.

Most often, the reasons for prematurity are unknown. Certain factors, however, place women at higher risk for premature delivery: (1) the mother's own prematurity or having given birth to a previous premature child, (2) poor medical or nutritional care, (3) age of the mother (under sixteen or over forty), (4) weight of the mother prior to pregnancy (under 100 pounds), (5) birth less than one year before present pregnancy, (6) mother's having a high-stress career that involves physical labor or standing or nervous tension, and (7) mother's cigarette smoking. Dr. Robert Creasy of the University of California at San Francisco states that the single most important factor is the mother's own obstetrical history—if she has given birth to one premature child, her risk of a second is about 40 percent.[3]

The infant's need for care will depend on how premature it is and whether it experiences complications. In general, the smaller the baby, the more problems he or she will encounter. This section cannot deal with all the complications and forms of treatment. Robin Henig and Dr. Anne Fletcher's book *Your Premature Baby* provides excellent descriptions in language parents can understand.[4]

Parents with a premature newborn face many problems. They must cope with their own worries about the child's health and survival. They must deal with a host of professionals—nurses, doctors of many kinds, technicians. They must deal with their feelings of guilt, responsibility, loss, and anger. They must find new ways to attach to a child who is not able to be cuddled, rocked, and nursed at the onset. They must handle the anxieties they may feel about being able to meet all the needs of this newborn. When they take their baby home, they must deal with uncertainties about its future development.

Following the sudden, unexpected birth, parents' first concern is for the survival of their child. This concern persists, or comes and goes as crises occur. As long as the baby's survival is at stake, it is difficult for parents to focus on other issues. They can only wait and be supportive to each other.

Once survival seems probable, parents must come to terms with the fact they have not had the birth process or the child they anticipated. As noted in earlier chapters, during pregnancy parents build images of their baby-to-be and of themselves as parents. Now they must accept that they have not had the healthy, full-term baby they looked forward to. If the baby has few complications and weighs enough to go home in a few days, this process may be a short one, as the reality has not been too different from that expected. However, if the baby has a very low birth weight and must stay in the hospital for two months undergoing many procedures, then the birth and baby are very different. Parents must become aware of feelings of guilt. They may wonder what they did to cause the prematurity. They may review past events, wondering whether there was too much physical exertion, sexual activity, emotional stress that may have triggered the labor. The mother may have underlying feelings of inadequacy—everyone else can produce a healthy child, but she cannot. Parents may feel angry at the unexpected loss, cheated of what everyone else has experienced.

When parents do not deal with disappointment, they are less active in the care of the infant.[5] They stay aloof. Yet continuing interaction with the child, seeing the child's health stabilize and the child grow, also helps disappointment decrease.

Parents need to talk to each other, discuss their feelings and have mutual acceptance of what the other parent feels. There is no right or wrong way to feel, and feelings change. Being able to express how one feels and listening carefully to how the other person feels are important skills at this time. Parents need not feel the same way, but knowing that the partner understands and accepts one's own feelings is a source of support.

Robin Henig and Dr. Anne Fletcher describe four stages of premie parenthood.[6] Parents work through these stages at different rates as each forms a close relationship with the new baby. The first is **anticipatory grief**—parents withdraw from the child until they are certain he or she will survive. The second, **facing up**, occurs as parents accept their inability to deliver a healthy, full-term baby. As already noted, mothers may feel especially inadequate, but both parents must become aware of any feelings of guilt about the early birth and accept the fact that the birth has occurred as it has. Once they have grieved for the loss of the full-term child, they can turn their attention to the newborn and begin the third stage of **bonding and attachment.**

Because the premie may be very sick, in an incubator or in a warming bed, hooked up to elaborate equipment with several tubes and wires, parents cannot pick up and hold or cuddle their child. It may not look like a baby, resembling more the fetus in the womb, with downy hair, transparent skin that quickly changes color, and little fat. So the baby is physically inaccessible and lacks the appealing babyish qualities of a rounded, pink body. As the baby begins to recover, is safe and able to come home, parents begin to believe the baby will be theirs and bond to it.

In the fourth or **learning stage**, parents acquire knowledge and information about their baby and skill in handling him or her. They recognize that though the baby has special needs at present, these needs will disappear with time.

Robin Henig and Dr. Anne Fletcher discuss in detail how parents bond to the premie.[7] They suggest that parents photograph their child so that if the child has to be transferred to another hospital, they at least have a picture. They should visit the intensive care nursery as soon after birth as possible. If the baby is in another hospital, the father may start visiting alone while the mother remains in the hospital. Some fathers feel close to their premie children because they began the bonding process with the child. Parents should touch their premie as soon as possible. The extremities are not as sensitive as the trunk, so parents can start by stroking an arm or leg. Even if you can only reach through a window and stroke a little, it is important to do this. Research indicates that premies who are touched 20 minutes a day beyond routine care fare better physically. They gain weight better, have less apnea (breathing stoppages) and score better on tests of development in later years than premies who don't receive this attention.

These authors also suggest talking to your child. Talking, combined with touching, enables the premature baby to incorporate stimulation from two senses. Because the baby is already familiar with parents' voices from pregnancy, these voices may be very soothing as they are associated with pleasant times. When parents are not there, they can leave a tape with their voices singing lullabies, reciting rhymes, for the nurse to play occasionally.

Parents are wise to take over as much of the care of their premature newborn as possible and start as soon as the child is out of danger. Doing routine care cements the bond between parent and child and helps parents feel more like parents. Some hospitals have arranged rooming-in for premies and mothers before they go home. When mothers have the opportunity to be completely responsible for care while still being able to ask questions, their skills and self-confidence increase.

Premature infants' motor behavior, visual and auditory behavior, and spontaneous motility all increase with age to a significant degree during the period from thirty-two conceptual weeks to full term.[8] During this period of development, premature babies also express individual differences in their behavior that are stable, just as full-term babies do. Mothers and fathers of preterms show the same sex differences in relating to infants that the parents of full-terms show. Mothers are more active, nurturant caregivers and fathers will engage in play and stimulation when appropriate.[9]

The fact that preterm infants grow and develop skills is heartening to parents. There are few signs of disabilities in mental development or expressive or receptive language development at age two and just slightly poorer motor skills.[10] When intervention programs have helped the mothers become sensitive to their babies' needs, there are no cognitive differences between preterm and full-term babies at age 4.[11] These children will be followed into school, and it will be important to see whether the intervention program, carried out at birth with the mothers, continues to have an effect. Preterm babies whose mothers did not have such help did not catch up with full-term babies and at age four remain slightly below in overall cognitive level, though they may catch up later.

Looking at preterm infants' cognitive development over time and the supports that facilitate it emphasizes the very powerful role that the mother's attitude has on the baby's growth. Mark Greenberg and Keith Crnic found that the attitudes mothers of full-term babies had about themselves, their babies, and husbands were only moderately related to their babies' growth; but in the preterm sample, mothers' attitudes were very strongly related to the baby's progress.[12] When mothers in this sample felt that their role was important and that they were doing a good job, when they felt positively about the baby, their husband, and life in general, then their babies developed well.

It is important for parents of premature babies to understand their strong and important role and the child's capacity for healthy growth, for our culture seems to hold subtle negative beliefs about preterms. A study of prematurity stereotyping found that labeling a child "premature" brings a host of negative qualities.[13] When mothers were told an unfamiliar six-month-old baby was premature, they were more likely to rate the child as smaller, less cute, and less likable, even when the child was actually full-term. In brief interactions, they touched the child less and offered a more immature toy for play. What is startling is that the babies' behavior changed with these women, and they became less active. College students watching videos of the interactions could tell immediately whether the child was described as full-term or preterm.

This negative view of premature babies may not affect the parents directly because they are influenced by their daily contact with the child. Such stereotypes, however, may influence friends and relatives of the parents, and they, in turn, affect the par-

486

CHAPTER 15
Parenting
Children
with Special
Needs

INTERVIEW
with Anneliese Korner

Anneliese F. Korner is Professor of Psychiatry and the Behavioral Sciences Research at Stanford University School of Medicine. She has studied infant development for the last thirty years, and in the last seven years has collected data and developed a test, The Neurobehavioral Assessment of the Pre-Term Infant. This test assesses a premature baby's progress in the early weeks of life.

You have done research with infants, particularly premature infants, for many years. What would you say are the important things for parents to do that will be helpful for their premature child?

To hang in there! One of the things that many, many studies have shown, not mine because I do not follow the infants beyond the hospital, is that when premies go home, they usually are not as rewarding to parents, in the sense that they get easily disorganized with too much stimulation, and they are not as responsive as full-term babies. Particularly if a mother has already had a full-term baby, she will find that the premie whom she is bringing home, who may have been very sick, may not give her the rewards that a full-term would. Sometimes parents begin to feel rejected, and a vicious cycle is set up. The less the baby responds, the more the mother tries; she overstimulates the child further, and the baby turns away even more. It takes sometimes as much as five to eight months for a baby to become more responsive; by that time many parents have become rather discouraged. It is exactly at that time when they really should be responding to the baby. One can't blame them because they have had this history of trying so hard and not getting anywhere and feeling discouraged. Kathy Barnard, for example, has said this is when parents need help. They are turned off, unrewarded, and the baby really needs them at that age, so parents need encouragement to get reinvolved.

Currently, we are about to begin a new study. What we have done over the last seven years is to develop a maturity test called The Neurobehavioral Assessment of the Pre-term Infant. We have seen some 500 babies over this time! About one-third were longitudinally examined from thirty-two weeks to thirty-seven weeks conceptual age. We were very hard-nosed, insisting on psychometric soundness—test-retest had to be very high, which is hard to achieve with little ones. The items we included had to be developmentally valid in that there would have to be age changes. Since we now have seven clusters that show significant age changes, we are using the test as a sort of therapeutic tool in showing parents that, over weeks, they can see their baby is really making progress. If I were a mother of a premie, being concerned about its development, seeing that the baby actually changes for the better over time would be tremendously reassuring.

What qualities do you think help parents to cope well with premature children?

Well, one thing that is helpful in the first few months is for parents to understand the

ents. Cynthia Zarling, Barton Hirsch, and Susan Landry found that although mothers of both full-term and preterm infants had equivalent support from relatives and friends, the effect of such support differed in the two groups.[14] Mothers of full-term infants were more sensitive in their caregiving when they had a closely knit support group. Mothers of preterm infants were less sensitive caretakers when surrounded

behavioral cues of the child. For example, it is better not to feed the child when the baby is in deep sleep. It would be better not to interrupt the baby's deep sleep and let him gradually wake up to feed. Respond to what the baby is conveying as much as possible because the baby can in some ways convey his needs. This is true of full-term babies also.

Are many premies irritable for a period of time?

That depends. When a baby is irritable and cries, that is actually an achievement because the younger babies cannot muster the strength to cry. When a baby cries lustily, that's a good sign. But it is true that premies have been described as more restless and more irritable, and that can test any mother's patience.

The parent who has more information and is really skilled with babies has an advantage in reading the baby's cues. The more children one has, for example, the better one is able, usually, to see individuality.

The important thing to know is what state the baby is in. Before the parents take the baby home, someone needs to explain that and there isn't always someone available. Have you ever seen a baby in REM sleep? They grimace a lot, they open and close their eyes a lot, their eyes dart all over the place. It has happened that, not knowing the state of the baby, people think the baby is convulsing. This is a total misreading. Someone needs to explain the infant's state to parents. Some hospitals have rooms for parents and before they go home, parents learn to take care of the baby for a day or two under the supervision of nurses. That is a wonderful luxury that few hospitals have.

Can a parent spoil a child with a lot of picking up?

Certainly not in the early months. The early months are spent in being a shield for the baby, and certainly if the baby is very uncomfortable, restless, or is crying, the idea of picking him up also gives him the feeling of being able to have an effect on people. He's not spinning his wheels; he's trying to communicate, and he is successful. One hears less about spoiling babies these days.

One of the most important things for a relationship is to enjoy each other. It is infinitely more important than pushing a child to achieve. In other words, there is so much richness in the parent's responding with joy to what a baby does and in the normal give-and-take that is part of the early relationships that the interchange is a rich source of stimulation and gratification for both participants. A mother is an infinitely complicated stimulus for a baby. Enjoying the child, being reciprocal, just being there, is what it is all about.

with such a network. The authors speculate that the distress which relatives and friends feel over the unexpected prematurity is conveyed to mothers frequently and serves to disrupt their mothering. Another study on the support provided to mothers as they make the transition to home care indicates that mothers who do well tend to adopt and nurture an optimistic attitude about the long-term outcome for the

488

CHAPTER 15
Parenting
Children
with Special
Needs

child. Professional support that discusses possible difficulties and coping strategies is at times disruptive for these mothers, although such help is useful to women who feel under stress with their infants.[15]

Although the long-term cognitive outlook is good for premature babies, there are differences in the emotional reactivity in the first year or two that make parenting difficult and the need for effective support strong.[16] Premature babies are initially more irritable, quicker to become overstimulated, and less interactive with parents. Parents', particularly mothers', initial reactions are to become more active and more stimulating, but then the child turns off and retreats to avoid further stimulation. Parents can be soothing and moderate in their interactions to their premature infants. Expressing interest in what the infant does seems to help the child reach a more positive state. Tendencies to become easily overstimulated, especially in the face of mild stress, continue into the second year.

As the child grows and develops in the first year, parents must remember the child's age is not measured from the actual birthday. If the premie was born on July 7, eight weeks premature, he or she is not the same age as a full-term baby born on that date. Because the last two months of development that would have occurred in the womb took place after birth for the premie, the child is always about two months behind full-term children born on the same date and two months must always be deducted from the chronological age to get the child's true age. It is important for parents to keep this fact in mind when looking at developmental milestones in the first year. Premie babies are expected to be slower to sit, crawl, stand, and verbalize, depending on the number of weeks of prematurity. By age two or three, however, these differences are not so important.

Because premie babies start life with special problems, their parents often become overprotective. Parental overprotectiveness is not unusual in the first several months as the child grows and becomes stronger. If overprotectiveness persists after the first year or exceeds what the pediatrician considers reasonable, however, parents have developed a problem. They may be so fearful, as a result of their initial worries about the child's survival, that they are not permitting the child opportunities for exploration, independence, or contact with children. Overprotectiveness can cover anger, too. All children can be demanding, irritable; and all parents at one time or another have had fleeting feelings of anger at the demands made on them. When they cannot accept this anger, they sometimes cover it with a layer of overprotectiveness to demonstrate how much they love and care for the child.

Because overprotectiveness, as noted, robs the child of opportunities for growth, parents must learn to grit their teeth and let their initially vulnerable babies take a few tumbles and some hurts. Giving children freedom to grow also gives parents free time to spend with each other. Sometimes they may choose to get a babysitter and go out. This is important. As we have discussed in Chapter 6, parents must make time to nourish the marital relationship if they are to develop a close, satisfying family life.

Having a premie baby is a stressful experience. Parents' feelings are intense, and they have much to do. Knowing that most babies grow and develop with few scars from their early entry into the world can be reassuring. Through the difficult experience, parents may gain a greater confidence in their abilities to cope and a special closeness grows among the family members who have shared the crisis and grown from it.

CHILDREN WHO ARE ADOPTED

Adoption is defined as taking a child into one's family through legal means and raising the child as one's own.[17] In the vast majority of cases, relatives—for example, stepfathers—adopt a child. It is not known precisely how many children are adopted each year because the U.S. government no longer collects statistics from individual states. In 1974, however, it was estimated that about 149,000 children were adopted, 36 percent by nonrelatives.[18] Other figures suggest there are about 5 million adopted children in the United States, half of these under the age of eighteen.[19]

Adoption occurs in many ways—through an agency in this country, through private individuals, through an agency bringing in children from other countries. Although emphasis is on adopting children as newborns or as close to that age as possible, children can be adopted at any age. This section is written for parents forming families by the adoption process, and especially for adoptive parents who are not related by blood or marriage to the child. Issues relating to stepparenting and stepparent adoption are covered in Chapter 14. Here we cover preparing for parenthood, the bonding and attachment process, and issues about adoption as the child grows and matures.

Most parents seek to create a family by means of adoption when they cannot have biological children. Infertility or genetic problems leading to child death are major reasons for adopting. Though a small group adopt because they want a child of a certain sex or because of belief in the importance of adoption, parents usually come to adoption with feelings of loss or inadequacy because they cannot produce biological children. As they prepare for parenthood, they must deal with their feelings of guilt, inadequacy, loss, and sadness before they adopt. Professionals believe adopting parents must acknowledge and accept such feelings before adoption so they do not use the adoption to deny the feelings of loss.

As they accept the fact they cannot have biological children, parents may ponder again whether they want to have children at all. Choosing not to have children occurs more frequently now because both men and women have many avenues for expressing creativity. Parents should consider how important it is to have a child and how they feel about raising a child who is not their biological offspring. Many persons feel an adult can create meaningful and important bonds with any child, but a smaller number may find biological connections essential.

If a couple decide to adopt, they can approach an agency to begin proceedings. Unlike a pregnancy, there is no definite nine-month period in which to prepare for parenthood. Parents may have to wait months or years, never knowing if or when a child may come. They are often so worried about whether they are going to get a child that they cannot go through the process of planning to be parents. They do not think about the kind of parent they want to be or wonder about their competence

490

CHAPTER 15
Parenting
Children
with Special
Needs

until the question of having a baby is settled. When that occurs, the baby is already there and parents are coping with all the adjustments of new parenthood at once. The image making that frequently occurs in a leisurely way during pregnancy occurs rapidly while the family members make many other adjustments and is an added stress to the initial parenting experience.

Dorothy Smith and Laurie Nehls studied the bonding process in adoptive families and described three states—(1) before entry (preadoption), (2) entry into the family (adoption), and (3) after entry.[20] As noted, before adoption, parents are less likely to fantasize about the coming baby and themselves as parents. Sometimes they tell no one they are trying to adopt because their hopes may not be actualized. They do not get informal support from relatives, friends, and their place of work. There is no routine maternity leave for mothers before or after adoption, nor do many adoptive parents have the experience of showers that give feelings of support.

The entry phase may be stressful. Although babies ideally come to the adoptive home from the hospital, this may not occur. Infants may arrive from foreign countries, weak and tired, unfamiliar with the language and culture. Or babies may arrive sad at losing foster parents who have cared for them while their biological parents were making decisions about adoption. Older children may have already experienced several different households and so come with feelings of insecurity, frustration, anger. Instead of rejoicing family and friends, adoptive parents may meet with a series of questions—"Where did you get the child?" "Who are the biological parents?" "How do you feel about taking care of another person's child?" As they rush to explain everything and stop the questioning, they may say more than is wise. They may discuss circumstances of the adoption and details that are really only the business of the close family and the child. Parents need to think in advance about how they will respond to others' requests for explanations.

As with biological children and parents, feelings of warmth and love may not arise immediately when the baby enters the family. These feelings build in the third stage, after adoption. As parents care for their children, learn their characteristics and moods, their love grows. When older infants and children are adopted, however, they may not return the parents' feelings. They may be sad, frightened, and rebellious because of past disappointments. Parents can be understanding of children's reactions and use active listening skills to deal with them. Being able to give children a prolonged time to settle into a new family helps both children and parents.

As attachment grows between parents and children and parents' confidence in their parenting skills grows, they steel themselves for the day their child will ask questions and need to be told he or she is adopted. Before deciding exactly what to say, parents need to understand their own feelings about being adoptive parents. If they feel comfortable about adoption and believe they are true parents because they are nourishing and protecting their child, helping him or her grow, then they convey a sense of confidence and security about the adoption process to the child. When parents feel secure, they neither overemphasize the fact of adoption nor hide it. They can explain the different ways to form a family as follows: Most often, mothers and fathers produce biological children whom they live with. Sometimes when parents divorce, a new parent enters the family and later becomes the adopted parent of the child even though they are not biologically related. Still other times, neither biological parent is in a position to care for the child, and so unrelated couples who want very much to have a child adopt the child into their family. The child is part of that family no matter how he or she was born.

The general advice is to tell children before their fifth birthday. Adoption, however, is not something you explain once or twice when the child is young and then forget about. Recent research evidence suggests that most preschoolers are unlikely to understand what adoption is even when parents have explained it to them and they refer to themselves as adopted.[21] Preschoolers confuse adoption and birth, making no distinction between the two ways of having children. By the age of six, most children can understand that there are two paths to parenthood—birth and adoption—and they understand that adoption makes the child a permanent member of the family.

Just as in most other areas of knowledge, children's conceptions of adoption broaden in the eight to eleven age period. Children begin to understand that adoption is not the usual way families grow. They become more aware that their biological parents exist somewhere, and many children become concerned that their biological parents may return and take them away from their adoptive families. By the end of this period, children return to a belief in the permanence of adoption even though it is not until early or middle adolescence that they understand it is a legal process.

Young children think adoption occurs because adoptive parents have strong needs to love and care for children, providing them a good home. In elementary school, between eight and eleven, children recognize that parents adopt children for additional reasons such as infertility, family planning needs, and the welfare of children. Very young children do not wonder why they needed to be removed from their biological parents. With increasing age, children distinguish financial reasons, parental death, and their biological parents' immaturity as reasons for adoption.

This research suggests that even though it may be wise to introduce the concept of adoption early, when children ask if their mothers carried them inside like other mothers they observe, children comprehend adoption only in the vaguest terms at this time. Parents will have to explain the concept many times as their children get older, and they should wait for direct questions or indirect hints that children want information on the topic.

Often the question first arises in the preschool years when children are curious about pregnancy and wonder if they grew in their mother's womb like some other baby they know. Parents can say, "No," and wait for the next question before volunteering the whole story. Often when children ask, they are focused on the idea of growing in a womb and getting out, and are not so curious about whose womb they grew in. When they ask whose womb they grew in, or why didn't they grow in the adoptive parent's womb, the parent can say that for physical reasons, they could not have a child that way. There were other parents who could bear a child, but were not in a position to care for the child when he or she was born, so they were able to adopt and have the child in their family.

Once children know of their adoption, parents can tell them how it occurred. Children often enjoy hearing the details of the parents' coming to get them at the hospital or the airport. If parents have kept baby books, they can show children pictures. Some professionals recommend baby books modified for adoptive families.

492

CHAPTER 15
Parenting
Children
with Special
Needs

Others, however, recommend a regular baby book if the child has entered the family as an infant. Baby books focus on the child's development, and if the parent has adopted the child at the earliest age, he or she can observe and record what is happening. The child's growth is the issue, not how the child got into the family. When children are adopted at an older age, an adoptive baby book may be more appropriate.

As children grow, and are in contact with other children, they may be teased or taunted: "You're adopted—your own mother didn't want you," or "Your parents weren't even married and you have to live with someone else." Adoption gets attention from teachers and other adults. Some teachers may wish to know details in order to understand the child. One mother refused to give detailed information about the biological parents, saying the agency would not approve; the information was for the child alone. Newspapers and television also present information and attitudes about adoption.

It is important for adoptive parents to be as aware as possible about what their children are experiencing in these ways. They can then talk about children's reactions to teasing, to other people's attitudes about adoption, to what they see on TV. For example, one boy saw a TV western showing a home delivery.[22] He said to the mother he knew now why she did not have babies—it hurt too much. That mother can explain it was not the pain of childbirth but some other physical problem. She can also put labor pain in perspective for the boy, saying it is intense but ends with birth, and most mothers forget it and go on and have several children.

Children may resent being different from other children who live with their biological parents. Active listening can draw out children's special concerns about being different. Parents can validate that it is hard to be different in that way. Most people, however, are different from others in one way or another and must accept the differences.

As children grow older, questions may center on the biological parents, especially the mother. It is best to use the term *biological parent* rather than *natural* or *real parent*. An adoptive parent is a real and natural parent, but is not a biological parent. Children usually want to know who the parent was, why they gave the child up for adoption, and whether the biological parent loved the child. Parents need to be sensitive to whether the questions are ones of curiosity, wanting information about the person, or ones reflecting emotional feelings of rejection. If the child is seven or eight, parents can say sometimes people get pregnant but cannot take care of a child. When mothers know they cannot provide good homes, they find parents who want children but cannot have biological children. Those parents adopt the child, and the child has a family who can care for him or her. As children get older, parents give specific information (if this is known) about why the biological mother could not care for the child—she was too young, a student without money. Parents often do not have many facts but perhaps can approach the adoption agency to learn anything available in the records.

Parents can counteract their children's feelings of rejection when they emphasize that their biological parents loved them even though they could not care for them. Linda Burgess, an experienced adoption worker, quotes an effective response by a mother to her son's statement that his mother didn't want him. "Your first mother

BOX 15-1
HOW CHILDREN EXPLAIN ADOPTION

One couple had five children, all of whom were adopted from different biological parents. Because they moved, the adoptive parents got their information about the biological parents from different agencies that gave varying amounts of detail. When the children asked why their mothers gave them up, the mother did not know what to say. She had information on only two situations and wanted to treat all the children alike. She decided to turn the question back to the children.

"I don't know why your mothers didn't keep you, but maybe each of you can think of some good reasons."

Mrs. Bartlett was taken aback by the offhand way in which the children pondered what was to her a solemn matter. From each child a spontaneous explanation came forth.

"I bet they were killed in an auto accident," said the ten-year-old auto buff.

"Mine had too many babies already," announced the eight-year-old, jealous of her younger brother.

"That's silly. My mother and father just weren't married," retorted the practical thirteen-year-old.

"I don't think they had enough to eat," said the hungry six-year-old.

"Well I know for sure my mother thought I was too ugly to keep," the self-deprecating fifteen-year-old declared.

The rejection of her children by their birth mother seemed to Mrs. Bartlett a tough and everlasting injury from which her adopted children would forever suffer. She had vowed to cushion them as much as she could from the hurtful consequences. As her children described their trials by rejection, Mrs. Bartlett's solicitude dissolved into amused appreciation as she listened to each of them mirror their own self-absorbed individuality. They seemed less concerned by the rejection than she was by the concept of it.

From Linda Cannon Burgess, *The Art of Adoption* (New York: W. W. Norton, 1981), p. 102.

was unable to care for you at the time you were born, and although she tried, she could find no way to keep you. People's lives can be so difficult and confusing that it seems there is no way to do what one would like most to do."[23] For another mother's response to this question, see Box 15-1

When children become teenagers, their questions about adoption may focus on identity issues. "What was my biological family like?" "What are my roots in this world?" "Who am I really?" "How am I like my biological parents?" As sexual interest increases in adolescence, children's interest in their own conception and birth may increase. They fantasize about their biological parents—usually as either inferior or superior beings. Though the fantasies start in earlier childhood, perhaps with ideas of being an abandoned member of royalty, in adolescence the fantasies become more specific and tied to real possibilities—being the product of a rape or an affair with

494

CHAPTER 15
Parenting
Children
with Special
Needs

a married man. Adolescent girls may worry that they are going to follow in their biological mother's path and conceive a child who will be put up for adoption. Girls and boys may wonder whether they have inherited an overly sexual nature that they cannot control.

As feelings intensify and their control over them wavers, teenagers may lash out at adoptive parents. Being rebellious, they may challenge the parents' authority with statements like, "You are not my real parents and you can't tell me what to do." "If you were my real parents, you'd love and understand me. You would let me do more." They may accuse their adoptive parents of never really wanting them. They may threaten to run away and find their biological parents.

As we can see, the fact of adoption can color all feelings and changes in adolescence. Just as biological parents have to try to understand and listen, send active I-messages, and set limits, adoptive parents must act similarly. It is especially stressful when adolescents lash out on a sensitive area like adoption. Parents' best protection and soundest guide is self-confidence in their own parenting skills and their wisdom to know when to listen and when to set limits. When teenagers carry on too long about the problems of having adoptive parents, parents have to set limits with firm I-messages of discomfort at what is said. They can always be willing to talk when such statements stop.

As adopted children get older, parents may face the possibility at some point that their children will want to seek out their biological parents. Many do this not because they are unhappy with their adoptive parents, but because they want a greater sense of their genetic history and an understanding of their social roots inherited from the biological parents. They want to understand their biological connections in the world. Adoptive parents cope best when they can sympathize with their children's desires, when they see the search as a reflection of the child's basic need for as complete a sense of identity as possible. Parents have the greatest difficulty coping when they see the search as a reflection on their adequacy as parents. Sometimes parents discourage the search for fear children will learn unpleasant facts. But in many instances actual knowledge, even of an unpleasant sort, is more welcome than the unknown or imagined.

Many states are beginning to set up clearinghouse agencies where adopted children and biological parents can register if they are interested in contact with the other person; in this way both parties can be sure the other wishes to meet. Currently, groups are run for biological parents and adopted children who meet so they can discuss their feelings and deal with them.

Though the process of parenting usually involves biological parents and child, it need not. Like stepfamilies, adoptive families are a testament to the human capacity to form strong, caring bonds that last a lifetime, even though children are not biologically related.

CHILDREN WHO ARE PHYSICALLY ILL

One of the hardest tasks in life is caring for children when they are physically ill, particularly when they are seriously ill. The work itself is not the problem, it is rather

seeing a child in pain or discomfort and not being able to remove the pain. Fortunately, most parents' experience with such tasks are confined to occasional bouts
of flu, colds, infectious diseases like mumps or measles, a broken bone. A significant
number of children, however—5 to 20 percent, depending on the exact definition—
are considered to have a chronic physical illness or handicap that lasts for months
or years, involves some decrease in functioning, and may or may not result in
an early death. The most common forms of such illnesses in children under eighteen are asthma (2 percent), epilepsy (1 percent), cardiac conditions (0.5 percent),
orthopedic illness (0.5 percent), and diabetes mellitus (0.1 percent).[24]

Parents must cope not only with episodes of acute illness, but also with the problems that result when a child has a chronic physical problem that affects the daily
regimen of all family members as well as the sick person. In this section we present
information about children's conceptions of their bodies and the nature of illness
and cure as such ideas influence response to treatment. Parents may incorrectly
assume that children understand much more about their bodies than they do; in
fact, patient explanations and repetitions of the causes and factors involved in physical illness are usually required. Then we describe parenting techniques in the case
of acute and chronic conditions.

Children's Conceptions of Their Bodies and Illness

Children's earliest conceptions of themselves are in terms of their physical
characteristics—their sex, their eye and hair color. As in other areas of thinking about
the world, however, children's understanding of their bodies is initially rudimentary.
From about ages four to eight, concepts are vague and few in number. Between ages
eight and ten, there is a leap in the complexity and accuracy of ideas concerning the
contents and functioning of the body, and by ages eleven to thirteen, conceptions are
fairly accurate.

Preschool and early elementary school students refer to parts of the body they see
or feel—their eyes, nose, skin, bones.[25] They tend to see the body as a large cavity
filled with food, bones, and blood. At early ages, they see all parts of the body as
equally important to life, and the loss of any part—for example, a tooth—may be
considered a major trauma. As they get a little older, children view as most important
those parts they see or feel most directly—their hearts, eyes, legs.

Young children get their ideas about the body from colloquial expressions.[26] For
example, nerves make you nervous or mad, or keep you from being a coward. Ideas
come, too, from cultural or religious sayings—one child thought humans are made
of dirt and return to dirt when they die. Children also get ideas from their physical
sensations; they describe bones where they feel them. Finally, they base their ideas
about the importance of body parts on the amount of time and attention given to
them. For example, one girl thought hair was the most important part of the body.

With increasing age, children's concepts of their body become more accurate and
detailed.[27] Still, their notions of how the body works remain rudimentary even in
early adolescence. Though young children understand air is important to life, it is
not until about age fifteen that they understand the role lungs play in breathing. One
thirteen-year-old thought lungs were in the throat—one was for breathing and one

496

CHAPTER 15
Parenting
Children
with Special
Needs

for eating. Children have a clear idea of where the heart is early on, and 50 percent of four-year-olds know it is essential to life. The heart is related to circulation but is primarily seen as the organ of feeling and affect. The doctor listens to your heart to be sure you are happy; the heart makes you dream. Sometimes religious thoughts are considered physical explanations—the heart is where God lives. Even young children know the brain is for thinking, but it is not until they are older that they link it with control of other bodily functions like movement.

Although eating and elimination are both important aspects of life, children know more about elimination than digestion, perhaps because as a culture we put so much emphasis on cleanliness. Children are not so aware of their stomachs as we would expect. In one study, no children under thirteen named the stomach spontaneously as a part of the body though it clearly gives many positive sensations.[28] Children focus more on elimination and tend to overestimate the number of bowel movements people have. Forty-three percent thought that between three and ten was the daily average for the population. Children know less about the bladder and urination.

Since it is not until children are twelve or thirteen that accurate ideas about the body develop, parents and health professionals must not overestimate children's understanding of their bodies and what is happening to them at times of illness. Parents can explore with children all their ideas about their physical functioning since often truths and half-truths are joined happily together in their minds.

Just as children's ideas about their bodies develop, so their conceptions of illness expand with development.[29] In the early years, children think of an illness in terms of a single symptom that is caused by a vague event. They can, however, understand that they can catch a cold from someone else or get a scraped knee from an accident.[30] In these early years, children sometimes describe illness as the result of an immoral act—you are bad and get punished. Parents must be aware of this tendency and seek to reassure their young child, who may wonder frantically what he or she has done to deserve this illness. Young children see cure as an instantaneous process; once the medicine has gone down, the person is well.

As children move into the elementary school years (ages seven to ten), they think illness consists of several symptoms that include reference to external parts and some internal organs. Illnesses are caused by germs, dirt, and—still—bad behavior. Direct contact with germs is needed to cause illness. The cure comes from surface contact with the curing agent whether it be ointment, person, or activity. The child feels more in control because illness can be avoided if you stay away from direct contact with the invading agent.

Children ages eight to ten see the person's physical condition as playing a role in causing the disease. The external germs invade the body, and the body is receptive to them. External agents are seen as sources of cure, but children believe that in many cases the body heals itself. For example, no one takes medicine for measles, they go away. Children assume other illnesses follow this same pattern.

In Piaget's stage of formal operations (when children are twelve or older), they think in more abstract terms. They understand there are more causes of illness—internal organs malfunction, for example. There are as many sources of illness as there are parts of the body that malfunction, and there are many kinds of cures. In the most advanced stage, adolescents view psychological factors as important influences on bodily functioning.

Changing conceptions of illness give children a greater sense of control over what is happening to them. In the early years, children may feel especially vulnerable because they believe even distant events like the sun can cause an illness, and there is little they can do about that. As they grow more mature, they realize that external agents must have direct contact with the body and produce some physical change. Attention centers on cures as well as ways to prevent illness by avoiding contact with germs. As children get older, they become more concerned with promoting health by following a healthy diet, getting exercise, and other activities. Children are not so dependent on medicines as they come to believe the body can heal itself. In the final stages, multiple causes of illness imply multiple ways to prevent it and reinforce the importance of developing a healthy, tension-free lifestyle.

How do children tell when they are ill? At first they determine illness by very subjective feelings:[31] "I don't feel good." Gradually they talk about pains and symptoms that are vague and not clearly defined. As children grow older, they know they are sick because of definite physical symptoms they can pinpoint in a specific place: "My head throbs," "Stomach aches." Children then develop a definite idea about illnesses—appendicitis, chicken pox. The symptoms are directly related to the illness. In the most advanced stages, also found in adults, the individual's overall mood and ability to function are used as criteria for determining sickness. If mothers can still carry out their tasks, they tend not to think of themselves as sick even though they may not feel well. We can see that with increasing age, signs for determining whether illness is present become more objective. Subjective feelings are the first basis, then come definite symptoms, then interference with one's daily activities.

Parents have an important role to play in helping younger children to understand and integrate the experience of poor health so they do not feel so vulnerable.

Routine Medical and Dental Visits

Since children do not conceive of their bodies or medical procedures the same way adults do, very routine events can have special significance. In preparing children for visits to the doctor and dentist, honest answers are most helpful. When children are old enough to have a sense of time, it is wise to start a short time in advance by saying that an appointment has been made for a regular checkup. If the child asks about shots or painful procedures, the parent gives information as honest as possible. If a parent knows a shot will be given and the child says he or she does not want one because of the pain, a parent can agree that it is painful for a very brief period, but the pain is worth it because the shot prevents illness that might be much worse. A tone of voice that accepts the fear as natural, but the shot as a necessity to be safe against other disease, helps keep the situation calm. When a child learns at the doctor's office that a shot is to be given, Lee Salk recommends that a parent say, "You are going to get an injection, and it is probably going to hurt; if you want to cry, that's all right, because when something hurts, it may make you cry."[32] If the child cries,

498

CHAPTER 15
Parenting
Children
with Special
Needs

the parent can respond sympathetically, "Yes, I know, it hurts—that's why you're crying." If the child doesn't cry, a parent can comment on the child's bravery. This technique is useful for any hospital procedure, too.

Behaviorists recommend parents associate medical visits with pleasurable events. Thus, having routine visits with no illness and only occasional shots help the child become comfortable in the medical setting. Doctors and dentists often give a reward at the end of the visit—a balloon, a plastic toy—to link pleasure with the visit. Parents can also arrange a special treat after the visit.

Acute Illness

Acute illnesses are time-limited medical problems that may require a few days or up to a few months for recovery. Although severe acute illnesses can lead to chronic problems, usually the child returns to his or her previous level of functioning. In the course of acute illness, four problems besides the fear covered in the previous section emerge: (1) ensuring that the doctor's orders on medicine and rest at home are followed; (2) filling the time so that children do not become too bored; (3) handling the child's immature behavior that often crops up in the face of stress; and (4) minimizing the aftereffects of an illness. Hospitalization, which an acute illness may require, is covered in the next section.

We know that children's concepts of treatment and cure are vague and sometimes magical. They may be reluctant to take any medicine, particularly if the medicine has an unpleasant taste. Careful explanations of the purpose of the medication can be repeated, if necessary, to reduce an unfavorable reaction, but such explanations may not remove all affect. Trying to disguise the medicine in food like ice cream sometimes works, but often simply approaching the child straightforwardly and assuming the child will take it once the purpose is known may solve the situation. If such an approach does not work, this is the one time, according to Thomas Gordon, that power is justified.[33]

When children are ill, their behavior is likely to become more immature, wanting parents to do things for them that they have done for themselves—feed them, dress them. This is not surprising since many adults crave similar kinds of tender, loving care when they are ill. Illness, however, usually increases irritability and a child may be less satisfied with parents' efforts. Expecting that a child will be demanding, anticipating that he or she may be more babyish and wanting more signs of affection, helps parents to respond with minimal difficulty. Sometimes a child may insist on many privileges and gifts, and a parent does not want to comply. In such cases a parent can accept the feelings while not complying with the request.

Boredom is a problem when children are recovering from illness. Joan Beck in *Effective Parenting* has many suggestions for helping children pass the time happily.[34] Time spent reading to the child, listening to the child's records, talking, playing simple board and card games are all useful devices. If children feel well enough, they can engage in simple craft activities—coloring, molding figures from play dough, making simple puppets from felt. Parents can be available to entertain the child for specific periods, and then leave a tape recorder so children can record anything they want to tell parents while they are off doing something else. Special foods and unusual ways of serving them also break the monotonous routine of an illness.

When children are ill, accepting the child's feelings, handling his or her fears openly, being supportive but not indulgent are all tactics that prevent temporary problems from becoming long-lasting ones.

Arthur Parmelee believes acute illnesses like colds and stomach or bowel upsets can be beneficial to development because they help children learn the difference between physical and emotional distress and they give opportunities for empathy and caregiving.[35] Since the average child under five has between four and nine acute illnesses a year, and the average family of four has about twenty, children experience their own illnesses and witness the illnesses of others fairly frequently.

Going to the Hospital

Occasionally an acute or chronic illness requires hospitalization. Preparation reduces anxiety, and that in turn helps healing. When hospitalizations are scheduled in advance, it is sometimes possible to tour the ward and meet the nurses ahead of time. This reassures children about the place.

In preparing children for the hospital, parents can use the guidelines researchers have developed to direct adults in time of emergency.[36] They recommend a message in simple words that tell: (1) what is happening, (2) why it is happening, and (3) what the person is to do. Incorporating these guidelines, a parent might say, "We are going to the hospital so the doctor can fix your foot (or whatever area is involved). You need this operation because your foot is not growing in the proper way (explain whatever the reason is) and the surgery will correct that. You will be there for a short time, and I shall be with you almost all the time you are there." A parent might want to repeat this statement—often the child cannot take it all in the first time—and then answer any questions. The parent's confidence and calmness will be a large factor in helping the child accept the procedures.

Along with reassurance that everything is expected to go well, the essential ingredient in helping the child master the experience is honesty about what is happening. One need not describe a procedure or the aftereffect in great detail, but if a child asks about pain or bleeding, a parent can say, "That may happen, but there are ways of taking care of it if it does." A child may have many questions, and all should be answered.

Many hospitals now permit parents to stay with their children around the clock, sleeping in chairs or cots, or in an adjacent room. Brazelton, an early supporter of parental participation in hospitalizations, describes the benefits as follows:

1. Children have less terror about what is happening, quicker recovery from surgery and acute illness, and better adjustment in the hospital.

2. Parents have less anxiety and guilt about the child's illness, better understanding of the illness and preparation for home care.

3. Hospitals benefit because of shorter stays and fewer demands from children.[37]

500

CHAPTER 15
Parenting
Children
with Special
Needs

Fears in the hospital vary according to the age of the child. Though children may have many different fears, very young children under three tend to fear separation from the parents; children between three and eight tend to worry about death.

Even if parents can stay in the hospital, they will need some time away from their child to eat or return home for brief periods. Being as honest as possible about when the parent will be there and when away helps the child. A young child will watch and wait for a parent to come for lunch and will become sadder with each passing moment that the parent is late. If parents cannot arrive on time, a phone call to the floor nurse who will inform the child eases the strain. When parents cannot stay overnight or must leave, they will ease the child and themselves if they are clear when they are leaving. Hoping to spare the child and themselves a parting scene, parents may tell a child they are going for coffee and not come back, or they may wait till the child naps and slip off without an advance statement about leaving. The child then becomes anxious, refusing to sleep when the parent comes again.

Accepting the child's feelings of pain and discomfort helps the child relax. A parent can point out that the pain of the surgery is temporary and will prevent physical problems from affecting the child in the future. The child who is able to accept pain will suffer less since fear intensifies the subjective experience of pain. In addition to reducing fear and pain by realistic preparation for what will happen, parents can help their child relax as much as possible by bringing along to the hospital a favorite possession like a blanket or stuffed toy, and by bringing books to read and a few toys for play when the child is alert. Talking to the child in a soothing voice about routine procedures as they are done will help the child relax as will holding and rocking when the child is young.

Parents' presence and participation in hospital care help reassure the child. Further, parents can help to interpret and explain what is happening in the hospital and get feedback from the child about his or her understanding, for, as we noted earlier, children think of illness and cure differently from adults. Having parents available to explain devices like intravenous tubes, catheters, and nose tubes helps children cope better. Parents' providing physical care for the child as well as supplying helpful information not only eases the strain of the entire experience, but also can increase the child's confidence that his or her parents are there when they are needed.

Chronic Physical Illness

The term **chronic illness** refers to many different physical conditions or illnesses. In all conditions, however, individuals must adjust to some long-term symptoms or problems that limit behavior or functioning to some degree and may or may not be life threatening. Children with mild handicaps may have more psychiatric problems than those with severe handicaps. The mildly handicapped child can still engage in many, but not quite all, previous activities, and this sense of being "not quite like everyone else but able to be with everybody else" may be more frustrating and irritating than having very definite limitations that remove the child from that setting.

Chronic illness may be particularly upsetting depending on the age of the child. Boys around eight to ten and adolescent girls may have the greatest difficulty in adjusting to physical limitations. The boys are in an age period in which they are concerned about their physical prowess, their ability to run and compete with other boys. Girls are most worried about illness when they are adolescents and increasingly concerned with physical attractiveness.

Parents help their children to cope in many ways. Jerome Schulman, a child psychiatrist, conducted interviews with parents and children who had a serious illness to determine what leads to successful coping. He summarized his impressions of factors that were important as follows:

1. Parents and children who cope well "are living by affirming life." They live one day at a time, take events as they come, and try to get some happiness each day.

2. Parents and children both have developed good self-concepts. They accept themselves as "satisfying human beings" and maintain self-esteem. This quality may not always have been there but people do develop it in adverse circumstances.

3. Ability to avoid a sense of guilt about the illness enables patients and parents to adjust to the illness. "Few can explain how their feelings of guilt disappeared," but it ceased to be an influence.

4. Religion is important to some families, but not all, and when it is important, it is of nonsectarian, nondogmatic kind.

5. Mutual support between husband and wife results in open acknowledgment and praise of each other's strengths with an absence of blame.

6. Emotional and practical support of relatives and friends provides a network of help for the family.

7. A major feature of the interviews is the openness and honesty that all family members show to each other and to relatives and friends.

8. Parents separate the illness from the child. They believe the sick child should be treated as nearly as possible like a healthy child, even if the child is dying. They have chores within their capacities, go to school, receive discipline as other children.[38]

As we can see from this list, the qualities that increase coping are those recommended for parenting healthy children as well—honesty, support as unique individuals, expecting participation and help in family activities within abilities. These are qualities researchers identified as characteristics of families with psychologically healthy children.

Illness: A Family Affair

A chronic illness is a family event of importance. The exact impact on the family depends on a variety of factors and what happens over time. Paula Beckman divides the many factors into two categories—constitutional and environmental factors.[39] Constitutional factors include characteristics of the person who is ill or disabled, the degree of caregiving required, the organization of the family, the characteristics of

502

CHAPTER 15
Parenting
Children
with Special
Needs

other family members and their relationships to each other. Environmental factors include the social status characteristics of the family and the support that it gets from other relatives and friends.

A major feature determining the stress on the family is the extra caregiving required for the ill or handicapped individual and the number of people to share the increased work. Perhaps most important is the emotional tone of the family members as they relate to each other and cope with all that has to be done. While the emotional tone can be strongly influenced by the amount of extra work, the tone need not be determined by it. When families recognize that more important than anything else is how they relate to each other emotionally, then they can take steps to have as positive an atmosphere as possible.

Siblings are often forgotten as individuals who bear part of the burden when a child is ill, and a recent study on their adjustment illustrates how important emotional tone is.[40] Children with disabled siblings were compared to children with healthy siblings in terms of extra work load and psychological well-being. Children with disabled brothers and sisters had more caregiving activities and spent more time doing them. They rated disabled siblings positively, however, and enjoyed their contact with them more than did children with healthy siblings. Girls did tend to feel more angry at disabled siblings at times, and both boys and girls felt they had more negative relationships with their mother.

Children with disabled siblings had more complaints of subjective distress. While their scores were generally in the normal range on mood tests, they reported more anxiety; girls reported more depression, and boys felt less competent. The number of complaints was related to the mother's negativity and not to the amount of caregiving. Mothers perhaps were more short-tempered because of the many responsibilities and had less time for their healthy children. So chronic illness affects each person in subtle ways. In this study there were no ratings with regard to fathers in the family, so their role was not known. We do know that maintaining as optimistic and happy a tone as possible is helpful for everyone. Reaching out for support from other family members and friends often gives the extra caring that helps everyone in the family.

Children Who Are Depressed

In the last fifteen years, mental health professionals have focused on depression in children. It used to be thought that young children could not be depressed. According to this reasoning, their thinking was not mature enough to produce negative self-evaluations and feelings of hopelessness much before early adolescence. Now we are aware that much younger children—five, six, and older—can be depressed and in need of treatment. Because depression is best treated in its early stages and because it can affect so many areas of life, this section describes what depression is, what seem to be the causes, and what parents can do about it. We focus first on the early years and then the adolescent period.

Depression is seen in human beings and animals alike. About 5 to 10 percent of children are thought to be depressed.[41] The essential features of depression are depressed mood and loss of interest or pleasure in usual pursuits. The depressed person may feel blue, down in the dumps, hopeless or helpless in dealing with the mood. Disturbances in sleep, eating, and activity patterns may or may not accompany the depressed mood. Sometimes people awake early in the morning and are unable to return to sleep. Their appetite decreases (some may eat compulsively and gain weight). Energy level drops, and people move more slowly and accomplish less than formerly. Sometimes depression is accompanied by loss of concentration and poor memory, so school performance may drop. Because they feel less interested and withdraw, depressed children may have fewer friends. These are the major markers of depression.[42]

In some cases, depression is a normal response to a loss—death of a parent, divorce of the parents, loss of an important pet, moving to a new location. Children may show signs of depression off and on for months following the event, depending on the severity of the loss. But gradually the depression will lift. Early adolescent years are times of mood changes, and many boys and girls find themselves blue. These moods are temporary and do not involve the global retreat from other people and decline in schoolwork that depression does.

Depression can be seen early in life. Infants and toddlers who lose or are deprived of a maternal caregiving figure become sad, uninterested in things, quiet, inactive. They may fail to grow and develop if deprived for an extended period, as in a hospital or orphanage. At about the age of four or five, when language and thought are more advanced, a specific diagnosis of depressive disorder can be made. A small number of children have depressed moods that alternate with periods of hypomanic behavior—high energy, overactivity, high productivity, aggressiveness.

In childhood, and to a greater extent in adolescence, depression can be accompanied by rebellious, acting-out behavior that masks the underlying condition. Some children who are serious discipline problems in school and become involved in drugs, alcohol, and risk-taking behavior are depressed. They lack self-esteem, feel hopeless about themselves and helpless to change.[43]

Many factors are thought to cause depressive states, including biological factors. A family history of depression in parents and close relatives indicates greater susceptibility to the disorder. Thirty percent of children with one depressed parent showed signs of depressed behavior, whereas only 10 percent of children with non-depressed parents showed such behavior. Research has tentatively identified some biochemical changes that may serve as markers or predictors of a depressed state, but this research is in very preliminary form.

Life events also contribute to depression. Loss of loved ones through death, divorce, or separations; family stresses that result in neglect, abuse, or rejection of the child; academic pressure on the child to perform in school; and emotional deficits in the family so the child does not learn to identify and express feelings in a healthy way are all possible factors contributing to depression.[44]

Nevertheless, no one kind of circumstance produces depression. Some depressed children come from disorganized families that have experienced multiple stresses. Some depressed children lack friends and do poorly in school, but other depressed children are highly successful and seem to have many friends and enjoy much success.

As a result of any combination of factors, children can become depressed and develop the hopeless feeling that they are confronted with an unresolvable problem that will continue. They blame themselves as incompetent, inadequate, unworthy in some way.[45] Prior to puberty, boys are more likely to be depressed; after puberty, girls are more likely to be depressed.[46]

Prior to puberty, suicide attempts are rare, but after puberty, the rate of suicide attempts skyrockets. An estimated 400,000 adolescents attempt suicide each year, and approximately 5,000 kill themselves.[47] Suicide is the third leading cause of death in teenagers and sometimes ties for second place.

Many signs can alert parents to the possibility of depression in their child. Depressed mood—feeling sad, hopeless, helpless—is a main indicator, as is loss of pleasure and interest in usual activities. Other signs include disturbance in eating and sleeping, lack of energy, falling grades because of poor concentration. Talking to children often reveals the extent of their depressed mood because children can be verbal about their feelings. When parents notice these signs, they should seek qualified professional help as outlined in Chapter 16. At the present time, there are no definitive studies on the best form of help for depression.[48] However, family therapies and therapies aimed at helping the child change the negative self-evaluations are useful. Medications are sometimes used as well. If parents are uncertain whether their concerns are justified, they can always consult a therapist by themselves to determine the severity of the depression and the need to bring the child in.

Once help has been obtained for the child and the family, parents can listen and accept all the child's feelings about being depressed. Many parents, eager to see their children feel better, try to argue the child out of the depression, pointing out all the reasons the child should not be depressed—these are the best years of their lives; children should enjoy them. Trying to argue someone out of depression, however, can make the individual even more depressed. He or she believes the other person is right: "I must be really weird for feeling this way."

Some parents minimize the importance of talk about suicide, saying those who talk about it don't do it, they must want attention. Never consider such talk only an attention getter. Even attention getting can be fatal, as those attempting to get attention sometimes kill themselves by mistake.

In addition to expressing concern and getting professional help, parents can act to boost the child's self-esteem and enjoyment in life. Arranging pleasurable outings with a parent or the whole family, arranging a special treat, can help. Parents need not expect an overwhelmingly positive response, but it is worth carrying through even in the face of protest. We have noted many times that pleasurable activities bring family members closer together. If teenagers are not interested in any special activity, they may well be open to conversation with parents on all manner of things, provided parents are available and forgo advice, criticism, or guidance. Just sitting and listening to the adolescent, reflecting love in your interest in what is said, are positive steps you can take during treatment.

505

Children
Who Have
Attention
Deficit
Hyperactivity
Disorder

CHILDREN WHO HAVE ATTENTION DEFICIT HYPERACTIVITY DISORDER

The old term for this problem was hyperactivity. Now the American Psychiatric Association has devised a new term—**Attention-deficit Hyperactivity Disorder (ADHD)** —which refers to children who display inappropriate impulsivity, overactivity, and inattention.[49] Children who have ADHD show inattention by being easily distracted, not seeming to listen or to complete tasks, not being able to concentrate on tasks or stick to play. Impulsivity is revealed in acting before thinking, shifting from one activity to another, needing a lot of supervision, having difficulty in organizing work or waiting turns at activities, calling out in class. Because of their impulsivity, their desire for attention, and their rule breaking, these children are often disliked by peers and teachers. They also tend to do poorly in academic work because of their inattention. As a result of all these accumulating problems, these children frequently suffer from low self-esteem and depressed mood.

Problems with ADHD can begin very early in life and are present by the age of seven. It is estimated that 5 to 10 percent of school-age children suffer from this problem. Since boys are about nine times more likely to be diagnosed with ADHD, however, 10 to 20 percent of boys may be diagnosed in this way. Originally, it was thought that children outgrew these problems, but recent follow-ups suggest that about one-third of children continue to have such difficulties in adolescence; and for some, the behavior may continue into adulthood.[50]

Several factors are identified as possible causes of ADHD—neurological, environmental, genetic, psychosocial, and biological. Reviewing all the evidence, Russell Barkley, a noted researcher in this area, concludes that children may inherit a temperamental tendency to be overly active and easily bored by repetitive tasks, and this tendency may simply be the high end of activity level.[51] There may be some immaturity in neurologic maturation of the brain so that these children are slower to develop the structure and brain organization to control certain behaviors. Birth complications may play a role as well. Environmental toxins and neurological damage are responsible for only a very small fraction of cases.

Psychological factors are associated with ADHD as well. Recent studies suggest that early caregiving behaviors play a role in increasing or decreasing activity level.[52] The relationship is a complicated one. Maternal stimulation that increases exploration and competence in less active toddlers decreases exploration in highly active toddlers. When mothers try physically and verbally to direct and guide highly active toddlers, the toddlers resist and become less active and less competent. What is helpful to other children interferes with the behavior of highly active children.

In a longitudinal study of children from birth to age six, Deborah Jacobvitz and L. Alan Sroufe found that when mothers are intrusive with their infants, interacting with them without regard for the babies' needs, and when mothers are overstimulating with their preschoolers, then their children are more likely to be labeled ADHD in kindergarten.[53] Jacobvitz and Sroufe speculate that when mothers are intrusive and too stimulating, then children experience sudden, unpredictable state changes that are hard to learn to regulate. Rather than soothing the child and getting him or her into a regulated state, intrusive mothers overexcite the child who cannot then learn to self-regulate.

Psychological changes occur as a result of ADHD too. Parents can become very frustrated with children who are inattentive and noncompliant. When children resist, parents yell and threaten yet use punishment inconsistently. Parents begin to fight with each other, and the family comes to resemble the families of aggressive children described by Gerald Patterson in Chapter 9. When children's behavior changes under medication, parents' behavior changes as well.

There are many strategies for dealing with ADHD syndrome. Parents, teachers, and authority figures can modify their behavior and increase the likelihood that children will comply. Reasonable goals, effective rewards, consistent negative consequences help to promote more attentive, controlled behavior on the child's part. Second, adults focus on dealing with academic problems that may increase high activity level. They can establish reasonable and achievable learning goals and reward achievements. As children achieve academic success, inattention and poor performance decrease. When these methods do not bring the problems under control, there is the possibility of medication. Certain medications help children focus their attention so that distractibility and impulsivity decrease. Different medications are available, but all have side effects. Teachers and parents report significant improvement in attention and ability to concentrate with these medications.[54] Further, when children take these medications, their social behavior improves, and they are not so disruptive, silly, and inappropriate. In fact, they resemble other children their age in social behavior.[55]

Diane McGuinness challenges the notion of such a syndrome as ADHD or hyperactivity.[56] She believes teachers and parents, as well as professionals, are too quick to apply the label *hyperactive* to children with high levels of activity and poorer performance on boring, repetitive tasks, since such labels apply to 10 to 20 percent of boys and few girls. Reviewing a wide variety of studies done in the last twenty years, she concludes that the main behavioral or physiological traits common to this group are not well established, in part because of poorly executed studies and in part because the hyperactive child does not differ from others when motivated to perform. She believes there is a group of children who are motorically active and bored by repetitive tasks. Often they have difficulty with school because of their boredom and fall behind. Their poor performance increases ADHD symptoms. She agrees with Barkley that these children are at the very high end of activity level and have inherited this temperamental quality, which they must learn to control. They do not have a disease or a disorder, and they do not need medication that does not improve schoolwork, though it makes children's behavior more acceptable to teachers.

Though there is a disagreement between McGuinness and other experts on ADHD, it is mainly in terms of whether a special syndrome can be identified and called a disorder when it applies to a significant number of boys and whether medication should be used. McGuinness, like other professionals, would rely on behavioral techniques to bring temperamental high activity under control.

In dealing with overly active children, parents first take several actions to spend more positive, rewarding time with their child. This tactic reverses the vicious cycle put into motion in which the child is noncompliant and parents are frustrated.

507

Children
Who Have
Attention
Deficit
Hyperactivity
Disorder

BOX 15-2
SPENDING ENJOYABLE TIME WITH HIGHLY ACTIVE CHILDREN

To reverse the vicious circle that can develop between parents and highly active children, parents are to spend free play time with that child daily in an activity of the child's choice. Choose 15 or 20 minutes in the afternoon or evening and tell the child you want to spend special time with him or her in an activity of the child's choosing. If other children in the family want special time, they can receive 15 or 20 minutes at another time; they are not allowed to participate in this child's time.

1. The child selects what he or she wants; you are not to help with the decision or to criticize it as long as the activity is within the bounds of generally approved activities.
2. In the beginning, say very little about the child's behavior and simply observe what is happening. Then enter into the activity by describing what the child does. "I see you are coloring (drawing, building with blocks, playing with trucks). You are using the red crayon . . . " Pretend you are a narrator describing what is happening.
3. Relax and enjoy the session. Do not ask questions or give suggestions. Do not criticize, label, judge, or make fun of what the child does.
4. Give no orders and make corrections of behavior only if large matters of discipline are involved (breaking items, hitting parent).
5. If the child begins to act up (yells, acts silly), ignore the child and pay attention to another positive event that is occurring—the child's actual production. If the behavior becomes more difficult, leave the room.

Adapted from Russell A. Barkley, *Hyperactive Children* (New York: Guilford, 1981), p. 307.

Parents begin by spending 15 to 20 minutes per evening playing with the child (see Box 15-2). Parents learn to pay attention when the child is compliant (see Box 15-3, p. 508). They also learn to give rewards when the child is not bothering them (see Box 15-4, p. 509). As a result of these actions, children will receive more positive attention and begin to get a sense of their good qualities.

Second, parents use all the techniques described in Chapter 4 to modify the child's behavior in the direction of greater control. Depending on the age of the child, suggestions for the difficult child in Chapter 8 and the aggressive child in Chapter 9 are appropriate.

Third, parents find ways to build the child's self-esteem. They find those areas of strength in the child and explore ways to get pleasure and satisfaction from them. For example, if the child is very athletic, sports of different kinds may channel the energy. If the child is creative, parents find an artistic activity like music or writing to focus energy on.

Parents also address other areas of special concern. Many ADHD children lack friends, and Barbara Henker and Carol Whalen in a recent review article state that the extent of the interpersonal problems ADHD children experience has become

508

CHAPTER 15
Parenting
Children
with Special
Needs

◆

BOX 15-3
PAYING ATTENTION WHEN YOUR CHILD IS COMPLIANT

Many parents of highly active children are so busy dealing with misbehavior and unplanned mishaps that they pay attention only when the child is doing something wrong. They fail to notice when the child is doing what they want. Thus, the child receives parental attention mainly when engaged in negative behavior, an effect that tends to reward negative acts. To reverse this process, parents are asked to send appreciative I-statements when the child behaves in a positive manner.

1. As soon as you make a request and the child follows through, compliment the child. "Thank you for making your bed. It looks nice and neat." "I like your taking the garbage out as soon as I ask because then I can forget about it."
2. Catch your child being good and compliment him or her for it. "It was thoughtful that you gave your little sister her bottle. She really likes that." "It's great when you get dressed and hurry right down for breakfast because then we have more time to eat and talk."
3. Look for positive behaviors that are pleasant but not required by rules and praise them. For example, when the child gives you a lively description of an event important to him or her, be interested and indicate your enjoyment of this skill by manner or words.
4. Log the number of times in a day that you praise your child.

Adapted from Russell A. Barkley, *Hyperactive Children* (New York: Guilford, 1981), p. 319.

clear only in the last decade.[57] These children are rejected in many social settings because of their disruptive, inappropriate actions. Parents can help children develop social skills of sharing, turn taking, and cooperative play. Suggestions for the isolated and shy child in Chapters 9 and 10 are useful for ADHD children.

Parents can forget labels and concentrate on all those techniques for dealing directly with the child's disapproved behavior. In the course of doing this, parents can become closer to their children and form more rewarding relationships as they work together to solve the problem.

CHILDREN WHO HAVE LEARNING DISABILITIES

Sometimes a child may do well in several school subjects but perform far below his overall ability in one or two special areas. Or a child may have so much difficulty with subjects like reading and writing that all school work is affected, even though the child seems to understand math or history. When this happens, parents should have the child tested for physical problems, like poor eyesight and poor hearing. If these are ruled out as causes of the child's problems, the parents need to consider the possibility of a learning disability.

Learning disabilities are difficult to define precisely. The National Advisory Com-

---

BOX 15-4
PAYING ATTENTION WHEN YOUR CHILD IS NOT BEING DEMANDING

There will be many times when you are on the telephone, having visitors, cooking dinner, or driving a car and you cannot pay direct attention to the child. Many children act up at precisely this time—when you are busy—to gain your attention.

When you are engaged in activities and the child is behaving well, stop the activity and go compliment the child. Tell him or her that you really like having the time to do your work without interruption—e.g., "I like it when you play quietly because then I can talk on the phone more easily. Thank you." "It's easier to drive when there is quiet, and I appreciate that."

In the beginning, do this every 5 to 8 minutes, and gradually increase the time between compliments. Eventually the child will go 45 minutes or an hour without disturbing you. Parents may object to interrupting their activity to talk to the child, but remember that if the child were misbehaving, you would also have to stop and talk to him or her.

If you have more than one child, pay attention to the one who is not bothering you and ignore the others.

Adapted from Russell A. Barkley, *Hyperactive Children* (New York: Guilford, 1981), p. 321.

---

mittee on Handicapped Children defines **learning disability** as one or more deficits in basic learning processes involving spoken or written language, reading, math, and spatial orientation.[58] The deficit results in a discrepancy between the child's overall ability and his performance in class. The discrepancy is not due to physical handicap, mental retardation, emotional disturbance, or educational deprivation.

We do not know how many children are affected with these problems or what causes them, but several possible causes have been suggested: (1) a genetic component, since learning disabilities tend to run in families and boys are affected more frequently; (2) prenatal, birth, and postnatal factors like prematurity, low birth weight, or poor oxygen supply during labor; (3) general immaturity or developmental lag; and (4) environmental factors like poor nutrition. Learning disabilities are not caused by low intelligence—children at all levels of intellectual ability have learning disabilities. Einstein and Edison were both thought to have learning problems, yet both were geniuses.

Diane McGuinness, a neuropsychologist, believes that teachers and parents use the term too quickly to refer to children who are simply slower to learn reading, writing, and math.[59] She believes that just as there are great individual differences in athletic and artistic abilities, there are great individual differences in the ease with which children master academic skills. Yet the schools make no provision for these individual differences. Children are expected to keep pace with their age mates; if they do not, they are labeled "learning disabled" and sent to special classes. She points out that no one talks about athletic or artistic disabilities; we expect and accept them as normal. So, differences in rates of learning must be accepted as normal.

510

CHAPTER 15
Parenting
Children
with Special
Needs

INTERVIEW
with Carol Whalen

Carol K. Whalen is professor and chair of the Department of Psychology and Social Behavior at the University of California at Irvine. With Barbara Henker, she is the editor of Hyperactive Children: The Social Ecology of Identification and Treatment.

You have done research on hyperactive children for many years. What do you think are the most important things for parents to do with regard to hyperactive children?

Well, the issue of medication comes up right away, and that is always a big problem for parents. It is hard. Some parents are totally antimedication from the beginning—it is a closed book before it ever got open. I don't think that is a very useful position. On the other hand, we have seen parents who say, "Oh, good! Is that the problem? Medication will solve it." They conscientiously go through a systematic assessment, but sometimes any effort to address other problems, like being behind in school, get lost because we now have the diagnosis and the treatment. Medication should not be the first resort, but also not the last either. It should not be ruled out as one of the possibilities.

I would suggest to parents that before they go to the physician for diagnosis they arrange to have the teacher rate the child's behavior at school. Schools usually have such forms, and most teachers are very willing to do this for the child's treatment. The diagnosis used to be based on the physician's tests and observations, but now the value of teachers' ratings in making the diagnosis is more widely recognized. Parents can go to the physician's office prepared with them and be assertive in insisting that they be included as important information.

When doctors are trying to figure out the effectiveness of medication and the proper dose, it is very helpful to have ratings on the child's behavior before and after the medication. When the ratings are done by the teacher who does not know whether the child is or is not taking the medicine, then you have some objective information on the effectiveness of the pills. It is important to repeat such a procedure about once a year because sometimes a child is put on medication, which is assessed as helping him, and it might just continue on and on for years. You don't really know whether or not it is continuing to help him or in what ways some things might be better without medication.

If medication is effective, it is important for parents not to attribute all of the positive outcome to the medicine. When things are getting better, a parent may be tempted to say, "Oh, your medication is working." It is better to avoid that kind of statement. I like the idea of explaining to the child that medication is like a pair of glasses. It will help you see and learn to read, but it does not do the seeing and reading for you. It is a help. We have seen children who think of the medication as the "spelling" pill or their "good behavior" pill, a magic pill idea. The medication may have a negative effect if the child attributes all the successful outcome to the pill rather than to the things he is learning to do and the competencies he is developing.

Related to this, parents should avoid saying frequently, "I can't stand the way you are acting. Are you sure you took your pill?" Over the weeks and years, the underlying message is, "I'm not counting on you or expecting you to do the right thing." That is telling the child there is an external source of control rather than an internal self-control.

A second thing parents need to consider is what J. McV. Hunt called the problem of the child-environment match. Hyperactive children might be more extreme on this dimension or that dimension, such as having trouble concentrating or being impulsive or highly active. But these are behaviors parents are used to coping with; the problem is the extent, it's being over and over, day to day, setting to setting. Sometimes some environmental changes really do have remarkable effects. In some schools, it may be a matter of changing the classroom environment or changing to a different classroom that is structured in a different way. Just exploring those possibilities, parents can be really creative if they have the notion of finding the right niche or the right match between the child's disposition and the environmental setting. I think that's a basic part of good parenting. There is more of a burden on parents with difficult children to work harder to optimize this match and to be more creative.

In one of your chapters, you comment that sometimes hyperactive children do well as long as they can go at their own pace, but as soon as they have to go faster, they feel pressured and have trouble.

That's true. It is good for parents to try changing pace or routine because parents have a certain routine in the family, and the other children adapt to it fine, but this child doesn't. Then being a little more flexible about when we do this or when that has to be done can help. But, the reason that I'm hedging a bit is that there is the other side to it. These children *do* need to have structure and rules to follow also.

We do not necessarily find that what works for a child in one context will work in the next context. If going at his own pace helps him to handle homework better, it may not necessarily be the best way for him to handle other situations. That is one of the puzzling things about hyperactivity, both in terms of what the children are like and in terms of medication effects. You think you understand what is going on right here, and then you change the task or change the situation, and it's different, even in the same child.

For example, today they may watch one video quietly, but not another, or yesterday they watched it quietly but not today. That is the puzzling part. Are the children really unpredictable or is it that the environment or setting changes and the child is less likely to change along with the environment? It is an intriguing question, and we do not have the answer.

It is difficult for hyperactive children because they eventually accumulate so many problems—school, peers.

Who knows what comes first and what is feeding into what. And now researchers are finding that these problems are not disappearing at adolescence. Some hyperactive children are hyperactive as young adults, and problems may continue all through their lives. The problems show up in different ways—auto accidents, job changes, marital difficulties, substance use. Adults are still reporting restlessness and difficulties concentrating, even though they are not running around the classroom or offices.

That is another thing parents must remember. This is a chronic condition, rather than a problem of diagnosing an illness and then taking a pill and getting better. We are really talking about a lifestyle, whether it is temperament or personality. We are talking about a long-term situation that you must adjust to and plan for.

We stress the cognitive-behavioral aspect of managing and guiding the behavior. When hyperactive children learn to control their behavior, they can be more productive and may feel better about themselves. They do not get in trouble as much and also they feel a sense of mastery that they should have, because this is a normal part of childhood but one that they have missed so often.

continued

512

CHAPTER 15
Parenting
Children
with Special
Needs

INTERVIEW

with Carol Whalen *continued*

There are all the other effects of failure in the classroom—school gets to be unpleasant, peers start to make fun of them, and they are chosen last to be on teams. I think the problems they have with peers have been underplayed because people have been so concerned, for good reason, with the school problems. Many of these children are not making it with peers even though they may seem dominant and in charge. These children often do not have friends, except perhaps younger ones, and it may not get better as they mature. Medication itself will not solve these problems.

With parents, there is the whole search for what went wrong. Most parents start out blaming themselves. There is such a need to figure out what caused the problems, and they often conclude that they are at fault—which is rarely the case. Sometimes even the diagnosis of hyperactivity, and certainly the prescription for medication is a positive event for parents because they think, "Oh, it wasn't my fault. The child was born with it." That can be an adaptive shift or transition as long as the parent does not also begin to feel, "Well, I didn't cause it and so there is nothing I can do about it."

One thing that is puzzling to people is the role of diet in children's behavior problems. It makes good sense to parents because the dietary problem is external to the child and to the parent, but yet they can control it. It is not their fault, and it is not the child's fault; and it is something they can change. So it is easy to see how people get hooked on diet changes or restrictions even though research has not supported these approaches.

Like all parents, those with hyperactive children have to be careful that they do not try too hard to protect their children from negative experiences or from situations they assume the child cannot handle. When they do, they can really circumscribe their child's learning. It is a matter of fine-tuning what you will encourage and what you will limit, and it is a process that all parents go through to one extent or another.

McGuinness believes sex differences in abilities in part account for some learning disabilities. Boys and girls learn in different ways, and these sex differences in learning predispose them to difficulties in certain areas. From infancy girls are skilled in verbal expression. They rely on verbal communication to learn, whereas boys learn about the world through direct action with objects. Their interaction with the physical world helps them develop the ability to visualize movement in space. When children come to the school experience, girls are more skilled in processing words and reading, and boys are later more skilled in higher mathematics. It is boys who are most frequently identified as having **dyslexia** (difficulty in reading) because they have poorly developed auditory and language skills. Girls do less well in higher math and are thought to have a math phobia.

McGuinness believes schools need to develop innovative programs that group children according to skill level rather than chronological age. Children work to achieve mastery of the material or blocks of information, then go forward at their own pace. She also believes there are better ways to teach basic subjects like reading and math. She points to the Patricia Lindamood reading technique that concentrates on sounds and the order of sounds in words. Using this technique has improved the reading of children dramatically. Patricia Davidson has developed a method of teaching math that combines the use of visual pictures with textbook work. Even children with poor spatial abilities gain a greater understanding of math as they see the math processes illustrated while they carry them out.

These new methods are just beginning to be used. It will be some time before they are available to all children. In the meantime, parents must get help for the disability and the accompanying behavioral problems, such as hyperactivity, poor attention span, and inability to delay actions. Here we focus on how parents can help children cope with the behavioral problems and with parents' and children's psychological reactions that accompany learning disabilities. Parents should consult teachers, educational therapists, or specialists in learning disabilities. Two outstanding books are available for parents—*Learning Disabilities: A Family Affair* by Betty Osman,[60] an educational therapist, and *The Learning Disabled Child: A School and Family Concern* by J. Jeffries McWhirter,[61] a counseling and educational psychologist.

Both Osman and McWhirter discuss parents' initial reactions of attempted denial, anger, guilt, and depression. In their disappointment, parents sometimes blame the child, but more often parents blame themselves. They sometimes feel guilty that they did not recognize the problem sooner. Parents need to accept not only their own feelings, but also the feelings and reactions of the child's siblings. Brothers and sisters are likely to resent the time and attention that go to the learning-disabled child.

After accepting their own mixed feelings, parents must explain to the child as clearly and honestly as possible what the problem is. We all have difficulties that we must learn to manage—a learning disability is one such difficulty. Children often realize, far sooner than their parents, that they have difficulty learning some kinds of material. They may ignore the problem, focusing instead on the things they do well. They may lose books, forget assignments, or tell parents that they have no homework.

Parents can help a learning-disabled child in several ways. First, they can show love and attention, regardless of the level of school work. They can value the child's feelings and encourage the expression of the frustration and anger felt at the extra effort required to do the work other children do easily. Anger at parents and teachers for setting firm limits and giving reminders of work is also felt and should be expressed as well.

Second, organizing the environment and establishing regular routines help such children to function more effectively. Box 15-5 contains suggestions for parents who want to structure the environment. Behavioral techniques described in Chapter 8 for the highly active child are also effective.

Third, parents can help by serving as a resource for the child, taking a more active role to show a child how to do a task. Osman says parents may have to show a child how to structure a book report or work a math problem the first time the task is assigned. The next time the child can do it alone. Help with homework must not become a routine, however. Equally important, parents can engage children in many games that will strengthen intellectual skills and help integrate motor and perceptual behavior. McWhirter's book contains many specific suggestions for toys, physical activities, board games, and card games that stimulate development and also are fun.

514

CHAPTER 15
Parenting
Children
with Special
Needs

◆

BOX 15-5
ORGANIZING THE ENVIRONMENT
FOR LEARNING-DISABLED CHILDREN

1. Hang a bulletin board in each child's room and in a central family area, like the kitchen, so schedules, chores, and reminders for important events can be posted.
2. Get in the habit of posting signs on mirrors, the refrigerator door, and the front door to remind children of special events or chores.
3. Have children leave messages of whereabouts or telephone calls in one place so each family member can check there.
4. Have the key to the house on a heavy string or bright ribbon that is hard to lose, and get a special hook in the child's room for it.
5. Identify all clothing with name tags so children can easily find lost items at school or friends' homes.
6. Write names and addresses on all notebooks and other possessions like eyeglass cases or backpacks in the event they are lost; keep identification in wallet or purse if carried.
7. Have bedroom furnished with plenty of cabinets or shelves for storage; have dividers in drawers to keep clothes separated.
8. Have a specific desk or study area for each child where the child can take books, notebooks, and papers immediately on returning home and where all school work can be done. It reduces the number of places you have to search for papers and books.
9. Try to organize a daily family routine, a regular time for getting up, eating meals, leaving the home and returning. Such a regular schedule helps to compensate for poor memory.

Adapted from Betty B. Osman, *Learning Disabilities: A Family Affair* (New York: Random House, 1979), p. 59.

Fourth, disciplinary techniques that anticipate and prevent problems from arising are useful. For example, if a child is easily excited, careful scheduling of events and monitoring of the amount of incoming stimuli, even in the home, can reduce emotional outbursts. If a parent sees a child building up a lot of irritation or frustration at a sibling, separation before a blowup is helpful.

Fifth, parents can help children build social skills. The experience of being a slow learner in one or more areas does little for one's self-esteem or feelings of confidence with peers. This is particularly true during the elementary school years, when it is so important to the child to be liked by everyone else. And so learning disabled children may become loners. Parents can help by arranging brief get-togethers with other children, for an hour or two. These will give the child valuable experiences that contribute to confidence. Parents also help by encouraging the child to develop a special skill that will bring recognition in the group. Osman makes suggestions for promoting social relationships (see Box 15-6).

◆
Box 15-6
PROMOTING SOCIAL RELATIONSHIPS
FOR LEARNING-DISABLED CHILDREN

1. Accept the child's statement of interpersonal troubles as valid. Empathy when a child is having trouble with friends is more valuable and helpful than criticism or denying the troubles exist.
2. Discuss how one goes about making friends. Asking children how they would feel if certain acts were done to them helps them to take the role of the other person.
3. Rewards might help the child get started with friendships, or serve as incentives to try extra hard to use control.
4. Recognize that some children mature more slowly and need more time before they are ready to sleep overnight at a friend's or develop deep friendships.

Adapted from Betty B. Osman, *Learning Disabilities: A Family Affair* (New York: Random House, 1979), pp. 77–78.

Parents must be careful neither to overindulge nor to overprotect a learning-disabled child. If parents feel guilty, they must deal with their own feelings so that they can be truly helpful to the child. Otherwise they may rob the child of the opportunity to develop competence and confidence.

CHILDREN WHO ARE GIFTED OR TALENTED

Parents often think how delightful it would be to have talented children. How enjoyable to sit back and see them excel in some activity—what a joy to see the talent unfold and the child express creativity! It *is* a pleasure to see, but this pleasure is accompanied by hard work of many years' duration, sacrifice on the part of the child and the family, and gradual attainment of outstanding skill. As we shall see, the process is much the same as that parents use in overcoming special difficulties.

In this section we look at the process of developing world-class abilities in the areas of athletics, artistic activities, and intellectual pursuits. We describe the parenting behaviors that contribute to success. We then look at the parenting behaviors useful in promoting success in general.

A University of Chicago team of researchers studied 120 young men and women who had achieved international levels of performance in their special areas, which included swimming and tennis in the athletic area, piano and sculpture in the artistic area, and neurology and mathematics in the intellectual area.[62] They interviewed the individuals, their parents, and in many cases their teachers and coaches to understand the process by which they earned success. Talent development, the researchers find, requires at least twelve to fifteen years of commitment. It can be divided into three stages—early, middle, and late years—with family and teachers

516

CHAPTER 15
Parenting
Children
with Special
Needs

providing essential support. Few of the outstanding individuals are identified as special in the beginning. It is the combination of individual commitment, family support, and outstanding instruction that lead to accomplishment.

In the early years, the parents are influential in introducing the child to the talent area though they do not select the exact activity. Parents may be athletic, musical, artistic, but the exact sport, instrument, or medium is the child's choice. Initially, the activity is one of enjoyment and fun and is pursued for pleasure. Parents select an early teacher who primarily works well with children and teaches basic skills. The teacher is easily available in the neighborhood, and the relationship between teacher and child is a comfortable one in which the child gets much positive feedback. Parents monitor progress. If a teacher does not seem to work out, they get another one. Parents also schedule daily practice of about an hour and make sure the child has prepared for lessons. They are supportive, encouraging, often helping solve difficulties though they may not be experts in the field. Most important, parents emphasize the ethic of hard work and doing one's best. They model this trait in their own lives as well as talk about it. Children are quick learners who easily absorb instruction and enjoy success at the activity.

In the middle years, after children have initial success in the area and make good progress with their initial teachers, parents begin to search for more skilled instruction and find an expert or special tutor to teach the child. This person usually lives some distance from the student and has a reputation for developing talent in that area. Children often have to demonstrate sufficient skill to be taken on as a student. These teachers are perfectionists who demand the highest level of performance from the child and expect superior accomplishment. It is unlikely that a child could start with this kind of instruction because of the demand placed on the child. At this time, children are expected to spend 3 to 5 hours a day at the activity, mastering and refining all the techniques.

Parents have an active role in this process. Financial expenses and time commitments increase. There is more driving, not only to lessons, but to competitions as well. The whole family's schedule changes to adapt to the child's training routine, and the child becomes identified as special within the family. Parents' responsibilities for monitoring the child's progress decrease as the teacher takes on this role, but parents do continue to see that practice schedules are maintained.

In the middle years, children make an increasing commitment to the activity. They begin to think of themselves as swimmers or pianists. Motivation becomes internal in that children strive to achieve their best. With the help of their teachers or coaches, they begin to set goals for themselves and to take pleasure in achieving them. They begin to enjoy the competitions and measuring their skills against others'.

In the later years, children make a complete commitment to the activity and plan ways to reach the highest level of achievement in their fields. They are perfecting the fine points of their skills and going beyond that to fashion their own style in carrying out the activity. They now receive instruction from master teachers who accept only a few students. The student now plays a greater role in planning his or her career with the advice of the teacher, who often makes contacts in the field at large for them.

The student has committed almost all waking hours to the activity. Relationships center on the activity, with major support coming from other students with whom he or she also competes. The parents' major role now is to provide financial resources and emotional support as needed. The student's motivation is completely internal. Public recitals and competitions serve as measures of achievement on the road to outstanding success.

Benjamin Bloom and his co-workers who carried out the research believe it is difficult to identify outstanding achievers early because what one does and learns at eleven or twelve is so different from what one learns and does ten years later. They write:

> The outstanding young student of mathematics or science (or music, art, tennis, or swimming) is a far cry from becoming an outstanding mathematician, neurologist, pianist, and so forth. And being good as a young student in the field is only in a small part related to the later development. In between is a long process of development requiring enormous motivation, much support from family, the best teachers and role models possible, much time, and a singleness of purpose and dedication that is relatively rare in the United States at present.[63]

Although this is a study of individuals who achieved world-class fame in their endeavors, the same principles apply to developing talent at any level. Parents and early teachers respond to the child's interest in an area and teachers give basic instruction. Children receive much support and external rewards of praise in the beginning. As children continue, though, they become more internally motivated, more interested in developing their talent to the highest degree, competing with others, mastering techniques of their discipline and then going beyond them. Finally, they impose their own style, plan their own career advances, and receive support and inspiration from others in their field.

Parents are early models of interest and enjoyment in a general field as well as models of hard work and achievement. In daily life, interacting with children, parents can be on the alert for special interests and skills and can encourage children to engage in these activities.

We have noted in earlier chapters what parents can do to provide optimal development of intellectual and other abilities. In infancy and toddler years, children's cognitive growth flourishes when parents are responsive, affectionate, interested in the children but not restrictive of them. When the home is organized and there are regular routines along with opportunities for variety in play, then intellectual growth is enhanced.[64] When parents are encouraging and give children a sense they can accomplish tasks, children are more willing to try and more likely to meet with success.

When children are young and primarily under parents' influence, parents have greater control of what opportunities their children have for learning and success. Special abilities can be encouraged and developed at their own rate. When children move into the school system, however, parents may have to become active advocates to ensure their children get the kind of educational experience best for them. Just as parents with children with special disabilities must push for special classes or arrangements that meet their children's needs, so must parents of children with spe-

518

CHAPTER 15
Parenting
Children
with Special
Needs

cial gifts. The school system is not necessarily organized to meet the needs of a gifted child. So, for example, if a child reads well before entering kindergarten, consultation with the school can provide a plan for meeting this child's needs for academic stimulation. He or she may go to the first grade for reading, may be put into a combination kindergarten–first grade class where he or she can easily join first graders for certain subjects. Specific arrangements must be made for each child because public schools usually have no classes for gifted and talented children before third grade.

Providing a broad array of activities in the early elementary school years enables children to find those interests and pursuits of greatest enjoyment to them. Parents can then seek out further activities in that area of special interest. Initially, parental support and encouragement are important; as children grow, their own motivation enables them to plan further development.

Parents not only help by providing activities of possible interest, but they also provide structure and discipline as children wish to learn more. They show children how to set up practice times and stick to them, how to seek out more information, how to solve problems as they arise. They model what they want their children to do in terms of striving for achievement. As parents do all these things, they provide the nurturing soil for all gifts to grow to mature expression.

Bloom and his co-workers emphasize the positive features of talent development. They believe all individuals have within them the potential for talented performance in some area and that some combination of home, school, and community enables individuals to manifest their talent. They wish to identify that combination of circumstances that promote talent so potential does not go undeveloped. Their study subjects reported few regrets about pursuing excellence. Individuals realized they gave up certain activities to pursue achievement and endured a great deal of frustration, but their interest in the field and their enjoyment of the activity outweighed negative features.

Many parents would question the wisdom of pushing children to make such demands on themselves. All know of some outstanding performer who sacrificed happiness and emotional well-being to achieve, and parents are reluctant to encourage their children to strive for outstanding levels of achievement. Certainly many creative, intelligent, gifted people enjoy the challenge of learning and are happy. If children seek out such activities and pursue them when opportunities are offered, parents can offer support. Parents, teachers, and coaches need not encourage children to go beyond certain limits in the pursuit of excellence. If children persistently and consistently voice doubts about what they are doing, if they push themselves with little joy in the activity, then parents and coaches may suggest a rest, a change in activities, and/or an opportunity for counseling when temporary discouragement becomes depression.

COMMON THREADS

In this chapter we have looked at children with special needs. Certain adaptive parenting behaviors are common to all special situations; indeed, these parenting behaviors are those already described as helpful to children in general. Parents' underlying positive regard for the child—seeing the child as important, competent, and special in his or her own way—is an essential ingredient in dealing with special needs. Though children may have difficulty in a certain area—a learning difficulty or overactivity—they are still competent in many ways, and the competence must be emphasized so that disability remains in proper perspective. The positive emotional tie between parent and child remains stable.

In dealing with difficulties or gifts, structured, organized routines and periods of practice help. Parents provide these and monitor children's adherence to them. Parents also become advocates for their child, relating to professionals and other adults such as teachers in the larger community to obtain the best possible care, the best possible education or instruction, for the child. The focus is always on providing for the child's particular strengths or traits needing improvement in a cooperative venture in which parents and other adults work together to foster growth.

So we can see that just as parenting under usual circumstances involves maintaining positive emotional ties and providing structure and organization, so these two parenting tasks are important with children with special needs. Getting support from the larger community network and working with other adults is useful under usual circumstances, but it is essential with children who have special needs. These needs force parents to relate more closely to other professionals and institutions in getting help for their children. As they do this, parents often form support groups of their own to address the problems of their children. These groups serve important functions. Parents who have been through similar difficult experiences understand each other and can offer support and advice in ways that are invaluable and impossible for professionals to duplicate. Cooperative ventures in meeting children's needs provide feelings of great satisfaction on everyone's part.

MAJOR POINTS OF CHAPTER 15

Children with special needs include:

- premature children, who are approximately 10 percent of new births
- adopted children who number about five million, half of whom are under eighteen
- children with chronic illness, who number between 5 and 20 percent of children, depending on the exact definition
- depressed children, whose exact number are unknown; but 400,000 teenagers attempt suicide each year
- hyperactive children, who number between 5 and 10 percent of children, 90 percent of whom are boys; so as many as 18 percent of boys may be considered hyperactive
- learning disabled children, whose exact numbers are not known
- talented and gifted children, whose exact numbers are not known

520

CHAPTER 15
Parenting
Children
with Special
Needs

Premature babies:

- are born before the thirty-seventh week of pregnancy
- fall into two groups—low-birth-weight babies (between 3 pounds 5 ounces and 5 pounds 8 ounces) and very-low-birth-weight babies (under 3 pounds 5 ounces)
- can have many or few problems; can be in intensive care nurseries or go home within a few days
- in most cases have a good outlook for long-term development

Factors that place women at risk for premature delivery include:

- mother's own prematurity or already having given birth to premature baby
- mother's poor medical/nutritional care during pregnancy
- mother's age (under sixteen and over forty)
- mother's low weight prior to pregnancy (under 100 pounds)
- birth less than one year before present pregnancy
- mother's having high stress/physically demanding work
- mother's cigarette smoking

Parents of premature babies face several problems:

- dealing with their own anxieties about baby's immediate and long-term future
- dealing with doctors, nurses, other hospital personnel
- dealing with one's own feelings of disappointment, sadness, anger, and possibly guilt
- learning to care for the child, who may need more than the usual amount of care

Premies' emotional reactivity involves:

- greater irritability
- being quicker to become overstimulated by parents
- being less interactive with parents

Parents' attitudes about the baby:

- are strongly related to the child's growth and progress
- may be influenced by negative stereotyping that premature babies are not as cute or as likable as full-term babies
- are affected by attitudes of those close to them

Children are adopted through:

- private individuals
- adoption agencies
- institutions/organizations in other countries

Preparing for adoption includes:

- accepting the fact that one will not/cannot have biological children
- accepting there is no definite period—like pregnancy—in which to prepare for parenthood
- recognizing that one may not have usual supports given to new parents of biological children—parties, help, leave from work

Entry phase of the bonding process includes:

- fact that infant can arrive with a history—previous placement in foster home, institution in another country, special physical problems
- little advance warning of the baby's arrival
- recognition that more explanation may be needed for casual friends—for example, where baby came from

Settling in after entry includes growth of:

- feelings of attachment and love
- feelings of confidence about adoption

Adoptive parents are usually advised that:

- they should tell the child about adoption by age five
- preschoolers may not really grasp concept of adoption even when explained
- explanations about adoption will have to be given several times, and child's questions may change with age
- parents' active listening helps children express their feelings about adoption so parents can give help

Initially, children's conceptions of their body:

- are vague and few in number and do not become accurate and detailed until early adolescence
- center on the parts of the body they feel most directly—heart, eyes
- are influenced by colloquial expressions
- focus on body parts that receive most time and attention

522

CHAPTER 15
Parenting
Children
with Special
Needs

Children's conceptions of illness:

- initially are of a single symptom caused by a vague event like being bad
- in the years seven to ten are of several symptoms that are caused by germs/dirt/bad behavior that can be avoided
- in the years eight to ten include the idea that the body may be receptive to illness and then cure itself
- in early adolescence become more abstract with recognition of more causes of illness and more forms of cure
- change with age and give children a greater sense of control
- are influenced by subjective feelings of distress—one is sick because he/she doesn't feel good

Acute illness:

- requires explanation several times to children
- decreases child's level of functioning
- increases child's desire for attention, affection, and entertainment
- can help children learn differences between physical and psychological distress
- of other family members gives children an opportunity to be empathic caregiver

Preparation reduces stress of:

- routine medical appointments
- dental appointments
- hospitalization

Children with chronic physical illness cope best when they:

- take one day at a time
- have positive self-concept
- avoid feelings of guilt
- gain support from parents and relatives
- live in an atmosphere of honesty and openness
- are allowed to live as much like healthy children as possible

Children who are depressed suffer:

- feelings of self-criticism, self-blame
- loss of interest in pleasures and usual activities
- feelings of helplessness and hopelessness
- loss of energy

- loss of sleep and appetite sometimes
- loss of memory and concentration sometimes

Factors related to depression include:

- biological factors as seen in increased risk of depression when there is a strong family history of depression
- life events—loss of loved ones, divorce, academic pressures, social pressures
- no one kind of circumstance—for instance, some depressed teens have no friends, some have many

Suicide:

- has a much lower rate prior to puberty
- increases dramatically after puberty
- is attempted by 400,000 teenagers per year with 5,000 killing themselves
- is the third leading cause of death among teenagers, and sometimes is tied for second place

When children are depressed, parents' tasks are:

- to get professional help for the child
- to cooperate with the recommendations of professionals, and if not satisfied with them, seek further professional advice
- to act to boost child's self-esteem
- to increase, where possible, enjoyable activities for the child

Children with ADHD have a number of the following characteristics:

- are easily distracted
- find it hard to focus attention on activity
- do not listen or complete tasks
- act before they think
- need a lot of supervision
- have difficulty organizing activity or task
- find it hard to wait for turns
- seem to need to be the center of others' attention

Children with ADHD often accumulate many problems:

- poor grades because of inattention
- dislike of peers and teachers because they do not follow rules or wait turns
- low self-esteem
- sometimes depressed mood

Several factors are thought to cause ADHD:

- neurological
- environmental
- genetic
- psychosocial
- biological
- temperamental

Help for children with ADHD consists of:

- cognitive/behavioral methods of behavior control first
- medication when behavioral controls are not sufficient
- social skill building
- activities to increase child's self-esteem

Children with learning disabilities:

- may perform below overall ability in one or two areas
- may have deficits in basic learning skills like reading that affect all work
- may have trouble in an area because of individual differences in ability, not because of special problem

Parents help children with learning disabilities in many ways:

- accept and love the child regardless of ability level
- organize the environment and daily routines
- serve as a resource to the child
- use disciplinary techniques that anticipate and prevent problems
- help children build social skills
- help children to put disability in perspective

Three stages of talent development include:

- early stage of introducing the child to the activity, having the child enjoy the activity, and teaching basic skills
- middle stage of getting more skilled instruction for child and establishing intense practice routine and involvement in task
- later stage when child makes a complete commitment to activity and is able to give own imprint or style to the activity

Common threads to all these areas include:

- parents' positive regard, acceptance, and support of the child's individuality

- establishing organized structure and routine to daily life so child can most easily learn and practice activity
- working with professionals in community to get best help for the child

Additional Readings

Bloom, Benjamin S., ed. *Developing Talent in Young People*. New York: Ballantine, 1985.

Jason, Janine, and Van Der Meer, Antonia. *Parenting Your Premature Baby*. New York: Henry Holt, 1989.

McCoy, Kathleen. *Coping with Teenage Depression: A Parent's Guide*. New York: New American Library, 1982.

Schaffer, Judith, and Lindstrom, Christina. *How to Raise an Adopted Child*. New York: Crown Publishers, 1989.

Taylor, John F. *Helping Your Hyperactive Child*. Rocklin, Calif.: Prima, 1990.

Notes

1. Robin Marantz Henig and Anne B. Fletcher, *Your Premature Baby* (New York: Ballantine, 1983).
2. Ibid.
3. Ibid.
4. Ibid.
5. Rachel Levy-Shiff, Haya Sharir, and Mario B. Mogilner, "Mother- and Father-Preterm Infant Relationship in the Hospital Preterm Nursery," *Child Development* 60 (1989): 93–102.
6. Henig and Fletcher, *Your Premature Baby*.
7. Ibid.
8. Anneliese F. Korner, Byron William Brown, Jr., Sue Dimiceli, Thomas Forrest, David K. Stevenson, Nancy M. Lane, Janet Constantinou, and Valerie A. Thom, "Stable Individual Differences in Developmentally Changing Preterm Infants: A Replicated Study," *Child Development* 60 (1989): 502–513.
9. Levy-Shiff, Sharir, and Mogilner, "Mother- and Father-Preterm Infant Relationships in the Hospital Preterm Nursery."
10. Mark T. Greenberg and Keith A. Crnic, "Longitudinal Predictors of Developmental Status and Social Interaction in Premature and Full-Term Infants at Age Two," *Child Development* 59 (1988): 554–570.
11. Virginia A. Rauh, Thomas M. Achenbach, Barry Nurcombe, Catherine T. Howell, and Douglas M. Teti, "Minimizing Adverse Effects of Low Birthweight: Four Year Results of an Early Intervention Program," *Child Development* 59 (1988): 544–553.
12. Greenberg and Crnic, "Longitudinal Predictors of Developmental Status and Social Interaction in Premature and Full-Term Infants at Age Two."
13. Marilyn Stern and Katherine A. Hildebrandt, "Prematurity Stereotyping: Effects on Mother-Infant Interaction," *Child Development* 57 (1986): 308–315.
14. Cynthia L. Zarling, Barton J. Hirsch, and Susan Landry, "Maternal Social Networks and Mother-Infant Interactions in Full-Term and Very Low Birthweight, Preterm Infants," *Child Development* 59 (1988): 178–185.
15. Glenn Affleck, Howard Tennen, Jonelle Rome, Beth Roscher, and Linda Walker, "Effects of Formal Support on Mothers' Adaptation to the Hospital-to-Home Transition of High Risk Infants: The Benefits and Costs of Helping," *Child Development* 60 (1989): 488–501.
16. Carol Zander Malatesta, Patricia Grigoryev, Catherine Lamb, Melanie Albin, and Clayton Culver, "Emotion Socialization and Expressive Development in Preterm and Full-Term Infants," *Child Development* 57 (1986): 316–330; Carol Z. Malatesta, Clayton Culver, Johanna Rich Tesman, and Beth Shepard, "The Development of Emotion Expression during the First Two Years of Life," *Monographs of the Society for Research in Child Development* 54 (1989): Whole Number 219.
17. William Morris, ed., *The American Heritage Dictionary of the English Language* (New

York: American Heritage Publishing Co., 1969).

18. Lois Gelman, *The Adoption Resource Book* (New York: Harper & Row, 1984).

19. Linda Cannon Burgess, *The Art of Adoption* (New York: W. W. Norton, 1981).

20. Dorothy W. Smith and Laurie Nehls, *Mothers and Their Adopted Children—The Bonding Process* (New York: Tiresias, 1983).

21. David M. Brodzinsky, Leslie M. Singer, and Anne M. Braff, "Children's Understanding of Adoption," *Child Development* 55 (1984): 869–878.

22. Burgess, *The Art of Adoption.*

23. Ibid., p. 106.

24. John E. Schowalter, "The Chronically Ill Child," in *Basic Handbook of Child Psychiatry,* vol. 1, ed. Joseph D. Noshpitz (New York: Basic Books, 1979), pp. 432–436.

25. Elizabeth Gellert, "Children's Conceptions of the Content and Functions of the Human Body," *Genetic Psychology Monographs* 65 (1962): 293–405.

26. Ibid.

27. Ibid.

28. Ibid.

29. Roger Bibace and Mary E. Walsh, "Developmental States of Children's Conceptions of Illness," in *Health Psychology,* ed. George C. Stone, Frances Cohen, and Nancy E. Adler (San Francisco: Jossey-Bass, 1979), pp. 285–301.

30. Michael Siegal, "Children's Knowledge of Contagion and Contamination as Causes of Illness," *Child Development* 59 (1988): 1353–1359.

31. John D. Campbell, "Illness Is a Point of View: The Development of Children's Concepts of Illness," *Child Development* 46 (1975): 92–100.

32. Lee Salk, *What Every Child Would Like His Parents to Know* (New York: Warner, 1972), p. 116.

33. Thomas Gordon, *P.E.T.: Parent Effectiveness Training* (New York: New American Library, 1975).

34. Joan Beck, *Effective Parenting* (New York: Simon & Schuster, 1976), pp. 180–187.

35. Arthur H. Parmelee, Jr., "Children's Illnesses: Their Beneficial Effects on Behavioral Development," *Child Development* 57 (1986): 1–10.

36. Elizabeth F. Loftus, "Words That Could Save Your Life," *Psychology Today,* November 1979.

37. T. Berry Brazelton, *Doctor and Child* (New York: Dell, 1978).

38. Jerome L. Schulman, *Coping with Tragedy* (Chicago: Follett, 1976).

39. Paula J. Beckman, "A Transactional View of Stress in Families of Handicapped Children," in *Beyond the Dyad,* ed. Michael Lewis (New York: Plenum, 1984), pp. 281–298.

40. Susan M. McHale and Wendy C. Gamble, "Sibling Relationships of Children with Disabled and Nondisabled Brothers and Sisters," *Developmental Psychology* 25 (1989): 421–429.

41. Donald H. McKnew, Leon Cytryn, and Herbert Yahraes, *Why Isn't Johnny Crying?* (New York: W. W. Norton, 1983).

42. Ibid.

43. Ibid.

44. Israel Orbach, *Children Who Don't Want to Live* (San Francisco: Jossey-Bass, 1988).

45. Ibid.

46. Michael Rutter, "Depressive Feelings, Cognitions, and Disorders: A Research Postscript," in *Depression in Young People,* ed. Michael Rutter, Carroll E. Izard, and Peter B. Read (New York: Guilford, 1986), pp. 491–519.

47. Kathleen McCoy, *Coping with Teenage Depression: A Parent's Guide* (New York: New American Library, 1982).

48. Maria Kovacs, "Affective Disorders in Children and Adolescents," *American Psychologist* 44 (1989): 209–215.

49. *Diagnostic and Statistical Manual of Mental Disorders,* 3d ed.–revised (Washington, D.C.: American Psychiatric Association, 1987).

50. Rachel Gittelman, Salvatore Mannuzza, Reginald Shenker, and Noreen Bonagura, "Hyperactive Boys Almost Grown Up: I Psychiatric Status," *Archives of General Psychiatry* 42 (1985): 937–947.

51. Russell A. Barkley, *Hyperactive Children: A Handbook for Diagnosis and Treatment* (New York: Guilford, 1981).

52. Mary Jane Gandour, "Activity Level as a Dimension of Temperament in Toddlers: Its Relevance for the Organismic Specificity Hypothesis," *Child Development* 60 (1989): 1092–1098.

53. Deborah Jacobvitz and L. Alan Sroufe, "The Early Caregiver-Child Relationship and Attention Deficit Disorder with Hyperactivity in Kindergarten," *Child Development* 58 (1987): 1488–1495.

54. Barkley, *Hyperactive Children.*

55. Carol K. Whalen, Barbara Henker, Julie Castro, and Douglas Granger, "Peer Perceptions of Hyperactivity and Medication," *Child Development* 58 (1987): 816–828.

56. Diane McGuinness, *When Children Don't Learn* (New York: Basic Books, 1985).

57. Barbara Henker and Carol K. Whalen, "Hyperactivity and Attention Deficits," *American Psychologist* 44 (1989): 216–223.

58. National Advisory Committee on Handicapped Children, *Special Education for Handicapped Children* (Washington, D.C.: United States Department of Health, Education and Welfare, Office of Education, January 31, 1968).

59. McGuinness, *When Children Don't Learn.*

60. Betty B. Osman, *Learning Disabilities: A Family Affair* (New York: Random House, 1979).

61. J. Jeffries McWhirter, *The Learning Disabled Child: A School and Family Concern* (Champaign, Ill.: Research Press, 1979).

62. Benjamin S. Bloom, ed., *Developing Talent in Young People* (New York: Ballantine, 1985).

63. Ibid., p. 538.

64. Robert H. Bradley, Betty M. Caldwell, and Richard Elardo, "Home Environment, Social Class and Mental Test Performance," *Journal of Educational Psychology* 69 (1977): 697–701; William J. Van Doorninck, Betty M. Caldwell, Charlene Wright, and William K. Frankenburg, "The Relationship Between Twelve-Month Home Stimulation and School Achievement," *Child Development* 52 (1981): 1080–1083.

INNER AND
OUTER RESOURCES

Healthy children develop occasional behavior problems as ways of expressing the tension that accompanies growth and life. The stress that occurs during times of transition is particularly likely to trigger such problems. Birth of a sibling; entrance into kindergarten and junior high school; separation, divorce, or remarriage of parents; and acute or chronic illness are among the events that can lead to behavior problems. Such problems are, however, usually temporary and decrease as the child adapts to the new situation.

What do you do when all your attempts at effective parenting do not resolve the child's problems? How do you decide whether to seek professional help? How do you decide what kind of help is needed? How do you go about finding the appropriate person or agency?

ASSESSING THE PROBLEMS

Parents can use the following guidelines in deciding whether the problems are sufficiently severe to need professional help. How *intense* are the problems? If a child has nightmares once or twice a week, parents might not seek help. If the child begins to have nightmares every night and cannot return to sleep for some time, parents might decide, after two or three weeks, that they need help.

How *long* have the behavior problems existed? A child who still has moderate problems several months after a new baby joins the household may need help. A child who cannot adjust to kindergarten four or five months after the school year has begun may need extra help.

What effects are the behavior problems having on a child's overall life pattern? Are the problems *preventing development?* For example, a child who has learning problems may come to hate not only schoolwork but also teachers, the principal, and other children at school. This hostility then cuts the child off from other people and gives him or her the additional problem of being a loner. Fearfulness and extreme self-consciousness produce the same results. Nervousness around others may prevent the child from developing friends and also hinder academic work at school because the child is afraid of criticism. When parents realize that a child is developing moderate to severe problems that are hampering several areas of functioning, they should take action to head off a vicious cycle of behaviors.

Are the problems having *negative effects* on other family members? Parents may find themselves so concerned about the problems and so affected by them that they feel professional help is required. For example, a teenager's acting out by getting poor grades may be so upsetting to the mother that it creates a rift between the parents and affects the other children in the family.

Does the child show a *dramatic change* in behavior for no apparent reason—behavior that does not disappear? If so, you may wish to seek help. If a child who has always been independent and self-reliant becomes dependent and clingy and does not reestablish previous patterns within a reasonable time, her parents may seek help, depending on how severe the behavior problem is and how appropriate it is for the developmental stage. A previously independent teenage girl who becomes more dependent on others, particularly peers, will arouse parental concern. But they are not likely to institute treatment because dependence on peers and conflicts around dependence on parents are typical of adolescence. However, if a previously independent third-grader suddenly develops fears and refuses to venture far from home, and there were no precipitating events, parents would be likely to seek help because children are usually increasing in independence at this age.

SOME SPECIFIC PROBLEMS

Lee Salk lists the following kinds of problems at different age periods as worthy of parental concern.[1] He cautions that no one of these problems alone is necessarily an indication of emotional disturbance. Rather, the persistence of problems and the number together will alert parents to possible trouble.

Preschool years: During these years parents should seek help if the child has continuous nightmares, wets the bed frequently after training is accomplished, masturbates excessively, shows total disregard for parental authority, is brutal toward siblings, is unable to get along with other children, is determined to cling to parents, or is withdrawn when with others.

School years: Salk focuses on school problems of all kinds—behavioral problems triggered by learning disabilities, including reluctance to go to school, truancy, bullying other children at school. You can add to this list such other problems as cruelty to children or animals, continual lying or stealing, and destructiveness. Increasing numbers of preadolescent children report marked depression, and some attempt suicide. Just as the quiet, withdrawn child goes unnoticed, so the depressed, tired, and uninterested child may go unnoticed because he or she makes no disturbance. Prolonged lack of interest and enthusiasm, poor appetite, poor sleep patterns, or withdrawal from friends indicate a need for professional help.

Adolescent years: Salk lists the acting-out problems associated with delinquency, rebelliousness, stealing, and breaking the law in other ways. Other similar problems are alcoholism, which is a growing problem among teenagers, sexual acting out, and depression. One form of adolescent behavior not quickly identified as depression, but containing an underlying depressive theme, is rebellious acting out. Rebellious teenagers are restless, vaguely unhappy persons who become uneasy if they are not in motion. They may drive poorly, drink excessively, and present a facade of delinquent characteristics. Yet they are basically depressed and discouraged. They seek the activity and trigger arguments with others to ward off the self-criticism and self-doubts that lie just under the surface.

HOW TO PROCEED

What should you do when you identify behaviors of concern? You can attempt to identify events that may be triggering and sustaining the problems. At times of transition you can expect behavioral reactions. Traumatic transitions include a move to a new school, loss of friends because the family moves, and changes in the family because parents separate. The first step is to see if the behavior subsides with time and support. Parents can offer understanding and seek ways to ease the path of growth. You can encourage new activities that will help the child meet new friends, for example. When a child has experienced a loss, you can help the child to find and enjoy pleasurable activities that are fun and help to balance the difficulties.

Parents can also examine strategies being used to see if some changes are needed. Nightmares may be helped by new bedtime routines and by helping the child to find acceptable ways to express aggression. You can ask other parents about their experiences with similar problems and get ideas about how to handle them.

As parents observe the child and try to understand the behavior, they need to realize that often a behavior problem is related to a series of different kinds of events, and interventions must occur at several levels. This was true of a four-year-old boy, Tim, whose parents took him to a therapist because he was having frequent nightmares. The parents had done everything they could think of, but they were losing too much sleep and becoming less able to function. So they sought help. This little boy was the middle of three children, with a younger brother about a year old. Tim was a slow-maturing, slender child who enjoyed physical affection and cuddling. Before the birth of his younger brother, Tim's parents had had more time and attention for him. Shortly after the birth, his mother went to work part-time in the late afternoon, so Tim had even less time with her. He had never been able to compete against his older, more competent sister, and he felt rejected and angry, but fearful of expressing these feelings. His nightmares expressed both the anger and the fear and, equally important, got his mother's attention for long periods as she tried to get him to sleep. As the parents began to give Tim more attention and to be firmer about a prescribed bedtime routine, the child settled down.

We can see from this example that the problem resulted from a combination of several facts—the child's slower rate of maturing and individual temperament, the arrival of a new sibling, the mother's going to work, and parenting strategies that had encouraged the problem. The parenting strategy was just one factor in the situation, although a decisive one for promoting change.

On occasion, parents will seek professional help for a child's problem and discover that the problem is their response to the situation, not the child. Stella Chess, Alexander Thomas, and Herbert Birch cite several examples of parents' unrealistic expectations for a child. This one is particularly helpful:

> Problems can develop if parents expect a child to act like some dream-child of their imagination instead of being *himself*. For example, a few years ago a mother consulted us about her five-year-old-son. She was afraid he was schizophrenic because he was quiet and withdrawn. He wouldn't play baseball or skate with the other children and was even reluctant to go outdoors.
>
> The boy looked like a handsome, solemn, quiet, hesitant youngster. We invited him into the playroom to see how he would adapt to a new situation and a new person, and how he would play.
>
> For a few minutes he sat quietly, looking around at everything in the room. Then he walked over to the blocks, carefully examined each size and shape, and then began to play, eventually bringing in dolls, cars, and so on. When he wanted to know what some unfamiliar object was or how to use it, he asked us without hesitating. Gradually he began to tell us what he played with at home and what he liked about the toys that were new to him.
>
> There was nothing at all the matter with the youngster. He was just not the ideal boy his mother had anticipated. She was a vigorous, active woman who had been a tomboy and couldn't wait to live vicariously a *real* boy's life, through her son. In her efforts to make him conform to her ideal, she had pressured him to become a bubbling, gregarious athlete. He had resisted, not by violent protests, but in his characteristic fashion by quiet retreat. It is possible that this retreat might eventually have made him a seriously withdrawn child.[2]

Some parents seek help with children's problems when, in fact, it is their own problems that are creating difficulties. One mother brought her thirteen-year-old daughter to a therapist because she was concerned about the girl being boy-crazy, rebellious, and depressed. During the interview, the therapist realized that the mother's depression was marked and that concern about her own sexuality was the major issue in her life. After the daughter was evaluated, it was the mother who became the patient.

When parents have doubts about the seriousness of the child's problems, they might seek consultation on that point as a couple. As noted, parents' problems are often the sources of children's difficulties. Growing children's confidence may be sapped by being identified as a patient when they are in fact not the problem. If parents are uncertain whether the child has a problem, they can seek help themselves first. Because family members live closely together and one person's problems affect everyone, it is wise to consider family therapy if problem solving in family councils is not sufficient to deal with the problems.

FORMS OF HELP

Most parents find it very difficult to face the idea that one of their children has problems they cannot handle. When we discover a child has a serious problem, we often feel guilty, wondering what we could have done to prevent it and how we have caused it. Professionals and parents are becoming increasingly aware that many kinds of factors and events influence a child's growth into adulthood. When parents understand this, they are likely to feel less guilty and more competent in helping the troubled child to cope.

It is natural to wait and hope these problems will go away. Sometimes they do. However, most severe problems lead to more difficulties, and consultation with a professional can be very useful. Where should you start? First, a pediatrician can determine if there is a physical reason for the child's behavioral problems. A thorough checkup may reveal physiological conditions that result in behavioral consequences. In this situation, treatment of the physical condition can alter the troubling behavior.

Parents may feel, after the child has been examined by the pediatrician, that additional help is needed. If so, the parent can call and get referrals from the pediatrician as well as from local professional societies—the medical, psychological or social work organizations—to the appropriate persons. If the child requires treatment that involves medical training and ability to prescribe medication, referral to a psychiatrist might be what is needed. If knowledge of healthy growth and development and awareness of behaviors associated with usual life crises are important, or if psychodiagnostic evaluation is required, referral to a clinical psychologist might be considered. If referral to a professional person with skills in mobilizing social support and help for families in crisis is required, a psychiatric social worker might be most helpful. Where family dynamics are interlocking and close and strong relationships enmesh several family members in the "child's" problem, family therapy may be most valuable. In getting any kind of referral, other parents or professionals who work with children can be sources of referrals.

When discussing a child's treatment with a professional, the parent should ask about the individual's educational and professional background. A professional is usually happy to answer such questions. The parent can ask about the likelihood of change and about the length of time needed to remedy the problems. A therapist who does not know the family or the situation in detail will probably be reluctant to make a very precise estimate of time or suggest particular techniques. Such specifics begin to be clear only when the therapist understands the situation better, perhaps after several sessions.

SOURCES OF STRENGTH

When children have problems, we can try to change our parenting strategies, we can get professional help, and we can try to change the balance of pressures so that coping and adaptation occur. Satisfactions that give pleasure also create strength. In *Anatomy of an Illness,* a discussion of his experience of a life-threatening collagen disease, Norman Cousins describes the healing, strengthening power of humor.[3] He found that watching old Marx Brothers films and reruns of *Candid Camera* brought release from pain and periods of relaxed sleep that increased his strength and powers of recovery. Cousins writes of the healing powers of laughter and of creativity. Help your child to find and engage in those activities most pleasurable for him, and you will be helping him to heal himself.

In helping children cope with problems, we have a great ally in the child's natural capacities. Jean Macfarlane, Lucile Allen, and Marjorie Honzik, concluding their study of the persistence of behavior problems, write:

> May we pay our respects to the adaptive capacity of the human organism, born in a very unfinished and singularly dependent state into a highly complex and not too sensible world. Unless handicapped by inadequate structure and health and impossible and capricious learning situations, he threads his way to some measure of stable and characteristic patterning. We see the variety of coping devices he uses for his complex set of tasks. He starts out with overt expression of his needs and feelings and attempts immediate and direct solutions to his problems. Many of his overt and direct problem-solving attempts are not tolerated, so he learns when necessary to sidestep, to evade, to withdraw, to get hurt feelings and, also, to submit overtly even while his releases and problem-solving continue internally until controls are established. If he is under fairly stable and not too discontinuous pressures and secures enough approval and support to continue his learning and enough freedom to work out his own compromise overt-covert solutions, he becomes, to use the vernacular, "socialized," and even without this optimum combination, he frequently arrives at stable maturity.[4]

Relying on the strengths of children and their drives to healthy growth, parents can move with greater confidence to carry out their role as prescribed by Selma Fraiberg:

> Man's consciousness of himself as a being, the concept of "I," of personal identity—the very center of his humanness—is achieved through the early bonds of child and parent. The triumph of man over his instinctual nature, his willingness to restrict, inhibit, even to oppose his own urges when they conflict with higher goals for himself, is again the product of learning, an achievement through love in the early years of development. Conscience itself, the most civilizing of all achievements in human evolution, is not part of the constitutional endowment, as any parent can testify, but the endowment of parental love and education.
>
> If we read our evidence correctly, it appears that parents need not be paragons; they may be inexperienced, they may be permitted to err in the fashion of the species, to employ sometimes a wrong method or an unendorsed technique, and still have an excellent chance of rearing a healthy child if the bonds between parents and child are strong and provide the incentives for growth and development in the child. For the decisive factors in mental health are the capacities of the ego for dealing with conflict, the ability to tolerate frustration, to adapt, and to find solutions that bring harmony between inner needs and outer reality. These qualities of the ego are themselves the product of the child's bonds to his parents, the product of the humanizing process.[5]

The parent-child relationship humanizes not only the child but the parent as well. As parents become nurturers, authority figures, interpreters of the world, helping children grow into independent maturity, they become deeper, wiser individuals who have often reworked some of their own heretofore unresolved childhood feelings. Further, children themselves often inspire their parents to take positive actions they have previously postponed. For example, some parents give up cigarettes to quiet their children's worries about their smoking. Other parents give up daily alcohol so they do not set a poor example for their children. And still others become selective television viewers and moderate exercisers to provide good models for their children. Children then force their parents to become good self-caretakers as well as effective child caregivers.

Children weave their parents more closely into communal social life. They stimulate parents' concerns about schools, safety in the community, programs that enhance physical, social, and artistic development. Parents learn to work with other parents and with community figures to provide the best environment possible for growth.

As children grow to maturity, then, they bring people together working interdependently to provide a healthy form of life for all. Parenting becomes a growth process for everyone—children, parents, and the community around them.

ADDITIONAL READINGS

Chess, Stella, and Thomas, Alexander. *Know Your Child*. New York: Basic Books, 1987.
Nelson, Jane. *Positive Discipline*. New York: Ballantine, 1987.

Notes

1. Lee Salk, *What Every Child Would Like His Parents to Know* (New York: Warner, 1972).
2. Stella Chess, Alexander Thomas, and Herbert G. Birch, *Your Child Is a Person* (New York: Penguin, 1976), pp. 188–189.
3. Norman Cousins, *Anatomy of an Illness* (New York: W. W. Norton, 1979).
4. Jean W. Macfarlane, Lucile Allen, and Marjorie P. Honzik, *A Developmental Study of the Behavior Problems of Normal Children between Twenty-One Months and Fourteen Years*, University of California Publications in Child Development, vol. 2 (Berkeley: University of California Press, 1954), pp. 220–221.
5. Selma Fraiberg, *The Magic Years* (New York: Scribner's, 1959), pp. 301–302.

INDEX